T0294517

LAW & ADVERTISING

ADVERTISING

"The worst nightmare of any advertising agency creative professional is having the company lawyer say 'Sorry, you can't use that.' So who better to write a book on advertising law than a veteran creative director who has been navigating the lawful boundaries of marketing communications for forty-five years? Dean Fueroghne has created an exhaustive resource for advertising law that both agency and client-side marketing professionals will find invaluable."

—Phil Odell, Casa Grande Communications

"*Law & Advertising* is an essential book for anyone in the field of advertising. Students to ad agency executives to brand managers will find the content accessible and valuable. I would have loved this as a resource while working as an account executive and dealing with everything from copyright and trademark issues to lottery guidelines and substantiation of ad claims. Today, it is a fabulous learning tool and resource for the future professionals in my undergraduate and graduate advertising courses. Eager to learn the key regulatory issues and common pit fall areas in advertising, readers are provided with conceptual definitions and multiple case examples to build understanding, solidify knowledge, and allow for future application."

—Carrie La Ferle, Temerlin Advertising Institute, Southern Methodist University

"Dean Fueroghne has long been not only a marketing guru to successful companies, but a highly sought legal expert witness about advertising. My firm has relied on his expertise in several class action cases. In this new book, he draws on his formidable experience to guide advertisers, marketers and designers through the legal issues they face."

—Adam Gutride, Esq., Gutride Safier LLP

"Dean Fueroghne has used his expertise and years of experience to write *Law & Advertising*, which is a thorough and thoughtful presentation of the law that regulates advertising. In this era of the internet, where fake news stories are being used to generate advertising revenue, this book has great importance."

—Mark A. Griffin, Esq., Keller Rohrback LLP

FOURTH EDITION

LAW &
ADVERTISING

A GUIDE TO CURRENT LEGAL ISSUES

DEAN K. FUEROGHNE

ROWMAN & LITTLEFIELD

Lanham • Boulder • New York • London

Senior Acquisitions Editor: Leanne Silverman
Assistant Editor: Carli Hansen
College Marketing Manager: Karin Cholak
Senior Marketing Manager: Kim Lyons
Interior Designer: Ilze Lemesis
Cover Designer: Meredith Nelson

Published by Rowman & Littlefield
A wholly owned subsidiary of The Rowman & Littlefield Publishing Group, Inc.
4501 Forbes Boulevard, Suite 200, Lanham, Maryland 20706
www.rowman.com

Unit A, Whitacre Mews, 26-34 Stannary Street, London SE11 4AB, United Kingdom

Copyright © 2017 by Rowman & Littlefield
First edition 1995. Second edition 2000. Third edition 2007.

This publication is designed to provide accurate and authoritative information with regard to the subject matter covered. It is sold with the understanding that neither the author nor the publisher is engaged in rendering legal, accounting, or other professional service. If legal advice or other expert assistance is required, the services of a competent professional person should be sought.
From a Declaration of Principles jointly adopted by a Committee of the American Bar Association and a Committee of Publishers.

British Library Cataloguing in Publication Information Available

Library of Congress Cataloging-in-Publication Data
Names: Fueroghne, Dean Keith, author.
Title: Law and advertising : a guide to current legal issues / Dean K.
   Fueroghne.
Description: Fourth edition. | Lanham, Maryland : Rowman & Littlefield, 2017.
   | Includes bibliographical references and index.
Identifiers: LCCN 2016048444 (print) | LCCN 2016048686 (ebook) |
   ISBN 9781442244887 (cloth : alk. paper) | ISBN 9781442244894 (electronic)
Subjects: LCSH: Advertising laws—United States.
Classification: LCC KF1614 .F84 2017 (print) | LCC KF1614 (ebook) | DDC
   343.7308/2--dc23
LC record available at https://lccn.loc.gov/2016048444

♾™ The paper used in this publication meets the minimum requirements of American National Standard for Information Sciences—Permanence of Paper for Printed Library Materials, ANSI/NISO Z39.48-1992.

Printed in the United States of America

Contents

Detailed Contents

Foreword

No employee is more reviled in an ad department or an advertising agency than the Legal person, since his or her job is to make the creative team stay within copy and layout guidelines to avoid lawsuits. I was that person for seventeen years at three top agencies: Doyle Dane Bernbach in New York City, and Wells Rich Greene and Ogilvy & Mather in Los Angeles. Later as a trademark lawyer I worked briefly at Young and Rubicam, NY, and in-house at a dental and household products company but it was not nearly as engaging as being on the firing line defending a position with a client, copywriter or art director who emphatically wanted NO changes to their commercial or print ad.

Imagine my surprise when a creative professional from another agency in Los Angeles called me to discuss his idea of publishing a comprehensive book on advertising regulation. Dean and I met and quickly became aware we were members of a very small tribe who actually cared about this topic. I had published a master's thesis on the Norman Lear lawsuit to end The Family Viewing Hour and had spent hundreds of hours researching the origins and permutations of broadcasting and advertising laws, but I thought my interest in this was peculiar. It turned out Dean had been interested in this topic for many years and wanted to know if I thought a detailed book was warranted. Sure, I said, knock yourself out and he wrote a terrific book I have kept in my study all these years.

Now almost three decades later Dean reached out to me to write the foreword for the fourth edition and I am truly flattered. This text has the same thoroughness of presenting all aspects of the topic with updated cases. Readers new to advertising regulation will be exposed to the origins and definitions concerning the subject which provides an important context whether you are a lawyer, law or communications student, an advertising or broadcasting professional, or a client. Those readers already familiar with that landscape will be able to fine-tune their knowledge on a variety of key topics such as copyright, trademark and the ever-increasing Internet issues of privacy, publicity and fair use. As an attorney licensed in California since 1987 most of my continuing legal education focuses on problems concerning the Internet and the availability of global information. Kudos to students and business professionals who recognize the need to delve into the laws and regulations of advertising and wisely bought this book to aid them in their education. You will not be disappointed and will keep this book on *your* shelves for years to come.

Laurel G. Phillips, Esq.

Advertising is a creative business but in the process of being creative, many agencies create more liability for themselves and their clients than awards for their ads. There are many examples of ads that don't adhere to the law. But just because someone gets away with robbing a liquor store, it doesn't make it legal for others to do it. In my experience, most advertisers feel that advertising laws (the few that they are aware of) restrict the power of their message. So the advertisers avoid dealing with the legal issues at all costs. What they're overlooking is that the laws don't restrict the power of the message—just the manner in which it's delivered. Nonetheless, anyone involved in advertising needs to understand these laws and their consequences.

The field of advertising is affected by legislation, statutes, court decisions, and consumerism. Unfortunately, legislative acts, statutes, and court decisions can be laced with unfamiliar words and complicated patterns of reasoning—making practical interpretation hard to understand. *Law & Advertising* provides a single accessible source of information about the laws that most directly impact the business of commercial advertising.

I wrote this book with three audiences in mind. First, it is addressed to all those who produce, distribute, and prosper from the business of commercial advertising—the account executive, the art director, the copywriter, the creative director, the advertising manager—whether in the advertising agency or an in-house advertising department. Second, it serves lawyers who may need or want a compilation of current advertising law in one accessible reference, as well as a book viable for CLE courses. Finally, it is also designed with the student in mind, whether in law school or in an advertising or communications law course. This book is not about public relations or ethics—I'll explain more about why that is in chapter 1. But now . . . how did I come to write this book in the first place?

I didn't plan my forty-five-year career in advertising; it just happened. What started out as an apprenticeship in the art department of the Bozell/Jacobs advertising agency eventually lead to becoming a creative director with DDB/Needham and Ogilvy & Mather, and later president of my own advertising agency. I also managed in-house stints as VP/general manager for McKesson as well as other companies. Over the past twenty-five years, I have also served as an expert witness on advertising-related litigation cases. So you could say I have vast real-world experience in all things advertising.

Early in my career I ventured into studying law at UCLA while working in advertising. One of the elective courses I opted for, because I worked in the advertising business, was Legal Aspects of Advertising (a course I would later teach at UCLA). The professor began the course by announcing that there was no required text for the course because none existed. Throughout that class I took copious notes and read every case I could photocopy at the law library. Not only because I loved studying the law, but also because this area was on point with my daily working career. It touched on issues I encountered every day in business. It also made me realize just how little my colleagues understood about the laws that affected advertising, and continue to increasingly affect it today.

I continued to research the laws that affected how I did my job and began organizing my notes into a personal reference. After many requests from colleagues for copies of my collected notes—and having seen so much naiveté about the implications of law in the advertising business—I created the first edition of this book in 1989. Today, there are a few other books on the market that cover this subject. What makes *Law & Advertising* different from those other books is that it was written by someone with the legal background, who also taught the subject at the college level, as well as someone who spent over four decades working daily in the advertising business. And the scope and expertise that comes with that unique combination of experiences is only available in *Law & Advertising.*

This fourth edition contains the clear explanations of how advertising and the law intersect that readers have so valued in its earlier iterations. At the same time, it provides a new structure to help organize those explanations more logically. First, chapter 1 serves as an overview of advertising regulation in general. The remainder of the chapters are now organized into thematic parts. Part I (chapters 2 through 5) follows with a discussion of the overall landscape of advertising law including general areas of law that impact all advertising, including the Federal Trade Commission, the business relationship between an advertiser and its agent, and advertising and the Internet. Part II (chapters 6 through 8) covers specific areas of law that can exist in advertising messages. Part III (chapters 9 through 13) discusses more specialized issues specifically related to advertising, including copyright and trademark, or warranties and contests. Second, this edition also covers new and updated areas of law, as well as looking heavily at the Internet and social media, and how they play into advertising regulation.

Structure and Organization

Now a little about the structure of the book. The chapters in this book are organized by "area of law" rather than type of advertising media for a specific reason. As an example, deceptive advertising regulation applies the same whether the deception occurs in a magazine ad or on a television commercial. A lawyer will understand this easily; a student or businessman maybe not so much. The legal theory, the reasoning, and the logic behind one area of law is often quite different from the legal theory, reasoning, and logic underlying another area of law. And yet, the regulation of, say, deceptive advertising applies the same whether the deception occurs on an outdoor billboard or on the Internet. Now consider "copyright and trademark law." I often hear people refer to these two in conversation as if they were part of the same whole, although they are not similar under the law. These two areas, like the others, cannot be studied together because the legal principles and reasoning behind each area is different; the laws are different, and so the understanding must be different. So what the reader may think are inconsistencies in logic from chapter to chapter are actually the variations in the different areas of law. The only exception to this is the chapter on the Internet. The reason being that there is so much recent activity in that area that is related specifically to the Internet.

I have tried to explain the legal principles as clearly as possible, believing that cases provide the best examples to illustrate each of the points. I've had to select the information and material that I felt was the most relevant, memorable, and interesting for all audiences. In some cases I've chosen examples and stories over in-depth legislative theory and history. In other cases I've used examples that were particularly ironic or entertaining. While many of the cases used in this book are older, there's a reason for that. It may seem hard for younger people and students to relate to, but I believe it's very important in order to understand the reasoning behind a law, to understand where it came from and why. Also laws, and as a result courts, work on precedent. Cases that change law set the precedent for that area of law for other courts to follow later. And those precedent-setting cases often remain in effect for many decades. The other reason is that only appellate-level cases are recorded in the official "reports" of the court. I do not reference lower court cases, which is where the most legal activity occurs on a current level because these cases are not reported, so they are not authoritative.

While I have tried to assure that the examples used in this updated fourth edition of *Law & Advertising* are current, the case law, statutes, and regulations should not be used as authoritative unless the user researches them at the time of use to determine their validity or any changes or modifications since the date of publication. And now for the obligatory legal disclaimer: This book is not intended to be construed as offering legal advice in any way. As with any legal problem, when in doubt, consult an attorney who specializes in that particular area.

To everyone I've worked with over the years in this business, who have provided the stories—sometimes humorous, sometimes sad—that have helped to illustrate the book, I extend my thanks. Many I have learned from; some I have walked away from shaking my head. But all have contributed to this book—some more than they would have liked.

Dean Keith Fueroghne
dean@deanfueroghne.com

An Overview of Advertising Regulation

1

People don't read advertising, they read what interests them. Sometimes it's an ad.

—*Howard Gossage*

The combined expenditure on advertising for the ten largest companies in the United States is greater than the gross national product of most nations.

In 2012, *Advertising Age* magazine reported that Apple spent $1 billion on paid advertising, Google spent $1.05 billion, Honda spent $1.4 billion, McDonald's $1.37 billion, Toyota $1.73 billion, Walmart $1.89 billion, Walt Disney Co. $2.12 billion, Ford Motor Co. $2.14 billion, AT&T $2.36 billion, Verizon $2.52 billion, General Motors $3.1 billion, and Proctor & Gamble tipped the scales at $4.9 billion.

A major national television commercial will be viewed by more people than the total number of people who have seen the entire *Star Wars* series. The average American adult is exposed to over five thousand advertising messages each day, according to market research firm Yankelovich. And that same person watches about twenty thousand television commercials each year, and their children see over fifty thousand a year. A major manufacturer will spend over a million dollars to produce a 30-second television commercial. And then there's the ever-increasing impact of "new media." While the national ad spending for TV, print, radio, and outdoor media increased in 2013 by 3.6 percent over 2012, the new media areas of digital, mobile, Internet, and social media have steadily increased their ad spending by 22.3 percent in 2012 to an expected 31.1 percent by 2017.

What this numbers' trivia illustrates is that advertising is a very expensive, very pervasive, very specialized, and very institutionalized segment of our social and economic environment. But have you ever wondered how all this advertising interacts with the rules that govern our society? Did you ever stop to ask yourself: How does advertising interact with the restrictions of society?

We generally accept that advertising is a part of the business process. Advertising goes hand in hand with moving products and services from the rawest of materials to the ultimate consumer. Advertising is, in essence, the catalyst that keeps a free enterprise market operating. Advertising is the process of creating messages (advertisements) that are placed in directly paid media—meaning any media form where an advertiser directly purchases space or time to display a message promoting a product or service.

As our economic system has grown over the years, it has become more complex by necessity. This complexity has forced the legal system to create an equally complex mechanism to maintain the delicate balance that exists between free enterprise and consumer protection.

On one side stand the advertiser and agency trying to display their product as favorably as possible. On the other side stands the consumer, guarded by a protective legal barrier which provides a sense of security in making purchasing decisions. The government has seen to that. Between these two constants lies a fine line. As you will see throughout the book, it is one beyond which neither side would be prudent to extend.

Throughout history, as promoters of products and advertising services have become more sophisticated and, indeed, cleverer, the legal system has had to keep pace. In the pages that follow, we will examine the relationship between advertiser and regulator, what brought it about, and its practical applications.

Because it is such a powerful marketing tool, and despite advertisers' ever-increasing awareness and emphasis on corporate social responsibility, advertising draws more than its share of criticism. Over the years, I have come to realize that consumer distrust of advertising is less about any specific claim made in an advertisement and more about advertising in general. Consumers generally believe that advertising, in general, lies. That advertising has the power to coerce people into buying products they don't need or want. Although that may be a naïve view, it's a pervasive one. Because of this, a major challenge for the advertising community is to restore the credibility of its product and to check public skepticism, lest it turn to cynicism. This can be accomplished, in large part, by following the law.

The demands of advertising professionals require that they keep current on all aspects of their profession. Law is one of those areas that has a powerful effect on advertising and how advertisers advertise. Therefore, the new policies dictated by regulatory agencies and the interpretations of court decisions must be well understood by advertising professionals, attorneys, and media, business and communications professors and students.

Many years ago, while in the Oval Office, Calvin Coolidge said that "advertising ministers to the spiritual side of trade." While some consumers have expressed a fear of—and others have indicated a hope for—the demise of advertising, it is still integral to our free-market environment. Advertising provides a valuable service to the seller, the buyer, and the public and serves the spirit of trade only so long as it remains truthful and honest.

Most textbooks teach that modern advertising began in the early 1900s. Greats like William Benton, George Batton, Albert Lasker, Chester Bowles, Bruce Barton, Leo Burnett, and David Ogilvy did not create the process of advertising, but they did pioneer the business of advertising. What we consider to be advertising in its purest sense has been around long before the time of these industry giants—long before the era of advertising depicted in *Mad Men*.

W. C. Crosby was an astute businessman. He understood all too well the power of advertising. Crosby had a knack for practicing the subtle art of persuasion. He knew how to pique a person's interest by using the right words: how to light a fire in the prospect, how to promote, how to sell—abilities that any great ad man must possess. He lived around the turn of the century (the twentieth century, that is), when he eloquently described his profession as "a business, like all business," which "takes rise from the conditions of life about it and adapts itself as does social life.

And . . . plays an invariable chord in the human make-up . . . according to the times and circumstances."

His was not a name that would go down in the history books as one of the great advertising giants. He would, however, be remembered as a craftsman of the art of persuasion. W. C. Crosby was a con man, and one of the best. He kept company with such colorful characters as Willie "The Sleepy Kid" Loftus, Jimmy McViccor, Charley (changed to Henry in the 1973 movie *The Sting*) Gondorf, "The Crying Kid," "Hungry Joe" Lewis, and "Big Joe" Turley.

The con man's migration to America was a natural occurrence. One frontier opened itself up to another. Long before the Civil War, the con man could be found in the Gold Rush shanty towns of California, riding the paddle-wheelers down the Mississippi to New Orleans, drifting through high society in the East, and riding the first railroads West.

W. C. Crosby and the others brought with them to America, the skills of the great European harbinger, Richard Town, who had so incurred the wrath of his victims that on May 23, 1712, in London, he was hanged. His open-air execution was viewed by a cheering throng of spectators. "My friends, this is my birthday," Town stated coolly. "I see you have come to help me honor it . . . my compliments, and thank you for coming to my adventure."

The Earliest Advertising Regulation

The Postal Fraud Laws

Where did it all begin? In 1872 stringent federal mail fraud laws were passed in order to wage war against the con man who was perpetrating his schemes through the mail. At that time, there was no Internet, no Google, no television—no radio even. And there were no laws against false advertising. The bulk of advertising was carried through local newspapers, the only widely-accessible and readily-available media. All that was required on the con man's part was the up-front capital to purchase relatively inexpensive newspaper space and postage stamps. Despite teeth-gritting indignation, the victims were virtually helpless against the guile of the con man.

Then as today, anyone who uses the U.S. mail in an attempt to engage in a fraud can be prosecuted under federal mail fraud law. And while enacting the mail fraud laws helped, they still did not do away with the con man overnight. Unfortunately, passage of these laws was only a small step toward stemming the ever-increasing tide of mail fraud in the United States. American con men still ran rampant among a gullible public—a public that responded to advertisements for mining rights, real estate, securities, inventions, cure-alls, and medicines of all types. The Post Office estimated that in 1911 alone, con men netted $77 million from duped investors in mail-order schemes. That would be about $2 billion by today's dollar.

Presidential Portraits and Home Remedies

When the mail-order fraud reached its peak, the perpetrators seemed to take a perverse pleasure not only in the fraud itself, but also in pouring salt into their victims' wounds. They often exhibited the sort of "I dare you" attitude that challenged their victims. One classic nose-thumber appeared in over two hundred newspapers in 1882—the year after President Garfield's assassination caused immense national grief (see box 1.1).

Box 1.1

Portrait of the President

I HAVE SECURED the authorized steel engravings of the late President Garfield, executed by the U.S. Government, approved by the President of the United States, by Congress, and by every member of the President's family as the most faithful of all the portraits of the President. It was executed by the Government's most expert steel engravers, and I will send a copy from the original plate, in full colors approved by the Government, postpaid, for one dollar each.

To each person sending in the required $1, the con man mailed the promised engraving of President Garfield–a 5-cent U.S. postage stamp.

Some fifteen years later, an offer appeared in newspapers promising a way to eliminate annoying moths (see box 1.2).

Box 1.2

DO THE MOTHS BOTHER YOU?
If so, send us fifty cents in stamps, and we will furnish a recipe CERTAIN SURE to drive the pests from furs or rugs or any other old things.

A few weeks later the consumer received the foolproof recipe, as advertised (see box 1.3). The reply read as follows:

Box 1.3

Dear Madam: Dampen the article in question in kerosene thoroughly (to soak it is even better) and add one lighted match. If the moths do not disappear, your money will be cheerfully refunded.   Yours truly, The Buncomb Company

Indeed, it was the era of the con man—of getting wealthy off the gullibility of the consumer. And some got very wealthy. In 1927 (his last year of operation), a con man named Hugh B. Monjar brought in a cool $7,666,631 before being sent to a federal prison for mail fraud.

In the late 1800s and early 1900s, the exploits of the con man were the main form of deceptive advertising. This is when consumers first learned to distrust all advertising—and while some may still argue that today's advertisers continue to prey upon consumers, times have changed: there are many more constraints in place to help protect consumers. No longer can the advertiser rampantly seek out the weaknesses in consumers and exploit them as easily as did early con men. The potent mail fraud laws still exist, but the consumer now has many additional advertising controls on his side. These controls have brought heavy restrictions for today's advertiser, who has to deal with the marketing dilemma of being heard in our overcommunicated society. Yet the advertiser must be very careful about how he gets the consumer's attention and what he delivers. The myriad issues the advertiser must consider today are far more serious than they were in earlier days.

With the advent of the Federal Trade Commission (FTC) in 1914, a force of **regulation**[1] against taking unfair advantage of the consumer began. Over the years since the inception of the FTC, the consumer has gained substantial protection. Protection from the FTC and from other bodies and areas of law as well. That's what the balance of this book will discuss.

The Advertising Landscape

What Constitutes Advertising?

An advertisement itself promotes a commercial message or proposition. Most commonly, this message is a direct offer to purchase the company's product or service. Sometimes it is more subtle than that, but the goal is the same: to benefit the advertiser by furthering their brand image, sales, and profits. Political advertising is an exception to this definition and has different protections which we'll discuss later.

So often we think of an advertisement as a promotional item in a magazine or newspaper, or on TV or the radio. But it's more than that. A freeway billboard is an advertisement. A sponsored message displayed on the side of a blimp is an advertisement. A website can be an advertisement. A digital sign in a shopping mall kiosk is also an advertisement. A message on the fold-down tray table on an airline seat is an advertisement. A banner on a website is an advertisement. A classified ad in the newspaper is an advertisement. A sign in a store window is an advertisement. A product brochure is an advertisement. A "sponsored" link on Google or Yahoo is an advertisement. The previews in movie theatres contain advertisements. "Suggested Likes" on Facebook could be an advertisement. Even some "editorial" looking articles can be considered advertisements (known as advertorials). There is no limit to the places and methods of placing an advertisement. So expand your thinking and keep in mind that the topics discussed here apply to any form, venue, or manifestation of advertisement.

Advertising is different than public relations (PR) however. Often in college communications courses, advertising and PR are lumped together because they are both forms of mass communication. But under the law they are very different. For that reason, PR issues are not covered in this book. PR is not considered "paid" advertising.

Who Regulates Advertising?

The FTC is primarily responsible for regulating advertising, but there are other federal governmental bodies as well. The Federal Drug Administration (FDA) regulates advertising as it relates to food and drugs. The Bureau of Alcohol, Tobacco and Firearms (ATF) regulates advertising in regards to alcohol, tobacco products, and firearms. In fact, almost every federal government agency, from the Federal Communications Commission (FCC) to the Department of Housing and Urban Development (HUD) to the Consumer Financial Protection Bureau (CFPB), has some level of regulation that relates to advertising. There are also federal quasi-governmental agencies—including the U.S. Postal Service, as noted above—that have regulations regarding advertising.

In addition to the federal government, each state government has regulations that often parallel the federal level.

Finally, the courts regulate advertising. Through their interpretation of legislation and the establishment of precedent, the state and federal court system is possibly the largest player in regulating the practice of advertising. In fact, the governmental agencies listed above often go through the courts to enforce their decisions.

---

[1]Bold type indicates a term that appears in the glossary at the back of the book.

Many self-regulatory bodies also exist such as the Advertising Self-Regulatory Counsel (ASRC) and the National Advertising Division (NAD) created by the Better Business Bureau, as well as industry-specific organizations. Although these groups don't have the power of law, they are often provide persuasive guidance.

Ethics and Advertising

There is no discussion of ethics in this book. I've kept ethics out of this volume for a reason. Ethics is about what you *should* do, and the law is about what you *must* do. Those are very different things. Ethics are defined as moral principles governing a person's or group's behavior. Ethics concerns itself with the basic concepts and fundamental principles of decent human conduct. Ethics are subjective, flexible, and malleable. Ethics are about values and behavior. The law, on the other hand, is defined and codified.

Let's say a woman asks me if she looks good in her recently-purchased dress. I reply "yes, you look beautiful" when I really *don't* think it makes her look beautiful. Was I being unethical by lying to her? Yes, because morally, I should have told the truth. But I lied so her feelings wouldn't be hurt (at least that's how I justify it in my mind . . . yet another ethical issue). However, let's say I persuade her to take off her new dress so she can try on another one that I tell her she'll look even more beautiful in, and then I sell the original dress to someone else. Now I've broken the law; it's called conversion, or the civil form of theft. In this book, I confine the discussion to the law and legal aspects of advertising.

The Creation of the Federal Trade Commission

The FTC was conceived by Congress in 1914 to enforce the country's faltering antitrust laws. Ironically, the first two cases it heard involved false advertising: *FTC v. Circle Cilk,* 1 F.T.C. 13 (1916) and *FTC v. Abbott,* 1 F.T.C. 16 (1916). The only intent of the FTC at that time was to preserve fair competition between businesses by preventing restraint of trade—that is, such acts as creating a monopoly, which reduce or eliminate competition. Although this concerned only how businesses dealt with each other, in essence, the Federal Trade Commission Act protected consumers because it protected sellers in their dealings with each other. This was an indirect consumer benefit at best.

Since its establishment, the scope of the FTC has been enlarged with the adoption of the Wheeler-Lea Amendments (52 Stat. 11) in 1938. These brought direct protection for the consumer into the picture by modifying the authority of the FTC. The commission was originally authorized to regulate "unfair methods of competition in commerce." The Wheeler-Lea Amendments, however, added to this definition the phrase ". . . and unfair or deceptive acts or practices in commerce," thus expanding the act's coverage to consumers, as well as to competitors. As a result, the emphasis shifted toward protecting the consumer against injury. This has been extended even further with the enactment of the FTC Improvement Act in 1975. We'll examine this act in more detail in chapters 2 and 3.

In 1962, President John F. Kennedy gave a special message to the Congress on the importance of protecting the consumer interest (88th Cong., 1st Sess., pt. 1, at 465 (1963)). He stated that every person, as a consumer, had four rights: To be informed; to be safe; to have a choice; and to be heard. And he promoted legislation to protect these rights.

This sparked the modern consumer movement. Since that time, major new legislation and amendments to prior regulation have been enacted. The FTC and the courts have dramatically increased their efforts to protect the consumer and to place him on equal ground with the advertiser.

The Long Arm of the FTC

The FTC, as a federal organization, is assigned the task of policing advertising on a national level under Section 5 of the act. As a result, Section 5 only covers advertising that promotes products involving interstate commerce—transactions between one state and another. The advertiser must realize, however, that he is not safe from the FTC if his products are sold only in his own state. Courts are broadly interpreting the act to also bring intrastate activities within the authority of the FTC. This means that if any part or ingredient of the product was manufactured or purchased out of state, the courts consider interstate commerce to be involved; therefore, the product and business falls within the control of the federal act.

The FTC's influence reaches into state activities in another way. Most states have laws that carry the same implications as the federal act. These are known as "Little FTC Acts" and Uniform Deceptive Acts and Practices Acts (UDAP), and are discussed in chapter 3. In fact, many of these state **statutes** direct the state courts to be guided by FTC decisions.

Disclosure of Information

An obvious element in creating advertising is determining what to say in an ad. The advertiser must determine which of all the facts and points about a product should be featured in the limited space of an ad. Generally, regulation of advertising addresses the availability of information and how it is presented. Enough information should be made available to the consumer for him to make an informed purchasing decision— one in which he gets everything he bargained for, without surprise or deception.

In recent years, legislation has required that accurate information be disclosed in many areas of the marketplace, including the durability of light bulbs, octane ratings for gasoline, mileage-per-gallon statistics for new automobiles, care labeling of all textile wearing apparel, many telemarketing activities, and the Internet. The list continues to grow.

The way in which the advertiser provides information and the relevance of that information are areas that must be carefully considered. Because of the competitive nature of the market system in the United States, every advertiser tries to show his product in the best possible light. As everyone in advertising knows, a good ad demonstrates the product's strengths while playing down its weaknesses. But when the strengths are distorted or when significant weaknesses are either played down or ignored altogether, a deception can be created.

Although it may be required, information disclosure creates certain problems simply by the nature of the marketplace. Well-established manufacturers may tend to avoid disclosing too much product information in their advertising for fear of opening opportunities for new competitors to enter or expand their market. An example of this situation is found in the history of the gasoline industry. Many years ago, gasoline manufacturers attempted to avoid disclosing gasoline octane formulation because this would have highlighted the fact that ratings of high-priced brands were substantially the same as those of low-priced, unadvertised brands. Since the survival of the small independent manufacturers depended largely on their ability to maintain a cost advantage, they could not have easily undertaken expensive advertising campaigns to inform consumers about comparative octane ratings.

In other product areas, information disclosure may create an industry-wide disadvantage for all sellers. A good example was the resistance in past years to an intensive advertising campaign promoting the smoking of low tar and nicotine cigarettes as a way to reduce health hazards. This would have obviously played up the fact that smoking any cigarette creates health problems. There was an obvious reluctance on the part of cigarette manufacturers to do this because total cigarette sales would suffer as a result.

Even after scientific evidence proved that smoking was harmful, advertisers of both low and high tar cigarettes played down negative comparison claims to avoid negative reactions toward other brands in their product lines. In fact, aggressive marketing of low tar, low nicotine brands has only recently occurred as a result of increased health issues and government pressure.

In December of 1970, cigarette manufacturers responded to threatened action by the government by voluntarily including the government test results for tar and nicotine contents in their advertisements. Soon after, television advertising of cigarettes ended. Cigarette advertising has come under intense pressure in recent years. We'll discuss cigarette, as well as alcohol, advertising and related issues in detail in chapter 13.

Another problem in gathering and disclosing accurate product information is the extreme expense, especially in certain industries. For example, technical data such as chemical formulas for over-the-counter (OTC) drugs probably have no meaning to the average consumer. Yet the cost of providing this information could, for many manufacturers, be prohibitive.

Unfairness Violations

In contrast to straight deception, the FTC has developed a category of unfairness violations. Unfairness takes into account whether a practice, which is not considered unlawful, offends public policy as established by statute, **common law**, or otherwise. A practice is also considered unfair if it is immoral, unethical, oppressive, or unscrupulous, or causes substantial injury to consumers, competitors, or other business people. This gives the FTC room to maneuver. It allows the commission to pursue activities that it couldn't under the principle of straight deception.

As the FTC has expanded the unfairness concept in recent years, it has determined that there are certain types of advertisements that can be considered nondeceptive, yet still be unfair. These include claims made without prior substantiation, claims which exploit vulnerable groups like children and the elderly, and where the advertiser fails to provide consumers with certain information about competing products. We will discuss unfairness issues in more detail in chapter 2.

Crime and Punishment: Deceptive Advertising

A major area of development since the advent of federal regulation of advertising involves sanctions for deceptive claims. Early on, the standard remedy for deceptive advertising was a **cease-and-desist order**. This consisted of an order to stop the action and not continue with the deceptive practice. Today, however, violation of the commission's cease-and-desist order can be quite expensive.

The original cease-and-desist order proved to be grossly inadequate. Advertisers, as well as their advertising agencies, routinely violated the law and went virtually unpunished, or more accurately, unnoticed. Advertisers were taking a calculated risk that the chance of being detected and ultimately prosecuted was extremely small, given the limited resources of the FTC and the tremendous amount of advertising that the commission was required to review.

However, in the years since, efforts by the FTC have focused on eliminating the gap in enforcement of sanctions for deceptive advertising violations. One development involves corrective advertising orders. These direct the guilty advertiser to spend a specific percentage of its future advertising budget to inform the public as to the false claim that was originally made. The reasoning behind corrective advertising was that it provided a way of dissipating the effects of a previously misleading advertisement since the original ad that misled could not be removed or discounted from the minds of the consumer. Yet, it could be counteracted (or at least neutralized) if the original deceiver was required to disclose information to "properly" inform the consumer. It was hoped that this corrective ad would offset the original inaccurate impression.

The price advertisers must pay under this sanction can be quite severe if they are found to have used misleading or deceptive advertising. For example, the manufacturer of Ocean Spray Cranberry Juice Cocktail was required to devote 25 percent of the company's advertising budget for one year to informing the public of a previous deception (Ocean Spray Cranberry, Inc., 80 F.T.C. 975 (1971)). The makers of Profile bread were required to expend 25 percent of their advertising budget for one year toward advertisements stating: "Profile bread will not engender weight loss," contrary to the claims of its previous advertising (ITT Continental Baking Co., 79 F.T.C. 248 (1971)).

In 1975 the Commission proceeded against Warner-Lambert and the advertising of its product Listerine mouthwash in: *Warner-Lambert Co.* (1973-1976 Transfer Binder) Trade Reg. Rep. (CCH) & 21, 066 (F.T.C. 1975), appeal docketed, No. 76-1138 (D.C. Cir., filed Feb. 13, 1976). Listerine's advertising had claimed that the product could prevent colds because it killed germs associated with colds. This was an unsubstantiated claim, which left an inaccurate message with the consumer. This case was the last time in which the Commission imposed the remedy of corrective advertising for the next twenty-five years.

This sanction lay unused since 1975, until 1999. The FTC imposed this sanction on Novartis Corporation (*Novartis Corporation et al.*, Docket No. 9279 (1999)) for making the unsubstantiated claim that their Doan's analgesic product was superior to other OTC analgesics in treating back pain. Corrective advertising is intended to prevent the harm to consumers and competition that is caused when a false belief engendered by prior deceptive advertising lingers. Novartis made an implied superior efficacy claim for Doan's through short television advertisements that have not been disseminated since May 1996. The Commission concluded that these advertisements caused a false superior efficacy belief that has lingered and is likely to continue to linger until the corrective advertising provision terminates in July 2000 or beyond.

Comparative Advertising

Other considerations for the advertiser lie in the area of **comparative advertising**. One form of this occurs when manufacturers go head-to-head to challenge each other's claims. Specific comparative advertising of products, if inaccurate, tends to open up the challenger to the possibility of a civil lawsuit or FTC intervention based on **deceptive advertising** practices.

Comparative advertising regulation stems basically from the Lanham Trademark Act of 1946, (15 USC, Section 1125a) Section 43(a). This Act allows a remedy for people or companies "likely to be damaged" by "false descriptions or representations" regarding comparisons of products or services. In other words, when Company X publishes an advertisement that compares its product to Company Y's product, and that ad proves to be untrue, Company X can be held liable.

Comparative advertising litigation concerns situations where a company implied a superiority of its own or an inferiority of the competitor's product. A good example of this can be found in *Smith* v. *Chanel, Inc.*, 402 F.2d 562 (9th Cir. 1968). In this case, the perfume manufacturer Smith claimed in an advertisement that its version of Chanel perfume was "equal to the original." That claim was found by the court to be false, and under the Lanham Act, Smith was held liable.

In situations where the comparative ad claim does not fall under the federal Lanham Act, **remedies** are available under state law as well. False statements of this nature may well be actionable under laws against unfair competition or under tort remedies of disparagement or libel. We will discuss the Lanham Act and its relation to advertising claims more thoroughly in chapter 6.

Advertising Industry Self-Regulation

Consumer abuse or exploitation from false, misleading, or deceptive advertising doesn't necessarily have to be controlled by the government alone. Deceptive advertising may also be controlled by the advertising industry through self-regulation. We look at these issues in more depth in later chapters.

Self-regulation of advertising can be accomplished through a number of avenues. The various industry trade associations have established codes of conduct or ethics. Within the advertising industry such agencies as the American Association of Advertising Agencies (AAAA), the American Society of Magazine Photographers (ASMP), the American Advertising Federation (AAF), the Graphic Artists Guild (GAG), the Screen Actors Guild (SAG), and the American Federation of Television and Radio Artists (AFTRA) have specific conduct requirements for their members.

In addition, the Advertising Self-Regulatory Council (ASRC), a creation of the National Advertising Review Board (NARB) inquiries into complaints, evaluates them on their merits, and negotiates agreements. The board can also establish an arbitration panel to handle appeals. Finally, the NAD/NARB can refer what it considers to be unlawful advertising to government agencies for action.

Forum to Challenge Deceptive Marketing

The ASRC is a forum administered by the NARB. Created by the advertising industry and the National Better Business Bureau to fight deceptive advertising and marketing practices. Since its inception in 2004, the ASRC/NARB has become an attractive alternative to challenge advertising and marketing practices that are not in compliance with the law.

The ASRC monitors and evaluates the truth and accuracy of product claims contained in direct response advertising. However, the ASRC interprets its **jurisdiction** broadly so that it includes any commercial message disseminated through any electronic media that: (1) prompts a consumer to make a purchase, or (2) requests the submission of additional information about the consumer. For example, the ASRC frequently reviews claims made through email or pop-up ads. The ASRC also reviews claims that are present in other traditional forms of media, such as print advertising, provided that they are related to the claims in an electronic media.

An ASRC review generally mirrors those of the ASRC's sister organizations, the NAD, the Children's Advertising Review Unit (CARU), and the Electronic Retailing Self-Regulation Program (ERSP) which oversees electronic retailing and direct response advertising. Consumers, trade associations, competitors, or the ASRC, acting on its own behalf, may initiate a review.

Once initiated, the ASRC relies heavily on standard advertising and marketing laws and principles to evaluate a claim or practice. Both from the FTC perspective, as well as federal and state false advertising cases.

While ASRC decisions are nonbinding, the organization commands a high degree of voluntary compliance. One current estimate places compliance with ASRC decisions at 90 percent. Such a high level of voluntary compliance is not surprising since the ASRC reserves the right to refer noncompliant parties to a relevant governmental agency, such as the FTC.

Media Regulation

The television networks also have rules about what they will and will not accept for commercials. Network clearance departments set standards that commercials must meet in order to be aired. These departments pass judgment on TV commercials, and will be discussed in more detail in chapter 13.

In his classic book on the ad agency business, *From Those Wonderful Folks Who Gave You Pearl Harbor* (1970), Jerry Della Femina says this about censorship (now referred to as "network clearance"): "One of the biggest problems that all agencies have is the headache of [network] censorship. There is simply no reason for it. Censorship, any kind of censorship, is pure whim and fancy. It's one guy's idea of what is right for him. It's based on everything arbitrary. There are no rules, no standards, no laws."

In many instances, censorship can get out of control. An example is the time the Ted Bates agency produced a TV commercial for a toy company. The spot showed a little boy playing with the toy machine gun. The scene was shot on a mound of dirt with the kid blasting away at whomever it was we were blasting away at in the late 60s—Vietcong maybe.

"This commercial is not acceptable," said the network censor. The agency was sure that the rejection had something to do with the portrayal of war and violence with children. Not so. "Well, it's obvious that the mound of dirt is part of the game," said the censor. "The kid will obviously think that it's part of the game since it's on the screen for the entire commercial, and the kid spends his time on the top of the mound of dirt." The network, fearing that kids would expect to get a mound of dirt with the toy machine gun, would approve the spot only if it ran with a line of copy on the screen telling kids that the mound of dirt was not included. When the agency tried to explain that a child wouldn't actually believe that the dirt came with the gun, the censor replied, "It's not the five-year-olds we're worried about. It's the one- and two-year-olds who might be swayed." The irony was that the network censor wasn't concerned with the five-year-old who might be deceived, but rather about younger children who couldn't read anyway.

The smaller independent stations also tend to follow the lead of the networks. If the networks won't clear the spot, then the local stations probably won't run it either.

Print media publishers have their own codes as well. Some years ago, I produced an ad for vitamins. The ad was to run in a series of health and fitness magazines. One of these rejected the ad because they had limits as to the levels of each ingredient, for example, if a multivitamin contained 500 mg of vitamin C, the maximum that could be claimed was 300 mg, even if the product contained a higher level. We had to produce a special ad for that magazine showing lower levels of the vitamins.

Factor into this the new player; social media. Yahoo, Google, AOL, Facebook, Twitter, and others are all technology media companies. They certainly have restrictions as to the content they will permit to be run. We will explore the nuances of the Internet in chapter 5.

While these self-regulation efforts don't have the force of law behind them, they have become an increasingly evident. They do place additional burdens on advertisers, and they are gaining in power. It's only when these efforts get overly aggressive and arbitrary that they lose credibility. Yet these are issues with which the advertiser must deal.

David versus Goliath: Consumer Action

It is also possible for consumer interests to be protected directly by the consumers themselves. The consumer can sue an advertiser directly, although this rarely occurs. The rare consumer suit against an advertiser typifies a larger pattern in our legal system—one where consumers find themselves powerless to take advantage of their legitimate legal rights. Most people simply cannot afford the often-prohibitive expense of a lawsuit, especially when battling the virtually unlimited resources of a major company.

In most cases, the deceptive practice involved a purchase of such small cost that it makes no practical sense to consider retaining an attorney to pursue the matter through the courts, other than for reasons of principle. Although fighting for a principle can be rewarding, it can also be very expensive.

The extent of consumer injury from a deceptive advertisement is difficult to prove, and the extent of the damage even more so. Unlike the FTC—who doesn't need to show that damage actually occurred (only a likelihood to deceive), the individual consumer has different burdens of proof in order to win an award. This adds to the complication and expense of a court battle.

As an alternative, class action suits are an available option. Class action suits have restrictions and minimum requirements that must be met in order to qualify as a "class." In addition to the federal courts, opportunities for consumers to pursue **class actions** in state courts exist as well. What this all boils down to is that even when consumers are aware that their rights have been violated—and that retribution is available on their behalf—they are often frustrated by the obstacles that lie in their path.

Finally, consumer protection organizations are a major force for advertisers to contend with in today's environment. As these organizations grow in strength, so does their power to effect change. The group Mothers Against Drunk Driving, for example, has had a tremendous impact on alcohol advertising practices in the United States.

Advertising's Role in Products Liability

There is another area of real concern to advertisers. Consumers are recovering substantial **damages** in products **liability** litigation. These are actions to recover damages when a defective product causes injury. For example, a car is intended to be safe to drive under normal conditions. If a consumer buys the car and gets injured when the car flips over after hitting a pothole, **products liability** may be involved, and the consumer can sue for damages. It may not be apparent how products liability is related to advertising though, but it is and advertising has begun to play a large role in products liability lawsuits. Product advertising can considerably influence liability. The problem occurs when the message created in an advertisement may not be supported by the product's actual performance. Courts assume that a product will perform as claimed. So does the consumer. When it doesn't and damage results, the advertising may be used as "evidence" in showing the advertiser's failure to "live up to" the product's claim.

The many areas of law that fall under "products liability" create an arsenal for the consumer who has been damaged from use of the product. As you can well imagine, cases of this nature can be a tremendous financial burden on an advertiser and its agency. chapter 8 is devoted exclusively to the subject of products liability and advertising's impact on it.

Other Areas of Law that Affect Advertising

There are many different areas of law beyond those obvious ones of false, misleading, and deceptive advertising. These include First Amendment issues of free speech and commercial. Copyright comes into play in areas of usage and rights of photography and other artwork in advertisements. Trademark laws can become a factor anytime a competitor's name or logo are used in an ad. The rights to privacy and publicity of individuals become involved when images of people are used in ads. And specific problems of advertising concerning warranties, guarantees, and contests exist. We explore these areas later in the book.

The relationship between an advertiser and his advertising agency is another area of concern. A client/agency relationship is one where an individual or company makes use of the services of another to accomplish things that could not be accomplished alone. When such a relationship is created—whether intentionally or implied by the law—it invokes a well-developed area of law. The law defines the rights and liabilities of the parties, their relation to each other, and their relation to third parties. Therefore, we have seen an increasing number of court actions in which the advertising agency is brought in with the advertiser and held jointly liable. In most cases, each party is liable for the actions of the other. The client–agency relationship will be discussed in detail in chapter 4.

And the newest area of regulation involves the Internet. The Internet is a new monster that grows and morphs almost daily. It has presented many new challenges to the legal community for one simple reason. Because of its nature, the Internet can (and does) change at will. By the time a situation arises, complaints are filed and a court hears the case . . . the world wide web has changed. In many situations the courts are ruling on conditions that don't exist at the time the rulings are handed down.

The Internet also poses situations that are, in many cases, very different from those of other areas of marketing and advertising. While the Internet, and all it brings with it, is a media as much as it is a technology, draws the attention of all areas of law. It has its own unique situations that the legal system has tried to keep pace with. As a result of this complexity, chapter 5 is devoted exclusively to the Internet.

Commercial Speech under the First Amendment

Although it has not always been that way, the Supreme Court now recognizes that "commercial speech" (advertising falls into this category) is protected under the First Amendment to the U.S. Constitution. This means, among other things, that certain advertising of products and services cannot be banned by the government. Today, advertising and other forms of commercial speech are still not held in the same high regard as political or religious speech. Yet, the good news is that because of this change, fewer restrictions are being placed on advertisers. Those restrictions that are in place, or are considered, continue to cause debate on First Amendment issues.

The New and Improved Commercial Speech Doctrine Until 1975 commercial speech was virtually unprotected by the First Amendment. However, in that year the

Supreme Court overturned a criminal conviction for violation of a certain statute on the books in Virginia making it a misdemeanor to distribute any publication that encouraged or promoted an abortion in Virginia. The case arose when a newspaper published an ad for legal abortions in New York.

The argument was that the ad was unprotected because it was a commercial message. However, the court held that the message that legal abortions were available in New York "did more than simply propose a commercial transaction. It contained factual material of clear 'public interest.'" The court continued by saying that the ad related to abortions, a service with which, generally, the state couldn't interfere.

Because of the Supreme Court's 1973 decision in *Roe* v. *Wade,* 410 U.S. 113, 93 S.Ct. 705, 35 L.Ed. 2d 147 (1973), the Virginia court did not need to decide the "precise extent to which the First Amendment permits regulation of advertising that is related to activities the State may legitimately regulate or even prohibit." The goal of protecting commercial speech was to provide the consumer with the same access to information as his or her access to political and religious debate. And this was good due the availability of information it provided consumers in the marketplace.

A year later the Supreme Court clearly settled the issue of whether there is an exception to First Amendment protection for commercial speech in a case involving a woman who was required to take prescription drugs on a daily basis. The Court ruled that commercial speech is protected under the First Amendment.

A Virginia law stated that a pharmacist licensed in Virginia would be guilty of unprofessional conduct if he "publishes, advertises or promotes, directly or indirectly, in any manner whatsoever, any amount, price, fee, premium, discount, rebate or credit terms . . . for any drugs which may be dispensed only by prescription."

The position was that prescription drug users would greatly benefit if advertising were allowed. The Virginia State Board of Pharmacy, however, argued that advertising prescription drug prices was not protected by the First Amendment because it involved commercial speech.

The Supreme Court, in *Virginia State Board of Pharmacy* v. *Virginia Citizens Consumer Council, Inc.* 425 U.S. 748, 96 S.Ct. 1817, 48 L.Ed. 2d 346 (1976), decided that advertising is valuable in that it provides information about who is producing and selling what product, why, and at what price. "So long as we preserve a predominantly free enterprise economy, the allocation of our resources in large measure will be made through numerous private economic decisions." The Court maintained that it was in the public's interest to aid in those decisions by being knowledgeable and well informed. "To this end, the free flow of commercial information is indispensable."

The Court went on to say ". . . that people will perceive their own best interests if only they are well enough informed, and that the best means to that end is to open the channels of communication rather than to close them." The end result was that Virginia could set whatever professional standards it wanted for its pharmacists; however, "it may not do so by keeping the public in ignorance of the entirely lawful terms that competing pharmacists are offering."

Limiting Commercial Speech: The Central Hudson Case While First Amendment protection now extends to commercial speech, it still earns less protection than other forms of expression like personal, political, and religious speech. The government can still limit First Amendment protection of some forms of commercial speech. In 1980 the Supreme Court created a four-part test to be used to determine if a certain restriction on commercial speech is allowed.

The New York Public Service Commission ordered electric utilities in the state to cease all advertising that "promot[ed] the use of electricity." This was put into place because New York did not have a sufficient fuel supply to meet the demands of the 1973–1974 winter, thanks in large part to the OPEC embargo.

Three years later the fuel shortage eased, and the commission proposed to continue the ban on promotional advertising. The Central Hudson Gas & Electric Corporation opposed the ban on First Amendment grounds.

The court in *Central Hudson Gas & Electric Corp.* v. *Public Service Commission*, 447 U.S. 557, 100 S.Ct. 2343, 65 L.Ed. 2d 341 (1980), recognized that commercial speech was entitled to First Amendment protection in some cases. However, the U.S. Constitution, the Court reasoned, affords less protection to commercial speech than to other constitutionally guaranteed forms of expression.

The First Amendment's protection of commercial speech is intended to allow and encourage the forms of advertising that provide consumer information. On the other hand, the Court ruled that there is no constitutional reason to support commercial messages that do not accurately inform the public about lawful activities. As a result, the government may ban communications that are more likely to deceive the public than to inform it. Governments may also ban commercial speech regarding an illegal activity (box 1.4).

> **Box 1.4**   **The Central Hudson Test**

The Court in the *Central Hudson* case established a four-part test for determining restrictions on commercial speech. This is known as the Central Hudson Test that courts follow:

- First, determine if the message qualifies for protection under the First Amendment, in that it must involve a legal activity and not be misleading;

- Second, determine whether the government's interest in restricting the commercial speech is substantial;

- Third, if the first two points are met, the courts must then determine that regulation of the message directly supports the government's interest; and

- Finally, the courts must determine whether regulating the message is more extensive than is necessary to further the government's interests.

The Court held that both the conservation of energy and the state's desire to keep rates fair both represented valid governmental interests.

The Court also looked at whether the commission's complete suppression of speech, which would ordinarily be protected by the First Amendment, was too extensive and went further than necessary to justify the state's interest in energy conservation.

The commission's order covered all promotional advertising regardless of its impact on overall energy consumption. Yet, this rationale did not justify suppressing information about electric devices or services that would not increase total energy use. The commission could have limited the format and content of Central Hudson's advertising and required ads to include information about the relative efficiency and expense of the service. The Court reasoned that a complete ban on advertising violated the First Amendment.

The Puerto Rico Casino Case With the Puerto Rico casino case, First Amendment protection for advertising took one step backward, temporarily. This was the first time a court upheld a government's ban on truthful advertising of a legal product. The Games of Chance Act of 1948, Act No. 221, May 15, 1948, P.R. Laws Ann., Tit. 15, §71 (1972), was a law in Puerto Rico that legalized certain forms of casino gambling. The intent of the law was simply to promote tourism. In addition, the law prohibited casinos from advertising or promoting themselves to the public of Puerto Rico.

This law also banned casinos from using the word "casino" in matchbooks, inter-office and external correspondence, invoices, brochures, menus, elevator cards, lobby cards, flyers, telephone books, directories, lighters, envelopes, napkins, glasses, plates, banners, paper holders, pencils, bulletin boards, or any other hotel object that could be accessible to the public.

The Condado Holiday Inn Hotel and Sands Casino filed suit claiming that the law suppressed commercial speech by violating the First Amendment.

Using the *Central Hudson* test, the U.S. Supreme Court ruled in 1986 that the Puerto Rico law did not violate the First Amendment. The government of Puerto Rico had an important interest in restricting the ads because it would reduce the demand for casino gambling by the residents of Puerto Rico. This constituted a substantial governmental interest.

The Court also found that this view directly advanced the government's interest, saying, "In our view, the legislature's separate classification of casino gambling, for purposes of the advertising ban, satisfies the third step of the *Central Hudson* analysis."

The fourth step of the *Central Hudson* test was satisfied because the ban was no more extensive than necessary to further the government's interest.

But what about cases in which the Supreme Court had struck down a ban on any "advertisement or display" of contraceptives and the one we just looked at in which it reversed a criminal conviction based on the advertisement of an abortion clinic? There was a difference between those cases and the casino case. In the two cases involving contraceptives and abortion the promoted activities were constitutionally protected and could not have been prohibited by the government. However, in the casino case, "the Puerto Rico Legislature surely could have prohibited casino gambling by the residents of Puerto Rico altogether." Gambling is not protected as a constitutional right. So, in the Court's opinion, "the greater power to completely ban casino gambling necessarily includes the lesser power to ban advertising of casino gambling."

The casino case, *Posadas de Puerto Rico Associates* v. *Tourism Company of Puerto Rico*, 478 U.S. 328, 106 S.Ct. 2968, 92 L.Ed. 2d 266 (1986), was heavily criticized, especially within the advertising community. This permitted virtually unlimited government regulation of commercial speech. This would all change in 1996, however.

The Liquormart Case One of the most significant changes in connection with the *Central Hudson* test addressed in a recent case concerned interpretation of the third and fourth elements of the test. These elements cover the extent to which the government must show that its restriction of the speech directly advances its interests and that the restriction is not more extensive than necessary.

In 1996 the Supreme Court reversed the position it held in *Posadas*. In *44 Liquormart, Inc.* v. *Rhode Island*, 517 U.S. 484, 116 S.Ct. 1495 (1996), the Court found that *Posadas* "clearly erred in concluding that it was 'up to the legislature' to choose suppression over a less speech-restrictive policy. The *Posadas* majority's conclusion on that point cannot be reconciled with the unbroken line of prior cases striking down similarly broad regulations on truthful, nonmisleading advertising when non-speech-related alternatives were available."

The First Amendment makes it clear that the Constitution presumes that efforts to regulate speech are more dangerous than efforts to regulate conduct. That reasoning is consistent with the role that the free flow of information plays in our society. The First Amendment, then, clarifies that the government may not suppress speech as easily as it may suppress conduct. Furthermore, restrictions on speech cannot be treated as simply another way for the government to achieve its desires.

Complaints from competitors about an advertisement placed by 44 Liquormart in a Rhode Island newspaper in 1991 led to this litigation. The ad did not state the price of any alcoholic beverages. In fact, it stated that "state law prohibits advertising liquor prices." The ad did, however, state the low prices at which other items were being offered. It identified many brands of packaged liquor and included the word "WOW" in big letters next to pictures of bottles of vodka and rum. Based on this implied reference to bargain prices for liquor, the Rhode Island Liquor Control Administrator assessed a $400 fine. The case ultimately ended up at the Supreme Court.

In *44 Liquormart*, the Supreme Court overturned the Rhode Island statute that banned all advertising of liquor prices outside a beverage store's sales premises. In 1956 the Rhode Island Legislature had enacted two separate prohibitions against advertising the retail price of alcoholic beverages. The first prohibits vendors from "advertising in any manner whatsoever" the price of any alcoholic beverage offered for sale in the State (other than displayed with the merchandise within licensed premises and not visible from the street). The second statute applies to the Rhode Island news media. It does not allow the publication or broadcast of any advertisements—even those referring to sales in other States—that "make reference to the price of any alcoholic beverages."

The Court reasoned that the ban did not directly advance the state's interest in reducing alcohol consumption. The Court also reasoned that the state has the burden of justifying a complete ban on speech. A blanket ban on commercial speech is not valid unless the speech is deceptive or promotes an unlawful activity.

The Court went on to say: Advertising has been a part of our culture throughout our history. Even in colonial days, the public relied on "commercial speech" for vital information about the market. Early newspapers displayed advertisements for goods and services on their front pages, and town criers called out prices in public squares. Indeed, commercial messages played such a central role in public life prior to the Founding that Benjamin Franklin authored his early defense of a free press in support of his decision to print, of all things, an advertisement for voyages to Barbados.

In accord with the role that commercial messages have long played, the law has developed to ensure that advertising provides consumers with accurate information about the availability of goods and services. In the early years, the common law, and later, statutes, served the consumers' interest in the receipt of accurate information in the commercial market by prohibiting fraudulent and misleading advertising. It was not until the 1970s, however, that this Court held that the First Amendment protected the dissemination of truthful and nonmisleading commercial messages about lawful products and services.

It's important to understand that the Court did not modify the *Central Hudson* test, yet it examined its interpretation of the third and fourth elements of the test. The Court required Rhode Island to show that the advertising ban significantly reduced alcohol consumption. It couldn't because truthful, nonmisleading speech does not relate to consumer protection. The Court also required that the restriction, although not perfect, must be reasonable and narrowly tailored to advance the government's interest. In this case, the ban only provides ineffective or remote support for the government's interest.

The Court said: In evaluating the ban's effectiveness in advancing the State's interest, we note that a commercial speech regulation "may not be sustained if it provides only ineffective or remote support for the government's purpose."

For that reason, the State bears the burden of showing not merely that its regulation will advance its interest, but also that it will do so "to a material degree." The need for the State to make such a showing is particularly great given the drastic nature of its chosen means—the wholesale suppression of truthful, nonmisleading information. Accordingly, we must determine whether the State has shown that the price advertising ban will significantly reduce alcohol consumption.

The Court went on: As is evident, any conclusion that elimination of the ban would significantly increase alcohol consumption would require us to engage in the sort of "speculation or conjecture" that is an unacceptable means of demonstrating that a restriction on commercial speech directly advances the State's asserted interest. Such speculation certainly does not suffice when the State takes aim at accurate commercial information for paternalistic ends.

In essence, the complete ban on liquor price advertising imposed by Rhode Island restricted speech under the First Amendment. Because Rhode Island failed to carry its heavy burden of justifying its complete ban on price advertising, it violated the First Amendment.

The Greater New Orleans Gambling Case More recently, two federal appeals courts each came to different conclusions regarding the *Central Hudson* test after the decision in *44 Liquormart*. Both of these cases involved a federal law that bans broadcast advertising for casino gambling, even in states where the practice of gambling is legal. In 1998 the Fifth Circuit in *Greater New Orleans Broadcasting Assn. v. United States*, No. 94-30732, 1998 U.S. App. LEXIS 17608 (5th Cir., July 30, 1998), held that the law (18 U.S.C. § 1304) was constitutional.

In the first case the Fifth Circuit in *Greater New Orleans* upheld the federal law banning radio and television advertising for casino gambling. The primary concern of the Fifth Circuit in *Greater New Orleans* was the test for determining whether the advertising restriction advanced the government's asserted interest. After *44 Liquormart*, determining what level of proof is required to demonstrate that banning a particular commercial speech directly advances a state's interest is unclear.

Concerning *Central Hudson's* forth element, the justices analyzed more carefully whether the state's ban of commercial speech serves the government's interests without unduly limiting free speech.

The court held that section 1304 passed both tests. Section 1304 prohibited broadcast advertising of "any advertisement of or information concerning any lottery, gift enterprise, or similar scheme, offering prizes depending in whole or in part upon lot or on chance . . ." There are exemptions to section 1304, including: fishing contests, wagers on sporting events, state lotteries, Indian gambling of all types, and charitable lotteries.

The court determined that while section 1304 allowed broadcast advertising of Indian casino gambling, the ban on advertising by private casinos directly advanced the government's interest in discouraging public participation in commercial gambling.

The court also found that the ban on broadcast advertising supported the policy of states, including Texas, that did not permit casino gambling.

The court reasoned that: The government may legitimately distinguish among certain kinds of gambling for advertising purposes, determining that the social impact of activities such as state-run lotteries, Indian and charitable gambling include social benefits as well as costs and that these other activities often have dramatically different geographic scope. That the broadcast advertising ban in [section] 1304 directly advances the government's policies must be evident from the casinos' vigorous pursuit of litigation to overturn it.

On another related issue, the court also reasoned that the ban was not broader than necessary to control participation in casino gambling. The court said: "*44 Liquormart* does not disturb the series of decisions that has found a commonsense connection between promotional advertising and the stimulation of consumer demand for the products advertised."

Section 1304, please remember, was not a complete ban on advertising. Other media including newspapers, magazines, and outdoor billboards all remained as options. The court went on, "Section 1304 simply targets the powerful sensory appeal of gambling conveyed by television and radio, which are the most intrusive advertising media, and the most readily available to children." The court determined that a nationwide ban on radio and television advertising for casino gambling also served to protect those states that allow non-casino gambling. "*Central Hudson*, as applied after *44 Liquormart*, does not inhibit all legislative flexibility in confronting challenging social developments."

The Valley Broadcasting Case Contrast to *Greater New Orleans*, in 1998 the Ninth Circuit held the federal law unconstitutional in *Valley Broadcasting Co. v. United States*, 107 F.3d 1328 (9th Cir. 1997), cert. denied 140 L.Ed.2d 114, 118 S.Ct. 1050 (1998).

Here, the court held an advertising ban was unconstitutional since it did not directly advance the government's interests. The court relied primarily on the exceptions in section 1304 that expressly allowed broadcast advertising for Indian-operated casino gambling, as well as other local charitable gambling. The court found these points inconsistent with the government's asserted interest.

In this case the government asserted two interests: first, an interest in reducing public participation in commercial lotteries; second, an interest in protecting those states that chose not to permit casino gambling. Certain states policies against casino gambling were of substantial interest. To support this, the government provided evidence that casino gambling attracted organized crime.

And, since broadcasts from states that permit casino gambling could be seen by people in other states that prohibited casino gambling, non-casino states would have no effective means to control the viewing of these advertisements by their residents.

The court, however, found that the restriction did not advance the government's interests. Section 1304 allowed broadcast advertising for such activities as Indian casino gambling, charitable gambling, state-run lotteries, and fishing contests. The court noted that the government had articulated its interest in reducing public participation in all commercial lotteries. The court reasoned that "because section 1304 permits the advertising of commercial lotteries by not-for-profit organizations, governmental organizations and Indian tribes, it is impossible for it to materially discourage public participation in commercial lotteries. To use the language from *Rubin v. Coors Brewing Co.*, 115 S.Ct. 1585 (1995), '[t]here is little chance that [the challenged restriction] can directly and materially advance its aim, while other provisions of the same act directly undermine and counteract its effects.'"

Determining Commercial or Noncommercial Speech under the First Amendment

Commercial and noncommercial forms of speech are granted different degrees of protection under the First Amendment. While the courts are becoming more liberal in their granting First Amendment protection of commercial speech (advertising), more latitude is still given to noncommercial speech. So, it is important to understand which speech falls into the commercial speech arena.

In *Bad Frog Brewery Inc.* v. *New York State Liquor Authority,* 134 F.3d 87 (2d Cir. 1998), the Second Circuit held that a beer manufacturer's bottle label that showed a frog, well, "giving the finger" was commercial speech and thereby protected under the First Amendment.

Bad Frog is a Michigan corporation that manufactures and markets several different types of beer products under the "Bad Frog" trademark. This case centers around labels used by the company for Bad Frog Beer, Bad Frog Lemon Lager, and Bad Frog Malt Liquor. The labels include an illustration of a frog making "the finger" gesture that is regarded as an offensive insult (the gesture of the extended middle finger is said to have been first used by Diogenes to insult Demosthenes), conveying a message that the company itself has characterized as "traditionally . . . negative and nasty." Versions of the label feature slogans including "He just don't care," "An amphibian with an attitude," "Turning bad into good," and "The beer so good . . . it's bad." Another slogan, originally used, but now abandoned, was "He's mean, green and obscene."

The New York State Liquor Authority (NYSLA) tried to ban the use of the offensive label in New York. The court held that the NYSLA failed to establish that the state's interest in protecting children from vulgar and profane advertising would be advanced by the ban.

Bad Frog contended that its beer label was noncommercial speech and, thus, afforded full First Amendment protection. Bad Frog argued that its labels did not purport to convey commercial information, but rather, communicated a "joke." Thus, the labels should enjoy full First Amendment protection, rather than the somewhat reduced protection accorded commercial speech.

Bad Frog contended that: Marketing gimmicks for beer such as the "Budweiser Frogs," "Spuds Mackenzie," the "Bud-Ice Penguins," and the "Red Dog" of Red Dog Beer [are] virtually indistinguishable from the Plaintiff's frog, promote intemperate behavior in the same way that the Defendants have alleged Plaintiff's label would . . . [and therefore the] regulation of the Plaintiff's label will have no tangible effect on underage drinking or intemperate behavior in general.

However, the NYSLA argued that the labels conveyed no useful consumer information and should not be protected under the First Amendment.

After considering the Supreme Court's position with regard to commercial advertising, the Second Circuit ruled that Bad Frog's labels were, in fact, commercial speech. As a result, they were subject to the *Central Hudson* test. The court concluded that:

> The Supreme Court has not explicitly clarified whether commercial speech, such as a logo or a slogan that conveys no information, other than identifying the source of the product, but serves, to some degree, to "propose a commercial transaction" enjoys any First Amendment protection. The Court's opinion in *Posadas*, however, points in favor of protection.

Bad Frog's label attempts to function, like a trademark, to identify the source of the product. The picture on a beer bottle of a frog behaving badly is reasonably to be understood as attempting to identify to consumers a product of the Bad Frog Brewery. In addition, the label serves to propose a commercial transaction. Although the label communicates no information beyond the source of the product, we think that minimal information, conveyed in the context of a proposal of a commercial transaction, suffices to invoke the protections for commercial speech articulated in *Central Hudson.*

Bad Frog then argued that its labels deserved full First Amendment protection because their "proposal of a commercial transaction" was combined with political or social commentary. The court agreed that there were forms of speech that combined both commercial and noncommercial elements. Whether a communication that combined those elements would be considered commercial speech depended on:

- Whether the message was an advertisement;
- Whether the message made reference to a specific product; and
- Whether the sender of the message had an economic motivation for the communication.

Clearly, these three elements existed in the beer label. Clearly, the labels were advertisements motivated by a desire to sell the product to which the labels were attached.

The court said: We are unpersuaded by Bad Frog's attempt to separate the purported social commentary in the labels from the hawking of beer. Bad Frog's labels meet the three criteria identified in Bolger: the labels are a form of advertising, identify a specific product, and serve the economic interest of the speaker. Moreover, the purported noncommercial message is not so "inextricably intertwined" with the commercial speech as to require a finding that the entire label must be treated as "pure" speech. Even viewed generously, Bad Frog's labels at most "link a product to a current debate," which is not enough to convert a proposal for a commercial transaction into "pure" noncommercial speech.

We thus assess the prohibition of Bad Frog's labels under the commercial speech standards outlined in *Central Hudson*.

Well then, how does the *Central Hudson* test apply to *Bad Frog*? As we have already discussed, *Central Hudson* establishes the guidelines for determining the government's restrictions on commercial speech.

The court held that the Bad Frog labels involved legal activity and were not misleading. "The consumption of beer (at least by adults) is legal in New York, and the labels cannot be said to be deceptive, even if they are offensive." The interests asserted by the NYSLA in protecting children from vulgar and profane advertising and promoting moderate and responsible use of alcohol among those above the legal drinking age and abstention among those below the drinking age were found to be substantial state interests.

The state failed, however, to show that a ban of the Bad Frog labels directly advanced its interests. "To meet the 'direct advancement' requirement, a state must demonstrate that the 'harms it recites are real and that its restriction will in fact alleviate them to a material degree.'" In fact, banning the Bad Frog labels would have made only a minute contribution to the state's interest in preventing exposure of children to vulgar advertising. The court stated:

> In this case, NYSLA endeavors to advance the state interest in preventing exposure of children to vulgar displays by taking only the limited step of barring such displays from the labels of alcoholic beverages. In view of the wide currency of vulgar displays throughout contemporary society, including comic books targeted directly at children, barring such displays from labels for alcoholic beverages cannot realistically be expected to reduce children's exposure to such displays to any significant degree.

A complete ban on the Bad Frog labels was also not narrowly tailored to achieve the state's asserted interest. Bad Frog suggested several less intrusive alternatives such as "the restriction of advertising to point-of-sale locations; limitations on billboard advertising; restrictions on over-the-air-advertising; and segregation of the product in the store." The court agreed that a complete ban on the labels was overbroad and not reasonable with the goal of protecting minors. The court stated, "NYSLA's complete statewide ban on the use of Bad Frog's labels lacks a 'reasonable fit' with the state's asserted interest in shielding minors from vulgarity, and NYSLA gave inadequate **consideration** to alternatives to this blanket suppression of commercial speech. [T]he government may not reduce the adult population . . . to reading only what is fit for children."

The court concluded that the NYSLA was prohibited from rejecting Bad Frog's label.

The First Amendment, Public Forum, and Prior Restraint Issues

Two other recent cases focused on the question of whether a government agency (in these cases, city public transportation authorities) had created a "public forum" for paid advertising on its city buses and stations. The cases further questioned whether restrictions on the content of those messages violated the First Amendment.

The Mayor Rudy Case In New York, an advertisement ran on the sides of MTA buses that featured the *New York Magazine* logo along with the headline, "Possibly the only good thing in New York Rudy hasn't taken credit for."

In 1998, in *New York Magazine* v. *Metropolitan Transportation Authority*, 136 F.3d 123 (2d Cir. 1998), the court held that the New York Metropolitan Transportation Authority's (MTA) refusal to continue to display on its buses a *New York Magazine* advertisement that referred to then Mayor Giuliani of New York City by his first name was an unlawful **prior restraint**.

New York Magazine had contracted with the MTA to place the ad on the side of MTA buses. Sometime later, the MTA removed the ad after receiving a complaint from the mayor's office, objecting to the use of the mayor's name to promote a commercial product, and claiming that the ad violated the mayor's rights under section 50 of the New York Civil Rights Law (N.Y.Civ.Rights Law § 50 (McKinney 1997)). Section 50 prohibited the use, for advertising purposes, of the name, portrait, or picture of a living person without their **consent**. However, *New York Magazine* argued that the ad was protected under the First Amendment.

A federal district court granted *New York Magazine* a preliminary **injunction** prohibiting the MTA from removing the advertisements. The district court held that the ad was commercial speech and that the buses constituted a public forum. The district court also held that the government's interest in upholding section 50 was not directly advanced by removing the ad. The appellate court affirmed the preliminary injunction on the grounds that the MTA's standards in reviewing the advertisement for violation of section 50 constituted an unconstitutional prior restraint on speech.

The MTA was a public benefit corporation created by New York state law that owned and operated the majority of public buses in New York City. The MTA raised revenues for its operation, in part, by leasing advertising space on the buses.

The MTA had adopted standards that governed its acceptance of advertising on its buses. The standards prohibited the display of advertising that "violates New York Civil Rights Law section 50." Section 50 provides in part: "A person, firm or corporation that uses for advertising purposes, or for purposes of trade, the name, portrait, or picture of any living person without having first obtained the written consent of such person . . . is guilty of a misdemeanor."

One issue here is that of public forum. A designated public forum is one opened by the government for use by the public for expressive activity. The court held that since the MTA (operated by the government) allowed both political and commercial advertising on its buses, it was the MTA's intent to create a public forum. Regulations based on the content of the message in a designated public forum are allowed only if narrowly drawn to support a compelling governmental interest. The purpose behind the MTA's regulations, in this case, showed that the MTA was acting as a regulatory agency. The court stated:

> [T]he MTA's exclusion is based on a general interest in upholding the law, and a corollary interest in avoiding litigation. The MTA articulates its interest as "seeing to it that commercial advertising appearing on buses complies with section 50, the statutory codification of the rights of privacy and publicity." There is no commercial reason why MTA has any special interest in the policy behind section 50; MTA's interest is only the interest in upholding the law because it is the law.

Given that MTA's standards allow both commercial and political speech, and given that the standard that MTA used to justify discontinuing the advertisement supports a legal characterization of MTA's action as regulatory, we conclude that the advertising space on the outside of MTA buses is a designated public forum.

Another issue in this case involves that of prior restraint. Having determined that the MTA intended to designate its advertising space as a public forum, the court reviewed MTA actions as an exercise of a prior restraint. The court held that the MTA's review of an advertisement for potential violation of section 50 was a prior restraint on speech that was more extensive than necessary to serve MTA's interest in avoiding litigation.

The court stated: In fact, the test that the Supreme Court regularly applies to commercial speech supports continuing to require procedural safeguards for prior restraints even where commercial speech is involved. That test requires us to consider "whether the regulation . . . is not more extensive than is necessary to serve [the asserted governmental] interest." If it is more extensive than necessary, the government's action fails. A prior prohibition of the Advertisement is certainly more extensive than is necessary to serve the governmental interest asserted here, particularly where this court found, when denying MTA's motion for a stay, that requiring MTA to display the Advertisement would not result in irreparable harm to MTA. In other words, we have already decided that applying section 50 before the Advertisement is displayed is more extensive than necessary. Because the advertising space is a designated public forum, MTA may not enforce section 50 through its advertising policy any more than a government agency, acting without procedural safeguards, could screen advertisements for violations of section 50 that private bus companies wished to display.

The result? Because the ad space is a designated public forum, the MTA may not enforce section 50 through its advertising policy. However, anyone (including Mayor Rudy) who feels his rights have been violated (under section 50) may bring an action privately under section 51 (N.Y.Civ.Rights Law § 51 (McKinney 1997)).

The Christ's Bride Case The Southeastern Pennsylvania Transportation Authority (SEPTA), an agency of the Commonwealth of Pennsylvania, operated buses, subways, and regional rail lines in and around the city of Philadelphia. It sold advertising space in its stations and on its vehicles. In 1995 Christ's Bride Ministries (CBM) began a public service campaign to alert the public to what it believed to be the increased risk of breast cancer among women who had abortions. CBM's advertisements offered the headline: "Women Who Choose Abortion Suffer More and Deadlier Breast Cancer."

After the CBM posters were in place in stations and on buses, Dr. Philip Lee, Assistant Secretary of Health in the United States Department of Health and Human Services, claimed that the ads were misleading, unduly alarming, and did not accurately reflect the link between abortion and breast cancer. In a letter, Dr. Lee stated that the studies showing a link between breast cancer and abortion suffered from methodological weaknesses, that there was no consensus on the theorized relationship between breast cancer and abortion, and that Dr. Lee knew of no evidence supporting the claim that abortion causes "deadlier" breast cancer. Based on Dr. Lee's letter, SEPTA removed the posters.

When the case went to the appellate court, the Third Circuit ruled that SEPTA could not remove advertisements from its buses. In *Christ's Bride Ministries, Inc.* v. *Southeastern Pennsylvania Transportation Authority*, 148 F.3d 242 (3d Cir. 1998), the appellate court summarized its thinking as follows:

> SEPTA has accepted a broad range of advertisements for display. These include religious messages, such as "Follow this bus to FREEDOM, Christian Bible Fellowship Church;" an ad criticizing a political candidate; and explicitly worded advertisements such as "Safe Sex Isn't" and an advertisement reminding viewers that "Virginity-It's cool to keep" and "Don't give it up to shut 'em up." Indeed, many ads address topics concerning sex, family planning, and related topics. Other examples include a controversial ad campaign on AIDS education and awareness, posters stating, "The Face of Adoption" "Consider Adoption" and "Every child deserves a family," and another ad reading "Pregnant? Scared? Confused? A.R.C. Can Help Call 1-800-884-4004 or (215-844-1082.)"

On the topic of abortion, SEPTA has accepted two ads. One read, "Choice Hotline, For Answers to Your Questions About: Birth Control * Pregnancy * Prenatal Care * Abortion * Adoption * HIV/AIDS * Sexually Transmitted Diseases (STDs), Call State Health Line 1-800-692-7254 For Free Booklet on Fetal Development." The other one addressed the health benefits of legalizing abortion: "When Abortion Was Illegal, Women Died. My Mother Was One of Them. Keep Abortion Legal and Safe. Support the Clara Bell Duvall Education Fund. 471-9110."

From the broad range of ads submitted, SEPTA has requested modification of only three. One was the large wrap-around bus ad for Haynes hosiery, which would have covered the entire bus with the picture of a "scantily clad" woman; it was too "risqué." The same ad was accepted as a smaller "poster" ad on the sides of buses. SEPTA also asked for modification of an ad depicting a gun with a condom stretched over it. The text of the ad, "Safe Sex Isn't," ultimately ran without the graphics. SEPTA also requested that an advertisement for a personal injury law firm delete references to rail accidents.

We conclude then, based on SEPTA's written policies, which specifically provide for the exclusion of only a very narrow category of ads, based on SEPTA's goals of generating revenues through the sale of ad space, and based on SEPTA's practice of permitting virtually unlimited access to the forum, that SEPTA created a designated public forum. Moreover, it created a forum that is suitable for the speech in question, that is, posters which presented messages concerning abortion and health issues. CBM paid for advertising space which had previously been used for ads on those topics.

The court went on by saying: In light of the other advertisements, including those relating to abortion, which SEPTA had previously permitted to run on its property, and in light of SEPTA's own purposes in using and leasing the space, we have determined that SEPTA intended to create a designated public forum. We find that SEPTA's action in removing the posters does not survive the strict scrutiny applied to speech within the parameters of a designated public forum; nor does it pass the reasonableness test applied where property of a governmental agency has not been designated a public forum.

As it relates to the public forum issue (like the Giuliani case), the court first determined whether the advertising space on SEPTA's buses and in its stations constituted a public forum. That is, whether SEPTA clearly and deliberately opened its advertising space to the public. Clearly, the court concluded that it did.

The main goal of SEPTA's advertising space was to generate money. Other than tobacco and liquor advertising, SEPTA accepted many types of advertising, including religious messages, political advertising, advertisements concerning sex issues, family planning, and others. On the topic of abortion, SEPTA had accepted two advertisements in the past.

SEPTA argued that it asserted "tight control" over the forum. However, because the forum was limited in one way (refusing to run ads related to tobacco or alcohol) did not disqualify it as a public forum regarding other categories of speech, the court held.

In removing the advertisement without giving CBM a chance to prove the accuracy of the representation, SEPTA acted unreasonably. According to the court, SEPTA became a censor, thereby limiting speech it felt was misleading. SEPTA then argued that it could not investigate the accuracy of medical claims in ads submitted for placement on its buses. For that reason, it relied on Dr. Lee's letter. While SEPTA was under no obligation to "hire its own cadre of experts to evaluate medical claims made in ads," it was SEPTA that accepted the ad and then decided that it was misleading.

The court reasoned: Having decided to exclude the posters on this basis, SEPTA did not act reasonably when it failed to ask CBM to clarify the basis on which the claim was made. This is all the more true where SEPTA has failed to explain how its content-based distinctions are related to preserving the advertising space for its intended use, and where SEPTA has in place no policy, old or new, written or unwritten, governing the display of ads making contested claims.

The First Amendment and Advancing Government Interests

In *Tillman* v. *Miller*, 133 F.3d 1402 (11th Cir. 1998), Georgia's Workers' Compensation Truth in Advertising Act of 1995, (O.C.G.A. § 34-9-31), was held to violate the First Amendment. This occurred because the Act did not advance the state's goal of deterring the filing of fraudulent workers' compensation claims and was too burdensome.

The Georgia statute provided:

Any television advertisement, with broadcast originating in this state, which solicits persons to file workers' compensation claims or to engage or consult an attorney, medical care provider, or clinic for the purpose of giving consideration to a workers' compensation claim or to market workers' compensation insurance coverage shall contain a notice, which shall be in boldface Roman font 36 point type and appear in a dark background and remain on the screen for a minimum of five seconds as follows: NOTICE-Willfully making a false or misleading statement or representation to obtain or deny workers' compensation benefits is a crime carrying a penalty of imprisonment and/or fine of up to $10,000,000.

The state claimed that the motive was "to assure truthful and adequate disclosure of all material and relevant information in advertising" for workers' compensation claims. However, the court reasoned that the state had not proven that advertising of legal services caused fraudulent workers' compensation claims to be filed or that the inclusion of the notice in advertisements would likely reduce fraudulent claims. "In such circumstances, Georgia is not justified in placing, on a television advertiser, the burden of the cost of educating the public," said the court.

The Chiropractor's Case In *Silverman* v. *Walkup*, No. 1:98-cv-208, 1998 U.S. Dist. LEXIS 15823 (E.D. Tenn., September 29, 1998), a Tennessee law that prohibited solicitation in person and by live telephone contact by chiropractors was also found to violate the First Amendment. Again, this was because the statutory restriction did not advance the state's asserted purpose of deterring "accident telemarketing."

The Tennessee law prohibited the "solicitation, in person or by live telephone contact, by a licensee, or by an agent, servant, employee, or independent contractor of a licensee, of a patient with whom the licensee has no family or prior professional relationship." Silverman was a chiropractor who alleged that the law violated his First Amendment rights.

In contrast, the State argued that the law prohibited "solicitation," not advertising by chiropractors. It argued this on the grounds that the statute did not ban chiropractors from talking to prospective patients on the street or at health fairs or shopping malls. However, the court found the statute was clearly broader than merely prohibiting "telephone solicitation." In fact, the state's own regulations defined advertising as including "business solicitation."

Having determined that the statute regulated advertising by chiropractors, the court found that the restrictions were not narrowly tailored to the state's asserted interests. The state had a substantial interest in protecting the "tranquility, and privacy of the home" from the intrusion of telephone calls using personal information gleaned from accident reports. In addition, the protection of people from overreaching and pressure at a time when their judgment could be impaired and establishing standards for professional chiropractors that protected the reputation of the profession were at stake. The blanket ban of both in-person as well as telephone solicitation was too broad, according to the court. The court granted the plaintiff a preliminary injunction on enforcement of the statute until a full hearing on the merits.

The Narrowing Bridge between Advertising and Editorial Content

As we have seen, the courts have clarified where commercial speech that has taken different forms. Generally, commercial speech is one that proposes a commercial transaction, whereas, editorial content (news articles, news reports, editorial opinions, etc.) is distinguished from commercial content. However that may be changing.

The United States Supreme Court has cautioned that statements may be considered as commercial notwithstanding the fact that they contain discussions of important public issues, and that advertising which links a product to a current public debate is not automatically entitled to the constitutional protection that is afforded noncommercial speech. In other words, advertisers should not be permitted to immunize false or misleading product information from government regulation simply by including references to public issues or by posing as "editorial" content.

A case in point, involved one of the most recognizable brands in the world: Nike. Most of Nike's products are made in China, Vietnam, and Indonesia by subcontractors. Many were surprised to learn that one of the most revered American brands was actually made in Asia. They would probably be even more surprised to learn that Nike's original shoe (under the company's original name, Blue Ribbon Sports) was made in Japan as well.

This suit *Kasky* v. *Nike, Inc.*, Cal. 4th 939 (Cal. 2002), was a California Supreme Court case involved Nike's subcontractors' labor practices. Activists repeatedly charged that subcontractors violated local labor and safety laws and provided unacceptable working conditions. Workers were paid less than the applicable local minimum wage; were required to work overtime; were allowed and encouraged to work more overtime than applicable law allowed; were subjected to physical, verbal, and sexual abuse; and were exposed to toxic chemicals, noise, heat, and dust without adequate safety equipment, violating applicable local occupational health and safety regulations.

In response to this adverse publicity, and for the purpose of maintaining and increasing its sales and profits, Nike made statements to the public that plaintiff alleges were false and misleading. Specifically, that Nike stated that workers who produced Nike products were protected from physical and sexual abuse, that they were paid in accordance with local laws and regulations governing wages and working hours, that they were paid on average double the applicable local minimum wage, that they received a "living wage," that they received free meals and health care, and that their working conditions were in compliance with applicable local laws and regulations governing occupational health and safety. Nike made these statements in press releases, in letters to newspapers, in a letter to university presidents and athletic directors, and in other documents for PR purposes. Nike also bought full-page newspaper advertisements that publicized a report by GoodWorks International. The report, prepared for and paid by Nike, found no evidence of illegal or unsafe working conditions at Nike factories in China, Vietnam, and Indonesia.

The plaintiff alleged that the corporation, in response to public criticism, and to induce consumers to continue to buy its products, made false statements about its labor practices and the working conditions in the factories that made its products. The issue in this case was whether Nike's allegedly false statements were commercial or noncommercial speech for purposes of constitutional free speech analysis under the California and United States Constitutions. Because the messages in question were directed by a commercial speaker (Nike), to a commercial audience, and because they made representations of fact about the Nike's own business operations for the purpose of promoting sales of its products, the court concluded that these messages were commercial speech.

The majority opinion stated: Because the messages in question were directed by a commercial speaker to a commercial audience, and because they made representations of fact about the speaker's own business operations for the purpose of promoting sales of its products, we conclude that these messages are commercial speech for purposes of applying state laws barring false and misleading commercial messages.

Summarizing U.S. Supreme Court precedent, the majority opinion identified three reasons for denying First Amendment protection for false advertising: (1) the speaker can more easily verify the accuracy of commercial speech, (2) commercial speech is "hardier" than noncommercial speech because the speaker wants to make a profit, and (3) the regulation of commercial speech may be intertwined with the government's authority to regulate the underlying commercial transaction.

Key Terms

THE GENERAL LANDSCAPE OF LAWS RELATING TO ADVERTISING

PART I

The Federal Trade Commission's Role in Advertising Regulation

2

Advertising works. But it has to be well done and enough people have to see it.

—Charles Osgood

In 1946 Frederic Wakeman wrote the classic novel about the exploits of an advertising agency and an arrogant client named Evan Evans. Since then, *The Hucksters* has become the public image of the advertising profession. In the movie adaptation, Clark Gable plays the part of the advertising account executive caught in a struggle of right and wrong with the ne'er-do-well soap king played by Sidney Greenstreet. As these two battles, symbols of good conscience and selfish motives dominate the screen. "Advertising," exclaimed the soap tycoon, "is nothing more than pompous ranting," which he relishes when accomplished with the poorest of taste.

George Washington Hill, the real-life Evan Evans and president of the American Tobacco Company, was well-known for his exaggerated advertising claims in the 1920s. When "creating" his own preference test statistics, Hill said, "I know the great preference for Lucky Strike is a fact, but the public won't believe it. Anyway, two-to-one has a better ring to it."

The Hucksters was written in an era when the advertiser took many liberties in selling his merchandise. For almost fifty years, however, moviegoers have overlooked the fact that Wakeman's book was a work of fiction. The book convinced the public that advertising flourished—with the consumer falling victim to the guile of the advertiser—in a sea of broken promises that were never intended to be kept. Unfortunately, this feeling has prevailed with help from more current movies like *Nothing in Common* (1986) and *Thank You for Smoking* (2005), and the hit TV series *Mad Men* (premiered in 2007). Today, the type of blatant deception demonstrated in movies and television is rigidly policed, primarily through the efforts of the Federal Trade Commission (FTC), which has successfully raised the standard of conduct of the advertising industry.

The Federal Trade Commission

As most advertising people already know, the FTC has the greatest control over advertising and the way it is produced. Yet few understand the extent of the

FTC's involvement. The formation of the FTC was an outgrowth of the Sherman Act, an antitrust law that prohibited conspiracies in restraint of trade and the formation of monopolies. The original mandate from Congress (under Section 5 of the Federal Trade Commission Act) was simple and straightforward: to prevent "unfair or deceptive acts or practices . . . [and] . . . unfair methods of competition."

In January 1914, President Woodrow Wilson addressed Congress calling for the creation of a FTC saying: "The businessmen of the country desire something more than that the menace of legal process in these matters be made explicit and intelligible. They desire advice, the definite guidance and information which can be supplied by an administrative body, an interstate trade commission."

"Constructive legislation, when successful, is always the embodiment of convincing experience, and of mature public opinion which finally springs out of that experience . . . . It is not recent or hasty opinion."

"The opinion of the country . . . would not wish to see it [the commission] empowered to make terms with monopoly or in any sort to assume control of business, as if the Government made itself responsible. It demands such a commission only as an indispensable instrument of information and publicity, as a clearing house of the facts by which both the public mind and the managers of great business undertakings should be guided, and as an instrumentality for doing justice to business where the processes of the courts are inadequate to adjust the remedy to wrong in a way that will meet all the equities and circumstances of the case."

In an early move, the Seventh Circuit of Appeals in 1919, stated its definition of the FTC's role in *Sears, Roebuck & Co.* v. *FTC*, 258 F. 307 (7th Cir. 1919), saying: "The commissioners, representing the government as parens patriae, are to exercise their common sense, as informed by their knowledge of the general idea of unfair trade at common law, and stop all those trade practices that have a capacity or tendency to injure competitors directly or through deception of purchasers, quite irrespective of whether the specific practices in question have yet been denounced in common-law cases."

The commission, as part of its scope, has the task of preserving a variety of marketplace options for consumers. Its efforts against deception help ensure that consumers will not make choices on the basis of misleading information. The ban on unfair practices also broadens the FTC's scope by protecting consumers from practices that are "exploitative or inequitable . . . morally objectionable, [or] seriously detrimental to consumers or others."

As we discussed earlier, Section 5 of the act, which was once considered only a tool against unfair methods of competition between businesses, was expanded in 1938 with the Wheeler-Lea Amendments to cover unfair and deceptive acts against individuals as well. While the rationale to abolish unfair methods of competition grew from the need to protect competitors from each other, the reasoning against unfair and deceptive acts and practices evolved out of the desire to protect the consumer from the advertiser.

While the Wheeler-Lea Amendments specifically gave the FTC jurisdiction in the consumer protection area, the commission continued its fight against unfair trade practices and monopolistic power. At times these divergent roles were in conflict.

The Reasoning behind the FTC Act and the Wheeler-Lea Amendments

Here, we will examine the different stages that the FTC has gone through in its development, and the reasoning behind these developments.

The FTC Act First, look at this excerpt from the Senate Committee on Interstate Commerce Report, 1914, supporting the enactment of a trade commission bill:

> The committee gave careful consideration to the question as to whether it would attempt to define the many and variable unfair practices which prevail in commerce and to forbid their continuance or whether it would, by a general declaration condemning unfair practices, leave it to the Commission to determine what practices were unfair. It concluded that the latter course would be the better, for the reason, as stated by one of the representatives of the Illinois Manufacturers' Association, that there were too many unfair practices to define, and after writing 20 of them into the law, it would be quite possible to invent others.

As we have seen, the original intent was to prohibit unfair trade practices as they existed between businesses.

The Wheeler-Lea Amendments Now, look at this excerpt from Senator Burton Wheeler in debate on the Wheeler-Lea Amendments, 1938 (Harris and Milkis 1989). "The Commission spent most of its time and most of its money allotted to it by the Congress, in running down the question of whether or not one man has lost some money by reason of unfair trade practices on the part of another. After all, Congress is not interested in whether John Smith lost some money as the result of the advertising complained of, but the question is whether or not the general public has been deceived or injured by reason of it. We are here to legislate with respect to that question."

This, then, also prohibited deceptive acts in commerce, thereby bringing consumer deception into the picture, and allowing the FTC to act on that as well. Truly, the Wheeler-Lea Amendments gave the FTC the consumer protection authority that it exercises today.

The 1975 FTC Improvement Act Essentially, the FTC Improvement Act of 1975 (P.L. 93-637, 88 Stat. 2183), modified section 5 of the FTC Act in one major way. It added the phrase "or affecting" to the existing phrase "in commerce." Now, as we'll see in the next section, the phrase reads "in *or affecting* commerce." This gives the FTC wider latitude in determining the existence of deception.

Key Sections of the FTC Act At this point, it may be valuable to look at the specifics of current key sections of the FTC Act.

Section 5. (a) (1) Unfair methods of competition in or affecting commerce, *and unfair or deceptive acts or practices in or affecting commerce* are hereby declared unlawful. (Underline added with Wheeler-Lea Amendments; bold added with 1975 FTC Improvement Act.)

Section 5. (b) Whenever the Commission shall have reason to believe that any such person, partnership, or corporation has been or is using any unfair method of competition or unfair or deceptive act or practice in or affecting commerce, and if it shall appear to the Commission that a proceeding by it in respect thereof *would be of interest to the public*, it shall issue and serve upon such person, partnership, or corporation a complaint stating its charges. (Italic shows concern for a public interest; bold added with 1975 FTC Improvement Act.)

Section 12. (a) It shall be unlawful for any person, partnership, or corporation to disseminate, or cause to be disseminated, any false advertisement.

(b) The dissemination or the causing to be disseminated of any false advertisement within the provisions of subsection (a) of this section shall be an unfair or deceptive act or practice in or affecting commerce within the meaning of section 5. (Section 12 added with Wheeler-Lea Amendments; bold added with 1975 FTC Improvement Act.) (box 2.1)

> ### Box 2.1   Key Events in the History of the FTC

The following list includes a history of events that have played an important role in the evolution of the FTC, many of which we will look at in this chapter.

1887	Interstate Commerce Commission created
1890	Sherman Antitrust Act passed
1903	Bureau of Corporations created
1914	FTC Act passed Clayton Antitrust Act passed
1918	Webb-Pomerone Act passed
1919	FTC v. Sears, Roebuck & Company
1920	FTC v. Gratz
1921	Packers and Stockyard Act passed
1922	FTC v. Winsted Hosiery
1929	FTC v. Klesner
1931	FTC v. Raladam
1934	FTC v. Keppel & Brothers, Inc.
1935	Humphrey's Executor v. United States
1936	Robinson-Patman Act passed
1938	Wheeler-Lea Amendments passed, amending the 1914 FTC Act
1939	Wool Products Labeling Act passed
1949	Hoover Commission Report
1950	Celler-Kefauver Antimerger Act passed Oleomargarine Act passed
1951	Fur Products Labeling Act passed
1952	McGuire Act passed
1953	Flammable Fabrics Act passed
1958	Textile and Fiber Products Act passed
1975	FTC Improvement Act passed
1984	Ruling in the Matter of Cliffdale Associates
1994	FTC Act Amendments on Unfairness passed

The FTC's Regulation of Advertising

Because the FTC's goal is to protect the consumer from false claims, deception, misrepresentation, and unfair acts and practices, the level of control it exerts over advertising has increased in recent years. The commission has gained increased authority and effectiveness for two reasons: first, through the cases it has heard and decided; and second, through the courts affirming the commission's decisions. In fact, courts have upheld the majority of the commission's decisions.

To begin, an advertiser must understand how the FTC views an ad. Overall, what deceptive qualities does it look for? What qualifies as a deceptive ad? Or an unfair one? How does the advertiser know if the ad he creates will be acceptable in the eyes of the commission?

As mentioned earlier, the FTC follows certain guidelines or principles where advertising claims are alleged to be unfair or deceptive. When deciding on a case before it, the FTC first examines the advertisement and all the information contained in it to determine if the ad is deceptive, or under current interpretation, if it is *likely* to deceive. The commission also looks at the net impression of the advertisement— the overall impression that the ad projects to the consumer. The commission views the materiality of all the representations in the advertisement and particularly the claims that are alleged to be false. The FTC also determines if the claims are simply sales exaggerations or puff.

The 1984 case, *In the Matter of Cliffdale Associates, Inc.*, 103 F.T.C. 110 (1984), (which we will examine later in this chapter), establishes the commission's current stance on deception. Exhibit 2.1 includes a copy of a letter from then FTC Chairman James C. Miller, III to the Committee on Energy and Commerce. This letter, written in October 1983, attempts to explain the commission's position and interpretation of deception. It's worth reading to hear it directly from the horse's mouth.

Now we'll examine each of the components of deception in more detail.

Exhibit 2.1

FEDERAL TRADE COMMISSION
WASHINGTON, D.C. 20580
October 14, 1983

The Honorable John D. Dingell
Chairman
Committee on Energy and Commerce
U.S. House of Representatives
Washington, D.C. 20515

Dear Mr. Chairman:

This letter responds to the Committee's inquiry regarding the Commission's enforcement policy against deceptive acts or practices. We also hope this letter will provide guidance to the public.

Section 5 of the FTC Act declares unfair or deceptive acts or practices unlawful. Section 12 specifically prohibits false ads likely to induce the purchase of food, drugs, devices, or cosmetics. Section 15 defines a false ad for purposes of Section 12 as one which is "misleading in a material respect." Numerous Commission and judicial decisions have defined and elaborated on the phrase "deceptive acts or practices" under both Sections 5 and 12. Nowhere, however, is there a single definitive statement of the Commission's view of its authority. The Commission believes that such a statement would be useful to the public, as well as the Committee in its continuing review of our jurisdiction.

We have therefore reviewed the decided cases to synthesize the most important principles of general applicability. We have attempted to provide a concrete indication of the manner in which the commission will enforce its deception mandate. In so doing, we intend to address the concerns that have been raised about the meaning of deception, and thereby attempt to provide a greater sense of certainty as to how the concept will be applied.

I. SUMMARY

Certain elements undergird all deception cases. First, there must be a representation, omission, or practice that is likely to mislead the consumer. Practices that have been found misleading or deceptive in specific cases include false oral or written representations, misleading price claims, sales of hazardous or systematically defective products or services without adequate disclosures, failure to disclose information regarding pyramid sales, use of bait and switch techniques, failure to perform promised services, and failure to meet warranty obligations.

Second, we examine the practice from the perspective of a consumer acting reasonably in the circumstances. If the representation or practice affects or is directed primarily to a particular group, the Commission examines reasonableness from the perspective of that group.

Third, the representation, omission, or practice must be a "material" one. The basic question is whether the act or practice is likely to affect the Consumer's conduct or decision with regard to a product or service. If so, the practice is material, and consumer injury is likely, because consumers are likely to have chosen differently but for the deception. In many instances, materiality, and hence injury, can be presumed from the nature of the practice. In other instances, evidence of materiality may be necessary.

Thus, the Commission will find deception if there is a representation, omission or practice that is likely to mislead the consumer acting reasonably in the circumstances, to the consumer's detriment. We discuss each of these elements below.

II. THERE MUST BE A REPRESENTATION, OMISSION, OR PRACTICE THAT IS LIKELY TO MISLEAD THE CONSUMER.

Most deception involves written or oral misrepresentations, or omissions of material information. Deception may also occur in other forms of conduct associated with a sales transaction. The entire advertisement, transaction or course of dealing will be considered. The issue is whether the act or practice is likely to mislead, rather than whether it causes actual deception.

Of course, the Commission must find that a representation, omission, or practice occurred. In cases of express claims, the representation itself establishes the meaning. In cases of implied claims, the Commission will often be able to determine meaning through an examination of the representation itself, including an evaluation of such factors as the entire document, the juxtaposition of various phrases in the document, the nature of the claim, and the nature of the transaction. In other situations, the Commission will require extrinsic evidence that reasonable consumers reach the implied claims. In all instances, the Commission will carefully consider any extrinsic evidence that is introduced.

Some cases involve omission of material information, the disclosure of which is necessary to prevent the claim, practice, or sale from being misleading. Information may be omitted from written or oral representations or from the commercial transaction.

In some circumstances, the Commission can presume that consumers are likely to reach false beliefs about the product or service because of an omission. At other times, however, the Commission may require evidence on consumers' expectations.

Marketing and point-of-sales practices that are likely to mislead consumers are also deceptive. For instance, in bait and switch cases, a violation occurs when the offer to sell the product is not a bona fide offer. The Commission has also found deception where a sales representative misrepresented the purpose of the initial contact with customers. When a product is sold, there is an implied representation that the product is fit for the purposes for which it is sold. When it is not, deception occurs. There may be a concern about the way a product or service is marketed, such as where inaccurate or incomplete information is provided. A failure to perform services promised under a warranty or by contract can also be deceptive.

III. THE ACT OR PRACTICE MUST BE CONSIDERED FROM THE PERSPECTIVE OF THE REASONABLE CONSUMER

The Commission believes that to be deceptive the representation, omission or practice must be likely to mislead reasonable consumers under the circumstances. The test is whether the consumer's interpretation or reaction is reasonable. When representations or sales practices are targeted to a specific audience, the Commission determines the effect of the practice on a reasonable member of that group. In evaluating a particular practice, the Commission considers the totality of the practice in determining how reasonable consumers are likely to respond.

A company is not liable for every interpretation or action by a consumer. In an advertising context, this principle has been well-stated:

> An advertiser cannot be charged with liability with respect to every conceivable misconception, however outlandish, to which his representations might be subject among the foolish or feeble-minded. Some people, because of ignorance or incomprehension, may be misled by even a scrupulously honest claim. Perhaps a few misguided souls believe, for example, that all "Danish pastry" is made in Denmark. Is it therefore an actionable deception to advertise "Danish pastry" when it is made in this country? Of course not. A representation does not become "false and deceptive" merely because it will be unreasonably misunderstood by an insignificant and unrepresentative segment of the class of persons to whom the representation is addressed. *Heinz W. Kirchner.*[27]

To be considered reasonable, the interpretation or reaction does not have to be the only one. When a seller's representation conveys more than one meaning to reasonable consumers, one of which is false, the seller is liable for the misleading interpretation. An interpretation will be presumed reasonable if it is the one the respondent intended to convey.

The Commission has used this standard in its past decisions. "The test applied by the Commission is whether the interpretation is reasonable in light of the claim." In the Listerine case, the Commission evaluated the claim from the perspective of the "average listener." In a case involving the sale of encyclopedias, the Commission observed "[i]n determining the meaning of an advertisement, a piece of promotional material or a sales presentation, the important criterion is the net impression that it is likely to make on the general populace." The decisions in *American Home Products, Bristol Myers*, and *Sterling Drug* are replete with references to reasonable consumer interpretations. In a land sales case, the Commission evaluated the oral statements and written representations "in light of the sophistication and understanding of the persons to whom they were directed." Omission cases are no different: the Commission examines the failure to disclose in light of expectations and understandings of the typical buyer regarding the claims made.

When representations or sales practices are targeted to a specific audience, such as children, the elderly, or the terminally ill, the Commission determines the effect of the practice on a reasonable member of that group. For instance, if a company markets a cure to the terminally ill, the practice will be evaluated from the perspective of how it affects the ordinary member of that group. Thus, terminally ill consumers might be particularly susceptible to exaggerated cure claims. By the same token, a practice or representation directed to a well-educated group, such as a prescription drug advertisement to doctors, would be judged in light of the knowledge and sophistication of that group.

As it has in the past, the Commission will evaluate the entire advertisement, transaction, or course of dealing in determining how reasonable consumers are likely to respond. Thus, in advertising the Commission will examine "the entire mosaic, rather than each title separately."

As explained by a Court of Appeals in a recent case:

> The Commission's right to scrutinize the visual and aural imagery of advertisements follows from the principle that the Commission looks to the impression made by the advertisements as a whole. Without this mode of examination, the Commission would have limited recourse against crafty advertisers whose deceptive messages were conveyed by means other than, or in addition to, spoken words. *American Home Products*.[28]

Commission cases reveal specific guidelines. Depending on the circumstances, accurate information in the text may not remedy a false headline because reasonable consumers may glance only at the headline. Written disclosure or fine print may be insufficient to correct a misleading representation.

Other practices of the company may direct consumers' attention away from the qualifying disclosures. Oral statements, label disclosures or point-of-sale material will not necessarily correct a deceptive representation or omission. Thus, when the first contact between a seller and a buyer occurs through a deceptive practice, the law may be violated even if the truth is subsequently made known to the purchaser. *Pro forma* statements or disclaimers may not cure otherwise deceptive messages or practices.

Qualifying disclosures must be legible and understandable. In evaluating such disclosures, the Commission recognizes that in many circumstances, reasonable consumers do not read the entirety of an ad or are directed away from the importance of the qualifying phrase by the acts or statements of the seller. Disclosures that conform to the Commission's Statement of Enforcement Policy regarding clear and conspicuous disclosures, which applies to television advertising, are generally adequate.[29] Less elaborate disclosures may also suffice.

Certain practices, however, are unlikely to deceive consumers acting reasonably. Thus, the Commission generally will not bring advertising cases based on subjective claims (taste, feel, appearance, smell) or on correctly stated opinion claims if consumers understand the source and limitations of the opinion. Claims phrased as opinions are actionable, however, if they are not honestly held, if they misrepresent the qualifications of the holder or the basis of his opinion or if the recipient reasonably interprets them as implied statements of fact.

The Commission generally will not pursue cases involving obviously exaggerated or puffing representations, i.e., those that the ordinary consumers do not take seriously. Some exaggerated claims, however, may be taken seriously by consumers and are actionable. For instance, in rejecting a respondent's argument that use of the words "electronic miracle" to describe a television antenna was puffery, the Commission stated:

> Although not insensitive to respondent's concern that the term miracle is commonly used in situations short of changing water into wine, we must conclude that the use of "electronic miracle" in the context of respondent's grossly exaggerated claims would lead consumers to give added credence to the overall suggestion that this device is superior to other types of antennae. *Jay Norris*. [30]

Finally, as a matter of policy, when consumers can easily evaluate the product or service, it is inexpensive, and it is frequently purchased, the Commission will examine the practice closely before issuing a complaint based on deception. There is little incentive for sellers to misrepresent (either by an explicit false statement or a deliberate false implied statement in these circumstances since they normally would seek to encourage repeat purchases. Where, as here, market incentives place strong constraints on the likelihood of deception, the Commission will examine a practice closely before proceeding.

In sum, the Commission will consider many factors in determining the reaction of the ordinary consumer to a claim or practice. As would any trier of fact, the Commission will evaluate the totality of the ad or the practice and ask questions such as: How clear is the representation? How conspicuous is any qualifying information? How important is the omitted information? Do other sources for the omitted information exist? How familiar is the public with the product or service?

IV. THE REPRESENTATION, OMISSION OR PRACTICE MUST BE MATERIAL

The third element of deception is materiality. That is, a representation, omission or practice must be a material one for deception to occur. A "material" misrepresentation or practice is one which is likely to affect a consumer's choice of or conduct regarding a product. In other words, it is information that is important to consumers. If inaccurate or omitted information is material, injury is likely.

The Commission considers certain categories of information presumptively material. First, the Commission presumes that express claims are material. As the Supreme Court stated recently, "[i]n the absence of factors that would distort the decision to advertise, we may assume that the willingness of a business to promote its products reflects a belief that consumers are interested in the advertising." Where the seller knew, or should have known, that an ordinary consumer would need omitted information to evaluate the product or service, or that the claim was false, materiality will be presumed because the manufacturer intended the information or omission to have an effect. Similarly, when evidence exists that a seller intended to make an implied claim, the Commission will infer materiality.

The Commission also considers claims or omissions material if they significantly involve health, safety, or other areas with which the reasonable consumer would be concerned. Depending on the facts, information pertaining to the central characteristics of the product or service will be presumed material. Information has been found material where it concerns the purpose, safety, efficacy, or cost of the product or service. Information is also likely to be material if it concerns durability, performance, warranties or quality. Information pertaining to a finding by another agency regarding the product may also be material.

Where the Commission cannot find materiality based on the above analysis, the Commission may require evidence that the claim or omission is likely to be considered important by consumers. This evidence can be the fact that the product or service with the feature represented costs more than an otherwise comparable product without the feature, a reliable survey of consumers, or credible testimony.

A finding of materiality is also a finding that injury is likely to exist because of the representation, omission, sales practice, or marketing technique. Injury to consumers can take many forms. Injury exists if consumers would have chosen differently but for the deception. If different choices are likely, the claim is material, and injury is likely as well. Thus, injury and materiality are different names for the same concept.

V. CONCLUSION

The Commission will find an act or practice deceptive if there is a misrepresentation, omission, or other practice that misleads the consumer acting reasonably in the circumstances, to the consumer's detriment. The Commission will not generally require extrinsic evidence concerning the representations understood by reasonable consumers or the materiality of a challenged claim, but in some instances extrinsic evidence will be necessary.

The Commission intends to enforce the FTC Act vigorously. We will investigate, and prosecute where appropriate, acts or practices that are deceptive. We hope this letter will help provide you and the public with a greater sense of certainty concerning how the Commission will exercise its jurisdiction over deception. Please do not hesitate to call if we can be of any further assistance.

By direction of the Commission, Commissioners Pertschuk and Bailey dissenting, with separate statements attached and with separate response to the Committee's request for a legal analysis to follow.

James C. Miller III
Chairman

Deceptiveness of an Advertisement

From 1914 until 1984, "tendency or capacity" to deceive was the FTC's benchmark. One early case that dealt with this concept of "tendency or capacity" to deceive was *FTC* v. *Raladam Co.*, 316 U.S. 149, 62 S.Ct. 966, 86 L.Ed. 1336 (1942). In that case the United States Supreme Court decided the issue of whether a cease-and-desist order by the commission (issued after a hearing in 1935) should stand. The case involved Raladam's product, Marmola. Marmola was a preparation for weight-reduction and was advertised as such. The company made claims in its advertisements that were misleading and deceptive, concerning the product's qualities as a remedy for obesity.

Raladam did not argue whether the statements were deceptive (they had been caught before in 1929 as well). Its argument was that no proof was offered to show that injury occurred. However, the court held that no actual injury need be proven, only a "tendency" to deceive. The court felt that it was impossible to determine whether any injury occurred, or would occur in the future, because of Raladam's false claims. In fact, one of the principles of the act was "to prevent potential injury by stopping unfair methods of competition in their incipiency."

There is an interesting side note from the history of the con man's role we discussed in early advertising. A man named Edward Hayes, a con man extraordinaire, marketed a product for years called Man Medicine. A turn-of-the-century version of Viagra, if you will. Hayes claimed his product would bestow the purchaser "once more with gusto, the joyful satisfaction, the pulse and throb of physical pleasure, the keen sense of man sensation." In reality, Man Medicine was merely a laxative that Hayes used to bilk millions of dollars from a susceptible male market.

Hayes was caught and brought to trial by the Postmaster General for fraud. He was found guilty in April 1914, fined $5,000, and made to promise never to get involved with such wild schemes again. Only months later, Hayes was back out in the market advertising a new miracle product—a foolproof cure for obesity. The product was called Marmola, the same product which, with its new owner Raladam, was taken to court in 1929 and later in 1935. Some people never learn.

Then in 1984, the pivotal case of *In the Matter of Cliffdale Associates, Inc.*, caused a change in the FTC's stance on deception. Still today, the FTC uses this standard to determine the existence of deception. "Tendency or capacity" to deceive has been replaced with "likely" to deceive. Since *Cliffdale*, the FTC takes a very close look at an advertisement to determine if a false representation or omission is "likely" to deceive a substantial number of consumers. As it was before 1984, actual deception is not necessary under the FTC act to constitute a violation.

In 1979 alone, Cliffdale Associates sold $692,998 in one of its products called the Ball-Matic Gas Saver Valve. The valve, what is commonly called an air-bleed device, was intended to be installed on an automobile engine to admit additional air into the engine to lean the air–fuel mixture, and thereby improve gas mileage. Ads promoted the sale of the Ball-Matic through mail order (box 2.2).

Box 2.2

GET UP TO 4 EXTRA MILES PER GALLON
– 100 EXTRA MILES BETWEEN FILL-UPS –
SAVE UP TO $200 A YEAR ON GAS.
GUARANTEED SAVINGS!

We firmly believe the Ball-Matic to be one of the best investments you can make to save money this year. The exact saving you will receive may vary significantly depending on the kind of car you drive, the condition of your engine, weather, your driving habits, and the amount of driving you do; however we guarantee that you MUST SAVE AT LEAST FIVE TIMES the amount you paid for your BALL-MATIC in the first year or you may return it for a full refund.

CONTROLLED TESTS CONFIRM BIG DOLLAR SAVING!

In the Spring of 1978, we arranged for a local Shell Service Station to conduct a controlled, supervised test using seven different cars owned and driven by non-professional drivers. Each car was fitted with a locked gas cap and the keys kept in the possession of the testers.

After establishing base mileage consumption data for the various cars, the BALL-MATIC was installed and miles-per-gallon figures were re-checked. Every single car in the test showed meaningful improvement.

IMPROVEMENT RANGE . . . 8% to 40%!

Yes, you can actually get up to 70 . . . 80 . . . 90 . . . even 100 extra miles from every single tankful. No matter how old or rundown your car may be . . . no matter how many gallons of gasoline it now devours each week.

READ THE RESULTS FOR YOURSELF!

"The BALL-MATIC (gas saver) that I purchased has proven itself. I drive a 1970 Oldsmobile, now I get four miles more per gallon."

C.T. –Orange, California

"I want to express my thanks for the BALL-MATIC. Since it has been installed in my car, my gas mileage has not been under 18 miles per gallon. This is an increase of 5.5 miles per gallon."

Rev. R.N. –Claremont, California

Cliffdale's ads guaranteed an increase in gas mileage of 8 to 40 percent or more with the Ball-Matic. Part of the convincing nature of these ads were the claimed scientific tests and the consumer endorsement letters—all of which turned out to be false and clearly deceptive.

When this case went to court, it was proven that no valid scientific tests had been performed on the valve. The endorsements used in the ads were deceptive since all but one letter was written by someone connected with the company. In addition, the Ball-Matic was proven to not provide any measurable increase in gas mileage when tested by a series of credible university facilities.

The commission, stated that it: ". . . will find an act or practice deceptive if, first, there is a representation, omission, or practice that, second, *is likely to mislead consumers acting reasonably under the circumstances*, and third, the representation, omission, or practice is material. These elements articulate the factors actually used in most earlier Commission cases identifying whether or not an act or practice was deceptive, even though the language used in those cases was often couched in such terms as 'a tendency and capacity to deceive.'" (Emphasis added.)

"The requirement that an act or practice be *likely to mislead,* for example, reflects the long established principle that the Commission need not find actual deception to hold that a violation of Section 5 has occurred." (Emphasis added.)

In this case, the commission went on to expand on yet another new reference, a "reasonably acting consumer."

They said that: "The requirement that an act or practice be considered from the perspective of a *consumer acting reasonably in the circumstances* is not new. Virtually all representations, even those that are true, can be misunderstood by some consumers. The Commission has long recognized that the law should not be applied in such a way as to find that honest representations are deceptive simply because they are misunderstood by a few . . . . [A]n advertisement would not be considered deceptive merely because it could be 'unreasonably misunderstood by an insignificant and unrepresentative segment of the class of persons to whom the representation is addressed.'" (Emphasis added.)

Now, the FTC has changed its requirement that a mere possibility of deception could occur, to a probability that deception will result from the claim. The new definition requires a higher degree of proof than the previous one. In essence, it provides less protection for the consumer than did the earlier "capacity or tendency" standard.

The change in the FTC's position on deception as a result of the *Cliffdale* case has been well articulated in the case's dissenting opinion of Commissioner Pertschuk:

> Under the guise of making the law more "clear and understandable," the [FTC] has actually raised the evidentiary threshold for deception cases. [We] have found it necessary to improve on language long understood by the courts and previous commissioners, by substituting the word "likely" for "tendency or capacity." "Likely to mislead," they insist, expresses more clearly the notion that actual deception need not be found! . . . the word "likely" suggests that some particular degree of likelihood of actual deception must be found. Therefore, it may create the impression, intentionally or not, that the burden of proof is higher than it has always been under the traditional "tendency or capacity" standard.

Commissioner Bailey also dissented in part to the *Cliffdale* decision, and stated: "The [FTC's] first criterion for deception is that there be a claim, omission, or practice that is 'likely to mislead' consumers. It is true that the courts have occasionally used this or similar phrasing, such as 'the likelihood or propensity' of deception, interchangeable with tendency or capacity."

Here, however, the majority makes unmistakable its intent to exchange the phrase tendency or capacity for the term likely, with only the brief explanation that it is meant to convey an understanding that "actual" deception need not be shown. As that was never in doubt, it does not explain the use of the term "likely" generally.

A standard Webster's definition of likely, "having a high probability of occurring or being true," suggests, however, that the purposeful substitution of this term for tendency or capacity may well be intended to raise, or may be construed so as to raise, the burden of proof the Commission must meet in demonstrating that deception has occurred.

The commissioner concluded by saying: "Thus, use of the term 'likely' here may be fairly perceived to be at least a partial retreat from the Commission's traditional position that it may on the basis of its own expertise determine what representations a seller has made to the public."

The Materiality Requirement

In order for the FTC to reach the conclusion that an ad is deceptive, the questionable representation (or omission) must also be a material one. A claim is material if it is likely to affect the consumer's choice of a product and his conduct in purchasing that product. In other words, it is material if it is important to the consumer in making his purchasing decision. Another way to understand this concept is in terms of injury to the consumer. Finding that a claim is material is finding that injury is likely, and injury exists if the consumer would have chosen differently had there been no deception. The consumer would be injured because he would be purchasing something other than what he thought he was purchasing. Thus, likelihood of injury and materiality are different sides of the same coin.

In most of the cases throughout this chapter and the next, we will see deceptions that are material.

An example of a material deception occurred in 1990. Volvo ran into major legal trouble over a television commercial that it aired to dramatically demonstrate the structural strength of its automobile. A thirteen thousand pound "monster truck" called "Bear Foot" was shown rolling over a line-up of cars. All of the cars shown were crushed under the weight of the truck except the Volvo station wagon.

Later it was discovered that additional steel supports had been welded into the Volvo to reinforce it against the monster truck's weight. The other cars, on the other hand, were weakened by having their roof supports cut with a saw to help them collapse under the weight.

As part of an out-of-court settlement, Volvo agreed to pull the commercial off the air and replace it with corrective ads. Volvo was also required to run newspaper ads apologizing to consumers for the deceptive advertising.

Scali, McCabe, Sloves in New York, Volvo's advertising agency for twenty-four years, and the creator of the commercial, resigned the $40 million account.

The commission feels that certain types of claims are unquestionably material in nature. Such claims include express claims; implied claims as intended by the advertiser; claims relating to health, safety, and other similar areas of concern to the consumer; claims that relate to the main characteristics of the product or service; claims establishing the purpose, efficiency, cost, durability, performance, warranty, or quality of a product; and statements regarding findings by a governmental agency concerning the product.

The *Cliffdale* case created much controversy in addition to new views on the three elements of deception; one of those being the materiality requirement. Commissioner Pertschuk, concurring in part and dissenting in part in the *Cliffdale* case, took exception with the new definition of materiality:

> The third element of deception is materiality. As the Supreme Court has explained, Section 5 prohibits the misrepresentation of "any fact which would constitute a material factor in a purchaser's decision whether to buy." Heretofore, any fact that is important to consumers has been considered material, regardless of whether consumer choices would actually turn on that fact. As the Commission has previously said, "[t]he fact that consumers were not harmed because they would have purchased the product anyway . . . is not relevant." The Commission has not required a showing of reliance or injury to establish deception.
>
> The majority opinion in this case [Cliffdale], however, suggests somewhat ambiguously that a misrepresentation is not material unless it is "likely to affect" consumers' conduct and "[c]onsumers thus are likely to suffer injury." Similarly, the October 14, 1983, Policy Statement on Deception states: "a finding of materiality is also a finding that injury is likely to exist . . . . Injury exists if consumers would have chosen differently but for the deception."

If the majority commissioners intend to require proof of actual or likely reliance on the misrepresentations of respondents in future cases, they have changed the meaning of materiality and made it more difficult to establish violations of Section 5.

Commissioner Bailey also dissented in part to *Cliffdale* by saying:

The Commission has long held that a challenged act or practice must be misleading in a material respect in order to be found deceptive. Just when all appears to be going well, however, the opinion . . . introduces a series of new concepts which appear to qualify standard principles of materiality in a restrictive fashion. At one point, the opinion seems to equate materiality with the actual effects of claims or practices on consumer conduct, and the Policy Statement expressly states that "injury and materiality are different names for the same concept' and that deception will be found where an act or practice "misleads . . . to the consumer's detriment." (Detriment is, of course, legally defined as injury.) The Policy Statement also notes that injury exists if consumers would have chosen differently "but for" the misleading act or practice, suggesting that reliance and causation are elements of materiality.

The commissioner went on to say: "Conclusions that injury and materiality are synonymous, that causation and reliance must be shown, or even that the likelihood of consumer detriment must be demonstrated in every case do not square with these accepted understandings of materiality."

"I have no quarrel with the conclusions reached in this case, but analyzing it by applying these new elements is a wholly unnecessary exercise which demonstrates, I fear, the serious evidentiary difficulties and the exercise of even greater analytical gymnastics that will be necessary in future, more complicated Commission cases."

It appears that the *Cliffdale* case has stirred up much dust which will not soon settle. However, the findings in *Cliffdale* still hold as true today as they did in 1984.

The Evolution of the "Reasonable Man" Standard

Another principle the FTC uses in determining deception is called the "Reasonable Man" standard. Although the courts refer to a reasonable or ignorant "man," the rationale equally applies to a woman as well. The court wasn't so politically correct back then. Although the standard has gone through much change from the "reasonable man" to the "ignorant man" and back, the FTC has settled on the reasonable man standard. Yet, today the level has been raised to a stricter scale since the opinion in the *Cliffdale* case.

The reasonable man standard was first mentioned in 1837 (*Vaughan* v. *Menlowe*, 3 Bing. N.C. 468, 132 Eng. Rep. 490 (1837)). He is a man of average prudence and ordinary sense, who uses ordinary care and skill.

To understand why the FTC has changed its stance over the years regarding the reasonable man standard, it is helpful to look at the way the standard evolved. Soon after the Wheeler-Lea Amendments to the FTC Act were passed in 1938, the reasonable man standard began to be replaced with a new ideology: the ignorant man standard. This new standard was based largely on a case concerning an encyclopedia company that had used many false statements in a sales campaign. These were not simply innocent misrepresentations, but rather blatant untruths intended to deceive potential buyers.

However, some or all of these falsehoods could have been detected by consumers. The case was *Federal Trade Commission* v. *Standard Education Society*, 302 U.S. 112, 58 S.Ct. 113, 82 L.Ed. 141 (1937). Now this case took place long before the Internet and Wikipedia, in 1937 to be exact, when actual bound encyclopedias were on many bookshelves and screamed prestige. In selling their *Standard Reference Work* and *New Standard Encyclopedia*, the company representative convinced the prospects that they had been selected because of their prestige and stature in the community from a small list of well connected, representative people in various areas. Allegedly, the company was presenting them with a "deluxe edition" of the encyclopedia free of charge. As the scheme developed, the representative would state that "they [were] giving away a set of books . . . free as an advertising plan . . . that the prospect [had] been specially selected, and that the only return desired for the gift [was] permission to use the name of the prospect for advertising purposes."

The prospects were told that they would only have to pay for the loose-leaf extension service, which was $69.50. This, the prospects were told, was "a reduced price and that the regular price of the books and the extension service is $150, sometimes even as high as $200." These statements were false and were part of the scheme. In fact, the $69.50 price was the regular price for both the encyclopedia and the loose-leaf extension. Clearly, it was the practice of Standard Education Society to mislead customers into believing that they were being given a free encyclopedia, and that they only were to pay for the extension service. The record in this case is chock-full of testimony from people in ten states that confirmed this.

What is interesting here is that the Circuit Court of Appeals for the Second Circuit (the lower court heard the case before the U.S. Supreme Court) had decided they could not seriously entertain the notion "that a man who is buying a set of books and a [ten] year extension service, will be fatuous enough to be misled by the mere statement that the first are given away, and that he is paying only for the second." Here the court felt that no "reasonable man" would believe the claim that he was getting one item for free if he paid for the other. The U.S. Supreme Court, however, felt—as did the FTC originally—that the lower court was wrong; an "ignorant man" could believe the claim.

To illustrate that point, Justice Black in the majority opinion authored by him in 1937 wrote: "The fact that a false statement may be obviously false to those who are trained and experienced does not damage its character, nor take away its power to deceive others less experienced. There is no duty resting upon a citizen to suspect the honesty of those with whom he transacts business. Laws are made to protect the trusting as well as the suspicious. The best element of business has long since decided that honesty should govern competitive enterprises, and that the rule of caveat emptor should not be relied upon to reward fraud and deception."

This case could have been interpreted in several ways, and it was by the appeals court. However, it was interpreted by the U.S. Supreme Court as having abolished the reasonable man standard altogether. In fact, it firmly entrenched the ignorant man standard, which would continue for some time.

The Ignorant Man Standard

During the decade that followed, the ignorant man standard flourished, as was illustrated in *Gelb* v. *FTC*, 144 F.2d 580 (2d Cir. 1944). The case concerned an advertising claim that, among other things, a shampooing and coloring preparation known as Progressive Clairol and Instant Clairol permanently colored hair. One of the questions in this case dealt with the standard of perception of the consumer—specifically, whether an order should be upheld that would enjoin Clairol from "representing that the effect produced upon the color of the hair by the use of said preparation is permanent."

Looking at the advertisements for Clairol literally, it is obvious that the preparation permanently colors hair to which it is applied. But the commission found (and this would seem obvious to a "reasonable" man) that the preparation has no effect on new hair as it grows in. Hence the commission concluded that the claim of the preparation "permanently" coloring hair was misleading. It seems absurd that any user of the preparation could be so simple-minded as to suppose that hair not yet grown out would be colored as well. (One witness was found who, after some prodding, finally testified "that you would think 'permanent' means you would never need to bother having it dyed again," although the witness knew better.) Yet the commission construed the advertisement as representing that it would do just that. Therefore, it ruled that the claim was false and deceptive.

The court, in this appeal from the earlier FTC ruling, validated the commission's earlier decision. Both the court and the commission reasoned that Section 5 of the act was designed for the protection of the blindly trusting, as well as the suspicious. The result of this case was that evidence of deception, regardless of how unintended or unreasonable, was sufficient for a finding of deceptive advertising, even if only a single person were deceived, and even if that person was incompetent or a complete babbling fool. The status quo at the time was that "people have a right to assume that fraudulent advertising traps will not be laid to ensnare them" (*Donaldson* v. *Read Magazine, Inc.*, 333 U.S. 178, 68 S.Ct. 591, 92 L.Ed. 628 (1948)). Yet it appears that, at that time, the concept was taken to its extreme.

Moving Back to the Reasonable Man Standard

Beginning in 1963 and modified in 1984, the FTC has moved back in the direction of a reasonable man standard of perception where it remains today. Thankfully, the commission withdrew from the concept that deception of a single consumer, no matter how foolish or imperceptive, constitutes a deceptive practice.

True, the commission's responsibility is to prevent deception of the gullible and credulous, as well as the cautious and knowledgeable. This principle, however, loses its credibility if it is pushed to an absurd extreme as it was with the "ignorant man" standard. It serves no public interest if an advertiser could be held liable for every misconception, however outlandish. His representations cannot be subject to interpretation by the foolish or feeble-minded—the "ignorant man." Some people, because of ignorance or incomprehension, may be misled by even a scrupulously honest claim.

Perhaps a few misguided souls believe that all Danish pastry is actually made in Denmark. Is it deceptive to call a bakery item "Danish pastry" if it is made in California? Of course not! There are product exceptions to this logic however. For example, Champagne is a term reserved (legally throughout the E.U. as of 1994) for a product made only in the Champagne region of France.

Under the reasonable man standard, an ad claim does not become false and deceptive merely because it will be misunderstood by an insignificant and nonrepresentative segment of people within the market that the ad addresses.

In 1973 the commission presented its opinion, *In the Matter of Coca-Cola Company*, F.T.C. Docket No. 8839. In this case the commission dealt with an issue involving the Coca-Cola Company's marketing of a drink called Hi-C. It had been advertised as "the sensible drink . . . made with fresh fruit . . . [and] . . . being high in Vitamin C, . . . [and that children] . . . can drink as much . . . as they like." Television commercials and some package labels showed oranges and other fruits, from which the juices are used to make Hi-C. The complaint in this case stated that these advertisements compared Hi-C with natural citrus juices by implication. Therefore it was deceptive.

The commission maintained that Hi-C advertisements implicitly compared Hi-C with natural citrus juices and with orange juice in particular. It was alleged that consumers would likely take the advertisement to mean that Hi-C was made from fresh orange juice and was equal to, or better than, actual fresh orange juice in nutritional value.

Here the advertising representations were "not reasonably likely to have communicated" characteristics of Hi-C which were contrary to fact. It is possible to agree that the statements were "not reasonably likely" to deceive based purely on the facts. However, the statement of Commissioner Jones (dissenting) brings into play the standard of perception model: "The commission's opinion ignores or perhaps reverses the standard model of the consumer as 'the ignorant, the unthinking and the credulous' consumer which the commission has been commanded to use in determining whether a particular act is unfair or deceptive. Instead, without any evidence in the record to support it, the commission implicitly adopts a new consumer model as its standard for interpreting whether a claim is likely to deceive."

This standard is actually one portraying the consumer as discriminating, sophisticated, and highly knowledgeable as well as skeptical and unbelieving. This consumer knows that fruit drinks are not the same as citrus juices despite what Hi-C ads said.

Because of that case, the commission has toughened its stance on the reasonable man standard as it exists today. The commission announced, through its 1984 *Cliffdale* decision, that only consumers "acting reasonably in the circumstances" were protected by the government. This new standard runs parallel with the "reasonableness" standard used in tort law negligence. Because of this, if the consumer is negligent in his behavior as a consumer, the FTC won't protect him.

It would appear then, that today the percentage of consumers affected would be required to be greater than with the earlier and original reasonable man standard. Perhaps we should call this the "prudent man standard." The main difference here is that in the past, the reasonable man standard was based on "a *reasonable person* in the situation," whereas now the issue involves "a consumer *acting reasonably*." (Emphasis added.) There is a difference.

In the *Cliffdale* case, much concern had been raised regarding the new direction that the commission had taken. Commissioner Pertschuk, concurring in part and dissenting in part to the *Cliffdale* decision, said that "[t]he new deception analysis has a more serious effect that is clearly not unintentional. That is, to withdraw the protection of Section 5 from consumers who do not act 'reasonably.'"

The Commissioner went on to say that: "The sad fact is that a small segment of our society makes its livelihood preying upon consumers who are very trusting and unsophisticated. Others specialize in weakening the defenses of especially vulnerable, but normally cautious, consumers. Through skillful exploitation of such common desires as the wish to get rich quick or to provide some measure of security for one's old age, professional con men can prompt conduct that many of their victims will readily admit—in hindsight—is patently unreasonable."

"Of course, what strikes me as 'unreasonable' consumer behavior may not seem so to other commissioners. The very subjective nature of the 'reasonable consumer' standard is cause for concern. How can consumer conduct be measured for reasonableness? I know of no test for it, and I am fearful of the *ad hoc* determinations that will be made in the future."

Also concurring in part and dissenting in part to *Cliffdale* was Commissioner Bailey. She had trouble with the new distinction as well.

Commissioner Bailey said: "The second requirement is that an act or practice be likely to mislead consumers 'acting reasonably under the circumstances.' Of the three newly introduced elements, I believe this is on its face the most divorced from prior precedent and also the most likely to produce troubling results."

She went on to explain that:

A claim or practice must deceive a "substantial number" of consumers in order to trigger a finding of deception . . . . Thus, while the Commission has indicated that it will not subject sellers to every interpretation made by an 'insubstantial and unrepresentative segment' of the seller's audience, it has at the same time faithfully adhered to the enduring proposition that consumers are entitled to take commercial representations at face value and need not mistrust them. I believe the imposition of a "reasonable consumer" test as an element of the legal standard for deception may seriously jeopardize this guiding principle of deception law, which has permitted and encouraged the Commission to spread its protective mantle over the uninformed and credulous, those with understandable but often unreasonable hopes, those with limited reasoning abilities, such as children, and even "average" consumers whose guard may be down or who may behave somewhat carelessly in the face of deceptive conduct.

Clearly, this element of deception has seen much activity and debate in cases to up to today.

Reasonable Basis Rule

This section is not to be confused with the reasonable man standard we just looked at. This is a different topic all together. Currently the FTC, and the courts, look to material claims of effectiveness in relation to whether there was a "reasonable basis" upon which the claims were made. In other words, was there adequate "credible" substantiation upon which to make the claim. The reasonable basis rule looks at the credibility of the support for claims used in an advertisement. This is a point all advertisers should take to heart.

A case in point, *Federal Trade Commission* v. *National Urological Group, Inc.,* 645 F. Supp. 2d 1167 (2008), discussed this point. National Urological Group (NUG) marketed a number of products, two of which were: Thermalean claimed to be an effective treatment for obesity and Spontane-ES claimed to be effective in treating erectile dysfunction. Many statements were made in the advertising upon which these claims were based.

The FTC argued, however, that the manufacturer made claims in its advertising that falsely represented that Thermalean was clinically proven to be an effective treatment for obesity and represented, without a "reasonable basis," and that Thermalean was an effective treatment for obesity. The FTC also argued that the Spontane-ES advertising, without a "reasonable basis," represented that Spontane-ES was effective in treating erectile dysfunction in 90 percent of users.

Under a "reasonable basis" theory, the advertiser must demonstrate a reasonable basis (or adequate substantiation) for asserting that the claim was true. The court said: "[I]n the case of health-related claims or claims concerning the efficacy or safety of dietary supplements, this reasonable basis must, at a minimum, consist of competent and reliable scientific evidence."

All of the products in this case are dietary supplements and compounds that are marketed as promoting health benefits in the form of weight loss and sexual enhancement. Therefore, all of the claims in this case must be supported by "competent and reliable scientific evidence." The FTC has defined competent and reliable scientific evidence as "tests, analyses, research, studies, or other evidence based on the expertise of professionals in the relevant area, that have been conducted and evaluated in an objective manner by persons qualified to do so, using procedures generally accepted in the profession to yield accurate and reliable results."

Let's take a look at one of the products, Thermalean for example. The ads claimed that a clinical test was performed on the product. However in court the defendants admitted that the products have not been clinically tested. The FTC further contended that the Thermalean advertisements falsely represent that Thermalean caused rapid and substantial weight loss, including as much as thirty pounds in two months.

In Thermalean advertising, a typical claim was made by Dr. Mark Wright, M.D. He stated that "Thermalean's scientifically proven formula has yielded the following results in independent university-sponsored trials: 42 percent reduction in body fat, 300 percent decrease in stored fat, 76.9 percent elevation in basal metabolic rate, 20 to 35 percent reduction in abdominal fat, 600 percent greater fat burning capabilities than placebo." The court concluded that this type of language clearly implies that the results were "clinically proven," and is satisfied that Wright made both of the asserted claims. However NUG provided no support for these claims.

The FTC cited that there was no evidence that the active ingredients used in Thermalean could provide anything close to the result claimed in the advertising. The defendants disputed this fact. However, rather than specifying the nature of their dispute, they simply pointed the court to an ambiguous reference to fifty "statements of fact." Even after reviewing these fifty statements of fact, the court found no support for their claims. The court said that ". . . the defendants' failure to combat the FTC's expert testimony with anything more than a vague reference to fifty paragraphs is the equivalent of sending the court on a snipe hunt through the defendants' evidence. It is not the role of the court to pinpoint the defendants' evidence for them; accordingly, the court concludes that there is no factual dispute and that the two representations at issue are false and likely to mislead."

Susceptibility of the Audience

In determining the consumer's interpretation of the message in an advertisement, the primary guideline is the susceptibility of the audience that the advertisement is directed toward. The level of susceptibility is flexible and is adjusted to the norm of the intended audience. It is different for children than for adults. It is also different for the elderly or terminally ill than for a healthy young adult. We find this condition often in the area of "unfairness" claims, which we will discuss later in this chapter.

In the case *In the Matter of Doris Savitch*, 50 F.T.C. 828 (1954), affirmed per curiam, 218 F.2d 817 (7th Cir. 1955), the commission measured the susceptibility of an audience to which the ad was directed. Personal Drug Co., owned by Doris Savitch and Leo Savitch, manufactured and advertised products under the names *Quick-Kaps* and *D-Lay Capsules*. Quick-Kaps were advertised as medication that would relieve a woman's overdue period (see box 2.3). Bear in mind that this took place in the mid-1950s when there was a vastly different mindset regarding pregnancy and abortion than there is today.

Box 2.3

PERIOD DELAYED?

(Overdue)

Don't Risk Disaster. Don't Worry

At last—it CAN BE SOLD, a new, extra effective, Doctor approved formula—"Quick-Kaps" capsules may relieve you of your biggest worry—when due to minor functional menstrual delay or borderline anemia. Scientifically prepared by registered Pharmacists, "Quick-Kaps" capsules contain only medically recognized drugs, having no harmful after effects—Complete supply—packed in a confidential box only $5.00. Send no money and we will mail C.O.D. plus small postal and C.O.D. charges or send $5.00 cash and we will rush AIR MAIL.

"Just the thing to have on hand

The implication here is strong: Relief from delayed menstruation due to pregnancy will be accomplished by using *Quick-Kaps*. The advertisements also represented that its use would provide relief from delayed menstruation due to "minor functional disorders and borderline anemia." The first problem here is with the causes of delayed menstruation. The biggest cause is pregnancy. A more infrequent cause is iron deficiency anemia. Borderline anemia is not a cause of delayed menstruation other than in those rare cases when it is due to iron deficiency anemia.

Let's take a look at some of the phrases used in the advertisement which are significant—for example, "Don't Worry"—"Don't Risk Disaster"—"May relieve you of your biggest worry"—"Medically recognized drugs having no harmful after effects"—"At last—it CAN BE SOLD, a new, extra effective, Doctor approved formula." The above-quoted phrase would seem to imply that, either because of a change in the law or recent medical discoveries, a new preparation was now being put on the market. This was not the case, and the ad was held to violate the FTC Act.

The commission felt that it was a commonly known fact that selling preparations or devices that would induce an abortion was prohibited by law. People looking for such a product would not expect to find it advertised as obviously and openly as products that were not prohibited. This advertisement seems to invite reading between the lines. It is reminiscent of bootlegging days when a knowing wink to a buyer implied that the "cold tea" being sold was in fact illegal liquor. Obviously, the implication about a product is as important as the literal truth of each sentence or picture. "The ultimate impression upon the mind of the reader (or viewer) arises not only from what is said, but also from what is reasonably implied."(*Aronberg, trading as Positive Products Company* v. *FTC*, 132 F.2d 165 (7th Cir. 1943)). We explore more on this area of interpretation of an ad later in this chapter.

The *Doris Savitch* case illustrates the condition of susceptibility of an audience to which an advertisement is directed. It is reasonable to say that a woman would worry about delayed menstruation and could believe that this was caused by pregnancy. If she wanted to alleviate that situation, the advertisement for *Quick-Kaps* might be interpreted as promising that relief (an abortion). In any event, the commission stated in its conclusion to the case: "the mental condition of such a person is an element to be considered in arriving at which construction might reasonably be put upon the advertisement."

Ads Directed at a Specific Audience

Let's take another situation. Suppose that an advertisement appeared in a medical journal. The ad was not deceptive to a physician. Yet it fell into the hands of a layman who was actually deceived. Under these circumstances would the advertisement be deceptive even though a different person/audience was actually deceived?

That was the situation in *Belmont Laboratories, Inc.* v. *FTC*, 103 F. 2d 538 (3rd Cir. 1939). Obviously false claims regarding the curing potential of Mazon, a soap and ointment, had been made. Keep in mind as you read the case that while this was in 1939, the theory still holds true today. In medical pamphlets addressed to doctors and nurses, Mazon claimed to permanently eliminate specific ailments (see box 2.4).

Box 2.4

Mazon—an ethical preparation compounded under the personal supervision of its originator—is the original treatment of its character for:

Eczema	Ring worm
Psoriasis	Athlete's foot
Head scalds	Barber's itch
Ivy poison	Other skin disorders

The colloidal nature of the base of Mazon and its strong penetrating characteristics, together with its healing and soothing ingredients, afford quick and permanent elimination of Eczema and other skin disorders. No other treatment for permanent cure has ever been discovered. Some of the best-known skin specialists in the city are using it exclusively and praise it highly.

The claims found in the example were medically untrue. A major problem was with the claim that the product "permanently eliminated" certain diseases. The copy tends to convey that by an external application of an ointment, internal disorders can be cured. It fails to recognize the need to apply internal remedies to diseases caused by internal problems.

Many of the diseases listed (eczema, psoriasis, etc.) are caused by internal disturbances. The application of an external remedy can do little more than alleviate the exterior symptoms. The ad also created an impression of newness. One may have a vision of thousands of doctors and druggists working diligently at hundreds of hospitals and laboratories to develop the new medical wonder—Mazon. This was certainly not the case.

These advertisements were found in pamphlets, which were circulated to the medical profession, and in a medical journal. Leaflets were also included inside the packages. The court said: "physicians and readers of professional journals are too smart to be deceived and that lay purchasers buy blind because the leaflet is inside the carton containing the ointment. We think that one position is untrue legally and the other factually."

In other words, the advertisements were blatantly untrue. Doctors and nurses would know that, but the consumer would not. The consumer would buy the product blindly because they could not read the leaflet, which was inside the package, until after he made the purchase.

The benchmark of this concept is: who is deceived? If a person of low intellect is deceived by an advertisement for a Tesla automobile, does this demonstrate "a likelihood" to deceive? The test for deception (or rather deceptiveness) is rooted in the market at which the advertisement is directed. However, if the advertisement reaches another market, the perception of that reader or viewer will be considered. Based on that reasoning, Belmont Laboratories lost.

The Issue of Net Impression

Whether an advertisement is deceptive must not be determined by viewing isolated parts of the advertisement (this has been alluded to earlier), but rather it should be based on the net impression of the entire ad. The net impression of the ad is the understanding that the reader walks away with after coming into contact with the advertisement, in total. Keep in mind the reader will be determined by the current reasonable man standard, as we have discussed earlier.

Directly on this issue are statements by FTC Commissioner Mary L. Azcuenaga during a speech to the American Advertising Federation, National Government Affairs Conference, in Washington, D.C., on March 8, 1994. She addressed the relationship between claims made in a headline and claims or qualifications made in the text of the ad.

Azcuenaga pointed out that: "it would not be good policy to condone advertisements that make strong false or misleading claims in a headline, only to disclaim them in what is referred to as 'mouse print.'" She went on to say: "In evaluating the impact of the headline, the Commission will consider the 'net impression' created by the advertisement. The meaning of the advertisement should be construed in the context of the advertisement as a whole, not by individual elements of the ad taken out of context."

One very well-established case (from the 1940s) that demonstrated the principle of "net impression" is *Zenith Radio Corp. v. FTC*, 143 F.2d 29 (7th Cir. 1944). In this case, the commission alleged two primary issues in a series of advertisements for Zenith radios to determine if they were deceptive. The first involved Zenith's assertion regarding the capacity of its radio to receive foreign broadcasts. The second assertion involved the number of tubes contained in its radio sets. These claims were found to be deceptive. The text of a typical advertisement appears in box 2.5.

Box 2.5

Europe is talking to you every night in English. Are you listening? With Zenith, the short wave radio that gives you Europe direct, you can hear all the leaders, all the daily news broadcasts. You need not depend on rebroadcasts which bring you only a small part. Europe, South America, or the Orient every day guaranteed or your money back on all short wave Zeniths. 1940 Zenith, the guaranteed short wave radio.

In truth, atmospheric conditions existed that made it impossible to receive satisfactory reception of foreign broadcasts. The Zenith radios were incapable of satisfactory reception of foreign broadcasts every day and under all conditions. The commission reasoned that the effect of the claims was to induce consumers to believe that radio reception problems would be completely overcome by using the Zenith radio. This is a good example of how deception was possible due to the consumers' lack of knowledge about the technical limitations of radio reception.

The second issue concerned the number of tubes contained in the radio. In the years before solid-state equipment was developed, radios used vacuum tubes.

The ads listed different models available with the following tubes:

6-Tube Superheterodyne Table Model
8-Tube Superheterodyne with Wavemagnet Aerial
10-Tube Superheterodyne with Rotor Wavemagnet Aerial
11-Tube Superheterodyne with Rotor Wavemagnet Aerial

The commission defined "tubes" as devices that perform "the primary function of detecting, amplifying, or receiving radio signals." However, some of the tubes contained in the Zenith radio, and which were included in the advertised tube count, had nothing to do with receiving radio signals. They were, in fact, used for tuning and converting alternating current into direct current, and therefore the commission determined that they did not qualify under its definition. The commission, after concluding that a large portion of purchasers believed that a radio was better and more powerful because of the number of tubes it contained, ruled against Zenith.

The point in the Zenith case was that while the statements about the number of tubes contained in the sets were accurate, viewed as a whole the ad was deceptive. The consumer couldn't determine the relevance of the number of tubes, other than "the more tubes, the better the set." As for the first issue in the case, reception capability, the consumer would believe that reception problems would be overcome with the Zenith set. The net impression created by the ad was, therefore, a deceptive one.

Distortion of Facts

Let's take a look at another situation. In *Lorillard Co.* v. *FTC*, 186 F.2d 52 (4th Cir. 1950), isolated segments of an article taken from *Reader's Digest* were used in an advertisement for Old Gold cigarettes. Lorillard attempted to use the argument that the ads merely stated what had been stated in that article. By examining the advertisements however, the court determined that the meaning of the *Reader's Digest* article had been distorted. In essence, it amounted to the "use of the truth in such a way as to cause the reader to believe the exact opposite of what was intended by the writer of the article."

By comparing the advertisement with the article, we see where the problem lies. The article, referring to results of independent laboratory tests of the leading brands of cigarettes, actually said:

> The laboratory's general conclusion will be sad news for the advertising copywriters, but good news for the smoker, who need no longer worry as to which cigarette can most effectively nail down his coffin. For one nail is just about as good as another. The differences between brands are, practically speaking, small, and no single brand is so superior to its competitors as to justify its selection on the ground that it is less harmful. How small the variations are may be seen from the data tabulated on page 7.

That table showed the insignificance of the difference in the tar and nicotine content of the various brands. While the tests did show that Old Golds contained less nicotine, tars, and resins than the others, the difference was so small as to be entirely insignificant to the smoker.

Yet the company advertised this difference as if it had been awarded a commendation for public health, rather than a slap in the face by *Reader's Digest* (see box 2.6 for one such advertisement). Almost anyone reading the ad would get an entirely different impression from the actual facts. A person would think that Old Golds were less irritating and less harmful than the other leading brands, all because of the *Reader's Digest* research. Few, in fact, would have bothered to look up the article. As we have seen, the truth was exactly the opposite.

Box 2.6

OLD GOLDS FOUND LOWEST IN NICOTINE

OLD GOLDS FOUND LOWEST IN THROAT-IRRITATING TARS AND RESINS

See Impartial Test by *Reader's Digest,* July Issue.

See How Your Brand Compares with Old Gold.

Reader's Digest assigned a scientific testing laboratory to find out about cigarettes. They tested seven leading cigarettes and *Reader's Digest* published the results.

The cigarette whose smoke was lowest in nicotine was Old Gold. The cigarette with the least throat-irritating tars and resins was Old Gold. On both these major counts Old Gold was best among all seven cigarettes tested.

Get July *Reader's Digest*. Turn to page 5.

See what this highly respected magazine reports.

You'll say, "From now on, my cigarette is Old Gold!"

Light one? Note the mild, interesting flavor. Easier on the throat? Sure. And more smoking pleasure? Yes. It's the new Old Gold—finer yet, since "something new has been added."

In this case, the court concluded by saying: In determining whether or not advertising is false or misleading . . . regard must be had, not to fine spun distinctions and arguments that may be made in excuse but to the effect which it might reasonably be expected to have upon the general public. The important criterion is the net impression which the advertisement is likely to make upon the general populace.

The Use of Visual Distortion

In addition to the blatant deception we saw in the Volvo case discussed earlier, the use of mock-ups (a model built to depict an actual situation) has also been an area of concern, particularly where photography and television are employed.

A problem can present itself due to certain limitations of visual reproduction. As we'll see, the deception issue arises when these limitations are overcome in a way that portrays the product as something it isn't.

In a landmark case, *In the Matter of Campbell Soup Co.*, 77 F.T.C. 664 (1970), the commission looked at advertisements that showed a bowl of Campbell's soup. To all appearances, the soup had been prepared according to the directions on the can and was shown in a "ready to eat" situation. By viewing the ad the consumer apparently saw the abundance of "solid ingredients" that were present in a typical bowl of Campbell's soup.

The commission stated the reality of the advertisement: "In truth and in fact, in many of the . . . advertisements, which purport to demonstrate or offer evidence of the quantity and abundance of solid ingredients in a can of Campbell soup, [the advertiser has] placed, or caused to be placed in the aforesaid bowl . . . a number of clear glass marbles which prevent the solid ingredients from sinking to the bottom, thereby giving the soup the appearance of containing more solid ingredients than it actually contains, which fact is not disclosed. The aforesaid demonstration exaggerates, misrepresents, and is not evidence of, the quantity or abundance of solid ingredients in a can of Campbell soup; therefore, the aforesaid advertisements are false, misleading, and deceptive."

In fact, Campbell Soup Co. had placed marbles in the bottom of a bowl of soup that was shown in the advertisement. This caused the solids in the soup to stay up at the surface. The respondent claimed that the limitations of the medium necessitated the use of this mock-up to portray the actual viscosity of the product. The commission didn't agree with that reasoning and ordered Campbell to stop using the ads. This case was settled by consent order; Campbell agreed to the commission's determination and consented to abide by it.

As seen in the above example, the reality of an advertisement's net impression must be considered carefully.

Unfairness Policy of the FTC

We touched on this earlier in chapter 1, and we should revisit the ever-expanding concept here. Due to a greater interest in privacy and new media technologies, it is becoming more common that the FTC will attack a claim under the unfairness theory, so the advertiser must understand its implications. Until 1994 there were few notable cases to review. The ones worth noting include: *FTC v. Sperry & Hutchinson Co.*, 405 U.S. 233, 92 S.Ct. 898, 31 L.Ed. 2d 170 (1972); *In the Matter of Pfizer, Inc.*, 81 F.T.C. 23 (1972); *In the Matter of I.T.T. Continental*, 90 F.T.C. 181 (1977); and, *In the Matter of International Harvester Co.*, 104 F.T.C. 949 (1984).

In 1980, the FTC issued a Policy Statement on Unfairness. The goal of the statement was to clarify the FTC's stance on unfairness violations. What follows is the bulk of that statement.

FTC Statement of Policy on the Scope of the Consumer Unfairness Jurisdiction

Section 5 of the FTC Act prohibits, in part, "unfair . . . acts or practices in or affecting commerce." This is commonly referred to as the Commission's consumer unfairness jurisdiction.

The present understanding of the unfairness standard is the result of an evolutionary process. The statute was deliberately framed in general terms since Congress recognized the impossibility of drafting a complete list of unfair trade practices that would not quickly become outdated or leave loopholes for easy evasion. The task of identifying unfair trade practices was therefore assigned to the Commission, subject to judicial review, in the expectation that the underlying criteria would evolve and develop over time. As the Supreme Court observed as early as 1931, the ban on unfairness "belongs to that class of phrases which do not admit of precise definition, but the meaning and application of which must be arrived at by what this court elsewhere has called 'the gradual process of judicial inclusion and exclusion.'"

By 1964, enough cases had been decided to enable the Commission to identify three factors that it considered when applying the prohibition against consumer unfairness. These were: (1) whether the practice injures consumers; (2) whether it violates established public policy; (3) whether it is unethical or unscrupulous. These factors were later quoted with apparent approval by the Supreme Court in the 1972 case of *FTC v. Sperry & Hutchinson Co.*, 405 U.S. 233, 249 (1972), [referred to hereafter as *S&H*]. Since then the Commission has continued to refine the standard of unfairness in its cases and rules, and it has now reached a more detailed sense of both the definition and the limits of these criteria.

Consumer Injury Unjustified consumer injury is the primary focus of the FTC Act, and the most important of the three S&H criteria. By itself it can be sufficient to warrant a finding of unfairness. The Commission's ability to rely on an independent criterion of consumer injury is consistent with the intent of the statute, which was to "[make] the consumer who may be injured by an unfair trade practice of equal concern before the law with the merchant injured by the unfair methods of a dishonest competitor."

The independent nature of the consumer injury criterion does not mean that every consumer injury is legally "unfair," however. To justify a finding of unfairness the injury must satisfy three tests. It must be substantial; it must not be outweighed by any countervailing benefits to consumers or competition that the practice produces; and it must be an injury that consumers themselves could not reasonably have avoided.

First of all, the injury must be substantial. The Commission is not concerned with trivial or merely speculative harms. In most cases a substantial injury involves monetary harm, as when sellers coerce consumers into purchasing unwanted goods or services or when consumers buy defective goods or services on credit but are unable to assert against the creditor claims or defenses arising from the transaction. Unwarranted health and safety risks may also support a finding of unfairness. Emotional impact and other more subjective types of harm, on the other hand, will not ordinarily make a practice unfair. Thus, for example, the Commission will not seek to ban an advertisement merely because it offends the tastes or social beliefs of some viewers, as has been suggested in some of the comments.

Second, the injury must not be outweighed by any offsetting consumer or competitive benefits that the sales practice also produces. Most business practices entail a mixture of economic and other costs and benefits for purchasers. A seller's failure to present complex technical data on his product may lessen a consumer's ability to choose, for example, but may also reduce the initial price he must pay for the article. The Commission is aware of these tradeoffs and will not find that a practice unfairly injures consumers unless it is injurious in its net effects. The Commission also takes account of the various costs that a remedy would entail. These include not only the costs to the parties directly before the agency, but also the burdens on society in general in the form of increased paperwork, increased regulatory burdens on the flow of information, reduced incentives to innovation and capital formation, and similar matters. Finally, the injury must be one which consumers could not reasonably have avoided. Normally we expect the marketplace to be self-correcting, and we rely on consumer choice—the ability of individual consumers to make their own private purchasing decisions without regulatory intervention—to govern the market. We anticipate that consumers will survey the available alternatives, choose those that are most desirable, and avoid those that are inadequate or unsatisfactory. However, it has long been recognized that certain types of sales techniques may prevent consumers from effectively making their own decisions and that corrective action may then become necessary. Most of the Commission's unfairness matters are brought under these circumstances. They are brought, not to second-guess the wisdom of particular consumer decisions, but rather to halt some form of seller behavior that unreasonably creates or takes advantage of an obstacle to the free exercise of consumer decision making.

Sellers may adopt a number of practices that unjustifiably hinder such free market decisions. Some may withhold or fail to generate critical price or performance data, for example, leaving buyers with insufficient information for informed comparisons. Some may engage in overt coercion, as by dismantling a home appliance for "inspection" and refusing to reassemble it until a service contract is signed. And some may exercise undue influence over highly susceptible classes of purchasers, as by promoting fraudulent "cures" to seriously ill cancer patients. Each of these practices undermines an essential precondition to a free and informed consumer transaction, and, in turn, to a well-functioning market. Each of them is therefore properly banned as an unfair practice under the FTC Act.

Violation of Public Policy The second S&H standard asks whether the conduct violates public policy as it has been established by statute, common law, industry practice, or otherwise. This criterion may be applied in two different ways. It may be used to test the validity and strength of the evidence of consumer injury, or, less often, it may be cited for a dispositive legislative or judicial determination that such injury is present.

Although public policy was listed by the S&H Court as a separate consideration, it is used most frequently by the Commission as a means of providing additional evidence on the degree of consumer injury caused by specific practices. To be sure, most Commission actions are brought to redress relatively clear-cut injuries, and those determinations are based, in large part, on objective economic analysis. As we have indicated before, the Commission believes that considerable attention should be devoted to the analysis of whether substantial net harm has occurred, not only because that is part of the unfairness test, but also because the focus on injury is the best way to ensure that the Commission acts responsibly and uses its resources wisely. Nonetheless, the Commission wishes to emphasize the importance of examining outside statutory policies and established judicial principles for assistance in helping the agency ascertain whether a particular form of conduct does in fact tend to harm consumers. Thus the agency has referred to First Amendment decisions upholding consumers' rights to receive information, for example, to confirm that restrictions on advertising tend unfairly to hinder the informed exercise of consumer choice.

Conversely, statutes or other sources of public policy may affirmatively allow for a practice that the Commission tentatively views as unfair. The existence of such policies will then give the agency reason to reconsider its assessment of whether the practice is actually injurious in its net effects. In other situations there may be no clearly established public policies, or the policies may even be in conflict. While that does not necessarily preclude the Commission from taking action if there is strong evidence of net consumer injury, it does underscore the desirability of carefully examining public policies in all instances. In any event, whenever objective evidence of consumer injury is difficult to obtain, the need to identify and assess all relevant public policies assumes increased importance.

Sometimes public policy will independently support a Commission action. This occurs when the policy is so clear that it will entirely determine the question of consumer injury, so there is little need for separate analysis by the Commission. In these cases the legislature or court, in announcing the policy, has already determined that such injury does exist and thus it need not be expressly proved in each instance. An example of this approach arose in a case involving a mail-order firm. There the Commission was persuaded by an analogy to the due-process clause that it was unfair for the firm to bring collection suits in a forum that was unreasonably difficult for the defendants to reach. In a similar case the Commission applied the statutory policies of the Uniform Commercial Code to require that various automobile manufacturers and their distributors refund to their customers any surplus money that was realized after they repossessed and resold their customers' cars. The Commission acts on such a basis only where the public policy is suitable for administrative enforcement by this agency, however. Thus it turned down a petition for a rule to require fuller disclosure of aerosol propellants, reasoning that the subject of fluorocarbon safety was currently under study by other scientific and legislative bodies with more appropriate expertise or jurisdiction over the subject.

To the extent that the Commission relies heavily on public policy to support a finding of unfairness, the policy should be clear and well-established. In other words, the policy should be declared or embodied in formal sources such as statutes, judicial decisions, or the Constitution as interpreted by the courts, rather than being ascertained from the general sense of the national values. The policy should likewise be one that is widely shared, and not the isolated decision of a single state or a single court. If these two tests are not met, the policy cannot be considered as an "established" public policy for purposes of the *S&H* criterion. The Commission would then act only on the basis of convincing independent evidence that the practice was distorting the operation of the market and thereby causing unjustified consumer injury.

Unethical or Unscrupulous Conduct Finally, the third *S&H* standard asks whether the conduct was immoral, unethical, oppressive, or unscrupulous. This test was presumably included in order to be sure of reaching all the purposes of the underlying statute, which forbids "unfair" acts or practices. It would therefore allow the Commission to reach conduct that violates generally recognized standards of business ethics. The test has proven, however, to be largely duplicative. Conduct that is truly unethical or unscrupulous will almost always injure consumers or violate public policy as well. The Commission has therefore never relied on the third element of *S&H* as an independent basis for a finding of unfairness, and it will act in the future only on the basis of the first two.

FTC Act Amendments of 1994

On August 26, 1994, the FTC issued certain amendments of the FTC Act. Of the numerous changes made were two areas that impact advertising directly. The first was a change in the definition of an unfair act or practice. The second involved rulemaking based on unfairness. Let's take a closer look at those two amendments.

Definition of Unfair Act or Practice

Section 5 of the FTC Act was amended to provide that in order for the FTC to determine that an act is unfair, three new requirements must be met:

1. The act or practice causes, or is likely to cause, substantial injury to consumers;
2. The injury, or likelihood of injury, is not reasonably avoidable by consumers; and
3. The injury, or likelihood of injury, is not outweighed by a benefit to consumers or to competition.

In addition, the amendment allows the FTC to consider public policy evidence in determining whether a practice in unfair. However, public policy evidence may not be the primary basis in determining unfairness.

Rulemaking Based on Unfairness

Until 1994, the Commission was banned from issuing industry-wide rulemaking that related to unfair advertising practices. However, with these amendments, Section 18(b) of the FTC Act was modified to end this ban. The amendment provides that the FTC may "rulemake" under the unfairness definition when there is reason to believe that the conduct is "prevalent" in the industry. "Prevalence" is defined as either:

1. Where the FTC has previously issued cease and desist orders relating to the challenged act or practice; or
2. Any other information that indicates a widespread pattern of unfair or deceptive acts or practices.

Restricting Nondeceptive, Truthful Advertising

In contrast to deceptive advertising is the issue of FTC restrictions on advertising that is truthful and not deceptive. The courts have addressed that situation as well. Here's a case in point.

In *California Dental Assn.* v. *FTC*, 128 F.3d 720 (9th Cir. 1997), the court held that the FTC's decision that the California Dental Association's (CDA) advertising rules unreasonably restrained trade and violated Section 5 of the FTC Act.

The CDA's advertising policies stated: "Any communication or advertisement which refers to the cost of dental services shall be exact, without omissions, and shall make each service clearly identifiable, without the use of such phrases as "as low as . . . and up," "lowest prices," or words or phrases of similar import."

"Any advertisement which refers to the cost of dental services and uses words of comparison or relativity—for example, "low fees" must be based on verifiable data substantiating the comparison or statement of relativity. The burden shall be on the dentist who advertises in such terms to establish the accuracy of the comparison or statement of relativity."

"Advertising claims as to the quality of services are not susceptible to measurement or verification; accordingly, such claims are likely to be false or misleading in any material respect."

The CDA's advertising rules about discount advertising required that advertisements disclose:

1. The dollar amount of the nondiscounted fee for the service;
2. The dollar amount of the discount fee or the percentage of the discount for the specific service;
3. The length of time that the discount would be offered;
4. Verifiable fees; and
5. Specific groups who qualified for the discount or any other terms and conditions or restrictions for qualifying for the discount.

Essentially, the CDA's advertising policy prohibited its members from making truthful, nondeceptive statements in advertising that related to offering volume discounts as well as statements describing prices as "low" or "reasonable." The court noted, "restrictions on the ability to advertise prices normally make it more difficult for consumers to find a lower price and for dentists to compete on the basis of price."

Limiting advertisements about quality, safety, and other nonprice aspects of dental services prevented the dentists from fully describing the services they offered. The CDA contended that claims about quality were inherently unverifiable and as a result misleading. The court, in reply, determined that this did not justify banning all quality claims without regard to whether they were, in fact, false or misleading.

In this regard, the court said: "Limiting advertisements about quality, safety, and other nonprice aspects of service prevents dentists from fully describing the package of services they offer, and thus limits their ability to compete. The restrictions may also affect output more directly, as quality and comfort advertising may induce some customers to obtain nonemergency care when they might not otherwise do so. CDA contends that claims about quality are inherently unverifiable and therefore misleading. While this danger exists, it does not justify banning all quality claims without regard to whether they are, in fact, false or misleading. Under these circumstances, we think that the restriction is a sufficiently naked restraint on output to justify quick look analysis. We also note in this regard the Supreme Court's repeated holdings that the scope of inquiry under the rule of reason is intended to be flexible depending on the nature of the restraint and the circumstances in which it is used. "

In upholding the FTC's ruling, the court further stated: "The Commission found that through its pattern of enforcement, the CDA went beyond the literal language of its rules to prohibit ads that were in fact true and nondeceptive."

The FTC correctly exercised its jurisdiction over the CDA. Substantial evidence supported the FTC's conclusion that the advertising rules of the CDA, as applied to truthful and nondeceptive advertisements, violate Section 1 of the Sherman Act and Section 5 of the FTC Act under an abbreviated rule of reason analysis.

On May 24, 1999, the U.S. Supreme Court unanimously upheld the FTC's jurisdiction over nonprofit professional associations but vacated and remanded to the court of appeals (*California Dental Association* v. *FTC*, U.S. Sup. Ct., No. 97-1625, cert. granted, 9/29/98).

The Issue of Puffery

Puffery is an area of advertising where the law allows the advertiser to make certain exaggerated statements or opinions about his product. Ivan Preston, in his classic book *The Great American Blow-Up: Puffery in Advertising and Selling* (2nd ed. 1996), defined puffing as the use of advertising that praises with "subjective opinions, superlatives, or exaggerations, vaguely and generally, stating no specific facts."

Similarly, Prosser and Keeton on Torts defines "puffing" as "a seller's privilege to lie his head off, so long as he says nothing specific, on the theory that no reasonable man would believe him, or that no reasonable man would be influenced by such talk." *Prosser and Keeton on the Law of Torts* ß 109, at 757 (5th ed. 1984).

Such statements as BMW's "The Ultimate Driving Machine," and Disney's "The Happiest Place on Earth" are perfect examples of puff. A certain degree of puffing has always been allowed in advertising. Yet, the tolerance for this practice is limited due to the inherent gray area in its use.

The use of puffing in advertising has generally been acceptable to both the FTC and courts, based on certain rationale. Courts have reasoned that consumers do not rely on expressions of opinion by advertisers about their products. Also, the FTC recognizes that certain statements of general praise are not likely to be relied on by consumers under its "capacity to deceive" standard. Finally, certain forms of superlative praise are permissible simply because there is no way to establish that they are false.

Legal Interpretation of Puffery

If the puff takes the form of a pure statement of opinion, and if the law prohibits only false factual statements, then it may be impossible for courts to prove that a false representation was made. While exaggerations, superlatives, and unsupported opinions in advertising have been tolerated, it is also clear that the extent of puffing has been reduced over the years. This is because of the increased desire of the FTC and courts to recognize that false factual representations can arise by implication, as we have discussed. This occurs in the use of some forms of puffing.

The commission investigated a situation of puffing in the case of *In The Matter of Dannon Milk Prods., Inc.*, 61 F.T.C. 840 (1962). Here, Dannon had made claims about its product, Dannon Yogurt. Specifically, Dannon claimed in advertisements, brochures, pamphlets, and radio broadcasts that "Dannon is known as nature's perfect food that science made better." Dannon argued that the perfect food claim was mere puffing. However, the commission reasoned that because of the present day emphasis on dieting, health, and nutrition, to make the claim that a food is perfect far exceeds puffing or exaggeration of qualities. It is a misrepresentation of a material fact.

The commission continued to develop the concept of puffing with their decision in *FTC* v. *Direct Marketing Concepts, Inc.*, 624 F.3d 1 (2010). The defendants in this case made millions off of infomercials shilling products that they claimed cured literally every disease, from cancer to Parkinson's to obesity. In particular, two products Coral Calcium and Supreme Greens were promoted through TV infomercials.

The infomercial for Coral Calcium relied on a purported expertise of Robert Barefoot. In the infomercial, Barefoot boasted a number of claims regarding coral-derived calcium and its supposed biological and medical healing properties. Barefoot claimed that all diseases are caused by a condition called acidosis. Barefoot then claimed that calcium derived from Okinawan coral cures these diseases including cancer, heart disease, Lupus and Parkinson's. During the period, from January 2002 to July 2003, the Coral Calcium infomercial generated $54 million in sales.

As with Coral Calcium, the Supreme Greens infomercials relied on the purported expertise of "Dr." Alejandro Guerrero. Like Barefoot, Guerrero claimed that many major diseases are caused by acidosis, and that these diseases can be prevented and cured by rendering the body more alkaline. Guerrero also claimed that Supreme Greens can cause weight loss by restoring alkalinity because "fat is your body's way of protecting itself from the acidic fluids." Guerrero was presented as a "Doctor of Oriental Medicine," but he had no medical degrees of any kind. During the period, August 2003 to June 2004, Supreme Greens generated $14 million in sales.

If you can believe it, the Defendants in this case actually claimed that their infomercials advanced no actual health claims but, instead, presented "only puffery which was further attenuated by the presence of general disclaimers." Now it's true that where a claim is merely "exaggerated advertising, blustering, and boasting upon which no reasonable buyer would rely," it may be unactionable puffery. However, "specific and measurable" claims and claims that may be literally true or false are not puffery, and may become the subject of deceptive advertising claims. In this matter defendants' infomercials presented specific and measurable health claims.

The court said: "These claims included definite statements that Coral Calcium cures cancer, autoimmune diseases, and pain by rendering acidic bodies more alkaline, as well as statements that Supreme Greens cure cancer, heart disease, and cause weight loss by rendering acidic bodies more alkaline. Due to their specificity and concreteness, such claims go far beyond puffery as a matter of law."

The FTC is not authorized to foreclose expression of honest opinion. The same opinion, however, may not be utilized to mislead or deceive the public or to harm a competitor. Because the dividing line between permissible puffery and implied deception is vague and because false implications of fact can be easily found, there is an increasing risk of liability from using puffery in advertising. The continued rise in consumerism has affected when puffery will be regarded as appropriate. A claim considered as opinion and puffery years ago could now be considered a deception.

Therefore, advertisers must be very careful in using hyperbole in their advertisements. The test is whether the average consumer will recognize or perceive the hyperbole for what it is or be deceived by it. Advertiser be warned: the puffing rule is not a license to lie. Terms like "best," "perfect," "prime," "exceptional," "original," "comparable in quality," "wonderful," and so on have been dealt with by the commission and the courts and do not qualify as puff. It should be obvious that puffing can cross over into deception very easily.

Specific Forms of Concern under the Federal Trade Commission Act

3

I know I waste half the money I spend on advertising.
The problem is, I don't know which half.

—*John J. Wanamaker*

In the previous chapter, we discussed the scope of the jurisdiction of the Federal Trade Commission. The theory and reasoning the Commission uses in its review of advertising was analyzed. In this chapter, specific forms of claims and the language used in advertising that can cause trouble are addressed.

We'll look at the types of advertising claims that the advertiser deals with almost every day, in almost every ad. We'll also review examples of untruthful ads and explore problems with pricing, labeling, and endorsements. Also, we discuss the uses and pitfalls of using qualified language and ads containing claims that a product is unique or will perform in a certain way. Such other problem areas as deception by implication or inference, use of technical language, vagueness, and deceptive truth are also presented. Parallel state laws and FTC industry guidelines are additionally addressed. First, let's examine the most obvious type of deceptive ad, one that is strictly untrue.

Untruth and Deception

This may seem to be contradictory, but an untrue claim is not, in and of itself, deceptive. The nature of the untruth must be explored to determine if it is deceptive. In simpler terms, there are claims that are factually untrue, but at the same time are certainly not deceptive.

Fantasy Claims

This type of claim is called fantasy advertising. While the Energizer claim "Keeps going and going and going" is clearly untrue, it is not deceptive because an ordinary consumer would not believe such a blatant claim.

As we have seen in chapter 2, these types of puff claims are not considered deceptive if we look to the "reasonable man" standard, that is, the perception of any ordinary, reasonable consumer. While fantasy claims are very similar to puffery, they are more than subjective opinion. They are blatant absurdities.

Literally False Advertising

Literal untruths in any other form are almost always deceptive. Early examples of some of the more blatant in advertising run the gamut. For example, Alix Cohn, a junk dealer, was sued in 1962 by the state of Connecticut for advertising his second-hand merchandise as being antique. The merchandise was certainly not "antique" in the true sense of the word (*State* v. *Cohn*, 24 Conn. Supp. 188, 188 A.2d 878 (1962)). In another case, a product designed to repair aluminum cookware, called So-Luminum, was advertised as being able to withstand a direct flame of 2,000 degrees Fahrenheit. The company's claim was absolutely untrue considering the melting point of aluminum is 1,221 degrees F (*In the Matter of Perfect Mfg. Co.*, 43 F.T.C. 238 (1946)). Advertisements were created that gave the impression that goods were made of leather when they were not. Duraleather—a material used in cars, suitcases, and upholstery—contained no leather but was painted and embossed with a grain to look like leather (*Masland Duraleather Co.* v. *FTC*, 34 F.2d 733, 2 U.S.P.Q. 442 (3d Cir. 1929)). In another example, a product called Sebrone claimed to permanently eliminate dandruff due to new discoveries of scientific research. In fact, the product only temporarily removed dandruff scales (*Sebrone Co.* v. *FTC*, 135 F.2d 676 (7th Cir. 1913)).

In one case, a company named Murry Space Shoes circulated reprints of a news article as an advertisement. The article claimed that the manufacturer's shoe would "cure many bodily ailments . . . correct foot deformities (and cure) . . . corns, fallen arches and bunions." Murry Space Shoes had no corrective or therapeutic value whatsoever and could not cure anything (*Murry Space Shoe Corp.* v. *FTC*, 304 F.2d 270 (2d Cir. 1962)).

To further illustrate untrue claims, let's take a more detailed look at two such cases where claims were considered to be plainly untrue. The first, *United States* v. *Hindman*, 179 F.Supp. 926 (1960), involved the manufacturer of military uniforms. Seymour Hindman had been promoting his uniforms as custom-made and custom-tailored. In fact, the uniforms were all mass produced. Hindman argued that the term custom-tailored did not mean that the uniform was made individually to fit, but that it was given "particularly fine stitching or other tailoring finish." The court felt that the average consumer would not agree with such a definition, but rather would believe that the uniform was made to order. Therefore, it was untrue that Hindman's uniforms were custom-made.

The second case, *National Commission on Egg Nutrition* v. *Federal Trade Commission*, 570 F.2d 157 (1977), involved the advertising of the National Commission on Egg Nutrition (NCEN) and their advertising campaign which made claims that there is no scientific evidence linking the eating of eggs to an increased risk of heart and circulatory disease. They essentially wanted to convey the message that eggs were harmless. NCEN claimed in their ads that there was no scientific evidence that eating eggs increases the risk of heart and circulatory disease, and that eating eggs does not increase the blood cholesterol. In fact, the NCEN ads claimed that there is scientific evidence that avoiding dietary cholesterol, including that in eggs, increases the risk of heart and circulatory disease. All of the NCEN's "expert" claims ran in the face of the large body of existing medical research that established the connection between egg consumption and cholesterol increases along with the increased risk of heart and circulatory disease.

The FTC said: "NCEN has done more than espouse one side of a genuine controversy. . . . It has made statements denying the existence of scientific evidence which the record clearly shows does exist. These statements are, therefore, false and misleading."

The irony of this case is that the very official-sounding NCEN, was actually formed by members of the egg industry, to counteract what the FTC described as "anti-cholesterol attacks on eggs which had resulted in steadily declining per capita egg consumption."

Under the FTC Act, the literal falsity of an advertisement is judged on the advertiser's reasonable basis, or lack thereof, for its claim. This is in comparison to a finding of falsity or a "likelihood to deceive consumers" that is required under the Lanham Act. Today, most of the FTC's actions here involve the existence and level of substantiation that supports the claim. Or lack thereof.

In 1983, the FTC developed *The FTC Policy Statement Regarding Advertising Substantiation* (CCH Trade Regulation Reports 139,060). Under this, advertisers must have a reasonable basis for advertising claims before the claims are made. With a claim like "tests show," "doctor recommended" or "studies prove," the advertiser must actually have literal, valid documented substantiation that supports these claims. The FTC looks to see that advertisers have a "reasonable basis" for their advertising claims even when no express or implied reference is made.

Consumer satisfaction also does not prevent an ad from being literally false. The court noted in *W.L. Gore & Assoc., Inc.* v. *Totes, Inc.*, 788 F. Supp. 800, 808 (D. Del. 1992), "[A] false claim is still a false claim, even if customers do not think the false claim is important enough to complain about it."

One area of heavy FTC activity in recent years involves health-related products. The manufacturers of self-help and health-related products have been rigorously investigated by the FTC for unsubstantiated claims. The FTC requires a high level of substantiation for any health- and safety-related claims. Generally, this would require reliable scientific evidence.

In a speech on February 29, 1996, Christine A. Varney, Commissioner of the Federal Trade Commission, outlined the FTC's stance on safety-related advertising. Here is an excerpt from that speech: "Some . . . examples of recent Commission action include a host of cases against companies making deceptive health claims, including health claims for diet and weight loss products, dietary supplements, hearing aids, arthritis treatments, baldness cures, and acne treatments. In addition, we have brought cases against various medical centers and clinics deceptively touting varicose vein treatments, impotence treatments, stop-smoking hypnosis seminars, and dyslexia diagnosis and treatment. Again, our focus is on those claims that can cause the greatest consumer injury."

"We routinely cooperate with other federal agencies, as well as state and local enforcement officials. This is particularly true in cases that involve health or safety claims, where we will rely on the expertise of such agencies as the CPSC, the EPA, and the FDA to help us analyze the validity of the underlying claim. Indeed, many of our cases are initiated by referrals from other agencies. For example, a case we settled last year with two marketers of home and office ozone generators was initiated in response to information submitted by the EPA. In that case, the companies marketed their products as the solution to "sick building syndrome," claiming their machines could clean the air of indoor pollutants, preventing allergies and relieving asthma. We alleged that these claims were unsubstantiated and, under the settlement, the companies are required to have competent and reliable scientific evidence to support such claims in the future."

A company's noncompliance with another agency's standards could, in some circumstances, also form the basis of a complaint. For example, under the Commission's unfairness jurisdiction, it might be possible to allege that a company that continues to market a product that was already the subject of, say, a CPSC recall is engaging in an unfair practice by selling an unsafe product. However, I expect that most of our cases will continue to focus only on the actual claims being made, and whether or not they are truthful and substantiated. And, as I just mentioned, we do try to coordinate our efforts with other agencies to avoid this sort of "double-whammy."

A Thin Case

Trendmark had promoted its weight-loss program called "Thin-Thin," and two weight-loss products called Nuero-Thin and Lipo-Thin.

Trendmark's advertising made a number of claims, including: Neuro-Thin controls appetite; taking Neuro-Thin and Lipo-Thin together will cause long-term or permanent weight loss; Lipo-Thin lowers LDL cholesterol and boosts HDL cholesterol; Lipo-Thin promotes the healing of ulcers and lesions; Lipo-Thin helps prevent irritable bowel syndrome; Lipo-Thin helps improve cardiovascular health; and that testimonials from "consumers" appearing in the Thin-Thin Diet ads are typical of those who use Neuro-Thin and Lipo-Thin (box 3.1).

Box 3.1

NEW ALL-NATURAL WEIGHT LOSS PRODUCT, NOW ON THE MARKET!!!

If you've heard about the new "Phen/Fen" Diet, and thought about trying it . . . DON'T!!!

With the ALL NATURAL "Thin-Thin Diet," you can achieve the same results, without the dangerous side-effect of Drugs! Eat the foods you want, and STILL lose 10 to 12 pounds per month!

Patent Pending Thin-Thin Diet works for you to lose weight and KEEP IT OFF.

The Thin-Thin Diet Program is a Nutritional Breakthrough Program with a NO DIET, NO WILL POWER, easy way to LOSE UP TO 20 POUNDS PER MONTH and KEEP IT OFF!!

Read what a few of the THIN-THIN DIET users are saying:

> "Because of the THIN-THIN Diet, I have reached my weight-loss goal and my diabetes is much less of a problem!"
>
> –Toni H., Ohio

> "After my husband died, I suffered from depression and gained 50 pounds. I tried several diets, but just couldn't lose any of the weight. I've lost 14 pounds already on the THIN-THIN DIET and feel great!"
>
> –Kay M., Tennessee

NEURO-THIN turns your "hunger switch" off.

NEURO-THIN help[s] balance the levels of serotonin and dopamine in your brain. The result? Food cravings and hunger pangs are eliminated . . . and . . . you'll be on the way to achieving your goal!

LIPO-THIN Features:

- Absorbs and binds fat.
- Inhibits LDL cholesterol and boosts HDL cholesterol.
- Promotes healing of ulcers and lesions.
- Helps prevent irritable bowel syndrome.
- Reduces levels of uric acid in the blood.
- Correlates with improved cardiovascular health.

LIPO-THIN eliminates fat before your body can absorb it. Forbidden foods that you craved before beginning your THIN-THIN DIET can still be eaten in moderation because the fat they contain is blocked by the chitin fiber found in LIPO-THIN. This remarkable, naturally occurring ingredient acts like a "fat magnet" or a "fat sponge" in your digestive tract. It forms a non-digestible gel that binds with fat molecules and prevents their absorption into your body.

This program works. The THIN-THIN DIET is based on the latest scientific studies. It stops cravings and blocks fat absorption.

According to the complaint, the defendants did not have substantiation for their claims that consumers would lose significant amounts of weight or that following the program would lower their cholesterol, promote the healing of ulcers, and improve cardiovascular health, all without any change in diet.

The FTC determined that Trendmark did not possess any credible studies relating specifically to the Neuro-Thin or Lipo-Thin products. The "studies" submitted by Trendmark were test tube studies of rats. In addition, the so-called consumer testimonials used in the ads were actually made by the company's distributors or their spouses.

In *TrendMark International, Inc.*, CCH Trade Regulation Reports ¶ 24,448, the company agreed to settle FTC charges that their advertising claims about the efficacy of the program and the scientific tests that allegedly supported those claims were unsubstantiated. The settlement agreement prohibited Trendmark from misrepresenting the health benefits, performance, or efficacy of the program or any food, drug, or device without competent and reliable scientific substantiation. In addition, Trendmark would be prohibited from misrepresenting the results of any test, study, or research, and would be required to disclose clearly and prominently any material connection between a product endorser and Trendmark.

An Itchy Treatment

Three producers of over-the-counter (OTC) head lice treatments agreed to change their advertising after they were found to have made false and unsubstantiated claims. The cases, *Care Technologies, Inc.*, CCH Trade Regulation Reports ¶ 24,502; *Pfizer Inc.*, CCH Trade Regulation Reports ¶ 124,503; and *Del Pharmaceuticals, Inc.*, CCH Trade Regulation Reports ¶ 24,504, all involved head lice shampoos that included a comb to remove lice eggs. All three companies made similar representations:

Their head lice products cured lice infestations with a single treatment;

The egg-removal comb was 100% effective;

Clinical studies proved the product cured lice infestations with a single treatment; and, Clinical studies proved that the egg-removal comb was 100% effective.

The FTC found the "single treatment" claim false since the pesticide used in the shampoo was not effective in a single treatment. Use of the shampoo required consumers to physically remove lice eggs and apply a second treatment in seven to ten days to kill any newly hatched lice. The study that the defendants relied on did not substantiate the claim because the study only used a single treatment.

As for the effectiveness of the egg removal comb, this could also not be substantiated. According to the FTC, lice eggs are difficult to see and remove. The effectiveness of the comb was largely dependent on the skill and tenacity of the user. As a result, the defendants could not make the blatant claim that the comb was 100 percent effective. Also, to substantiate the claim, the study relied on individuals trained in egg removal as opposed to an average consumer.

The cases were settled by consent order that required competent and reliable scientific substantiation for any effectiveness claims to be used in the future.

A Case to Clean the Air

Deception cases don't always involve small obscure companies. Sometimes even major manufacturers can fall into the trap. Honeywell, a manufacturer of room air purifiers (among other products), settled a case with the FTC for false advertising in *Honeywell, Inc.*, CCH Trade Regulation Reports ¶ 24,358.

Honeywell claimed that its product removed nearly all or "99.97 percent of the impurities from the air that people breathe, including dust mite allergens, mold spores, bacteria, and viruses." Honeywell also claimed that its air cleaners provided noticeable allergy relief.

In court, it was revealed that the 99.97 percent figure referred to the filter's expected efficiency in removing particles that actually pass through the filter. While the filter's efficiency was a factor in determining its effectiveness, the FTC alleged that this figure overstated the actual effectiveness of the air purifier itself in removing pollutants from the air in a user's environment, as was stated by the advertising. The actual effectiveness of an air purifier depended on the amount of air that the purifier processes, the type of pollutant, and the rate at which the pollutant is being introduced into the environment.

According to the FTC, Honeywell's allergy relief claims were overstated because there was no proof that allergy sufferers would enjoy a noticeable reduction in symptoms by using the air purifier. This would depend on many variables, including the source and severity of their allergies, the rate at which the allergens are emitted into the environment, whether the allergens tend to remain airborne, and other environmental factors.

Somebody Stop Me

The FTC ordered Brake Guard Products, Inc., in *Brake Guard Products, Inc.*, CCH Trade Regulation Reports ¶ 24,380, to stop advertising that its add-on braking system performed as effectively as factory installed antilock braking systems. The FTC also banned the company from using the term "ABS" in advertising. Because this case involved motor vehicle safety, the FTC took the case very seriously.

The FTC alleged that Brake Guard made false and unsubstantiated advertising claims by stating that its Brake Guard Safety System, also known as Advanced Braking System or Brake Guard ABS, was an antilock braking system as effective as manufacturer-installed ABS brakes; complied with a performance standard established by the Society for Automotive Engineers; would qualify a vehicle for automobile insurance discounts in a significant proportion of cases; complies with a performance standard pertaining to antilock braking systems as established by the National Highway Traffic Safety Administration; and reduces stopping distances by 20 to 30 percent.

Using Qualifying Language to Overcome Deception

Another area of concern is the use of a deceptive statement made in an advertisement with the advertiser trying to offset the deception by clarifying it elsewhere with other language; the proverbial "small print." The practice of clarifying a deceptive—or possibly deceptive—claim with other language is sound policy for the advertiser. However, if the potentially deceptive statement is more noticeable than the qualification, either intentionally or unintentionally, then the statement will still be considered by the FTC to be false and deceptive.

The idea here is that the qualifying statement (often referred to as a disclaimer) must relieve any misrepresentation made by the other statement. If this is effectively accomplished, deception has probably not occurred. But remember, this works only if the qualifying statement is made with the same weight and conspicuousness. But where the qualifying statement is made in an inconspicuous manner (compared to the qualified statement), then it has been held that deception probably exists.

Double Eagle Lubricants manufactured motor oil that was re-refined from previously used oil. The oil was displayed in the standard one-quart can, the type found in any auto parts store. The trade name of the product was printed on the front of the can. On the side of the can was printed a statement that the oil was re-refined.

The cans were intended for display with the fronts showing, stacked side by side on the shelf. The front of the can faced the prospective customer to attract his attention. By placing the clarifying statements on the side of the can, the customer would conceivably pick up the can and purchase it based on the face label. For there to be a clear and conspicuous disclosure, the clarifying statement should have appeared on the front panel of the can.

The case, *Double Eagle Lubricants, Inc. v. FTC*, 360 F.2d 268 (10th Cir. 1965), discussed this situation and the court found that the labeling practice was deceptive. We will see more on labeling requirements later in this chapter. True, Double Eagle had made a disclosure about the product, but not with enough weight to avoid a misinformed purchase. What was interesting in this case was that Double Eagle brought in witnesses who testified that the labeling did not deceive them. Yet the court, in deciding against Double Eagle, said: "Evidence of [actual] deception is not necessary where the exhibits themselves sufficiently demonstrate their capacity to deceive." Remember, the test is now "likely" to deceive.

The court went on to say: If the commission can find deception without evidence that the public was deceived, we believe that it can make the same finding on the basis of its visual examination of exhibits even though numerous members of the public have testified that they were not deceived.

As we discussed in chapter 2, actual deception is not required, only a likelihood of deception need be shown to satisfy the requirement of the FTC Act.

Visibility of a Qualifying Statement

In *Giant Food, Inc. v. FTC*, 322 F.2d 977 (D.C. Circuit 1963), *cert. dismissed*, 376 U.S. 976, 84 S.Ct. 1121, 12 L.Ed. 2d 82 (1964), the qualifying statement was not placed close to the statement that it was meant to clarify. This case dealt with the small print in an ad. Giant Food, Inc., a large eastern retail chain, advertised its products through the newspapers, printing its sale price along with what it referred to as a regular price. The regular price was derived from a manufacturer's suggested price list and was not indicative of prices that the merchandise was ever actually sold at in the area.

Box 3.2 shows a typical Giant Food ad which ran in three Washington, D.C., area newspapers. Giant Food used the phrase "Regular Price" in a way that led the consumer to believe that it had sold the product at that price "in the recent, regular course of its business." That was untrue. Giant Food argued that its advertising was not deceptive because a disclaimer in small print ran at the bottom of the ad. The disclaimer was worded in a rather lengthy and confusing manner. The witnesses who testified at the trial said that they would not normally read the disclaimer, or that they would have been more confused if they had read it. The court said, "that the disclaimer might engender confusion appears to us . . . to be an understatement."

Giant Food also used the phrase "Manufacturer's List Price," which represented to the consumer the price at which the product was usually and customarily sold at

Box 3.2

Procter Steam & Dry Iron #10010
Regular Price $15.95
Sale Price $8.47

retail. In fact, the manufacturer's list was substantially in excess of the usual and customary retail price. The way to look at this is if you state a "regular price" in an ad, the product must have actually been sold by you, at that price, generally within the previous thirty days. Specific pricing terms and their uses are discussed in more detail later in this chapter.

Prior Knowledge of a False Statement

What happens when the consumer knows that an advertisement is false? Simply because the consumer knows that a claim is false does not relieve the fact that its deceptive.

In *Heavenly Creations, Inc.* v. *FTC*, 339 F.2d 7 (2d Cir. 1964), knowledge of false statements was at issue. Although this case involved dealers, rather than consumers, the practice was still deceptive. Heavenly Creations sold a variety of products to distributors, jobbers, salesmen, and retailers. These products were then resold to consumers. The problem here was with the pricing of the manufacturer's product to its dealers.

Dealers knew that Heavenly Creations had a practice of preticketing goods at inflated prices. Heavenly, as a defense, tried to prove that there was a custom of fictitious pricing within the retail trade. However, the court maintained that "a practice does not cease to be . . . unfair because the falsity of the . . . representation has become so well-known to the trade that dealers . . . are no longer deceived."

Claims of Uniqueness

A claim of uniqueness about a product or service is another area of concern under Section 5 of the FTC Act. It is deceptive to state that a product has extraordinary features or is unique, if it is not. But what is considered to be a claim of uniqueness? Again, it's based on the average reasonable consumer of that type of product.

Fedders Corporation manufactured air conditioners and, in the mid-1970s, advertised them as being unique due to their having "reserve cooling power." This was a claim that could not be substantiated. *Fedders Corp.* v. *FTC*, 529 F.2d 1398 (2d Cir. 1976), they even admitted that the statement "reserve cooling power" was "intended to imply an unusual ability to produce cold air under extreme conditions of heat and humidity." The false claim that Fedders air conditioners possessed "reserve cooling power" implied to the consumer that some feature of the cooling, circulation, or dehumidifying systems in the air conditioner allowed them to outperform other brands in extreme temperature situations. In reality, Fedders air conditioners had no real technical advantage over its competitors' equipment.

The court ordered Fedders to cease and desist from making claims that its air conditioners were unique in any material respect, unless it was a fact that could be proven. In the commission's order, it prohibited Fedders from: "Making, directly or indirectly, any statement or representation in any advertising or sales promotional material as to the air cooling, dehumidification, or circulation characteristics, capacity or capabilities of any air conditioner, unless at the time of such representation [they] have a reasonable basis for such statement or representation, which shall consist of competent scientific, engineering or other similar objective material or industry-wide standards based on such material."

Performance Claims

There are specific problems inherent in performance claims. Specifically, these are claims about how a product will work or perform. They are claims that a product will do what the ad says it will do. The Fedders case we just looked at was a good example of this. In fact, a claim of uniqueness is also a claim of performance.

Substantiation of Performance Claims

In *Sears, Roebuck and Co.* v. *FTC*, 676 F.2d 385 (9th Cir. 1982), the claim that "our dishwasher cleans dishes so well that they do not have to be pre-rinsed" was an example of an absolute performance claim. If the claim were made that "our dishwasher cleans better than theirs," it would be considered as a relative or comparative performance claim. Sears, Roebuck & Co. is the largest retailer of general merchandise in the United States. In the early 1970s Sears devised a program to increase the sales of its "Lady Kenmore" dishwasher. Sears did not reengineer or redesign the product. Instead it attempted to change the image of—or reposition—the product. The objective was expressed by Sears advertising agency as seeking to "transform the consumer image [of the Lady Kenmore] from a price brand to a superior product at a reasonable price. Eventually, the brand should move from market leadership to market dominance as the market share increases."

Sears produced ads claiming that the Lady Kenmore "completely eliminated" the need for prescraping and prerinsing. Sears labeled the machine as the "Freedom Maker." Box 3.3 shows one example of the kinds of ads Sears ran in various media over a four-year period, and at a cost of over $8 million. As a result of the Lady Kenmore campaign, unit sales rose more than 300 percent from 35,029 units in 1971 to 105,570 units in 1973. Sears total dishwasher sales rose from $73.47 million to $94.5 million during that period.

Box 3.3

SEARS LADY KENMORE

THE DO-IT-ITSELF DISHWASHER

No scraping. No rinsing. Lady Kenmore has 6 powerful hot water jets for the bottom rack, surging hot water with enough force to scrub every dish, pot and pan really clean. Even baked-on food comes off. And the dishes on top get as clean as those on the bottom. With a Kenmore you'll never have to scrape or rinse again. Even dishes crusty with leftover food. Kenmore's 14 powerful hot water jets scour every dish clean . . . with no scraping or rinsing.

It's great!

You'll like the way it makes pre-rinsing and soaking of heavily soiled dishes, pots and pans a thing of the past. Gets even the messiest baking dishes and roasting pans spotlessly clean . . . without pre-rinsing!

Wouldn't the woman in your life love a Kenmore Dishwasher for Mother's Day? A Kenmore Dishwasher from Sears means no more dishpan hands, she'll never have to touch dishwater again!

Egg, lipstick, peanut butter, jelly, even spaghetti sauce come right off with no pre-rinsing.

Now let us look at the reality of the case. Sears "no scraping, no pre-rinsing" claim was simply not true, and it had no reasonable basis upon which to make the claim. In fact, the instruction manual, which customers could only get after their purchase, contradicted the claim. The manual specifically instructed the owner to presoak or lightly scour certain dishes.

What the commission ordered Sears to do in this case is worth noting. In addition to a cease-and-desist order, Sears was ordered to maintain written records "in connection with the advertising, offering for sale, sale, or distribution of dishwashers or other major home appliances." The records required included:

1. All materials that were relied upon in making any claim or representation in advertising . . . concerning the performance characteristics of any Sears . . . dishwashers or other major home appliances; and
2. All test reports, studies, surveys, or demonstrations . . . that contradict, qualify, or call into question any claim or representation in advertising . . . on behalf of . . . Sears, Roebuck & Co.'s dishwashers or other major home appliances . . . for a period of three years.

Requirements of Substantiation

The FTC has in recent years stepped up its activity regarding ad claim substantiation. Check the FTC's website at www.ftc.gov for the *FTC Policy Statement Regarding Advertising Substantiation.*

We've seen that if you make a claim in an ad, you must be able to substantiate it. And note that substantiation must exist prior to making the statement. In other words, an advertiser must be able to show that they had credible substantiation prior to making the claim. But what type of substantiation is acceptable? The courts have decided that the proof to support a claim must have a reasonable basis. Put another way, the proof can't be contrived, out of context, or based on distorted facts or statistics. This was discussed in *F.T.C.* v. *Pharmtech Research, Inc.*, 576 F. Supp. 294 (D.D.C. 1983).

In July 1983, Pharmtech Research aired a television commercial for a product called Daily Greens (box 3.4). Other advertisements ran in magazines, on the radio, and on television. Although each ad varied somewhat, they all claimed that by taking Daily Greens the consumer would reduce the risk of certain cancers. The claim was also made that using Daily Greens would contribute to building certain biological defenses.

Box 3.4

The following message concerns a revolutionary new concept in diet and nutrition. According to this report, commissioned by the National Cancer Institute, a combination of cruciferous and carotene rich vegetables, has been proven to help our bodies build certain important biological defenses. Of course, to get the most benefit from any vegetable, you should eat them raw. But that is difficult to do every day. So I'd like to introduce you to Daily Greens. Daily Greens are not just another vitamin pill. They're natural, fresh, cruciferous and carotene-rich vegetables, dehydrated and compressed, to give you the important nutritional supplements that could be so vital to your future health. So, if you're not getting enough raw vegetables, every day, rely on Daily Greens—to help your body defend itself.

The advertisements didn't claim that the use of Daily Greens would prevent cancer. Yet the problem stemmed from the fact that Pharmtech relied solely on a report published by the National Academy of Sciences entitled *Diet, Nutrition, and Cancer.* The report itself states: "These recommendations apply only to foods as sources of nutrients—not to dietary supplements of individual nutrients." The report also warned "that the removal of water which occurs during dehydration may alter the protective effect of nutrients and other compounds."

Pharmtech's ads represented that the use of Daily Greens was connected to a reduction in the risk of cancer. The Daily Greens ads were deceptive for two reasons. First, they misstated the findings in the report—that the use of supplements reduces the risk of cancer or the building of biological defenses. Second, they failed to disclose some important material facts, including that the report's findings did not apply to processed supplements, but only whole foods. In other words, the report was taken and used out of context. The advertisement's substantiation did not have a reasonable basis.

Deception by Implication or Inference

In ads that contain deception by implication or inference, there is no specific untruth, yet for various reasons the advertisement's net impression is not one of truthfulness. In 1884, Mark Twain wrote *The Adventures of Huckleberry Finn*. In Chapter One, Huck describes the way Twain had written about him earlier in *The Adventures of Tom Sawyer*. In Huck's honest opinion he said about Twain: "he told the truth, mainly. There was things which he stretched, but mainly he told the truth."

An ad can cause the same effect. Some mainly tell the truth while some are stretched quite a bit. But an ad is not a work of fiction. At least, it's not supposed to be. It's a commercial message that has to create an impression of truthfulness. And it has to live up to that impression. An important point is that an advertiser should not try to hide behind the excuse that there was no intention to deceive. A claim of an innocent deception is no defense. The ad clearly speaks for itself.

Innuendo that Creates Deception

Obvious misrepresentations are one thing. But deception through innuendo is much more subtle. The makers of Hollywood brand bread created the impression that its product was a low calorie food. Specifically, the Hollywood bread advertisements claimed that its product was lower in calories than ordinary bread and, that by using Hollywood in a normal diet, the user would lose weight or prevent a weight gain.

The ads for Hollywood bread showed a picture of a beautiful movie star in a sleek full-length pose. The ads also showed a picture of the product. The copy read:

> When a woman's Panther Slim, she's vital as well as slender. A good figure is more than luck when a lady watches her weight the famous Hollywood Way Hollywood Bread is high in protein, vitamins and minerals, yet has only 46 calories per 18 gram slice. Choice of Golden Light or Nut-like Dark Hollywood.

The court in *National Bakers Serv., Inc.* v. *FTC*, 329 F.2d 365 (7th Cir. 1964), found that the average consumer had no perception of the average caloric content or gram weight of a slice of bread. It also felt that the claim "only 46 calories per 18 g slice" was intended to, and did, convey the impression that Hollywood bread had fewer calories than other breads. The claim also implied that by eating the same amount of Hollywood bread as other breads, the consumer could lose weight.

In reality, there is no significant difference in the caloric content of Hollywood bread and other brands of commercial white bread. Both contain about 276 calories per 100 g. However, other breads are sliced into twenty 23-g slices while Hollywood is sliced into twenty-five 18-g slices. The only reason that Hollywood bread contains fewer calories per slice is that it is sliced thinner.

The ad was technically true in that there were no incorrect facts. Yet, innuendo created an impression that was not altogether truthful. Hollywood bread had no fewer calories than other commercial breads, and, in fact, its only usefulness in a diet came from the fact that its thinner slices meant the consumer would consume smaller individual portions and therefore fewer calories.

Implication that Creates Deception

Another area of concern under Section 5 of the act is deception by inference or implication. Telebrands markets a wide variety of products to consumers using direct-response advertising. You've probably seen some of Telebrands' more successful products, which include Ambervision Sunglasses, the Magic Hanger, Dental White Tooth Whitening System, the Safety Can Opener, the Audubon Singing Bird Clock, the Better Pasta Pot and the Roll-a-Hose Flat Hose.

In *Telebrands Corp.* v. *Federal Trade Commission*, 457 F.3d 354 (2006), the case revolved around Telebrands' expensive, nationwide advertising campaign for the Ab Force. The Ab Force included a small battery-powered control unit (EMS) held in place by an elastic belt worn around the waist. The control unit cycled an electric current into the abdominal muscles, causing them repeatedly to contract and release involuntarily. The belt was promoted as a method to lose weight and to gain well-defined abdominal muscles, all without the need for exercise.

When Telebrands introduced the Ab Force, several other EMS products were already on the market. Infomercials for three competing EMS abdominal belts, AbTronic, Ab Energizer and Fast Abs, were highly ranked before and during the time that the Ab Force was being marketed. The competitions infomercials promoted their belts as a method to lose weight, fat and inches, and to gain well-defined abdominal muscles, all without the need for exercise.

In their advertising, Telebrands elected not to make such claims expressly but suggested them implicitly by encouraging comparison to the products that did so. For example, Ab Force advertisements referenced "those fantastic electronic ab belt infomercials on TV." Television and radio advertisements for the Ab Force also described abdominal belts as "the latest fitness craze to sweep the country," and pointed out that the other belts "promis[e] to get our abs into great shape fast—without exercise." Fit, well-muscled models were shown using the Ab Force in the television advertisements.

Telebrands spent over $4 million on an advertising campaign for the Ab Force, which included spots that aired more than ten thousand times on cable, satellite and broadcast television outlets in major national markets. The campaign sold approximately 747,000 units with gross sales exceeding $19 million.

Telebrands, in its defense, claimed that it intended to make comparisons based solely on price and technology. In court, Telebrands argued that it avoided making explicit health claims, yet the court determined that Telebrands intended to make the same claims implicitly. The court said:

> Ab Force television and radio advertisements touted the device as being "just as powerful and effective" as the EMS abdominal belts sold in infomercials. Those same advertisements lacked any explicitly identified purpose for using the Ab Force. That omission left consumers to infer, based on knowledge of the infomercials for the other EMS abdominal belts and, in the case of the television advertisements for the Ab Force, the visual images of fit models with well-defined abdominal muscles using the device, the benefit associated with the Ab Force's power and effectiveness.

The Personal Computer Guarantee

Gateway 2000, a trendy manufacturer of personal computers from 1995 to 1998 (now Gateway, Inc. owned by Acer as of 2007), settled with the FTC on charges that it made numerous false statements in advertisements for its refund policy and its on-site warranty service in *Gateway 2000, Inc.*, CCH Trade Regulation Reports ¶ 24,467.

Gateway's advertising claimed that it would provide a "money-back guaran-tee" of a full refund. In reality, it deducted the cost of shipping the merchandise to consumers, of about $62. The advertising also claimed that consumers would be provided free on-site service upon request. In reality, the on-site service was not pro-vided unless the company diagnosed the problem over the telephone first.

The settlement in this case prohibited Gateway from failing to make a full refund under any money-back guarantee unless it clearly disclosed in close proximity to the guarantee any deductions that would be made. It also prohibited Gateway from promising free on-site service unless it disclosed any material limitations to that ser-vice up front.

Use of Technical Language and Vagueness

Another way deception can be accomplished through the use of technical language that the consumer is not likely to understand, or by making vague or ambiguous statements. Technical language or complicated verbiage cannot be expected to be understood by the average consumer, and it often causes liability issues.

Use of a Foreign Language

One of the obvious situations can involve using a foreign language reference in an ad. About 1840 Edouard Pinaud opened a business in Paris, France, to manufacture per-fumes. His goods, as well as his name, became very well known at the time and are still quite well known under the Ed Pinaud - Clubmen brand today. Monsieur Pinaud for many years built a reputation for the quality of his products. After Pinaud's death in 1868, the Koltz Company took over the Pinaud line.

From 1891 to 1895, a Mr. Hecht worked for Koltz. After leaving, Hecht began manufacturing, in the United States, his own line of toilet preparations. Hecht's bot-tles, contents, stoppers, and labels were all made in the United States. The labels, however, were printed in French. The labels contained the sentence:

Preparee par M. Hecht,
Dernierement avec Parfumerie Ed. Pinaud, Paris.

Roughly translated the line means "Prepared by Mr. Hecht, formerly with per-fumer Ed. Pinaud, Paris." The court in *Koltz* v. *Hecht*, 73 F. 822 (2d Cir. 1896), stated that using foreign words, although literally true, can be considered deceptive. Hecht admitted at the trial that it was, in fact, his intent to mislead the public into believing that his domestic perfume was made in France, therefore trading on the reputation of French perfume and the name of Ed. Pinaud. While it was true that nowhere on the bottle was it stated that the product was foreign made, Hecht inge-niously conveyed that impression through his labeling, especially if the purchaser was not fluent in French.

Deception by Implying a Technical Term

Let's look at another example. Box 3.5 shows the text of an ad placed in trade mag-azines (directed toward mattress manufacturers) by a manufacturer of mattress cloth. In *In the Matter of Blumenthal*, 43 F.T.C. 158 (1946), the use of the word "Ster-itized" created a problem for the advertiser because the buyer perceived the word to say "sterilized." This was a natural assumption. Why was this a problem if the fabric lived up to the claims? Well, here's the rub. It didn't. The steritized fabric didn't do any of the things that the ad claimed it could. It was not sterile, sanitary, antiseptic, odorless, bacteriostatic, bacteria-, germ-, or water-repellent. It would not prevent perspiration odors, wear longer, or guard against the spread of infection. People would believe that, by some new sterilizing process, the Blumenthal fabric could have all of the claimed qualities. Blumenthal simply made up a name for its product, which bore an amazing resemblance to another word.

Box 3.5

STERITIZED FABRIC has a proven sales idea, proven in shoes, proven in clothes, proven in hats. The sales appeal of a STERITIZED FABRIC has been proven in many other fields. We are not guessing when we say that what has been done in the shoe, the hat, and the dress industries can also be done in the mattress industry. In the Nation's Greatest Stores, other merchandise has shown sales jumps by using the same Germ-Repellent Method. STERITIZED FABRIC—Repellent to Bacteria. Repellent to Water. STERITIZED mattress ticking avoids perspiration, stains, and odor. STERITIZED FABRIC is absolutely noninjurious. STERITIZED FABRIC Repels Germs, Helps protect all the family against spread of infection, is positively nonirritating, guards against odors. STERITIZED Mattress Fabric . . . Tested under standards stated in Circular 198, U.S. Department of Agriculture, made by Blumenthal Print Works, New Orleans, U.S.A. Blumenthal Print Works, Converters of Cotton Cloth.

Deception through Technical Language

In *Chrysler Corp.* v. *FTC*, 561 F.2d 357 (D.C. Cir. 1977), we see an example of using confusing technical language. The 1973–74 energy crisis, fueled (excuse the intentional pun) by the OPEC embargo combined with President Nixon's decision to take the U.S. off the gold standard, created a change in the type of cars America needed to produce. Gone was the day of the gas-guzzler. As car manufacturers refocused their priorities, Chrysler ran ads for their new Dodge Dart. A typical ad promoted the fuel efficiency of Chrysler cars (see box 3.6). The asterisk in the ad referred to a disclaimer that read: "Gas mileage figures based on October 1973 *Popular Science* magazine. Tests performed by *Popular Science* for its report were conducted on '73 vehicles with figures adjusted by *Popular Science* for 1974 model changes and the results of EPA tests."

Box 3.6

THE SMALL CAR VS THE SMALL CAR
You can buy a Chevrolet Nova OR you can buy a small car that can beat it on gas mileage*. . . .

• • • • •

The answer is a small car at your Chrysler-Plymouth and Dodge dealers . . . .

• • • • •

See all the Darts at your Dodge/Dodge Trucks dealer.
See the Dusters and Valiants at your Chrysler-Plymouth dealer.

That was one of a series of ads, all with the same message. The *Popular Science* tests referred to in the ad showed that the Plymouth Valiant and Dodge Dart equipped with 6-cylinder engines got better gas mileage than a Chevrolet Nova equipped with either a 6-cylinder or a V-8 engine. The same report also showed that Valiants and Darts equipped with V-8 engines got worse mileage results than Novas equipped with V-8s or 6-cylinder engines. In essence, the ads claimed that, based on the magazine report, all Chrysler small cars got better gas mileage than all Chevrolet Novas. In reality, however, the report covered only those cars equipped with 6-cylinder engines. But that was not stated clearly in the ad.

The Dream Vacation

In *Design Travel*, CCH Trade Regulation Reports ¶ 24,491, the company used celebrities to promote luxury vacations in tropical settings. According to the FTC, consumers were promised "resort accommodations" and a "luxury cruise" with the payment of a small promotional fee. Those who took the trip found it was not the "world class" vacation they were led to believe. Others, faced with restrictions and extra costs, canceled their plans and lost their initial payment of up to $600.

Here's how it worked. Consumers were urged, at local fairs and trade shows, to "register" for a dream vacation. The names of those who registered were passed on to telemarketers. The telemarketers called these consumers and led them to believe they had won a vacation. The telemarketers persuaded the consumers to provide credit card information and pay $598 for a luxury cruise to the Bahamas. After providing the information, the consumers learned that there were additional charges for "port reservation processing fees." Consumers who tried to cancel the vacation were told that there was a no-refund policy.

At the request of the FTC, the federal district court in Pittsburgh, Pennsylvania, froze the assets of the companies and temporarily halted the deceptive practices pending trial.

Jodie Bernstein, Director of the FTC Bureau of Consumer Protection, said: "These are major players in the vacation certificate industry, but their 'dream vacations' were a nightmare." According to Bernstein, complaints about travel plans rank among the top received, and annual losses as a result of travel-related fraud are estimated to exceed $12 billion each year.

Deceptive Truth

Up to this point, we have dealt with obvious deceptive untruths. But what about situations where the truth is deceptive? There is a common element to all of the cases involving statements of deceptive, literal truth. That is, there is always some element missing, or a conclusion is inferable that is short of the truth.

In *Donaldson v. Read Magazine, Inc.*, 333 U.S. 178, 68 S.Ct. 591, 92 L.Ed. 628 (1948), the U.S. Supreme Court discussed ads that, as a whole, may be misleading even though every sentence taken separately is literally true. This can occur when things are omitted or when ads are composed in such a way that they mislead.

Donaldson, who was the Postmaster General, sued *Read Magazine* based on its puzzle contests. Donaldson sued because he felt that *Read's* contest was "a scheme . . . for obtaining money through the mails by means of false and fraudulent pretenses, representations, and promises."(39 U.S.C. 259, 732)

In 1945 *Read Magazine* advertised its *Facts Magazine* Hall of Fame Puzzle Contest. Customers were led to believe that they would be eligible to win prizes by paying a $3 fee. In reality, they would have to pay up to $42. Customers were also led to believe that the contest was a puzzle contest. It was not. The puzzles were so easy to solve that most people would solve all of them. The prizes were awarded, if the truth be known, based on a tie-breaking letter-essay contest.

Read Magazine argued that it had explained all of these facts in its ads. The ads contained wording that specified that the first $3 puzzles might result in a tie. This would require a second and third series of $3 puzzles. Ultimately, if no winner appeared, one would be selected based on essays on "The Puzzle I Found Most Interesting and Educational in This Contest."

There were sentences in *Read's* advertisements which, taken alone, would have conveyed to a deliberate reader all of these details of the contest. But they were not sentences standing alone. They were small and inconspicuous bits of lengthy descriptions. *Read's* ads were very long, and its form letters to contestants were even more lengthy.

In bold one inch type their ads barked:

$10,000 FIRST PRIZE PUZZLE CONTEST

Pictures of sample puzzles covered the page. The ads left little doubt that the contest presented an opportunity to win large prizes (remember, this was 1947) by solving the puzzles. In the lower left corner of the ad appeared the "Official Rules of the Contest." There were ten rules. Somewhere near the middle of the ninth rule appeared the only reference to the possible need for essay letters as a means of tie-breaking. While all of the information was in the ad, and no claims were made that were not factual, the ad in-total was still deceptive. Granted there is a fine line here, but there is still a line.

This case is used to illustrate the principles of deceptive truth. Regulations that specifically control the advertising of contests and sweepstakes are explained in chapter 11.

Rules for Specific Product and Service Advertising

In addition to the general laws we've examined up to this point, there are also heavy regulations regarding some specific product and industry areas. These include types of products like banking, real estate, jewelry, auto parts, and furniture, to mention a few. There are also areas which include pricing and credit advertising, which are important for advertisers to understand.

Specific information for the advertiser is available from the FTC, other government agencies, and industry trade associations. I would urge the advertiser or agency to familiarize yourself with the requirements of the particular area you're advertising, and you'll help avoid problems.

While most of these areas are covered by the FTC (under the auspices of policing deceptive and misleading advertising claims), other government agencies may also be involved in regulating advertising as well. Check with the appropriate group for information on the legalities of that specific trade or industry. The federal agencies listed here can be located through the Internet. In addition to the federal agencies listed, check with the applicable state government in the states where you advertise for specific local regulation information.

FTC Industry Guidelines

The Federal Trade Commission offers a series of guides, policy statements, and business education materials pertaining to the advertising, labeling and disclosure requirements of certain products and services. While these generally deal with misrepresentations and deceptions in advertising, they also provide information on other issues that are important to the advertiser.

Box 3.7	**Federal Agency List**

Here is a general reference list of the federal agencies that have an impact on advertising and marketing activities and the common products that each govern.

Federal Trade Commission: http://www.ftc.gov
Light bulbs, binoculars, audio systems, sewing machines, appliances, consumer products, foods, drugs, cosmetics, medical devices, wool, fur, textile products, cigarettes, telemarketing, the Internet.

Food and Drug Administration: http://www.fda.gov
Food, drugs, nonalcoholic beverages, cosmetics, medical devices, biological products, hearing aids, radiation emitting devices (microwaves).

Department of Housing and Urban Development: http://portal.hud.gov
Real estate, land, mobile homes, apartments.

Department of Transportation: http://www.dot.gov
Motor vehicles, tires, boats.

Department of the Treasury: http://www.treasury.gov
Imported goods, alcoholic beverages, tobacco products.

Department of Agriculture: http://www.usda.gov
Meat products, poultry products, eggs and egg products, fruits, vegetables, seeds.

Department of Commerce: http://www.commerce.gov
Seafood, fire detection devices, consumer products, fruits, vegetables.

Consumer Product Safety Commission: http://www.cpsc.gov
Consumer products, flammable fabrics, poisons, hazardous materials, bicycles, toys, refrigerators.

Department of Energy: http://energy.gov
Dishwashers, refrigerators and freezers, washers and dryers, water heaters, air conditioners, heating devices, televisions, stereos, furnaces, ovens and ranges, microwaves.

Environmental Protection Agency: http://www.epa.gov
Motor vehicles, engines, fuels and fuel additives, noise emitting devices, insecticides and pesticides, poisons, insect and rodent traps and repellents.

Recent FTC guides relate to subjects including telemarketing, the Internet, and advertising directed toward children. Contact the FTC or check the FTC web site at: www.ftc.gov for a current list of guides.

Certain products and services also require that certain information be included in ads, such as the country of origin. As examples, the advertising regulations for jewelry, household furniture, appliances, televisions sets, audio equipment, fur products, wool products, and textiles are outlined below. These will give you an idea of the type of information that needs to be typically covered in these product messages

Other, more complex product and service areas are discussed in detail in later chapters of this book.

Jewelry All forms of advertisement that mislead or deceive consumers about the type, quality, metallic content, size, weight, cut, and color of jewelry products are prohibited.

It violates the law to misrepresent (or withhold) the place of origin, production, or manufacture of any jewelry item (or major components). It violates the law to misrepresent gold, silver, precious, and semiprecious stones, as well as the use of quality designations such as "carat" and "sterling."

For example, it is illegal to use the word "gold" (or its abbreviation) to describe any product not composed throughout of fine (24-karat) gold.

Household Furniture This covers advertising of articles of utility, convenience, or decoration that are suitable for use as furniture. It is illegal to misrepresent or fail to disclose any material facts that would likely mislead or deceive consumers and, therefore, influence their purchase decision. This includes situations where deception may result from the appearance alone, which in the absence of affirmative disclosures, could have the capacity and tendency or effect of misleading or deceiving. For example, using veneers or simulated materials without disclosure is an unfair trade practice in violation of the FTC Act.

If an advertiser makes representations regarding test results or performance characteristics of fabrics, they must be prepared to submit substantiating data that existed prior to making the claims. Because of this, it is wise to keep documentation for three years after a representation is made. The FTC can demand to review the proof within that three-year period.

If furniture is made in the United States, it should not be advertised by terms that suggest a foreign origin, such as "Danish" or "French." Unless, that is, the fact that the furniture was made in the United States is clearly and conspicuously disclosed in the ad. The ad should contain a disclaimer, such as "made in the U.S.A." or "manufactured by Acme Co., New York, NY, U.S.A."

It also violates the law to represent, either directly or implicitly, that the advertiser is also the manufacturer or owns or controls the factory where the products were made if this is not true.

Appliances and Electronic Goods It is a violation of the FTC Act for an ad to represent the energy consumption of certain consumer appliances or the cost of energy consumed unless the product has been properly tested and the claim accurately portrays the results of the testing. This applies to refrigerators, refrigerator-freezers, dishwashers, water heaters, room air conditioners, clothes washers and dryers, and furnaces.

In order to comply, ads, brochures, and catalogs for appliances and electronic products must include the following information:

- The capacity of the model;
- Energy efficiency ratings for room air conditioners and furnaces;
- Estimated annual energy costs or energy efficiency ratings (as of the date of publication); and
- A clear and conspicuous statement that "Important energy information is available. Turn to page(s) 000." Or, "See your dealer for details."

Television Sets A major concern when advertising televisions sets involves the size of the viewable area of the picture tube. It is illegal to state the picture size of a television set unless it is the actual size of the viewable picture area as measured on a single plane basis.

If the stated size is other than the actual measurement of the set's picture area, the size designation must be accompanied by a clear and conspicuous clarification, in close connection and conjunction therewith. A footnote or other disclosure does not work. For example, making reference to a "19-inch diagonal picture tube" is acceptable, but "21-inch set" is not.

Home Entertainment Products When stating the power output ratings for stereo components, tape players, compact disc players, and component audio amplifiers, certain performance characteristics of the power amplification equipment must be made. If the ad doesn't include the required ratings, it is an unfair or deceptive ad. It is advisable to refer to the appropriate guide for details.

Textile Fiber Products Textile fiber products are governed by the Textile Fiber Products Identification Act (Textile Identification Act, 15 U.S.C. § 70). This governs the advertising of textile fiber products when a reference to the fiber content is made or the ad includes a "fiber trademark" (identification of a particular fiber, such as cotton, etc.). The ad will be considered deceptive if it does not identify any constituent fiber content of the product. Let's look at an illustration. If a garment is made of 100 percent cotton, this can be stated. However, if it is only 60 percent cotton, the actual content of the other fibers must be listed: 60 percent cotton, 40 percent rayon.

Ads must include a clear and visible statement of the product's origin. A clarification that the product was made in the United States, was imported, or both must be made in all advertising and labeling as well.

The requirements of the Textile Identification Act and its regulations do not apply to products regulated by the Wool Products Labeling Act of 1939.

Wool Products The Wool Products Labeling Act of 1939 (Wool Act, 15 U.S.C. § 68) relates to the labeling of fabrics composed of wool.

When a wool product is advertised, a statement of origin must be made which makes a clear and conspicuous statement that the product was either made in the United States, imported, or both. And, this statement must be consistent with the labeling on the actual product.

The Wool Act does not make any requirements for advertising other than those stated above. However, the FTC looks closely at advertising that violates the principles of the Wool Act and creates a deceptive or misleading claim.

Linings, paddings, stiffening, trimmings, facings (except where express or implied representations of fiber content are commonly made), or other products whose fiber content is customarily stated or whose fiber content is insignificant, do not fall under the Wool Act.

Fur Products Advertising for furs and fur products must be in line with the Fur Products Labeling Act (Fur Act, 15 U.S.C. §§ 69-69j). This act prohibits deceptive advertising, and specifically governs misrepresentation of pricing.

A statement of the country of origin is also required in an ad for imported furs and fur products. If the ad shows a group of fur products made in more than one country, a statement such as: "Fur products labeled to show country of origin," is acceptable. This does not apply, however, to catalogue, mail-order, Internet, or other types of advertising where the purchaser cannot inspect the product and label before buying. In this case, a clear origin reference must be made in the ad.

Advertising Price Issues

Use of the Word "Free"

Probably the single word that has caused the most anguish for advertisers is "free." Just plug the word "free" into an ad and you're asking for trouble. It is important for the advertiser to understand how the word "free" can be used and what bargain must be lived up to when it is. Indeed the guidelines in this area are quite clear-cut. The simplest form of free offer is a gift or sample truly given without any strings attached. The operative word here is *any*. The word "free" means the consumer pays nothing and is required to do nothing.

Often an advertisement offers a free sample that will be sent to the consumer for paying a small amount to cover mailing and handling. This is acceptable only if the amount requested is no more than the actual cost to the advertiser of the handling and mailing. But if the consumer must pay more than the actual cost, the offer is improper.

Mark Twain once said, "Few things are harder to put up with than the annoyance of a good example." So here is one. It involves a major furniture retail chain where I was once employed. The company found out what can happen when the word "free" is used too loosely.

These folks had been running advertisements for appliances. In their ads a simple, direct statement was made: "FREE DELIVERY." Things were going along fine, for many years in fact, until one day we got a call from a distraught older woman. She had not received satisfaction from our local store, so she called the general offices. She had purchased a new refrigerator at a competitor's store and wanted us to pick it up and deliver it to her home. After all, our ad did say "free delivery" and she wanted her refrigerator delivered—free.

The more we discussed it with her, the worse it got. We finally passed her off as a trouble-maker out to get a free ride, no pun intended. Sometime later we were contacted by the FTC, and they wanted some answers. Unfortunately the ones we gave them weren't the right ones. The statement had to be lived up to—literally—or be changed.

From that day on the ads read: "FREE DELIVERY INCLUDED." You had to buy *our* merchandise to get *us* to deliver it free of charge. Granted, the average consumer understands that we will only deliver our own merchandise. But the problem went beyond that because "free delivery" is a deceptive claim. The delivery is not actually free. The consumer has to do something—usually buy the merchandise. In basic contract law this action is called consideration. In this case delivery is not free; it is included in the price of the merchandise. You don't pay extra to receive it, but the point is, you do pay for it because it is built into the price.

A Free Offer Must Contain No Consideration As we have just seen, consideration is the legal term for payment. But payment can be in forms other than the commonly used version; money. Consideration can be any action that induces someone into a contract. It can be a price, or an action, or a motive, or a forbearance (an agreement not to do something). *Black's Law Dictionary* defines consideration as: "Some right, interest, profit, or benefit accruing to one party, or some forbearance, detriment, loss, or responsibility, given, suffered, or undertaken by the other." In other words, an item is not free if it is given with some other consideration.

Along the same lines, *FTC* v. *The Book of the Month Club*, 202 F.2d 486 (2nd Cir. 1953), dealt with the use of the word "free." In this case the Book-of-the-Month Club had published advertisements that read:

FREE TO NEW MEMBERS
OF THE BOOK-OF-THE-MONTH CLUB

The "free" was another book. At the bottom of the ad was a coupon that the consumer filled out and sent in. This constituted a contract with the new member. The coupon stated that the consumer would receive the designated book free of charge, and that that person agreed to purchase at least four additional books a year from the club. However, in the court's opinion, there was no free book. If the member failed to buy the four other books within the year's time, the club would demand payment for the "free" book. The book was not a gift. And it was not free.

In deciding this case the court looked at the definition developed by the FTC on January 14, 1948 (Federal Register, January 14, 1948, Administrative interpretations with reference to the use of the word *free* and words of similar import under certain conditions to describe merchandise). The definition read as follows: "The use of the word 'free' or words of similar import, in advertising to designate or describe merchandise . . . that is not in truth and in fact a gift or gratuity or is not given to the recipient thereof without requiring the purchase of other merchandise or requiring the performance of some other service . . . is considered by the commission to be a violation of the Federal Trade Commission Act."

"Free With Purchase" Offers An offer of one item for "free" with the purchase of another item indicates to the consumer that they are paying nothing for the "free" item and not more than the regular price for the other item. The term "regular price" is taken to mean the price at which the advertiser has actively sold the same product, in the same market area. This must have occurred within a recent span of time and for a reasonably substantial period (usually thirty days).

The rationale is, a purchaser has a right to believe that the merchant will not directly and immediately recover, in whole or in part, the cost of the free merchandise or service by marking up the price of the article which must be purchased, by substituting inferior merchandise or services.

When creating a free offer, it is important to prevent the likelihood that the consumer might misunderstand the terms of the offer. To accomplish that, the FTC wants free offers to "set forth clearly and conspicuously at the outset of the offer" all limitations and conditions.

There are a few considerations for the timing and repetition of offers, as well. A "free" offer should not be advertised for more than six months in any twelve-month period. No more than three identical offers in the same area should be made in any twelve-month period, and at least thirty days should elapse before another such offer is promoted in the same area.

For another example of how not to use the word "free," let's look at *FTC v. Mary Carter Paint Co.*, 382 U.S. 46, 86 S.Ct. 219, 15 L.Ed. 2d 128 (1965). Here, Mary Carter Paint had a practice of advertising that for every can of paint purchased the buyer would get a free can of equal quality. However, Mary Carter Paint Co. did not have a history of selling single cans of paint. In fact, it only sold two can sets. The company claimed in its advertising that the usual and customary retail price of each single can of paint was $6.98. This was actually the price needed to cover the cost of two cans of paint. What Mary Carter did, in essence, was double the retail price of its paint, sell the cans in twin sets, and then offer one of the cans as "free." Clearly Mary Carter's practice was deceptive and violated the FTC Act.

It's not what you call it, it's what it *is* that counts.

Comparative Pricing and "Sale" Terminology

Advertisements that make price or value comparisons or that offer "sale" merchandise fall under the FTC's guides.

Pricing guides cover only "the most frequently employed forms of bargain advertising" (16 C.F.R. § 233.5).

Yet "variations which appear from time to time . . . are . . . controlled by the same general principles." When advertising any bargain offer, the guides amplify the point that "advertisers should make certain that the bargain offer is genuine and truthful."

Advertising Price Reductions A company may advertise that an item is being offered at a reduced price, if the former price "is the actual, bona fide price at which the article was offered to the public on a regular basis for a reasonably substantial period of time." But beware: the FTC has not defined a "reasonably substantial period of time."

One illegal tactic is to state an unusually high price to give a misleading impression of an actual saving and later reducing it to a "sale" price. To avoid this, it's important that the former price listed in the ad is not a fictitious one. Even if it's accompanied by terms like "regularly," "usually," or "formerly," make sure that the former price is not a false one.

The FTC guides state that a "former price is not necessarily fictitious merely because no sales at the advertised price were made." Yet, be very careful that the former price is one that was "openly and actively offered, for a reasonably substantial period of time, in the recent, regular course of business, honestly and in good faith—and, of course, not for the purpose of establishing a fictitious higher price on which a deceptive comparison might be based." If substantial sales were not actually made at the former price, the advertiser "should scrupulously avoid any implication" that the former price is a "selling price" (e.g., with language such as "Formerly sold at $000") as opposed to an "asking price."

What if the former price or the amount or percentage of the price reduction is not disclosed? When an ad simply states "sale," the amount of the reduction cannot be so insignificant as to be meaningless. The issue here is whether the price difference is large enough that the consumer, if he knew the difference, would believe that he was getting a genuine bargain or saving. That should be your guideline.

Using Phrases like "Formerly," "Originally," "Regularly," and "Usually"
Using phrases like "formerly," "originally," "regularly," and "usually" in relation to an advertised sale will project a certain impression to the consumer. Because of this, it is important that these terms are used properly, so as not to mislead the consumer.

"Originally," is defined as the advertiser's own original customary price offered in the recent, regular course of business. A price no higher than the first price used in the current selling season. If the original price is not the most recent price, it should be made clear along with any intermediate price reductions. One way to overcome this is to make a statement such as, "40 percent Off Original Prices (intermediate markdowns taken)," or, "Originally $299, Formerly $185, Now $149."

Terms like "formerly," "reduced," "Was $80, Now $60" or "$80 radio $60," convey to the consumer that this was the last, most recent previous price for the same article. As always, truth is the benchmark.

Using the term "regularly" means the last previous price. Using "regularly" also implies that the item will later return to that regular presale price. This needs to be the truth.

"Usually" is taken to mean the current or last previous price. This term may also mean the advertiser's own customary price for the same article or the usual customary price for the same article in the area. Therefore, it is wise for the ad to clearly disclose the basis used for the comparison.

Value Comparisons It is a common practice for one company to advertise the same goods at prices lower than their competition in the area in which both companies do business. This is acceptable if the advertised higher price is based upon fact (not fictitious or misleading) and the advertiser is reasonably certain that the claimed competitor's price does not appreciably exceed the price at which substantial sales of the item are being made by typical sellers in the same area.

It is acceptable to show comparisons of prices charged by others in the same market for comparable goods, if such goods are of essentially similar quality and are obtainable in the area. It must be clear in the ad that a comparison is being made. However, as with comparisons of the same merchandise, the advertiser must be certain that the advertised price of comparable or competing goods does not exceed that at which it is being sold by other retail outlets in the area.

Advertising Manufacturer's Suggested Retail or List Prices

Another common practice involves advertising price reductions based on a "manufacturer's list price" or "suggested retail price." This won't cause a problem if the listed price is the amount at which substantial (not isolated or insignificant) sales are made in the area in which the advertiser does business.

This general rule applies to national companies, regional manufacturers, mail-order catalog and Internet distributors who deal directly with the public, or a local retailer. In other words, any company, any advertiser.

The key here is to determine whether the manufacturer's list price is actually the price regularly charged by other outlets in the area. This must be done before advertising the list price comparison. If the business operates on a large regional or national basis, they may advertise a suggested list price if the main retail outlets in a significant number of representative areas are selling the product at that price. To sum up, the retailer who engages in advertising a list price must act honestly and in good faith, and not with the intention of establishing a basis for a deceptive comparison in any trade area.

Bargain Offers Requiring the Purchase of Other Merchandise

Ads that offer a bargain if another item is purchased by the consumer, must clearly state all of the terms and conditions of the offer. For example, by using language such as "Free," "2-For-1 Sale," "Half Price Sale," or "Buy One-Get One Free." This must be done clearly in the ad and not in an attempt to mislead the consumer. Refer back to the *FTC* v. *Mary Carter Paint Co.* case that we discussed earlier in this chapter.

As stated in the *Mary Carter* case, a deception that violates the FTC Act would occur "[w]here the seller, in making such an offer, increases his regular price of the article required to be bought, or decreases the quantity and quality of that article, or otherwise attaches strings (other than the basic condition that the article be purchased)."

Introductory Sales

An introductory or "advance" sale may be promoted when the advertiser expects in good faith to increase the price at a later date. There is no requirement that the price in fact be raised later, but the intent must be made in good faith. It would be deceptive to advertise an introductory sale, while intending to keep the price at that level later.

"Cents-Off" and Other Savings Offers

Advertising that makes "cents-off" or other price representations may be required to comply with the Fair Packaging and Labeling Act and the FTC's regulations under the Fair Packaging Act (15 U.S.C. §§ 1451-1461 (1982); 16 C.F.R. §§ 502.100-.102 (1987)), or with regulations under the federal Food, Drug and Cosmetic Act (16 C.F.R. § 1.35). The regulations under the two statutes require similar disclosures in advertisements and impose similar conditions. Let us take a closer look.

"Cents-Off" Promotions A "cents-off representation" is any message content consisting of the words "cents-off" or similar words placed on any ad, label or packaging stating or implying that a consumer commodity is being sold at a price below the "customary retail sale price."

"Cents-off" representations are prohibited unless the labeled item has, recently and during regular business within the area, been sold at an ordinary and customary price and is currently sold at a reduction from the ordinary price in an amount at least equal to the "cents-off" amount that is shown on the package or label.

The "cents-off" claim must be marked as a savings from the retailer's regular price, such as, "Price Marked is 00¢ Off the Regular Price." The regular price must be clearly and conspicuously displayed on the package or label, or on a sign, placard or shelf-marker along with the display.

Within any twelve-month period, "cents-off" promotions for the same size item in the same trade area must not be initiated more than three times, extended more than six months, or exceed fifty-percent of the item's total sales volume. At least thirty days must have passed between each promotion. Invoices or other records should be maintained for at least one year following the twelve-month period in which the promotion occurred.

A "cents-off" representation cannot be made where it is known or should be known that it will be used to deceive, for example, where the retailer charges a price which does not fully pass on to the consumers the represented price reduction or fails to post the regular price, as required.

Introductory "Cents-Off" Offers "Cents-off" representations made in connection with introductory offers are prohibited unless:

- The item is new, introduced into a new area for the first time, or has been substantially changed;
- The offer is clearly and conspicuously qualified as an "Introductory Offer;" and
- The offer does not continue within the area for more than six months.

At the time the introductory offer is made, the advertiser must intend in good faith to offer the item, alone, at the anticipated ordinary and customary price for a reasonably substantial period of time after the introductory promotion ends.

The term "economy size" or similar words should not be used unless the advertiser simultaneously offers the same brand of that commodity in at least one other size or form, and only if one size of the item is labeled "economy size." The item labeled "economy size" must be sold at a price-per-unit of weight or other measure which is substantially reduced, that is, at least 5 percent.

The Federal Food, Drug, and Cosmetic Act The Federal Food, Drug, and Cosmetic Act also regulates "cents-off" and other savings claims used on labeling for food, drug, cosmetic products, or devices.

"Cents-off" representations may be made for an item if it has been openly and actively sold in the recent and regular course of business in the market area for at least thirty days, and if the selling price, "has been reduced by at least the savings differential represented on the package or labeling."

Sponsors of "cents-off" promotions, as well as persons involved at all other levels such as wholesalers and jobbers, must keep records of all promotions within any twelve-month period. These must be kept for at least twelve months after the end of the year in which the promotion occurs to document that the retailer has passed the represented savings on to the purchaser, should the FTC ask. And they just might.

Other savings offers, such as "two-for-one" or "one-cent" sales, which appear on the label or labeling of food, drug, or cosmetic items or devices "shall include all material facts relative to the offer and shall in no way be misleading."

Bait-and-Switch Advertising

Bait-and-switch advertising is stringently prohibited. The FTC has defined bait-and-switch advertising as: "An alluring but insincere offer to sell a product or service which the advertiser in truth does not intend or want to sell. Its purpose is to switch consumers from buying the advertised merchandise, in order to sell something else, usually at a higher price or on a basis more advantageous to the advertiser. The primary aim of a bait advertisement is to obtain leads as to persons interested in buying merchandise of the type so advertised."

Remember, showing actual sales of the advertised items doesn't necessarily prove that a bait-and-switch scheme did not exist. The commission has determined that, on occasion, an actual sale is a "mere incidental by-product of the fundamental plan and is intended to provide an aura of legitimacy to the overall operation." Therefore, the FTC advises, "[n]o advertisement containing an offer to sell a product should be published when the offer is not a *bona fide* effort to sell the advertised product."

The ad must not create a false impression of the product or any of its characteristics, such as grade, make, color, availability, or otherwise misrepresent the product so that, "on disclosure of the true facts, the purchaser may be switched from the advertised product to another."

To determine whether the advertiser has created a bait-and-switch scheme, the FTC examines each of the following criteria:

- Refusal to demonstrate or sell the product as offered;
- Disparagement of the product as advertised, or features such as the guarantee or credit terms;
- Failure to meet reasonable demands for the advertised product unless the ad "clearly and adequately" discloses that "supply is limited" or item is "available only at designated outlets;"
- Refusal to accept orders for the advertised item, for delivery within a reasonable period;
- Showing an item that is "defective, unusable or impractical" for its advertised purpose; or
- Use of a sales program or compensation method that is designed to prevent, discourage, or penalize employees from selling the advertised product.

Attempts by a company to "unsell" merchandise or to sell other merchandise instead, is also prohibited. The FTC will consider that a sale was not made in good faith, but rather was a scam to sell other merchandise if it finds:

- Acceptance of a deposit for an advertised product and then switching the buyer to a more expensive item;
- Failure to deliver an advertised product within a reasonable time, or failing to offer a refund;
- Disparagement of the advertised product or any characteristic connected with it; or,
- Delivery of the product in a condition that is defective, unusable, or impractical for its advertised purpose.

The Mail, Internet, or Telephone Order Rule

The FTC's Mail, Internet, or Telephone Order Merchandise rule (Mail Order Rule) controls advertising of all merchandise that is ordered from a seller by mail, telephone, fax, or over the Internet. The federal Mail Order Rule overrides any state law, municipal ordinance, or other local regulation that does not provide equal or greater rights to the buyer.

The Mail Order Rule states that it is "an unfair or deceptive act and practice" for a seller "[t]o solicit any order for the sale of merchandise to be ordered by the buyer through the mails unless, at the time of the solicitation, the seller has a reasonable basis to expect he will be able to ship [the] ordered merchandise to the buyer." The order must be shipped within the time specified in the ad or, if no date is specified, within thirty days after receipt of the order from the buyer.

More on this in chapter 5, on the Internet.

Credit "Truth in Lending" Advertising

The federal Truth-in-Lending Act (15 U.S.C. §§ 1601-1614,1661-1665a (1987).), controls all advertising of consumer credit. That means credit offered to a consumer "primarily for personal, family, or household purposes." Anyone who advertises consumer credit in any form, must comply with the act's consumer credit regulation, also known as "Regulation Z" (12 C.F.R. pt. 226 (1987).

The FTC oversees and enforces Regulation Z as it applies to retailers, real estate developers, consumer finance companies, nonbank credit-card issuers, and all creditors not regulated by other agencies.

It would be advisable for anyone offering credit in an advertisement to get a copy of Regulation Z, and study its terms.

Definition of Consumer Credit

The Truth-in-Lending Act defines two forms of consumer credit: "open-end" and "closed-end."

Open-end consumer credit generally includes credit cards and revolving charge accounts. It is extended in one of the following situations where:

- The creditor reasonably anticipates repeat transactions;
- The creditor may impose a finance charge from time-to-time on any outstanding balance; or
- The amount of credit that may be extended to the consumer during the term of the plan (up to the limit set by the creditor) is generally based upon how any outstanding balance has been repaid.

"Closed-end" credit, on the other hand, covers any other form of consumer credit.

Terms that Trigger Disclosure

The Truth-in-Lending Act includes a list of certain "triggering" terms. If any of these terms are used in an advertisement, the act requires certain additional disclosures to be made.

Triggering terms for open-end credit include any reference to one of the following:

- The circumstances when a finance charge will be imposed and an explanation of how it will be determined;
- A statement of when the finance charge begins to accrue, including any "free ride" period;
- The periodic rate used to calculate the finance charge, the range of balances to which it applies, and the annual percentage rate;
- The method used to determine the balance on which the finance charge is computed;
- The method used to determine the amount of the finance charge, including a description of how any finance charge (other than periodic rate) will be determined;
- Any amount, other than a finance charge, that may be imposed, or an explanation of how the charge is determined. Examples include application fees charged to credit applicants, late and delinquent payment amounts, and annual or periodic charges;
- If the creditor has or will acquire any security interest in the property purchased under the plan, or in any other property; or
- A statement outlining the consumer's rights and the creditor's responsibilities.

If any triggering terms are used in an advertisement, it must also clearly and conspicuously explain each of the following points:

- Any minimum, fixed, transaction, activity, or similar charge that may be imposed;
- Any periodic rate that may be applied, shown as an annual percentage rate; and
- Any membership or participation fee that may be imposed.

Triggering terms for closed-end credit include any reference to one of the following:

- The amount or percentage of any down-payment;
- The number of payments or period of repayment;
- The amount of any payment; or
- The amount of any finance charge.

If any closed-end triggering terms are used in an advertisement, it must also clearly and conspicuously explain all of the following points:

- The amount or percentage of any down-payment;
- The terms of repayment; and
- The "annual percentage rate," using that term, and the details, if the rate may be increased.

In the case of a multipage advertisement only one set of disclosures is required if a table or schedule fully explains each type of credit. If there is a triggering term anywhere in this type of promotional material, there must also be a reference to the page on which the table or schedule is located.

Consumer Leasing

In addition to the above, the Truth-in-Lending Act requires certain disclosures in ads promoting consumer lease transactions. The consumer leasing disclosure provisions of the Truth-in-Lending Act are implemented by "Regulation M" (12 C.F.R. pt. 213. (1987)).

A "consumer lease" is "a contract in the form of a bailment or lease for the use of personal property by a natural person primarily for personal, family, or household purposes, for a period of time exceeding four months, for a total contractual obligation not exceeding $25,000, whether or not the lessee has the option to purchase or otherwise become the owner of the property at the expiration of the lease." Excluded from this section are leases that otherwise fall under the definition of a credit sale and therefore are controlled under Regulation Z.

As with consumer credit advertising under Regulation Z, certain triggering terms used in an ad for a consumer lease require that disclosures be made. In an ad for a consumer lease, triggering terms include any reference to the following:

- Statements as to the amount of any payment;
- The number of required payments; or
- Any or no down-payment, or other payment, is required upon entering into the lease.

Ads that include any triggering terms listed above must also clearly and conspicuously state all of the following:

- That the transaction advertised is a lease;
- The total amount of any required payment such as a security deposit or capitalized cost-reduction required at the execution of the lease, or that no such payments are required;

- The number, amounts, due dates, or periods of scheduled payments, and the total of such payments under the lease;
- If the lessee has the option to purchase the leased property and at what price and in what time. A statement of the method of determining such price is acceptable; and
- The amount (or method to determine it) of any liabilities the lease imposes upon the lessee at the end of the lease. Also required is a statement that the lessee shall be liable for the difference, if any, between the estimated value of the property and its actual value at the end of the lease.

As in the case of consumer credit examined earlier, a catalog, brochure, or multipage ad used to promote a consumer lease requires only one set of clear disclosures for the triggering terms. If a triggering term appears on other pages, a clear reference must be made to where the table or schedule begins.

In the case of point-of-sale tags (for items that include triggering terms) there must be a clear and conspicuous reference to where a table or schedule of the additional terms can be found.

Endorsements and Testimonials in Advertising

The FTC monitors testimonials and endorsements as part of its enforcement of the Federal Trade Commission Act. Another sticky area to pay close attention to.

The FTC defines an endorsement as: "Any advertising message (including verbal statements, demonstrations, or depictions of the name, signature, likeness or other identifying personal characteristics of an individual or the name or seal of an organization) which message consumers are likely to believe reflects the opinions, beliefs, findings, or experience of a party other than the sponsoring advertiser (16 C.F.R. § 255.0(a) (1987)."

The FTC provides many examples of the type of representations it considers to be endorsements or testimonials. As an example, a film critic's excerpted statements regarding a specific film which were put into an ad would be considered an endorsement. This is because the consumer would readily believe that the statement is the critic's view rather than the view of the advertiser. Let us take another example: a television commercial for baseball bats showing a well-known professional ballplayer hitting balls would qualify as an endorsement, even if the professional makes no actual statement in the commercial.

On the other hand, an advertisement for a pain reliever using a long-standing spokesperson as the announcer would not be considered an endorsement by the spokesperson. The reasoning here is that the audience would recognize the announcer as a representative of the drug company and not a neutral and unbiased expert.

Please note: An endorsement or testimonial can be created by any person; it does not need to be a celebrity. The FTC looks at any endorsement or testimonial regardless of who makes it. The fame (if any) of the person making the claim only affects how closely the FTC's magnifying glass is held to the issue.

FTC Principles

In order to be acceptable under the FTC's guidelines, testimonials and endorsements must accurately portray the honest beliefs and experiences of the endorser. Furthermore, the endorser cannot make any representation that the advertiser could not directly make on its own. This means that the endorser cannot make any representation that would be deceptive or unsubstantiated even if it is his own belief.

We looked at the *Cliffdale* case in chapter 2. We'll revisit it here. In *In the Matter of Cliffdale Assocs., Inc.*, 103 F.T.C. 110 (1984), the FTC issued a complaint alleging Cliffdale, a mail-order company, with misrepresenting the value and performance qualities of an automobile engine part called the "Ball-Matic Gas Saver Valve." The advertisements stated that the Ball-Matic was "the most significant automotive breakthrough in the last ten years," that "every car needs one," and that car owners could "save up to 20 percent and more" in gasoline costs.

Several of these advertisements included consumer "test results" showing gasoline savings of 8 to 40 percent. Some ads included testimonials by consumers reporting gasoline savings of two to six miles per gallon. These claims were highlighted in a heavy-bordered box in the ad asking readers to "read the results for yourself."

It's of little surprise that the FTC ruled the Ball-Matic ads to be false and deceptive. After reviewing the substantiation provided by Cliffdale and the results of tests conducted by the FTC, they found that "even under conditions most likely to produce benefits from the Ball-Matic," the fuel savings did not even approach those claimed in the alleged consumer test or testimonials.

This points out that the advertiser is required to possess a reasonable basis for claims contained in testimonials, even if the testimonials reflect the honestly held views of the testifier. The commission rejected Cliffdale's argument that the testimonials, in and of themselves, validated the claims. The FTC stated that "consumer tests and testimonials . . . are not a recognized way of testing fuel economy." As the FTC stated, "irrespective of the veracity of the individual consumer testimonials, [the] use of the testimonials to make underlying claims that were false and deceptive was, itself, deceptive."

Cliffdale made substantial use of consumer endorsements to make performance claims about its product. About this, the commission said: "The clear impression created was that the quotes came from actual, current users of the Ball-Matic." For example, several advertisements quote phrases such as "Now I get four miles more per gallon," and, "Now that I have installed your unit . . ." Furthermore, the wording conveyed a sense that the testimonials were given voluntarily: "It gives me great pleasure to express to you my satisfaction," and "Just a short note to inform you of the performance of your Ball-Matic."

In truth these claims were false, and the testimonials were not what they appeared to be.

In another case, *In re Cooga Mooga, Inc.*, 92 F.T.C. 310 (1978), the FTC ordered the manufacturer of a topical acne medication to prohibit celebrity Pat Boone from representing (as it had in the ads) that all of his daughters used the medication with favorable results, unless those statements were true. The FTC reasoned that since not all of Boone's daughters used the acne medication, the statements were materially false and misleading.

If a person states in an ad that she uses a certain product, the advertiser may run the advertisement only if it knows that the endorser actually uses the product. In addition, an expert or celebrity can serve as an endorser only during the time when the endorser "continues to subscribe to the views presented."

Requirement that Endorsements Must Be Typical

The FTC will examine an ad that represents a consumer's experience regarding a material attribute of the product. Furthermore, the consumer claim must be representative of what an ordinary consumer will experience when using the product. Therefore, an advertiser should not employ endorsements in an ad unless it can adequately verify that the endorser's experience is representative of what will generally be achieved by others.

The *Cliffdale* case discussed above illustrates this requirement well. In this case, the advertiser stated that the claimed experiences were typical because the consumers (endorsers) represented a variety of locations, makes of cars, and occupations. In addition, the ads claimed "over 100,000 in use."

The commission, however, presumes that viewers will accept consumer testimonials as representative experiences, unless there is a clear disclaimer to the contrary. The scientific record in *Cliffdale* revealed the typical fuel economy improvement was, in the very best case, half that claimed in the consumer endorsements. The commission said: "We have already found that no competent scientific test supports respondents' performance claims." Therefore, the FTC ruled that the testimonials were deceptive since, "even if the individual experiences were accurate, they cannot be typical experiences. . . ."

Use of Disclaimers

The guides make it clear that, unless the endorser's experience is typical of what other consumers may generally expect to realize with the advertised product in actual use conditions, the advertiser must disclose the performance that would generally be found in similar circumstances or in the limited applicability of the endorser's experience. In other words, clarify the facts.

The FTC guides warn that "[t]he mere disclosure that 'not all consumers will get this result' is insufficient because it can imply that while all consumers cannot expect the advertised results, a substantial number can expect them." The FTC provides no general rule concerning how specific the disclaimer must be, so it would be wise to err on the safe side.

Advertisements for LaSalle Correspondence School (owned by Macmillan, Inc.) offered numerous testimonials of graduates reporting stunning careers and salary advances. Some ads did, in fact, imply that the testimonials were "exceptional cases" of "more successful graduates." However, the FTC found in *In re Macmillan, Inc.*, 96 F.T.C. 208 (1980), that the advertisements promoted an image that similar success could be readily expected by the reader. The commission, therefore, required all unrepresentative testimonials to be accompanied by the specific disclaimer: "This testimonial does not reflect the typical and ordinary experience of LaSalle students," in typeface that is as large as the testimonial itself.

Use of Actual Consumers

Clearly, the advertiser should use actual consumers if it implies in an advertisement that the endorser is an actual consumer. To do otherwise would violate Section 5 of the FTC Act by creating a false and deceptive impression that is likely to mislead consumers.

Use of Consumer Endorsements in Drug Ads The manufacturer of a drug product should not use a lay person's endorsement in its ads unless: (1) the advertiser possesses comprehensive scientific substantiation to prove the validity of its claims, and (2) the claims do not violate any FDA regulation regarding the drug or device.

Going back to an earlier case *In re Cooga Mooga, Inc.*, 92 F.T.C. 310 (1978), the FTC ordered the advertiser of acne medication to possess reliable information, tests, or studies that substantiated any results claimed in its consumer testimonials. Cooga Mooga, through the endorsement by Pat Boone, had falsely represented that its product penetrated the pores of the skin and cured acne. Nevertheless, the FTC permitted Cooga Mooga to rely solely on the personal experiences of the endorsers when the product or service was not related to health and safety and "where the evaluation of such products or services, for purposes of any endorsement, requires no professional expertise and such products or services can be reasonably evaluated through lay use."

In *American Home Prods. Corp.* v. *Johnson & Johnson*, 654 F. Supp. 568 (S.D.N.Y. 1987), the court upheld American Home Product's (AHP) television advertisements in which an actor depicted as "a typical Anacin user" stated: "My headache's gone, and Anacin didn't upset my stomach."

The defendant had alleged that such statements falsely implied that "Anacin," an aspirin product, caused less stomach upset than ibuprofen or acetaminophen. The court rejected McNeil's (manufacturer of Tylenol and a subsidiary of Johnson & Johnson) claims, stating that the only message the "Anacin" advertisement "literally communicates is that one user got pain relief without stomach upset."

The court further stated that while aspirin-based products are the most likely OTC analgesics to produce gastric discomfort, AHP's commercial made no implied claim that "Anacin" caused less stomach discomfort than nonaspirin pain relievers. The court reasoned that "Anacin's 'no stomach upset' advertising is within the acceptable and expectable limits of commercial puffery and is therefore unlikely to mislead consumers."

Endorsements by Experts

When using an expert to endorse a product or service, the expert must actually evaluate the product or service he or she is endorsing. It cannot be a blind claim where the endorser has not actually used and evaluated the product. Furthermore, the evaluation must be "as extensive as someone with the same degree of expertise would normally need to conduct in order to support the conclusions presented in the endorsement."

Any endorsement made in the ad must be clearly supported by the endorser's actual evaluation. It also must be relevant to his area of expertise. This, however, does not prevent an expert from expressing a personal opinion about a product as long as it involves matters outside his area of expertise. But, as always, this situation (as an opinion) must be clear in the ad.

Another area where problems can arise involves comparisons of products. In cases where an endorsement is used, the expert endorser relying upon his expertise must have concluded that the endorsed product and the competitor's product are essentially equal. If the ad creates the impression that the endorsed product is superior to the competitor's product, it must be clear that it is the expert (not the advertiser) that concluded the product is superior to the competitor's product. An expert may not be used in an ad to falsely imply that he is endorsing a product.

When an endorsement is made by an organization that is claimed as an expert it must be based upon recognized experts within the organization, or by documented standards (that are suitable for evaluating the products) previously in existence within the organization. We'll look more into endorsements by organizations later in this chapter.

What Is required to be considered an Expert If an ad claims or implies that the person giving the endorsement is an expert, the endorser must actually possess qualifications as an expert in that area. Dan Mar Products manufactured and advertised a product called the G.R. Valve. This was an automotive retrofit device advertised as a product to improve fuel economy. NASA astronaut Leroy Gordon Cooper (flew on Mercury 9 and Gemini 5 missions) gave endorsements, as an expert, in ads for the G.R. Valve. In large part Cooper's credibility came from his fame as an astronaut and the implied scientific knowledge that went with that position.

In the case *In re Cooper*, 94 F.T.C. 674 (1979).the FTC held that NASA astronaut Leroy Gordon Cooper was not qualified to represent himself as an expert with respect to fuel saving devices for automobiles. The commission held that "Gordon Cooper does not have the education, training, and knowledge to qualify him as an expert in the field of automotive engineering."

The commission reasoned that the ad falsely represented, either directly or by implication, that Gordon Cooper was a qualified expert in the field of automotive engineering. In fact, he was not.

Product Efficacy Claims

Dr. Bricklin, a professor of clinical psychology, had developed the basic "rotation" diet principles that were the basis for a weight reduction program marketed by Buckingham Productions, Inc. He also served as director of the company. In addition, Dr. Bricklin personally participated in the promotion of the diet by appearing in print ads as an expert endorser.

The FTC initiated an action in June 1985 against Dr. Barry Bricklin, an expert endorser, as well as against Buckingham and others, claiming that ads for the so-called "rotation" diet plan made false and deceptive claims about typical weight losses achieved, ease of dieting, permanence of results, and the energizing, hunger-inhibiting, and fat-burning properties of the wafers and tablets used in the diet.

The FTC in *In re Bricklin*, 106 F.T.C. 115 (1985), alleged that by virtue of his expert endorsements, Dr. Bricklin claimed he had a "reasonable basis" for his representations. Yet no such basis existed. A "reasonable basis" would consist of testing of the product and programs involved, which would support the conclusions presented in the endorsement. This is the standard required by the FTC in its guides.

The FTC prohibited Bricklin from representing in ads that consumers can lose weight without disclosing that weight loss depends on an overall reduction in caloric intake, and that a comparable weight loss can be obtained from any weight-control program. That is, unless these claims can be supported by a competent, reliable survey or other scientific evidence that substantiates the representation.

Implied Endorsements

"I want a pain reliever I can really trust," said the young lady. "When I sprained my ankle and went to the hospital, they gave me Tylenol. I learned that Tylenol is the pain reliever hospitals use most. Hospitals trust Tylenol. Last year, hospitals dispensed ten times as much Tylenol as the next four brands combined. If hospitals trust Tylenol, shouldn't your choice be Tylenol?" AHP, makers of Anacin, challenged the above ad for Tylenol.

The court in *American Home Prods. Corp.* v. *Johnson & Johnson*, 654 F. Supp. 568 (S.D.N.Y. 1987), examined the assertion that the advertisement presented an implied expert endorsement. If you'll recall, we looked at another element of this case earlier.

AHP objected to the advertisement on the basis that it gave the false impression that hospitals use more Tylenol than other analgesics because Tylenol is a superior pain reliever. According to AHP, the real motivation in dispensing more Tylenol was that McNeil (a subsidiary of Johnson & Johnson) supplied Tylenol to them at extremely low prices.

The court reasoned that the Tylenol ad was not false or unfair, because hospitals would, in fact, not use Tylenol if it were ineffective or unsafe. The court said; "At worst, the statement is a half-truth, in that it omits to mention that hospitals choose Tylenol for the additional reason that it costs less than competitive analgesics."

In its counterclaim, McNeil complained of an AHP ad that used a similar marketing tactic. In response to McNeil's "hospitals trust" advertisements, AHP conducted a campaign in which it mailed free samples of Anacin-3 to 250,000 doctors with attached postage prepaid postcards, which when returned entitled doctors to additional free samples. AHP then surveyed a sample of the 108,000 doctors who returned the cards and computed a percentage from the sample of those who responded that they had recommended Anacin-3. AHP then multiplied the percentage by the 108,000 total responses to arrive at its advertising claim that 70,000 doctors recommended Anacin-3. McNeil complained that this advertisement falsely implied that most doctors recommend "Anacin-3" when 70,000 doctors represented only about ten percent of the doctors in the United States.

The court rejected McNeil's argument. Assuming that AHP's extrapolation was reliable, it held that AHP could say that "70,000 doctors recommend Anacin-3" whether or not most laymen understood the percentage of doctors that figure represented.

In addition, the court noted that the more problematic issue was that "the 70,000 doctors did not spontaneously recommend Anacin-3 [but v]ery likely, all that most of them did was to pass on to patients free samples which AHP had furnished them." It concluded that AHP had, in effect, carried "McNeil's scheme to its logical extreme" by reducing the price of Anacin-3 to zero. The court accordingly held that AHP's campaign was not false or "unacceptably misleading" since 70,000 doctors impliedly recommended Anacin-3.

Endorsements by Groups and Organizations

An organization's endorsement must fairly reflect the collective view of the group. This is because consumers view endorsements by organizations as a collective judgment, free from the sort of subjective influences inherent in an individual's judgment.

In the case *In re Biopractic Group, Inc.*, 104 F.T.C. 845 (1984), the commission ordered the manufacturer of a treatment for arthritis and musculoskeletal ailments called "Ice Therapy" to stop representing that the treatment had been endorsed by various medical organizations and athletic groups. Biopractic's advertisement stated that "[d]octors, medical pain centers, physical therapists, health clinics, professional athletic teams, U.S. and Russian Olympic Track Teams Praise Ice Therapy." The commission alleged that no such medical or athletic organizations had given Biopractic the endorsements and found the ad to be false and misleading.

In another case, *In re Estee Corp.*, 102 F.T.C. 1804 (1983), the FTC ordered the maker of a fructose-sweetened food product to stop representing that its products had been recommended by the FDA or the American Diabetes Association when no such endorsements had been made. And in *In re Bristol-Myers Co.*, 102 F.T.C. 21 (1983), *aff'd*, 738 F.2d 554 (2d Cir. 1984), cert. denied, 469 U.S. 1189, 105 S.Ct. 960, 83 L.Ed. 2d. 966 (1985), the FTC ordered a drug manufacturer to stop representing in its ads that doctors recommended Bufferin more than any other pain reliever, without a reasonable basis for the claim.

In *In re Emergency Devices, Inc.*, 102 F.T.C. 1713 (1983), the commission ordered the manufacturer of a gas mask to stop ads containing an approval by any municipal, state, or federal agency when such an endorsement was not true. The ads had included statements such as "[t]ested and approved! In the U.S. and Canada, the mask has undergone vigorous testing by fire officials" and "[t]he filtering system was evaluated by an independent chemical testing lab, approved by OSHA and the California State Health Department." This was not true.

Disclosure of a Business Connection Any connection between the endorser and the advertiser, which cannot reasonably be recognized by the audience, that might materially affect the credibility of the endorsement, must be fully disclosed.

Consumers expect an advertiser to pay an expert or a well-known personality for an endorsement, but they do not expect such a payment for a noncelebrity endorsement. Therefore, if an advertiser is paying a noncelebrity for an endorsement, the compensation must be conspicuously disclosed in the advertisement.

The FTC reiterated its position concerning the disclosure of business connections in *In the Matter of Cliffdale Assocs., Inc.*, 103 F.T.C. 110 (1984), a case which we looked at earlier. The FTC held that Cliffdale implied that the consumer endorsements in its advertising were "freely given by individuals who were unrelated to the marketers of the Ball-Matic" on the basis of specific language in the testimonials such as, "It gives me great pleasure to express to you my satisfaction" and "Just a short note to inform you of the performance of your Ball-Matic." In fact, many testimonials were solicited by Cliffdale employees from business associates.

As the commission states in their guidelines, when a connection exists between the endorser and the advertiser that might affect the weight and credibility of the endorsement, the connection must be disclosed. The FTC found the connection between the endorsers and Cliffdale to be material because potential purchasers would have difficulty evaluating the Ball-Matic on their own and would therefore be apt to rely heavily on endorsements of other users. The FTC also reasoned that the language used by the endorsers specifically implied that their testimonials had been unsolicited.

In another case we have looked at already, *In re Cooga Mooga, Inc.*, Pat Boone also had a financial interest in the advertised product, Acne-Statin. In fact, Boone had the majority control of the company. The commission maintained that "if a material connection exists between the endorser and the advertiser or its advertising agency, such connection must be disclosed in the advertisement(s) which contain the endorsement." The commission went on to further explain that: "A 'material connection' shall mean, . . . any financial interest in the sale of the product or service which is the subject of the endorsement or any familial connection between the endorser and the advertiser or its advertising agency."

However, the FTC guides do not require the disclosure that a testimonial is solicited.

Labeling

A number of labeling laws affect a wide variety of products. As an example, various provisions of the federal Food, Drug, and Cosmetic Act regulate labeling for those products. These regulations are administered by the Food and Drug Administration (FDA). Other examples include wool products (regulated by the Wool Products Labeling Act of 1939), textile products (regulated by the Textile Fiber Products Identification Act), and fur products (regulated by the Fur Products Labeling Act). These various acts outlaw mislabeling, which is often referred to as "misbranding" and are administered by the Federal Trade Commission.

The Relationship between the FDA and the FTC Concerning Labeling

As a general rule, the FDA maintains jurisdiction for labeling of food, drug and cosmetic products, whereas the FTC has jurisdiction over the truth or falsity (and likelihood of deception) of any advertising used in relation to these products.

In the absence of an express agreement between the two agencies to the contrary, the FTC will exercise primary jurisdiction over all matters regulating the truth or falsity of advertising of food, drugs (with the exception of prescription drugs), devices, and cosmetics.

The Food and Drug Administration

The FDA controls labeling under the federal Food, Drug, and Cosmetic Act, 15 U.S.C. §§ 301-392, (FDC Act), and the Fair Packaging and Labeling Act, 15 U.S.C. §§1451–1461, (FPL Act). Both acts apply to foods and drugs for humans, as well as animals, cosmetics, and medical devices.

In addition, many states have similar laws modeled after the FDC Act. Among other things, this act is designed to insure that labeling and packaging is truthful, nondeceptive, and informative. On the other hand, the FPL Act controls the location and contents of information on packages and labels.

Basically, the FDC Act forbids distribution within or importation into the United States of products that are adulterated or "misbranded." In this context, "misbranding" includes statements, designs, or pictures on labels that create a false or misleading impression. It also covers failure to display required information in labeling.

The FDC Act contains detailed definitions of "misbranding." For example, the FDC Act states that a product is "misbranded" if its label is false or misleading in any manner. As an example, use of testimonials constitute misbranding if the impression given is that the drug is effective for a particular condition when it isn't, or hasn't been proven effective for that condition.

The FDC Act defines "labeling" as all labels and other written, printed, or graphic matter accompanying the product. You should be aware that the FDA, and the courts, will interpret "accompanying" in very broad terms. Therefore, "labeling" may also include items that help identify the article, its uses, and give directions, even if it is not actually included with the product. Under this definition the FDA can proceed against a false or misleading food or drug ad. If the FDA believes a threat to the public health may exist in such an ad, they can attempt to link the ad with the product to give the agency the authority to act.

In 1981 then FDA Commissioner, Dr. Arthur Hull Hayes, Jr., stated in a speech to the American Advertising Federation Conference that: "The line between advertising and labeling sometimes is very thin. In certain cases, advertising may become labeling when it accompanies a product. For example, tear sheets from newspapers or magazines, when they are placed on the counter next to the product, are labeling. Catalogues may be labeling, as may brochures used to promote a product. Courts have held that written, printed or graphic promotional material accompanying a product is labeling, regardless of the nature of the material, or the manner in which it became associated with or accompanies the article."

Dr. Hayes also provided three examples of situations where the FDA might take action against an ad:

• A drug or medical device product is legally misbranded if its advertising contains conditions, purposes, or uses for which the labeling does not bear adequate directions for use;

- A drug or product may not be promoted, in either its labeling or advertising, with any representation or suggestion that approval by FDA is in effect; or
- A drug or medical device is illegally misbranded if its advertising is false or misleading in any way.

State Law Parallels to the FTC Act

In addition to the federal regulations under Section 5 of the FTC Act just discussed, there are also state statutes and regulations. You should research and understand the unfair and deceptive acts and practices (UDAP) statutes that exist in the states where you plan to advertise.

In the past most states have developed some type of consumer protection law. Many of these statutes parallel the Federal Trade Commission Act and are appropriately called "Little FTC Acts" or "Mini FTC Acts." However, unlike the FTC Act many of these statutes afford consumers the right to bring a civil action for damages. There are four types of UDAP statutes which we will discuss in the following sections:

Unfair Trade Practice and Consumer Protection Laws

This type of UDAP statute follows a form drafted by the Federal Trade Commission in association with the Committee on Suggested State Legislation of the Council of State Governments. There are three versions of this model that are used in various states:

- Pure "Little FTC Acts" specifically outlawing unfair methods of competition and unfair or deceptive acts or practices. These have been adopted in states including: Connecticut, Florida, Hawaii, Illinois, Louisiana, Maine, Massachusetts, Montana, Nebraska, North Carolina, South Carolina, Vermont, Washington, and West Virginia;
- Acts prohibiting certain specific practices, in addition to any other practice that is essentially unfair or deceptive. These are found in states including: Alabama, Alaska, Georgia, Idaho, Maryland, Mississippi, New Hampshire, Pennsylvania, Rhode Island, and Tennessee; and
- Acts prohibiting false, misleading, or deceptive practices. These statutes are found in states including Kentucky and Texas.

Uniform Consumer Sales Practices Acts Developed by the American Bar Association and the National Conference on Uniform State Laws, this act applies only to consumer transactions and makes deceptive and unconscionable practices illegal. This act has been adopted by states including Kansas, Ohio, and Utah.

Uniform Deceptive Trade Practices Acts This type of act gives businesses the right to take action against a competitor that uses deceptive techniques to attract customers. In addition, the act has also been applied to consumer cases. This act in different forms is in effect in: Colorado, Delaware, Georgia, Hawaii, Illinois, Maine, Minnesota, Nebraska, New Mexico, Ohio, Oklahoma, and Oregon.

Consumer Fraud Acts The Consumer Fraud Acts forbid misrepresentation, fraud, deception, and unfair or unconscionable acts. States that employ such acts include: Arizona, Arkansas, Delaware, Indiana, Iowa, Michigan, Missouri, Nevada, New Jersey, New York, North Dakota, South Dakota, Virginia, Wyoming, and the District of Columbia.

State Law Cases

Failure to Disclose

We've seen recent cases that revolve around a failure to disclose facts. As a result, failure to disclose a fact may or may not be considered false advertising depending on the particular state's law. Take two cases that occurred in 1998, each involving AT&T's failure to disclose its practice of "rounding up" to the next full minute the cost of long distance telephone service. A New York court held that this was not false advertising under New York law, and a California court held that AT&T's omission was false advertising under California law.

The subject of a number of false advertising/deceptive practices actions in recent years, "rounding up" occurs when a long distance phone conversation lasts for one minute and ten seconds, and the customer is charged for two minutes of time. A typical defense against any request for monetary relief in such actions involves the filed rate doctrine. Telecommunications companies are required to file their rates with the Federal Communications Commission (FCC). As long as the company does not deviate from those rates, no civil action (based on rates) may be brought against the company. The theory here is that once the rates are filed, they become public record and therefore the public is presumed to be informed.

In *Marcus* v. *AT&T Corp.*, 136 F.3d 46 (2d Cir. 1998), AT&T's failure to disclose its rounding up practice in its advertising was not considered false advertising under New York law. AT&T did disclose its rounding-up practice when it filed with the FCC.

Under New York's false advertising statute (N.Y. Gen. Bus. L., §§ 349-350 (McKinney's 1988 & Supp. 1996)), a plaintiff must allege that the defendant made a material false misrepresentation, including how the advertising failed to reveal material facts.

The court stated: "[T]he statutes are meant to protect the public from a wide spectrum of improper conduct in advertising. They may be invoked where the advertising complained of is not actually false, but thought likely to mislead or deceive, or is in fact false. By their breadth, the statutes encompass not only those advertisements which have deceived or misled because they are untrue, but also those which may be accurate on some level, but will nonetheless tend to mislead or deceive."

The court in this case determined that since the phone cards were prepaid and the packaging of the cards did not reveal the practice of rounding up, AT&T's advertising was likely to mislead.

Specifically, the plaintiff argued that AT&T, who sells the prepaid phone cards, does not "reveal to the consumer, prior to purchase, that calls made with these cards are, in fact, rounded up to the next higher minutes." As an example, on the packaging of its "PrePaid Card" AT&T states the card is "worth 10 minutes of phone calls in the U.S." and that "1 minute of calling time requires 1 unit when calling within the U.S."

Based on the advertising, a consumer would not know that rounding up was done until the card was purchased.

The court reasoned: "The State of California has no requirement that common carriers disclose their rates anywhere other than in the rate schedules filed with the PUC. Nonetheless, businesses are prohibited from engaging in advertising practices which are potentially misleading to the public, so that if they choose to promote their rates, they must do so with sufficient accuracy that they did not risk misleading or deceiving the consumer. We hold that under California's unfair business practices and deceptive advertising provisions, respondents are prohibited from disseminating misleading or deceptive packaging materials with their prepaid phone cards."

The court continued by stating: "We hold that the policies which are furthered by the California statutes would be undermined by the filed rate doctrine's presumption of a consumer's omniscience of filed rates, and the resulting immunity to common carriers, regardless of any advertising deception used to lure the consumer."

Here, the court viewed *Marcus* differently because consumers were able to read their phone bills and see the rounding up practice.

The court specified: "We decline to conclude on the facts alleged here that no reasonable consumer of prepaid phone cards would be likely to be misled or deceived by respondents' practices. The rationale of the holdings in . . . *Marcus* rested in part upon the consumers' ability to read the phone bills provided by the respondents there. With this document before them, they could see that only full minutes had been charged, but could not reasonably believe that each call they had made had been in increments of precise minutes."

While in *Day*, the packaging of the phone cards did not discuss rounding up. Also, in *Day*, the court refused to consider the filed rate presumption of consumer knowledge.

In another case we see a contrast to the previous two cases. In *Tenore* v. *AT&T Wireless Services*, No. 65609-6, 1998 Wash. LEXIS 593 (Wash S. Ct., September 10, 1998), the Washington Supreme Court held that AT&T Wireless could be liable for false advertising under Washington's consumer protection law for not disclosing its practice of rounding up.

There the court stated:

Respondent AT&T engaged in "deceptive, fraudulent, misleading and/or unfair conduct" by not disclosing its practice of "rounding" airtime in order to "induce cellular customers to use its cellular service, and/or in order to unfairly profit." "Rounding," "rounding up," or "full minute billing" is a common billing practice in the cellular and long distance telephone industry where fractions of a minute are rounded up to the next highest minute. For example, a call that lasts one minute and one second is charged as a two-minute call, but the subscriber is not informed of the actual duration of the call. Appellants claim this billing practice "results in millions of dollars of excess billing . . . all at the expense of the unwary customer." Appellants additionally claim this practice is "contrary to the 'Service Agreement' . . . which states that the customer is billed only for 'the time you press send until the time you press end.'"

The court added: "Appellants claim cellular customers do not receive the full minutes they have contracted for at a fixed rate under their service plan because of rounding. For example, all subscribers are required to choose between plans that offer varying specified minutes of airtime, such as 30, 60, or 100 minutes, for a fixed monthly rate, beyond which calls are billed at a specified per-minute rate. But a 30-minute plan may not in fact provide 30 full minutes because of rounding. This is what Appellants claim AT&T should have disclosed."

The essential difference in *Tenore* was that AT&T Wireless Services was a cellular service provider. These providers are exempt from the FCC tariff filing requirements. *Marcus* and *Day* were long distance telephone service providers that were considered "common carriers" under the Federal Communication Act, which required the filing of tariffs. Since they weren't, AT&T Wireless could not use the filed rate doctrine as a defense. The court then looked at whether the doctrine of primary jurisdiction required the issues in the case to be decided by the FCC.

AT&T Wireless argued that finding false advertising under Washington's consumer protection statutes required a court to engage in rate regulation in determining a reasonable charge for partial minutes of airtime. Thus, the matter should have been referred to the FCC, which had special competence and expertise in rate regulation.

The court disagreed, relying primarily on the Supreme Court decision in *Nader v. Allegheny Airlines, Inc.*, 426 U.S. 290 (1976). In that case, a plaintiff brought actions against an airline for not disclosing its overbooking practices. The plaintiff had been "bumped" from a flight on which he had a confirmed reservation. The Supreme Court held that the doctrine of primary jurisdiction did not require the misrepresentation claim to be referred to the Civil Aeronautics Board.

The Court in *Nader* stated: "The action brought by petitioner does not turn on a determination of the reasonableness of a challenged practice—a determination that could be facilitated by an informed evaluation of the economics or technology of the regulated industry. The standards to be applied in an action for fraudulent misrepresentation are within the conventional competence of the courts, and the judgment of a technically expert body is not likely to be helpful in the application of these standards to the facts of this case."

The plaintiffs were not challenging AT&T Wireless' practice of rounding up, but rather its failure to disclose the practice. The Washington Court reasoned that a court could award damages without it constituting rate-making.

A Few Final Words on the Subject

Having now studied the various problem areas involving the Federal Trade Commission Act and state parallels, the advertiser should be better equipped to avoid creating a deceptive ad. Advertisers and their agencies, with this knowledge in mind, must carefully and objectively evaluate their advertising to avoid trouble.

You should study the following document, reproduced in full in Exhibit 3.1, which was originally created in 1975 by the Federal Trade Commission. It contains a series of questions that the Commission uses to investigate advertising cases.

Exhibit 3.1	**Federal Trade Commission Policy Planning Protocol for Deceptive and Unsubstantiated Claims**

These questions which follow are not cumulative. The answer to less than all of them may indicate the need for action. Moreover, answers to certain of these questions will frequently not be available at all, or may not be available except at considerable cost and delay. Answers to these questions therefore should not be required where obtaining the answers would be unduly burdensome or speculative, or where the answers to other of the questions indicate that the action proposed is a particularly good one, or, of course, where the answers could be obtained only by compulsory process and the action which the Commission is being asked to take is to authorize such process.

A. Consumer Interpretations of the Claim

1. List the main interpretations that consumers may place on the claim recommended for challenge, including those that might render the claim true/substantiated as well as those that might render the claim false/unsubstantiated.

2. Indicate which of these interpretations would be alleged to be implications of the claim for purposes of substantiation or litigation. For each interpretation so indicated, state the reasons, if any, for believing that the claim so interpreted would be false/unsubstantiated.

B. Scale of the Deception or Lack of Substantiation

3. What is known about the relative proportions of consumers adhering to each of the interpretations listed above in response to question 1?

4. What was the approximate advertising budget for the claim during the past year or during any other period of time that would reflect the number of consumers actually exposed to the claim? Is there more direct information on the number of consumers exposed to the claim?

C. Materiality

5. If consumers do interpret the claim in the ways that would be alleged to be implications, what reasons are there for supposing that these interpretations would influence purchase decisions?

6. During the past year, approximately how many consumers purchased the product [refers to the particular brand] about which the claim was made?

7. Approximately what price did they pay?

8. Estimate, if possible, the proportion of consumers who would have purchased the product only at some price lower than they did pay, if at all, were they informed that the interpretations identified in response to question 2 were false.

9. Estimate, if possible, what the advertised product would be worth to the consumers identified by question 8 if they knew that the product did not have the positive (or unique) attributes suggested by the claim. If the claim can cause consumers to disregard some negative attribute, such as a risk to health and safety, to their possible physical or economic injury, so specify. If so, estimate, if possible, the annual number of such injuries attributable to the claim.

D. Adequacy of Corrective Market Forces

10. If the product to which the claim relates is a low ticket item, can consumers ordinarily determine prior to purchase whether the claim, as interpreted, is true or invest a small amount in purchase and then by experience with the product determine whether or not the claim is true? Does the claim relate to a credence quality, that is, a quality of the product that consumers ordinarily cannot evaluate during normal use of the product without acquiring costly information from some source other than their own evaluative faculties?

11. Is the product to which the claim relates one that a consumer would typically purchase frequently? Have product sales increased or decreased substantially since the claim was made?

12. Are there sources of information about the subject matter of the claim in addition to the claim itself? If so, are they likely to be recalled by consumers when they purchase or use the product? Are they likely to be used by consumers who are not aggressive, effective shoppers? If not, why not?

E. Effect on the Flow of Truthful Information

13. Will the standard of truth/substantiation that would be applied to the claim under the recommendation to initiate proceedings make it extremely difficult as a practical matter to make the type of claim? Is this result reasonable?

14. What are the consequences to consumers of an erroneous determination by the Commission that the claim is false/unsubstantiated? What are the consequences to consumers of an erroneous determination by the Commission that the claim is true/substantiated?

F. Deterrence

15. Is there a possibility of getting significant relief with broad product or claim coverage? What relief is possible? Why would it be significant?

16. Do the facts of the matter recommended present an opportunity to elaborate a rule of law that would be applicable to claims or advertisers other than those that would be directly challenged by the recommended action? If so, describe this rule of law as you would wish the advertising community to understand it. If this rule of law would be a significant precedent, explain why.

17. Does the claim violate a Guide or is it inconsistent with relevant principles embodied in a Guide?

18. Is the fact of a violation so evident to other industry members that, if we do not act, our credibility and deterrence might be adversely affected?

19. Is there any aspect of the advertisement – e.g., the nature of the advertiser, the product, the theme, the volume of the advertising, the memorableness of the ad, the blatancy of the violation—which indicates that an enforcement action would have substantial impact on the advertising community?

20. What, if anything, do we know about the role advertising plays (as against other promotional techniques and other sources of information) in the decision to purchase the product?

21. What is the aggregate dollar volume spent on advertising by the advertiser to be joined in the recommended action?

22. What is the aggregate volume of sales of the advertised product and of products of the same type?

G. Law Enforcement Efficiency

23. Has another agency taken action or does another agency have expertise with respect to the claim or its subject matter? Are there reasons why the Commission should defer? What is the position of this other agency? If coordination is planned, what form would it take?

24. How difficult would it be to litigate a case challenging the claim? Would the theory of the proceeding recommended place the Commission in a position of resolving issues that are better left to other modes of resolution, for instance, debate among scientists? If so, explain? Is there a substantial possibility of whole or partial summary judgment?

25. Can the problem seen in the ad be handled by way of a rule? Are the violations widespread? Should they be handled by way of a rule?

H. Additional Considerations

26. What is the ratio of the advertiser's advertising expense to sales revenues? How, if at all, is this ratio relevant to the public interest in proceeding as recommended?

27. Does the claim specially affect a vulnerable group?

28. Does the advertising use deception or unfairness to offend important values or to exploit legitimate concerns of a substantial segment of the population, whether or not there is direct injury to person or pocketbook, e.g., minority hiring or environmental protection?

29. Are there additional considerations not elicited by previous questions that would affect the public interest in proceeding?

4 The Client–Agency Relationship

Advertising may be described as the science of arresting human intelligence long enough to get money from it.
—*Stephen Butler Leacock*

A common practice in Italy around 1,250 was to sell wine by the flask. Many unscrupulous wine merchants filled the bottom of their bottles with wax, thereby reducing the amount of wine in the bottle and improving the profit margin substantially. When the public found out about this deception, wine sales dropped rapidly. So the legitimate wine merchants banded together and began sending agents out into the streets promoting wine with placards saying "Sine Cere," which means "without wax." From this Italian phrase comes our word "sincere," and from this practice comes one of the earliest examples of an organized advertising agency.

Volney Palmer was simply a small business owner struggling to make a profit in a city crippled by unemployment and debt brought on by the Panic of 1837. Yet Palmer did, in fact, forever revolutionize American business in 1841.

The son of a newspaper entrepreneur, Palmer was no stranger to the business. In 1841, Palmer moved to Philadelphia and established a real estate office in the city. Between 1841 and 1842, Palmer expanded his real estate business to include other services. One of which was the establishment of his advertising business. As a result, he created the country's first formal dedicated advertising agency.

Early advertising agents were merely buyers of large blocks of newspaper space. They would then resell that space in smaller increments to local businesses. They were essentially media space brokers.

Although the original advertising agency established in 1841 by Palmer ceased to exist after his death, it would evolve into *N. W. Ayer & Son, Inc.* In 1869, Francis Wayland Ayer was an ambitious young schoolteacher who persuaded his father, Nathan Wheeler Ayer, to join him in business. With an initial investment of $250, *N. W. Ayer & Son* would grow into owning the claim of being the oldest advertising agency in the United States. It would also become one of the largest and best-known agencies in the world.

Immediately after the purchase of Palmer's agency, Ayer pioneered the "open contract," a revolutionary change in the method of billing for advertising that became the industry standard. He also included the use of art in advertising and made use of a full-time copywriter, thereby forming the beginnings of a creative department.

From those early days of the advertising agency business, the media has not resisted the temptation to use the advertising agency as a source of drama and entertainment. Movies like: *The Hucksters* (1947), *Mr. Blandings Builds His Dream House* (1948), *Will Success Spoil Rock Hunter?* (1957), *Putney Swope* (1969), *Kramer vs. Kramer* (1979), *Mr. Mom* (1983), *Nothing in Common* (1986), *Crazy People* (1990), and *What Women Want* (2000), fueled a portrayal of the unscrupulous, manipulative and corrupt ad agency business that lingers today.

The Advertising Agency

In this chapter, we'll discuss the business relationship between an advertising agency and its client. Generally this involves one businesses relationship with another business. But it can apply to individuals as well when they act in the same roles.

A professional agency is a business (or it can be an individual as well) that acts on behalf of others. Attorneys, accountants, brokers, factors, auctioneers, and, yes, advertising agencies may fall into this category. Any profession—if it acts as an agent—is regulated by the same laws. As a result, some of the cases we examine in this chapter do not involve advertising agencies, but the principles are binding on any agency relationship.

First, there are a couple of terms that need to be clarified. An *agent* can be an individual alone, a group of people, a large corporation, or a full-time employee. A principal can be a client or an employer. But for purposes of clarity, we refer to a principal as the *client* throughout this chapter.

One distinguishing feature between an "agent" and "independent contractor" is the amount of control retained by the client over the physical conduct of the person performing the service. The independent contractor obligates herself or himself to produce a result and is free to pursue her or his own methods in the performance of the work.

For example, if Acme Company wants a new machine, it can use its own employees to build it. Or it can contract with Bosco Corporation to build the machine according to Acme's specifications and at an agreed-on price. If Acme hires Bosco to build the machine, Bosco is an independent contractor. Bosco has been hired to produce a result: a specific machine at a specific price. Acme has no physical control over how Bosco produces the machine.

However, in most (but not all) cases advertising agencies are true agencies in the legal sense. They don't have the independent contractor's freedom of control. The ad agency is subject to direct control by the client. In the advertising business, most clients reserve the right to select, approve, confer, and be advised of the work of their advertising agencies during every stage of the process. Anyone who has ever worked in an agency can vouch for that.

When an Advertising "Agency" Is Not an Agent

Advertising agencies that want the legal benefits of being an agency must abide by the duties that go along with the title. Simply calling a company an "advertising agency" does not mean that it is an agent, legally. The legal relationship is what exists, not what is claimed.

Now, you may ask why ad agencies are called "agencies" if they are not always. It's more out of tradition than for any other reason. The title creates a trade name more than an establishment of legal status. It is actually a misnomer; a throwback from the early "space-broker" days when advertising agencies were merely brokers of media space as we saw at the beginning of this chapter.

The alternative to being an agency is being an independent contractor. Here's an example to illustrate. A person owns a Chevrolet dealership in Los Angeles. This dealer sells Chevrolet cars and trucks, and the business is referred to as a Chevrolet agency. However, this dealer is not an agent. The person simply sells Chevrolet products as an independent contractor, he or she does not work on behalf of others.

In the case of an advertising agency, this can often occur when the agency produces work on a speculative basis (spec work). This is a fairly common practice in the advertising business. It commonly happens when an advertising agency creates work on its own; its own time, its own money, its own efforts.

Let's say an advertising agency wants to pitch a new account. In order to do this they research, create and develop an ad campaign. They mock it up (comps) to show the potential client. The client hasn't paid anything, or committed to buying the work. If the client buys the ad campaign, they get paid for their time and costs. But if the client doesn't buy the campaign, the advertising agency absorbs the costs it expended as a loss. In cases like this, the advertising agency is not an "agent" of the client. It is operating under its own control. The same situation occurs when a client asks an advertising agency to "show us what you can come up with." It is a very common practice for a potential client to request a few ad agencies to submit their "ideas" in a speculative pitch for the business. The client will then pick the one it likes best. Situations like this are purely speculative and fall into the independent contractor realm.

The balance of this chapter will look at situations where the advertising agency is operating as an agent of the client.

Duties of the Advertising Agency

When an advertising agency does work as a true agent, the following issues must be considered by both parties.

An advertising agency is able to commit the client to contracts, and at the same time it owes a duty of confidence and trust (fiduciary) to the client. Duties that the agency owes to the client fall into one of two areas: specific duties that are spelled out in a written contract and duties that are imposed by law. Specific duties can be anything so long as they do not violate a law and that the client and agency want to make a part of the contract.

Even if no written contract exists between the client and agency, the agency's duties imposed by law still exist. These include the following:

- High level of skill required of agency;
- Full disclosure to client;
- Obligations regarding competitive accounts;
- Trustee of client and handling of funds;
- Accountability to client;
- Duty to cooperate with client;
- Obligation to preserve trade secrets; and
- No undisclosed interest in suppliers.

Now let's look at each of these duties in more detail.

High Level of Skill Required of Agency An advertising agency represents itself as being an expert in its field. When an ad agency makes a presentation to a prospective client, it goes out of its way to impress upon the client that it possesses a tremendous degree of skill in both the area of advertising and that of the client's product. Once stated, the agency is then obligated to deliver. It must not merely show a general level of skill, but it must demonstrate the level of a highly skilled professional.

It is not enough that an advertising (or any other) agency apply the usual degree of care to the business entrusted it by its client. It must put forth its best efforts using its skill, experience, and knowledge to the best of its professional ability. When an agency fails to deliver on this, breach of contract may exist. The breach may be cause for the client to terminate the contract, or in some cases, bring suit for damages.

On the other hand, it is true that an agency is not required to guarantee the success of the advertising that it produces, only to put forth all of its best efforts toward the success of it. That means not doing anything that would diminish its chance for success.

Full Disclosure to Client An agency owes its clients complete loyalty. This may seem simple to accomplish, but it can affect an agency in many ways. Part of this loyalty includes a responsibility to inform the client of any fact or occurrence that affects the client in any way. For instance, if the agency has been late in paying a supplier, who in turn threatens to cut off services, the agency is under a duty to inform its client. As unpleasant as this may be, the client is legally entitled to be informed quickly and thoroughly on all such matters.

Let me give you a good example. The disclosure required of an agent was discussed many years ago in *Crocker* v. *United States*, 240 U.S. 74, 36 S.Ct. 245, 60 L.Ed. 533 (1916). Frank Crocker owned a company, which had a contract to furnish mail-carrier satchels to the U.S. Post Office. His company did so, but something happened to cause the Postmaster General to rescind the contract and refuse to pay for the satchels.

Two employees of Crocker, Mr. Lorenz and Mr. Crawford, made a secret agreement with Mr. Machen, who was superintendent of the division that needed the satchels. Machen arranged for the contract to go to Crocker's company in exchange for half of the profits. Crocker got the government contract, with Machen getting half the profits from the sales. The company furnished over ten thousand satchels before the Postmaster General learned of the collusion.

Lorenz and Crawford were agents of Crocker, and were acquiring the contract at the company's request. They were trying to secure the government contract by working out a fraudulent deal with Machen. By virtue of the agency relationship, Crocker in essence sanctioned what they did. Because the contract was obtained fraudulently, Crocker lost his claim for payment.

Obligations as to Competitive Clients A problem arises when an agency tries to serve two clients who are in competition with each other. The agency can't serve both unless it has the consent of the two parties in advance. This became the issue in *Joyce Beverages of New York, Inc.* v. *Royal Crown Cola*, 555 F.Supp. 271 (1983).

Joyce Beverages was a licensee, and as such an agent, of several soft drink manufacturers, including Royal Crown Cola, 7-Up, Diet 7-Up, A&W Root Beer, Sugar-Free A&W, Perrier, Nestea, Hawaiian Punch, and Nehi drinks. Royal Crown's licensing agreement with Joyce stated that Joyce must use its best efforts to build, maintain, and expand the sales of the Royal Crown drinks to Royal Crown's satisfaction.

The contract between the parties would not allow Joyce to distribute any soft drinks that were "substantially or reasonably similar" to Royal Crown products. The contract further provided that "any cola shall be deemed substantially or reasonably similar to any . . . cola [and] any diet cola to any . . . diet cola."

One of the ways Joyce could breach this agreement was to take on a competing drink. That's exactly what it did. In 1982 Joyce began marketing "LIKE," a decaffeinated cola drink manufactured by the 7-Up Company.

By handling another competitive cola in its market area, Joyce created "inevitable and corrosive divided loyalty and effort and made impossible a continued relationship . . . of confidence and cooperation." In essence, Joyce would be selling a new product to old customers, with advertising and promotion practices that it established for the old product. This breaches the duty of an agent not to handle competing clients without consent.

Joyce argued, in its defense, that Royal Crown would not be put in a position to "sink or swim" by itself. Joyce also claimed that Royal Crown wouldn't "go down the drain." This points out a common misconception, that is, Joyce's duty to its client is to vigorously promote the product—to expand its market share, not simply to keep it alive. The court agreed and allowed Royal Crown to rescind the contract.

Sometimes it is not easy to determine whether two clients compete with each other. Clients compete, basically, when their products are similar or interchangeable or where one product may replace the need of the other. Such products that could replace the other might be toothpaste and dental cleaning powder, floor wax and a product that eliminates the need to wax, or bandages and a cut spray that replaces a bandage.

Another area of competition is situations in which products are advertised and sold in different geographic areas. In these cases there may be no direct competition of products, yet clients may not be pleased. Clients may claim that information obtained from one company is being used to benefit the other. While this may not violate any duty, the ad agency could have some very irritated clients on its hands. The best practice is to inform the agency's existing client and get its approval beforehand.

However, many agencies do represent different clients in competition for the same market. These agencies promote the fact that they specialize in a certain area: banking, real estate, or healthcare, for example. In many fields, this agency specialty is preferred by clients. In these cases, clients who know of this are considered to have consented to the agency's representing other competitors. If the client is told about representing other competitors in the same field before it becomes a client, it will have very little to complain about later. The point is that the client must be made aware of, and give its consent to, this multiple representation.

Trustee of Client and Handling of Funds *Handling of Funds* The financial aspect of a client–agency relationship can be a major source of aggravation for both, especially in the area of commingling of funds, that is, mixing the money that belongs to the agency with that which belongs to the client. The agency is the trustee of the funds taken in on behalf of the client and must treat that money accordingly.

Basic agency law requires that an agent must keep money belonging to its client separate from its own. The only time that this does not need to happen legally is when the client has knowledge and has consented in advance.

The common practice, however, is to the contrary for a number of reasons. When a client sends money to the agency, rarely does it identify what it should be applied to. It is very uncommon that a client will send a separate check for each type of payment. However, payments intended to cover the agency's fees and costs need not be kept separately. But, money that merely flows through the agency on the way to suppliers (like photographers, printers, production companies, etc.)

or media, less commissions, should not be mixed with the agency's money. To avoid problems later, this subject should be specifically addressed in the client–agency contract.

The best way to protect the agency is to have separate bank accounts: one as a trust account for the client's money, which can be drawn on as needed, and another for the agency's money, which is not subject to accountability to the client.

Trustee of Rights and Materials Everything that the agency creates for its client belongs to the client; the agency holds these items in trust for the client. This could include such materials as photographs, artwork, videotapes, or rights such as copyright, trademark rights, or rights of publicity.

The agent does not own these items or rights, but it has a duty to guard them for its client. Here's an example which occurred between the Molle Company and its agency, Stack-Goble Advertising, in 1933.

Molle manufactured shaving cream and, through Stack-Goble, wanted to develop radio advertising. Stack-Goble hired Sedley Brown to produce and direct a program with Molle as the sponsor. We must remember that years ago it was common for advertisers to sponsor shows by themselves (it's not common today however), and it was the job of the advertising agency to put the shows together. For example, "Amos 'n Andy" sold Pepsodent, "The Story of Mary Marlowe" sold Kleenex, "Fibber McGee and Molly" sold Johnson's Glo-Coat floor wax, "The Rhythm Boys" (featuring a youngster named Harry Lillis Crosby, later to be known as Bing) sold M. J. B. Coffee, and the list went on and on.

But back to Molle. As part of producing the show, Brown created a jingle out of Molle advertising slogans and set the words to the music of E. L. Gruber's "West Point Caisson Song" (see box 4.1). Okay, so it's not Justin Bieber, but this was 1933 after all. Brown produced the first radio show on September 25, 1933, and continued to do so until late December when he left the show. The show, along with the theme song, continued to air without any protest from Brown. In April 1934, Brown filed a copyright for the words to the song and gave notice to Molle of his claimed ownership in September of that year.

Box 4.1

Mo-lle, Mo-lle,

The way to start your day,

As your razor goes sliding along,

Over cheek, over chin,

You don't have to rub it in,

As your razor goes sliding along.

Then it's sing, boys, sing,

Good-bye to pull and sting,

Your whisker troubles quickly fade away,

You can shave close and clean with this

brushless shaving cream,

So remember the name

Molle, Molle.

When Molle refused to acknowledge his claim, Brown brought suit for copyright infringement in *Brown* v. *Molle Co.*, 20 F.Supp 135 (1937), claiming ownership of the rights to the jingle. While it was true that the words were written by Brown, they belonged to Stack-Goble, who held them as trustee for Molle. Brown was employed by Stack-Goble to produce the program, including the theme song. Brown was an employee of Stack-Goble, and as such, anything he created as part of his duties became the property of Molle. When an agent creates work for, and at the direction of the client, it gives up, along with the work, any right to the work. Brown lost his case.

Accountability to Client An agency is under a strict duty to account for all funds passing through the agency, or controlled by it, on behalf of its client. The client has the right to inspect books, records, papers, invoices, orders, receipts, and any other items that apply to its account with the agency. These must be made available to the client, at any time, for its inspection. Along these lines, the client can demand an accounting of all commissions or discounts, received from or credited by third parties (suppliers, media, etc.) to the agency on the client's account.

One major problem area regarding accountability involves hidden profits. This constitutes a serious breach of the agency's duty. Legally, this is called "fraudulent concealment." I have known of a few agencies that made a practice of stating in their contracts that they charged a 17.65 percent markup on third-party bills. Yet, the estimates and invoices given to clients actually included an undisclosed and considerable markup in excess of 30 percent.

If an agency makes a purchase for a client based on an estimate, and the actual billing comes in lower, the agency must pass this savings on to the client. It cannot legally keep the difference. At some agencies, the policy is to estimate a job and get the client to sign the estimate. Then the agency prebills the client for that amount before beginning the project, often receiving payment before the project is completed. Sometimes the final cost of the project comes out lower than the estimate. If the ultimate costs are lower than the estimate, and the difference is not returned to the client, the agency is breaching its duty.

If prebilling must be done, the best practice is to provide a reconciliation of the project showing any amounts billed in excess of the estimate and credit them back to the client.

Purchase Orders Another important duty is that the agency should document all purchases for its client with a written purchase order. The purchase order must establish what has been ordered and what will be paid. It should also establish that the order is being placed on behalf of the client.

Duty to Cooperate with the Client Rarely do we hear mention of the duty of obedience when discussing the relationship between an agency and client. This may be due to the fact that advertisers are usually inclined to bow to the expertise of the agency. Or it may be attributable to good business sense on the part of the agency. Whatever the reason, this is an area that needs to be discussed, nonetheless.

An advertising agency has a duty to do its best to cooperate with the client. Sometimes this can be difficult when an agency is determined to sell a campaign to its client. Let's say that the agency submits a campaign plan to its client. The client has the right to disapprove of the campaign plans—media, copy, art, or any other proposals of the agency—simply because it does not like them. An agency cannot force the client to produce advertising that it does not like or has not approved. The client cannot be deprived of the right to reject the agency's creative work in a campaign or in an individual ad. I can testify that, after fifty-four years in the business, this is a major point of contention between ad agencies and their clients. It is the reality of the business.

Such a situation became the subject of *Medivox Productions, Inc.* v. *Hoffman-LaRoche, Inc.*, 107 N.J. Super. 47, 256 A.2d 803 (1969). Hoffman-LaRoche, a well-known pharmaceutical manufacturer, entered into a contract with Medivox Productions as its agent in the production of a series of radio programs entitled "Milestones of Medicine." The contract called for 260 programs to be created and produced during one year at a total cost of $140,000. These programs were to be dramatic episodes depicting important medical events in history. Hoffman-LaRoche was to have a credit line in each episode. The intent was that of enhancing the public's image of those connected with medicine and health, while at the same time promoting the importance of pharmaceutical drugs.

The contract stated that before being produced and broadcast, scripts would be submitted to Hoffman-LaRoche for their review and approval. Even without a contract this would be required. By the time Medivox had produced 135 of the programs (which the client had approved), Hoffman-LaRoche terminated the contract, having paid only $63,000. Medivox sued for breach of contract and sought to be allowed to complete the shows and receive the balance due on the contract. Hoffman-LaRoche claimed that they were entitled to terminate the contract because Medivox produced poor quality scripts.

Hoffman-LaRoche was dissatisfied with the scripts because they were inaccurate factually, and many of them discussed events that were not in keeping with the "Milestones of Medicine" theme. Medivox failed to satisfy its client, and as a result, Hoffman-LaRoche terminated the relationship. The court ruled that Medivox could not force the continuation of the relationship (legally this is called "specific performance") or collect the balance due on the contract. However, Hoffman-LaRoche could not recover the money that it had paid Medivox because it had accepted, used, and received the benefits of the 135 programs.

The client has the right, in an agency relationship, to approve or reject the work of its agency. Termination of the relationship, then, is based on the genuineness of its dissatisfaction, not necessarily on the reasonableness of it. Generally, the client makes this determination. Keep in mind, when the client expects satisfaction, the agency must allow the client to be the sole judge of its satisfaction.

The agency also has a duty to obey the instructions of its client in all but extreme situations. Yet the agent has the right to refuse under certain extreme conditions without liability for damages. However, the client also has the right to terminate the contract if the agent does refuse to perform.

The four situations when the agent can legally refuse to obey its client are listed below.

1. The instructions are unlawful:
   The agency has the right to refuse to produce advertising that is illegal—that is, advertising that violates any rights of others (including such things as publicity rights, copyrights, and trademarks), or when it would be engaging in unfair methods of competition or deception.

2. The instructions conflict with other duties of the agency:
   The agency may refuse to perform any instruction, such as the client's demand that the agency hold off paying certain media bills. Yet, this would be valid only if it would be a conflict of an agency duty. The agency may also refuse if the client demands that the agency take on a new product made by the existing client, which competes with another existing client of the agency.

3. The instructions defeat the agency's right to protect its own interests:
   A good example would be demanding the agency accept work on a speculative basis, with payment contingent on the client's sales or profits.

4. The instructions are unreasonable:
   This fourth area may cause some problems, as we saw in the earlier Medivox case. What is considered unreasonable becomes the tough question. In many situations agencies feel that creating an ad it knows to be ineffective is unreasonable. An agency is hired for its expertise in a certain area and should be allowed to use its judgment. Logically, this may be true; legally, it may not.

Basic agency law states that, barring one of the above exceptions, an agent must obey the instructions of its client. Failure to abide by the instructions of the client could result in agency liability for damages. On the other hand, the agency may terminate the relationship at any time, with proper notice given, if it does not want to abide by the instructions.

The Obligation to Preserve Trade Secrets Frequently it is necessary for a client to familiarize its agency with many matters it desires to keep secret. An advertising agency is under an obligation, both during and after its employment, to preserve those trade secrets, that is, secrets that were disclosed or learned during the relationship.

Originally the issue was discussed in *E. I. Du Pont de Nemours Powder Co.* v. *Masland,* 244 U.S. 100, 37 S.Ct. 575, 61 L.Ed. 1016 (1917). A former employee, Mr. Masland (an agent), was sued to prevent him from disclosing or using secret trade processes learned while in the employ of Du Pont. Masland intended to open a company to manufacture artificial leather. He admitted that he intended to use processes related to those learned while employed with Du Pont. Masland's former employer did not want any of its secret trade processes divulged, and it had the right to enforce this. Masland had learned the facts about Du Pont's processes through a confidential relationship.

It is difficult to define what a trade secret is (and too much discussion is beyond the scope of this book). However, some examples would include a specialized manufacturing process as we just saw, or special ingredients in a product such as Coca-Cola or Monster Energy drink that it seems that courts are more interested in the unfair use of the information than by the nature of the information itself.

The best story I can recall about trade secrets occurred a number of years ago. I was working for an agency that handled the Mitsubishi Electronics account. One day we got the news that two Mitsubishi executives had been arrested by the FBI. Evidently, Mitsubishi had paid $26,000 to undercover FBI agents who posed as grey-market electronics dealers. The money was paid in exchange for confidential trade secrets about IBM's newest computing products. This event was dubbed "Japanscam" by the press.

Note that any information that is easily accessible through other sources cannot be considered a trade secret. Lists of customers would be a good example. As a general rule these are not considered trade secrets because they are readily obtainable through such other public sources as trade publications.

There is another area to consider. Some years ago, Chiat/Day Advertising was in the running for the Godfather Pizza account. In order to prepare a "speculative" presentation to Godfather, the agency was given access to confidential information by the restaurant chain. A number of Chiat/Day employees were given this information, which contained many trade secrets.

Before the presentation was made to Godfather, Chiat/Day declined the account in favor of the Pizza Hut account. At that point, Godfather went to court to stop the use of the confidential information that Chiat/Day had obtained. The California Superior Court judge granted an injunction against Chiat/Day stating stated that Chiat/Day could not use any of the confidential information it obtained from Godfather. In addition, the injunction banned the Chiat/Day employees involved in the Godfather presentation from being involved in any way with the Pizza Hut account. The point here is that, even at the presentation stage, the duty to preserve trade secrets is in force, and courts are backing this up by issuing injunctions.

Finally, the agency has a continuing duty, even after termination, not to disclose or use trade secrets or other confidential information obtained during the course of its professional relationship. This can be a real problem area for ad agencies. Often when one client is lost the agency will pursue another client that is a competitor. Using the experience from one client to pitch another client. That industry learned experience is a valuable sales tool for ad agencies, and it is a huge part of the ad agency business model. But, agencies must be careful what information they use and disclose.

No Undisclosed Interest in Suppliers Another area of concern involves suppliers, vendors, or media that provide work for the agency's clients. The agency cannot have an undisclosed financial interest, such as part ownership, kickback arrangement, and so on, in these companies. Let's say that Acme Advertising produces brochures for its client, ABC Company. Bogus Photography Studio photographs ABC's products for the brochure. However, Acme Advertising owns 33 percent of Bogus Photography, and ABC doesn't know it. This would breach Acme's duty as an agency and make it impossible for the agency to make decisions in the client's best interests, so the theory goes. The agent cannot perform as a true, impartial, and unbiased agent for its clients. Or at least it couldn't convince a court that it could.

Two other areas of this type of conflict of interest need to be discussed. First, the agency must not contract with suppliers who use them as their agency. To go back to our earlier example, if Bogus Photography uses Acme Advertising as its agency, Acme cannot let ABC Company's brochure be photographed by Bogus. Second, the agency must not perform work itself that it has been instructed to contract out. Again, let's say Acme is told by ABC Company to have Bogus photograph its brochure. Acme Advertising cannot photograph ABC's brochure itself, in-house.

Although these types of situations do exist, it is usually without the client's knowledge. If the agency has the client's consent, in writing, then it is not a breach of the agency's duty, since no trust has been violated.

Duties Owed to the Advertising Agency by Clients

Yes, clients do actually have duties to their agencies as well. The most important duty the client has to its agency is to make the payments it owes to the agency. There are other duties, however, such as furnishing information to the agency and approving or disapproving programs or ads. The client must perform its duties within a reasonable time so as not to cause the agency additional delay and expense. It should make its decisions based on reason and good faith, not on a whim. Furthermore, as seen earlier, the client does not have a right to demand the agency produce advertising that violates any laws. Finally, the client is bound by any contracts made by the agency on its behalf, again, provided the agency acted within the scope of its authority.

Let's take an example from the story that opened this chapter. One of N. W. Ayer's clients, Devlen, manufactured Dent's Toothache Gum. In 1905 Devlen instructed Ayer to place an advertisement in daily newspapers. He also informed Ayer that he wanted "full position" (meaning that only editorial would be around the ad) for his small-space ad. Ayer informed its client that it was impossible to guarantee full position for a very small ad, and that in some papers such position was available only at an increased rate.

As the ad began to run, Devlen noticed that he was not getting full position in all newspapers. He complained to Ayer about this, but the ads continued to run for many months. Devlen also continued to make payments for the ads that ran.

In October 1907 Ayer terminated the contract with Devlen and in *Ayer* v. *Devlen*, 179 Mich. 81, 146 N.W. 257 (1914), and asked the court for damages of $3,801.22 for the balance of the media charges. Devlen had wanted his ads to receive a certain position in newspapers, and although he had been told that this was not possible in most cases, he authorized the placement of the ads for some time while still demanding full position. The main issue here was whether Devlen had a contract for his ads to be placed in full position only. The court decided that Devlen did not, and he was ordered to pay the back media charges.

Client–Agency Contract Issues

In the most simplistic terms, a contract is based on a promise or promises. When the promise is broken, a breach of contract can exist and a lawsuit may result. The client–agency contract can be breached when either party fails to perform in some area. For the agency, this can occur when it fails to comply with a duty; written in the contract or required by law. Placing an ad that the client had not approved or taking more than the amount of commission stated in the contract are examples of this. The client can also breach the contract if it fails to live up to its duties. Failure to pay the agency's bills is the most obvious example.

Generally, remedies for a breach of contract claim are recision (canceling the contract), damages, specific performance (forcing the other to fulfill the contract), or termination. Specific performance does not apply to personal service situations; that is called slavery, and there are laws against that now. The two main remedies left are recision and damages. A party may find that recision is more realistic than seeking damages. And termination is always a remedy available to both parties.

In breach of contract cases the most common problem is not whether the contract has been breached, but rather determination of the amount of damages. Here's a good example of a breach of contract situation.

An ad agency, William B. Tanner Company, bought space from Action Transit Ads. Action sold space on buses and subways in New Jersey. Tanner, at the request of its client, Tanya Hawaiian Tanning Oil, entered into a contract for three years, 1969 through 1971. The contract provided for three things: the advertising was for Tanya, the agency would receive a 15 percent commission, and the contract could be canceled at the end of each year.

In mid-1971, another contract was entered into between Tanner and Action for Tanya for the years 1972 through 1974. As with the previous contract, Action was to be paid $22,500 per year. However, the difference here was that Tanner did not have the permission of its client to enter into this new contract. At the end of 1972, when Tanya refused to pay the bills, Tanner notified Action that it was terminating the contract. As a result, Action sued in *Action Ads, Inc.* v. *William B. Tanner Co.*, 592 S.W.2d 572 (1979).

William Tanner was authorized by Tanya to purchase the transit ads for the first three years, 1969 through 1971. However, it was not authorized by Tanya to make the second three-year contract. Because of that, Tanner was acting on its own when it entered into the 1972 through 1974 contract. Tanner had breached its contract with its client and was itself liable for the $22,500 for the 1972 contract with Action.

Elements of the Client–Agency Contract

Although it is not imperative that a written contract be created, it is the much wiser option. When the rights, duties, and intentions of both parties are fixed in writing, there is less interpretation and guesswork involved if a problem arises.

There are certain considerations that should be addressed when the contract provisions are made. The following list includes the most important ones:

* Appointment as the agency;
* Nature and extent of services to be provided;
* Compensation (commission, fees, etc.);
* How supplier contracts are to be handled;
* Rights upon termination of contract;
* Indemnity against claims;
* Handling of competitive clients; and
* Liability to media.

Duration of Contracts

In all written contracts, the length of time that the agreement is to run must be stated. If it is indefinite, that should be stated as well. Common sense dictates that all contracts between advertising agencies and clients should be in writing. Oral contracts are not a good idea for a variety of legal reasons, mainly because they can be found to be unenforceable in many situations. And it is difficult to prove what the terms of the agreement were since there is no written documentation.

Termination of Contracts

Notice of Termination When a contract is terminated, the first thing to consider is the amount of time that must be given to the other party as notice. This "grace period" is typically built into client–agency contracts to allow the agency time to restructure staff and overhead in anticipation of the change, and for the client to settle its business with the agency. In other words, no undue hardship should be placed on either party.

The length of the notice period, according to industry trade custom, is usually sixty to ninety days, although it can be any period of time that both parties agree to. (A trade custom is considered as law because of the length of time that the practice has been accepted and used.) To be on the safe side, the notice period should be stated in the contract. On this subject, Doyle Dane Bernbach tried to recover $126,729 for advertising from a former client, Avis Flowers, in *Doyle Dane Bernbach, Inc.* v. *Warren E. Avis*, 526 F.Supp. 117 (1981).

Doyle Dane also handled the Avis Rent-A-Car account, which was started in 1948 by the owner of Avis Flowers, Warren Avis. Avis Rent-A-Car Avis put the agency on notice that it had to choose between the two clients due to the similarity in names and identity. Obviously, Doyle Dane opted to keep the Avis car account.

When Doyle Dane terminated the agreement with Avis Flowers in November 1977, it gave 90 days' notice. During the notice period, Doyle Dane contacted the flower company to arrange for the transfer of the account to another agency. Even though it had given a notice of termination, Doyle Dane continued to handle the Avis Flowers account through the end of 1977, placing ads in *People* magazine that had been approved prior to when notice was given.

Avis Flowers claimed that Doyle Dane placed the ads after termination (breach of contract) and, therefore, was liable for any media charges incurred after the agency gave notice for those insertions. In fact, there was no written contract, so there was no stated notice period. However, the ninety-day notice period is standard in the advertising industry and is accepted as a trade custom—one that Avis should have been well aware of. Doyle Dane gave Avis a sufficient amount of notice—the standard amount in the industry—and continued to perform through the notice period. As a result, Avis was required to pay the media fees incurred during the ninety-day period.

Commissions Due After Termination As just illustrated, certain postcontractual liabilities and duties are imposed on both parties. If the agency had entered into contracts with third parties on behalf of the advertiser before the relationship was terminated, the agency would be entitled to the commissions that it would have received.

In 1952 Hansman-Joslyn Advertising entered into a contract with the Uddo & Tormina Company, makers of Progresso Italian foods (now owned by General Mills). Hansman, as its agent, entered into a contract with WBOK radio. The one-year radio contract with Progresso was canceled after only a few months, causing the radio station to charge a "short rate" amount for the time because the full contract period was not used. The short rate policy is a trade custom in the advertising business.

In *Hansman* v. *Uddo and Tormina Co.*, 76 So.2d 753 (La. App. 1955) the court said: "Contracts made with any kind of advertising media . . . providing therein a short rate cancellation, that is to say, the advertiser contracts to use the media for a stated length of time at a certain rate . . . if the advertiser sees fit to cancel the contract prematurely, then he is obligated to pay the rate which would be applicable had the contract . . . been for the number of advertisements actually used."

Ultimately, Uddo was ordered to pay the amount actually due for the media. Now, let's look at the case of media contracts that were entered into by a previous agency. If the client takes its business to a new agency, the client is liable to the previous agency for the media commissions, unless a contract agreement covers this occurrence.

To illustrate, let's go back to the hypothetical situation used earlier. Acme Advertising had purchased media for an ad for its client, ABC Company, in *American Widget Monthly* magazine. A week later ABC notifies Acme that it is moving its account to a new agency, Dinkum Advertising, in ninety days. Even though Dinkum produces the ad and coordinates with the magazine, ABC must still pay Acme the amount of commission it would have received.

Here is a question though. What if the client uses material from the former agency in preparation for another advertising campaign, after the termination of the relationship? If that material was never used or paid for, the client must compensate the original agency for its efforts. It cannot use the fruit of the agency's labor for future advertising without paying for it. In legal terms this principle is known as *quantum meruit*. In simpler terms; you can't get something for nothing.

When ABC Company transferred its account over to Dinkum Advertising, it also gave them campaign concepts and layouts that were developed by Acme Advertising. Acme had prepared the campaign on a speculative basis, but it was never approved by ABC. Since ABC never paid for the concepts and layouts, if it produces the campaign through Dinkum, it must compensate Acme for the work. On the other hand, if ABC had paid for the campaign to be created, the company would be free to produce it without further compensating Acme.

Soliciting New Accounts after Giving Notice of Termination When notice of termination has been given, can the agency service a competing account? It is certainly free to do so after termination. What is doubtful, though, is whether the agency is free to associate with prospective new clients who are in competition with the current client before termination becomes effective. The best advice would be that the agency should not jeopardize itself by creating a potential liability.

Limit to Use of Information Gained We touched on an element of this earlier. But in the natural course of the advertising business an agency often becomes familiar with the workings of its clients. It obtains a certain amount of expertise in each client's line of business. There can be no doubt, however, that intimate knowledge of a client's trend of thought and method of doing business can become part-and-parcel of the agency's general knowledge and expertise.

Therefore, the postcontractual duty not to divulge or use details of the client must be restricted to actual trade secrets and the kind of confidential information that is separate from the general knowledge about a trade or business.

Here's a strong case in point. Murray Salit and other employees of Irving Serwer Advertising were sued by Serwer in *Irving Serwer, Inc. Advertising* v. *Salit*, 17 A.D.2d 918 (1963). This occurred after the employees left the agency to open their own shop, Salit & Garlanda Advertising. Serwer claimed that Salit and the others had taken accounts over to the new agency by obtaining confidential information while in its employ and that they "entered into a course of conduct and conspiracy to destroy [Serwer's] business." However, the court held that simply gaining information about clients while working for an agency does not, in and of itself, constitute learning trade secrets or confidential information. As a result, Serwer lost his case.

Although this situation involves employees of an agency, this reasoning applies to agencies who use knowledge gained from other clients. If the information does not constitute a trade secret and is not confidential (as discussed earlier), the agency cannot be stopped from making use of the knowledge.

Liability to Media

Is a client liable for media commitments made by the agency? There is a conflict here, but the general feeling is that the ultimate liability is on the advertiser. In essence, if the media knew who the client was and knew that the agency was acting on its behalf, any claims would be against the client. The agency would not be liable on the contract as long as it entered into the agreement with the client's knowledge and consent. One exception to this is a sole liability clause, which we'll discuss later in this chapter.

American Manufacturers Mutual Insurance contracted, through its agency Clinton E. Frank Advertising, to sponsor a news broadcast entitled "ABC Evening Report." At the end of one broadcast on November 9, 1962, a promotional announcement was run that displeased American Manufacturers. The announcement promoted a show called "The Political Obituary of Richard M. Nixon." American Manufacturers terminated its sponsorship of the "ABC Evening Report" and refused to pay the media fees.

American Broadcasting Company filed suit for the amount due for media charges: *American Broadcasting-Paramount Theatres* v. *American Manufacturers Mutual*, 42 Misc.2d 939, 249 N.Y.S.2d 481 (Sup.Ct. 1963), aff'd 251 N.Y.S.2d 906, aff'd 17 N.Y. 2d 849 (1966). In this case, Clinton E. Frank Advertising was named as one of the defendants, but was held not to be liable for the media fees. Even though Clinton Frank was the agency and placed the order, it was not liable for any damages because ABC knew Frank was acting as the agency for American Manufacturers. ABC also knew that the agency had entered into the contract on behalf of its client. ABC won the suit for breach of contract, and American was liable for the media.

The important point is that the client–agency relationship may exist only with the knowledge and consent of both parties. The client who hires an agency voluntarily empowers it to bind the client to contracts with others. Simply put, when someone hires an agency it creates an implied acknowledgment that the client intends to be bound by any contract or transaction that the agent must enter into to fulfill its agency duties. Parties who deal with a known agent generally assume that the client intends to be bound by the agency's commitments.

In 1971 Lennon & Newell was the ad agency for Stokely-Van Camp foods company (now Van Camp, owned by ConAgra since 1995), as it had been for the previous seventeen years. Lennon & Newell had purchased media space for Stokely on CBS. In 1967 the agency began to suffer substantial losses and by 1970 was in severe trouble. It had been paid by Stokely for media billings but had not, in turn, paid the media. By the end of 1971 Lennon owed CBS $714,000 out of total payables of $3 million and could not make its payments. About that time, Lennon & Newell filed for bankruptcy.

Because of the situation, CBS filed suit, in *Columbia Broadcasting System, Inc.* v. *Stokely-Van Camp, Inc.*, 522 F.2d 369 (1975), directly against the client. This was a case of liability when an agent goes bankrupt owing money to media. Does the media have a claim against the client? In this case, it did even though the client had paid the agency for the media.

In 1978 Sander Rodkin/Hechtman/Glantz Advertising purchased television time for its client Climate Control, an air conditioning distributor. At the time, Sander was having financial problems. When the agency received money from Climate Control for media, it did not pay the media. Climate Control, however, had paid its total bill and documented each payment. The final payment for $15,000 was designated as "final payment for WLS-TV air time."

WLS-TV was, and still is, the local ABC affiliate in Chicago. It sued Climate Control for the amount due in *American Broadcasting Companies, Inc.* v. *Climate Control Corporation*, 524 F.Supp. 1014 (1981). It was not until December 1979 that ABC contacted Climate Control and told them that it was liable for the unpaid balance. Right after that, this lawsuit was initiated.

In this case, Sander was the agency for Climate Control, and as such, bound Climate Control to any contracts it had made for the client. The result: Climate Control was liable for the unpaid balance to ABC. Sander Rodkin went out of business.

Sole Liability Clauses

As alluded to earlier, the advertising agency is directly liable to the media under certain conditions. One of those conditions occurs when the agency voluntarily agrees to be directly liable for media bills. The other is when the media contract contains a "sole liability" clause to which the agency has committed. In both cases, the agency accepts full liability for media costs.

The sole liability clause, which is included in many media contracts today, says that the agency is solely liable for the debts incurred on behalf of the client. As a consequence of the sole liability clause, the agency can impose on the client a duty to pay the media charges to the agency prior to the media's due dates. Failure to make these payments on time can easily lead to cancellation of the media space, as well as substantial damage claims by the agency against the client.

Liability for Advertising

As seen in other chapters of this book, the agency can be liable along with the client for the advertising it produces. If the advertising makes deceptive or unfair claims, the agency as well as the client can be held liable for those claims. This has been proven many times in court. Claiming, as many agencies do, that they only did what the client told them to do does not relieve the agency's liability. The courts generally consider that an advertising agency should know what its clients are doing.

Other areas where the agency can be liable involve defamation (libel and slander), copyright and trademark infringement, violation of privacy and publicity rights, in addition to others. In general, advertising agencies must realize that the courts look on them as the skilled and knowledgeable professionals. This idea goes back to the "higher degree of skill" concept discussed earlier. More and more, agencies are being held liable for the joint actions stemming from the client–agency relationship. It is very important that agencies understand this idea.

Examples of Joint Liability

A manufacturer of automobile windows set about to demonstrate how much clearer its windows were, compared to those of its competition. The commercial exaggerated the demonstration by distorting the competition's windows with a coat of Vaseline. The clarity of the advertiser's windows was additionally enhanced by simply rolling down the window during the filming of the commercial.

When the FTC filed an action, the manufacturer's defense was that it had instructed its advertising agency to "present a fair commercial." The court reasoned, when it upheld the FTC's previous ruling in *Libbey-Owens-Ford Glass Co.* v. *FTC*, 352 F.2d 415 (6th Cir. 1965), that this statement did not allow the advertiser to escape liability by delegating the responsibility for the commercial to its agency. In fact, the agent was the agent of the client.

Situations like the one above can also occur between a publisher, who acts as the advertising agent, and their client. This can happen, when the publisher advises the client on advertising strategy and content as well as creates, designs, and produces the advertising for the client directly. In other words, when they act as the advertising agency as well as being the publisher. A case in point was *Knepper* v. *Brown*, 345 Ore. 320; 195 P.3d 383 (2008). This case was a common-law fraud action where Mrs. Knepper, a patient of Dr. Timothy Brown, obtained a $1.5 million judgment against the publisher, DEX Media and Dr. Brown, based on the publisher's involvement in creating and publishing a Yellow Pages advertisement that misrepresented Dr. Brown's qualifications.

Dr. Timothy Brown was a licensed medical doctor who held certifications from the American Board of Medical Specialties in dermatology and anatomic and clinical pathology. Dr. Brown started a dermatology practice in Oregon in 1985 and advertised in Dex's Yellow Pages directory, under the heading "Physicians and Surgeons" and the subheading "Dermatology".

In 1996, Dr. Brown placed advertisements in Dex's Yellow Pages under the subheading "Surgery, Plastic and Reconstructive." The ad stated that Brown performed liposuction, wrinkle treatments, and sclerotherapy. It also stated that Brown was "Board Certified."

The advertisements were created at the urging of the Dex sales representative. Dex "mocked up" a new advertisement and advised Dr. Brown that the "plastic and reconstruction surgery" subheading in the Yellow Pages would be the best place to reach his target market. Dex's sales representative also recommended that the advertisement should identify Dr. Brown as "board certified," because "patients were expecting a [board certified] plastic surgeon to do these techniques." However, Dr. Brown's board certification was in dermatology, not plastic and reconstructive surgery. Yet Dex's sales representative continued to push for a nonspecific "board certified" designation under the "Surgery, Plastic and Reconstructive" category. Dr. Brown, who had final approval, acceded to Dex's advice.

Early in 1997, Mrs. Knepper was considering cosmetic liposuction surgery and wanted to be treated by a plastic surgeon. She consulted the "Surgery, Plastic and Reconstructive" subheading in the Dex Yellow Pages and saw Dr. Brown's advertisement and believed him to be a board certified plastic surgeon.

Dr. Brown, performed a liposuction procedure on her in December 1997. And after the procedure, Mrs. Knepper complained about pain. As a result Dr. Brown performed two more liposuction procedures in an unsuccessful attempt to repair the damage. Knepper eventually filed suit against Dr. Brown and Dex, claiming medical malpractice, fraud, conspiracy to commit fraud, and loss of consortium.

Mrs. Knepper's fraud claim revolved around a few issues: that Dex knew that Brown was not board certified in plastic and reconstructive surgery; that Dex and Brown together designed and developed an advertisement that falsely implied that Brown was a board-certified plastic surgeon; that Knepper wanted a board-certified plastic surgeon to perform liposuction surgery on her; that Knepper relied on the misleading Dex advertisement and had Brown perform liposuction surgery; that if Knepper had known the truth about Brown's true credentials, she would not have consented to surgery by him; and that Brown caused injury by performing the liposuction negligently.

During the trial, Dex argued that courts must recognize that "publishers require some additional protection from claims arising out of false or misleading advertisements, and cannot be held liable for the publication of such advertisements unless the publication is done maliciously or with intent to harm another or in reckless disregard of that possibility." However, the court reasoned that "This is not a case of the unwitting publication of an advertisement that turns out to be false. It is, instead, a case in which the publisher took a knowing and active part in the perpetration of the fraud."

Employee Relations within the Agency

One of the areas that ad agencies need to be aware of involves situations when an employee leaves and takes accounts with them, without the agencies consent. Sometimes this happens when an employee wants to take an account she has been working on to a new employer. Other times it can happen when one or more employees leave and take an account to start their own ad agency. Account piracy is a growing internal problem for ad agencies, and many agencies are dealing with the problem by adopting restrictive covenants in employment contracts to prevent this.

Let's say that you own the Acme Advertising agency and your employees become increasingly dissatisfied with you and the way you run the agency. Some of the key people get together and decide that they will give you an ultimatum: sell them the agency and get out, or they will leave and take some of the accounts with them. Is this legal?

Let's take a look at just that type of situation to find the answer. The Duane Jones Company was an ad agency founded in 1942 by Duane Jones, who was the president and operating head of the agency until August 1951. At that time, the agency billed $9 million annually from about twenty-five accounts. But what happened in August 1951 threw a wrench into the machinery of the agency.

About that time the agency lost three accounts and $6.5 million with them. Along with that, three executives and numerous staff people resigned from the agency because, as the employees claimed, Duane Jones "had been guilty of certain behavioral lapses at his office, at business functions, and during interviews with actual and prospective customers. As a result . . . several of [Jones's] officers and directors expressed dissatisfaction with conditions—described as 'intolerable.' "

In June 1951 a private meeting had been held at a hotel in Manhattan between a number of the agency's officers, directors, and employees, led by one of the officers, Mr. Hayes. It was decided that these people would make an ultimatum to Jones: either sell them the agency or they would resign "en masse." Hayes told Jones of this plan and informed him that certain clients of the agency had been presold on the idea of leaving with the employees. Jones responded, "In other words, you are standing there with a Colt .45, holding it at my forehead, and there is not much I can do except to give up?" Hayes replied, "Well, you can call it anything you want, but that is what we are going to do."

At first, Jones decided to accept the buyout of the agency, but negotiations fell through in August 1951. That same month, six officers and directors resigned from the agency. A few days later the former employees of Jones opened a new agency; Scheideler, Beck & Werner, Inc. This agency employed 71 of the 132 Duane Jones employees. Within a few weeks, the new agency had as accounts Manhattan Soap Co., Heublein, International Salt, Wesson Oil, C. F. Mueller Co., The Borden Co., Marlin Fire Arms, McIlhenny Corp., Haskins Bros., and Continental Briar Pipe—all former clients of Duane Jones.

When one acts as an agent or employee—the legal relationship is the same for either—a duty of loyalty, trust, and good faith is owed to the client or employer. We discussed this duty earlier. As a result, Duane Jones filed suit in *Duane Jones Co. v. Burke, et al*, 281 N.Y.A.D. 622, (1953), aff'd 306 N.Y. 172 (1954).

The court awarded damages to Jones and said: "defendants . . . while employees of [Jones], determined upon a course of conduct which, when subsequently carried out, resulted in benefit to themselves through destruction of [Jones's] business, in violation of the fiduciary duties of good faith and fair dealing imposed on defendants . . . ."

There are situations in which taking accounts away from a former employer is acceptable, however. One example of such an occurrence is found in the case of *Nationwide Advertising Service, Inc. v. Kolar*, 329 N.E.2d 300 (1975). Here, Nationwide sued a former employee, Martin Kolar, and his new employer, Bentley, Barnes & Lynn, for acquiring former accounts of Nationwide. Not until after Kolar left Nationwide and became employed with Bentley did he solicit accounts of Nationwide. This was acceptable.

One of the issues in this case involved an implied covenant binding Kolar not to compete with his former employer. But this covenant covered only confidential information gained through his employment, and then used for his benefit, and to the detriment of the employer. This was not the case here.

Granted, an agency's interest in its clients is proprietary by nature, but this is valid only when the client–agency relationship is near permanent. In the advertising business, this is a rare claim. Furthermore, Nationwide's client list was not confidential, and no trade secrets were used to solicit the accounts. Kolar did not solicit any accounts until after leaving the employ of Nationwide. The court held that no breach of trust or confidence occurred; Nationwide lost the case.

Restrictive Covenants

Restrictive covenants in written employment contracts are the best solution to dealing with account piracy by former employees. This is the only way to legally enforce damages against former employees for account piracy.

Under an agreement containing a restrictive covenant, the employee agrees not to serve or contact any client of the former agency for a specific period of time. It is crucial that a specific period of time be stated in the agreement; otherwise it will be unenforceable. Also, the time must be reasonable, usually one to two years.

Restrictive covenants must be agreed to at the beginning of the employment. If an agency wishes to add restrictive covenants to existing employment situations, some additional consideration must be given. This can be any valuable offering: extension of employment, stock options, money, and so on.

Other Areas that Can Impose Agency Liability

This is a very important subject for advertisers and their agencies. There are a number of situations where liability can occur. We'll look at those here.

First we'll look at kids. Almost every ad agency has dealt with children in the course of producing an ad, television commercial, billboard, or brochure. Anytime an agency that works with children it needs to understand the applicable restrictions and requirements.

The Problem with Children

You're at the photo studio to photograph a client's project. Everything is going fine. The set looks good, the kids are great in their costumes, and the collie is behaving just fine. All of a sudden, the photo assistant kicks a light stand and the dog, startled, turns and bites one of the children. The child falls, knocking over a prop stand causing the entire set to crash down on top of another child. About then you wonder what else could go wrong.

Well, if the children were working without a valid work permit, you've only begun to hear your world come crashing down around you. If you, or your client, did not have the proper work permits, you could face criminal or civil prosecution, resulting in lawsuits, fines, and even jail. If the child is working without the proper permits, liability insurance could be useless. Insurance companies can deny coverage if a law was violated that led to the injury.

This was something movie director John Landis learned the hard way. Landis was the director of such well-known movies as *National Lampoon's Animal House*, *An American Werewolf in London*, *Trading Places* and *The Blues Brothers*, in addition to Michael Jackson's music video *Thriller*. In 1982, while filming the movie *Twilight Zone*, two child actors Myca Dinh Le (age 7) and Renee Shin-Yi Chen (age 6), and actor Vic Morrow were killed when a helicopter crashed. The children were employed illegally for four reasons. First, they were working at 2:30 a.m. Second, they were in an extremely dangerous situation. Third, the children did not have work permits as required by California law. Fourth, no social worker was present. Had one been, the filming would probably not have been allowed. Had the laws been obeyed, the accident would not have killed the children or Morrow, since they would not have been on the set at that time.

Landis and four other crew members were charged with involuntary manslaughter.

The prosecutors attempted to show that Landis was reckless, and had not told the parents or others of the children's proximity to explosives and helicopters and of limitations on their working hours. He admitted that he had violated the California law regulating employment of children, by using the children after hours, and conceded that that was "wrong." But he denied culpability. Numerous members of the film crew testified that the director was warned, but ignored these dangers. After a nine-month jury trial in 1986 and 1987, Landis, represented by criminal defense attorney Harland Braun, and the other crew members were acquitted of the charges.

Landis was later reprimanded for circumventing the State of California's child labor laws in hiring the two children. This tragedy resulted in stricter safety measures and enforcement of child labor laws in California. The parents of the children sued, and eventually settled out of court with the studio for $2 million per family. Morrow's children, one of them being actress Jennifer Jason Leigh, who was twenty at the time, also settled out of court for an undisclosed sum.

Child Labor Laws In the early 1900s child labor laws were created in response to an increase in serious injuries of children. Most of these injuries were the result of severe conditions in mills, sweatshops, and mines where children were used as cheap labor.

Child labor laws created restrictions on minimum wages, hours of employment, and working conditions. While some laws are federal, the most important are state statutes. The individual states have become more involved in this area and have adopted very stringent laws to protect children. New York and California are at the head of this list.

Note: anyone can be held liable—the photographer, the director, the ad agency, or the client. Each must protect itself by making sure that the proper permits are obtained and working conditions are met.

Guidelines for Working with Children

- **Check with the state agency** that oversees child labor laws to determine the state's requirements. For example, in California, it is the California Division of Labor Standards.
- **Obtain the proper permits** from the state where the photography takes place.
- **Abide by the hours of employment** allowed by law. For example, in California, children six to eighteen years old can only work a maximum of four hours a day and not after 6:30 p.m. A one-hour lunch break must be provided no later than 1 p.m. For sessions out of the studio, lunch must be provided free to the child and teacher or welfare worker.
- **Provide the required supervision**. Again, in California, a studio teacher or welfare worker must be hired and present during any session.
- **Check insurance coverage**. Make sure that the photographer has valid workers' compensation and liability insurance.
- **Report any injury** that occurs to a child immediately to the insurance carrier and the state Workers' Compensation Board.
- **Provide medical attention**. Make sure that the child gets immediate medical attention.
- **Parents cannot waive liability**. Remember, a parent or guardian cannot give a release of liability by law. Even a written release will not protect you.

The Chilko River Incident

Over the years, Al Wolfe organized fishing and river rafting trips for many of his employees and clients. As Wolfe would later say of his trips: "If you could get away from the titles and pretense and really get to know each other, there would be a bond formed."

In 1987 Wolfe put together one such trip while he was the president of DDB Needham Worldwide's Chicago office. The plan was to take a group of eleven friends and business acquaintances for a weekend fishing and rafting trip on the Chilko river in British Columbia, Canada.

On a Saturday in August, the group set off down the Chilko, some of the roughest rapids in the world. Suddenly, after entering a stretch of river known as the "White Mile," the raft hit a rock and overturned. Five of the eleven perished in the river.

Those who never returned included Robert Goldstein, VP/advertising for Procter & Gamble; retired agency executive Richard O'Reilly; retired DDB Needham Senior VP James Fasules; Stuart Sharpe, Senior DDB Needham VP account manager; and, Gene Yovetich, Senior DDB Needham VP account manager.

The disaster, dramatized in the 1994 HBO movie *White Mile*, affected not only the participants but the agency as well. DDB Needham was sued by Mr. Fasules' family for his death due to the inadequate safety precautions and the negligence of Wolfe (in his capacity as president of DDB Needham). Fasules was not an employee of the agency at the time, and therefore the family could bring a negligence suit directly against DDB Needham. The agency employees, however, were limited to recover damages under workers' compensation actions. While the U.S. District Court determined that Fasules was 45 percent responsible for his own death, they also found that DDB Needham was 55 percent responsible. The court awarded Fasules's family $1.1 million in damages to be paid by DDB Needham.

The Chilko case illustrates how an action can bring liability to an agency, even if it did not actually involve work within the agency. Agencies (like any other company) can be held liable for the actions of their employees, at any time, when they are acting within the course and scope of their employment.

Avoiding Liability for Use of Unsolicited Ideas Submitted by Outsiders

Occasionally, someone outside an agency or client may approach the company with an offer of a new idea for the company. While this is a common occurrence for advertising agencies, these situations present risks since subsequent use of the ideas can lead to an obligation to reasonably compensate the person who submitted the idea. This applies to creative ideas for ads, as well as marketing and product development ideas.

A good example involves the famous "Yo Quiero Taco Bell" Chihuahua campaign of the late 1990s. The tiny 12-pound spokesdog, whose real name was Gidget (yes "he" was a "she"), captured the heart of American TV viewers for a number of years touting the Taco Bell brand channeled through the voice of Carlos Alazraqui.

Here's a little history. In June 1996, Ed Alfaro, who was a licensing manager at Taco Bell, attended a trade show in New York where he noticed a cartoon of a Chihuahua dog character (Psycho Chihuahua) being marketed by its creators: Tom Rinks and Joe Shields of Wrench LLC. Alfaro told Rinks and Shields that he wanted to explore the use of Psycho Chihuahua by Taco Bell.

During late 1996, Wrench provided Taco Bell with items bearing Psycho Chihuahua's image. From then through June 1997, Alfaro tried to build support within Taco Bell management for use of Psycho Chihuahua in its advertising. He showed the goods to Taco Bell's senior managers and their advertising agency at that time, Bozell Worldwide. As a result, Taco Bell conducted a focus group study including Psycho Chihuahua and several other ideas. Alfaro reported to a senior Taco Bell executive that Psycho Chihuahua was the most popular of all the ideas.

In November 1996, Taco Bell and Wrench's licensing agent, Strategy Licensing, discussed the possible use of Psycho Chihuahua as Taco Bell's mascot. Taco Bell asked to see a proposal for the use of Psycho Chihuahua. On November 18, 1996, Strategy Licensing submitted a proposal but Taco Bell did not accept it. Taco Bell clearly understood that if it decided to use the character, they would have to pay Wrench for such use.

In February 1997, Pepsi Co. (Taco Bell's then-parent company), made a presentation to Taco Bell's marketing department regarding the possible use of Psycho Chihuahua in a Taco Bell "Cinco de Mayo" promotion. Taco Bell conducted additional focus group studies on Psycho Chihuahua all of which resulted in positive consumer response.

In March 1997, Taco Bell changed advertising agencies from Bozell to TBWA Chait/Day and Taco Bell charged TBWA with creating a new ad campaign for 1998. Between February and April 1997, Alfaro continued to work with Wrench to promote Taco Bell's use of Psycho Chihuahua.

In May 1997, TBWA presented approximately thirty advertising ideas to Taco Bell for its new campaign. One idea involved a male Chihuahua dog passing by a female Chihuahua dog to get to Taco Bell food. They chose that as the center of its new advertising campaign starting in January 1998.

The court stated: "Alfaro believed the character Wrench had created from the original Psycho Chihuahua closely resembled the TBWA Chihuahua to be used in Taco Bell commercials. He alerted Taco Bell's in-house counsel that Wrench would likely sue because of the similarities between the characters. Alfaro drafted a memorandum . . . describing the parallel path he had taken with Wrench and their idea of using a Chihuahua to advertise Taco Bell food."

By January 1998, Taco Bell began airing the Chihuahua campaign. Wrench then sued Taco Bell, claiming that Taco Bell was using Psycho Chihuahua in its advertising without providing compensation to Wrench. *Wrench LLC* v. *Taco Bell Corp.*, 51 F. Supp. 2d 840 (W.D. Mich. 1999).

In its defense in *Wrench*, Taco Bell claimed that "there was no contract with Wrench because Alfaro had no authority to bind the company, the Chihuahua character used by Taco Bell was not Psycho Chihuahua, and the Chihuahua character used by Taco Bell was independently created by TBWA."

TBWA created and broadcast over forty more Chihuahua commercials between January 1998 and June 2000. In June 2003, the *Wrench* jury determined that Taco Bell had breached an implied contract by using Psycho Chihuahua without compensating Wrench. A judgment was entered against Taco Bell in the amount of $42 million.

Taco Bell requested full indemnification from TBWA for its liability to Wrench. Within weeks of the *Wrench* trial, Taco Bell filed this lawsuit in *Taco Bell Corp.* v. *TBWA Chait/Day Inc.*, 552 F.3d 1137 (2009), suing it for breach of the Agency Agreement, express indemnification, and declaratory relief. Taco Bell lost because the court concluded there was only evidence of Taco Bell's fault in its liability to Wrench.

On the other hand, unsolicited ideas do not always result in liability. Here's another case that happened around the same time. In *Burgess* v. *Coca-Cola Company*, 245 Ga. App. 206; 536 S.E.2d 764 (2000), Robert L. Burgess sued The Coca-Cola Company ("Coca-Cola") for allegedly taking his creative ideas and using them in a commercial that featured anthropomorphic polar bears drinking Coca-Cola.

Let's start at the beginning. Burgess approached Coca-Cola in January 1989 and pitched a concept he referred to as "The Fantastic World of Coca-Cola." The presentation included seven storyboards that depicted various aspects of the concept. This "Fantastic World," as Burgess explained, "was an imaginary world located inside a Coca-Cola vending machine and populated with a wide variety of Coca-Cola characters, including, as shown by one of the storyboards, a family of white bear-like 'cola bears' making ice to cool the Coca-Cola." Burgess was told they were not in a position to help him.

In July 1991, Coca-Cola hired Creative Artists Agency (CAA), to develop new advertising. Coca-Cola executives did not participate in any aspect of CAA's creative process and they only reviewed the final submissions. According to the court: "One of the many concepts approved and ultimately made into a commercial was 'Bears at the Theater.' This commercial featured a family of anthropomorphic polar bears who were drinking Coca-Cola while they watched the aurora borealis." The commercial was the brainchild of Ken Stewart, the husband of a CAA executive. The evidence shows that "Stewart came up with the idea on his own, free from any input from Coca-Cola personnel. He was unaware of any of Burgess' ideas. In fact, Stewart was inspired by his Labrador Retriever puppy, who apparently looked like a polar bear." Burgess presented no evidence in court from which a jury could reasonably infer that Stewart's idea for the "Bears at the Theater" commercial was created using Burgess' "Fantastic World" concept or any of its parts, including the cola bears.

The "Bears in the Theater" commercial, first broadcast in 1993, was one of twenty-seven commercials aired as part of Coca-Cola's "Always" campaign.

Burgess claimed that the CAA polar bear, with its human attributes and family values, was taken from the cola bears he had envisioned in his Fantastic World. Not only did Coca-Cola produce evidence showing that the CAA polar bear was independently created by Stewart, it introduced evidence showing that the use of a polar bear "spokescharacter" was not unique or novel. Coca-Cola demonstrated a long history of companies using animated anthropomorphic animals as product spokescharacters, including Kellogg's Tony the Tiger, Star Kist's Charlie the Tuna, and Nine Lives' Morris the Cat. In fact, the Icee Company had an animated polar bear representing its frozen drink products since the 1960s. Finally, Coca-Cola has used anthropomorphic bears, including polar bears, in its own advertising since 1923. The Coca-Cola company had used an anthropomorphic white bear named "Teddy Snow Crop" to market its Minute Maid frozen orange juice in 1961.

However, the court ruled, "even if Coca-Cola had made use of Burgess' cola bears idea, which the evidence does not support, Burgess' claim fails because using an anthropomorphic polar bear to sell a soft drink is not a novel idea."

The court stated: "To be novel the concept must be peculiar and not generally available or known to others in the trade. To be protected, an idea must possess genuine novelty and invention, which it cannot have if it merely is an adaptation of existing knowledge, albeit a clever, useful, or sensible adaptation."

Although subsequent use by a company of information or ideas submitted to it is always somewhat risky, use of the information is not invariably illegal. Before liability is imposed, courts will insist that the outsider's idea be both novel and concrete; liability will not be imposed for use of vague and general ideas (unless, of course, there is a clear, express contract covering the matter). While the line between concrete and vague ideas is ambiguous, it's more prudent to err on the safe side to avoid the problems that can result from accepting unsolicited idea submissions. Formal records should be kept as to the date the idea was received and its specific content. Also, a written response should be made to the person submitting the idea explaining the company's position on not accepting unsolicited outside ideas.

If an outside submission is accepted, it is wise to make a specific written agreement between the parties as to the use of, and compensation for, any ideas to be submitted. If an outside person submits an idea that had already been developed internally, there is no liability to compensate for the same suggestion. However, to guard against a possible argument that subsequent use of an internally developed idea actually came from an outsider, firms should keep accurate records as to the time and place of, and employees involved in, the discovery and development of new ideas and trade secrets.

Arbitration of Disputes

The pay-for-litigation phenomenon is a nationwide big-business that generates hundreds of millions of dollars a year. But it's most prevalent in California, where a largely unregulated private system litigates more commercial cases than does the state court system.

Congress enacted the Federal Arbitration Act in 1925, making arbitration agreements enforceable like other contracts, and arbitration has long been a tool in labor disputes. But it wasn't until the mid-1970s that private judging began to take a more popular position. What started the arbitration craze in earnest began with two Los Angeles-area attorneys, Hillel Chodos and Jerome Craig, who were representing opposing sides in a complicated case involving a medical billing firm and its lawyers. They found an obscure 1872 California law that authorizes litigants to have any civil case heard by hired referees, who need not be judges or even lawyers. The pair signed up a retired judge and got the approval of then Presiding Judge Richard Schauer of Los Angeles County Superior Court. Within seven months they had a final decision on their case. Its relative speed saved their clients some $100,000 in attorneys' fees.

Retired judges would sometimes act as arbitrators back then, and most charged little or nothing. Chodos and Craig concluded that it wasn't fair to ask them to serve for free when they were getting hundreds of dollars an hour. So the lawyers paid the arbitrator "lawyer's wages."

The judge "was like a kid with a new toy," Chodos said. "He never made any money on the bench. It was a brand-new idea. He kept giggling about it." Chodos said, "I feel like I created a Frankenstein."

And a monster it has indeed become. As the courts become ever more crowded it often takes five years for a civil case to find its way to trial. The demand for alternatives intensified and companies such as the American Arbitration Association (AAA) and Judicial Arbitration and Mediation Service (JAMS) went into business managing the cases and brokering the arbitrator's services. . . . for a very substantial fee.

In today's business environment, it's become popular to try to push litigation into arbitration as a way of speeding up the process and saving legal fees. The original concept of arbitration wasn't all bad. The idea was to provide a less formal, more streamlined and economical process of deciding cases. Because the proceedings were held outside the courts, arbitrators didn't have to follow formal, complicated—and often needless—rules. What's more, private judges could be counted on to give the case something all too rare in the harried courts, their full attention.

In recent years it has become more popular to submit conflicts to binding arbitration and the advertising business follows along. This is generally done, either by mutual agreement of the parties, or by a mandatory arbitration clause in the client–agency contract. However, use of these clauses in client–agency contracts to force dispute resolution into arbitration may cause many more problems than they solve. Why is that? Well, the arbitration arena is in effect a gated community. It's largely undocumented, unregulated and biased in favor of big business and against the little guy.

Once the rose-colored glasses are removed, here are some of the major problems with arbitration.

First, arbitration cases are decided out of public view, leaving no public record of what went on in the proceedings, or legal precedent for others to follow. There is no public register where cases can be read and reviewed.

Second, when private judges are deciding between a big company and a small one, which way do you think they tend to lean? "Private judging is an oxymoron because those judges are businessmen. They are in this for money," said J. Anthony Kline, a state appellate justice in San Francisco. "In this state, there are tens of thousands, probably hundreds of thousands and, for all I know, millions of disputes that are being resolved by decision makers who are not truly independent."

If arbitrators try to be truly neutral and unbiased, the risk is obvious. They may not get hired again. So if they're going to be neutral, they'll most likely be more neutral for some, than others.

Third, arbitrators aren't required to follow the law. A simple but oppressively important shortcoming with arbitration. In a crucial 1992 decision, *Moncharsh v. Heily & Blase*, 3 Cal. 4th 1, 10 Cal. Rptr. 2d 183, 832 P.2d 899 (1992), the California state Supreme Court held that an arbitrator's award is not subject to review even if it is "legally wrong" and causes "substantial injustice."

The fact that arbitration decisions are almost never overturned may seem contrary to justice. Yet, another reason judges are reluctant to vacate arbitration decisions (even when they are clearly wrong or unjust on their face) might be that those same judges will most likely be looking for future employment from the arbitration system itself. Why would they rule against a system that will be a future nest egg . . . and a very profitable one at that?

Fourth, there is virtually no possibility of appeal or having an arbitration decision overturned, even if there is severe error in the validity of the arbitrator's reasoning, or the sufficiency of the evidence that supports the arbitrator's decision. The result is that we now have a second legal system where arbitrators can rule based on tea leaves. The fact is that arbitrators make mistakes . . . and there is virtually no appeal right if they make a stupid or diabolical mistake, or one that is made in bad faith. The parties are on their own and are stuck with the decision. Only under very rare circumstances where corruption can be shown or that the arbitrator exceeded his powers, can the decision possibly be overturned.

Fifth, the inbred environment of the system creates a situation where the arbitration arena draws its manpower from the courts. Four years after the Supreme Court handed down its ruling in Moncharsh, the opinion's author, former state Chief Justice Malcolm Lucas, went to work for JAMS. He charges $6,500 a day, according to a company fee schedule (as of January 2006). Former Justice Edward A. Panelli, who also signed the decision, is now at JAMS too and his rate is $7,500 a day. For a system that is supposed to be easier, faster and cheaper . . . arbitration rarely is.

When a party feels it has been wronged, it first researches the law. It reviews current precedent, statutes and case law to determine if it has a realistic case. Then when that case if filed in arbitration, all the relevant law, precedent, and legal argument can be discarded by the arbitrator. Public policy favors upholding arbitration awards and consequently an arbitrator can rule in any way he wants, whether it is legally or factually valid or not. An arbitrator's decision is binding and can't be corrected even if the decision is based on laws from the planet Pluto, rather than the United States.

Arbitration, in reality, is a system that is out of control and not governed by any accountability.

The Internet 5

Progress is man's ability to complicate simplicity.
                    —Thor Heyerdahl

It was the 1960s. The era of the Beatles, Flower-Power, audio cassette tapes, the Hippies, and the Zodiac Killer. The Peace Corps was created. Ebbett's Field was torn down. Gasoline was less than fifty cents a gallon, Toyota sold its first car in the United States, and the Eagle landed at Tranquility Base. John F. Kennedy was elected the thirty-fifth president of the United States, and assassinated three years later. It was the time of the cold war between the Soviet Union and the United States. Both countries built more and more atomic weapons, and both had the power to wipe out the entire planet.

So America's premier Cold War thinking machine, the Rand Corporation, approached a strategic problem. If one computer in a network was destroyed, communication was also. And if there was a central hub, it would surely be the first target for an atomic attack. So how could the United States authorities successfully communicate after a nuclear attack? (Now we'd call it a terrorist attack.) RAND invented a new kind of network in 1964 that would have no center—all the nodes would be equal in status, each could send and receive messages. That means that if one node was destroyed, the rest of the nodes would still be able to communicate.

The first test network built on these principles was installed in National Research Laboratory in Great Britain in 1968. Soon after, the Pentagon's Advanced Research Projects Agency (ARPA) installed a more advanced network based on the same principles. The network consisted of four high-speed computers. In 1969, the first node was installed at UCLA.

Then in 1972, Ray Tomlinson of BBN invented the first e-mail program. But why is this that important? Well, over the years an odd fact became clear. Instead of using the Internet for long-distance computing, the scientists used it to communicate with each other—for sharing results of their experiments—but mainly for gossiping.

In 1989, the WWW was invented by British scientist Tim Berners-Lee at CERN. CERN (Conseil Européen pour la Recherche Nucléaire), or European Council for Nuclear Research, in Switzerland is a provisional body that was founded in 1952. The institute has revolutionized the world of physics recently through its Large Hadron

Collider studies of particle physics, antimatter, and the standard model. Originally, WWW was developed only for high energy physics (for world-wide communication).

The first website in the world was hosted on Berners-Lee's NeXT computer. The original website described the basic features of the web; how to access other people's documents and how to set up your own server. The NeXT machine (the original web server) is still at CERN today. As part of the project to restore the first website, in 2013 CERN reinstated the world's first website to its original web address.

In 1993, the first browser, Mosaic, was released and since then the growth rate of the Internet has grown at an alarming rate. Just look at how much the Internet has proliferated in twenty-five short years. Dial-up came and went. And the online experience went from your desktop computer to your cell phone.

Very recent developments tell us that we may soon find out exactly how the FCC proposes to regulate the Internet as if it was a utility. If they have their way, ISPs would be reclassified and regulated under "Title II" of the Telecommunications Act. That's the law that would be used to govern Internet companies, instead of classifying them as "information services," as they have been to date. What can we say about the future of the Internet? One can only guess what it will look like ten years from now.

Since the 1995 edition of *Law & Advertising*, the Internet has provided the largest amount of new activity in the area of advertising law. In fact, the Internet was not included in early editions of this book, since advertising on the Internet only began in 1994 when the first banner ads were sold. As television was forty years ago, the Internet is the "new media" du jour.

As one court *Digital Equipment Corp.* v. *Altavista Technology, Inc.*, 960 F. Supp 456, 462 (D. Mass.) (1997), so well put it: "The Internet has no territorial boundaries. To paraphrase Gertrude Stein, as far as the Internet is concerned, not only is there perhaps 'no there there,' the 'there' is everywhere where there is Internet access. When business is transacted over a computer network via a Web-site accessed by a computer in Massachusetts, it takes place as much in Massachusetts, literally or figuratively, as it does anywhere."

Law and the Internet

The first thing that needs to be pointed out is this. The Internet is a media (or perhaps medium) for personal communication, educational dialog, editorial content, and commercial marketing (and that includes a subset of marketing; advertising). The bulk of this book contains chapters that discuss different areas of law, but unlike the rest of this book, this chapter discusses an area of media. What this means to you is that all of the principles, all of the analysis, and all of the laws in all of the other chapters of this book also apply to this chapter.

I wrote, at the beginning of this book, that the chapters were broken down by "area of law." That was done because each area of law is based upon different rules, different reasoning and different histories. This chapter, however, is unique in that it deals with the Internet; a media, a venue for communication if you will. While there are laws and legislation that apply specifically to the Internet, all of the other areas of law apply as well. All the information about the Federal Trade Commission (FTC) applies to the Internet. All the laws that apply to copyright apply to the Internet. All the laws that apply to trademark apply to the Internet. All the laws that apply to privacy and publicity rights also apply to the Internet. While this chapter primarily will limit itself to the laws that apply specifically to the Internet and situations that are unique to that media, all the other areas of law apply here too.

The Internet is a constantly developing and evolving technology that continually fuels new forms of innovation, interaction, content, and political activity. The reality of the Internet is it has the potential to transform our economy, society and political system in ever-changing ways. As is has exponentially for two decades.

The physical components of communications such as cable and telephone networks, in addition to communication services that are provided over them, have become one of the most rapidly active areas of laws that affect our information-highway dependent world. And the debates over whether network providers should be able to restrict the content that their Internet users can access are examples of this trend. At the same time, the Internet's ability to support a variety of different communications services such as telephone, information services or video over the same physical network challenges the existing communications law. This had always been based on the know-outdated assumption that different physical systems offer different communications services.

So now we'll dig in and take a look at the current interconnection between advertising and the Internet.

The FTC's Role

As with other forms of advertising, the same FTC regulations apply to Internet marketing. A claim may be considered misleading if relevant information is left out or if the claim implies something that is untrue.

In 2014, in *FTC v. Ross*, 743 F.3d 886, U.S. App. LEXIS 3476, 2014-1 Trade Cas. (CCH) P78,686, 93 Fed. R. Evid. Serv. (Callaghan) 1031 (2014), the court demonstrated the FTC's involvement in Internet advertising issues. Section 5 of the Federal Trade Commission Act was violated as a result of representations that were made to consumers through Internet-based ads and software-generated reports that induced consumers to purchase IMI's computer security products. Specifically, the Defendants (both IMI corporate, and Ross individually) developed a series of software advertisements. These ads appeared in the form of "popups" and "warnings" on a consumer's computer, claiming to have discover malicious software (malware) and offering to provide a "cure" at a cost ranging from $30 to $100. Essentially, these deceptive advertisements, some of which included sham "system scans," had the effect of convincing Internet users that their computers contained malicious software, "illegal" pornography, or critical system errors, and that to fix these problems they needed IMI's repair software. The repair software sold by IMI included WinFixer, WinAntiVirus, WinAntiVvirusPro, WinAntiSpyware, Popupguard, WinFirewall, InternetAntispy, WinPopupguard, ComputerShield, WinAntispy, PCsupercharger, ErrorSafe, SysProtect, DriveCleaner, SystemDoctor, and ErrorProtector.

As it turned out, both the advertisements and the repair software were deceptive. In fact, the number of errors found on any given computer was predetermined by IMI. As a result, more than one million consumers purchased IMI's products, and approximately three thousand customers filed complaints with the FTC. On top of this sham, every major computer security vendor considered these products to be system threats.

Here's how it worked. In October 2004, Ms. Ross opened fifty-four individual password-protected accounts with MyGeek, an Internet advertising company that would later become known as AdOn. She used these accounts to place Flash advertisements for IMI products including Winfixer, DriveCleaner, FreeRepair, WinAntivirus, WinAntispyware, System Doctor and others. These ads reached customers over six hundred million times. She also personally funded the advertisements placed at MyGeek for up to approximately $23,000. The court said: "In total, Kristy Ross placed $3.3 million of advertisements for Defendants' products with MyGeek."

Clearly IMI's advertising was deceptive under the FTC Act. However this case went deeper than that. The evidence presented in this case demonstrated that Ms. Ross had actual knowledge of the deceptive marketing scheme. The court said: "She wrote, edited, reviewed, and participated in the development of multiple advertisements. She instructed developers to make the advertisements more aggressive and on at least two occasions ordered them to remove the term 'advertisement' from certain ads. She funded the accounts through which the ads were disseminated to consumers. She was fully aware of the many complaints from consumers and ad networks and was in charge of remedying the problems. Moreover, she had the marketing expertise and was trusted by her partners because of that expertise."

Even if Ms. Ross, despite exercising significant control over the advertisements, had not had actual knowledge of the advertising's deceptive nature, it was clear that at the very least she was recklessly indifferent or intentionally avoided the truth. It gets worse; it was found that Ms. Ross was romantically involved with another defendant, Mr. Jain since before the creation of IMI. In 2006, she became romantically involved with another IMI executive, defendant Mr. D'Souza.

The court, having previously determined that the amount of damages calculated by the FTC was a reasonable approximation of consumer damages, this court held that Ms. Ross was personally liable along with IMI for over $163 million.

Disclaimers on Internet Advertising

Advertising a product or service on the Internet will be subject to the same standards as advertising in other media. However, the FTC maintains that there are some issues that are unique to the Internet and that require special rules or guidance.

The FTC investigates the use of disclaimers in advertisements that appear on the Internet as they would other media. In print advertisements, for example, disclaimers usually appear in smaller print than the rest of the ad copy. In television commercials, a disclaimer might be made through the voice-over. Where, and in what form, should an advertisement disclaimer be used on an Internet website so that it is clear and conspicuous to the reader? As with other forms of advertising, the FTC views the disclaimer in the context of all of the other elements of the ad to determine whether it is effectively communicated. "Ordinarily, a disclosure [disclaimer] is clear and conspicuous, and therefore is effectively communicated, when it is displayed in a manner that is readily noticeable, readable and/or audible (depending on the medium), and understandable to the audience to whom it is disseminated." (63 Federal Register 25002, May 6, 1998.)

However, applying this standard to Internet ads involves several issues that are unique to Internet advertising.

The FTC stated the issues as follows: "Many Internet advertisements, for example, include scroll bars to maneuver down pages that usually exceed one screen in length. They also often include hyperlinks, both to other pages on a website as well as directly to other websites. On the Internet and in other electronic media, new graphics technologies create messages that scroll, blink, spin, pop-up, relocate, and so on. These unique features may require the Commission to give special consideration to certain factors in determining whether a disclosure is effectively communicated on electronic media. As is true for any medium, the specific elements necessary to effectively communicate a disclosure may vary depending on the nature of the advertisement and the nature of the claim" (63 Federal Register 25002, May 6, 1998).

The FTC recommends that disclaimers in Internet ads should be very apparent to "reasonable" consumers. Consumers should not have to take any special action to see the disclaimer, such as scrolling down a page, clicking on a link to other pages, activating a "pop-up," or entering a search term. The Commission also feels that the disclaimer should be accessible at all times. In other words, a consumer who follows a hyperlink to another page should not be prevented from going back to the page containing the disclaimer. The disclaimer should also be close to the representation that it clarifies.

The FTC also suggests that if the representation is made visually, the disclaimer should be made visually also. The same standard applies for audio representations.

Credit Repair Programs

This is an area that has seen a fair amount of activity on the Internet, and the FTC has pursued the issues.

In its first case targeting advertising on the "information superhighway," the Federal Trade Commission charged a Sacramento, California, man with making false claims in the course of promoting his credit-repair program online. In *FTC v. Corzine*, (FTC File No. 9423295, 1995), the FTC charged Brian Corzine, doing business as Chase Consulting, for promoting his scheme on America Online. The program advised consumers to take steps to repair their credit records, while representing that it is "100% legal."

According to then FTC Chairman Janet D. Steiger: "As these computer networks continue to grow, we will not tolerate the use of deceptive practices here any more than we have tolerated them on other recently-emerged technologies for marketing products and services to consumers."

Consumers were instructed to contact Chase Consulting through the computer service. Corzine allegedly enticed consumers through statements such as:

FOR JUST $99.00 WE WILL SHOW YOU

HOW TO CREATE A BRAND NEW CREDIT FILE

AT ALL 3 OF THE MAJOR CREDIT BUREAUS:
100% LEGAL AND 200% GUARANTEED.

Consumers who contacted Chase Consulting by computer were instructed to obtain a "taxpayer identification number" from the Internal Revenue Service and then to use this number in place of their Social Security number on credit applications. The complete "file segregation" program included a booklet which instructed consumers to obtain two new addresses: one for use on their driver's licenses and one for use on credit applications. Corzine allegedly represented that the program is legal. However, consumers who falsify statements on certain loan and credit applications or falsify their Social Security number would violate one or more federal criminal statutes.

Spam: Unsolicited Electronic Mail

Spam is the bane of our Internet experience, and it is growing at an alarming rate. The FTC has a "long history of promoting competition and protecting consumers in new marketing media." Door-to-door sales, television and print adverting, direct mail marketing, pay-per-call number sales, and telemarketing were all marked by early struggles between legitimate merchants and fraud artists battling for potential profits of the new marketplace. Spam is the evil that lurks within the World Wide Web.

The FTC monitors deceptive, unsolicited electronic mail, commonly called "spam." Then FTC Commissioner Shelia F. Anthony told the Senate Commerce, Science and Transportation Committee on June 17, 1998, that the Commission views the problem of deception as a significant issue in the debate over unsolicited e-mail and other Internet schemes. The Commission closely monitors e-mail for deception and fraud.

It might shock you to know that spam amounts to 14.5 billion messages globally, per day! In other words, spam makes up 45 percent of all e-mails. Spam e-mail makes up an even greater portion of global e-mails, some 73 percent in fact. Not surprisingly, the United States is the number one generator of spam e-mail, with Korea clocking in as the second largest contributor of unwanted e-mail.

Let's take a look at a few more statistics for perspective. Advertising-related spam e-mail accounts for approximately 36 percent of all spam messages. The second most common category of spam is adult-oriented (read: pornography) and makes up roughly 31.7 percent of all spam. Spam related to financial matters is the third most popular form, at 26.5 percent.

Amazingly, scams and fraud comprise only 2.5 percent of all spam e-mail today. However, identity theft (known as "phishing") makes up 73 percent of that.

Because spam has permeated the personal and corporate worlds of e-mail, it has affected the way that individuals and companies communicate.

In the first law enforcement action targeting fraudulent, unsolicited commercial e-mail, the FTC charged a company using unsolicited, false, and misleading commercial e-mail, or "spam," to induce consumers to advertise on its Internet newspaper sites. According to the charges, the company claimed that investors in the Internet "billboards" could sublease advertising space and earn a guaranteed return on their investment. The company claimed that purchasers could reasonably expect to sublease 25 percent of their billboard, realizing earnings up to $800 per month. In fact, the FTC alleged, few purchasers achieved the levels of earnings claimed and the company did not provide a refund as promised. In addition, the business ventures sold by the company were franchises, and the company failed to make complete and accurate disclosures as required by the FTC's franchise rule.

Jodie Bernstein, former Director of the FTC's Bureau of Consumer Protection, stated: "The rules for advertising by e-mail are the same as the rules for advertising through the regular mail: don't mislead or lie to consumers, or the FTC will come after you." (*Maher*, CCH Trade Regulation Reports ¶ 24,397.)

CAN-SPAM Act

CAN-SPAM stands for "Controlling the Assault of Non-Solicited Pornography and Marketing." The act went into effect in January 2004, to establish requirements for those sending out commercial e-mails, define penalties for spammers, and give consumers the right to ask e-mailers to stop spamming them.

The law covers e-mail that's primary purpose is to advertise or promote a product, service, or website. Personal e-mails and e-mail updates and advertisements that have been consented to are not covered under this law. Also not covered are "transactional or relationship messages," which are e-mails that pertain to agreed-upon transactions or e-mails that update customers in an existing business relationship. That is because these types of e-mails are not technically spam—they are a result of previous consent or a business relationship. However, if these types of e-mails contain false or misleading information they are in violation of the CAN-SPAM Act.

The CAN-SPAM Act is enforced by our friends at the FTC, and the Department of Justice has authority to enforce its criminal sanctions. Other federal and state agencies can also enforce the law in their jurisdictions. Internet service providers (ISPs) can also sue violators directly.

Requirements and Prohibitions of CAN-SPAM

The CAN-SPAM Act has four main provisions:

False and misleading header information is banned. This means that an e-mail's "From," "To" and routing information, including the originating domain name and address, must be accurate and identify the sender.

Deceptive subject lines are prohibited. The subject line cannot mislead the receiver of the message to open it under false pretenses, thinking it's something else. The receiver must not be mislead as to the contents or subject matter of the e-mail.

Opt-out methods must be provided. A response mechanism must be provided for the receiver to opt-out of any future commercial messages from the sender. In addition, opt-out requests must be processed for at least thirty days after the initial commercial e-mail was sent, and senders have ten business days after an opt-out request to stop sending messages to that address. Messages cannot be sent to the opt-out requestor on behalf of the sender by any other entity.

Commercial e-mail must be identified as an advertisement and it must include the sender's valid physical postal address. The receiver must be clearly informed that the message is an advertisement or solicitation, he must be told he can opt-out of future mailings, and a valid physical postal address must be included in the message.

Receivers must be warned of sexually explicit material. For any message that contains sexually explicit material, the warning "SEXUALLY-EXPLICIT" must be contained in the subject line.

The FTC is also currently looking into establishing a National Do Not E-mail Registry, much like the existing National Do Not Call Registry, that would prohibit senders of commercial messages from targeting anyone who puts themselves on the list.

Violation of the provisions of the CAN-SPAM Act are subject to fines of up to $11,000. Deceptive commercial e-mails are also subject to laws relating to false or misleading advertising.

The Mail, Internet, or Telephone Order Rule

The FTC's Mail, Internet, or Telephone Order Merchandise rule (Mail Order Rule) controls advertising of all merchandise that is ordered from a seller by mail, telephone, fax, or over the Internet. The federal Mail Order Rule overrides any state law, municipal ordinance, or other local regulation that does not provide equal or greater rights to the buyer.

The Mail Order Rule states that it is "an unfair or deceptive act and practice" for a seller "[t]o solicit any order for the sale of merchandise to be ordered by the buyer through the mails unless, at the time of the solicitation, the seller has a reasonable basis to expect he will be able to ship [the] ordered merchandise to the buyer." The order must be shipped within the time specified in the ad or, if no date is specified, within thirty days after receipt of the order from the buyer.

What happens if the seller can't ship the ordered items before the thirty-day period or by the specified shipping date? Then the company must (without the consumer demanding) offer the buyer the option to either agree to a delay in shipping the item or cancel the order and receive a prompt refund.

The Not-So-Sweet Suite

Dell Computer Corporation, agreed to pay a civil penalty of $800,000 to settle charges that it violated the FTC's Mail Order Rule in *Dell Computer Corp.*, CCH Trade Regulation Reports ¶ 24,411. The penalty was the largest ever paid (to date) by a single defendant for violating the Mail Order Rule.

The "Dell Software Suite" was advertised as being a part of the Dell Dimensions system. The FTC alleged that consumers who called to purchase a Dell Dimension system were not informed that the Dell Software Suite would not be included when their product was shipped. Instead, the company included a coupon for the software "when available." In reality, consumers did not receive the software for quite some time. Also, Dell did not offer purchasers the option of accepting the delay or canceling their orders and receiving a prompt refund, which was required by the rule.

Internet Service Providers

In March 1998 the FTC settled a case against America Online, Inc., Prodigy Services Corp., and Compuserve, Inc., for their "free trial" offers that actually resulted in charges to consumers. The FTC claimed that the three ISPs had not made it clear that consumers had an affirmative obligation to cancel before the trial period ended. So, as a result, consumers that did not cancel were automatically enrolled as members and were charged monthly service charges. The provisions of the consent order stop the companies from misrepresenting the terms or conditions of any trial offer. They must also not represent that the service is free without disclosing clearly any obligation to cancel or state action that must be taken to avoid charges. The case was *America Online, Inc.*, CCH Trade Regulation Reports ¶ 24,260.

The Illinois Attorney General (and attorneys general for the states of Alabama, Arizona, Arkansas, California, Connecticut, Florida, Georgia, Idaho, Illinois, Indiana, Kansas, Kentucky, Louisiana, Maine, Maryland, Massachusetts, Michigan, Mississippi, Missouri, Nebraska, Nevada, New Jersey, New Mexico, New York, North Carolina, North Dakota, Ohio, Oklahoma, Oregon, Pennsylvania, Rhode Island, South Carolina, Tennessee, Texas, Utah, Vermont, Virginia, Washington, West Virginia, and Wisconsin) settled with American Online (AOL) in *In The Matter of America Online, Inc.*, 98-2-131837SEA, Assurance of Voluntary Reliance, King County Wash. Sup. Ct., May 28, 1998. This settlement provides new protections when prices or services are altered.

The settlement provides the following:

> *Disclosures for Free Offers.* Under the terms of AOL's "Free Trial Offer," the company must make new disclosures, including that the fifty-hour free trial must be used within a month, that the consumer must cancel the trial to avoid billing, and that consumers should be careful to determine if AOL maintains a local access number in their area to avoid long-distance charges. If consumers cancel their AOL service, procedures must be explained clearly in AOL under "Keyword: Cancel" and "Terms of Service." The company also must mail a notice of cancelation.
>
> *Disclosures Concerning Pricing.* If AOL increases its monthly fees or otherwise modifies its contract, it must provide clear notice of the change at least thirty days in advance. The notice must describe the change, state its effective date, and direct the subscriber to an area where the change is described in greater detail. If such notice is not delivered, a subscriber is entitled to a refund on any price increase.
>
> *Disclosures Concerning Premium Areas.* AOL has agreed to notify all consumers, via pop-up screen, when they enter a game or other premium service area where

charges are incurred beyond the monthly fee. The pop-up box will state the rate per minute of the extra charges.

Disclosure Regarding Advertising to Minors. In advertisements for AOL service directed toward persons under the age of 18 or which are placed in a medium directed or disseminated primarily to persons under the age of 18, AOL shall: (1) use language generally understandable to the youngest age group to which the advertisement is directed; (2) present disclosure information in such a manner to attract the attention of the youngest age group; and (3) explain that a person must be 18 years or older to subscribe to AOL, if that is AOL's policy.

AOL agreed to two earlier settlements in 1996 and 1997 with numerous states regarding the company's $19.95-a-month unlimited service promotion.

"We are demystifying the relationship between consumers and online services," said then, Illinois Attorney General Ryan. "Under this settlement AOL must notify consumers in advance whenever there is a price increase or substantial service change. The notification must be clear and direct. The goal is to make sure that consumers know all the facts so they can make informed choices." (Ryan Leads 44-State Settlement with America Online That Provides New Protections For Consumers, Illinois Attorney General Press Release, May 28, 1998. Communications Decency Act (CDA) of 1996.)

In February of 1996, Congress chose to "promote the continued development of the Internet and other interactive computer services and other interactive media" and "to preserve the vibrant and competitive free market" for such services, largely "unfettered by Federal or State regulation . . . ." (47 U.S.C. § 230(b)(1) and (2)).

It effectively immunized providers of interactive computer services from civil liability in tort with respect to material disseminated by them that was actually created by others. By recognizing the speed of information and the near impossibility of controlling information content, Congress decided not to treat providers of interactive computer services like newspapers, magazines, and television and radio stations. All of these may be held liable for publishing or distributing obscene or defamatory material written or prepared by others. While Congress could have made a different policy choice, but because of the uniqueness of the Internet it choose not to hold interactive computer services liable for their failure to edit, withhold, or restrict access to offensive material disseminated through this medium.

Section 230(c) of the CDA of 1996 (which we'll look at later) provides: "No provider or user of an interactive computer service shall be treated as the publisher or speaker of any information provided by another information content provider."

In another case, the court, in *Zeran* v. *America Online, Inc.*, 129 F.3d 327 (4th Cir. 1997), stated:

> The purpose of this statutory immunity is not difficult to discern. Congress recognized the threat that tort-based lawsuits pose to freedom of speech in the new and burgeoning Internet medium. The imposition of tort liability on service providers for the communications of others represented, for Congress, simply another form of intrusive government regulation of speech. Section 230 was enacted, in part, to maintain the robust nature of Internet communication and, accordingly, to keep government interference in the medium to a minimum.

None of this means, of course, that the original culpable party who posts defamatory messages would escape accountability. While Congress acted to keep government regulation of the Internet to a minimum, it also found it to be the policy of the United States "to ensure vigorous enforcement of Federal criminal laws to deter and punish trafficking in obscenity, stalking, and harassment by means of computer" Id. § 230(b)(5). Congress made a policy choice, however, not to deter harmful online speech through the separate route of imposing tort liability on companies that serve as intermediaries for other parties' potentially injurious messages.

The Communications Decency Act

Inside the CDA of 1996 is one of the most valuable tools for protecting freedom of expression and innovation on the Internet: Section 230 (also known as the Cox-Wyden Amendment).

Surprisingly, the original intent of the legislation was to restrict free speech on the Internet. The Internet community as a whole objected strongly to the CDA, and the anti-free speech provisions were struck down by the Supreme Court.

Section 230 states that "No provider or user of an interactive computer service shall be treated as the publisher or speaker of any information provided by another information content provider" (47 U.S.C. § 230). In other words, online services that host or republish speech are protected against legal liability for what others say and do. The protected services include not only regular ISPs, but also a range of "interactive computer service providers," including essentially any online service that publishes third-party content. Although there are important exceptions for certain criminal and intellectual property-based claims, Section 230 establishes broad protection allowing free speech online.

This legal policy allows YouTube and Vimeo users to upload their videos, Amazon and Yelp to post unlimited user reviews, Craigslist to host classified ads, and Facebook and Twitter to post social comments to hundreds of millions of people on the Internet. Section 230 may well be the most effective protection that has allowed the Internet to thrive since 1996.

Section 230 also shields bloggers who act as intermediaries by hosting comments on their sites. Under the law, bloggers are not liable for comments left by readers, the work of guest bloggers, tips sent via e-mail, or information received through RSS feeds. This legal protection still exists even if the blogger is aware of the objectionable content.

While the legal protections provided by Section 230 only apply to the United States, most online services are based there. This is mainly because Section 230 makes the United States a safe haven for websites that want to provide a platform for controversial or political speech and a legal environment favorable to free speech (box 5.1).

Box 5.1   **The Communications Decency Act: 47 U.S. Code § 230**

It's worth reading the full text of Section 230, so here it is:

(a) Findings

The Congress finds the following:

(1) The rapidly developing array of Internet and other interactive computer services available to individual Americans represent an extraordinary advance in the availability of educational and informational resources to our citizens.

(2) These services offer users a great degree of control over the information that they receive, as well as the potential for even greater control in the future as technology develops.

(3) The Internet and other interactive computer services offer a forum for a true diversity of political discourse, unique opportunities for cultural development, and myriad avenues for intellectual activity.

(4) The Internet and other interactive computer services have flourished, to the benefit of all Americans, with a minimum of government regulation.

(5) Increasingly Americans are relying on interactive media for a variety of political, educational, cultural, and entertainment services.

(b) Policy

It is the policy of the United States:

(1) to promote the continued development of the Internet and other interactive computer services and other interactive media;

(2) to preserve the vibrant and competitive free market that presently exists for the Internet and other interactive computer services, unfettered by Federal or State regulation;

(3) to encourage the development of technologies which maximize user control over what information is received by individuals, families, and schools who use the Internet and other interactive computer services;

(4) to remove disincentives for the development and utilization of blocking and filtering technologies that empower parents to restrict their children's access to objectionable or inappropriate online material; and

(5) to ensure vigorous enforcement of Federal criminal laws to deter and punish trafficking in obscenity, stalking, and harassment by means of computer.

(c) Protection for "Good Samaritan" blocking and screening of offensive material

(1) Treatment of publisher or speaker

No provider or user of an interactive computer service shall be treated as the publisher or speaker of any information provided by another information content provider.

(2) Civil liability

No provider or user of an interactive computer service shall be held liable on account of:

(A) any action voluntarily taken in good faith to restrict access to or availability of material that the provider or user considers to be obscene, lewd, lascivious, filthy, excessively violent, harassing, or otherwise objectionable, whether or not such material is constitutionally protected; or

(B) any action taken to enable or make available to information content providers or others the technical means to restrict access to material described in paragraph (1).

(d) Obligations of interactive computer service

A provider of interactive computer service shall, at the time of entering an agreement with a customer for the provision of interactive computer service and in a manner deemed appropriate by the provider, notify such customer that parental control protections (such as computer hardware, software, or filtering services) are commercially available that may assist the customer in limiting access to material that is harmful to minors. Such notice shall identify, or provide the customer with access to information identifying, current providers of such protections.

(e) Effect on other laws

(1) No effect on criminal law

Nothing in this section shall be construed to impair the enforcement of section 223 or 231 of this title, chapter 71 (relating to obscenity) or 110 (relating to sexual exploitation of children) of title 18, or any other Federal criminal statute.

(2) No effect on intellectual property law

Nothing in this section shall be construed to limit or expand any law pertaining to intellectual property.

(3) State law

Nothing in this section shall be construed to prevent any State from enforcing any State law that is consistent with this section. No cause of action may be brought and no liability may be imposed under any State or local law that is inconsistent with this section.

(4) No effect on communications privacy law

Nothing in this section shall be construed to limit the application of the Electronic Communications Privacy Act of 1986 or any of the amendments made by such Act, or any similar State law.

(f) Definitions

As used in this section:

(1) Internet

The term "Internet" means the international computer network of both Federal and non-Federal interoperable packet switched data networks.

(2) Interactive computer service

The term "interactive computer service" means any information service, system, or access software provider that provides or enables computer access by multiple users to a computer server, including specifically a service or system that provides access to the Internet and such systems operated or services offered by libraries or educational institutions.

(3) Information content provider
The term "information content provider" means any person or entity that is responsible, in whole or in part, for the creation or development of information provided through the Internet or any other interactive computer service.

(4) Access software provider
The term "access software provider" means a provider of software (including client or server software), or enabling tools that do any one or more of the following:

(A) filter, screen, allow, or disallow content;

(B) pick, choose, analyze, or digest content; or

(C) transmit, receive, display, forward, cache, search, subset, organize, reorganize, or translate content.

Section 230 in Practice

The case we're going to look at to see how Section 230 is interpreted, stems from a dangerous, cruel, and highly indecent use of the internet for the apparent purpose of revenge.

Late in 2004, Cecilia Barnes broke off a relationship with her boyfriend. The ex-boyfriend then posted profiles about Barnes on a website run by Yahoo!, Inc. (Yahoo). Barnes did not authorize her former boyfriend to post the profiles, and it's obvious why. The profiles contained nude photographs of Barnes and her boyfriend, taken without her knowledge, and some kind of open solicitation to engage in sexual intercourse. The ex-boyfriend also created discussions in Yahoo's online "chat rooms," posing as Barnes and inviting male readers to the profiles he had created. The profiles also included contact information about Barnes' place of employment. Before long, . . . well you can imagine what happened.

Following Yahoo's policy, Barnes mailed them a copy of her photo ID and a signed statement denying her involvement with the profiles and requesting their removal. One month later, Yahoo had not responded and the undesired advances from unknown men continued. Barnes again asked Yahoo by mail to remove the profiles. Nothing happened. Another month passed and Barnes sent Yahoo two more mailings. During the same period, a local news program was preparing to broadcast a report on the incident. A day before the air date of the broadcast, Yahoo broke its silence and promised that they would take care of it. Another two months passed without action from Yahoo, so Barnes filed this lawsuit, *Barnes* v. *Yahoo!, Inc.*, 570 F.3d 1096, U.S. App. LEXIS 20053, 37 Media L. Rep. 1705, 47 Comm. Reg. (P & F) 1028 (2009), against Yahoo. Shortly thereafter, the profiles amazingly disappeared from Yahoo's website.

According to Yahoo's Member Directory, "[a] public profile is a page with information about you that other Yahoo! members can view. You[r] profile allows you to publicly post information about yourself that you want to share with the world. Many people post their age, pictures, location, and hobbies on their profiles."

In this case the court said: "Leaving no stone unturned, Barnes reminds us that the statutory purpose of the Amendment is to encourage websites affirmatively to police themselves, not to provide an excuse for doing nothing. This argument from statutory purpose has more force to it, because section 230(c) is, after all, captioned 'Protection for 'good samaritan' blocking and screening of offensive material.' " They went on further by explaining: "It would indeed be strange for a provision so captioned to provide equal protection as between Internet service providers who do nothing and those who attempt to block and screen offensive material. As the Seventh Circuit has recognized, if section (c) did provide equal protection, then '[Internet Service Providers] may be expected to take the do-nothing option and enjoy immunity' because "precautions are costly."

From a closer look at the whole of section 230(c), the court stated:

Subsection (c)(1), by itself, shields from liability all publication decisions, whether to edit, to remove, or to post, with respect to content generated entirely by third parties. Subsection (c)(2), for its part, provides an additional shield from liability, but only for "any action voluntarily taken in good faith to restrict access to or availability of material that the provider . . . considers to be obscene . . . or otherwise objectionable." Crucially, the persons who can take advantage of this liability are not merely those whom subsection (c)(1) already protects, but *any* provider of an interactive computer service. Thus, even those who cannot take advantage of subsection (c)(1), perhaps because they developed, even in part, the content at issue, can take advantage of subsection (c)(2) if they act to restrict access to the content because they consider it obscene or otherwise objectionable. Additionally, subsection (c)(2) also protects Internet service providers from liability not for publishing or speaking, but rather for actions taken to restrict access to obscene or otherwise objectionable content.

Now, the court decision here and in other cases, clearly confirms that ISPs are treated as a publisher or speaker of third-party content and therefore not liable for the content.

However the court clarified the point by stating:

many causes of action might be premised on the publication or speaking of what one might call "information content." A provider of information services might get sued for violating antidiscrimination laws; for fraud, negligent misrepresentation, and ordinary negligence; for false light or even for negligent publication of advertisements that cause harm to third parties. Thus, what matters is not the name of the cause of action (defamation versus negligence versus intentional infliction of emotional distress) what matters is whether the cause of action inherently requires the court to treat the defendant as the "publisher or speaker" of content provided by another. To put it another way, courts must ask whether the duty that the plaintiff alleges the defendant violated derives from the defendant's status or conduct as a "publisher or speaker." If it does, section 230(c)(1) precludes liability.

In the summer of 2005, Jane Doe lied about her age and claimed that she was eighteen years old, and created a profile on MySpace.com. In fact, she was thirteen at the time. By claiming that she was eighteen this allowed her to circumvent all safety features of the MySpace.com site and resulted in her profile being made public. Nineteen-year-old Pete Solis, another member of MySpace.com, was able to initiate contact with Jane in April 2006 when she was fourteen. The two communicated offline on several occasions after Julie provided her telephone number. Ultimately they met in person in May 2006, at which time Solis sexually assaulted Jane.

Although MySpace.com employs a computer program designed to search for clues that underage members have lied about their age to create a profile on the website, no current technology is foolproof. All members are cautioned regarding the type of information they release to other users on the website, including a specific prohibition against posting personal information such as telephone numbers, street addresses, last names, or e-mail addresses. MySpace.com members are also encouraged to report inaccurate, inappropriate, or obscene material to the website's administrators.

This situation was the subject of *Jane Doe* v. *MySpace Inc.*, 528 F.3d 413; U.S. App. LEXIS 10612; 36 Media L. Rep. 1737; 45 Comm. Reg. (P & F) 321 (2008). I reference this cased because, while MySpace was protected from liability, the court made a distinction by pointing out that while the "publisher" may not be liable the third-party user often is.

The court clarified by stating: "Parties complaining that they were harmed by a website's publication of user-generated content have recourse; they may sue the third-party user who generated the content, but not the interactive computer service that enabled them to publish the content online. None of this means, of course, that the original culpable party who posts defamatory messages would escape accountability . . . Congress made a policy choice, however, not to deter harmful online speech through the separate route of imposing tort liability on companies that serve as intermediaries for other parties' potentially injurious messages."

There is one other aspect of Section 230 that is worth discussion. We just looked at situations where an ISP is except from liability for third-party content posted on its site. This protection also extends to its ability to refuse to run advertising on its site. In *Langdon* v. *Google, Inc.*, 474 F. Supp. 2d 622, U.S. Dist. LEXIS 11902, 35 Media L. Rep. 1567 (2007), this issue was addressed.

Christopher Langdon had two Internet websites; www.NCJusticeFraud.com and www.ChinaIsEvil.com. He alleged that the NCJustice website exposed fraud perpetrated by various North Carolina government officials and employees, and that the China website delineates atrocities committed by the Chinese government. Langdon claimed that Google refused to run ads on the two websites.

Langdon argued that Google gave a fraudulent excuse for not running the Cooper ads that the reasons for refusal do not appear in its website or in its ad content policy. He claims that Google gave no reason for not running the China ad. His suit included other defendants: Microsoft refused to run his ads and gave no reason for its refusal; Yahoo refused to run his ads because his websites were not hosted by Yahoo. Langdon alleged that the defendants' refusal to run his ads violated his First and Fourteenth Amendment rights under the U.S. Constitution.

Langdon argued that Google's content policy was "part of its pattern of fraud, deceit, and misrepresentation regarding its advertising policies and search engine results. He alleges that "the rejection or acceptance of ads is based upon whether the political viewpoint of the ad and the related website agree with those of Google's executives and employees, all in contravention of its 'fraudulent content policy.'" His argument went further in that Google engaged in fraud when it encouraged advertisement and then disallowed ads for reasons that are contrary to its content policy, while at the same time allowing ads that do not comply with its content policy. While Google's practice may be contrary and capricious, they are allowed to be.

Section 230 provides immunity from civil suits as follows: "No provider or user of an interactive computer service shall be held liable on account of . . . any action voluntarily taken in good faith to restrict access to or availability of material that the provider or user considers to be obscene, lewd, lascivious, filthy, excessively violent, harassing, or otherwise objectionable, whether or not such material is constitutionally protected." This applies as much to allowing ads to appear on its site as it does to controlling third-party content. In other words, Section 230 provides immunity to publishers or speakers of information originating from another information content provider. The court ruled: "The provision 'precludes courts from entertaining claims that would place a computer service provider in a publisher's role,' and therefore bars 'lawsuits seeking to hold a service provider liable for its exercise of a publisher's traditional editorial functions - such as deciding whether to publish, withdraw, postpone, or alter content.'"

The Internet and Comparative Advertising

We will look at comparative advertising in detail in the next chapter. However, here is a good example of how it applies to Internet issues, so it makes sense to touch on it here.

In *Trafficschool.Com, Inc.* v. *Edriver Inc.*, 653 F.3d 820, U.S. App. LEXIS 15536, 99 U.S.P.Q.2D (BNA) 1628, 2011-2 Trade Cas. (CCH) P77, 637 (2011), the Lanham Act played into a case involving two websites.

TrafficSchool.com, Inc. and Drivers Ed Direct, LLC market and sell traffic school and driver's ed courses directly to consumers. They also compete with DMV.org for referral revenue. They claim that defendants violated the Lanham Act by actively fostering the belief that DMV.org is an official state Department of Motor Vehicles website, or is affiliated or endorsed by a state DMV. They were right.

Drivers Ed owned and managed DMV.org, a for-profit website with an intent to save you "time, money, and even a trip to the DMV!" DMV.org. Consumers visited DMV.org for help renewing driver's licenses, buying car insurance, viewing driving records, beating traffic tickets, registering vehicles, and even finding DUI/DWI attorneys. The court explained: "The more views DMV.org attracts, the more money defendants earn from selling sponsored links and collecting fees for referring site visitors to vendors of traffic school courses, driver's ed lessons and other driver-related services. This seems like a legitimate and useful business, except that some visitors mistakenly believe the site is run by their state's department of motor vehicles (DMV)."

Courts generally presume commercial injury exists when defendant and plaintiff are direct competitors and defendant's misrepresentation has a tendency to mislead consumers. Competitors "vie for the same dollars from the same consumer group," and a misleading ad or website (remember, a website can be an advertisement) can upset their competitive positions.

As we will study in chapter 6, The Lanham Act permits "any person" to sue if he "believes that he . . . is *likely* to be damaged." Because a likely injury is far less certain than an actual injury, plaintiffs need not prove the latter to establish the commercial injury necessary to bring a Lanham Act suit.

In this case the court discussed several facets of the website that were likely to mislead consumers into thinking DMV.org was affiliated with a government agency. At the time plaintiffs filed their suit, anyone in California who googled (when did Google and Photoshop become verbs?) "dmv" or "drivers ed" would see sponsored listings for "ca.dmv.org" or "california.dmv.org," respectively. Clicking those listings would take the consumer to DMV.org. "While there's nothing inherently misleading about sponsored search results, they *can* mislead if they are named so as to give a false impression as to the likely sponsorship of the website to which they refer," said the court. The use of the "ca." and "california." prefixes obviously was designed to suggest an affiliation with the State of California. To make it worse, DMV.org's site design also mimicked an actual DMV site by copying slogans and state symbols, and by linking to web pages elsewhere on the site that helped consumers complete DMV-related transactions like applying for a license, registering a car and signing up for traffic school. While DMV.org did disclaim any connection with state DMVs, this disclaimer was easy to miss because it was displayed in a small type at the bottom of each page, where many consumers would never scroll.

Trafficschool.Com also introduced evidence of actual consumer confusion. They provided two declarations from individuals who confused DMV.org with an official DMV site and hundreds of e-mails sent by consumers who contacted DMV.org thinking it was their state's DMV. Some of these e-mails contained sensitive personal information that the typical consumer wouldn't share with a commercial website. Here's an example: "My boyfriend George [redacted] . . . got a ticket in South Carolina in 2006 . . . . Mr. [redacted] driver's license number is [redacted]. His date of birth is [redacted]. I have his social security number if needed, but I don't want to put all of his personal information on this e-mail if possible . . . . I was told by Central

Court for Lexington County in South Carolina that if we contacted the Arkansas DMV that y'all would be able to tell us what court this is in and where to pay the ticket."

Other e-mails were sent by law enforcement officials and state DMV employees who were similarly confused by DMV.org. For example, a Washington state trooper e-mailed DMV.org asking: "Dear Oregon DMV, I am currently involved in a DUI case in which a driver used his friends ID but I remember it having his picture. It is an Oregon ID in the name of [redacted]. I would like to see if I can get a copy of the picture/ID e-mailed to me for identification purposes. The DUI arrest occurred on September 16, 2006 in Snohomish County, WA."

Plaintiffs also produced evidence that two California cities, a private law firm in Texas and a number of newspapers mistakenly linked their websites to DMV.org instead of a state DMV website.

Civil Lawsuits

EarthLink Goes to Court

In *Earthlink Network, Inc.* v. *Cyber Promotions, Inc.*, BC 167502, Cal. Sup. Ct., March 30,1998, spam e-mail was the focus. EarthLink had charged Cyber Promotions with falsely labeling messages with EarthLink's addresses and clogging members' mailboxes with thousands of unwanted e-mails. Cyber Promotions settled the $2 million case, with the following provisions. In addition to writing a formal letter of apology to EarthLink and its members for the inconvenience it may have caused, Cyber Promotions was prohibited from:

1. Causing, authorizing, participating in, or intentionally or recklessly assisting or enabling others in the sending of any commercial or promotional messages or solicitations through e-mails to any EarthLink e-mail address without the express permission of the EarthLink subscriber. "Express permission" shall mean (1) written permission sent by some means other than e-mail; and/or (2) e-mail permission, if, and only if, prior to the transmission of the commercial or promotional message, the user allegedly granting permission affirmatively responds to a separate request for confirmation of the permission (i.e., the validity of the user's request is confirmed via a "three-way handshake").
2. Intentionally or recklessly assisting or enabling others in the use of any false or misleading reference to EarthLink, an EarthLink e-mail address, EarthLink equipment, or EarthLink's computer system or resources in the header of, or in connection with in any way, any electronic message or newsgroup posting.
3. Causing, authorizing, participating in, or intentionally or recklessly assisting or enabling others in the modification, disguise, elimination, or erasure of the identification of the originating address and/or header of or for any e-mail sent to an EarthLink subscriber.
4. The sale, offer or other distribution of any e-mail address of any EarthLink subscriber and/or any list of e-mail addresses that contains the address of any Earthlink subscriber.

Cyber Promotions would also be liable for up to $1 million if it violates the settlement agreement.

The Hotmail Case

Hotmail was owned by Microsoft (in 2013 Hotmail was rolled into Microsoft's Outlook browser) and provided free e-mail to hundreds of millions of subscribers. Every e-mail sent by a Hotmail subscriber automatically displayed a header depicting

Hotmail's domain name, "hotmail.com," and a footer depicting Hotmail's "signature" at the bottom of the e-mail, which read: "Get Your Private, Free E-mail at http://www.hotmail.com." To become a Hotmail subscriber, the consumer agreed to abide by a service agreement that specifically prohibited subscribers from using Hotmail's services to send unsolicited commercial bulk e-mail, or "spam," or to send obscene or pornographic messages.

Hotmail found out that several individuals were sending spam e-mails which contained Hotmail's return address to thousands of Internet users. The spam messages advertised pornography, bulk e-mailing software, and "get rich quick" schemes. Hotmail also discovered that a number of Hotmail accounts were created to collect responses to these e-mails and "bounced back" messages to a "drop box" whose contents were never opened, read, or responded to. These Hotmail accounts were used as return addresses instead of actual return addresses.

As a result, Hotmail was inundated with hundreds of thousands of misdirected responses, including complaints from Hotmail subscribers. The overwhelming number of e-mails took up a substantial amount of Hotmail's computer space, threatened to delay Hotmail's subscribers in sending and receiving e-mail, and resulted in significant costs to Microsoft in dealing with the problem. It also damaged Hotmail's reputation and goodwill. In fact, a hotmail.com e-mail address long ago became a mark of grandmas and other schemers. Asking someone to contact you at Hotmail was an invitation for ridicule.

Typical of the spamming that went on were the following that were stated in the complaint:

Hotmail discovered a spam e-mail message advertising pornographic material that was sent by ALS. While this spam originated from ALS and was transmitted through an e-mail provider other than Hotmail, ALS falsely designated a real Hotmail e-mail address as the point of origin. The e-mail address chosen for this purpose was "geri748@hotmail.com."

Hotmail discovered a number of spam e-mail messages advertising pornographic material that were sent by LCGM. While these spam e-mails originated from LCGM and were transmitted through an e-mail provider other than Hotmail, LCGM falsely designated a number of real Hotmail e-mail address as the points of origin. The e-mail address chosen for this purpose was "becky167@hotmail.com" [etc.].

Hotmail discovered a spam e-mail message advertising pornographic material that was sent by Moss. While this spam originated from Moss and was transmitted through an e-mail provider other than Hotmail, Moss falsely designated a real Hotmail e-mail address as the point of origin. The e-mail address chosen for this purpose was "rebecca_h19@hotmail.com."

Hotmail discovered a spam e-mail message advertising a cable descrambler kit that was sent by Palmer. While this spam originated from Palmer and was transmitted through an e-mail provider other than Hotmail, Palmer falsely designated two real Hotmail e-mail addresses as the points of origin. The e-mail addresses chosen for this purpose were "kelCA@hotmail.com" and "angiCA@hotmail.com."

Hotmail discovered a spam e-mail message advertising a service that matches people seeking cash grants that was sent by Financial. While this spam originated from Financial and was transmitted through an e-mail provider other than Hotmail, Financial falsely designated a real Hotmail e-mail address as the point of origin. The e-mail address chosen for this purpose was "order_desk66@hotmail.com."

Hotmail discovered a number of spam e-mail messages advertising pornography that were sent by Snow. While this spam originated from Snow and was transmitted through an e-mail provider other than Hotmail, Snow falsely designated several real Hotmail e-mail address as the point of origin. The e-mail addresses chosen for this purpose were "bettyharris123@hotmail.com," annharris123@hotmail.com, "cindyharris123@hotmail.com," "wilmasimpson@hotmail.com," "rw3570@hotmail.com;" "rw3560@hotmail.com," and "jw2244@hotmail.com."

The court in *Hotmail Corp.* v. *Van Money Pie, Inc.*, No. C98-20064 JW, 1998 U.S. Dist. LEXIS 10729, 47 U.S.P.Q.2D (BNA) 1020 (N.D. Cal., April 30, 1998), granted Hotmail a preliminary injunction for unfair competition under the Lanham Act and for violation of the Computer Fraud and Abuse Act (18 U.S.C. § 1030). The court found that the defendants' use of Hotmail's domain name and return address was likely to cause consumers to believe that the defendants were somehow associated with or sponsored by Hotmail.

Under the federal dilution statute, ownership of a famous mark and dilution of the distinctive quality of that mark, regardless of whether consumers are confused about the parties' goods, is actionable (15 U.S.C. § 1125(c)(1)). And, under the California dilution statute, actual injury or likelihood of confusion need not be shown; plaintiff need only show its business reputation is likely to be injured or the distinctive value of its mark is likely to be diluted (Cal. Bus. & Prof. Code § 14330).

Here, the court stated: "[T]he evidence supports a finding that plaintiff will likely prevail on its federal and state dilution claims and that there are at least serious questions going to the merits of these claims. First, there is sufficient evidence to lead to a finding that plaintiff's trademark is "famous" within the meaning of 15 U.S.C. § 1125(c)(1) and also that it is entitled to state dilution protection. Plaintiff's mark is distinctive, has been advertised and used extensively both nationally and internationally in connection with plaintiff's services, and has established considerable consumer recognition. Moreover, the use of identical marks by defendants who are sending e-mails to thousands of e-mail users across the country and the world through identical trade channels threatens to dilute the distinctiveness of plaintiff's trademark and threatens to harm plaintiff's business reputation."

The Computer Fraud and Abuse Act prohibits any person from knowingly causing the transmission of information which intentionally causes damage, without authorization, to a protected computer.

In supporting its computer fraud claim, the court stated:

> The evidence supports a finding that plaintiff will likely prevail on its Computer Fraud and Abuse Act claim and that there are at least serious questions going to the merits of this claim in that plaintiff has presented evidence of the following: that defendants knowingly falsified return e-mail addresses so that they included, in place of the actual sender's return address, a number of Hotmail addresses; that such addresses were tied to Hotmail accounts set up by defendants with the intention of collecting never-to-be-read consumer complaints and "bounced back" e-mails; that defendants knowingly caused this false information to be transmitted to thousands of e-mail recipients; that defendants took this action knowing such recipients would use the "reply to" feature to transmit numerous responses to the fraudulently created Hotmail accounts, knowing thousands of messages would be "bounced back" to Hotmail instead of to defendants, and knowing that numerous recipients of defendants' spam would e-mail complaints to Hotmail; that defendants took such actions knowing the risks caused thereby to Hotmail's computer system and online services, which include risks that Hotmail would be forced to withhold or delay the use of computer services to its legitimate subscribers; that defendants' actions caused damage to Hotmail; and that such actions were done by defendants without Hotmail's authorization.

Copyright Issues Applied to the Internet

In *Playboy Enterprise, Inc.* v. *Frena*, 839 F. Supp. 1552 (M.D. Fla. 1993), Playboy sued an online service provider because a subscriber of the service downloaded digital copies of copyrighted Playboy photographs.

The Court held the online service provider directly liable for the distribution of unauthorized copies on the service as well as the display of unauthorized copies to subscribers even though the provider did not have knowledge that the subscriber had downloaded the photographs.

The Court further stated that "[i]t does not matter that [the online service provider] may have been unaware of the copyright infringement . . . . Intent or knowledge is not an element of infringement, and thus even an innocent infringer is liable . . . ."

This decision seems to impose a next-to-impossible burden on an online service provider to screen all uploaded information and material. The problem is that an online service provider has no way of knowing whether the information or material is subject to copyright protection. The courts have justified imposing this heavy burden by relying on the fact that the Copyright Act gives courts the discretion to consider the innocent intent of the infringer in determining the amount of damages to be awarded.

Protection against Infringement

An online service provider may protect itself by having a written, signed contract with its subscribers. The contract should state that:

1. The subscriber acknowledges that the ISP does not regulate the content of its online service.
2. The subscriber acknowledges that the information it is downloading will be considered in the public domain.
3. The subscriber warrants that it has all rights necessary to submit such information it is downloading.
4. The ISP will not take any responsibility to determine what information is protected nor will it be responsible for the use of the information by other subscribers.

In addition, the contract should include an indemnity clause which requires the subscriber to indemnify the online service provider against actions brought by a third party alleging improper use, publication, distribution or display of the protected material. This is not absolute protection, but it should help the online service provider if a legal action is ever brought for posting copyrighted materials.

Another option is including a disclaimer on the front screen every time a subscriber logs on. This should also be used by online service providers who already have written contracts with their subscribers. The disclaimer should simply incorporate the elements listed above. However, this type of disclaimer offers much less protection than a written contract.

The Digital Millennium Copyright Act

In October of 1998 Congress passed the Digital Millennium Copyright Act (HR 2281, 17 USC 1), which was signed into law by President Clinton on October 28, 1998. The Act establishes limitations on the liability of Internet and online service providers for copyright violations by their subscribers, provided that certain conditions are satisfied. The Act immunizes an Internet or online service provider from claims for its storage of infringing materials on its system at the direction of the user of those materials. ISPs are also shielded from claims based on their referring or linking users to a site containing infringing materials. These limitations on liability do not apply, however, if the provider knew or had reason to know that the materials were infringing, derived a financial benefit from the infringing activity, or failed to remove the infringing materials expeditiously upon notice (box 5.2).

Box 5.2 The Digital Millennium Copyright Act

Section 512 of the Act states:

Limitations on liability relating to material online include:

(a) TRANSITORY DIGITAL NETWORK COMMUNICATIONS—A service provider shall not be liable for monetary relief, or, except as provided in subsection (j), for injunctive or other equitable relief, for infringement of copyright by reason of the provider's transmitting, routing, or providing connections for, material through a system or network controlled or operated by or for the service provider, or by reason of the intermediate and transient storage of that material in the course of such transmitting, routing, or providing connections, if

(1) the transmission of the material was initiated by or at the direction of a person other than the service provider;

(2) the transmission, routing, provision of connections, or storage is carried out through an automatic technical process without selection of the material by the service provider;

(3) the service provider does not select the recipients of the material except as an automatic response to the request of another person;

(4) no copy of the material made by the service provider in the course of such intermediate or transient storage is maintained on the system or network in a manner ordinarily accessible to anyone other than anticipated recipients, and no such copy is maintained on the system or network in a manner ordinarily accessible to such anticipated recipients for a longer period than is reasonably necessary for the transmission, routing, or provision of connections; and

(5) the material is transmitted through the system or network without modification of its content.

(b) SYSTEM CACHING:

(1) LIMITATION ON LIABILITY—A service provider shall not be liable for monetary relief, or, except as provided in subsection (j), for injunctive or other equitable relief, for infringement of copyright by reason of the intermediate and temporary storage of material on a system or network controlled or operated by or for the service provider in a case in which:

(A) the material is made available online by a person other than the service provider;

(B) the material is transmitted from the person described in subparagraph (A) through the system or network to a person other than the person described in subparagraph (A) at the direction of that other person; and

(C) the storage is carried out through an automatic technical process for the purpose of making the material available to users of the system or network who, after the material is transmitted as described in subparagraph (B), request access to the material from the person described in subparagraph (A), if the conditions set forth in paragraph (2) are met.

(2) CONDITIONS—The conditions referred to in paragraph (1) are that:

(A) the material described in paragraph (1) is transmitted to the subsequent users described in paragraph (1)(C) without modification to its content from the manner in which the material was transmitted from the person described in paragraph (1)(A);

(B) the service provider described in paragraph (1) complies with rules concerning the refreshing, reloading, or other updating of the material when specified by the person making the material available online in accordance with a generally accepted industry standard data communications protocol for the system or network through which that person makes the material available, except that this subparagraph applies only if those rules are not used by the person described in paragraph (1)(A) to prevent or unreasonably impair the intermediate storage to which this subsection applies.

Privacy Issues and the Internet

One of the major concerns of the Internet involves the amount of privacy protection consumers have when using the Internet. Especially when it involves children.

Former FTC Chairman Robert Pitofsky, before a House subcommittee on July 21, 1998, pointed out: "The Commission believes that, unless industry can demonstrate that it has developed and implemented broad-based and effective self-regulatory programs by the end of this year, additional governmental authority in this area would be appropriate and necessary." To date, however, few have come to pass.

Privacy issues regarding the Internet push some of the hottest buttons in today's society. Not just in the United States, but worldwide. The scope of this book is limited to those controls that are directed at advertising however. Almost all companies today have a website as part of their advertising and marketing function. In operating a website there are regulations that affect how it deals with privacy issues.

FTC Enforcement

GeoCities settled FTC charges that it misrepresented why it collected personal identifying information from children and adults. This was the first FTC case involving Internet privacy. Under the terms of a proposed consent order, GeoCities would be required to post on its site a clear and prominent privacy notice. Consumers would need to be notified of the information that was being collected and the purpose, who it will be disclosed to, and how to access and remove the information. GeoCities also would have to obtain parental consent before collecting information from children twelve and under.

Jodie Bernstein, then Director of the FTC Bureau of Consumer Protection, stated: "GeoCities misled its customers, both children and adults, by not telling the truth about how it was using their personal information."

Through an online registration process, GeoCities created a database that included e-mail and postal addresses, member interest areas, and demographics including income, education, gender, marital status, and occupation. GeoCities told consumers that its membership application form was used only to provide members the specific advertising offers and products or services they requested and that "optional" information (education level, income, marital status, occupation, and interests) would not be released without the member's permission. However, this personal identifying information of children and adults was released to third-party marketers. The FTC complaint also charges that GeoCities engaged in deceptive practices relating to its collection of information from children (*GeoCities*, CCH Trade Regulation Reports ¶ 24,485).

Children's Online Privacy Protection Act

Bill S. 2326 was introduced on July 17, 1998, and was adopted as part of the Omnibus Spending Bill that was approved by Congress. Moving quickly, the Children's Online Privacy Protection Act (COPPA) was signed by the President in October 1998. The Act took effect on April 21, 2000. The Act requires operators of websites (or online services) directed at children under thirteen to provide notice on the website of what personal information is collected, how the information will be used, and the disclosure practices for the information. The Act also requires that verifiable parental consent be obtained before collecting information (known as the "opt-in" requirement) from children under thirteen.

Personal information means individual information such as first and last name, home address, e-mail address, and social security number. A clearly labeled link to the notice of the site's children's information practices policy must be clearly and prominently placed (1) on the home page and (2) on every page where personal information is sought or collected from a child. If the website is a general audience site with a separate children's area, the site must post the link on the home page of the children's area.

The notice of children's information practices must contain specified information. The contact information for all of the website operators collecting or maintaining personal information must be included in the notice. The type of personal information that will be collected, the manner in which it will be collected, and how such information will be used must also be disclosed. The notice must state whether and for what purposes the personal information will be disclosed to third parties. In addition, it must be disclosed that parents are able to review the personal information collected from their children and prohibit further use or collection of such by the site and/or third parties. The notice must also state the procedures to follow. Finally, the notice must expressly inform parents that operators cannot condition a child's participation in an activity on the provision of more personal information than is reasonably necessary for the activity.

According to the Act, "verifiable parental consent" means any reasonable effort to ensure that a parent gets notice of the collection, use, and disclosure practices, and authorizes that collection, use, and disclosure. This must be done before any personal information is collected. The Act has not defined "reasonable effort," however. Yet, the FTC suggests some methods of satisfying this requirement. For example, the site could require a parent to print out a consent form and return it to the sponsor, or a toll-free number may be provided for the parent to call and confirm authorization.

There are several exemptions to the prior consent issue. It is not required where online contact information is used only one time in responding to a child, or where a child's or parent's online contact information is requested only for the purpose of obtaining parental consent or notice under the Act, and it is not maintained. Prior consent is also not required where online contact information is gathered more than once from a child in response to the child and is not used beyond that purpose so long as after the initial response to the child, the service uses reasonable efforts to provide notice to the parents that the information is being collected, how it is being used, and provide an opportunity for the parent to stop its use.

If a website collects information from a child who is under thirteen (without prior verifiable parental consent), in order to respond to a specific request from the child more than once, the operator must make reasonable efforts to ensure that the parent receives notice immediately after the first response. The notice must include all the information required in the website's information collection practices notice. In addition, the service must state that information has been collected from the child, that the service has contacted the child once, and that it needs to contact the child again to respond to the child's request. The notice must also provide the parent with the opportunity to request that the operator cease using the information and delete it. The information collected in this manner cannot be used for any purpose other than to send the parental notice and to respond to the child's request. Until verifiable consent is obtained, the website cannot respond to any more requests from the child. However, if the parent fails to respond to the notice, the information may be used for the purpose stated in the notice.

The act also requires that a service provide to a parent whose child has given personal information a description of the specific types of personal information gathered from the child and a reasonable means for the parent to obtain that information. Under the "opt-out" rule, any parent may, at any time, refuse to permit further use of the information or future collection of information.

For more information, see the FTC website at: http://www.ftc.gov/ enforcement/rules/rulemaking-regulatory-reform-proceedings/childrens-online-privacy-protection-rule

Internet Search Engines and Metatags

Quite simply, a metatag is a word or phrase that is embedded in the hidden source code of a website. When a person types a phrase into a search engine (such as Google or Yahoo) the engine uses an algorithm to search the Internet looking for web pages containing those particular keywords. The greater the number of times a term appears in metatags and in the text of the webpage itself, the greater the chance that a search engine will be listed higher in the search results. We've all done this. For years search engine optimization, or SEO, has been an important step in marketing a company's website. The problem here occurs when one company uses the trademark of their competitor in their metatags.

Let me be really clear though, use of another's trademark as a metatag is not the same as using another's trademark as your domain name. The point being, it's clearly illegal to use another company's trademark or trade name as your website domain name.

Currently, the legality of unauthorized use of trademarks in metatags is not clear. The area of metatag usage comes out of trademark law, which we will look at in detail in chapter 10. A claim of trademark infringement requires a showing that another's mark was used in commerce and that that use likely confused consumers as to which company was actually selling that service or those goods. Since a metatag isn't visible on a web page, courts haven't agreed whether a metatag is "used or displayed in the sale or advertising of a service rendered in commerce" or "placed in any manner" on a good transported in commerce.

Courts and legal analysts have taken different—and often contradictory—approaches regarding the use of trademark terms in metatags, making the doctrine something of an ongoing quagmire. While the courts are starting to move toward some agreement there is still a very decided split in decisions. The use of trademarked terms in metatags presents a difficult proposition for marketers and the courts. While metatag use does not seem analogous to traditional trademark use, and search engines do not seem analogous to supermarket shelves, it is not clear that trademark law should be completely inapplicable. In attempting to understand metatags and find their place within trademark law, courts and commentators have employed metaphors. The use of these metaphors to work through novel legal claims is not bad in and of itself. But, many of the metaphors that have been used for metatags are considerably off the mark and very outdated. The result is that these improper metaphors are being used to support questionable rulings. And the battle rages on.

Some argue that the proper metaphor for a keyword metatag is a voluntary consumer questionnaire. And the proper metaphor for a search engine listing is a bin. And that the proper metaphor for a description metatag is a product label.

To be precise there are two different forms of metatags, but both involve code that is hidden in the invisible part of a web page. It is invisible to the viewer, but readable by search engines. The "keyword metatag" allows web designers to code-in relevant search terms that would be recognized by search engines and directories. The keyword metatag, in theory, increases search engine accuracy by offering information about the contents of a site. Search engines also read "description metatags." The description metatags allow authors to give a brief description of the contents of their website pages in plain language.

The purpose of these metatags is to communicate with search engines that index the web. Just like traditional road maps, the web needs directories and search engines to aid travelers through cyberspace. Unlike their counterparts, however, the cartographers of the web face substantial obstacles. Every day their geography drastically expands and distorts. And, as a result, courts are making rulings on technology that is long past by the time decisions are rendered.

There are essentially two search engine models that index the web, though almost all search engines these days partake of both models. The first model, commonly associated with Yahoo, is human-centered. Although Yahoo has mechanical search engine capabilities, a methodical, labor-intensive process primarily builds its directory of websites. Companies such as Bing, AltaVista, and Google exemplify the second model. In their search engine model, massive computer databases continually search and read as many web pages as they can manage. These web indexing programs are known as "spiders," "robots," and "crawlers."

As I said earlier, the crucial factor therefore becomes search engine "ranking," or in other words, how high up in a list of returned results a particular site listing appears. Most search engines attempt to rank sites by relevance, but the formula for determining relevance varies by search engine. In the "no there, there" of the web, every site is equally accessible if a user can locate it. As a result, the fight to be located is fierce.

The Battle over Metaphors

Building metaphors is a natural reaction to new situations, and discussion of the Internet has always been filled with metaphors. The metaphors that have been used for metatags are also less than perfect. Some courts and commentators have referred to metatags as "signposts" and "billboards" that direct traffic on the information superhighway. Others have referred to metatags as "invisible infringers." These metaphors evince confusion: How can a signpost be invisible?

So far, the only federal court to address metatag issues in detail was the Ninth Circuit in *Brookfield Communications* v. *West Coast Entertainment Corp.*, 174 F.3d 1036, 1064 (9th Cir. 1999). In that case, Brookfield and West Coast, two film industry companies, were in litigation over rights to the mark "moviebuff." The court enjoined West Coast video from using "moviebuff" as a metatag, using a billboard metaphor to describe metatags. The court felt that while metatags are not well suited to standard infringement analysis, they could infringe by causing "initial interest confusion" among the public. The court said:

> Suppose West Coast's competitor (blockbuster for example) puts up a billboard on a highway reading— "West Coast Video: 2 miles ahead at Exit 7"—where West Coast is really located at Exit 8 but Blockbuster is located at Exit 7. Customers looking for West Coast's store will pull off at Exit 7 and drive around looking for it. Unable to locate West Coast, but seeing the Blockbuster store right by the highway entrance, they may simply rent there.

This discussion might be persuasive if metatags were billboards, but simply they are not. Problems with the metaphor were evident in the landmark case of *Playboy* v. *Netscape*, 55 F.Supp. 2d 1070 (C.D. Cal. 1999), aff'd, 202 F.3d 278 (9th Cir. 1999). The suit concerned the practice (common among search engine companies) of "keying" search terms to advertising banners. The search engine programmed results pages to display a particular set of advertisement banners whenever "playboy" was entered as a search term. In its complaint, Playboy cited Brookfield and alleged that these banners constituted infringement and dilution of the Playboy mark.

The judge found that the use of the term "playboy" was noncommercial and did not constitute infringement or dilution of Playboy's mark. In order to do this, she was forced to grapple with the Brookfield billboard and somehow reshape it to fit the decision. The court's opinion stated: "Here, the analogy is quite unlike that of a devious placement of a road sign bearing false information. This case presents a scenario more akin to a driver pulling off the freeway in response to a sign that reads 'Fast Food Burgers' to find a well-known fast food burger restaurant, next to which stands a billboard that reads: 'Better Burgers: 1 Block Further.'"

Though the final ruling in *Playboy* v. *Netscape* makes sense, the supporting logic has nothing to do with the billboard metaphors bandied about by both courts.

Since courts continue to use metaphors in order to rule on metatags, more accurate and useful metaphors may be the best solution. It has been suggested that a better metaphor for a search engine would be a thrift store with very large bins—the kind of bins that some people might rummage through for hours in search of some rare bargain buried near the bottom. Each of these metaphorical discount bins is marked with a search term, such as "Nike" or "Amy Pascal+Sony" or "How do I get to Albuquerque?" The bins are filled with everything that could be vaguely related to the keyword or phrase. The thrift store tries its best to make sure that the most relevant objects stay on top, but this is a professed goal much more than an actual state of affairs.

Using Metatags in a Website

No discussion of metatag litigation would be complete without mentioning one of the best-known and longest-litigated metatag battles, *Playboy Enters.* v. *Welles*, 7 F. Supp. 2d 1098 (S.D. Cal. 1998), aff'd 162 F.3d 1169 (9th Cir. 1998).

The Welles decision involves competitor and editorial use of both keyword and description metatags. The Welles case also demonstrates that at least some courts are searching for ways to limit the ability of trademark owners to control the use of particular words in metatags.

Terri Welles was Playboy's Playmate of the Year for 1981. In June 1997, she opened up a website "www.terriwelles.com." The site contained information about Welles and some nude photographs. Throughout the site were references to *Playboy* magazine. In addition, "PMOY "81" was repeated throughout the background of the page, and the title of the page was "Terri Welles - Playboy Playmate of the Year 1981." The site did, however, bear a disclaimer that read, "This site is neither endorsed, nor sponsored by, nor affiliated with Playboy Enterprises, Inc. PLAYBOY, PLAYMATE OF THE YEAR and PLAYMATE OF THE MONTH are registered trademarks of Playboy Enterprises, Inc." Most importantly, Welles used the words "Playboy" and "Playmate" in both her keyword and description metatags. When Playboy unsuccessfully attempted to convince Welles to let Playboy host her website, Playboy sued Welles claiming state and federal trademark infringement, dilution, and "passing off" claims.

In the first round of litigation, Judge Judith Keep denied Playboy's motion for a preliminary injunction against Welles, upholding Welles' use of the Playboy marks throughout the site under the "fair use" doctrine. The court stated that Welles "was and is the 'Playmate of the Year for 1981'" and that, as such, the title had "become part of [her] identity." Moreover, Welles had "minimized her references to Playboy on her website" and had "not attempted to trick consumers into believing that they [were] viewing a Playboy-endorsed website." On the issue of Welles's metatags, the court stated that Welles had "used the terms Playboy and Playmate as metatags for her site so that those using search engines on the web [could] find her website if they were looking for a Playboy Playmate." The court addressed the issue of metatags further:

> Much like the subject index of a card catalog, the metatags give the websurfer using a search engine a clearer indication of the content of a website. The use of the term Playboy is not an infringement because it references not only her identity as a "Playboy Playmate of the Year 1981," but also it may also reference the legitimate editorial uses of the term Playboy contained in the text of defendant's website.

When the Welles case came again before the district court, on a motion for summary judgment by Welles, the *Brookfield* hypothetical had become a reality, as the Welles website now had a substantial editorial section devoted to the Playboy case. The top of Welles's main page, in fact, bore the heading "Playboy vs. Welles: Playboy Sues Playmate." Ironically, Playboy's suit against Welles contributed to making Welles's use of the Playboy mark legitimate. The court awarded summary judgment to Welles and noted that "[Welles] has links to and references about articles regarding the litigation on her website, and sometimes makes critical, albeit editorial, comments about Playboy."

The court also found no evidence that Welles intended to divert Plaintiff's customers to her website by trading on Playboy's goodwill. Summarizing its discussion of the metatag issue, the court quoted Justice Oliver Wendell Holmes: "When the mark is used in a way that does not deceive the public we see no such sanctity in the word as to prevent its being used to tell the truth."

Through not a result of the case, Terri Welles eventually shut down her website on October 31, 2006.

The Welles opinion shows the uneasiness that some courts feel about granting rights in keyword metatags to trademark owners, even in the case where a direct competitor is using a famous mark without license. This uneasiness has led two courts to suggest an approach to keyword metatags that might be called a "dictionary doctrine." Put simply, the dictionary doctrine would appear to protect the keyword metatag use of any word that appears in a dictionary. The theory behind this seems to be that the necessary descriptive words of the English language can be found in dictionaries, and those which are not in dictionaries can only describe a trademark owner's product. It is encouraging to see courts trying to find more breathing space for keyword metatags, but this approach is probably not ideal either.

Metatags in Other Keyword Search Formats

Google's AdWords program enabled advertisers on their site to trigger display of their ads when users performed a matching Google keyword search. Based on Google policy, advertisers may trigger their ads on arbitrary keywords, including trademarked keywords that they do not own. This allowed competitors of American Blinds to place their ads alongside American Blind's ads when a user searched for "American Blind," "American Blinds." or "Decoratetoday"—all of which are registered trademarks of American Blind. Google places ads in specially marked "Sponsored Links" sections of its webpage to set them off from other web content, and prohibits unauthorized trademark use in the ad content. But despite requests from American Blind and others, Google refused to discontinue its use of trademarks to trigger the ads.

In *Google Inc.* v. *American Blind & Wallpaper Factory, Inc.*, 2007 U.S. Dist. LEXIS 32450 (2007), American Blinds alleged that Google sold these terms to American Blinds's competitors. Google acknowledges that it does this and has a stated procedure for handling trademark complaints. That procedure states: "When we receive a complaint from a trademark owner, we will only investigate whether the advertisements at issue are using terms corresponding to the trademarked item in the advertisement's content. If they are, we will require the advertiser to remove the trademarked term from the content of the ad and prevent the advertiser from using the trademarked term in ad content in the future. *Please note that we will not disable keywords in response to a trademark complaint.*"

American Blinds provided no evidence that contradicts Google's description of the placement and identification of sponsored links. The Court concluded that Google's use of American Blind's trademarks was a use under the Lanham Act, for two reasons. First it was bound by the precedent set in *Playboy* v. *Netscape*, where Netscape's practice of keying searches to trademarked terms was deemed a use of Playboy's marks. The court notes that although use was not explicitly established in the Playboy ruling, the Playboy court focused heavily on the question of confusion, thereby implicitly signaling that use was established. Second, the Court pointed out that precedent set in other circuits also agree that keying is use. For example, in *800-JR Cigar, Inc.* v. *GoTo.com, Inc.* the court concluded that "by accepting bids from those competitors of JR desiring to pay for prominence in search results, GoTo trades on the value of the marks," and hence "uses" the mark as defined in the Lanham Act.

This Court concluded, as did the courts in *GEICO, 800-JR Cigar, Humble Abode, Edina Realty,* and *Wentworth,* that the sale of trademarked terms in the AdWords program "is a use in commerce for the purposes of the Lanham Act. While the Second Circuit's decision in *1-800 Contacts* and the subsequent district court decisions may cause the Ninth Circuit to consider this issue explicitly, the lengthy discussions of likelihood of confusion in *Brookfield* and *Playboy* would have been unnecessary in the absence of actionable trademark use. Accordingly, while Google's analogies to trademark infringements outside the digital realm are attractive, the Court will deny Google's motion for summary judgment to the extent that it is brought on the basis of an asserted absence of trademark use."

This case explored all aspects of trademark law and infringement issues and related them to keywords and metatag use. We will delve into the intricate details of trademark law in chapter 10.

BROAD ISSUES RELATING TO ADVERTISING

PART II

Comparative Advertising 6

*Imagination is one of the last remaining legal means you
have to gain an unfair advantage over your competition.*
—*Ed McCabe*

The year was 1949, June to be exact. At 350 Madison Avenue in New York, Ned
Doyle, Maxwell Dane, and William Bernbach, along with thirteen employees, started
an ad agency with a simple philosophy of Bernbach's: "Don't be slick. Tell the
truth." Bernbach had a clear and deliberate approach to advertising. He felt that
most advertising was dull and failed to motivate the consumer. "Business is spending
money for advertising," he would say, "and is achieving boredom with typical American efficiency."

Doyle Dane Bernbach has produced its share of memorable ad campaigns over
the years since its inception. In the beginning, the agency took on prestigious clients
of the day like Ohrbach's, Levy's Rye Bread, Polaroid, El Al Airlines and in 1959,
Volkswagen. Doyle Dane Bernbach created the Volkswagen campaign that stands as
one of the industry's best.

Then, in the fall of 1962, Avis moved its $1.5 million account from McCann-
Erickson to Doyle Dane Bernbach. At that time Hertz was the car-rental leader and
pulling way ahead of Avis (Today, Enterprise Rent-A-Car is the largest in the United
States.). So, Doyle Dane Bernbach gathered art director Helmut Krone and copywriter Paula Green together. They came away with the first of a new series of Avis ads
(see box 6.1).

Before the client was shown the new ad, Bernbach commissioned a consumer
survey to pretest the ad. It scored very poorly. Nonetheless, Bernbach sold the client
on the ad. Two years later Avis had increased its market share by 28 percent.

While Avis never mentioned who it tried harder than, everyone knew. Hertz was
the number one car rental company at the time. Because of this, the Avis ads have
become acknowledged as the first major comparative advertising campaign . . . even
before direct comparative advertising was allowed.

While the Avis campaign might have been the first comparative ad campaign,
many more have followed, and they have run the gamut. My personal favorite started
life in the late 1970s. The commercial depicted a small, bulbous store owner standing in his electric light bulb store. On the phone he proclaims: "If those bulbs aren't

here tomorrow morning, I am out of business!" In the next scene, Dingbat Air Freight pulls up in front of the store, two days late. The courier scurries around frantically looking at the front door. A sign across the front of the store reads: "OUT OF BUSINESS."

Federal Express took on the giants of air freight, Emery, United Parcel, and even the United States Postal Service. Its slogan, "Twice as good as the best in the business," became fighting words for Federal Express. The company started in 1971, and promptly fell $30 million into debt. But by 1983 Federal Express (now simply known as FedEx) had rebounded and broken the $1 billion mark in annual revenue. Those early Federal Express ads, created by Ally & Gargano Advertising, were classics of comparative advertising. They did the job and did it very well.

In recent years, comparative advertising has flourished.

Pepsi and Coke have been taking aim at each other since the 1970s, but the most widely remembered advertising battle between the two was called the "Pepsi Challenge" in 1975. Pepsi paraded around its taste test victories for years. This prompted Coca-Cola's response including the horrific New Coke debacle in 1986. Since then, these two marketing giants have continued the battle into all media from TV to social media.

The two fast food giants Burger King and McDonalds have taken shots at each other for decades. In 2009, Burger King's "Whopper Virgins" campaign put the two brands' signature products (The Whopper and Big Mac) to a taste test featuring people in remote places around the world.

Then there's the classic battle between Mac and PC. It all started in 2006 with the "Get A Mac" campaign depicting the eternal Mac versus PC battle. Ads featuring Apple's benchmark all-white background with actor, Justin Long, presenting "Hello, I'm a Mac," and actor John Hodgman, presenting himself as "And I'm a PC."

Then there's the decade-old rivalry between Xbox and PlayStation. In October 2013 Microsoft's Xbox One and Sony's PlayStation 4 were about to be released. To combat Sony, Microsoft released their "Invitation" ad to promote the Xbox One. Even though Microsoft enlisted the help of soccer star Steven Gerrard, Star Trek actor Zachary Quinto, and others, Sony's ad still generated twice the amount of hype.

The feud between Mercedes-Benz and Jaguar heated up in 2013. Mercedes-Benz started a viral ad campaign showcasing their Intelligent Drive Magic Body Control (which ensures optimum driving comfort). The message they wanted to get across was "What do chickens and Mercedes-Benz have in common? Stability at all times." Three months later, Jaguar challenged Mercedes-Benz's chicken ad with their "Jaguar vs. Chicken" ad. Their concept of a chicken showed its stability throughout the video but with a twist at the end: "Magic Body Control? We prefer cat-like reflexes, don't you?"

Then there are competitors Microsoft and Google. Constantly looking for angles to best one another, in 2013, Google produced an ad entitled "Chrome: Now Everywhere" to promote their browser. Two months later, Microsoft came up with their retort campaign entitled "Scroogled" cautioning Chrome users that Google is breaching their privacy. Microsoft parodied Google Chrome's ad by responding with an ad entitled "Microsoft Internal Google Chrome Bouncing Ball Now Everywhere," claiming that Chrome tracks everything they do. By late 2013, Microsoft's "Scroogled" campaign even sold merchandise with anti-Google messages. Google responded, saying "Microsoft's latest venture comes as no surprise; competition in the wearables space is really heating up." Google proposed that, while Microsoft was busy trying to sell t-shirts, Google was hard at work on Google Glass.

As we've seen in the examples above, when a company compares its product to another, both are identified either by name, implication, or reputation. The use of another company's identity involves the use of its image, trademark, or trade name. If this use is truthful, honest, and accurate the law allows products to compare themselves. On the other hand, if Bunko Company compares its product as being superior to Binko's product and a deception results, the image and therefore value of Binko's trademark can suffer. As we will see in chapter 10, a company's trademark is of great value, and can be protected by its owner under the law.

Therefore, comparative advertising is based on trademark law. In fact, deceptive comparative advertising is controlled by a section of the Trademark Act, which we'll delve into in this chapter. You may be asking why this type of false advertising falls under the Trademark Act. Simply because when one company compares its product to another company's, it is actually comparing one brand (or brand name) against another. And a brand is based upon the company's trademark.

Under this law there is nothing illegal about comparing a product to that of a competitor, in fact it's encouraged, unless a deception is created. When this happens, there are basically two avenues of court action for victims. One is under federal law: Section 43(a) of the Lanham Act (15 U.S.C., Section 1125(a)). The other is under state law: Antidilution statutes. We examine both in this chapter.

The Development of Comparative Advertising

Today, comparative advertising bombards the consumer. But this hasn't always been the case. For the most part, comparative ads were not used prior to the 1970s. One main reason was that mentioning a competitor's name gave recognition to it and, in effect, free publicity. For this reason, major companies rarely had any interest in comparative ads. These companies felt that nothing was to be gained from mentioning competitors.

Many companies also felt that showing a competitor in a bad light would create consumer sympathy for the competitor, thereby causing consumers to buy its products. As a result, companies did not want to be pictured as a "big bully picking on the little kid."

Taking part in comparative advertising was also considered by many advertising agencies to be unethical, hitting below the belt so to speak. Many advertisers and their agencies also shied away from this practice for moral reasons. The main deterrent, however, was that the FTC and the television networks would not allow comparative ads.

There was a concern over the use of advertisements that compared products. Until 1972 two of the television networks and some major print publications banned comparative ads altogether. But in 1972 the FTC came out in favor of direct comparative ads, and the media changed its stance and accepted comparative advertisements. The FTC proclaimed that by having the ability to compare the features of various products, the consumer could make a more informed and intelligent purchasing decision, as long as the comparison was fair and accurate. But, as the bard would tell us, therein lies the rub.

The FTC Policy Statement established the commission's position on comparative advertising. The commission has supported the use of brand comparisons where the bases of comparison are clearly identified. Comparative advertising, when truthful and nondeceptive, is a source of important information to consumers that assists them in making rational purchase decisions. Comparative advertising encourages product improvement and innovation, and can lead to lower prices in the marketplace (S. Kanwit, *Regulatory Manual Series*, Federal Trade Commission, Section 22.17 n. 13 (1985)).

Suave Shampoo's comparative advertising is a good example of the FTC's position. Ads for Suave compared it to other leading brands and claimed that Suave performed as well, but at half the price. The consumer benefited because that person could purchase a product that would do the same job at a lower cost. Because of its campaign, Suave Shampoo increased its sales from $10 million to $50 million in just four years.

Comparative advertising also contributed to a 20 percent increase in sales in one month, and 31 percent increase annually for Wendy's Restaurants. Wendy's superb 1984 "Where's the Beef?" campaign compared its single to McDonald's Big Mac and Burger King's Whopper.

Wendy's debuted its now-iconic "Where's the Beef?" commercial, featuring Clara Peller as an old lady demanding more meat from her fast-food hamburger. And a classic 1980s catchphrase was born. The ad, the brainchild of agency Dancer Fitzgerald Sample, featured three white-haired grannies examining a burger—with a tiny patty and a huge bun. While the other two women admired the "big, fluffy bun," Peller demanded: "Where's the beef?" The catchphrase was a sharp jab at competitors Burger King and McDonalds, allowing Wendy's to trumpet the fact that their burgers had more beef than the Whopper or Big Mac.

The phrase became part of our lexicon when it made its way into the 1984 presidential campaign as Walter Mondale queried "Where's the Beef?" to attack Gary Hart's lack of substance during the Democratic primary.

Comparative advertising can have positive benefits for both the consumer and the advertiser, but it must be fair, truthful, and accurate. Otherwise it can be a dangerous instrument. This is why the FTC and the courts keep a very watchful eye on comparative ads.

The television networks, to help assure truthful comparative advertising, have established guidelines for advertisers to follow as well. Included in these guidelines are the requirements for comparative advertising. A list of comparative advertising guideline sources for the major networks are listed in the Index of Sources for this book.

Before we get into the details of the Lanham Act, it's important to keep in mind that there are basically two forms of comparative ads as you read through the balance of this chapter. The most obvious form includes ads that specifically name the competitor and the product. The second form of comparative ad is more subtle. It does not name the competitor, but rather implies it. The Avis ad campaign discussed earlier falls into this area because Avis does not name the competitor, but the implication is understood by everyone; there's no doubt that it's Hertz.

The Lanham Act

The federal government has developed a policing resource through private court action that can overcome the inherent drawbacks to an FTC suit for deception. Section 5 of the FTC Act allows the government to sue companies for deceptive advertising. And, like a Section 5 claim, comparative advertising complaints do also involve a deception. But, under the Lanham Act, the deceptions are specifically through comparison of one company (or its product) to another.

The Lanham Act allows one company to sue another company directly for damages due to deception and also serves as a way of avoiding the red tape, time, and expense of an FTC action. However, to qualify under the Lanham Act, the deceptive claim must involve a comparison of products. The Lanham Act provides for private litigation for "all actions...without regard to the amount in controversy or to... the citizenship of the parties" (Section 39 of the Lanham Act, 15 U.S.C. Section 1125(a)).

Congress passed Section 43(a) of the Lanham Act in 1946 providing: "Any person who shall . . . use in connection with any goods . . . any false description or representation, including words or other symbols tending falsely to describe or represent the same, and shall cause such goods or services to enter into commerce . . . shall be liable to a civil action by . . . *any person who believes that he is or is likely to be damaged* by the use of any such false description or representation." (Emphasis added.)

The real power here is in the phrase, "believes that he is or is likely to be damaged." The important word is "likely." Unlike many other areas of law, the Lanham Act does not require that proof of actual damage be shown, only that damage is likely. This is a very broad concept, which gives the act tremendous strength.

Another benefit to the Lanham Act is expressed in the phrase "any person." This means Section 43(a) actions are available not only to companies who are in competition, but individual consumers as well. For this reason, advertisers must be very aware of the Lanham Act and its provisions. The reasons a company may decide not to sue a competitor, even if it is the victim of a deceptive comparison, usually won't apply to the consumer. Deceived consumers, now, are a concern to advertisers.

The courts originally placed severe limitations on actions brought under Section 43(a) of the Lanham Act. As we have seen before, it takes time for courts to adjust to new legislation. Just as water seeks its own level, laws also need a period of adjustment to find their level in society. For example, the courts initially refused to act unless thirty or more cases were reported against an advertiser. However, all this changed in 1954 when the Lanham Act found its level as a result of the following case.

In the 1950s, L'Aiglon Apparel manufactured and sold a distinctively styled ladies dress for $17.95. In its advertisements, L'Aiglon pictured its dress along with the price. This combination of picture and price became very identifiable with the public at the time.

Lana Lobel, a retailer, sold a different dress of much lower quality. Lobel advertised its dress in a national magazine for the price of $6.95, available through mail order. The Lobel ad showed an actual photographic reproduction of the L'Aiglon dress. This fraudulently represented to the buying public that the L'Aiglon dress was being sold at $6.95—a representation that was not true.

Lobel's ads provoked L'Aiglon to sue in *L'Aiglon Apparel, Inc.* v. *Lana Lobel Inc.*, 214 F.2d 649 (3rd Cir. 1954). L'Aiglon alleged that two forms of damage existed. First, Lobel's misrepresentation "caused some trade to be diverted" from L'Aiglon to Lobel. And, second, other trade was lost by L'Aiglon because of the inaccurate impression given to the public that L'Aiglon had been unfairly selling a dress worth only $6.95 for $17.95.

The resulting lawsuit was filed under Section 43(a) of the Lanham Act. And, the court gave a new and clear interpretation for future cases to follow.

The court said: "It seems to us that Congress has defined a statutory civil wrong of false representation of goods in commerce and has given a broad class of suitors injured or likely to be injured by such wrong the right to relief in the federal courts."

This case interpreted the Lanham Act to mean that a single individual or company could bring suit. The earlier requirement that there be a minimum of thirty victims before a suit could be initiated was abolished. L'Aiglon won its case against Lobel and helped establish the Lanham Act as a versatile tool against deceptive comparative advertising.

The Trademark Law Revision Act of 1988

On October 19, 1988, Congress passed the Trademark Law Revision Act of 1988. Although the 1988 act deals primarily with trademark matters, it also changed comparative advertising law in several respects. Certain changes may prove significant, but whether they will actually have a material affect on advertising litigation remains an open issue (box 6.2).

Box 6.2   The Trademark Law Revision Act of 1988

Section 43(a) of the Lanham Act has been amended to read:

(a) Any person who, on or in connection with any goods or services, or any container for goods, uses in commerce any word, term, name, symbol, or device, or any combination thereof, or any false designation of origin, false or misleading description of fact, or false or misleading representation of fact, which:

(1) is likely to cause confusion, or to cause mistake, or to deceive as to the affiliation, connection, or association of such person with another person, or as to the origin, sponsorship, or approval of his or her goods, services, or commercial activities by another person, or

(2) in commercial advertising or promotion, misrepresents the nature, characteristics, qualities, or geographic origin of his or her or another person's goods, services, or commercial activities, shall be liable in a civil action by any person who believes that he or she is or is likely to be damaged by such act.

As amended, section 43(a) will make illegal any advertising that disparages "another person's goods, services, or commercial activities." This change was intended to circumvent decisions in cases holding that section 43(a) extended only to false statements concerning the advertiser's own products and did not apply to claims that merely disparaged the products of another.

Disparagement (often referred to as trade libel or injurious falsehood) is a false and deliberate attack on the advertiser's product. This disparagement tends to diminish the respect, confidence or esteem in the product that is attacked. Disparagement exists where the quality of the advertiser's product is impugned, and violates the Lanham Act. While this is a new element in section 43(a), it is one that the advertiser must be aware of.

Another change to section 43(a) was its application to false representations pertaining to, among other things, the "commercial activities" of the advertiser or of another person. Section 43(a) previously applied only to false representations pertaining to the "inherent quality or characteristics" of the defendant's "goods." After the 1988 amendment, however, the section applies to false representations pertaining to any commercial activities."

Failure to Disclose in Comparative Advertising In connection with the 1988 amendment of section 43(a) of the Lanham Act, Congress considered including a section that made actionable a failure to disclose. The section was eventually not included in Section 43(a) and the Senate report stated: "To respond to concerns that it could be misread to require that all facts material to a consumer's decision to purchase a product or service be contained in each advertisement...the committee does not through the deletion indicate that it condones deceptive advertising, whether by affirmative misrepresentations or material omission, and leaves to the courts the task of further developing and applying this principle under section 43(a)." *Gillette Co. v. Norelco Consumer Products Co.*, 946 F. Supp. 115, 132 (D. Mass. 1996) (CCH 1996-2 Trade Cases 171,657).

For example, in *McNeilab, Inc. v. American Home Products Corp.*, 501 F. Supp. 517, 532 (S.D.N.Y. 1980), the court, in interpreting an alleged omission in an advertisement under the Lanham Act, stated "a failure to inform consumers of something, even something that they should know, is not *per se* a misrepresentation actionable under Section 43(a) of the Lanham Act."

Under state law, failure to disclose a fact may or may not be false advertising, depending on the particular state law. For example, in two cases that involved a claim by consumers that AT&T failed to disclose its practice of rounding up to the next full minute the cost of long distance telephone service, a New York court held that the failure to disclose was not actionable under New York law, while a California court held that AT&T's omission was false advertising under California law.

The Federal Trademark Dilution Act of 1995 We will discuss the Dilution Act in detail in chapter 10 on trademark. While literal trademark cases are where this act will have the most impact, it will nonetheless spill into the comparative advertising realm. In an effort to confront First Amendment concerns, the Dilution Act explicitly exempts certain trademark uses from liability. Congress carved out "fair use" of a mark in comparative advertising, "noncommercial" use of a mark, and news reporting and commentary from the universe of actionable uses.

While the following case was decided under a state dilution statute, it shows the reasoning of how the Dilution Act can impact comparative advertising directly.

State Dilution Actions Here's an example of a case that was decided under state dilution statutes. In *Deere & Co. v. MTD Prod., Inc.*, 41 F.3d 39, 32 U.S.P.Q. 2d 1936 (2nd Cir. 1994), the court found that New York's Anti-Dilution statute applies to situations where a competitor's alteration of a company's well-known trademark does not necessarily result in the blurring or tarnishment of the mark.

Deere owns a trademark for a deer design (Deere Logo). MTD, the defendant, manufactures and sells lawn tractors that compete with products sold by Deere & Company. MTD ran an advertising campaign in which the Deere Logo was depicted in unflattering ways. In one of the commercials, the deer was running in fear, while being chased by a dog and an MTD tractor. Deere brought suit under the New York Anti-Dilution statute.

The district court ignored the federal trademark infringement claim that was part of the suit and ruled that the plaintiff had demonstrated a probability of prevailing on its state dilution count under "dilution by blurring." The district court issued a preliminary injunction limited strictly to activities within New York state.

The Second Circuit affirmed the district court's finding of a likelihood of dilution, but for different reasons. The Second Circuit did not believe that the defendant's use of the Deere Logo gave rise to a likelihood of dilution by blurring because such use posed a slight, if any, risk of impairing the identification of Deere's mark with its products. The court also did not think that such use constituted dilution by tarnishment since, according to the court, tarnishment is usually found where a mark is depicted in a context of sexual activity, obscenity, or illegal activity.

The Second Circuit found that the New York Anti-Dilution statute includes an undefined cause of action which protects trademark owners from attempts by others to increase sales of competing products by altering and satirizing the trademark. According to the court, defendant's use of the Deere Logo fell within the proscribed range since it altered a well-known mark for the sole purpose of promoting a competing product rather than to make a social comment for its own sake.

The court did note that a seller of commercial products may, without violating the New York Anti-Dilution statute, use a competitor's mark to identify the competitor's product in a comparative advertisement. Provided "the mark is not altered, such use serves the beneficial purpose of imparting factual information about the relative merits of competing products and poses no risk of diluting the selling power of the competitor's mark." In addition, a satirist may lawfully use another's mark in a parody to make a point of social commentary, so long as the satirist is only selling the publication that contains the parody and not another product. The case illustrates the growing strength of state dilution law. It also, however, illustrates the potential First Amendment concerns that arise under anti-dilution statutes.

Standing to Sue under the Lanham Act

As mentioned earlier, under the Lanham Act any "person" may bring a civil suit "who believes that he is or is likely to be damaged by the use of any such false description or representation." This broad definition creates a huge group of people who are potential litigants. Under the Lanham Act the term "people" covers businesses, groups, or individuals. In the following sections we will examine consumer and business groups separately.

Standing to Sue under "False Association" Prong Although an individual consumer may bring suit under the Lanham Act, in practice, this is not very common, mainly because the cost of a court battle is so high.

Some, but not all, courts feel that individual consumers must show a "commercial interest" in order to bring suit. In the case that follows we see how the court dealt with both issues.

Arneson, an inventor, brought suit against the Raymond Lee Organization, a patent service. The suit claimed that Raymond Lee had lured clients through misleading advertisements under a "false association." The case was *Arneson* v. *Raymond Lee Organization, Inc.*, 333 F. Supp. 116 (C.D. Cal. 1971). The court felt that the wording in the act should be taken literally, that is, "any person" could bring an action under the Lanham Act. Arneson was "any person" and was allowed to sue Raymond Lee. That is what the act says, and that is what it means. After all, consumers can be injured by deceptive comparative advertising as well as competitors. An ad can clearly compare two products, pointing out the flaws in one but if this is done through incorrect, misleading, or deceptive statements, the consumer will be damaged when the claim is relied on to make the purchase. As a result, the consumer will purchase the product based on incorrect information, and a commercial interest will become involved.

The "false association" clause of the Lanham Act requires that a plaintiff need only allege commercial injury based upon the deceptive use of a trademark or its equivalent to satisfy standing requirements.

...nding to Sue under "False Advertising" Prong In contrast to the false associ-... prong discussed above, this situation illustrates something different. This case ...from a philosophical disagreement between groups of well-intentioned people ...ted to the breed of dog known as the Jack Russell Terrier. Georgia Fisher and ...Sprague, two of the plaintiffs, were former Jack Russell Terrier breeders who ...nned from competing in Jack Russell Terrier Club of America (JRTCA) sanc-...ials after registering their dogs with the American Kennel Club (AKC). In ...o being denied access to JRTCA dog trials and shows, the JRTCA "black-...mbers who registered with the AKC by listing them in the JRTCA's bi-...agazine dedicated to Jack Russell Terriers, *True Grit*. Both Fisher and ...e "blacklisted" by advertisement that ran in *True Grit*. The plaintiffs al-...er the advertisement ran other Jack Russell Terrier owners and breeders ...ociate with Fisher, breed with her dogs, or buy her puppies.

...hat followed was *Jack Russell Terrier Network of Northern California*
...*nnel Club, Inc.*, 407 F.3d 1027 (2005). The court concluded that,
...listing" advertisement in *True Grit* constituted commercial speech
...late the Lanham Act, the JRTCA's actions did not violate the
...its actions were targeted at the AKC, not the Plaintiffs. The court
...JRTNNC was not a commercial competitor of the JRTCA, and
...nding to bring a Lanham Act 'false advertising' claim."

...the Lanham Act prohibits the use of false designations of origin,
...false representations in the advertising and sale of goods and
...plaintiff's argued that "the publication of the former JRTCA
...tered with the AKC was a false advertisement that misrepre-
...ir Jack Russell Terriers by falsely implying that JRTCA-only
...l other Jack Russell Terriers and falsely implying that those
...et JRTCA standards." This "blacklisting" may cause eco-
...ders depend on their dogs' reputation of quality and on
...CA events to sell and breed their dogs.

...t the JRTNNC is not a direct competitor with the
...t that standing of noncompetitors has been recognized
...hey also argued that breeders Sprague and Fisher, as
...ets of the JRTCA "blacklist," had standing to bring

...ed: "We have said that different causes of action
...subsections of *15 U.S.C. § 1125(a)* have different
...es plaintiffs cited involved the "false association"
...hich a plaintiff need only allege commercial injury
...trademark or its equivalent to satisfy standing
...say: "That the parties be competitors 'in the tra-
...other hand, for standing pursuant to the 'false
...a plaintiff must show: (1) a commercial injury
...product; and (2) that the injury is 'competi-
...to compete with the defendant."
...false advertising. The JRTNNC was not a
...ed a competitive injury. Nor does the fact
...f the *True Grit* advertisement make them

competitors with the JRTCA that have suffered competitive injuries. The court ruled that plaintiffs lacked standing under the Lanham Act.

A Company's Standing to Sue The most common Lanham Act issue involves direct competitors in business. In other words companies having a commercial interest that is directly threatened by deceptive comparative advertising. Situations that are most likely to create court actions involve companies or products that compete directly for the same market. We see this in most of the cases illustrated throughout this chapter.

A company may, however, have a commercial interest even though it does not compete directly with the other company. As an example, two companies may be in totally different industries, selling to completely separate markets. Yet, one company may create a deception that affects the other company's name or image.

The best example I can recall to illustrate this point occurred in 1978. This is also one of the more unique cases we discuss in this book. In November of that year, Pussycat Cinemas began showing an X-rated movie called *Debbie Does Dallas*. Remember th the Internet wasn't around yet and much of the world's supply of pornography was se in actual movie theaters. This film was described by the court as "a gross and revo ing sex film whose plot, to the extent that there is one, involves a cheerleader at a tional high school, Debbie, who has been selected to become a Texas Cowgirl." (Co sometimes make editorial opinions.) The movie ends with a scene showing Debb a cheerleader's uniform bearing a striking resemblance to the outfit worn by the a Dallas Cowboys Cheerleaders. In fact, twelve minutes of the film shows Debbie e ing in various sexual acts while wearing all, or part, of the uniform.

The movie was promoted with a poster showing Debbie wearing the same that is, a combination of white boots, white shorts, blue blouse, white star-studd and belt, all of the same style and cut as that used by the Dallas Cowboys Cheerl

As soon as the Dallas Cowboys Football Club learned of the movie, the or tion filed suit under the Lanham Act in *Dallas Cowboys Cheerleaders, Inc.* v. *Cinema, Ltd.*, 604 F.2d 200 (1979), seeking an injunction to prohibit th bution and showing of *Debbie Does Dallas* because of the movie's use of th Cowboy's image and trademark. Remember too that this was the heyda Dallas Cowboys. During the 1970s, the Cowboys won 105 regular seaso more than any other NFL franchise during that span. And they appeared i won two Super Bowls.

The actual Dallas Cowboys Football Club employs thirty-six womer form as the Dallas Cowboys Cheerleaders. *The Dallas Cowboys Cheerlea Cowgirls*, and *Texas Cowgirls* are all registered trademarks. The group worldwide exposure (excuse the pun) and has made many public appea side of football stadiums. Some notable alum include; Lee F. Jackson, fc County Judge and Texas State Representative, currently Chancellor of North Texas (2002–present), all the way to Erica Kiehl Jenkins, singer of The Pussycat Dolls.

As a result, the Dallas Cowboys organization has earned substantial its commercial ventures involving the Cheerleaders.

The Dallas Cowboys wanted the movie banned because it felt t was likely to be deceived by the representations in the movie and pron Pussycat claimed, as a defense, that the public would not be confuse gin of the film. Such confusion is a requirement the courts look for actions. Yet, the court said about the existence of consumer confusi lic's belief that the [trademark's] owner sponsored or otherwise app the trademark satisfies the confusion requirement."

Simply put, the issue here was the association between *Debbie Does Dallas* and the Dallas Cowboys Football Club—or, more accurately, the assumed association between the two. In fact, a commercial interest existed even though the two "products" did not directly compete. The movie did create a confusion in the consumer's mind and injured the Dallas Cowboys' business, name, and reputation. The Dallas Cowboys Cheerleaders won their case.

Required Elements that Create a Lanham Act Violation

The concept of the Lanham Act is very simple. When an ad claims a superiority over another product, a comparison is used. This occurs many times in today's advertising—Nissan compares itself against Toyota, Hebrew National against Oscar Mayer, and Apple against Microsoft.

However, if the comparison is disparaging, deceptive or misleading, a lawsuit may be brought by the victim. But certain specific conditions must exist in order to create a violation of the act. In fact, there are five elements that must exist:

* A false statement about the product must be made.
* The advertising must have actually deceived or have the tendency to deceive.
* The deception must be material.
* The advertised product must have entered interstate commerce.
* There must be injury or a likelihood of injury.

One case where all of these requirements developed involved two power tool manufacturers, Skil and Rockwell. The two companies manufacture portable electric drills and jigsaws for sale to the consumer. In 1973 Rockwell began a major national advertising campaign using television, magazine, and newspaper. It was estimated that the campaign reached approximately eighty million people.

The Rockwell campaign revolved around a comparison of product testing, which had been done by an independent testing lab. Under "supposedly normal-use situations," Skil, Rockwell, and other manufacturers' tools were tested. The results of this independent testing was used in Rockwell's ad campaign. In the ads, Skil products were clearly shown and were identifiable by their labels.

The Lanham Act was violated because Rockwell's ads were not factually accurate regarding the performance of the Skil product line. Mainly, the test results used to compare product performance were biased. The testing was not conducted under normal-use conditions. The Skil products were put through much more demanding test conditions than would have been encountered in normal use, which was not disclosed in the advertising.

As a result, Rockwell used false, misleading, deceptive, and incomplete claims in its ads about Skil. When Skil realized the content of Rockwell's ads, it filed suit in *Skil Corp.* v. *Rockwell International Corp.*, 375 F. Supp 777 (N.D. Ill. 1974).

Skil not only sought an injunction against Rockwell, it also wanted damages for its loss of profits and damage to its name, which would affect future earning power. This one case developed the guidelines for the five elements required to bring a lawsuit under the Lanham Act. Now let's examine each requirement.

1. Making False Statements about a Product The first requirement to bring suit under the Lanham Act is that the ad must create a deception in one form or another by making disparaging, false or partially correct claims, or failing to disclose material facts about its product.

Going back to our case, Rockwell made false statements about the performance qualities of Skil tools. The facts used in its ads were supposedly the result of testing the tools under normal-use conditions. This was not the case, however, so the results used in the ads were clearly false, misleading, and deceptive.

2. Requirement that Advertising Actually Deceived or Has a Tendency to Deceive The second element required is that the advertisement actually deceived consumers or had a tendency to deceive a substantial portion of the intended audience. This also refers to the confusion requirement we saw in the *Dallas* v. *Pussycat* case. Confusion is another way of saying "tendency to deceive."

Consumers who buy power tools base their decision on many factors: price, the features of the tool, performance, and durability. If a consumer buys a Rockwell power tool over a Skil tool, it would be for one or more of these reasons. If, as in this case, the consumer buys the Rockwell product based on the performance features it claims to have over Skil, the consumer has been clearly deceived. Since the Rockwell ads gave factually incorrect information in the comparison of Skil products, actual deception occurred.

3. The Deception Must Be Material The third requirement necessary to bring suit is that any deception created must be a material one. That is, it must have been likely to have influenced the purchasing decision. We saw this in chapters 2 and 3 in the discussion of deception and the FTC Act. The same reasoning applies here.

In the Rockwell case, its false and misleading claims involved the performance of Skil products. This is a primary criterion for purchasing a power tool, as discussed in the previous section. Statistics about the durability and performance of a power tool would weigh heavily in the consumer's decision to purchase or not to purchase a specific brand of product. Rockwell's deceptive statements were, without question, material.

4. The Advertised Product Must Have Entered Interstate Commerce The fourth element required under the Lanham Act is that the goods advertised were involved in interstate commerce. Simply, the product must have been engaged in commerce between two or more states. At first glance this may seem to disqualify many products. However, the courts feel that if any portion of the product—during any stage of its manufacture—crossed state lines, or even if the product has an "effect" on interstate commerce, then the product is considered to have entered interstate commerce.

It is not just the final product that can meet the interstate requirement. If any part of the tool, say the power cord, is purchased out of state, then interstate commerce is involved. This means that many more products qualify under the interstate commerce requirement than would first appear.

In the case of Rockwell, both its and Skil's finished products were sold in every state and therefore were clearly involved in interstate commerce; there was no need to look into the manufacturing of either product to see if a more subtle form of interstate commerce was involved.

5. Injury or Likelihood of Injury Must Exist The final requirement that must be present in order to sue under this act is that the advertisement has injured, or is likely to injure. Actual injury can result either from the diversion of sales or by the weakening of goodwill belonging to the product or service.

In the Rockwell case actual injury occurred in both forms. For Skil, the injury involved sales (lost profits) that were lost due to the deception. Skil also suffered potential future injury because, in the consumer's eye, Skil products were of a lesser quality as a result of Rockwell's deceptive advertising. In essence, the future selling power of Skil's long established name and reputation had been diminished. By the way, Skil won its case. It received an injunction and was awarded damages.

Types of Claims that Violate the Lanham Act

As the use of comparison advertisements grew, certain types of claims began to appear. Of those, a certain group has emerged that can violate the Lanham Act—claims that a product does something that others don't do. If the product claims are true, accurate and can be supported, this is legal.

However, claims that unjustifiably attack another product's qualities or performance or do so without support are another matter. There are a few different forms that this can take. The claim may be implied or it may be created, for example, through the use of a survey, disclaimer, or trademark.

Literally False Claims

A High-Pressure Example Let's look at a literally false claim. K&M Plastics, Inc., was a manufacturer of fiberglass pressure tanks for use in the water treatment industry. K&M mailed advertising to customers stating that K&M was "the only manufacturer with NSF certification" and that it had a pending application for National Sanitation Foundation (NSF) certification for its pressure vessels. NSF certification indicated that it had been deemed suitable for holding drinking water. K&M's competitor, Park, claimed that the statements were false and misleading because it and other manufacturers in the industry were, in fact, NSF certified.

The court in *K&M Plastics, Inc.* v. *Park International, Inc.*, No. 97C8018,1998 U.S. Dist. LEXIS 456 (N.D. Ill., January 7,1998), found that K&M's representations violated both the Illinois Deceptive Trade Practices Act and the Lanham Act because they suggested that Park was not NSF certified when, in fact, it was.

K&M was enjoined from using advertising that implied that it was the only manufacturer of pressure tanks in the water treatment industry with certification by the NSF; that it had obtained certification for products when it had not; and that its competitor (Park International Corp.) did not have NSF certification for its products.

A Fitting Example Kimberly-Clark makes a line of diapers called Huggies "Natural Fit." Among the distinguishing qualities were sides that were contoured toward the center. According to Kimberly-Clark, being contoured between the baby's legs, the diapers have a more "natural" fit than diapers that are not contoured.

Kimberly-Clark's advertising for its Huggies products included television, print and the Internet, claimed a more natural fit. The advertising campaign at issue here was the "Brick Baby" campaign. The commercial referred to the fact that in Kimberly-Clark's television ad the voice-over humorously suggested that Kimberly-Clark's diapers were designed for "babies of the human variety" juxtaposed with a scene implying that other diapers are designed to fit the shape of a brick.

The case was *The Procter & Gamble Company* v. *Kimberly-Clark Corp.*, 569 F. Supp. 2d 796 (2008). Needless to say, Procter & Gamble did not appreciate Kimberly-Clark's humor. In particular they objected the suggestion that other leading brands of diapers (particularly Pampers and Luvs, which were not named but were the clear target of the ads) fit less naturally compared to Huggies. In fact, Procter & Gamble argued that Kimberly-Clark's claim that Huggies "fit more naturally" because of the contoured shape is false. Huggies' contoured shape, Procter & Gamble claimed, is irrelevant to how a diaper fits. Both sides produced consumer studies to support their arguments.

The court reasoned that: "If subjectivity plays a role in deciding what it means to 'fit more naturally,' it plays an even stronger role in *measuring* the 'natural fit' of a diaper. That is, even if we could all agree on what it means (in the abstract) for a diaper to fit more naturally, our conclusions as to which diaper actually fit more naturally would be based on purely subjective judgments."

In deciding in favor of Kimberly-Clark, the court believed that the consumer studies expressed the impressions of the consumer rather than of the baby actually wearing the diapers. They said:

> To the extent the "fit" of a piece of clothing is measurable, one would think it is primarily a question put to the wearer rather than a third party. Because the studies here are based on perceptions of third parties, at best they can be deemed advisory rather than dispositive. In summary, Procter & Gamble asks the Court to find Kimberly-Clark's natural fit claim false even when: (1) people cannot agree on what factors make a diaper fit more naturally; (2) the measurement of any of the possible factors is based on subjective consumer perception; and (3) the perception about fit does not even come from the wearer of the diaper itself.

For all of these reasons, the court concluded that Procter & Gamble can't prove that Kimberly-Clark's statements about natural fit are actionable statements under the Lanham Act.

Implied Claims

Certain claims are literally true but create a misleading impression, as seen in the FTC's interpretation of deceptive advertising. This can also occur from a comparative advertising standpoint. In this section, I'm giving you a number of examples to illustrate the various forms that an implied comparative claim can take.

A good example can be seen in a series of ads run by Hertz in early 1984 (see box 6.3).

Box 6.3

HERTZ HAS MORE NEW CARS THAN AVIS HAS CARS.

If you'd like to drive some of the newest cars on the road, rent from Hertz. Because we have more new 1984 cars than Avis or anyone else has cars—new or old.

Hertz. The #1 way to rent a car.

The ad was produced by Hertz's ad agency Scali, McCabe & Sloves. Obviously, the objective of the ad was to lure renters away from Avis and to Hertz. The lure was based on the claim that Hertz had more cars available for rental. Therefore, Hertz implied that it had an advantage over Avis, an advantage that consumers should exploit. The reality though was quite different. While the statements were literally accurate, they painted an inaccurate picture for the consumer.

Here's the problem. As of the time the ad ran, Hertz had a total of 97,000 (1984 model) cars. Avis, on the other hand, had a total of 95,224 (1984 model) cars. So, literally, the claim that Hertz had more 1984 model cars than Avis was true. However, of the 97,000 Hertz cars, only 91,000 were available for rental: The others were part of Hertz's licensee fleet. Although Hertz did own them, these cars were not part of the cars available to rent.

When an "apples-to-apples" comparison was made (that is, cars available for rental), Hertz had only 91,000 compared to Avis' 95,224. That is why the claim was misleading. The ad claimed that Hertz "has more new cars." But the impression on the potential car renter—to whom the ad was directed—was that Hertz "has more *rental* cars" than Avis. Because of this ad campaign, Avis sued Hertz for violation of the Lanham Act in *Avis Rent-A-Car* v. *Hertz Corp.*, 782 F.2d 381 (2nd Cir. 1986). Avis won.

The Directions Example American Express complained about a MasterCard television commercial entitled "Directions." The humorous commercial depicted a man trying to find a location where he could get cash with his American Express Card. After asking seven people for directions, and receiving a variety of responses, he was left at the end of the commercial cashless and frustrated. Meanwhile, the MasterCard holders depicted were able to access cash as the voice-over stated "with MasterCard, you can get cash just about anywhere. At nearly 200,000 bank branches and 60,000 ATMs."

First, American Express alleged that "Directions" implied that it was difficult to get cash with the American Express Card. American Express pointed to the sequence where, in response to the question "Cash?" by the man holding up an American Express Card, a woman responds: "You know, the thing is, not with that card. That's the problem."

Second, American Express alleged that the voice-over's statement: "Looking for cash without MasterCard can lead you nowhere," coupled with the accompanying scene of the man driving across a bridge over river heavily lined with trees, falsely indicates that it is virtually impossible to get cash with the American Express Card.

Third, American Express complained that the commercial falsely implied that an American Express card holder needed to travel to remote locations to get cash with her card. Besides the depiction of the bridge, American Express cited one set of directions given to the man to "go through a corset store" where "in back, there's a dirt road."

Fourth, American Express alleged that the advertisement falsely implied that it is difficult to get cash with the American Express card, because the locations were hard to find and because it was hard to find directions to the locations.

In *American Express Travel Related Services Company, Inc.* v. *Mastercard International Incorporated*, 776 F. Supp. 787 (1991), the court agreed with American Express. They said: "an advertisement can be false, and thus violative of the Lanham Act, in two ways: (1) it can be explicitly false or (2) it can be ambiguous on its face, but implicitly misleading to consumers as evidenced by the consuming public's reaction to it. In a case such as this, where an advertisement makes a comparison between competing products, irreparable injury will be presumed if the advertisement is found to be false and misleading, either explicitly or implicitly. Likelihood of success of on the merits is found if the court finds a commercial explicitly false or plaintiff proves through a consumer reaction survey that it is implicitly false."

Antibiotic Drug Example Eli Lilly claimed that its competitor, Roussel, was stating that cefaclor (a generic antibiotic drug) was an "alternative to brand name drugs." The implication according to Lilly was that the drug was approved by the Food and Drug Administration (FDA). While Roussel had originally received FDA approval for distribution of the drug in the United States, that approval was withdrawn by the FDA when it found misrepresentations in the application.

In *Eli Lilly and Co.* v. *Roussel Corp.*, No. 97-2009 (JAG), 1998 U.S. Dist. LEXIS 10063 (D.N.J., July 1, 1998), the court held that simply placing a drug on the market did not act as an implied representation that the FDA approved it. Such violations would need to be dealt with under the Federal Food, Drug, and Cosmetics Act (FFDCA). However, under the FFDCA, no private right of action existed, so Eli Lilly couldn't directly pursue action there. On the other hand, allowing Eli Lilly to proceed on a Section 43(a) basis (merely by placing its drug on the market) would permit Eli Lilly to enforce the Food, Drug, and Cosmetics Act, the court reasoned. Without any statement or representation in the competitor's advertising that declared that it had obtained "proper FDA approval," that portion of Eli Lilly's complaint was dismissed.

The Insulin Example Novo Nordisk manufactured an insulin pen injection system for personal use by diabetics. Novo's system consisted of three parts: the actual pen, a disposable needle, and an insulin cartridge. The needle and the cartridge were replaceable. The system was designed as a convenient way for diabetics to administer insulin themselves.

The problem arose when Novo ran advertisements that stated that the pen injection system was to be used only with Novo disposable needles. And on the package for the pen system it also stated: "Use with Novolin PenFill cartridges and NovoFine disposable needles only."

Becton, a competitor, also sold disposable insulin needles, and charged that Novo's ads gave the impression that Becton's disposable needles were not compatible with the Novo's system. However, clinical tests showed that Becton's needles were compatible with the Novo system.

In *Novo Nordisk AIS* v. *Becton Dickinson and Co.*, 997 F. Supp. 470 (S.D.N.Y. 1998), Novo claimed that these statements were merely sales statements and were not literally true or false.

However, the court reasoned that: "Becton has submitted consumer survey evidence, as discussed below, that supplies 'the causative link between the advertising and [Becton's] potential lost sales.'" Becton submitted three clinical tests that proved that its needles were, in fact, compatible with Novo's system.

Becton also submitted the results of a survey that included over two hundred diabetics and one hundred pharmacists. This consumer survey looked at Novo's statement that the pen system should only be used with Novo disposable needles. The results showed that 48 percent of the diabetics and 56 percent of the pharmacists said that the pen system could be used only with Novo needles. When asked directly if the pen system could be used with other needle brands, 90 percent of the diabetics and 96 percent of the pharmacists said no. The court found the survey reliable and held that Novo's "use only with" claim misled consumers to believe that other brand needles were incompatible with the Novo.

Initially, the court agreed with Novo that, considering that Novo's statement is a directive, it can't be deemed literally true or false. On its face, Novo's statement makes no factual claim. Taken literally, Novo's statements merely request diabetes patients to buy NovoFine needles. A sales recommendation, as long as it is nondeceptive, is proper and shows only that Novo is interested in promoting its product over others, the same as any other company.

The court said: "The real issue before the Court is whether the 'to be used only with' statement is deceptive, or implicitly false, such that it is likely to mislead and confuse consumers. Had Novo included the word 'recommended' before its statements or deleted the word 'only,' the Court has little doubt that Novo's advertisements would be lawful." However, since Novo chose neither of these options, the Court was left to consider whether Novo's statements convey a misleading or confusing message.

[T]he "to be used only with" language is understood in the diabetes treatment industry to mean that other needles are incompatible. Based on this evidence, Becton has demonstrated a likelihood that Novo's advertisements convey a message of incompatibility.

The court went on further to reveal: "In addition . . . Becton points to litigation in Europe that resulted in Novo being enjoined from making analogous statements. There, a German court and the Commission of the European Communities found that Novo's advertisements were misleading because Becton's needles were compatible with Novo's pens. While this Court is not bound by the European findings, it does believe that these findings support Becton's current claim of compatibility."

The court granted Becton a preliminary injunction to keep Novo from making its claims.

The Unsafe, Safe Can Opener Example Telebrands sold a patented hand-held can opener named "Safety Can." Their device opened cans by cutting through the rim of the lid so that no sharp edges were left either on the lid or on the rim of the opened can.

The Media Group, a competitor, also sold a can opener that it advertised as leaving the lid of the can smooth.

The Media Group's can opener was advertised on television, showing a woman opening a can with its can opener. The woman then rolled the lid of the can across her arm. The announcer claimed: "Sharp lids become a thing of the past . . . ." What was not clear in the ad was that the can opener cut through the side of the can beneath the rim, leaving the rim of the can as sharp as a lid cut with a conventional top-cutting can opener.

This case is a good example of an implicitly false claim. The ad was challenged by Telebrands.

In *Telebrands Corp.* v. *The Media Group, Inc.*, CCH 1998-1 Trade Cases 172,042, Telebrands claimed that the statement about sharp lids and the shots of the woman rolling the lid across her arm implied that a person using the Media Group's can opener would be handling cans that were left in a safe condition.

To make its point Telebrands conducted the following consumer survey:

The first question asked the respondents what the main message of the commercial was.

The second question asked: "[D]id the [commercial] say anything about the safety of the can opener, or was this not mentioned, or do you not recall what was said." If a respondent answered that the commercial did mention the safety of the can opener, that person was asked what the commercial said specifically.

The third question asked if the commercial mentioned anything about the availability of the can opener in different colors.

The fourth question asked: "[D]id the [commercial] say anything about the edge of the can after it has been opened, or was this not mentioned, or do you not recall what was said." If the respondent answered that the commercial did mention the edge of the can, that person was asked what the commercial said specifically.

Finally, the fifth question asked: "[D]id the video say anything about the edge of the lid after the can has been opened, or was this not mentioned, or do you not recall what was said." If the respondent answered that the commercial mentioned the lid, that person was again asked what the commercial said.

In response to the first question, 20 percent of the respondents answered that the main message was "will not cut yourself/can't cut yourself."

The court determined that some consumers came away with the impression that use of the safety can opener would leave the lid and the rim of the can smooth. In other words, a user would not get cut. In reality, Media Group's can opener left the rim of the can as sharp as the lid of a can opened with a traditional top-cutting can opener. The court concluded:

> The context in which consumers are likely to view the commercial confirms the reliability of the survey's conclusion that some consumers were misled by defendant's advertising. Prior to Safety Can's introduction to the market, hand-held can openers opened cans in a manner that almost universally left a lid with a sharp edge and a can with a smooth rim. Defendant's advertisement informs the public that its "amazing new" hand-held can opener leaves a safe lid, but does not warn the public that by doing so, the can rim, which is left smooth by an ordinary hand-held can opener's operation, is now sharp. No warning of this situation is given to the consumer viewing the advertisement. Accordingly, the consumer is misled into believing the sharp lid problem, associated with the use of traditional can openers, has been remedied while the smoothness of the rim remains unaffected. Therefore, the evidence that some respondents took away from the message that they "will not cut [themselves]/can't cut [themselves]" is not unsupportable.

Media Group contended that the order of some of the questions rendered the survey results unreliable. The court agreed that the order of the questions, especially four and five, could produce misleading results. Therefore, the court based its opinion that the advertisement was misleading on the responses to question one alone. As the court noted: "[E]ven recognizing the survey's limitations, the Court cannot conclude that it does not merit consideration."

As in this case, false advertising is not confined to literal falsehoods. It also encompasses claims that are literally true, but have a tendency to deceive when considered in the overall context of the message. In *American Home Products Corp. v. Johnson & Johnson*, 577 F.2d 160 (2d Cir. 1978), the court stated that the fact that: "[S]ection 43(a) of the Lanham Act encompasses more than literal falsehoods cannot be questioned . . . Were it otherwise, clever use of innuendo, indirect intimations, and ambiguous suggestions could shield the advertisement from scrutiny precisely when protection against such sophisticated deception is most needed. It is equally well established that the truth or falsity of the advertisement should be tested by the reactions of the public."

First, the actual message or the message conveyed by the advertisement is examined. Next, it must be determined whether the claim is likely to mislead a consumer. Typically, these determinations are made by looking at consumer surveys, market research, or clinical tests, although direct consumer testimony may also be used. As the court stated in *American Brands, Inc.* v. *R.J. Reynolds Tobacco Co.*, 413 F. Supp. 1352 (S.D.N.Y. 1976), under the Lanham Act: "The question in such cases is what does the person to whom the advertisement is addressed find to be the message?"

Campaign Slogans and Comparative Advertising

Just like specific claims an ad campaign slogan can have an effect in comparative advertising situations. In 2000, the case of *Pizza Hut, Inc.*, v. *Papa John's International, Inc.*, 227 F.3d 489 (2000) brought this issue out.

Pizza Hut is owned by Yum! Brands, and with over 7300 restaurants it's the largest pizza chain in the United States. In 1984, John Schnatter founded Papa John's Pizza in the back of his father's tavern. Papa John's has about 4500 locations, making it the third largest pizza chain in the United States.

Since 1995, Papa John's has invested hundreds of millions of dollars building its trademark "Better Ingredients. Better Pizza." The slogan has appeared on signs, shirts, menus, pizza boxes, napkins and other items, and has regularly appeared as the "tag line" in Papa John's radio, television and print advertising.

In 1997, Pizza Hut launched its "Totally New Pizza" campaign. This campaign was the conclusion of "Operation Lightning Bolt," a nine-month, $50 million marketing campaign where Pizza Hut declared "war" on poor quality pizza. From the deck of a World War II aircraft carrier, Pizza Hut's president, David Novak, declared "war" on "skimpy, low quality pizza." National ads aired during this campaign touted the "better taste" of Pizza Hut's pizza, and "dared" anyone to find a "better pizza."

Right around the same time, Papa John's launched its first national ad campaign. The campaign was directed at Pizza Hut's "Totally New Pizza" campaign. In a pair of TV commercials featuring Pizza Hut's cofounder Frank Carney, he extolled the superiority of Papa John's pizza. Although Carney had left the pizza business in the 1980s, he returned as a franchisee of Papa John's because he liked the taste of Papa John's pizza the best. The ad campaign was remarkably successful, showing a sales increase of 11.7 percent.

In February 1998, Papa John's launched a second series of ads touting the results of a taste test where consumers were asked to compare Papa John's and Pizza Hut's pizzas. In the ads, Papa John's boasted that it "won big time" in these taste tests. The ads were a response to Pizza Hut's "dare to find a better pizza" campaign. Taste tests showed that consumers preferred Papa John's traditional crust pizzas over Pizza Hut's.

Then Papa John's ran a series of ads comparing specific ingredients used in its pizzas with those used by its "competitors." In the ads, Papa John's promoted the superiority of its sauce and dough. During the sauce campaign, Papa John's claimed that its sauce was made from "fresh, vine-ripened tomatoes," that were canned using a "fresh pack" process while its competitors (including Pizza Hut) made their sauce from remanufactured tomato paste. Papa John's also stated that it used "clear filtered water" to make its pizza dough, while the "biggest chain" used "whatever comes out of the tap." Papa John's also stated that it gives its yeast "several days to work its magic," while "some folks" use "frozen dough or dough made the same day." In each of the ads, Papa John's punctuated its ingredient comparisons with the slogan "Better Ingredients. Better Pizza."

Pizza Hut filed suit charging Papa John's with false advertising in violation of Section 43(a)(1)(B) of the Lanham Act. During the many-faceted trial Pizza Hut did not contest the truthfulness of the claims made by Papa John's ads. Pizza Hut argued, however, that its own independent taste tests and other "scientific evidence" showed that filtered water makes no difference in pizza dough, that there is no taste difference between Papa John's sauce and Pizza Hut's sauce, and that fresh dough is not superior to frozen dough.

The court looked at a number of issues related to the Lanham Act. The court questioned whether the evidence established that Papa John's slogan "Better Ingredients. Better Pizza." was misleading and violated section 43(a) of the Lanham Act. They also questioned whether the slogan was tainted, and therefore actionable, as a result of its use in a series of ads comparing specific ingredients used by Papa John's with the ingredients used by its "competitors."

The court reasoned: Bisecting the slogan "Better Ingredients. Better Pizza.," it is clear that the assertion by Papa John's that it makes a "Better Pizza." is a general statement of opinion regarding the superiority of its product over all others. This simple statement, "Better Pizza," epitomizes the exaggerated advertising, blustering, and boasting by a manufacturer upon which no consumer would reasonably rely.

Keep in mind that, during this same period, Pizza Hut used the slogan "The Best Pizza Under One Roof." Similarly, other nationwide pizza chains employed slogans touting their pizza as the "best;" Domino's Pizza used the slogan "Nobody Delivers Better."; Danato's used the slogan "Best Pizza on the Block."; Mr. Gatti's used the slogan "Best Pizza in Town: Honest!"; and Pizza Inn used the slogan "Best Pizza Ever." and "The Best Tasting Pizza."

When the slogan was used as the tag line in the sauce and dough ads it may have been factually misleading (but not false) literally. However, in order for the combined message to be actionable under the Lanham Act, the court must determine whether reasonable consumers would have a tendency to rely on this misleading statement of fact in making their purchasing decisions. They concluded that Pizza Hut failed to produce evidence that the misleading statements of fact conveyed by the ads and the slogan together was material to consumers. Consequently, there was no evidence of materiality which was necessary to establish liability under the Lanham Act.

Using Consumer Surveys and Test Results
To Demonstrate Deception

One of the difficulties in succeeding in a Lanham Act case involves proving that a comparative ad is deceptive, or is likely to deceive. One method is by using market research or consumer surveys as evidence to prove that the consumer was deceived or is likely to be deceived. For this reason consumer surveys are widely used in Lanham Act cases.

A good case in point involved Coca-Cola. In early 1984 Tropicana Products began airing a television commercial for its orange juice product. 1976 Olympic Gold Medalist in the decathlon, Bruce Jenner (now arguably even more famous as Caitlyn Jenner) was shown squeezing an orange and claiming: "It's pure, pasteurized juice as it comes from the orange." In the next scene, Jenner poured the fresh-squeezed juice into a Tropicana carton while continuing: "It's the only leading brand not made with concentrate and water."

When the ad came to their attention, Coca-Cola the makers of Minute Maid orange juice filed suit in *The Coca-Cola Company* v. *Tropicana Products, Inc.*, 690 F.2d 312 (1982). In this case, Tropicana's claim was blatantly false. The ad claimed that Tropicana contained unprocessed, fresh-squeezed juice. In fact, it was pasteurized (heated to 200 degrees) and then frozen prior to being packaged. In the commercial, Jenner claims that Tropicana is "pasteurized juice as it comes from the orange." Well, pasteurized juice doesn't come from oranges. The representations in the commercial were clearly untrue.

Tropicana and Minute Maid, at the time, were the top selling ready-to-serve orange juices on the market. If Tropicana's advertising were allowed to mislead consumers into believing that its juice was better because it was fresh-squeezed and unprocessed, then Minute Maid would lose a significant share of the market.

Prior to the trial, Coca-Cola commissioned a consumer reaction test to be conducted by ASI Market Research, Inc. to measure consumer recall of the commercial. At trial, Coca-Cola produced this evidence showing that a "significant number of consumers would be likely to be misled" by the Tropicana ad. The court ruled in favor of Coca-Cola.

This does not mean that any survey can be used effectively in court. On the contrary, courts are very critical about the credibility and thoroughness of any survey brought into court as evidence. The intent of the court is to make certain that damage amounts are calculated accurately. Surveys are acceptable as evidence only if they accurately reflect typical consumers' true impressions.

The Feminine Hygiene Example Smithkline redesigned its feminine hygiene douche, Massengill, and began an advertising campaign to promote it. In the advertising, Smithkline claimed that its Massengill douche was "Now Designed for Better Cleansing" (the claim was based on its improved design). C.B. Fleet, the manufacturer of a competing product, Summer's Eve, filed suit against Smithkline in *C.B. Fleet Co., Inc.* v. *Smithkline Beecham Consumer Healthcare, L.P.*, 131 F.3d 430 (4th Cir. 1997). The issue here involved whether the claim was literally false.

After Smithkline began claiming an "improved design," it conducted several tests to study the new design against the old design. And also against the Summer's Eve product. Here's where it gets tricky: Regarding the "improved design" claim, the tests showed that the new Massengill design outperformed the Summer's Eve product, but that its old Massengill design outperformed its new Massengill design.

This case involved a comparative superiority claim. Smithkline claimed that its "improved design" claim wasn't false even though the tests showed that its previous design was better than its new design. Smithkline's experts described the new nozzle design and emphasized those features that improved its mechanical performance "overall" over the old model. The court agreed with Smithkline that its "improved design" claim referred to the entire new design and not just its cleansing capabilities. The court found that the claim was not literally false.

The court held that C.B. Fleet had to prove that the claim was literally false. The fact that no clinical tests had been done did not matter because the advertisement made no claim that the statement was based on any tests. There is a difference between advertising that implies a claim that is favorable and which is supported by tests, and an ad that makes no actual reference to tests but simply asserts a favorable fact (a "bald" claim). In these different situations, the burden of proof is different. When a "tests show" claim is challenged, the challenger must prove only that the referenced test did not validate the claim. When a "bald" claim is challenged, the challenger has the more difficult task of proving that the favorable fact asserted is itself false.

The court put it this way:

> As to the "improved-design" claim, SmithKline witnesses described the new nozzle design, emphasizing those features that improved its mechanical performance over that of the old model. Specifically, they noted that it has deeper side channels which improved outflow, a more rounded tip which made insertion easier, and improved flow dynamics which made the douching process more gentle and, possibly, safer. As to its actual cleansing properties, as measured by the blue-dye studies, they conceded that it did not perform better than did the earlier design (as they had hoped it would) though, per those studies, it did still outperform the Summer's Eve douche in this respect.

In this case the court stated: "[T]he relevant question for determining the required proof is whether the advertisement made an assertion of test-validation to the consumer public. If it was not asserted in the advertised claim, it was not made part of the claim being challenged as false. If it is later revealed, through discovery or otherwise, that the claim was test-based, the claimant obviously may challenge the test's reliability in attempting to prove false the advertised fact, but falsity of that fact remains the required object of proof."

Fleet argued that the superiority claim implied that it was based on clinical tests. The court disagreed because the advertising claim made no express claim of test validation and there was no language in the ad that implied testing. The court reasoned that "because the 'comparative superiority' claim was not a 'tests show' type, Fleet's burden was to prove affirmatively that the advertised claim of 'comparative superiority' was literally false."

After hearing testimony from experts on both sides, the court held that the tests conducted by Smithkline did support its superiority claim.

I Know What You Did Last Summer Here's a case that examines implicitly false advertising in a campaign for the horror movie *I Know What You Did Last Summer*. The ads claimed that the movie was by the same creator as the motion picture *Scream*, and was determined to be implicitly false in *Miramax Films Corp.* v. *Columbia Pictures Entertainment, Inc.*, 996 F. Supp. 294 (S.D.N.Y. 1998).

Miramax, the creator of the highly successful horror movie *Scream*, claimed that Columbia's advertising campaign for the movie *I Know What You Did Last Summer* (*Summer*) falsely created the impression that the two movies came from the same "creator," namely, Wes Craven, the director of *Scream*.

Columbia's advertising campaign used statements such as "From The Creator of *Scream* . . . Last Time He Made You Scream, This Time You Won't Have The Chance," and "From the Creator of *Scream* Comes A New Chapter in Terror."

In truth, the only connection between the two movies was the screenwriter Kevin Williamson. Williamson wrote the original screenplay for *Scream*. The screenplay for *Summer* was adapted from the novel by Lois Duncan. In the television and print ads, Williamson's name appears in small print but he's never named or otherwise identified as the "creator," as the advertisements referred.

Miramax submitted two consumer surveys to prove that consumers believed that the movie *Summer* was created by or somehow associated with Wes Craven. The first study surveyed consumers who saw *Summer* during its opening weekend. The second study surveyed consumers standing in line to view the movie *Summer*. Both surveys included 15-to-40-year-olds and were taken in the top 180 motion picture markets in the United States.

In the first study, 17 percent of the consumers responding to open-ended questions believed either that (1) *Summer* was a sequel to *Scream*; (2) the creator of *Summer* produced *Scream*; (3) the creator of *Summer* directed *Scream*; or (4) the creator of *Summer* was Wes Craven. Only 2 percent of the consumers thought that the advertising for *Summer* communicated that *Summer* was by the writer of *Scream* or by Kevin Williamson. According to the second study, the results were 20 percent and 1 percent, respectively.

Based on this evidence, the court held that the *Summer* advertising was likely to mislead potential viewers into believing that *Summer* came from the same source as *Scream*. The consumer surveys proved that, based on the advertising, an appreciable number of consumers held the false belief that there was a significant connection between the two films. The advertisements failed to name Kevin Williamson, or the writer of the movie script, as the only link between the two films. Columbia allowed the advertisements to imply that the films were more closely related.

As Comparison

Until now we've looked at surveys as a way of showing the existence of deception. However, surveys can also be used in an ad as a way of comparing products. Using consumer-survey information as part of a comparative advertisement may create a deception. This can occur if the results or methodology are misrepresented.

In the mid-1970s, two of the leading cigarette manufacturers in the United States were Phillip Morris and Lorillard (which was owned by Loew's Theatres). In 1972 Phillip Morris introduced Marlboro Lights, and in 1975 it introduced Merit. Merit was supported by an intensive ad campaign pushing a claim of good taste in a low-tar cigarette. In 1979 Lorillard began marketing its low-tar brand, Triumph.

In April of 1980 Lorillard hired SE Surveys to conduct "A National Taste Test: Triumph Menthol versus Winston Lights, Marlboro Lights, Vantage and Merit Non-Mentholls." The results of that test were used in Triumph's advertising (see box 6.4).

Box 6.4

TRIUMPH. NATIONAL TASTE TEST WINNER.

Triumph tastes as good or better than Merit, or . . . Marlboro Lights. In rating overall product preference, more smokers independently chose Triumph over Merit, or . . . over Marlboro Lights.

As a result of these ads, Phillip Morris filed suit for an injunction. The case was *Phillip Morris, Inc.* v. *Loew's Theatres, Inc.*, 511 F. Supp. 855 (S.D.N.Y. 1980). At the time of the trial, Merit was the largest selling low-tar cigarette in the United States, generating over $350 million in revenue. About $80 million was spent on advertising that one brand alone.

The actual issue in this case revolved around the use of a taste test. Lorillard claimed that its brand Triumph was the "National Taste Test Winner." Yet, actual test results revealed that 36 percent preferred Triumph over Merit for taste; 24 percent considered the two brands to be equal; 40 percent preferred Merit.

Obviously, from the test results, Merit not Triumph was preferred for taste. The ad failed to inform the consumer that, based on the same criteria, 64 percent stated that Merit tastes as good or better than Triumph. In other words, Triumph stated a statistic, which was true, and implied that the figure made it the winner. In reality, the other brand scored higher, which the ad failed to report.

Obviously, the results of the taste test were not used accurately in the Triumph advertisements. Phillip Morris submitted evidence at trial that consumers believed credible tests had proven that Triumph tasted better than Merit. As a result, the court stated: "[T]here is convincing evidence that consumers are being deceived by Triumph's false claim of taste superiority."

The Roach Bait Example A television commercial for Maxattrax, entitled "Side by Side," depicts a split-screen view of two roach bait products on two kitchen countertops. On the left is the Maxattrax box; on the right, a generic "Roach Bait" box that bears a vague similarity to the Combat brand sold by Clorox. The announcer asks: "Can you guess which bait kills roaches in 24 hours?" The camera moves past the boxes to reveal a clean, pristine kitchen, uninhabited by roaches, on the Maxattrax side. On the other side, the kitchen is in a chaotic state: cupboards and drawers are opening, items on the counter are turning over, paper towels are spinning off the dispenser, a spice rack is convulsing and losing its spices, apparently the result of a major roach attack. The message "Based on lab tests" is shown at the bottom of the screen. The two roach bait boxes then reappear on the split-screen, and several computer-animated roaches on the "Roach Bait" side appear to kick over the generic box and dance happily upon it. The final scene shows only the Maxattrax box, with the announcer concluding: "To kill roaches in 24 hours, it's hot-shot Maxattrax. Maxattrax, it's the no-wait roach bait."

In this case, *United Industries Corp.* v. *The Clorox Co.*, 140 F.3d 1175 (8th Cir. 1998), we find another example of a claim that was not literally false.

Scientific testing by both companies showed that Maxattrax contained a fast-acting nerve toxin that actually killed roaches within twenty-four hours from the time they made contact with the product.

The court explained:

The district court determined that the Maxattrax commercial conveyed an explicit message that the product killed roaches in 24 hours and found that this message was literally true. The court concluded that scientific testing performed both by United Industries and Clorox sufficiently demonstrated that Maxattrax, which contains the fast-acting nerve toxin known as chlorpyrifos or Dursban, will actually kill a roach within 24 hours of its coming into contact with the product. In response, Clorox argues that the district court erroneously "ignored the explicit visual statements in United's advertising that, as a matter of law, combine with its express audio statements to determine its literal meaning."

Our review of the record satisfies us that the district court's determination that the commercial was literally true is not clearly erroneous. The court was clearly correct in its assessment that the audio and print components of the advertisement are literally true. The scientific evidence and expert testimony contained in the record satisfactorily established that Maxattrax roach bait "kills roaches in 24 hours." Clorox protests that this statement is literally true only in circumstances where a particular roach actually comes into contact with the product. This complaint rings hollow. The requirement that roaches must come into contact with the poison for it to be effective is the central premise of the roach bait line of products. We will not presume the average consumer to be incapable of comprehending the essential nature of a roach trap.

Combat argued that the commercial also projected three literally false messages: (1) that Maxattrax controlled roach infestations in consumers' homes within twenty-four hours; (2) that Combat, and others, were ineffective in consumers' homes within twenty-four hours; and (3) that Maxattrax provided superior performance in consumers' homes in comparison to Combat and other brands.

The court disagreed since the evidence, which included clinical tests and expert testimony, established that the twenty-four-hour claim was literally true and that the ad did not make any claims about complete infestation control.

The court reasoned:

> The depiction of a Maxattrax box in a pristine, roach-free kitchen, coupled with the depiction of a kitchen in disarray in which animated roaches happily dance about on a generic roach trap, is not sufficient, in our view, to constitute literal falsity in the manner in which it was presented. When the context is considered as a whole, moreover, the audio component of the advertisement, emphasizing only the 24-hour time frame and quick roach kill with no mention of complete infestation control, fosters ambiguity regarding the intended message and renders the commercial much more susceptible to differing, plausible interpretations. Thus, in our view, the district court's finding that the commercial did not explicitly convey a literally false message that Maxattrax will completely control a home roach infestation within 24 hours is not clearly erroneous.

The Resource versus Ensure Example In *Abbott Laboratories* v. *Gerber Products Co.*, 979 F. Supp. 569 (W.D. Mich. 1997), an advertisement that claimed a liquid dietary supplement was "preferred" by consumers over a competitor's product became the point of contention. This case considered whether consumer test results were reliable. Gerber's advertising campaign for its nutritional supplement called Resource claimed: "America Prefers Resource over Ensure" and "National Preference Winner Resource Beats Ensure." The maker of Ensure (Abbott Laboratories) filed suit for false advertising, arguing that Gerber's tests did not substantiate its advertising claims.

The court stated: In the case at issue, Abbott argues that Gerber's claim that Resource is preferred over Ensure is literally false, and, therefore, Abbott need not show consumer confusion. This Court agrees that if Abbott can establish that Gerber's claim is literally false, that evidence of consumer confusion is not needed.

Abbott asserts that Gerber's claim is false in two ways: (1) the tests Gerber relies upon to support its claim were conducted as taste tests and not as tests indicating overall preference and (2) these tests do not show that Resource tastes better or is preferred over Ensure.

During the trial, the court found that Gerber's preference claim was in reality a taste claim. During the trial, experts established that the nutritional supplements of both brands were nutritionally the same. In fact, most consumers used the products for medical reasons and would chose the product that tasted better.

The "product preference test" conducted by Gerber included 4,000 consumers over the age of 55 who were users or potential users of a nutritional supplement. The test showed that consumers preferred Resource over Ensure in every category tested.

The court went on to state: "This Court finds Gerber's use of test participants over the age of fifty-five, whether users or potential users, was appropriate. NSBs [nutritional supplement beverages] are in a dynamic market. Consumers are entering and leaving the market at a very high rate. Furthermore, consumers are in the market for a very short period of time, making it necessary for companies who market NSBs to reach potential users. If Gerber wanted to limit the test participants to users and potential users, the only way to limit the participants would be to have a requirement that test participants be over the age of fifty-five since a majority of the users of NSBs are over the age of fifty-five. Gerber limited its test participants to those most likely to have used or will use NSBs in the relatively near future. Furthermore, Gerber qualified its claim so that consumers would know that the test was limited to test participants over the age of fifty-five."

As we can see, the court rejected Abbott's contention that the test participants should have been restricted to consumers who actually used a nutritional supplement. The court determined that users as well as potential users of a product were acceptable participants in consumer tests.

The consumer tests conducted by the defendant were sufficiently reliable to substantiate the advertising claim.

Use of Disclaimers in a Comparative Ad

There are situations in which an advertiser adds a disclaimer to an advertisement to offset what would otherwise be a deceptive claim. In 1984 the FDA authorized the sale of the drug ibuprofen in over-the-counter 200-mg tablet form. American Home Products marketed the aspirin substitute under the brand name "Advil." A competitor, Upjohn, marketed the drug under the brand name "Nuprin." Prior to the over-the-counter release of ibuprofen, Upjohn manufactured and sold ibuprofen only as a prescription under the trademark of "Motrin." Now, who's on first?

American Home Products produced an ad campaign for Advil through its ad agency, Young & Rubicam. The campaign included magazine ads and television commercials. In the ads, an Advil tablet was shown. The tablet was orange in color and the same size and shape as the prescription drug Motrin. Copy in the ads exclaimed: "ADVIL contains ibuprofen, the same medicine as the prescription drug MOTRIN now in nonprescription strength."

When Upjohn learned of the ads, it contacted American Home Products requesting that it change them to avoid any confusion for the consumer. American Home Products changed the color of its Advil tablets to brown. It also changed the disclaimer used in its ads to read: "ADVIL contains a nonprescription strength of ibuprofen, the medicine found in the prescription brand, MOTRIN." American

Home Products also added a visible line of copy to the television commercial that Advil is from Whitehall (a division of American Home Products) and that Motrin is manufactured by another company (see box 6.5 for copy used in the revised print ads).

Box 6.5

ADVIL IS ADVANCED MEDICINE FOR PAIN

ADVIL isn't Tylenol and it isn't aspirin.

Advil contains ibuprofen—the medicine in the prescription brand Motrin, the product of another company. Now ibuprofen is available in nonprescription strength in Advil. Ibuprofen has been proven so effective in relieving many types of pain that doctors have already prescribed it over 130 million times.

After American Home Products made these changes and added the disclaimers, Upjohn went to court requesting an injunction in *Upjohn Co.* v. *American Home Products Corp.*, 598 F. Supp. 550 (S.D.N.Y. 1984). Upjohn felt that the consuming public would still be misled and confused by American Home Product's ads for Advil. Upjohn wanted to stop any implication that Advil tablets were the same color as Motrin, that Advil was manufactured by Upjohn, that Advil was the equivalent of Motrin, or that the ingredient in Advil was Motrin.

The court examined these issues and determined that the new changes and disclaimers used in the Advil ads were sufficient. For the trial, consumer reaction surveys were instituted to determine the effect of the revised ads on the public. The surveys found that a higher percentage of consumers polled recalled the disclaimers as opposed to those who felt that Advil and Motrin were made by the same manufacturer. The court said: "[S]uch disclaimers are preferred to an absolute prohibition of the potentially misleading reference as a means of alleviating consumer confusion . . . "

The important point to remember is that consumer confusion can be alleviated through the use of disclaimers or qualifying language. However, if this is challenged in court by the competitor, consumer surveys will be relied on and the survey will be used to determine whether use of the disclaimer alleviates the majority of consumer confusion.

Fair Use of Trademarks in Comparative Ads

There is nothing illegal *per se* in referring to another company's trademark. But this is true only if the use is informational and not likely to cause confusion about the source of the product or its qualities. We see many instances where an ad will make reference to, or show another company's product. In most cases this is done fairly and to compare qualities or features that one product has making it distinctive from the other. These comparisons must be true and accurate. Comparisons must not be deceptive or mislead the consumer, and proof to support the claim must exist prior to making the claim.

Here is another example of deceptive comparisons. Johnson & Johnson Company, founded in 1886, is a major manufacturer of products including Johnson's Baby Oil, Johnson's Baby Powder, and Johnson's Baby Shampoo. Quality Pure, a lesser-known company, also manufactured skin oil, skin powder, and shampoo. Its products are packaged in containers that exhibit an amazing resemblance to the J & J products. In fact, at a quick glance, the competing product packages look the same. Such similarity can be an infringement of trademark. This close similarity, known as "palming off" involves the use of another company's trademark to cause a likely confusion as to the origin of the product.

As an example, let's look at the shampoo products. The Johnson & Johnson Baby Shampoo bottle is elongated and made of clear plastic. The clear, yellow shampoo can be seen through the container. The Quality Pure shampoo package was almost identical to J & J's, down to the style and color of label. The J & J label contained a tear drop with the slogan "No More Tears," while the Quality Pure label used three tear drops on the label with the words "Tear Free."

The packaging of all of the Johnson & Johnson products was distinctive and unique. Suffice it to say that Quality Pure was in competition with Johnson & Johnson. But the competitor is not allowed to package its product so as to ride on the coattails of the image, reputation, and goodwill built over many years by Johnson & Johnson.

Quality Pure produced and aired a thirty-second commercial to promote its new line of products. In its commercial, an actress, Jane Paley, claimed that Quality Pure Shampoo "gave me the same lather" as Johnson & Johnson Baby Shampoo. The commercial also claimed that "both were extremely mild." The gist of the commercial was that while the products gave the same results and had the same qualities, Quality Pure was cheaper than Johnson & Johnson.

As a result Johnson & Johnson brought suit in *Johnson & Johnson* v. *Quality Pure Mfg., Inc.*, 484 F. Supp. 975 (D.N.J. 1979). Two items were at issue in this case: the similarity of the packaging and the advertising claim of equal performance and lower price. The court expressed its opinion that competing on a price level is perfectly acceptable. Yet it is not acceptable to "sell a competing product on the basis of a lower price and at the same time use [packaging] designed and calculated to fool the customer into the belief that he is getting someone else's product."

Furthermore, Quality Pure had no basis for the claims used in its commercial. Quality Pure conducted a "survey" by handing out samples of competing shampoos to shoppers at shopping centers. The competing shampoos were unidentified except for a mark on each bottle, either X or Y. Then Jane Paley was given the samples and, after using them, scored them as equal. This result is what appeared on the television commercial.

The problem rests on the credibility of the "survey." There was no way of determining which brand of shampoo was in which bottle, or even if the products were different. The test was rigged and without any substantiation, and in the court's eye "had far too much resemblance to three-card monte to be accepted . . . ."

Celebrity Look-Alikes and the Lanham Act

In chapter 7 look-alikes that can violate a celebrity's right of publicity or privacy will be discussed. However, in 1985 the issue of look-alikes was taken one step further. It crossed over into the comparative advertising realm.

Early in 1984 a man named Phil Boroff appeared in ads for National Video, a video rental service. Boroff was hired through his agency, Ron Smith's Celebrity Look-Alikes in Los Angeles, California, because he bore a striking resemblance to Woody Allen.

In the National ads, Boroff appeared behind the counter where two of Woody Allen's films were displayed. The headlines for two of the ads claimed:

We'll Make You Feel Like A Star. You Don't Need A Famous Face To Be Treated To Some Famous Service.

These ads ran in national magazines including National Video's own publication and *Video Review* magazine. In the *Video Review* issues the ad carried the disclaimer: "Celebrity double provided by Ron Smith's Celebrity Look-Alikes, Los Angeles, Calif."

Allen was not amused by this. He filed suit in *Allen* v. *National Video, Inc.*, 610 F. Supp. 612 (S.D.N.Y. 1985). What made that case unique was that it was the first time that a suit of its type succeeded under the Lanham Act. Allen claimed a violation of Section 43(a). He argued that a likelihood of confusion existed between Boroff and himself.

Even if some consumers realized that the person in the ad was not Allen himself but a look-alike, these same people most probably will assume another possibility. That is, the public "may be led to believe by the intentional reference to [Allen] that he is somehow involved in, or approves of their product."

You might say that there was a disclaimer in the ad stating that the person was a double for Allen. Yet, a small disclaimer at the bottom of an ad was not sufficient to offset an overall deceptive advertisement.

The result of this case was that an injunction was issued, stopping the use of any of the ads with Boroff as Woody Allen. National Video paid Allen $425,000, and Boroff was barred from appearing as a look-alike for Allen in any advertising that "creates the likelihood that a reasonable person might believe that he was really [Allen] or that [Allen] had approved of the appearance."

The court order requires TV commercials or print ads featuring Boroff to carry disclaimers proclaiming that Allen has no connection to and has not "authorized or approved" the product or service advertised. For print ads, the disclaimer must be in bold-face type equal to or larger than the type in the copy. Boroff also must submit a copy of the court order to any prospective employer and advise them that they must abide by it. "The restrictions are so strict," Boroff said, "that people just don't use me."

When interviewed by the L.A. Times in December, 1986, Mr. Boroff said he's never imitated Woody, even when starring locally in the Allen-penned play *Play It Again, Sam* (which uses a Bogart imitator, as does the film version). "I don't know how to do an impression. I don't mimic him in any way. I just happen to look like him."

Jacob Laufer, Allen's attorney said: "It was not our intention to impact (Boroff's) career. Our intention was to stop him from profiteering on Woody Allen's image. And I hope we've accomplished that." Apparently so.

While this case is relatively revolutionary, it shows a trend. The Lanham Act was effectively used to stop the use of a look-alike who in essence created a false impression by comparing Boroff to Allen. And after all, that's what the Lanham Act was created for. The moral of this story is that the deceptive comparison can be one involving people as well as of products.

Labeling and Its Relationship to the Lanham Act

While most of the cases that we've looked at here have arisen as a result of problems with advertising, the Lanham Act also applies to labeling. In fact, the statute specifically provides:

Any person who shall affix, apply, or annex, or use in connection with any goods or services, or any container or containers for goods, a false designation of origin, or any false description or representation, including words or symbols tending falsely to describe or represent the same, and shall cause such goods or services to enter into commerce, and any person who shall with knowledge of the falsity of such designation of origin or description or representation cause or procure the same to be transported or used in commerce or deliver the same to any carrier to be transported or used, shall be liable to a civil action by any person doing business in the locality falsely indicated as that of origin or in the region in which said locality is situated, or by any person who believes that he is or is likely to be damaged by the use of any such false description or representation.

A Regular Example Keeping this in mind, what if you wanted to make reference to a competitor's trademark on your own product label? You can, if your label reference is truthful, according to a decision in *C. D. Searle & Co.* v. *Hudson Pharmaceutical Corp.*, 715 F.2d 837 (3rd Cir. 1983).

The case was brought under Section 43(a) of the Lanham Act and involved a vegetable laxative marketed and sold by two competitive pharmaceutical firms. Since 1934 Searle marketed a laxative product containing psyllium hydrophilic mucilloid using the registered trademark METAMUCIL. In 1964 Hudson Pharmaceutical Corp. marketed a laxative containing the same psyllium hydrophilic mucilloid, under the registered trademark name REGACILIUM.

Hudson had developed a comparative advertising campaign that ran for many years, not only in trade publications but also in point-of-purchase materials. Since 1972 Hudson had included in its comparative ads the claim that REGACILIUM is "Equivalent to METAMUCIL."

Until 1980 both of these companies' competitive products were packaged very differently. In that year, however, Hudson changed its product's packaging to resemble the METAMUCIL packaging. In addition to the ads, Hudson's new package label contained the statement Hudson had long used in trade catalogs and point-of-purchase advertising: "Equivalent to METAMUCIL."

The new packaging with its comparative statement brought on the lawsuit. Searle sued Hudson to halt any mention of METAMUCIL on the REGACILIUM container. The court held that Hudson could not make further reference to METAMUCIL on the REGACILIUM container, stating:

> Unless the defendant's container is changed such that "METAMUCI" appears in type no larger than the word "Equivalent" and in green letters on the white background. Defendant shall place an asterisk next to the METAMUCIL mark and shall state adjacent to said mark the statement "a product of G.D. Searle, not a Hudson product."

It was "proper for Hudson, on its REGACILIUM container, to truthfully characterize REGACILIUM as 'Equivalent to METAMUCIL.'" The court said: "Whether one is entitled to refer to a competitor's trademark depends not on where the reference appears, but on whether the reference is truthful."

A Joint Example A recent case involved Rexall (originally founded in 1902), a national chain of drug stores and Perrigo (originally founded in 1887), a multinational generic pharmaceutical company. Rexall sold a number of nutritional supplements under the brand name Osteo Bi-Flex, which were designed to promote joint health. Perrigo on the other hand sold competing store-brand (or "generic") joint-care supplements.

In *Rexall Sundown, Inc.* v. *Perrigo Co.*, 707 F. Supp. 2d 357 (2010), Rexall claimed that Perrigo's use of statements such as "Compare to Osteo Bi-Flex Glucosamine Chondroitin MSM with Joint Shield Ingredients," "Compare to Osteo Bi-Flex Ingredients," "Compare to Ingredients of Osteo Bi-Flex," or "Compare Osteo Bi-Flex," on the packaging of the Perrigo products implied that their products contained the same ingredients as Osteo Bi-Flex or had the same effectiveness. Rexall argued that neither of these implied messages was accurate and that, the "Compare To" claims constituted false advertising under the Lanham Act. The court agreed.

As damages for Perrigo's Lanham Act violation, Rexall sought Perrigo's profits from the sale of the products. Section 35(a) of the Lanham Act, provides that: "a plaintiff who establishes that a defendant has willfully violated one of several Lanham Act provisions is entitled to recover, *inter alia*, the defendant's profits." The statute goes on to state that "[i]n assessing profits the plaintiff shall be required to prove defendant's sales only; defendant must prove all elements of cost or deduction claimed."

Remedies Available under the Lanham Act

Originally, there were essentially three remedies available under the Lanham Act: an injunction against the deceptive ad, corrective advertising by the company that ran the deceptive ad, and monetary damages. In order to recover damages or require corrective advertising, however, it must be shown that the buying audience was actually deceived. If only a likelihood of deception can be shown, an injunction is the sole remedy allowed.

The 1988 act made the damage remedies set forth in section 35 of the Lanham Act applicable to actions under section 43(a).

Section 35(a) provides as follows: "When a violation of any right of the registrant of a mark registered in the Patent and Trademark Office, *or a violation under section 43(a)*, shall have been established in any civil action arising under this chapter, the plaintiff shall be entitled...subject to the principles of equity, to recover (1) defendant's profits, (2) any damages sustained by the plaintiff, and (3) the costs of the action." (Emphasis added.)

Prior to the amendment, most courts that had considered the question held that section 35(a) applied to actions under section 43(a), although most of those cases involved unregistered trademarks rather than advertising issues.

The 1988 act authorizes courts to apply the remedies provided in section 35, and provides damages and profits should continue to be "rarely assessed" in actions under section 43(a). The 1988 act also makes the remedies provided for in section 34 (injunction) and section 36 (destruction of infringing copies) applicable to actions under section 43(a). Injunctions, however, have always been available in false advertising cases.

Injunction This is the most common (and quickest) remedy under the Lanham Act. Essentially, an injunction bans the ad from running. The most important function of an injunction is that it stops the publication of the deceptive ad.

Most people have the view that the legal system moves very slowly. It may be refreshing to learn that a preliminary injunction can be obtained within months or even weeks of filing a complaint. This can be a major consideration to the company who is the victim of an advertisement showing its product in an unfavorable, disparaging or misleading way.

Discussed earlier, one of the features of an injunction is that it stops continuing damage. The negative side, though, is that it does not remove the deception already created. Further, an injunction does not compensate the victim for injury either.

In order to be granted an injunction, the person or company requesting one must show the court that irreparable damage will be suffered if the injunction is not issued. Actual lost sales need not be proved, but it must establish that there is more than a belief of injury. If the advertising claim is explicitly false, no other proof is required. However, if the advertisement is less than explicit, some other evidence must be shown that establishes that the claim is likely to deceive the consumer.

The Toro Company and Jacobsen Manufacturing (a division of Textron) were manufacturers of various labor-saving machines for consumer use. Around 1980 a controversy arose when Jacobsen produced an ad directed toward dealers. The ad showed a performance comparison between its Sno-Burst snow thrower and Toro's Snow Master. In the ad Jacobsen's Sno-Burst appeared to come out ahead in the categories rated.

When Toro learned of this, it filed suit seeking an injunction against the ad. Toro obviously felt the ad was deceptive. The court, in *Toro Co.* v. *Textron, Inc.*, 499 F. Supp. 241 (D. Del. 1980), discussed whether the ad misled dealers about the features of both machines. The ad headline claimed: "The New Jacobsen. You Get More To Sell." The ad then proceeded to compare categories such as reserve power, engine size, starter priming, gas–oil ratio, wheel size, snow-throwing distance, fuel capacity, auger housing, handle adjustment, and warranty.

The basis for Jacobsen's comparison, however, proved to be insignificant and arbitrary. Here are some examples. Regarding the category under "starter," Jacobsen claimed that its machine didn't need to be primed to start, while the Toro did. The court found that, in fact, the Jacobsen required pulling the starter cord a number of times before the machine would start, just as with the Toro model. This, the court reasoned, constituted priming. The comparison was considered false.

Some of the other claims by Jacobsen were literally true, but they were insignificant as a valid comparison. Jacobsen claimed that its handle was adjustable and Toro's was not. A true statement. However, on closer examination, the Jacobsen handle was only adjustable one inch. The claim that the handle on the Jacobsen was adjustable was truly misleading.

As is clear, a number of the compared features between the two machines were found to be false or so insignificant that there was a likelihood of confusion of the buyer. While Toro could not show that purchasers were actually deceived (a requirement for damages), it could show that the ads had a tendency to deceive. In order to obtain an injunction, "[Toro] need only show that the misrepresentations of which it complains 'have a tendency to deceive' . . . [T]he three claims found to be false do have a tendency to mislead consumers into purchasing a Jacobsen rather than a Toro, and injunctive relief is, therefore, appropriate."

Toro was granted an injunction against Jacobsen for making the deceptive claims.

Corrective Advertising This type of remedy is essentially an award of money. The company who created the deception is ordered by the court to use its own money to produce advertising that will offset the originally deceptive ads.

The intent of corrective advertising is for the new ads to correct the confusion created by the deceptive ad. The company must produce its own ads with a message that effectively counters the previous, deceptive message, much like a public apology.

Durbin Brass Works is a manufacturer of brass lamps, selling its lamps through, among other outlets, The Sharper Image stores and catalog. In the early 1980s, Richard Schuler also sold lamps of the same style and design as Durbin's. The Schuler lamps were sold through, among other outlets, the American Express Company catalog. Schuler's lamps were manufactured in Taiwan as opposed to Durbin's lamps, which were manufactured in the United States.

Durbin filed suit in *Durbin Brass Works, Inc.* v. *Schuler*, 532 F. Supp. 41 (E.D. Mo. 1982), claiming that Schuler's lamps caused a decline in sales of its lamps because of consumer confusion between the two manufacturers. In other words, due to the identical appearance of the two brands of lamp, consumers were drawn to buy the cheaper version while believing that they were buying the original Durbin lamp.

Schuler sold over $60,000 worth of imitation lamps before Durbin brought suit. The court agreed with Durbin that these sales were a result of the public's confusion. Durbin testified at the trial that it would cost his company $10,000 in advertising to offset the deception created by the Schuler ads. The court concluded that Schuler's actions created actual consumer confusion, and therefore an award of corrective advertising was appropriate. Durbin was awarded $10,000 as damages plus court costs. It was ordered, by the court, that the $10,000 be spent by Schuler on corrective advertising to offset the deception that it had originally created.

Monetary Damages Until the early 1980s no court had awarded monetary damages to a plaintiff under Section 43(a) of the Lanham Act. All prior awards were either injunctions or corrective advertising. This, however, was to change when a case came to court that was able to prove a direct loss of sales or potential sales. In seeking damages, two things must be shown: actual consumer deception and consumer reliance on the false claim.

Another section of the Lanham Act, Section 35, has been utilized in comparative advertising cases. This has given even more punch to an already strong law by expanding the damages allowed. Under Section 35, the lost profits, actual damages, and the cost of the lawsuit may be recovered. Treble (three times) damages and attorney's fees may also be recovered in certain extreme cases.

Ryder System was in the car and truck rental business (and they still are). In the mid-1970s, James A. Ryder began to lose control of the company that he had begun. New internal management had largely ignored him for a few years.

Even though Ryder was over sixty years old, he decided to leave Ryder System and start a new company to compete with Ryder. The new car and truck rental company was originally named "Jarpool," but was later renamed Jartran. Originally Jartran, with only mediocre results, leased large truck and trailer units to businesses. Seeing the potential in consumer rentals, Mr. Ryder wanted to expand into the self-move rental field. This would bring the new company directly into competition with the leader, U-Haul.

In order to put his plan into motion, Mr. Ryder went heavily into debt to acquire the vehicles that he needed. Once Jartran obtained its vehicles, it needed to get them on the road fast. And that meant competing head-to-head with U-Haul for customers. As anyone in advertising knows, it is extremely difficult to dislodge the number one company in any field. But Jartran was determined to do it.

So, Jartran, through its ad agency Sandra C. Tinsley Advertising, created an ad campaign to generate consumer rentals. The campaign was designed to compete on a price advantage over U-Haul. Did the campaign work? Jartran's gross revenues in 1979 (its first year) were $3 million. In 1980, however, gross revenue rose to $58 million, and in 1981 to $95 million. Yes, I'd say it worked. Within months Jartran had taken over more than 10 percent of the market.

The campaign worked so well that it won the Gold Effie award from the American Marketing Association for "its overall marketing effectiveness." In Mr. Ryder's opinion the campaign "knocked the competition (U-Haul) on their ass."

How did this affect U-Haul? In 1979 U-Haul had almost all of the self-move rental business in the United States. Others had entered the field over the years but with very little effect. U-Haul's largest competition came, coincidentally, from Ryder System in 1979. However, U-Haul's revenue began to decrease after Jartran's campaign broke. In 1981 U-Haul saw, for the first time, its revenue decrease with a loss of $49 million. To stem the tide, U-Haul tried to counteract Jartran's efforts with $13.6 million spent on advertising between 1981 and 1982.

Without its concentrated and comparative ad campaign directed at U-Haul, Jartran would not have gained the market share that it did. The ads were simple. The headlines claimed:

> U-Haul It to Dallas for $0000.... Jartran It to Dallas for $000. Save big money ... to almost any city.

The price stated for Jartran was always less than the stated U-Haul price. In the ads, a picture of each company's rental truck was shown. However, the size of the U-Haul truck used in the ad was smaller to make it look less attractive.

In June 1980 U-Haul filed suit to stop Jartran's campaign. *U-Haul International. Inc.* v. *Jartran, Inc.*, 601 F. Supp. 1140 (D. Az. 1984), was the case. U-Haul claimed that Jartran's price comparison ads were false and that Jartran knew it. The court agreed.

The Jartran rental prices shown in the ads were "special promotion prices," although this very important point was never mentioned. The intent, which worked, was to convey that the advertised price was Jartran's regular price. Actually, the rates advertised were considerably lower than those stated on Jartran's one-way price sheet. Conversely, the price Jartran quoted for U-Haul rentals was its regular price plus a distribution fee. Again this was not disclosed in the ad. In fact, a distribution fee is charged in only certain unique rental cases.

The price claims that Jartran made were blatantly false and were intended to mislead the consumer into renting from Jartran instead of U-Haul. A series of consumer surveys were used as evidence to substantiate that: "The false and deceptive statements contained in the Jartran ads were material in influencing rental decisions of a substantial segment of the public interested in renting self-move equipment."

The claims in the Jartran ads were published deliberately. They were known by Jartran to be false, and they were intended to damage U-Haul by taking business away through deception. Under the Lanham Act, "a court may award additional damages, up to three times the amount awarded for actual damages according to the circumstances of the case."

In this case, the court awarded actual damages of $20 million to U-Haul. In addition, the court felt that Jartran's advertising was "willful, malicious or in reckless disregard of the rights of [U-Haul]," and an additional $20 million was awarded— $40 million in all. U-Haul was also awarded court costs and attorney's fees.

Jartran filed for bankruptcy in 1986.

Antidilution Statutes: State Action and Comparative Advertising

What we've seen up to now is federal control over comparative advertising. But many states have also become involved by enacting what are termed "dilution statutes." In practice, through use of these statutes, each state controls deceptive comparative advertising within its borders. Since these are state laws, the necessity for interstate commerce is not a requirement.

Dilution is defined basically as any whittling away or general eroding of the trademark's selling power. In other words, any nonowner use of a trademark or trade name that diminishes the selling power of that mark violates the statute. As we saw with the Lanham Act, a comparative ad, if untrue, can diminish the selling power of the competitor's trademark.

Dilution actions can take place under three situations: generic usage, unrelated usage, and comparative advertising. The first is generic usage. This situation exists when a competitor uses another trademark to denote a class of product. In other words, using another's mark as if it were the generic type of product.

The second area, unrelated usage, covers use of a trademark on products that do not compete and have no connection. Here again this type of use erodes the value of the mark. We saw this earlier in *Dallas Cowboys Cheerleaders, Inc.* v. *Pussycat Cinema, Ltd.* Although that case was brought under the Lanham Act (federal law), the principle is the same.

The final area involves literal comparative advertising. As in federal cases, comparative advertising can injure a product's selling ability by redirecting the trademark's image to another company's product. This violates antidilution statutes because consumers no longer associate the reputation of the trademark exclusively. In other words, a dilution of the mark has occurred.

Twenty-five states have enacted dilution statutes. In general, the states have patterned their law after the Model State Trademark Bill, § 12 (USTA 1964), which in part provides: "Likelihood of injury to business reputation or of dilution of the distinctive quality of a mark registered under this Act, or a mark valid at common law or a trade name valid at common law, shall be a ground for injunctive relief notwithstanding the absence of competition between the parties or the absence of confusion as to the source of goods or services."

The Rights of Privacy and Publicity 7

Who the hell wants to hear actors talk?
—H. M. Warner (1927)

The year is 1913. The place was an empty horse barn recently converted into a "factory where pictures that move are made." It's daytime, but the inside of the big empty barn is dark. Only bright sunlight streams through a window at the end of the room. A few stagehands move camera equipment around in the distance. The air is dusty. The floor is covered with straw.

As the television commercial we're watching continues, a man's feet step into view. A megaphone sits on the floor in front of his feet. The name "Mr. DeMille" is stenciled on it. The legendary director rocks in place in his knee-high riding boots, tense in anticipation.

The camera moves around him while he clutches a pair of leather gloves behind his back. His hands squeeze the gloves with nervous excitement. DeMille takes in the activity happening within the room. We see, almost as if a ghost, the image of an early 1900s train approaching from the distance. Then we see the image of an early 1900s camera crew on the set.

We hear a resonant voice: "In 1913 a young director prepared to step off the train in Flagstaff, Arizona. But it was raining. So he stayed on to the end of the line and shot his feature-length Western in a rented barn in a quiet farming town . . . called Hollywood."

The last of the crew members have moved away and the director moves out of the picture. Through the stark light of the window emerges the figure of a man. He walks toward us and becomes recognizable as Gene Barry, the late actor of the 1950s and 1960s. "Now, at the barn where it all began, you can relive those early days when Hollywood first met the movies." He turns toward DeMille. "Ready, Mr. DeMille" the actor concludes.

This was a television commercial that I produced many years ago promoting the site of the first feature-length motion picture—a little yellow barn, located in Hollywood, California, and preserved as a historical landmark. The place where, literally, "Hollywood" began (instead of Flagstaff).

I've used this example because the commercial involves the subject of this chapter—the right of publicity and the right of privacy. Both rights protect a person against the unauthorized use of his or her identity. As we see in this chapter, each area of law covers different injuries and promotes different values. Whenever an advertiser uses an image, likeness, or name of another person in an ad or for trade, certain rights must be considered. Here, we explore two of these rights: The right of privacy and the right of publicity.

The Right of Privacy

We start with the oldest of the two rights; the right of privacy. The concept of a specific right of privacy began to take shape in the late 1800s to protect individuals who truly desired privacy, mainly private citizens.

Here's a little sociology lesson. Individuals, by becoming a part of a society, give up many rights and privileges that they would be free to exercise in nature. In exchange for this, they receive the benefits of being part of a society. But all rights are not given up. There are matters that are private that any intelligent member of a society can recognize, and there is a right of privacy in those matters.

The intent of the right of privacy laws is to protect the essence of the individual person. To put it another way, privacy laws protect his or her persona from being taken and used without his or her knowledge or permission for the profit of another.

The words Shakespeare wrote for Iago were straight to the point:

> Good name in man or woman, dear my lord,
> Is the immediate jewel of their souls;
> Who steals my purse steals trash;
> 'tis something, nothing;
> Twas mine, 'tis his, and has been slave to thousands;
> But he that filches from me my good name
> Robs me of that which not enriches him,
> And makes me poor indeed.

Individuals have the right to live their lives in any way they see fit so long as it does not invade the rights of others or violate public laws or policies. People may make themselves visible to the public when they desire and may withdraw from the public when they wish.

In Roman law we see the beginnings of what would become the right of privacy. Anyone who brought public attention to another on a public road or on the other's own private grounds would be punished. Shouting until a crowd gathered or following an honest woman or child were banned under Roman law. In those days the law recognized a right "to be let alone." Even though, at the time, it was considered a property right, and property was an extremely valuable commodity then.

In *Semayne's* case (5 Coke, 91), 1 Smith's Lead. Cas. 228, one of the oldest English cases to be reported, we find the first legal maxim applied that "the house of every one is to him as his castle and fortress, as well for his defense against injury and violence as for his repose." Today, we find Semayne's maxim recognizable in our phrase "every man's home is his castle."

The unreported case of *Manola* v. *Stevens*, heard before the Supreme Court of New York in 1890, was the first case in this country where the right of privacy idea was used in an attempt to persuade the court that the lawful right existed. The complainant claimed that while the plaintiff performed on the Broadway stage in tights, she was photographed with the use of a flashlight. This was done without her knowledge or consent by the defendant sitting in a box seat. While the court permanently enjoined the display of the unauthorized photo, they steered clear of labeling this a right of privacy.

The Early View

In 1902 the New York Court of Appeals rejected the existence of a common law right of privacy in *Roberson* v. *Rochester Folding Box Co.*, 171 N.Y. 538, 64 N.E. 442 (1902), Abigail Roberson—at the time a child—sued for the unauthorized use of her photograph in posters (promoting a flour product) that were displayed in stores, warehouses, saloons, and so on. Even though the posters were complimentary—describing her as "The Flour of the Family"—the publication of the photo subjected her to "scoffs and jeers . . . causing her great distress and suffering both in body and mind."

In spite of this, the court refused to rule in favor of Roberson. They feared that this would open the floodgates once the principle of a privacy right was established. The court said: "[T]he so-called right of privacy has not yet found an abiding place in our jurisprudence, and, as we view it, the doctrine cannot now be incorporated without doing violence to settled principles of law by which the profession and the public have long been guided."

However, the public reacted very strongly to what it considered to be an injustice and demanded that the legislature change the law. The New York legislature quickly enacted a statute prohibiting the use of a person's name, likeness, or picture, without prior written permission, for trade or advertising purposes (1903 N.Y. Laws Ch. 132, sections 1-2 (codified as amended; N.Y. Civil Rights Law sections 50-51 (1976)). This became the model law that other states have since followed.

The Right of Privacy Becomes Law

The first court case to specifically recognize the right of privacy was *Pavesich* v. *New England Life Ins. Co.*, 122 Ga. 190, 50 S.E. 68 (1905). Paolo Pavesich's picture was published in a life insurance company's ad that had run in the *Atlanta Constitution* newspaper. His picture, that of a healthy and well-dressed man, appeared next to one of a sickly and badly dressed one. The caption above Pavesich read: "Do it now. The man who did." Above the sickly person ran the caption: "Do it while you can. The man who didn't." Below both pictures was the statement, "These two pictures tell their own story." Under Pavesich's picture was the following copy:

> In my healthy and productive period of life I bought insurance in the New England Mutual Life Insurance Co. of Boston, Mass., and today my family is protected and I am drawing an annual dividend on my paid-up policies.
>
> – Thomas B. Lumpkin, General Agent.

The photo was used without Mr. Pavesich's knowledge or consent. The statement under his picture was also false; he never had a life insurance policy with the company. Pavesich asked for $25,000 in damages. He got it. In essence, the court allowed Pavesich to recover damages for injured feelings.

The Pavesich case established for the first time the precedent for future actions under a right of privacy, and the court, in an opinion over thirty pages long, addressed the issue in detail. In its conclusion to the case it said: "So thoroughly satisfied are we that the law recognizes within proper limits, as a legal right, the right of privacy, and that the publication of one's picture without his consent by another as an advertisement, for the mere purpose of increasing the profits and gains of the advertiser, is an invasion of this right, that we venture to predict that the day will come when the American bar will marvel that a contrary view was ever entertained by judges of eminence and ability."

Since the time of the *Pavesich* decision and the passage of the New York statute, every state has developed (in one form or another) a right of privacy. The U.S. Supreme Court, in fact, established that the right of privacy stems from the specific guarantees in the Bill of Rights (See *Griswold* v. *Connecticut*, 381 U.S. 479, 85 S.Ct. 1678, 14 L.Ed. 2d 510 (1965)).

All right of privacy laws protect against one of four forms of violations:

* The unauthorized use of another person's name or likeness for another's benefit;
* The invasion into an individual's seclusion;
* The public disclosure of embarrassing private facts; and
* The presentation of an individual in a false light in the public view. The common denominator between these four is the right to be left alone.

Waiver of Privacy Rights The right of privacy, like every other right of an individual, may be waived by voluntarily allowing one's image to be used in an ad. An advertiser must get written permission for such use in order to avoid a violation. A person may also imply that he or she waives privacy rights. A good example of this occurs when a private citizen runs for public office. Here, the person's rights are waived in order to allow the public to investigate how the candidate's private life is conducted. This is allowed to determine the person's qualifications for the office that the candidate wishes to hold. But the waiver of rights applies only to matters that affect competency for the office being sought. This type of implied waiver, however, is rarely involved in advertising situations.

Depiction that Can Cause Privacy Liability What type of depictions can cause trouble for advertisers? As we'll see, there are many. There is a difference between the right of privacy and the right of publicity regarding what depictions create a problem. The right of privacy is very specific.

Upholding Privacy Rights Requires Recognizability The right of privacy generally requires that a visually recognizable likeness of the person is used even if the name is not. This right is narrower in scope than publicity rights because it protects citizens where there is a recognizability by others.

What constitutes a recognizable likeness? The New York Court of Appeals defined that in *Cohen* v. *Herbal Concepts, Inc.*, 63 N.Y.2d 379, 472 N.E.2d 307 (1984).

In 1977 on the July 4th weekend, a woman and her daughter were photographed while bathing in a stream in Woodstock, New York. The photo of Susan Cohen and her four-year-old daughter, Samantha, was photographed from behind while they bathed nude in the stream located on their friend's private property. Ira Cohen, the husband and father, saw the photographer taking pictures, became incensed, and chased him away. However, the photographer printed and sold the photos.

The photo showed the nude mother and daughter from behind and to the right in a full-length pose. The shot did not show their faces, but their backs and right sides are clearly visible, as was the mother's right breast. The photo later appeared in ads that ran in *House and Garden, House Beautiful,* and *Cosmopolitan* magazines.

The ad for Au Naturel, manufactured by Herbal Concepts, promoted a product intended to help eliminate body cellulite. As the ad said: "those fatty lumps and bumps that won't go away." While leafing through one of the magazines that contained the ad, Ira Cohen "recognized [his] wife and daughter immediately."

The issue here was whether a photograph of the nude mother and child constitutes a sufficiently identifiable likeness without showing their faces. The court established that it does. Features such as the mother's and child's hair, bone structure, body shape, stature, and posture all together could make the people in the photograph identifiable by someone familiar with them. The court ruled that the photo need not show their face. The plaintiff need only show that the photograph is reasonably recognizable. The photo was clear and sharp with no objects blocking the subjects. In New York, privacy claims are based on sections 50 and 51 of the Civil Rights Law. This statute, as with many other states, was designed to protect not only name, portrait, or picture, but a person's identity. The plaintiff must be "identifiable." The fact that Susan and Samantha were identified by Ira Cohen was acceptable.

Privacy and the Internet

In recent years much has been made about consumer privacy issues and the Internet. This discussion revolves around marketers (in fact anyone) who accesses "personal" data about people so they can direct advertising toward them. For example, if an advertiser knows that you just had a home foreclosure, or recently purchased a new car they can show you ads related to those situations. The argument follows, that due to the data-intense nature of the Internet, advertisers have access to mounds of personal data about consumers and their activities.

Recent cases, including *LaCourt* v. *Specific Media, Inc.*, 2011 WL 1661532 (C.D. Cal. 2011), address consumer issues over the business of delivering targeted advertisements from cookies used to track consumers and develop individual behavioral profiles. These allow marketers to target specific messages to specific consumers.

In re DoubleClick Privacy Litigation, 154 F. Supp. 2d 497 (S.D.N.Y. 2001), is another example of recent class-action litigation. DoubleClick, now a subsidiary of Google, provides Internet advertising products and services in the world. DoubleClick specializes in collecting, compiling and analyzing information about Internet users through proprietary technologies and techniques, and using it to target online advertising. They have placed billions of advertisements on their clients' behalf and its services reach the majority of Internet users in the United States.

When a user visits any DoubleClick-affiliated website, a "cookie" is placed on their hard drives. Cookies are computer programs commonly used by websites to store information such as usernames, passwords, and preferences that make it easier for users to access web pages. However, Plaintiffs in this case complain that DoubleClick's cookies collected "information that Web users, including plaintiffs . . . consider to be personal and private, such as names, e-mail addresses, home and business addresses, telephone numbers, searches performed on the Internet, web pages or sites visited on the Internet and other communications and information that users would not ordinarily expect advertisers to be able to collect."

Here's how it works as stated by the court. "In Step One, a user seeks to access a DoubleClick-affiliated website such as Lycos.com. The user's browser sends a communication to Lycos.com (technically, to Lycos.com's server) saying, in essence, 'Send me your homepage.' In Step Two, Lycos.com receives the request, processes it, and returns a communication to the user saying 'Here is the Web page you requested.' The communication has two parts. The first part is a copy of the Lycos.com homepage, essentially the collection article summaries, pictures and hotlinks a user sees on his screen when Lycos.com appears. The only objects missing are the banner advertisements; in their places lie blank spaces. The second part of the communication is an IP-address link to the DoubleClick server. This link instructs the user's computer to send a communication automatically to DoubleClick's server."

"In Step Three, as per the IP-address instruction, the user's computer sends a communication to the DoubleClick server saying 'I am cookie # 0001, send me banner advertisements to fill the blank spaces in the Lycos.com web page.' This communication contains information including the cookie identification number, the name of the DoubleClick-affiliated website the user requested, and the user's browser-type."

"Finally, in Step Four, the DoubleClick server identifies the user's profile by the cookie identification number and runs a complex set of algorithms based, in part, on the user's profile, to determine which advertisements it will present to the user. It then sends a communication to the user with banner advertisements saying 'Here are the targeted banner advertisements for the Lycos.com homepage.' Meanwhile, it also updates the user's profile with the information from the request."

Now the Plaintiffs contend that they have suffered economic damages including the value of the opportunity to present plaintiffs with advertising; and the demographic information DoubleClick has collected. Essentially, they argued that because companies pay DoubleClick for plaintiffs' attention to advertisements and demographic information, the value of these services must, in some way, have rightfully belonged to plaintiffs.

However, the court reasoned that "[e]ven assuming that the economic value of plaintiffs' attention and demographic information could be counted towards the monetary threshold—a dubious assumption—it would still be insufficient. We do not commonly believe that the economic value of our attention is unjustly taken from us when we choose to watch a television show or read a newspaper with advertisements and we are unaware of any statute or case law that holds it is. We see no reason why website advertising should be treated any differently. A person who chooses to visit a web page and is confronted by a targeted advertisement is no more deprived of his attention's economic value than are his off-line peers. Similarly, although demographic information is valued highly (as DoubleClick undoubtedly believed when it paid over one billion dollars for Abacus), the value of its collection has never been considered an economic loss to the subject. Demographic information is constantly collected on all consumers by marketers, mail-order catalogues and retailers. However, we are unaware of any court that has held the value of this collected information constitutes damage to consumers or unjust enrichment to collectors. Therefore, it appears to us that plaintiffs have failed to state any facts that could support a finding of economic loss . . ."

While these are growing issues with the Internet and its viral nature, they are not actually issues of advertising. And they are certainly not new issues. Target marketing has been around almost as long as advertising has been. Direct mail houses have been able to access specific demographic names and addresses for many years prior to the Internet. Retailers have built and purchased specific lists of potential customers for just as long. None of this is new. What is new is the speed with which it's accomplished today and the pervasiveness. Because of this, it's a current hot topic with those who distrust advertising in general.

What I said earlier though, about this problem not being an issue of advertising, is true. It is an issue of media however. For that reason the subject won't get much attention in this book other than this overview. The laws that are brought into play by the topic involve computer and Internet laws, the Electronic Communications Privacy Act, the Stored Communications Act, and many are trying to include it in the right to privacy. But this book is about advertising law, not media, publishing, marketing research or data acquisition. And it is about the right to privacy, but only as it applies to creating and producing advertising. The issue here is about what a company says in a banner ad, not how they figured out whom to show the banner ad to.

The Right of Publicity

The right to privacy had its limitations. As years progressed, many people actually wanted publicity, not privacy. The right of publicity grew out of the need to aid people such as celebrities, entertainers, and athletes who wanted to protect the "use of their marketable image."

Development of a Right of Publicity

Prior to the establishment of a right of publicity, it was not illegal for others to freely use entertainers' names or likenesses. Because entertainers sought publicity; they were making their lives public, and as such, waived their rights to privacy, it was felt.

In *O'Brien* v. *Pabst Sales Co.*, 124 F.2d 167 (5th Cir. 1941), a well-known football player claimed a violation of his right of privacy after Pabst Brewery used his picture on a calendar promoting its beer. While at Texas Christian University, David O'Brien was selected by Grantland Rice for his *Collier's* All American Football Team in 1938. O'Brien was probably the most publicized football player of the 1938–1939 season. After graduating from TCU, he would play professionally for the Philadelphia Eagles.

Pabst Brewing Company, at the time based in Milwaukee, published a popular calendar every year with the schedule of the entire football league included. Inland Lithographing Company printed 35,000 calendars for 1939 that used the picture of O'Brien in uniform. The headline read, "Pabst Blue Ribbon Football Calendar, 1939."

O'Brien claimed that he had not given his permission for the use of his picture. In fact, he did not even know that it had been used until quite some time after the calendar was released to stores. He claimed that he was greatly embarrassed by the publication of his picture in connection with the sale of beer, a product he personally was against using.

The court, however, stated that: "[A]s a result of his activities and prowess in football, his chosen field, and the nationwide and deliberate publicizing with his consent and in his interest, he was no longer . . . a private but public person, and as to their additional publication he had no right of privacy."

The court decided that O'Brien had no case. He could not recover under a right of privacy claim because O'Brien was a famous National Football League figure and had purposefully publicized his name and photos. Because of this, he had waived his right of privacy. In fact the court said, "the publicity [he] got was only that which he had been constantly seeking."

Establishment of the Right of Publicity as Law

Essentially, celebrities had little chance of recovering damages for the appropriation of their names or likenesses for commercial use. However, this dim outlook was soon changed by the Court of Appeals for the Second Circuit. For the first time, a right of publicity was recognized in *Haelan Laboratories* v. *Topps Chewing Gum, Inc.*, 202 F.2d 866 (2d Cir. 1953).

Haelan was a chewing gum company that had obtained the exclusive right to use a baseball player's photograph in connection with the sale of gum. The defendant

Topps, a competing chewing gum company, claimed that it had a contract for the use of the same ballplayer's photograph during that same time. Topps had, in fact, deceptively persuaded the ballplayer to enter into a contract with it while he was still bound by the contract with Haelan.

In this case, the court admitted that, in addition to rights of privacy, a person has a right of publicity. It protects a person's commercial interest in his or her identity, and that person has the right to authorize the publication of a picture of that identity. When this happens, it is an exclusive grant, and other advertisers are not allowed to use the picture. Haelan won its case because it owned the publicity rights to the ballplayer. Topps' contract was invalid.

Public Figures Do Not Waive Their Right of Privacy

Public figures who do not market themselves commercially may suffer injury by being associated with commercial products. These people have not waived their rights of privacy simply by being public figures.

A good example of this occurred when the late Jacqueline Onassis, former First Lady and widow of President John F. Kennedy, won an action under a right of privacy claim in *Onassis* v. *Christian Dior, New York, Inc.*, 122 Misc.2d 603, 472 N.Y.S.2d 254 (Sup. Ct. 1984). What made the case unique was the way that Dior violated her right of privacy. Dior, through its ad agency, J. Walter Thompson, produced a campaign of sixteen ads. Dior spent $2.5 million in publications including *Esquire, The New Yorker, Harper's Bazaar*, and the *New York Times*.

The ads featured a trio known as the Diors (one female and two men) who were to be the essence of the idle rich, decadent, and aggressively chic. The intent was to develop a group of characters that would become the most memorable personalities since Brooke Shields refused to let anything come between her and her Calvins in 1980. The copy for one of the ads read "When the Diors got away from it all, they brought with them nothing except *The Decline of the West* and one toothbrush." The ads led the reader through a progression of various situations that would include the marriage of two (but not the exclusion of the third), the birth of a baby, and their ascent to Heaven.

One ad, for the wedding (see box 7.1 for copy), showed the trio along with their wedding party. Included in the group were movie critic Gene Shalit, model Shari Belafonte Harper, actress Ruth Gordon, and a secretary named Barbara Reynolds, who bears an amazing resemblance to Jacqueline Onassis. All were obviously delighted to be at the event.

Box 7.1

CHRISTIAN DIOR
SPORTSWEAR FOR WOMEN AND CLOTHING FOR MEN.
The wedding of the Diors was everything a wedding should be: no tears, no rice, no in-laws, no smarmy toasts, for once no Mendelssohn. Just a legendary private affair.

Dior knew that there was no chance of Ms. Onassis consenting to being in the ad. She has never permitted the use of her name or picture to be used in connection with the promotion of any commercial products, but only for public service, art, educational, or civic projects. So, the agency and photographer Richard Avedon contacted Ron Smith Celebrity Look-Alikes to supply someone who resembled Onassis. That they did with Barbara Reynolds. As we saw with the Woody Allen case in chapter 6, the use of look-alikes requires the permission of the actual celebrity, nonetheless.

Even though Onassis' name was not used in the ad, and the image was not actually of Onassis, the public would naturally assume that it was Onassis. In essence, a visual pun was used to catch the reader's eye and draw attention to the ad. What they had was a recognizable likeness, which was not consistent with reality.

Dior also contended that having Onassis attend the wedding of the Diors was "no more than a touch of humor" and therefore was protected as a form of free speech. However, simply claiming that a statement was intended to be funny does not make it permissible to make the statement. In this case, the humor was used only to promote Dior products, so absolutely no freedom of speech privilege existed to justify its use.

What is ironic about this case, as the court noted, was that Dior was attempting to "pass off the counterfeit as a legitimate marketing device," when it had in the past, so adamantly tried to prevent others from deceptively obtaining the "fruits of another's labor." For example, in a previous case, *Dior* v. *Milton*, 9 Misc.2d 425,155 N.Y.S.2d 443, aff'd. 2 A.D.2d 878, 156 N.Y.S.2d 996 (1956), Dior complained bitterly of the misappropriation of its good name and reputation that had taken so long to develop. Now the shoe was on the other foot.

Although Onassis was a public figure, even a celebrity, she purposely avoided any connection with commercial products. Embarrassment and annoyance were her injury rather than loss of economic opportunity.

Publicity Rights Do Not Apply to Corporations

"Bear Foot" was the name of a monster truck that competed in monster truck races across the country. Bear Foot, Inc., the owner of the truck, complained that while it participated in a monster truck show on November 28, 1987, in Houston, Texas, footage of Bear Foot's performance in a videotape was used by Robert Chandler and Bigfoot 4X4, Inc. (Bigfoot). "Bigfoot" was a competing monster truck.

There were two issues in this case. The first was a breach of contract claim, which was dismissed. The second was a right of publicity claim, which we'll discuss here.

Here is another example of state interpretation of right of publicity issues. In *Bear Foot, Inc.* v. *Chandler*, 965 S.W.2d 386 (Mo. Ct. App. 1998), the court held that corporations did not have a right of publicity. Under Missouri law, the right of publicity provided for a person to recover damages for pecuniary gain through misappropriation of the person's likeness. Essentially, the statute protected a person from losing the benefit of his or her work by developing a publicly recognizable person.

In contrast to the right of privacy, the right of publicity does not intend to protect the person's feelings, but rather provided remedy for the misappropriation of the person's valuable public persona or image. The court stated that "[w]hile some states have recognized a right of publicity in individuals or the deceased, we do not believe that a corporation has such a right. The right of publicity creates a cause of action only for misappropriation of a person's likeness."

On this issue, the court went further: Missouri courts have not addressed the "right of publicity" of a corporation. The right of publicity is frequently recognized as a cause of action distinct from the right of privacy. The right of publicity allows a person to recover damages for pecuniary gain from misappropriation of their likeness. It protects a person from losing the benefit of their work in creating a publicly recognizable persona. In contrast to the right of privacy, the right of publicity is not intended to protect the person's feelings, but provides a cause of action where a defendant has been unjustly enriched by misappropriation of the person's valuable public persona or image.

In holding against Bear Foot, the court ruled that: "Since there is no right of publicity in a corporation, Bear Foot failed to state a claim upon which relief could be granted."

Descendibility of Publicity Rights

The right of publicity is a property right, separate and distinct from the right of privacy. The right of privacy is a personal right and is nondescendible; it terminates at death. The right of publicity is a property right, on the other hand, and can be inherited by or assigned to someone.

Although some courts disagree, the trend is clearly toward descendibility. Since it is a property right, it survives after the death of the owner. A valid reason exists for recognizing this survivability. It motivates celebrities' efforts and creativity in encouraging them to develop their image so that their heirs will also benefit. It's money in the bank, so to speak. It may take many years to develop a talent, ability and reputation that will create large economic returns. Along those lines, nonrelated persons should not be able to benefit from the efforts celebrities put into developing their own images.

In practice, the various state courts have adopted one of three views regarding descendibility. One view says that the commercial use of the person's name or likeness shifts to the public domain after death. In other words, the right of publicity is never descendible.

Another view recognizes descendibility only if the right of publicity has been sufficiently exploited before death. What constitutes sufficient exploitation? Generally, it must be exploited by the celebrity through the creation of a second business or through the use of his or her name or likeness in connection with a product or service promoted by the person.

Finally, some courts recognize the descendibility of the right of publicity without any other conditions. In fact, one state allows the right of publicity to extend up to seventy-five years after the death of the individual.

Let's take a closer look at the three views. It is important to remember that the theory that applies to each case is determined by the state law used to decide that case.

Nonsurvivable Theory: The Statue of Elvis The strict view of descendibility is illustrated in *Memphis Development Foundation* v. *Factors Etc. Inc.*, 616 F.2d 956 (6th Cir. 1980), an example of when the right of publicity is not descendible. Under Tennessee law the courts hold the opinion that the celebrity's right of publicity is not inheritable.

Elvis Presley died on August 16, 1977, in Memphis. In his honor, the Memphis Development Foundation, a nonprofit corporation, wanted to build a large bronze statue of Elvis in downtown Memphis. The foundation would collect the needed money from contributions. Contributors of $25 or more received an eight-inch pewter replica of the full-size statue.

The defendant, Factors Etc., was the assignee of Presley's right of publicity, and the company claimed that Memphis Development had taken away its right to market Presley's name and likeness. Memphis claimed that Factors' license did not allow for the distribution of the statuettes.

The court decided that, based on Tennessee law, Factors could not inherit Presley's right of publicity. It reasoned that "the basic motivations are the desire to achieve success or excellence in a chosen field, the desire to contribute to the happiness or improvement of one's fellows, and the desire to receive the psychic and financial rewards of achievement." Essentially, the court felt that this right should not be survivable to the heirs because the celebrity alone did not have complete control over developing the notoriety in the first place.

The court felt that the public was an integral element in the creation of an image. Therefore it had "serious reservations about making fame the permanent right of a few individuals to the exclusion of the general public." In conclusion, the court said: "Fame falls in the same category as reputation; it is an attribute from which others may benefit but may not own."

In other words, the right of publicity is not descendible, but rather becomes public domain after death. At least this is the case in Tennessee and other states that have adopted the same philosophy.

Descendibility If Exploited During Life The second option is where there is no descendibility unless the right was sufficiently exploited during the person's life. To illustrate, let's look at a case involving Bela George Lugosi and his well-known character, Count Dracula, the legendary character created in 1897 by author Bram Stoker. In September of 1930, Lugosi entered into an agreement with Universal Pictures to star in the lead role in the film classic, *Dracula*.

The case was *Lugosi* v. *Universal Pictures*, 25 Cal.3d 813 (1979), during which Justice Mosk rather sardonically stated, "not unlike the horror films that brought him fame, Bela Lugosi rises from the grave 20 years after death to haunt his former employer."

In this case, the heirs of Lugosi, his son and widow, claimed that Universal had taken property rights that the studio had not been given in the agreement for the production of *Dracula* in 1930. Between 1960 and 1966 Universal licensed many companies to manufacture items using the Count Dracula character. There was no doubt that the merchandising of the Count Dracula character was patterned after the likeness of Lugosi. It may well be true, also, that Lugosi is readily recognized as having been Count Dracula, even though Max Schreck, Christopher Lee, John Carradine, Lon Chaney, and others also have appeared in the role.

Yet, Lugosi never exploited the character of Dracula commercially during his lifetime. He also never exploited his own identity commercially. Let's assume, for the sake of argument, that Lugosi had opened a company named Lugosi/Dracula Enterprises. This company made T-shirts and hats with a picture of the actor made up as Dracula. Under the picture was printed "Dracula Lives . . . signed Bela Lugosi." This product created a large public awareness of the business. If the business existed and had not been sold before Lugosi's death in 1956, his heirs may have had a claim if the Dracula image was later misappropriated.

However, under California law at the time, the right to profit from one's name and likeness was personal and had to have been be exercised during lifetime in order for the right to survive after death. Since Lugosi hadn't used his name or likeness as Count Dracula in association with any business, service, or product (other than the part in the movie), he had no claim under the California interpretation of publicity rights. As a result, his heirs lost the case.

It is important to note that this case does not concern Lugosi's right of publicity for his likeness, but rather that of a character he played. Unless there is a contract to the contrary, merely playing a role creates no inheritable property rights—any more than George C. Scott has any rights to the character of General Patton, Jesse Eisenberg to that of Mark Zuckerberg, Leonardo DiCaprio to that of Howard Hughes, or Will Smith to that of Muhammad Ali.

The United States Court of Appeals for the Second Circuit agreed with the Lugosi decision when it decided a case involving three brothers Adolph, Julius, and Leo Marx. This case concerned the brothers' public image for which they were known as Harpo, Groucho, and Chico, respectively. The case was *Groucho Marx Productions, Inc.* v. *Day and Night Co., Inc.*, 523 F. Supp. 485 (S.D.N.Y. 1981), rev'd, 689 F.2d 317 (2d Cir. 1982).

At the New End Theatre in London, a play opened in January of 1979 called *A Day in Hollywood/A Night in the Ukraine*. In May of 1980, it came to Broadway. The second half of the play featured performers who simulated the Marx Brothers' unique style, appearance, and manner.

The Marx Brothers had assigned the rights to their names, likenesses, and style prior to their deaths; and subsequently their heirs transferred that right to Groucho Marx Productions, the plaintiff. The Marx Brothers, it can be said, made a profession of capitalizing on the unique characters they had created. Their fame arose directly from their efforts to create their instantly recognizable characters. The Marx Brothers' characters bore little resemblance to their actual personalities. This was a key issue in the case.

The Marx Brothers had capitalized on the commercial value of the artificial personalities they created. Every appearance and advertisement they took part in demonstrated their awareness of the commercial value of their images as Chico, Harpo, and Groucho. In fact, the Marx Brothers had promoted many products during their lifetimes, including Plymouth cars and Smirnoff vodka.

The play created a duplication, as faithfully as possible, of the Marx Brothers' performances. Granted, it devised a new situation and used new lines. But the essential style of humor of the Marx Brothers was accurately reproduced. The court said:

> Although the [plaintiffs] may have intended to comment "about 1930s Hollywood, its techniques, its stars, and its excesses," . . . the content of the relevant portion of the play attempts to accomplish that objective exactly as would the Marx Brothers themselves.

The court found that indeed the Marx Brothers had established a commercial use of their names, likenesses, and images during their lifetimes. This allowed their right of publicity to survive them; to be passed on to their heirs. They had won their case.

Always Descendible Theory The third approach makes the right of publicity always descendible. The case we see here was easier to determine than the Lugosi case because it featured actors playing themselves. Stanley Laurel and Oliver Hardy developed their own characters, which were theirs alone and certainly not fictional.

The heirs of Laurel and Hardy brought suit for $250,000 against Hal Roach Studios, which claimed that the studio had been given the exclusive rights to the Laurel and Hardy characters. Roach contended that the rights had been acquired through contracts between the studio and the comedy team in 1923. However, the specific rights acquired were those of copyright for the Laurel and Hardy films, not the unlimited usage of the Laurel and Hardy names and likenesses. We'll look more closely at copyright in chapter 6.

Roach also claimed that the names and likenesses of the comedy team are in the public domain. The court, in *Price* v. *Hal Roach Studios, Inc.*, 400 F.Supp. 836 (S.D.N.Y. 1975), disagreed. Its only question was whether the right of publicity terminated on the death of Laurel and Hardy or was it descendible.

The court felt that there was no reasonable basis to assume that the right was not assignable or that it should terminate with the death of the person. The court decided that the heirs of Laurel and Hardy were entitled to the commercial rights to the names and likenesses of the team. It also reasoned that the heirs were entitled to the actual damages sought in the lawsuit—for the appropriation of that right by Roach.

A further extension of the right of publicity for celebrities involved the late Dr. Martin Luther King, Jr., a public figure but not a celebrity. From 1955, Dr. King was the prime leader of the civil rights movement in the United States. For his efforts, he was awarded the Nobel Peace Prize in 1964. On April 4, 1968, Dr. King was assassinated.

American Heritage Products manufactured plastic products. It developed the idea of marketing a bust of the late Dr. King. Although the company had asked permission for the endorsement of the product of the Martin Luther King, Jr. Center for Social Change (the nonprofit corporation that holds the rights to the King estate), the center refused to participate.

Despite the lack of endorsement, American Heritage hired an artist to produce a mold for the bust. It also hired an agent to promote the product. American bought two half-page ads in the November and December 1980 issues of *Ebony Magazine* (see box 7.2).

Box 7.2 **American Heritage Products Ad**

AN EXCLUSIVE MEMORIAL.

An opportunity to support the Martin Luther King, Jr. Center for Social Change.

A contribution from your order goes to the King Center for Social Change.

American also printed 80,000 brochures that were inserted in newspapers across the country. Two hundred busts had been sold with orders for twenty-three more when the lawsuit was initiated in *Martin Luther King, Jr. Center for Social Change, Inc.* v. *American Heritage Products, Inc.*, 694 F.2d 674 (11th Cir. 1983).

Generally, the right of publicity is the distillation of celebrities' exclusive rights to the use of their names and likenesses. These celebrities are most often actors, musicians, athletes, comedians, or other entertainers. Although Dr. King was none of these, he still had the right to control the use of his image for trade purposes and advertising.

Indeed a public figure, Dr. King avoided having his name exploited during his life, and he was protected from having it exploited after death. Under Georgia law, individuals do not have to commercially exploit their names or likenesses during their lifetimes in order to have the right of publicity extend beyond life to their heirs. The Center won its case against American Heritage.

Forms of Use that Deal with Publicity Rights

As for publicity rights, almost any form that can be devised can potentially cause trouble. Because of this, the advertiser must be very careful when using any form of celebrity or public figure in an ad. Name, image, likeness, voice imitations, commonly associated phrases, look-alikes, cartoons, and even identifiable situations are potential problem areas. Now, let us explore some of these areas in detail.

Use of a Name Ferdinand Lewis Alcindor played basketball at Power Memorial Academy High School in Manhattan, winning seventy-one consecutive games in the 1960s. After high school "Lew" Alcindor went to UCLA where, from 1967 to 1969, he played under coach John Wooden, contributing to the team's three-year record of eighty-eight wins and only two losses.

Drafted by the one-season-old Milwaukee Bucks in the 1969 NBA draft as the first overall pick, Alcindor spent six seasons in Milwaukee. After winning his first NBA championship in 1971, at age twenty-four, he opted to record the name "Kareem Abdul-Jabbar" under an Illinois name recordation statute. From then on Kareem Abdul-Jabbar played basketball (he remains the all-time leading scorer in the NBA) and endorsed products under that name. He has not used the name "Lew Alcindor" for commercial purposes since he changed to Kareem Abdul-Jabbar.

During the 1993 NCAA men's basketball tournament, GMC aired a television commercial: A voice asked, "How 'bout some trivia?" This question was followed by the words, "You're Talking to the Champ." The voice then asked, "Who holds the record for being voted the most outstanding player of this tournament?" A title followed, "Lew Alcindor, UCLA, '67, '68, '69." Next, the voice asked, "Has any car made the 'Consumer Digest's Best Buy' list more than once? The Oldsmobile Eighty-Eight has." A film clip of the GMC, with its price, followed. During the clip, the voice said, "In fact, it's made that list three years in a row. And now you can get this Eighty-Eight special edition for just $18,995." At the end of the clip, a message appeared in print on the screen: "A Definite First Round Pick," accompanied by the voice saying, "it's your money." A final title appears: "Demand Better, 88 by Oldsmobile."

In *Kareem Abdul-Jabbar* v. *General Motors Corporation*, 85 F.3d 407 (1996), GMC had not obtained Abdul-Jabbar's consent, nor did it pay him, to use his former name in the commercial. The court announced its ". . . that plaintiff has abandoned the name Lew Alcindor, and has abandoned the right to protect that name, and the right to assert any other rights that flow from his having had that name at one time in the past." This finding forms the basis for the district court's decision to grant summary judgment in favor of GMC.

The court ruled that GMC was entitled to summary judgment on both the statutory and common law causes of action. The court reasoned that: (1) Abdul-Jabbar had abandoned his former name and (2) GMC did not "use" plaintiff's name because Abdul-Jabbar "did not [at the time of the ad] and does not have the name used." While the court found that GMC knowingly used the name Lew Alcindor for commercial purposes without obtaining plaintiff's consent, it concluded that GMC had not used plaintiff's name because he no longer bore that name.

Use of a Phrase The use of a familiar phrase can be an infringement. In 1962, long before Jay Leno, Conan O'Brien and Jimmy Fallon, Johnny Carson began hosting *"The Tonight Show"* for NBC Television. Carson was introduced five nights a week with the phrase "Heeeeere's Johnny." Johnny Carson is a well-known entertainer, and a large segment of the television viewing public associated him with the particular phrase.

In 1967 Carson authorized the use of this phrase by another business. He allowed it to be used by a restaurant chain called "Here's Johnny Restaurants." In 1970 Carson formed a clothing manufacturer and used the phrase "Here's Johnny" on its clothing and in its advertising. And in 1977 Carson authorized Marcey Laboratories to use the phrase as a name for a line of toiletries.

However, in 1976 a Michigan corporation was formed to rent and sell a product it called "Here's Johnny" portable toilets. The owner developed a clever tag line for the product: "Here's Johnny Portable Toilets. The World's Foremost Commodian." The owner claimed that this made "a good play on a phrase."

Not long after this, Carson brought suit for, among other things, infringement of his right of publicity in *Carson* v. *Here's Johnny Portable Toilets, Inc.*, 698 F.2d 831 (6th Cir. 1983). This was a case of an appropriation of Carson's identity without the use of his name—the phrase is so recognizable that when the public heard it, no one else but Carson came to mind. The phrase "Here's Johnny" is a symbol of Carson's identity, just as is a name or picture. The president of the toilet company even admitted that he used the name because it identified Carson.

A celebrity's right of publicity is invaded when his identity is intentionally appropriated for commercial purposes. The fact that the defendant did not use Carson's last name did not lessen the offense. In fact, no violation would have occurred if his name had been used.

The court gave as examples of names that would not have violated Carson's right of publicity: "J. William Carson Portable Toilet," "John William Carson Portable Toilet," and "J. W. Carson Portable Toilet." The reason that these uses of his name would not have been violative of Carson's right is simple—there would have been no appropriation of Carson's identity as a celebrity. Even if his real name was used, the public would not have associated the two as the same person.

Carson's full real name was not recognizable by the public any more than James Smith would be for LL Cool J's real name, or Peter Gene Hernandez for Bruno Mars, or Thomas Mapother for Tom Cruise, or Stefani Germanotta for Lady Gaga, or even Katheryn Hudson for Katy Perry.

Use of an Object Here's another example of appropriation of an identity without the use of a name. This case involved an object commonly associated with a celebrity.

Lothar Motschenbacher was an internationally known race car driver competing in NASCAR. He competed in one Sprint Cup Series event in his career. That came in 1970, when Motschenbacher raced in the season opener at Riverside. Motchenbacher was best known for his racing in the SCCA Can-Am series in the late 1960s and early 1970s.

Part of his income came from product endorsements. Since 1966 all of Motschenbacher's cars had been individualized to set them apart from other cars and to make them more recognizable as his. Each was red with a narrow white pinstripe, unlike any other car. The white background of his racing number 11 was always an oval, unlike the circular ones on other cars.

In 1970 R. J. Reynolds Tobacco Company and its agency William Esty produced a television commercial that used a stock photo showing several race cars on the track.

Motschenbacher's car was in the foreground. The driver could not be identified in the photo because of the helmet and driving suit.

The ad agency altered the photograph for the commercial. They changed the numbers on all of the cars; Motschenbacher's number 11 was changed to 17. A spoiler (wing) was attached to the car, displaying the name of the product, Winston. All other product names were removed from the other cars.

The agency then filmed the slide, adding a series of comic book-type balloons with messages. Over Motschenbacher's car the balloon said: "Did you know that Winston tastes good, like a cigarette should?" The commercial was broadcast nationally.

Motschenbacher filed suit in *Motschenbacher* v. *R. J. Reynolds Tobacco Co.*, 498 F.2d 821 (9th Cir. 1974). The court agreed that the plaintiff himself was not recognizable. However, the decoration of the car in the picture left little doubt that the car was Motschenbacher's, and implied that he was driving. Because of this, R. J. Reynolds lost the case.

Use of a Performer's Style Appropriation of a performer's style is another way that one's right of publicity can be violated. Guy Lombardo had invested forty years in developing his image as "Mr. New Year's Eve." Add to this the combination of New

Year's Eve, balloons, party hats, and "Auld Lang Syne" in the right context and you have an image that is unmistakable, and one that can be exploited commercially.

Doyle Dane Bernbach, the ad agency for Volkswagen at the time, entered into negotiations with Lombardo in late 1974 to obtain his appearance in a television commercial. The negotiations, however, fell through but the agency went on to produce the commercial featuring several products of the car manufacturer all set against the background of a New Year's Eve party.

Lombardo's name was never mentioned, but the actor used to portray the bandleader conducted the band using the same gestures and choice of music. Even the set resembled the one that Lombardo had become so closely associated with as "Mr. New Year's Eve." The case that resulted was *Lombardo* v. *Doyle Dane Bernbach, Inc.,* 58 A.D.2d 620, 396 N.Y.S.2d 661 (App. Div. 1977). Lombardo won.

Use of Three-Dimensional Objects Eleanor Brown Young was, in 1941, a professional model of junior misses' clothes. She was employed by a department store and was asked to pose for the making of a mannequin. She allowed Greneker Studios to mold the mannequins in her image—her form, features, and likeness—for the exclusive use of her employer—the department store.

Later, it was learned that Greneker sold the mannequins to others. *Young* v. *Greneker Studios, Inc.,* 176 Misc. 1027, 26 N.Y.S.2d 357 (Sup. Ct. 1941), was the case that followed. Young alleged that Greneker manufactured and sold mannequins in her likeness, without her permission, for the purposes of trade.

Under New York Civil Rights Law, section 51, an action may be brought by "any person whose name, portrait, or picture is used . . . for advertising purposes or for the purposes of trade without the written consent first obtained." Even though Young gave her permission for her employer to make and use the mannequins in her image, she had not given permission to the company who manufactured them to sell them to anyone else.

What this case points up is that the courts give broad latitude to what form constitutes a "portrait or picture" of a person. As we have seen a picture is not limited only to a photograph of the person, but to any representation of that person. The representation can be two-dimensional or, as in this case, three-dimensional. The words "picture" and "portrait" are general enough to encompass any form of an image, from a photograph to a painting to a sculpture.

Use of Illustrations Donald Newcombe was a major league baseball all-star from 1949 until 1960. He pitched for the Brooklyn Dodgers and other teams during that time, and previously had played in the so-called Negro leagues. Newcombe was one of the first African-American players in the major leagues after Jackie Robinson broke the color barrier in 1947. Newcombe is the only player in major league history to have won the Most Valuable Player Award, the Cy Young Award, and the Rookie of the Year Award. He was a four-time member of the National League All Star Team, batted over .300 in four separate seasons, and had the most wins of any pitcher in the National League in 1950, 1951, 1955, and 1956.

Newcombe's baseball career was cut short due to a personal battle with alcohol. He is a recovering alcoholic, and he has devoted a substantial amount of time using his fame to advocate the dangers of alcohol, including serving as a spokesperson for the National Institute on Drug and Alcohol Abuse. At the time of trial in this case, Newcombe was the Director of Community Relations for the Los Angeles Dodgers, where he maintains an active role in battling alcohol abuse.

An advertisement in the February 1994 *Sports Illustrated* "swimsuit edition" for Killian's Irish Red Beer (manufactured by Coors) featured a drawing of an old-time baseball game. The drawing filled the left side of the full-page ad, while the right side was a picture of a glass of beer.

The court described the image in the ad: "The baseball scene focused on a pitcher in the windup position and the background included a single infielder and an old-fashioned outfield fence. The players' uniforms did not depict an actual team, and the background did not depict an actual stadium."

However, Newcombe, along with family, friends and former teammates, immediately recognized the pitcher featured in the advertisement as Newcombe in his playing days.

While denying that the pitcher in the advertisement was a "likeness" of Newcombe, Coors admitted that the drawing was based on a newspaper photograph of Newcombe pitching in the 1949 World Series. In reality, the drawing and the newspaper photograph were virtually identical.

In *Newcombe* v. *Adolf Coors Co.*, No. 95-55688, U.S. App. LEXIS 23308 (9th Cir., September 22, 1998), the court determined that there was an issue of fact regarding whether Newcombe was readily identifiable as the pitcher in the advertisement. Under both California statutory and common law, to prove a cause of action for commercial misappropriation, the plaintiff must prove that his or her likeness or identity had been used.

To accomplish this, the court looked to the statute's definition that a person is considered readily identifiable from a photograph "when one who views the photograph with the naked eye can reasonably determine that the person depicted in the photograph is the same person who is complaining of its unauthorized use."

In determining that Newcombe's image had been appropriated, the court stated: "Having viewed the advertisement, we hold that a triable issue of fact has been raised as to whether Newcombe is readily identifiable as the pitcher in the advertisement. Initially, we note that the drawing in the advertisement and the newspaper photograph of Newcombe upon which the drawing was based are virtually identical. The pitcher's stance, proportions and shape are identical to the newspaper photograph of Newcombe; even the styling of the uniform is identical, right down to the wrinkles in the pants. The defendants maintain that stance alone cannot suffice to render a person readily identifiable, and that even if it could, the drawing of the pitcher in the advertisement was essentially generic and could have been any one of thousands of people who have taken to the pitcher's mound to throw a baseball. We disagree."

It may be the case that Newcombe's stance is essentially generic, but based on the record before us, Newcombe is the only one who has such a stance. The record contains pictures of other pitchers in the windup position but none of these pitchers has a stance similar to Newcombe's, thus giving us no basis to reach the conclusion proposed by the defendants that the pitcher in the advertisement is "generic." Furthermore, Matthew Reinhard, the Art Director at [Foote, Cone,] Belding, declared that a prior work of Cassidy's, which depicted former San Francisco Giant pitcher Juan Marichal in his unorthodox high-leg-kick windup, would not have been suitable for the advertisement at issue because Marichal's windup was too distinctive. Reinhard's admission that a pitcher's windup could be so distinctive so as to make that player readily identifiable, regardless of the visibility of his face or the markings on the uniform, bolsters our determination that there is a genuine issue of material fact as to whether Newcombe's stance was so distinctive that the defendants used his likeness by using a picture of Newcombe's stance.

In addition to the identifiability of the pitcher in the advertisement as Newcombe based on the pitcher's stance, the pitcher's skin is moderately dark, which is quite similar to Newcombe's skin color. A jury could rationally find from this that Newcombe was readily identifiable, even though his facial features were not entirely visible.

Furthermore, while the drawing in the advertisement was slightly altered from the newspaper photograph, that does not alter our conclusion that there is a genuine issue of material fact as to whether the advertisement made use of Newcombe's likeness. For example, the uniform number in the advertisement ("39") is only slightly different than Newcombe's number ("36")—the first number is the same and the second number is simply inverted and the advertisement utilized the same block style numbers that were used on Newcombe's jersey—and it is arguable that the similarity in numbers could either consciously or subconsciously conjure up images of Newcombe. Also, we do not find persuasive the fact that the coloring of the bill of the hat in the advertisement is different, in light of the fact that the rest of the uniform is identical to the uniform in the newspaper photograph of Newcombe.

Use of Photo-Illustrations Another form that can create a problem involves photorealistic illustrations. On February 15, 1978, Leon Spinks defeated Muhammad Ali in a 15-round split decision. Until then, Ali had been the heavyweight boxing champion of the world. In the February 1978 issue of *Playgirl* magazine a picture ran with an article entitled "Mystery Man," showing a nude black man seated in a corner of a boxing ring. The illustration fell somewhere between cartoon and realistic art. The article was not editorial, but rather fictional writing, using, as the court determined, the picture of Ali solely "for the purposes of trade."

There was no question that the portrait was of Ali. In the court's words: "The cheekbones, broad nose, and wide-set brown eyes, together with the distinctive smile and close-cropped black hair are recognizable as the features of...one of the most widely known athletes of our time." In *Ali* v. *Playgirl, Inc.*, 447 F. Supp. 723 (S.D.N.Y. 1978), the court agreed that Ali's right of publicity had been violated.

One important thing to note here is that not only was the magazine liable for the violation of the right of publicity, but the artist who drew the portrait was named as a defendant as well.

Use of Modified Photos When a photograph or picture is modified or altered slightly, but still identifiable as a specific person, a problem can result. A situation such as this happened quite some time ago in 1917 when Gladys Loftus, a twenty-two-year-old Ziegfeld Girl, appeared in the rose garden scene in *Midnight Frolics* wearing a special costume known as "the rose costume," made by Lady Duff-Gordon.

Loftus had her picture taken wearing the rose costume by Alfred Johnson, a photographer employed to take pictures of some of the girls in the play, while in costume. Loftus became readily recognizable in her costume, and the public became very familiar with Johnson's photograph of her.

Sometime later The Greenwich Lithographing Company, a designer of theatrical and movie posters, was hired to produce a poster for the photoplay, *Shame*. The posters, which printed the name *Shame* in very large type, were distributed throughout the city of New York (see box 7.3).

On the poster was a picture of a man pointing his right hand in scorn at a woman who had her head slightly bowing. Greenwich admitted that it had copied the photograph of Loftus to use as the model of the woman in the poster.

Box 7.3

Shame Poster

Coming Soon to your local theatre John W. Noble presents the photoplay of the hour *SHAME* featuring Zena Keefe (A story of the world's unjust condemnation.)

The artist, Ira Cassidy, used the rose costume picture when he painted the poster art for *Shame*, making only slight variations:

* Changing the tilt of the head;
* Lowering the hair;
* Altering the outline of the nose, chin, and neck; and
* Removing the right arm from view.

All other aspects of the photo were duplicated in the final painting.

The court determined in *Loftus* v. *Greenwich Lithographing Co., Inc.*, 192 A.D. 251, 182 N.Y.S. 428 (App. Div. 1920), that the poster was not a direct copy of the photo, but the image of Loftus was duplicated in such a way as to make it easily identifiable as being Loftus. Loftus won her case.

Use of a Voice Impersonation In 1985 Ford Motor Company, through it agency Young & Rubicam, Inc., developed a campaign using the song "Do You Want To Dance?" After getting permission to the copyright of the song, they hired a backup singer to record the song. They wanted to get a singer that could match singer Bette Midler's voice and style as close as possible. They did. The fact that the rendition of the song sounded exactly like Midler allowed her to win in court. When a distinctive voice that is widely known and recognized is deliberately imitated to sell a product, that person's identity is pirated.

Bette Midler v. *Ford Motor Company*, 849 F.2d 460 (1988) resulted.

Midler is a nationally known actress and singer. She won a Grammy in 1973 as the Best New Artist of that year. Midler has been nominated for two Academy Awards, and won three Grammy Awards, four Golden Globes, three Emmy Awards, and a special Tony Award. She has sold over thirty million records worldwide and along with that has also received four gold, three platinum, and three multiplatinum albums.

When Ford's ad agency, Young & Rubicam, presented the commercial to its client it played an edited version of Midler singing "Do You Want To Dance," taken from the 1973 Midler album, "The Divine Miss M." After the client accepted the commercial idea, the agency contacted Midler's manager, Jerry Edelstein. Here's how the conversation went: "Hello, I am Craig Hazen from Young and Rubicam. I am calling you to find out if Bette Midler would be interested in doing . . .?" Edelstein: "Is it a commercial?" "Yes." "We are not interested."

Undeterred, Young & Rubicam hired Ula Hedwig who had been one of "The Harlettes," the backup singers for Midler for ten years. Hedwig was told by Young & Rubicam that "they wanted someone who could sound like Bette Midler's recording of Do You Want To Dance." At the direction of Young & Rubicam, Hedwig recorded the song for the commercial.

After the commercial aired Midler was told by "a number of people that it sounded exactly like her record of 'Do You Want To Dance.' Hedwig was told by 'many personal friends' that they thought it was Midler singing the commercial."

Keep in mind that neither the name nor a picture of Midler was used in the commercial. And Young & Rubicam had a license from the copyright holder to use the song. (But the song and the performance are different.) At issue in this case is only the protection of Midler's voice. The court described the defendants' conduct "as that 'of the average thief.' They decided, 'If we can't buy it, we'll take it.'"

Use with Merchandising Agreements In *Allison* v. *Vintage Sports Plaques*, 136 F.3d 1443 (11th Cir. 1998), the plaintiffs were Elisa Allison, the widow of a well-known race car driver, Clifford Allison, and Orel Hershisher, the famous baseball pitcher.

Clifford Allison had a licensing agreement with Maxx Race Cards (MAXX) whereby Maxx would manufacture and market trading cards bearing his likeness for a royalty of 18 percent of sales, which is now paid to his estate. Orel Hershisher (Hershisher) has a licensing agreement with the Major League Baseball Players Association (MLBPA) that grants MLBPA the right to use and license his name and image for commercial purposes in exchange for a pro rata share of all revenues derived therefrom. MLBPA has licensed Hershisher's name and image to various trading card companies.

Vintage Sports purchased trading cards from manufacturers and (without modifying the cards at all) mounted them under acrylic on a wood board. Vintage then labeled each plaque with the celebrity's name. They market each plaque as a "Limited Edition" and an "Authentic Collectible." Vintage is not a party to any licensing agreement and has never paid a royalty or commission for the use of the celebrity's name or image. However, pursuant to their respective licensing agreements, royalties from the card manufacturers and distributors for the initial sale of the cards to Vintage were received.

Mrs. Allison, on behalf of her husband's estate, claimed that the resale of the cards violated her husband's right of publicity. The court held that while Alabama had never recognized a right of "publicity," the Alabama right of privacy contained an analogous right. The court found that the right of privacy included the appropriation of some element of the plaintiff's personality for commercial use. The court stated: "We read Alabama's commercial appropriation privacy right, however, to represent the same interests and address the same harms as does the right of publicity as customarily defined. Indeed, the elements of Alabama's commercial appropriation invasion of privacy tort, bases liability on commercial, rather than psychological, interests."

Having decided that Alabama law recognized publicity rights, the court then determined that the first-sale doctrine precluded Mrs. Allison's claim. The court explained:

> The first-sale doctrine provides that once the holder of an intellectual property right "consents to the sale of particular copies . . . of his work, he many not thereafter exercise the distribution right with respect to such copies . . . " Any other rule would extend the monopoly created by the intellectual property right so far as to permit control by the rightholder over the disposition of lawfully obtained tangible personal property.

The court went on to discuss the impact of ignoring the first-sale doctrine. They reasoned that:

> Accepting appellants' argument would have profoundly negative effects on numerous industries and would grant a monopoly to celebrities over their identities that would upset the delicate balance between the interests of the celebrity and those of the public.

Such a holding presumably also would prevent, for example, framing a magazine advertisement that bears the image of a celebrity and reselling it as a collector's item, reselling an empty cereal box that bears a celebrity's endorsement, or even reselling a used poster promoting a professional sports team. Refusing to apply the first-sale doctrine to the right of publicity also presumably would prevent a child from selling to his friend a baseball card that he had purchased, a consequence that undoubtedly would be contrary to the policies supporting that right.

The court rejected Mrs. Allison's argument that the first-sale doctrine should not apply. She argued that the right of publicity protected "identity," whereas the others protected "a particular photograph or product." The court found that accepting this argument would profoundly affect numerous industries, and would bestow a monopoly to celebrities over their identities that would upset the delicate "balance between the interests of the celebrity and those of the public." Not to apply the first-sale doctrine to the right of publicity would make the resale of sports trading cards and memorabilia actionable in court.

By applying the first-sale doctrine, however, the celebrity would continue to control the right to license his or her image initially and still have the ability to determine when, or if, that image could be distributed. The court reasoned:

> Because the application of the first sale doctrine to limit the right of publicity under Alabama law will maintain the appropriate balance between the rights of celebrities in their identities and the rights of the public to enjoy those identities, we conclude that the Alabama Supreme Court would apply the first-sale doctrine in this case and the district court properly so applied it.

Allison and Hershisher cannot win a commercial appropriation action if Vintage merely resells the trading cards that bear their likenesses, because the resale of licensed images falls under the protective scope of the first sale doctrine as we have seen.

So, the district court ruled correctly, and observed: "Vintage would probably violate the right of publicity if [it] attached a trading card to a baseball glove and sold it as 'an official Orel Hershisher glove' or if [it] affixed a Clifford Allison card onto a model car and sold it as 'an official Clifford Allison car.' Thus, this court must decide if the Vintage Clocks and plaques are more like reselling the trading cards or more like using Plaintiffs' names and likenesses to sell frames and clocks, similar to selling an Allison car or a Hershisher glove."

The district court concluded that Vintage was selling the trading cards after putting them in a more attractive display. Because the first-sale doctrine permits such resale, the court granted summary judgment on the right of publicity claim.

Implied Editorial Jamie Messenger, a teenage fashion model from Florida, posed for photographs for the magazine *Young and Modern*. The photographs were used to illustrate a love and sexual advice column that was a monthly feature of the magazine. The column contained a letter from a teenager, signed as "Mortified," who sought advice because she had had sex with three boys and was then ostracized by her friends. The column, entitled "I got trashed and had sex with three guys," was illustrated by three provocative photographs of Messenger in various stages of undress.

The court rejected the publisher's argument that the photographs were "newsworthy" and, as a result, exempt under Sections 50 and 51 of the New York Civil Rights Law, in *Messenger* v. *Gruner & Jahr USA Publishing*, 994 F. Supp. 525 (S.D.N.Y. 1998), Messenger claimed that the publisher created the false impression that she was the author of the letter, and therefore the use of the photographs violated the New York right of publicity law. In contrast, the publisher argued that its use of the photographs was not for trade or advertising purposes, but was used in connection with editorial: a matter of public interest.

The court reasoned that the use of a photograph to illustrate an article on a topic of public interest was not actionable unless the photograph had no relation to the article or unless the article was actually an advertisement. However, if the use of the photograph was false or misleading in connection with the article, this could be a violation of the person's right of publicity.

The court found that readers of the sex advice article could interpret the accompanying photographs to be of the writer of the "Mortified" letter. Thus, the publisher's "newsworthy" privilege could be lost.

The court stated:

> The fundamental issue is whether the publication created the impression that Messenger had had the experiences that were the subject of the column, a matter that turns on the interpretation that would be given to the column by readers. The problem is

analogous to that presented in libel cases where the question is whether the accused publication is defamatory, and the mode of analysis is the same. The Court initially must determine as a matter of law whether readers reasonably could construe the article in the manner alleged by the plaintiff. If they could, the issue whether they actually did so is for the trier of fact. Although the defendants have pointed out several substantial indications that arguably would lead a reader to conclude that the photographs of Messenger were those of a model and not in fact of "Mortified," the purported author of the letter, the Court is not prepared on this record to say that this was the only reasonable conclusion.

Commemorative Messages On September 11, 2009, Michael Jordan was inducted into the Basketball Hall of Fame. To honor the occasion, Time, Inc., the publisher of *Sports Illustrated*, produced a special edition of *Sports Illustrated Presents* to celebrate Jordan's legendary career, entitled "Jordan: Celebrating a Hall of Fame Career." The commemorative issue was not distributed to regular *Sports Illustrated* subscribers, but rather was sold separately in stores.

Michael Jordan led the Chicago Bulls to six National Basketball Association championships, winning myriad awards and countless accolades as the best player in the game. Jordan led the NBA in scoring in ten seasons (NBA record) and tied Wilt Chamberlain's record of seven consecutive scoring titles. He retired with 32,292 points in regular season play, placing him fourth on the NBA's all-time scoring list behind Kareem Abdul-Jabbar, Karl Malone, and Kobe Bryant. Jordan's yearly income from his endorsements (including Nike's Air Jordan) is estimated to be over $40 million.

A Time sales representative contacted Jewel Food Stores to offer free advertising space in the commemorative issue in return for a promise to sell the magazines in its stores. Jewel agreed to the deal and designed a full-page color ad. The ad featured a photo of a pair of basketball shoes, each bearing Jordan's number "23." The headline of the ad read: "A Shoe In!"

To Jordan the ad was not a celebratory gesture but a misappropriation of his identity for the supermarket chain's commercial benefit. He responded with a $5 million lawsuit in, *Michael Jordan* v. *Jewel Food Stores, Inc.*, 743 F.3d 509 (2014).

Jewel argued that its ad didn't propose a commercial transaction and therefore flunks the leading test for commercial speech. But the court said: "As we have explained, the commercial-speech category is not limited to speech that directly or indirectly proposes a commercial transaction. Jewel nonetheless places substantial weight on this test."

The court continued:

> It's clear that the textual focus of Jewel's ad is a congratulatory salute to Jordan on his induction into the Hall of Fame. If the literal import of the words were all that mattered, this celebratory tribute would be noncommercial. But evaluating the text requires consideration of its context, and this truism has special force when applying the commercial-speech doctrine. Modern commercial advertising is enormously varied in form and style.
>
> We know from common experience that commercial advertising occupies diverse media, draws on a limitless array of imaginative techniques, and is often supported by sophisticated marketing research. It is highly creative, sometimes abstract, and frequently relies on subtle cues. The notion that an advertisement counts as "commercial" only if it makes an appeal to purchase a particular product makes no sense today, and we doubt that it ever did. An advertisement is no less "commercial" because it promotes brand awareness or loyalty rather than explicitly proposing a transaction in a specific product or service. Applying the "core" definition of commercial speech

too rigidly ignores this reality. Very often the commercial message is general and implicit rather than specific and explicit.

Use of an Expression In September 1997, Dillard Department Stores ran a newspaper advertisement for a shirt known as a "henley." The ad showed a photograph of a man wearing a henley shirt with copy reading: "This is Don," beside the picture, and an arrow pointing toward the man's head. Underneath the words was the copy, "This is Don's Henley" in the same size print, with an arrow pointing to the shirt.

Donald Hugh Henley, is a critically acclaimed rock and roll musician began his music career in 1970. He had moved to Los Angeles to record an album with his early band, Shiloh, while living at the home of fellow Texan, Kenny Rogers. Soon after, Henley met Glenn Frey and they both became members of Linda Ronstadt's backup band. After touring with her, two months later they, along with Bernie Leadon and Randy Meisner, became *The Eagles*. After *The Eagles* broke up in 1980, Henley maintained a very successful solo career by continuing to produce platinum-selling albums and perform at concerts around the world.

The result of the "This is Don's Henley" ad was *Donald Hugh Henley* v. *Dillard Department Stores*, 46 F. Supp. 2d 587 (1999). Typically, in a Right to Publicity case the defendant has "appropriated to his own use or benefit the reputation, prestige, social or commercial standing, public interest or other values of his name or likeness." However a person's right of publicity may be violated when a defendant uses a version of that person's persona in a manner that symbolizes or identifies the person, "such as the use of a name, nickname, voice, picture, performing style, distinctive characteristics, or other indicia closely associated with a person." This manner of appropriation can become actionable when it is used to "advertise the defendant's business or product." The court said: "A violation can occur simply in the use of a phrase that clearly identifies the celebrity. It is not fatal to a plaintiff's claim that the defendant did not use the plaintiff's 'name.'" That is in the context of a name.

The issue was to determine whether Dillard actually appropriated Henley's name or likeness. Dillard used Don Henley's name by using the expression "Don's henley." In advertising parlance we call this technique "borrowed interest." You just have to be careful who's interest you borrow. Henley argued that, at a minimum, his likeness and identity were "borrowed" (the law calls it "appropriated") by Dillard for its ad.

During her deposition in the case, Lisa M. Robertson, the creator of the ad said:

Q: Well, what prompted you to come up with the idea "This is Don. This is Don's Henley"?

A: Well, I was trying to find a play on words to use for the ad.

Q: And there's no doubt that when you were using the words "This is Don. This is Don's henley," the Don Henley wordplay meant Don Henley the recording artist, not some other person named Don Henley?

A: Well, obviously the name -- yes, I mean I knew it was Don Henley; that was where it came from. But it wasn't, you know, to imply that he was a part of it.

Q: I think you said earlier that by using the word -- by using the headline "This is Don. This is Don's henley," you intended a wordplay, correct?

A: Yes.

Q: And so it was your intention for consumers to recognize this advertisement as a wordplay."

A: Yes.

Q: And for the wordplay to work, the consumer had to recognize the name Don Henley, right?

A: Well, you'd have to know who he was to get it, yes.

Q: So for it to work or for them to get it, they must recognize the similarity between the words "This is Don. This is Don's Henley" and the name of the recording artist Don Henley, correct?

A: Yes.

While use of the expression "Don's Henley" is arguably the use of Plaintiff's name, a genuine issue of fact exists as to whether that expression is, indeed, Plaintiff's name. However, Courts have recognized that a defendant may be held liable for using a phrase or image that clearly identifies the celebrity, in addition to finding liability for using a plaintiff's precise name.

A Recent Change in Right of Publicity Cases . . . Profits as Damages

Russell Christoff posed for a two-hour photo shoot in 1986 for Nestle and was paid $250. He signed a model release stating that he would be paid an additional $2,000 if Nestle's Canadian division used his likeness in its marketing. Years later, while shopping in a Rite-Aid store, Mr. Christoff, now fifty-eight years old and a kindergarten teacher, noticed his image on a Taster's Choice coffee jar. It was now 2002. Claiming that he was never paid the $2,000 as stated in his original release, Mr. Christoff filed a lawsuit *Christoff* v. *Nestlé USA, Inc.,* 47 Cal. 4th 468 (2009) against Nestle, the makers of Taster's Choice, under California Civil Code Section 3344.

Section 3344 is violated when a person "knowingly uses another's name, voice, signature, photograph, or likeness, . . . for purposes of advertising or selling, . . . without such person's prior consent." To sustain a cause of action for commercial misappropriation under Cal.Civ. Code Section 3344, a plaintiff must prove: (1) the defendant's use of the plaintiff's identity, (2) the appropriation of the plaintiff's name or likeness to the defendant's advantage, commercially or otherwise, (3) lack of consent, and (4) resulting injury. If a plaintiff prevails on a Section 3344 claim, he may be able to recover significant damages. Specifically, the statute provides that "the person who violated the section shall be liable . . . in an amount equal to the greater of seven hundred fifty dollars ($750) or the actual damages suffered by him or her as a result of the unauthorized use, and any profits from the unauthorized use that are attributable to the use and are not taken into account in computing the actual damages. Punitive damages may also be awarded [and the] prevailing party . . . shall also be entitled to attorney's fees and costs."

During discovery, Mr. Christoff learned that Nestle's Canadian company began using his image in 1986, and that from 1997 to 2003, Nestle used his image on coffee labels in the United States, Mexico, South Korea, Japan, Israel and Kuwait. Nestle offered $100,000 to settle the dispute, and rejected Mr. Christoff's counteroffer of $8.5 million. After a six-day trial, the jury decided that Nestle should have paid Christoff $330,000 for the use of his likeness. And that Mr. Christoff should receive damages equal to 5 percent of Nestle's profits from Taster's Choice sales between 1997 and 2003.

On January 27, 2005, a California jury awarded $15.6 million to Mr. Christoff. This is an important development and should be a warning about the substantial damages a defendant faces if the appropriate permission for use is not obtained.

California's right of publicity statute significantly differs from other states' right of publicity statutes in that it allows for the recovery of a defendant's profits. (This remedy is typically reserved for copyright and trademark actions.) Section 3344 provides that in seeking to recover the defendant's profits, "the injured party or parties are required to present proof only of the gross revenue attributable to such use, and the person who violated this section is required to prove his or her deductible expenses."

Thus, under Section 3344, the burden of proof on the plaintiff is relatively minimal—he is only required to show the defendants' gross revenues. The defendant, however, bears a significant burden of establishing all of its deductions and expenses and establishing what elements of its profits are due to matters other than the infringement.

Right of Publicity and the Lanham Act

Many of the cases that are brought for right of publicity issues also claim a cause of action under the Lanham Act. We clearly saw this in *ETW Corp.* v. *Jireh Publishing, Inc.*, 99 F. Supp. 2d 829 (2000), where Tiger Woods sued Jireh Publishing under the Lanham Act, in a trademark infringement lawsuit arising out of the sale of a print that used the name, image or likeness of him. In this case, defendant's motions for summary judgment were granted and plaintiff's motions were denied. Woods failed to establish the validity of its claim to trademark rights in the image of Tiger Woods. There was no evidence that plaintiff actually used the allegedly infringing image of Tiger Woods as a trademark, as would be required. Furthermore, defendant's print was an artistic creation seeking to express a message, and was protected under the Constitution.

The Lanham Act has been unsuccessfully relied upon in right of publicity cases (to protect one's likeness) for some time in relation to publicity rights. In fact, the right of publicity is currently controlled under state law, as we have seen. Yet, many have recommended that the Lanham Act be amended to create, in effect, a federal right of publicity.

The International Trademark Association (INTA) along with the American Bar Association adopted a resolution in its Request For Action By The INTA Board Of Directory, Federal Right of Publicity, March 3, 1998, calling for the introduction of legislation, in the form of an amendment to the Lanham Act, for a federal right of publicity. INTA formed a subcommittee in 1994 to address the issue, and the committee presented its recommendations in a report on March 3, 1998. There is a variance in the right of publicity laws from state to state, and the subcommittee felt that there was a need to create a consistent standard on a national level.

The subcommittee created a working draft of the proposed statute. They feel that a federal right of publicity is needed to bring uniformity and predictability to this area. As of the date of the report, seven states had recognized the right exclusively by statute. Eleven states recognized the right by common law. Eight states recognized both a common law and a statutory right of publicity.

Whether the right of publicity survived the death of the holder was a point of sharp division among the various states, as we discussed earlier. Some states limit publicity rights to the lifetime of the person, in effect, making them nondescendible. Other states treated the right as descendible. Some states differed on the duration of descendible rights.

The subcommittee also proposed that the federal law be designed to accommodate First Amendment constitutional and fair use principles as well. It also considered using "aspects of a persona" as they relate to matters of public interest.

While the above action clearly shows that a consistent (federal) right of publicity is desirable, no such change has occurred to date.

Problems Relating to Consent for Usage

The most appropriate method of avoiding lawsuits involving the right of publicity and the right of privacy is to obtain the person's prior consent. Generally, this consent must be in writing, and it involves more than just the authorization to use a person's name, likeness, or image. Involved are questions of how the image is used, the media, the form, where and when it is used, and so on. The advertiser must make certain that these questions are answered by the consent release to avoid liability later. For an interesting development in the area of consent and liability, see also the *Christoff* v. *Nestle USA* case that is discussed in this chapter.

Let's look at the different areas where consent problems are common.

Consent for a Specific Use

As one of the world's most famous fashion models, Christie Brinkley has appeared on the covers of many major magazines, including *Mademoiselle, Ladies Home Journal, Harper's Bazaar*, and *Sports Illustrated* in a career that spanned over thirty years. Early in her career, in September of 1979, John Casablancas, the president of Elite Model Management in Paris (Brinkley's agent), signed a licensing agreement with Galaxy Publishing. The agreement was to produce a series of posters of several models, including Brinkley.

Brinkley verbally agreed to the project and picked her own makeup artist, hairstylist, and bathing suit for the photo session. Photographer Michael Reinhardt photographed Brinkley for the poster. Cable TV network HBO (back then it was called Home Box Office) filmed the photo session for use in a special entitled: "Beautiful, Baby, Beautiful," on the careers of this country's top models. Brinkley gave her written permission to appear in the broadcast in the same pose and suit that was to be used for the poster.

After the session, Brinkley reviewed the photos and requested some retouching be done on the specific shot she had intended for the poster. This was back in the days when celebrity retouching wasn't the controversial act it is today, and before the advent of Photoshop in 1990. At that point, Galaxy proceeded to print the posters. The problem was that Brinkley never signed a model release authorizing the publication of her pictures in a poster. Brinkley stated that she "agreed to participate in a shooting from which a poster *may* have been the result, depending of course on my final judgment of the final product." She claimed that the printing and distribution of pinup posters was an unauthorized exploitation, for commercial purposes, of her name and image. The court agreed.

In *Brinkley* v. *Casablancas*, 80 A.D.2d 428, 438 N.Y.S.2d 1004 (App. Div. 1981), Brinkley's consent for the use of her photo for a cable television show did not include consent for a poster of a different photo taken at the same session. There was no written permission given for that particular photo to be used as a poster.

Consent for a Specific Length of Time

Another area where a problem can arise is the length of time allowed for the usage. In 1973 actor Charles Welch appeared in a television commercial for Mr. Christmas, a manufacturer of artificial Christmas trees. Welch was paid the sum of

$1,000 for the commercial. According to the contract the $1,000 fee allowed the commercial to be run for no more than one year. However, the contract further provided for an additional year's option with the payment of an additional $1,000. Although Mr. Christmas had not paid Welch the additional fee to exercise the option for the second year, it allowed its distributors to air the commercial in 1974.

Welch found out about this and agreed to a financial settlement for the 1974 option. In March of 1975 Mr. Christmas was contacted by the Screen Actors Guild and cautioned that the spot could not be aired any longer without further negotiations. In spite of this warning, the commercial aired during 1975.

In the lawsuit that resulted, *Welch* v. *Mr. Christmas Inc.*, 57 N.Y.2d 143, 440 N.E.2d 1317 (1982), the plaintiff was awarded compensatory damages of $1,000 and exemplary damages of $25,000. Here, the time limit was part of the original consent agreement. Using the commercial after the authorized period expired is the same as airing the commercial with no consent at all.

Mr. Christmas claimed as a defense that it did not use the commercial, claiming that its dealers were expected to purchase their own air time and that it did not know or have control over the spots used by them. However, Mr. Christmas encouraged its dealers to get the maximum use of the commercial, and made no attempt to notify the dealers that the usage period had ended. All of this made Mr. Christmas liable.

As we have seen before, not taking action when you have a responsibility to do so is also negligent. Since the agreement was with the actor and Mr. Christmas, those are the parties who are responsible to each other. If the dealers had aired the spot after they were notified in writing by Mr. Christmas not to do so, the situation may have been different.

We'll discuss such responsibilities in greater detail in chapter 11, The Client/Agency Relationship.

Use in a Medium that Was Not Authorized

Frank Dzurenko is a model who participated in a photo session for Jordache jeans. At the end of the photo session, Dzurenko signed a model release inserting the phrase "magazine ad use only." His reason for adding the limitation was that in the photos he had posed with a female model who was wearing only a pair of jeans.

After the session one of those photos was blown up and produced as a poster, which was then distributed to retailers. This violated Dzurenko's right of publicity because the photo's use exceeded the limitations of the release. In *Dzurenko* v. *Jordache, Inc.*, 59 N.Y.2d 788, 451 N.E.2d 477 (1983), the court determined that a release can cover not only the use of a name, picture or likeness, but also the time, form, and media of its use. Dzurenko won the case.

Another interesting issue brought as a defense was that Dzurenko didn't sign the release with the limitation until after the photos had been taken. However, the court held that this didn't matter. Dzurenko had the absolute right to limit the usage of the photos in any way he desired, regardless of when the release was signed.

When Parental Consent Is Revocable

Another problem regarding consent can occur when a child's parent gives consent and then the child, on becoming an adult, attempts to withdraw it. This can pose a unique problem for advertisers. That was exactly what happened with Brooke Shields and Garry Gross.

In 1975 Brooke Shields was ten years old. At the time she was registered with the Ford Model Agency, working as a child model (and a very famous one at that).

One of the jobs she did was for Playboy Press that required her to pose nude in a bathtub. The intent was that the photos would be published in a publication called *Sugar and Spice.*

Before the photo session, Teri Shields, Brooke's mother, signed a consent for the photographer Garry Gross to "use, reuse and/or publish, and republish" the photos. Brooke's photos appeared in *Sugar and Spice,* as well as on posters and in other publications. Brooke even used the photos in a book about herself with the permission of the photographer. Gross, in fact, had shot Brooke on many occasions for *Penthouse* magazine, *New York Magazine*, and advertising for the Courtauldts and Avon Company.

In 1980 Brooke learned that the *Sugar and Spice* photos had appeared in the French magazine, *Photo*. At that point, she became disturbed by the publication of the photos and attempted to buy the negatives (long before the impact of digital photography) from Gross.

When that failed, she brought suit: *Shields* v. *Gross*, 58 N.Y.2d 338 (1983). The suit claimed, among other things, that her right of privacy had been violated and sought to cancel the consent given by her mother in 1975.

According to New York's Civil Rights Law, section 50, once the written consent is obtained, the photos can be published as agreed. If that person is a minor, his or her parents may give the consent.

Under common law, infants can disaffirm their own or their guardian's consent. However, where a specific statute permits a class of agreements to be made by a child, the discussion is ended, and the agreement is valid. Consent had been given, and it would stand under its original terms. Brooke lost her claim.

The First Amendment's Relation to Privacy and Publicity

When Freedom of the Press Outweighs the Rights of Privacy and Publicity

In 1978, the movie *Magic* was released and subsequently grossed over $23 million (from a $7 million budget). The movie starred Anthony Hopkins and Ann-Margret. For only the second time in her career (the first time was in the 1971 movie *Carnal Knowledge*), Ann-Margret appeared in a nude scene. She made the decision to disrobe for artistic reasons, agreeing to do so only if there was a minimal crew at the filming and if no still photos were taken.

High Society magazine runs photographs of well-known women caught in revealing situations. In one particular issue, five pages were devoted exclusively to Ann-Margret. One of the photos was taken from the movie *Magic* and showed her nude from the waist up. After learning of this photo, suit was brought in *Ann-Margret* v. *High Society Magazine, Inc.*, 498 F.Supp. 401 (1980), for violation of her right of privacy and right of publicity.

There was no doubt that Ann-Margret was considered a celebrity, in fact one of the most famous sex symbols of the 1960s and 1970s. But simply because she was a celebrity she has not given up her right to privacy. However, she chose to appear in the motion picture, partially nude, knowing that the public would see her performance. The reproduction of scenes from that performance were faithful and accurate and not distorted, and therefore were not an invasion of her privacy.

The court said: "Undoubtedly, the plaintiff is unhappy about the appearance of her picture in [the] magazine. And while the court can sympathize with her feelings, the fact that she does not like either the manner in which she is portrayed, or the medium in which her picture is reproduced . . . [does] not expand her rights or create any cause of action . . .”

As far as her claim of violation of her right of publicity, the court felt that it also had no merit. There is only an action when the use is for “advertising purposes or for the purposes of trade.” The fact that the magazine is sold for profit does not constitute such a use. The mere use of the photos in an editorial context was acceptable according to the court. The case was dismissed.

When the Right of Publicity Exceeds Freedom of the Press

“Ladies and gentlemen, children of all ages, I present the great Zacchini.” Hugo Zacchini practiced a form of entertainment developed by his father and performed by his family for over fifty years. Zacchini was a human cannonball, and over the years he performed at many public fairs and events.

In August and September of 1972, Zacchini performed his act at the Geauga County Fair in Burton, Ohio. The performance took place in a fenced area surrounded by grandstands. He was shot from a cannon into a net two hundred feet away, and the performance lasted fifteen seconds.

A freelance reporter for Scripps-Howard Broadcasting, owner of the local television station, visited the fair on August 30, 1972, where Zacchini was performing. Zacchini spotted the reporter carrying a video camera and requested that he not tape the performance, but on the next day the reporter returned and videotaped the feat anyway. The event was broadcast on the 11 o’clock news along with a commentary, which was very complimentary.

When Zacchini learned of the unauthorized broadcast, he sued for damages for showing and commercializing his act without his consent. This was the first case involving the right of publicity to reach the United States Supreme Court: *Zacchini v. Scripps-Howard Broadcasting Co.*, 433 U.S. 562, 97 S.Ct. 2849, 53 L.Ed 2d 965 (1977).

Scripps-Howard argued that its broadcast of the event was protected under the 1st and 14th Amendments—freedom of the press. The TV station had the right to broadcast items of legitimate public interest. However, the TV station broadcast the entire act, from start to finish, along with a description of the event. If the station had broadcast that Zacchini was performing at the fair, commented on the performance, and showed his picture on TV, this could have been a very different case.

But as the Court said, Zacchini: “[H]ad a right of publicity that gave him personal control over commercial display and exploitation of his personality and the exercise of his talents. This right...was said to be such a valuable part of the benefit, which may be attained by his talents and efforts, that it was entitled to legal protection.”

Zacchini did not sue to stop the broadcast of his performance; he simply wanted to be paid for it. The Court agreed that Zacchini’s commercial interest in his act was protected under his right of publicity.

The Three Stooges Case and the “Transformative” Test

The Supreme Court of California eventually dealt directly with the tension between The First Amendment’s protection of an artist’s use of an image and the subject’s right of publicity. In *Comedy III Productions, Inc.* v. *Saderup*, 25 Cal. 4th 387 (2001), the defendant, who was an artist, sold lithographs and T-shirts showing the Three Stooges. The image was reproduced from a charcoal drawing he had made. Initially, the Court reasoned that because Saderup’s drawing was an “expressive” work (and not simply an advertisement or endorsement of a product) it was entitled to a higher level of First Amendment protection. Then, the Court found that celebrities have a public meaning, and that using their likeness in art helped express viewpoints or to promote debate on public issues. The Court also stated that works of art are protected under the First Amendment even when expressed in nontraditional forms, which includes T-shirts.

The Court then went on to balance the First Amendment issues against the subject's right of publicity. The Court held that depictions of celebrities "amounting to little more than the appropriation of the celebrity's economic value are not protected expression under the First Amendment." To put it another way, a simple reproduction of the celebrity's likeness, no matter how skilled, does not qualify for First Amendment protection.

However, even while acknowledging the economic impetus behind the right of publicity, the Court declined to adopt the test used in the Zacchini case, by which economic harm would simply be weighed against First Amendment concerns to determine if a particular use of an image was precluded by the right of publicity. The Saderup Court, instead, determined that the test in determining if a work of art depicting a well-known figure deserves First Amendment protection is: if the work is "transformative" in nature. According to the Court, a work is transformative if, in the artwork, "a celebrity's likeness is so transformed that it has become primarily the defendant's own expression rather than the celebrity's likeness."

The Saderup Court went on to explain its newly formulated rule. It stated that to be transformative, the use of the likeness by the artist must create something recognizably his own. The artist must contribute something more than a mere trivial variation to the work. Potentially adding to the confusion, the Court also observed that in determining whether a work is transformative, courts should consider whether or not the marketability and economic value of the work comes from the fame of the celebrity shown.

Here's an example. With Andy Warhol's work, the Court stated that through "distortion and the careful manipulation of context, Warhol was able to convey a message that went beyond commercial exploitation of celebrity images" and, as a result, had created works that would likely receive First Amendment protection.

In this case, the Court held that because it did not find any ". . . significant transformative or creative contribution" in Saderup's rendition of the Three Stooges, the work was not entitled to First Amendment protection and was in violation of California's right of publicity statute.

New York's New Rule In *Hoepker* v. *Kruger*, 200 F. Supp. 2d 340 (2002), a federal court in New York decided whether a photograph of the plaintiff, cropped and used as part of a collage, violated her rights under the New York right of publicity statute.

The court first held that a collage, like a drawing or painting, was a form of art entitled to full First Amendment protection. The court then acknowledged that under California's *Saderup* test, the collage was transformative enough to be afforded First Amendment protection. Even so, New York court refused to adopt the *Saderup* test, stating that courts "should not be asked to draw arbitrary lines between what may be art and what may [not be]."

So instead, the court offered a different approach, requiring a determination of whether the collage had primarily a "public interest" aspect or a "commercial" aspect. This means that if the value of the collage can be found primarily in its social usefulness as a work of art, it will receive First Amendment protection (in New York at least). On the other hand, if its primary value lies in generating sales through the popularity of the depicted celebrity, the artist may be liable for a violation of the right of publicity statute.

In spite of their different approaches, both the *Hoepker* and Saderup tests contain essentially the same element. They grant or deny First Amendment protection based upon a court's determination of the artistic nature of the work.

The Tiger Woods Case

ETW Corp. v. *Jireh Publishing, Inc.*, 99 F. Supp. 2d 829 (2000), is a recent case that has provided the latest ground for the debate between the First Amendment and the right of publicity. In ETW Corp., Rick Rush, a "sports artist," created a painting that was sold as a limited edition print and a large edition lithograph. The painting featured Tiger Woods (whose full name is Eldrick "Tiger" Woods; thus ETW Corp.) in the center in several poses, including one "displaying that awesome swing" according to the artist's accompanying text.

The painting, which memorialized Woods' 1997 victory in the U.S. Open, also depicted several past winners of the tournament superimposed over the leader board in the background, a caddie and a golf scoreboard. Tiger Wood's exclusive licensing agent sued, claiming in part that the print violated Tiger Woods' right of publicity under Ohio law.

The Ohio federal court rejected Wood's argument that the print was "merely sports merchandise" unworthy of First Amendment protection. Instead, the court found that the print sought to convey a message, and that message was a unique expression of an idea, rather than the mere copying of an image. As a result, the court decided that the print was protected by the First Amendment, and dismissed the case. The case was appealed, and the decision was upheld by the Sixth Circuit Court of Appeals in 2003.

In light of the cases, it is clear that artists do enjoy the right to use a celebrity's image as part of their artistic creations. The lesson to be learned from this recent activity? The more the art focuses and depends on the celebrity image, the more likely it will to run afoul of right of publicity statutes. On the other hand, the more clearly the work expresses an artistic theme and uses the celebrity image as part of that expression, the greater the reliance that the artist's work is protected by the First Amendment.

The Hollywood Studio Museum Commercial

At the beginning of this chapter, I wrote about a television commercial that had been produced for The Hollywood Studio Museum. Now that you have read the chapter, I'm sure that you can see why I used the story to begin.

Let's analyze that commercial to see if and where a problem could arise. First, there is the image of the famous director C.B. DeMille. Do we have to be concerned with invasion of his privacy rights? What about his rights of publicity? Secondly, we must consider the rights of the actor who played DeMille in the commercial, Gene Barry. Think about these issues for a moment.

Let's start with DeMille. His privacy rights ended at the time of his death, so there is no problem in that area. Regarding publicity rights, did we need the permission of the DeMille heirs to use his name and likeness? As we know, publicity rights are survivable under certain conditions. Under California law (that's where jurisdiction would have been), the publicity right is descendible, but only where it was exploited commercially during life. DeMille did, in fact, exploit his name and likeness during his life for commercial purposes. He was a very famous motion picture director, and his name alone sold many movies. Permission of the DeMille heirs was required and obtained.

As for actor Gene Barry, consent was of course required. A veteran of a fifty-five-year acting career, Mr. Barry had starred in the original movie *War of the Worlds* (1953) as well as the Steven Spielberg remake in 2005. A very recognizable actor from the 1950s and 1960s, he also starred in the popular TV western *Bat Masterson* (1958–1961) the fictionalized recounting of the life of the real-life U.S. Marshal, gambler, and gunman. Obviously, his appearance in the commercial was evidence of his consent to have his name and image used. He also signed a talent release and usage agreement. However, there were questions of usage. Barry, through the Screen Actors Guild (SAG), authorized use for only one year. The consent was for television and radio (the voice portion) use only. Another required restriction imposed by Mr. Barry was that we clearly identify the spot as "a public service message." This was to clarify that he had donated his time and name and thereby not diminish his worth for commercials other than public service messages.

Noncompliance with any of these restrictions could give rise to a lawsuit for breach of his publicity rights and consent agreement.

As you can see, using a person's identity, and how it is used, brings with it many issues which must be considered.

Advertising's Role in Products Liability

8

The purpose of advertising is to heighten our expectations.
—Hal Riney

"This is a stickup. Open the safe." Startled, John Klages turned toward the voice from the other side of the registration counter. Klages worked as a night clerk at Conley's Motel in Hampton Township, Pennsylvania. It was about 1:30 a.m. on an otherwise quiet March morning, and two armed men stood across the counter. Klages indicated that he didn't have the combination to the safe. In an instant, one of the robbers pointed a gun at him and fired.

The gun, fortunately, was only a starter pistol, and Klages suffered only minor injuries.

The day after the robbery attempt, Klages decided that he needed something to protect himself from future holdups. After reading some literature, a fellow employee, Bob McVay, suggested that they investigate mace as a weapon. McVay gathered four brochures from Markl Supply Company. The manufacturer of one of the mace weapons was General Ordnance Equipment Corporation. Klages selected the MKII model because it was easy to conceal yet, reassured by the literature (see box 8.1), it had the stopping power he needed. McVay and Klages read the brochure and, after discussing it with their boss, purchased an MKII mace weapon from Markl Supply.

Box 8.1 Markl Supply Company Brochure

Rapidly vaporizes on face of assailant effecting instantaneous incapacitation . . . It will instantly stop and subdue entire groups . . . Instantly stops assailants in their tracks . . . An attacker is subdued—instantly, for a period of fifteen to twenty minutes . . . *Time* magazine stated the chemical mace is "for police the first, if not the final, answer to a nationwide need . . ." A weapon that disables as effectively as a gun . . . and yet does no permanent injury. The effectiveness is the result of a unique incapacitation formulation (patent pending) projected in a shotgun-like pattern of heavy liquid droplets that, upon contact with the face, cause extreme tearing, and a stunned, winded condition, often accompanied by dizziness and apathy.

About 1:40 a.m. on the morning of September 22, 1968, two men entered the motel office where Klages was again on duty. The two men requested a room. Klages handed them a registration form and turned to reach for the room key. One of the men announced that it was a holdup, pulled out a gun, and demanded that Klages open the safe.

Klages moved behind the cash register where the mace was kept and, using the register as a shield, squirted the mace directly into the robber's face. Klages quickly ducked behind the counter. Unfortunately, the robber followed and shot him in the head—this time with a real gun, with real bullets. He survived the attack, but the bullet wound left Klages blind in his right eye.

Klages sued General Ordnance for damages. On March 4, 1974, a jury trial began in *Klages* v. *General Ordnance Equipment Corp.*, CCH Prods. Liab. Rep. Paragraph 7664 (Pa. Super. 1976). When it was over, the jury ruled in favor of Klages, awarding him $42,000.

This case is an example of products liability. Granted, the advertising did not cause the injury. It wasn't about a deceptive ad. Or, a false or misleading message. This area is very different from the other advertising issues covered.in this book.

Here's how it works. The manufacturer made a product for a specific purpose. The consumer purchased the product for that purpose. When the product failed to live up to it, the manufacturer was liable for the injury that resulted. Advertising was the machinery that created the image in the mind of the consumer—an image that painted a clear picture that the product would perform in a certain way.

A manufacturer, through its advertising, implies that its product is safe—and will perform—for its intended use. The manufacturer makes a promise or representation about his product. In the Klages case the manufacturer sold a product designed solely as a device to deter would-be assailants. Its sole use was to protect the purchasers from harm under extremely dangerous conditions. Klages bought the product with these specific purposes in mind. The product failed to live up to its promise, and the injury that resulted made the manufacturer liable.

Products Liability and Its Impact on Advertising

Products liability is an area of law that deals with a product's failure to perform whatever function for which it was sold. In this chapter we explore the connection between a company's advertising and products liability lawsuits.

In the 1950s, a product called Toni Home Permanent opened the door for women who wanted a permanent hair wave without going to a beauty salon. Since its introduction, Toni Home Permanent was going head to head with the perms that were done professionally at beauty salons (and other competitors).

In order to get the word out, radio personality Bill Cullen described the classic advertising campaign. The ad promotion featured identical twin sisters who had identical looking waves. One twin had her hair done professionally at a beauty salon; the other twin used Toni. The classic question Cullen asked the listeners was, "Which twin has the Toni?" Now bear in mind, the cost of perms at the time was about $15 from a professional salon and $2 for a Toni kit. Unless the people were told, it was inconclusive which twin had used which method. For women who wanted a professional looking wave, it was easy to use Toni at home and save the money.

"The Toni Twins" promotion was so popular, the phrase "Which Twin Has the Toni?" became a part of our 1950s vernacular, just like Nike's "Just do it!' is now.

In *Rogers* v. *Toni Home Permanent Co.*, 167 Ohio St. 244, 147 N.E. 2d 612 (1958), Ms. Rogers purchased a Toni Home Permanent set marked "Very Gentle." She bought the product because of the manufacturer's claims in its advertising and on its packaging. After following the directions supplied with the kit, Rogers' hair became "cotton-like . . . and . . . gummy." Her hair would not dry, and when the curlers supplied with the kit were removed, her hair fell out, leaving only one-half-inch of hair remaining.

This 1958 case is important because it was the first time the court made an effort to change how a manufacturer's liability was viewed. Originally, a consumer could sue only the retailer of a product for breach of warranty. It was considered that a contract did not exist between the ultimate consumer and the manufacturer, and therefore no warranty existed. The only contract was between the consumer and the store where the item was purchased. The manufacturer could not be sued directly, except in cases of negligence.

Because of the *Rogers* case, however, the courts have taken the position that the consumer can sue the manufacturer directly for breach of warranty actions (otherwise known as products liability). The court said:

> Today, many manufacturers of merchandise, including the defendant here, make extensive use of newspapers, periodicals, signboards, radio, and television to advertise their products. The worth, quality, and benefits of these products are described in glowing terms and in considerable detail, and the appeal is almost universally directed to the ultimate consumer. Many of these manufactured articles are shipped out in sealed containers by the manufacturer, and the retailers who dispense them to the ultimate consumers are but conduits or outlets through which the manufacturer distributes his goods. The consuming public ordinarily relies exclusively on the representations of the manufacturer in his advertisements. What sensible or sound reason then exists as to why, when the goods purchased by the ultimate consumer on the strength of the advertisements aimed squarely at him do not possess their described qualities and goodness and cause him harm, he should not be permitted to move against the manufacturer to recoup his loss. In our minds no good or valid reason exists for denying him that right. Surely under modern merchandising practices the manufacturer owes a very real obligation toward those who consume or use his products. The warranties made by the manufacturer in their advertisements and by the labels on their products are inducements to the ultimate consumers, and the manufacturer ought to be held to strict accountability to any consumer who buys the product in reliance on such representations and later suffers injury because the product proves to be defective.

Advertising as Evidence in Products Liability Cases

How does advertising play into this? Products liability cases can be made using the advertising as proof of what the consumer expected from the product. Since advertising imparts an image, that image can become a large aspect of what the consumer expects when he or she purchases the product. If it fails, the advertising can be used to substantiate what the consumer expected. And, it can also confirm that the manufacturer is liable for any injury that resulted.

I've heard a number of comments that products liability isn't part of advertising law. I've heard that cases involving advertising and products liability are rare. Neither argument is true or accurate. In fact, products liability is just as relevant to the business of advertising as is copyright or trademark, or privacy or publicity rights.

The reality is that more and more products liability lawsuits involve the product's advertising. And the advertiser's advertising agency is being included as a defendant in many recent cases. Based on our discussion in chapter 4, I'm sure you can see why that is. In fact, there has been a steady rise in products liability cases that involve the plaintiff's advertising in recent years. Another reason for the recent increase in products liability cases in general is simple. Consumers are readily able to bring products liability lawsuits, as opposed to FTC Section 5 actions. Sections 5 and 12 actions do not provide consumers a private cause of action, only businesses and the government. And, additionally, Lanham Act claims also are limited to competitors in business, not individual consumers.

The manufacturer's advertising or promotion may be a direct reason to bring suit or it may be used as evidence during a suit; evidence that can establish what the consumer expected from the product. The advertising may demonstrate the manufacturer's inability to live up to the representations made in the advertisement.

In the eyes of the law, a manufacturer is liable for any deficiency in its product. And the content in advertisements is playing an increasingly larger role in products liability lawsuits. In some cases, consumer expectations about how a product should perform under specific conditions includes advertising and promotional materials that demonstrates what the ordinary consumer was led to expect in regard to the product's performance. This was exactly the situation with Mr. Klages.

Theories of Products Liability

To assess the role advertising plays in products liability litigation, we should understand that there are a number of legal theories under which a products liability lawsuit can be brought. Those theories are briefly described below with specific illustrative cases, which you'll find discussed later in the chapter.

Negligence exists when there is a failure to exercise reasonable care to protect others against high risks.

A manufacturer may be negligent for an act (such as poor quality control) or for a failure to act (such as not testing the product).

Deceit occurs when there is intent to mislead regarding the existence or non-existence of a material fact, the consumer relies on the misleading information and damages result.

Fraudulent concealment covers situations in which the manufacturer withholds information when he has a duty to speak.

Negligent misrepresentation allows the consumer to bring suit when the manufacturer's statements become misrepresentations that he should have known were untrue or inaccurate. Again, this deals with the duty of reasonable care.

Strict liability holds the manufacturer liable for a consumer's physical injury resulting from a misrepresentation about the product. In these cases the consumer does not need to prove that the misrepresentation was made negligently or fraudulently.

Express warranty occurs when any specific warranty that becomes a part of the purchase. Any act, representation, affirmation of fact, or promise made by the manufacturer about the product becomes a part of the bargain (Uniform Commercial Code, Section 2-313). This creates an express warranty that the product will live up to the act, representation, and so on.

Implied warranty exists by operation of law. Simply stated, it is implied in the sale of the product. One such warranty is for merchantability (Uniform Commercial Code, Section 2-314), which means that the product is fit for the purpose for which it was sold. There is also a warranty of fitness for a particular purpose (Uniform Commercial Code, Section 2-315. Restatement of Torts (Second), Section 402A).

Strict tort liability occurs when the product is defective and that defect causes injury or damage. It is not necessary to prove that the manufacturer or seller was negligent (Restatement of Torts (Second), Section 402A).

These theories form the basis for all of the cases in this chapter. In one form or another, all products liability litigation stems from these areas of law. What's universal is how these theories are supported by the manufacturer's advertising.

Advertising Claims

It's important to start off with a discussion of situations that present unique and challenging issues in relation to products liability and advertising's impact on that area of law.

An Example of *Lack of Liability*

In 2003, Roberta Pelman and Israel Bradley alleged that the practices of McDonalds, in making and selling their fast food, was deceptive and that this deception has injured their children. The children were consumers who had purchased and consumed the McDonalds' products and, as a result, became overweight and developed diabetes, coronary heart disease, high blood pressure, elevated cholesterol levels, and other detrimental and adverse health effects.

In *Pelman* v. *McDonald's Corporation*, 237 F. Supp. 2d 512 (2003), questions of personal responsibility, common knowledge and public health were presented, as was the role of society and the courts in addressing these issues. The plaintiffs contended that all the health damage done to the children was the result of McDonalds' actions. Those were:

1. McDonalds failed to adequately disclose the ingredients and/or health effects of ingesting certain of their food products with high levels of cholesterol, fat, salt and sugar. And that they described their food as nutritious, and their advertising and marketing enticed consumers to purchase "value meals" without disclosing their detrimental health effects.
2. McDonalds was negligent in selling food products that were high in cholesterol, fat, salt and sugar.
3. McDonalds failed to warn consumers that the ingredients, quantity, qualities and levels of cholesterol, fat, salt and sugar content and other ingredients in their products, and that such a diet could lead to obesity and health problems.
4. McDonalds acted negligently in marketing food products that were physically and psychologically addictive. And, that their advertising and marketing was geared toward inducing children to purchase and ingest McDonalds' food products.

In what might be called the "McLawsuit" the court said: "The issue of determining the breadth of personal responsibility underlies much of the law: where should the line be drawn between an individual's own responsibility to take care of herself, and society's responsibility to ensure that others shield her? Laws are created in those situations where individuals are somehow unable to protect themselves and where society needs to provide a buffer between the individual and some other entity—whether herself, another individual or a behemoth corporation that spans the globe."

A reasonable person should know that eating huge amounts of supersized McDonalds' products is unhealthy and may result in weight gain and other health problems (because of the high levels of cholesterol, fat, salt and sugar). It is not the law's place to protect them from their own excesses. Nobody is forced to eat at McDonalds. Even more relevant, nobody is forced to supersize their meal or choose less healthy options on the menu. Coincidentally, Morgan Spurlock's film *Super Size Me* was released a year later, in 2004.

This case points out the type of situation where the company's advertising didn't contribute to products liability. The case was dismissed in its entirely.

An Example of Supporting Liability

Unlike the McDonalds case above, the balance of this chapter will focus on products liability claims where the advertising was held to be related to the damage.

One evening in May 1995, Linda McCathern and her daughter, together with her cousin, Sanders, and her daughter, were riding in Sanders's 1994 Toyota 4Runner. Sanders was driving, McCathern was in the front passenger seat, and the children were in the back seat. Everyone was wearing their seatbelt while riding in, what was then, a vehicle made by the largest car manufacturer in the world.

While the group was traveling south on Highway 395 in Oregon at approximately 50 MPH, an oncoming vehicle veered into Sanders's lane. Sanders steered to the right onto the paved shoulder to avoid a collision, then steered back to the left onto the highway. At that point the 4Runner began to rock from side-to-side as she turned to the right again to return to the south-bound lane. Right at that point the 4Runner rolled over and landed upright on its four wheels. During the rollover, the roof collapsed and McCathern sustained serious, permanent injuries. The other passengers sustained only cuts and bruises. The vehicle that had veered into Sanders's lane didn't stop.

In *McCathern* v. *Toyota Motor Corporation*, 332 Ore. 59; 23 P.3d 320 (2001), one expert stated that the accident was caused solely by the geometry of the 1994 4Runner, as opposed to any other tripping hazard.

As for Toyota's advertising, the court said it: ". . . did not attempt to communicate to consumers the rollover risk attendant with the vehicle's height. When presented with an example of a television commercial depicting the 4Runner performing evasive maneuvers similar to those that occurred in plaintiff's accident, [their expert] admitted that, under certain conditions, the maneuvers being depicted in the commercial might cause the vehicle to roll over." Toyota's expert was also shown several Toyota advertising brochures and he testified that he was "not really sure" if the 1994 4Runner could perform the maneuvers shown in the brochures safely.

If the visuals used in Toyota's company advertising, brochures and TV commercials had been consistent with what the car could safely do, this case could have turned out much differently. Instead, the jury returned a verdict in favor of plaintiff and awarded damages totaling $7.65 million.

Since the concept of *caveat emptor* (buyer beware) was first created, the complexity of doing business has undergone many changes. Advertising has become a major factor in creating the demand that causes goods to flow from manufacturer to ultimate consumer. As we discussed earlier, the manufacturer is bound to a form of strict liability to the buyer. Strict liability places absolute liability on the manufacturer for a consumer's (usually physical) injury resulting from a misrepresentation about the product as in the case we just examined. The manufacturer can be held liable to the buyer based upon representations that are proven to be false whether in advertisements, literature, or in a document that is passed along to the consumer by a dealer.

Let's look at a hypothetical situation. Acme Company manufactures hoists for cars. Acme distributes a manual that contains statements about the hoist's strength, lifting capacity, and so on. Mr. Jones goes into a local auto parts store and, after reading the literature, buys an Acme hoist. Jones uses the hoist to lift his car. The hoist does not have the lifting capacity that was stated in the literature, and as a result, the car crashes to the floor, injuring Mr. Jones. Acme is subject to strict liability to Jones.

Similar situations may occur in almost any situation; the form that the representation takes is not important. In fact, a representation may be in the form of an advertisement on the television, in the newspaper, on the manufacturer's website, or in other literature (labels on the product, packaging material, etc.). It can be written or oral. For strict liability to exist, there must be an issue of fact in the advertising claim. In other words, the representation that the consumer relied on must be presented as a fact. This type of claim is more than just puffing, fantasy advertising, and the like.

Claims of Quality Construction

In *Greenman* v. *Yuba Power Prods., Inc.*, 377 F.2d 897 (Cal. Sup. Ct. 1963), claims that a power tool was rugged were discussed. Mr. Greenman saw a demonstration of a product called a "Shopsmith." The Shopsmith was a combination power tool used as a drill, saw, and wood lathe. After studying a product brochure, Mr. Greenman decided that he wanted a Shopsmith. He told his wife this, and she purchased one for Christmas in 1955.

In 1957 Greenman purchased an attachment that would allow him to use the Shopsmith as a wood lathe. While working on a wood piece, it suddenly flew out of the lathe, striking Greenman in the head and causing serious injuries.

The jury returned an award of $65,000 in favor of Greenman after determining that Yuba Power Products had negligently constructed the Shopsmith. Expert witnesses testified that the set screws used to hold sections of the machine together were not adequate. Normal vibration would cause the screws to loosen, allowing the tailpiece of the lathe to move away from the spinning piece of wood, eventually allowing the wood to fly out of the lathe at high speed.

Here again, we see that the statements made in the manufacturer's product brochure (see box 8.2) were instrumental in determining the nature and extent of any express warranty that Yuba had made to the potential purchaser. As we saw earlier, an express warranty is created when any description, sample, model, fact, or promise is made by the seller to the buyer that relates to the goods and becomes part of the basis of the bargain. The express warranty is that the goods will live up to the promise. It does not matter that the advertiser knew or should have known that the express warranty was a misrepresentation.

Box 8.2 **Yuba Power Products Brochure**

When Shopsmith is in Horizontal Position—Rugged construction of frame provides rigid support from end to end. Heavy, centerless-ground steel tubing ensures perfect alignment of components. SHOPSMITH maintains its accuracy because every component has positive locks that hold adjustments through rough or precision work.

In this case, the court said: "A manufacturer is strictly liable . . . when an article he places on the market, knowing that it is to be used without inspection for defects, proves to have a defect that causes injury to a human being." Simply because the

Shopsmith was placed on the market, the consumer could assume that it was safe for the jobs for which it was built.

Those jobs were detailed in the product brochure on which the consumer who purchases the product would rely. It does not matter that the manufacturer did not intend to mislead or cause harm. The harm occurred, and the manufacturer was liable. This holds true as long as the injury results from a defect in the product that appears when the product is being used as intended.

Liability for Commercial Loss

In February of 1962, Mr. Lonon purchased a Fordson Major Diesel tractor from the Haywood Tractor Company. Lonon was a farmer and needed a large tractor capable of performing certain tasks. He had visited the Ford tractor dealers in the area and had read the sales literature. He also had seen the many advertisements Ford published in farm magazines and ran on television. The literature contained information about the live power take-off, the power steering lift, and other full specifications.

Over a period of time the tractor failed to perform the functions that were claimed it could perform. The tractor was taken in for repairs on many occasions with no effect. It was defective from the time that it was purchased. Lonon sued Ford after failing to receive any satisfaction. In *Ford Motor Co.* v. *Lonon*, 398 S.W.2d 240 (Tenn. 1966), the jury award of $4,000 was upheld. Lonon received $4,000 plus court costs for a tractor that originally cost him $4,243.10.

What makes this case interesting is that, unlike other products liability cases, there was no physical injury to the plaintiff. Most of the decisions hold the manufacturer liable for physical injury that was a direct result of the manufacturer's breach of warranty. In this case, we see that the courts can apply the same principle to commercial losses (losses of time and business as opposed to physical injury) that result from a defectively manufactured product or product part.

Liability for Implied Claims

Clifford King was at a friend's house when he dove into an above-ground swimming pool. The pool was only four feet deep and as he leveled off near the bottom of the pool, he struck his head on the drain outlet that protruded from the bottom. King had only swum once or twice a year in the five years before the accident. He was not an expert swimmer or diver, and he had only swum in an above-ground pool once before. He had seen other people, including his brother, dive into the pool and didn't consider that such a dive could cause so severe an injury. As the result of this final dive, King became a quadriplegic.

During the trial in *King* v. *Kayak Manufacturing Corporation*, 182 W. Va. 276; 387 S.E.2d 511 (1989), he testified that he had not seen the two "No Diving" signs, which were approximately six inches long and two and one-half inches wide. Kayak's, the defendant, main defense was that King used the pool on several occasions shortly before his final dive and was aware of the shallow depth and either assumed the risk or was contributorily negligent. That argument didn't work.

Here's where a big part of the problem came in. Kayak published advertisements showing people diving into similar above-ground pools. They also knew that many people did not appreciate the risks of death or paraplegia associated with diving. They sold this type of above-ground pool primarily to recreational, untrained divers. At the trial "defendants admitted it to be foreseeable that users of the pool might employ the manufacturer-supplied deck as a diving platform; [and] . . . they did not provide the type of warning signs recommended by the American National Standards

Institute." They did have warning signs on the pool but they were very small and not clearly visible.

As for the relevance of the advertising, the court said: "In a product liability case, the manufacturer's advertising or promotional material concerning the uses of the product are a part of reasonable use of the product and may be admitted into evidence even though the user is not aware of the material." The amazing thing is that, if Kayak knew that diving into their pool was dangerous, and went to the effort to place warning signs on the pool, why would they show a picture of someone diving into the pool in their advertising?

Liability for Performance Claims

Richard Beck, the baseball coach at Oak Hill High School in Marion, Indiana, would not allow his players to wear sunglasses because he thought they were too dangerous. Yet, before the 1966 season he read about Rayex sunglasses in *Sporting News* (see box 8.3). The product packaging stated: "Simply flip . . . for instant eye protection," and "Rayex lenses are guaranteed for life against breakage."

Box 8.3

PLAY BALL!

and Flip for Instant Eye Protection with

RAYEX

Baseball

SUNGLASSES

Professional

FLIP-SPECS

Scientific lenses protect your eyes with a flip from sun and glare anywhere . . . baseball, beach, boat, driving, golfing, fishing, just perfect for active and spectator sports— world's finest sunglasses.

After reading the advertisement and packaging, coach Beck purchased Rayex flip-down sunglasses for his team. One of the teenage boys on the team, Michael Filler, wore the glasses while playing in a game. A batted ball struck the boy in the face, breaking the glasses. The shattered glasses splintered and damaged one of the boy's eyes so badly that it had to be removed. The court in *Filler* v. *Rayex Corp.*, 435 F.2d 336 (7th Cir. 1970), in awarding damages in excess of $101,000, said about the product: "Since they lacked the safety features of plastic or shatterproof glass, the sunglasses were in truth not fit for baseball playing, the particular purpose for which they were sold."

There was no explicit advertising claim about the shatterproof quality of the glasses. The ad copy referred only to protection against sun and glare. But they were advertised in a sporting magazine, directed to athletes, and stated that they were safe for use in baseball. The obvious implication was that they were safe for use in that sport, even though the manufacturer had not made adequate tests to support that claim. This was a case of a safety claim being implied, but a safety claim nonetheless. Along with the sale, an implied warranty was created.

Regarding a point that we covered earlier, an implied warranty means that the warranty is implied with the sale of the product. As we have discussed, there are warranties of merchantability and fitness for a particular purpose. Merchantability refers to the fitness of the product for the ordinary purposes for which such goods are used. Fitness for a particular purpose implies a specific use by the buyer which is peculiar to the nature of his business.

Liability for Reasonably Anticipated Use

The Missouri Supreme Court upheld a $94,000 award in *Blevins* v. *Cushman Motors*, 551 S.W. 2d 602 (Mo. 1977), involving a man who was pinned under a golf cart that had overturned. Advertisements had appeared in golfing magazines promoting the Cushman golf cart (see box 8.4).

Box 8.4   **Cushman Golf Cart Ad**

TALK ABOUT A TURNED ON RIDE. SMOOOOTH.

With a beefier, low-slung three-point rubber suspension. New rubber suspensions between power frame and main frame lets the GC tool through turns with super ease, super safety, super stability. Low ground-hugging center of gravity makes for wide stance, razor-honed handling. Fat, ground-gripping, turf-protecting 9.50 x 8 Terra Tires are standard. This baby floats the course.

On the afternoon of July 15, 1969, Albert Blevins and a friend met for a round of golf at the Stayton Meadows Golf Course. The two men began play using their Cushman Golf Cart. On the thirteenth hole, the cart was being driven at about five miles per hour when it crossed a wet, shaded area. The cart skidded and turned over, throwing Blevins' friend clear of the cart. Blevins, however, fell on the ground and was pinned and injured by the overturned cart.

In order to win his case, Blevins needed to establish that the accident and damage resulted from a use of the product that was "reasonably anticipated." Blevins was required to show that the golf cart was used as that—a golf cart which could negotiate a golf course. Here the advertising clearly convinced the court that that use was not only anticipated but encouraged. The advertising showed a "justified use and reliance by the driver" of the cart. In fact, the advertising tended to draw the purchaser into a false sense of security as to the use of the cart and its safety.

Punitive Damages

Increasing indications show that advertising is being considered heavily as an influential factor in imposing punitive damages in certain lawsuits. Punitive damages are awarded to punish the wrongdoer. They are also a strong deterrent for others to consider.

In *Leichtamer* v. *American Motors Corp.*, 424 N.E. 2d 568 (Ohio 1981), a four-wheel-drive vehicle overturned while going down an incline. On April 18, 1976, Paul Vance and his wife Cynthia invited Carl and Jeanne Leichtamer to go for a ride in the Vances' Jeep CJ-7. The Vances belonged to an off-road club located near Dundee, Ohio, which had been converted from an old strip mine.

While the Vances' Jeep was descending a double-terraced hill, the vehicle's rear end pitched over. The Jeep had cleared the first embankment; and after clearing the second, it landed on the front wheels. At that point, the rear end continued over the front end of the Jeep. The Jeep landed upside down pointing back up the hill. Paul and Cynthia Vance were killed. Carl Leichtamer sustained a skull fracture, and Jeanne Leichtamer became a paraplegic.

During the trial it was acknowledged that Paul Vance's negligence caused the accident. However, it was claimed that the Leichtamers' injuries were "substantially enhanced, intensified, aggravated, and prolonged" as a result of the failure of the factory-installed roll bar on the Jeep. The roll bar was offered as optional equipment on the Jeep CJ-7 and was promoted solely for protection in the event of a rollover. The roll bar was not structurally sound enough to withstand the pitchover that the Vances went through.

Jeep, then a division of American Motors Corporation, had produced a multimillion dollar television campaign that encouraged people to buy a Jeep:

> Ever discover the rough, exciting world of mountains, forests, rugged terrain? The original Jeep can get you there, and Jeep guts will bring you back.

This case illustrates the role advertising can play in the imposition of liability. Certain expectations that the consumer develops about the safety of a product are formed largely through the product's advertising. The manner in which a product's use is advertised is relevant to the use that the product is intended for.

The Jeep commercials depicted its qualities and safety in an off-road situation and stressed the Jeep's ability to negotiate steep hills. One particular spot challenged a young man, accompanied by his girlfriend (see box 8.5). In fact, the advertising clearly depicted the Jeep going up and down steep and rugged terrain safely. Even the owner's manual claimed that the Jeep could "proceed in safety down a grade which could not safely be negotiated by a conventional 2-wheel drive vehicle."

Box 8.5

"You guys aren't yellow, are you?

Is it a steep hill?

Yeah, little lady, you could say it is a steep hill.

Let's try it.

The King of the Hill is about to discover the new Jeep CJ-7."

The court felt that the advertising was a significant factor in supporting a finding for punitive damages since it showed the probable use of the vehicle while ignoring the danger that could likely result from that use saying: "The commercial advertising clearly contemplates off-road use of the vehicle."

The salesman's guide to the vehicle described the roll bar in the following terms: "Surround yourself and your passengers with the strength of a rugged, reinforced steel roll bar for added protection. A very practical item, and a must if you run competition with a 4WD club. Adds rugged good looks, too."

Given the foreseeability of roll-overs and pitch-overs, the failure of appellants to test to determine whether the roll bar "added protection" represents a flagrant indifference to the probability that a user might be exposed to an unreasonable risk of harm. For appellants to have encouraged off-the-road use while providing a roll bar that did little more than add "rugged good looks" was a sufficient basis for an award of punitive damages.

The Ohio Supreme Court granted a $2.2 million damage award in the case. Over half of the damages were punitive.

The Extent of Punitive Damages

In 1982, the California Supreme Court affirmed a $9.2 million award in *Hasson* v. *Ford Motor Co.*, 19 Cal. 3d 530 (1977), CCH Prods. Liab. Rep. Paragraph 9398 (Sept. 16, 1982). About $4 million were in punitive damages. The case developed because of a catastrophic brain injury suffered by the driver of a 1965 Lincoln Continental when the brakes failed on a hill. The driver established that the manufacturer failed to warn dealers and owners of a known (to Ford) problem with the brakes, and how to correct it, because it was protecting the model's reputation among customers. The manufacturer deliberately failed to test for the problem with the brakes and subsequently failed to install a dual master cylinder, which would have overcome the defect.

Deceit and fraudulent concealment—which we discussed at the beginning of this chapter—occur when the advertiser intends to mislead the consumer regarding a material fact about the product and the consumer relies on that information to his detriment. If the advertiser expressly misstates a fact, it is deceit. If the advertiser withholds information when he should give it out, it is fraudulent concealment.

The issue here was Ford's knowing disregard for the safety of the vehicle, something that its advertising convinced otherwise. Ford management had a policy of advertising that the Lincoln Continental was free from the need for service for a large portion of its components.

SPECIFIC ISSUES RELATING TO ADVERTISING

PART III

Copyright Regulation

Experience is the name everyone gives to their mistakes.
—*Oscar Wilde*

In March 1998, Larry Page had been working on his dissertation thesis as a Ph.D. student at Stanford University. Page was considering exploring the mathematical properties of the World Wide Web. In fact, his highly successful "PageRank" algorithm had been developed two years earlier.

Page's supervisor, Terry Winograd, encouraged him to go with his idea in what Page later described as "the best advice I ever got." His project focused on the problem of discovering which web pages linked to any other given web page. He wanted to develop an effective system that would overcome this problem inherent in the web.

Page was joined by fellow student Sergey Brin. Both Brin and Page had been working on the Stanford Digital Library Project, the goal of which was "to develop the enabling technologies for a single, integrated and universal digital library" and it was funded through the National Science Foundation, in addition to other federal agencies.

"We chose our system's name, Google, because it is a common spelling of googol, or 10^{100} and fits well with our goal of building very large-scale search engines" they said. As of 2014, according to the Interbrand ranking, Google had become the second most valuable consumer brand in the world (right behind Apple) with a value of $107.4 billion.

In its original mission statement Google's intent was "to organize the world's information and make it universally accessible and useful," and its unofficial slogan was "Don't be evil." Which, appropriately, brings us to the Google Books case.

In 2004 Google announced that it was partnering with several research universities around the world to scan their entire library collections. Harvard University, Oxford University, Stanford University, the University of California, the University of Michigan and the New York Public Library agreed to have their books scanned.

Google would then make the digitized copies available for search online. To date Google has scanned about thirty million books out of a potential thirty-seven-plus million. Scanning a book is copying a book without permission from the publisher or author. That violates the Copyright Act, at least it has for over three hundred years (since 1790 when the Act was first created by Congress).

Soon after Google's announcement, publisher and author groups claimed their rights had been violated. Google needed to ask their permission and pay for the rights. Didn't they? Well, Google argued that scanning the books was "fair use" under the Copyright Act. Their rationale was that, while all books would be indexed and searchable on the Google Books site, users would only be able to access the full text of books that were out of copyright and in the public domain. Otherwise a search would only return a small "snippet" of text, not the whole book. That's like saying it's okay to steal a part of something. According to Google that was okay.

By mid-2005, *Authors Guild Inc. et al* v. *Google Inc.* (U.S. District Court, Southern District of New York, No. 05-08136), was filed to stop Google. If Google had lost they would have had a $3 billion damage hit. Subsequently, the Author's Guild's case was certified as a class-action lawsuit. The downside to Google's class-action certification was that all authors who had published a book would be part of the class and would be bound by the result of the case, even if they weren't aware of it.

Fast forward three years: after extensive negotiations, the parties announced they had reached a settlement. Google would pay $125 million up front and would then be allowed to continue scanning books and making them available online. More importantly, Google would be allowed to offer not just snippets, but it would be allowed to sell entire books. The copyright holder would get about two-thirds of the revenues and Google would keep one-third.

The Google Books settlement bound all authors—known and unknown. Google could proceed to scan orphan works (items for which the copyright holder is no longer clear, even if they are technically still covered by copyright) without having to worry. If an author later surfaced who didn't want his book used, he could no longer sue Google. He could opt-out of the program and claim a check for the revenues associated with his book, but no more.

However, in late 2014, the settlement agreement was rejected by the court. Google won dismissal of the long-running lawsuit. U.S. Circuit Judge Denny Chin accepted Google's argument that its scanning of (at that time) more than 20 million books, and making "snippets" of text available online, constituted "fair use" under U.S. copyright law.

The decision, if it survives the certainly expected appeal, would let Google continue expanding the library, which it said helps readers find books they might not otherwise locate. But what about authors who deserve to get paid for their work?

Judge Chin wrote that "the scanning makes it easier for students, teachers, researchers and the public to find books, while maintaining 'respectful consideration' for authors' rights."

He also said Google's digitization was "transformative," meaning it gave the books a new purpose or character, and could be expected to boost rather than reduce book sales. "In my view, Google Books provide significant public benefits," Chin wrote, "Indeed, all society benefits."

"Google made unauthorized digital editions of nearly all of the world's valuable copyright-protected literature and profits from displaying those works," the Authors Guild said. "Such mass digitization and exploitation far exceeds the bounds of the fair use defense." This matter is far from over.

While Google has thrown a wrench into the Copyright Act, it illustrates the ongoing debate over, and interpretation of, copyright protection. Since forewarned is forearmed, let's now take a look at the areas of copyright law affecting advertisers. Keep in mind as you read this chapter, and the next on trademark, the differences between copyright and trademark law. Each is based on different principles and, therefore, must be thought of separately.

The Copyright Act

The Copyright Act of 1976 protects the creators of artistic works as an incentive to pursue their creative talents. The United States Constitution—Article 1, Section 8, provides that Congress shall have the power: "To promote the Progress of Science and useful Arts, by securing for limited Times to Authors . . . the exclusive Right to their . . . Writings . . .." The original Copyright Act was passed by the first Congress in 1790, shortly after the signing of the Constitution. The act has been amended over the years in 1831, 1870, 1909, and most recently in 1976.

In 1976 Congress updated the Copyright Act, which went into effect on January 1, 1978. Any work produced after that date was covered by the new law. Works created prior to that date are covered by the Copyright Act of 1909. In this chapter we deal with the current act.

Requirements to Qualify for Copyright Protection

It is important to understand what can qualify to be copyrighted. There are conditions that must be met in order to apply for protection under copyright law. To qualify, a work must be the product of the original author and meet the requirement of originality. It must also be considered a "writing" and be fixed in a tangible medium. Let us look at each of these requirements separately.

Definition of a "Writing" To be eligible for copyright protection an item must be put in a written form, referred to as a "writing"—but bear in mind that the common definition of "a writing" is much different than the legal definition. Under the Copyright Act, what is meant by "a writing" is quite broad, encompassing anything that is "fixed in any tangible medium of expression, now known or later developed, from which [the original] can be perceived, reproduced, or otherwise communicated, either directly or with the aid of a machine or device" (17 U.S.C. section 102(a) (1982)).

At the time the Copyright Act was first drafted, about the only means of performance was the stage. There were, of course, newspapers, books, maps, and so on, which were specifically listed in the original act. But other than those forms of creative expression, the stage was all that was left. No YouTube or Vimeo. No DVRs, in fact no TV. In those years, the only medium to "record" a stage performance was the mind of the audience. Today, a performance can be recorded in many ways that allow it be perceived by others after the fact, with incredible realism in high definition. Protection of the creative work, therefore, has had to expand to keep pace with the times and the current technology

Here's an example to illustrate the point. Between 1970 and 1971, Mr. Goldstein and his associates purchased copies of record albums or tape cassettes at local record stores, duplicated them on tape, and distributed them to retail stores for sale to the public. This took place long before Napster or iTunes. In fact long before digital audio files were available for download and copying. Goldstein never asked for permission from, and made no payments to, the artists, writers, performers, producers, or any other person involved with the original recordings. No payments were made for the use of the artists' names or the titles of the original albums.

Eventually the state of California, where this occurred, arrested and prosecuted Goldstein in *Goldstein* v. *California*, 412 U.S. 546, 93 S.Ct. 2303, 37 L.Ed.

2d 163 (1973), for record piracy: the unauthorized duplication of major artists' performances. In this early case, the United States Supreme Court established that a writing covered "any physical rendering of the fruits of creative, intellectual, or aesthetic labor." Records and tape recordings certainly qualified under this heading. As do digital video and photographs, and ".mp3", ".aiff" or any other form of digital audio file.

Fixed in a Tangible Medium In order for an original work to be considered a writing, the work must exist in some tangible entity. Today a tangible entity can be paper, video tape, film, any digital file, record, flash drive, CD or DVD, or almost anything else capable of maintaining its form. Under the copyright statute, material is protected when it is created and fixed into a concrete medium so that it can be perceived by others.

David Brown wrote a term paper for Professor Hagendorf's law course in 1977. In the fall of 1978, Hagendorf copied large sections of Brown's paper to use in an article he wrote for Commerce Clearing House, a legal publisher. Brown's term paper was fixed in a tangible medium. Hagendorf's version was also fixed in a tangible medium when it was published in the magazine. Since both papers were in tangible mediums, they were both protected by, and subject to, copyright law. Brown sued—and won—for copyright violation in *Hagendorf* v. *Brown*, 699 F.2d 478 (9th Cir. 1983).

Even a term paper can be protected by copyright. It is a tangible form that can be perceived by others.

Definition of Author Only the original author of a work can receive copyright protection. This was first discussed in *Burrow-Giles Lithographic Co.* v. *Sarony*, 111 U.S. 53, 4 S.Ct. 279, 28 L.Ed. 349 (1884). In this case, photographer Napoleon Sarony took a picture of Oscar Wilde in January of 1882. In those days, photographers often paid their celebrity models to pose for them and received a model release. The photographer then retained the rights to the photograph as well as the rights to use the person's image in the photo Sarony photographed American Civil War General, William T. Sherman (he was on the winning side), authors Samuel Clemens (Mark Twain) and Oscar Wilde (*The Picture of Dorian Gray* and *The Importance of Being Earnest*). Sarony reportedly paid famed stage actress Sarah Bernhardt $1,500 to pose for his camera, the equivalent of more than $20,000 today.

Sarony claimed that he was the author of one Oscar Wilde picture entitled, "Oscar Wilde No. 18" and printed a notice on each copy of the photograph which read: "Copyright, 1882, by N. Sarony."

Burrow-Giles had printed reproductions of the Oscar Wilde picture without Sarony's permission. Burrow-Giles argued that a photographer cannot be considered an author and therefore cannot hold the copyright to the photo. However, the Court disagreed and awarded Sarony $610 in damages (remember, this was 1883), the current equivalent of just over $14,500. At the time of this case, photography was a rather new medium and did not exist at the time the original copyright act was created.

This case defined an author as the person "to whom anything owes its origin; originator; maker . . ." The Court in its opinion restated Lord Justice Cotton's earlier definition of an author: "In my opinion, author involves originating, making, producing, as the inventive or master-mind, the thing which is to be protected, whether it be a drawing, or a painting, or a photograph."

On appeal, the U.S. Supreme Court affirmed this decision. Sarony later photographed the Supreme Court itself, to celebrate the centennial of the federal judiciary in 1890.

The author of a work protected under copyright has a variety of rights. These include the right to make and distribute copies of the work, to create adaptations, and to publicly display and perform the work.

Requirement of Originality Copyright protection is available only to original works. But what is the definition of original? An original work must be the result of an independent effort. The test of originality is known as the "scènes à faire" doctrine. Scènes à faire means "scene to be made" in French, and refers to elements of a work that are not protected if the common idea is only capable of expression in a more or less stereotyped form. In other words, copyright does not cover ideas, procedures or concepts. It only covers the literal expression of the idea or concept.

The NuWave halogen oven was produced by Hearthware and was sold through television infomercials. Their commercials were copyright protected. The NuWave infomercials opened with a flurry of incentives for potential buyers, including a two-year warranty and free items such as a blender/food processor. The product's benefits were explained by an upbeat host, who presented the product with the assistance of a "TV Cooking Expert." The two hosts sampled food cooked in the NuWave oven and explained how the product improves the lives of those who own one. The video was intermixed with enthusiastic testimonials, demonstrations, and reminders of the bonus offer. The infomercial was full of scenes of different types of food cooking dramatized using time-lapse footage.

In 2010, E. Mishan & Sons, Inc., entered the halogen oven market too. Emson hired a production company to produce an infomercial for its Super Wave oven. The competing infomercials shared a number of similarities. Both had a brisk, energetic tone. Both showed many of the same foods being prepared and used time-lapse footage to demonstrate the cooking process. Both suggested their respective products may be used in a recreational vehicle, a dorm, or on a boat. Both featured a host knocking frozen food against a hard surface to prove that it was frozen. Both noted that the ovens were able to broil, roast, grill, bake, barbecue, steam, dehydrate, and air fry. The Super Wave infomercial touted "tri-cooking technology" while the NuWave infomercial promised "triple-combo cooking power." Both brands used on-camera presenters that were chipper, the testimonials enthusiastic, and the virtues of the product emphatically conveyed.

In *Hearthware, Inc.* v. *E. Mishan & Sons, Inc.*, 2012 U.S. Dist. LEXIS 113932; 104 U.S.P.Q.2D (BNA) 1207 (2012), Hearthstone sued Mishan for copyright infringement. Hearthware alleged that the Super Wave infomercial essentially copied the NuWave infomercials, and therefore created an infringement. This was all because of the overall similarity of the commercials, not due to any literal copying.

Mishan had produced evidence that the similarities cited by Hearthware were commonplace in halogen oven infomercials. For each element allegedly copied, Mishan presents a comprehensive list of infomercials that used the idea prior to Hearthware's copyrighted infomercials.

The court stated: "Mishan argues that the similar scenes cited by Hearthware are unprotectable 'scènes à faire'. The 'scènes à faire' doctrine prevents a plaintiff from establishing infringement by pointing to features that are so standard or unavoidable that they fail to distinguish works within a certain class. Elements of an original work are not protected if the common idea is only capable of expression in a more or less stereotyped form.

The court referred to *Reed-Union Corp.* v. *Turtle Wax, 77 F.3d 909 (7th Cir. 1996)*, which illustrated how the "scènes à faire" doctrine applies to advertisements. The court said:

> In *Reed-Union*, the plaintiff produced a car polish called NU FINISH. A NU FINISH TV commercial featured a beat-up car in a junkyard. After NU FINISH was applied, the revived vehicle was subjected to 52 car washes. The shine remained. The commercial also featured the results of independent lab tests. In 1991, defendant Turtle Wax introduced a competing car polish, FINISH 2001. One FINISH 2001

TV commercial featured a car surrounded by strewn-about spare parts and also featured lab test results. Another FINISH 2001 spot featured before-and-after shots of polished cars and then subjected one vehicle to 104 car washes. The shine remained. The FINISH 2001 commercials did not infringe on the NU FINISH spot because the use of "hackneyed ideas," such as polishing up old cars, washing the polished cars, and citing lab tests, was not protectable.

Derivative Works

As we just saw, what is required for a new work to be copyrightable is enough expressive variation from public-domain or other existing works to enable the new work to be readily distinguished from its predecessors. This standard does not require a high degree of originality to be copyrightable, but it must contain some substantial, not merely trivial originality. The level of originality required for copyright in a derivative work is the same as that required for copyright in any other work.

HIT Entertainment owned the copyright to the popular "Thomas & Friends" train characters, and it licensed Learning Curve International to make toy figures of its characters. Learning Curve then hired Daniel Schrock, a professional photographer, to photograph the toys. Learning Curve used Schrock's services on a regular basis for about four years and after that continued to use some of his photographs in its advertising and on product packaging. Schrock invoiced Learning Curve for this work, which included "usage rights" limiting Learning Curve's use of his photographs to two years. Learning Curve paid the invoices in full, totaling more than $400,000. After the two-year usage rights expired, Learning Curve stopped giving him work but continued to use his photos. Schrock registered his photos for copyright protection (an author has five years after the work is created to file for and receive copyright registration) and sued Learning Curve and HIT for infringement. The case was *Daniel P. Schrock v. Learning Curve International, Inc.*, 586 F.3d 513 (2009). This case discussed the issue of derivative work and its relationship to copyright protection. Learning Curve argued that Schrock had no standing to sue for infringement since his photos were merely depictions of the toy figures that Learning Curve already owned the copyright to.

A "derivative work" is, by definition, a work based upon one or more preexisting works, such as a translation, musical arrangement, dramatization, fictionalization, motion picture version, sound recording, art reproduction, abridgment, condensation, or any other form in which a work may be recast, transformed, or adapted. A work consisting of editorial revisions, annotations, elaborations, or other modifications which, as a whole, represent an original work of authorship, is a "derivative work."

The court here explained that:

> In many cases, the photographer does not invent the scene or create the subject matter depicted in it. Rather, the original expression he contributes lies in the *rendition* of the subject matter—that is, the effect created by the combination of his choices of perspective, angle, lighting, shading, focus, lens, and so on. Elements of originality in a photograph may include posing the subjects, lighting, angle, selection of film and camera, evoking the desired expression, and almost any other variant involved. Most photographs contain at least some originality in their rendition, except perhaps for a very limited class of photographs that can be characterized as "slavish copies" of an underlying work.

The court referred to an example to illustrate in *Bridgeman Art Library, Ltd. v. Corel Corp., 25 F. Supp. 2d 421 (S.D.N.Y. 1998)* "finding no originality in transparencies of paintings where the goal was to reproduce those works exactly and thus to minimize or eliminate any individual expression."

In the case of Schrock's photographs, however, they did not fall into the narrow category of photographs that can be classified as "slavish copies," that lacked any independently created expression. On the contrary, the photographs were accurate depictions of the three-dimensional "Thomas & Friends" toys, using Schrock's artistic and technical choices to create a two-dimensional image that is subtly but nonetheless sufficiently his own. This was confirmed in Schrock's testimony where he described his creative process. He used various camera and lighting techniques to make the toys look more "life like," "personable," and "friendly." He explained how he tried to give the toys "a little bit of dimension" and that it was his goal to make the toys "a little bit better than what they look like when you actually see them on the shelf."

As to this case, the district court correctly classified Schrock's photographs as derivative works. It does not follow, however, that Schrock needed authorization from Learning Curve to copyright the photos. As long as he was authorized to make the photos (and he was), he owned the copyright in the photos to the extent of their incremental original expression. The court said: " . . . copyright in a derivative work arises by operation of law—not through authority from the owner of the copyright in the underlying work—although the parties may alter this default rule by agreement. Schrock created the photos with permission and therefore owned the copyright to the photos provided they satisfied the other requirements for copyright and the parties did not contract around the default rule."

The court concluded:

> We also take this opportunity to clarify that "a derivative work must be substantially different from the underlying work to be copyrightable." This statement should not be understood to require a heightened standard of originality for copyright in a derivative work. We have more recently explained that the only "originality" required for [a] new work to be copyrightable . . . is enough expressive variation from public-domain or other existing works to enable the new work to be readily distinguished from its predecessors. Here, Schrock's photos of Learning Curve's "Thomas & Friends" toys possessed sufficient incremental original expression to qualify for copyright.

The Scope of Copyright Protection

Anyone who deals with advertising needs to understand copyright law and what it protects. Certain works can be copyrighted, others cannot. Now we take a closer look at what can and cannot be protected.

Under the current definition, almost any form of expression can be covered under the Copyright Act. For the advertiser, the most common forms of copyrighted works include:

- Photographs, television commercials, videos, digital files and images;
- Illustrations, renderings, cartoons, prints, charts, models, mock-ups, drawings;
- Sound recordings, radio commercials, music;
- Advertisements, billboards, brochures, displays, packages, signs;
- Literary works; and
- Websites.

Generally, items that are not eligible to be copyrighted include the following:

- Works that have not been fixed in a tangible form. For example, if a person creates a song in his mind, it must be put in writing or some other tangible form to be copyrighted. The thought is not tangible because others cannot perceive it;
- Titles, names, short phrases and slogans, symbols, or design elements. These items could be protected under trademark law in certain cases however; see chapter 10;
- Ideas, procedures, methods, systems, processes, concepts, principles, discoveries, devices, and machines. These would be protected under patent law, if the item qualified; and
- Works that are only common property information and have no original authorship. This includes items such as calendars, measurement rulers, public lists, and so on.

Copyright Protects Only a Specific Item Copyright, as we have seen, protects work from unauthorized duplication or copying. The work might be in any form, from a brochure to a photograph, a drawing, a banner ad, a music video or a television commercial. However, copyright protects only the tangible medium used.

This situation occurred in *Webloyalty.Com, Inc.*, v. *Consumer Innovations, LLC*, 388 F. Supp. 2d 435 (2005). Webloyalty is the owner of U.S. Copyright for material titled "Reservation Rewards 'COF'—Coupon" and "Special Offer Banner."

On November 24, 2003, Webloyalty began using its website "sell page" and "banner ad" to market its Reservation Rewards program in the following way: Webloyalty displayed its banner on Walter Drake's sales confirmation page so that the banner was visible to consumers after they made a purchase from Walter Drake. The banner read in part "Click here to claim your Special Offer," and, if consumers clicked the banner, they were directed to the Webloyalty sell page where they could sign up for Webloyalty's program.

In late 2003, Consumer Innovations (CI) was approached by List Services. They told CI about a potential marketing opportunity with Walter Drake. Walter Drake would give CI the opportunity to connect its own sell page to the Walter Drake confirmation page, setting up a head-to-head test between the sell pages of CI and Webloyalty.

The final version of CI's web sell page that was connected to the Walter Drake site was written in a manner that made the text in certain portions virtually identical to the Webloyalty sell page. To connect Walter Drake customers to the CI sell page, CI used a banner that was identical to the Webloyalty banner in all respects except that "Reservation Rewards" was replaced by "Traveler Innovations."

The evidence was overwhelming that CI actually copied Webloyalty's sell page and banner ad. The court said:

> Large sections of the CI Sell Page are identical to the Webloyalty Sell Page. The identical language in the final versions of the two Sell Pages reveals a probative similarity—and this, coupled with CI's access to the Webloyalty page, is sufficient to show that CI engaged in actual copying. The presence of Webloyalty's telephone number on the CI first draft is compelling additional evidence of copying; in fact, copying is the only reasonable explanation for the phone number to appear on CI's draft. As noted at the bench trial, CI was caught "red-handed." The CI Banner is identical to the Webloyalty Banner, except for the substitution of the words "Traveler Innovations" for the words "Reservation Rewards." This identity obviously reveals a probative similarity. Coupled with CI's access to the Webloyalty Banner, this probative similarity is sufficient to show that CI engaged in actual copying of the Banner.

Copyright Protects Only the Visual Depiction The case we just looked at brings up an important point worth discussing here regarding visual depictions. To be clear, a photograph of a building is copyrighted, but the building that is depicted in the photograph is not. This is an important issue that I hear about often. There are the rights to the photograph, and separately there are the rights to what's shown in the photograph. These are two distinct things that are often incorrectly interchanged. Often people incorrectly believe that if they buy and own a photograph, they also own rights to everything that is depicted in the photograph.

So to clarify, a photograph is protected under copyright. However that does not give any legal rights to what is shown in the photograph. Whatever is shown in a photograph often involves other legal rights of ownership, distinct from the copyrights to the photograph. If there is a person in the photo, publicity or privacy rights belong to the person unless they signed an agreement (see chapter 7). If there is a building in the photo, property or trademark rights may be involved (see chapter 10).

The same reasoning applies to music. A person may own the rights to a piece of music; the lyrics to a song for example. However, the actual recording involves other rights including the singers and musicians, composers and lyricists, and so on.

The point here is just because you own the rights to a specific aspect of a copyrighted work, doesn't mean you own rights to other aspects or elements of the work.

Objects of Use Are Not Copyrightable Items that do not in and of themselves convey information are considered "objects of use".

Objects which are only objects of use may not be copyrighted. Things like time cards, account books, diaries, bank checks, score cards, address books, and order forms fall into this category. Devices, machines, tools and such are not copyrightable. These items may qualify under patent law however.

In *Joshua Ets-Hokin* v. *Skyy Spirits, Inc.*, 225 F.3d 1068 (2000), the court dealt with a photograph of a Skyy Vodka bottle. The photographer, Ets-Hokin, filed a copyright infringement suit against Skyy for a photograph he took of their blue bottle. As one part of the case, Skyy claimed that their bottle was protected under copyright and, as such, Ets-Hokin's photo was merely a "derivative" work.

In order for a work to be derivative, the work must be based on a preexisting work that is copyrightable. However, the Skyy vodka bottle was a utilitarian object that is not protected by copyright.

Under the Copyright Act, the design of a useful article, such as a bottle, is not protected unless the design includes features that exist separately from utilitarian ones.

The court stated: "Such works shall include works of artistic craftsmanship insofar as their form but not their mechanical or utilitarian aspects are concerned; the design of a useful article, as defined in this section, shall be considered a pictorial, graphic or sculptural work only if, and only to the extent that, such design incorporates pictorial, graphic, or sculptural features that can be identified separately from, and are capable of existing independently of, the utilitarian aspects of the article."

We'll discuss more aspects and details of this Skyy Vodka case later in the chapter under Copyright and Protection of Ideas.

Copyright of Compilations and Collections Collective works also include periodicals, anthologies, or encyclopedias, where a number of separate works are brought together into one entity.

A compilation is a collection or assemblage of preexisting works. According to the Copyright Act, a compilation is "data that are selected, coordinated, or arranged in such a way that the resulting work as a whole constitutes an original work of authorship." (17 U.S.C. section 101). It is important to keep in mind that in order for the derivative work or collection to be copyrighted, it must have enough originality in itself to merit protection. Also, it must not infringe any other existing copyrights. To avoid violations, permission must be obtained from the original authors of the individual pieces.

A person who assembles these separate works into one unit would be considered the author of the collective work, and, if the work is copyrighted, that person would be the owner of that copyright. But the owner of the collection of works only owns the rights to the *collection*, not to the individual works composing the collection.

Rand McNally, in 1978 and again in 1982, produced the *Rand McNally Mileage Guides* for sale to the public (long before GPS). These guides listed mileages between various cities throughout the United States. Rand McNally gathered the distance figures for its guide from various city, county, and state maps in the public domain. It also examined road conditions, compensated for variations between map sources, and broke down the distances into smaller segments. Unavailable mileage figures between some cities were developed from scales between other cities. *Rand McNally Mileage Guides* were compilations and were copyrighted. As we saw earlier, individual facts cannot be copyrighted, yet certain compilations of facts can be protected under copyright.

A problem arose when Fleet Management System copied virtually all of the figures listed in the *Rand McNally Mileage Guides* to produce mileage guides of its own. This all came to light in *Rand McNally & Co.* v. *Fleet Management Sys. Inc.*, 600 F.Supp. 933 (N.D. Ill. 1984), where the court determined that Rand McNally held valid copyrights to the compilation and that Fleet Management had infringed on its copyright. Keep in mind that it was not the individual figures that were protected under the copyright but the collection of data that had been copied almost in total that constituted the violation.

Protection of Copyright

To be protected by copyright, the author must abide by certain rules.

Notice of Copyright When something is considered important enough to protect, it should be identified by a copyright notice. The notice must consist of three items: a "C" with a circle around it for visual works or a "P" with a circle around it for audio works (or the word "copyright" may be used), the year of first publication, and the copyright owner's name. Under the Copyright Statute, the following format should appear:

- Copyright 1987, John Doe & Company. All Rights Reserved; or
- ©1987 John Doe & Company. All Rights Reserved.

The phrase "all rights reserved," is not required in the United States, but is necessary for protection in foreign countries as part of the Berne Convention. Ideally, each copy of the material should bear this notice clearly and conspicuously. Proper notice shows the world that the owner claims the copyright to the work. Typically, copyright notice should be placed on:

- A photograph—printed on the print;
- A digital file—included in the meta data;

- A TV commercial or video—legibly displayed on the screen at the beginning or end of the spot for at least two to three seconds;
- A magazine or newspaper ad—printed legibly in the corner of the ad;
- A radio commercial—printed on the box label and tape reel or included in the meta data of a digital file;
- Original artwork—printed on the back of the original; and
- A book, report, or other literary work—printed on the title page (or the page immediately following) at the front of the work.

Publication of Copyrightable Work Publication is defined legally as "the distribution of copies . . . of a work to the public by sale or other transfer of ownership, or by rental, lease or lending. The offering to distribute copies . . . to a group of persons for purposes of further distribution, public performance, or public display, constitutes publication." (17 U.S.C. section 101).

However, the Copyright Act doesn't give any clarification as to how this applies to works displayed on the Internet. For other media, when someone gives a copy of an original work to another, the original is considered published, so it is important that the original and any copies clearly display the copyright notice. In the case of a book it's clear when it has been published. The same for a DVD. But as with everything else, the Internet has added a wrinkle to the issue of registration which affects photos as well as websites themselves. Specifically, is posting an image on the Internet considered published under copyright? Well it's still in debate. In *Rogers* v. *The Better Business Bureau of Metropolitan Houston, Inc.,* No. H-10-3741 (Aug. 15, 2012), the court provided some analysis. In this case, the defendant challenged the copyright because Rogers had registered his webpages as unpublished. The defendant claimed that the webpages were in fact published so registration was invalid. The court cited the cases below.

In *Getaped.com, Inc.* v. *Cangemi,* 188 F. Supp.2d 398, 402 (S.D.N.Y. 2002), the district judge found that a website, similar to photographs, music files, or software, was published when posted on the Internet. The court said: "By accessing a webpage, the user not only views the page but can also view—and copy—the code used to create it. In other words, merely by accessing a webpage, an Internet user acquires the ability to make a copy of that webpage, a copy that is, in fact, indistinguishable in every part from the original. Consequently, when a website goes live, the creator loses the ability to control either duplication or further distribution of his or her work."

A 2006 opinion from of the same court *Einhorn* v. *Mergatroyd Prods.,* 426 F. Supp.2d 189, 197 (S.D.N.Y. 2006), stated that, assuming that posting a digital file on the Internet of a show performance constituted distribution, it lacked the element of commercial exploitation required for publication.

More recently, the same district court stated in *McLaren* v. *Chico's FAS, Inc.,* No. 10 Civ. 2481(JSR), 2010 WL 4615772, (S.D.N.Y. Nov. 9, 2010), that posting images on a website was not publication.

In 2009, another district court avoided the issue in *Moberg* v. *33T LLC,* 666 F. Supp.2d 415, 422 (D. Del. 2009), finding it to be "unsettled."

The Northern District of California in *Sleep Science Partners* v. *Lieberman,* No. 09-04200 CW, 2010 WL 1881770, at *6 (N.D. Cal. May 10, 2010), was of the opinion that making a website available to the public through the Internet was publishing.

The Southern District of Florida in *Kernal Records Oy* v. *Mosley,*794 F. Supp.2d 1355, 1364 (S.D. Fla. 2011), determined that the creator of a music file "published" the file when he posted it on the Internet because it could be downloaded and copied by members of the public.

The court in Rogers summarized the issue by holding that whether the work was published depended on whether the facts indicated that the website users were authorized to make copies, i.e., whether a distribution occurred.

So is an item on the Internet considered published? Well it's a firm possibility of a definite maybe.

Registering for Copyright Ideally, a copyright should be registered as soon as the work is fixed in a concrete, tangible form, but in any case, must be registered with the Copyright Office within five years of the date of first publication to be protected. Publication without displaying a copyright notice does not necessarily invalidate a copyright registered within five years however. If notice was not placed on the work, the author must make a reasonable attempt to add the notice to all works distributed after discovery of the omission.

Although registering a work is not required to secure protection under copyright, there are valid reasons why the author should do so. Most importantly, registration of the copyright protects the author by providing evidence of ownership. This is a crucial point for legal support of an author's claim to copyright protection. If a work is infringed upon, prior registration is required before a lawsuit may be initiated.

Registration is a prerequisite to filing an infringement action, but registration may be obtained any time during the copyright term. To register a copyright, the appropriate form must be completed. This form, along with copies of the work and a fee are sent to the Register of Copyrights, Copyright Office, Library of Congress, Washington, D.C. 20559.

Copyright can also be filed online. The U.S. Copyright office has a website set up where items registration can be done over the Internet through their eCO (electronic Copyright Office) website. The Index of Sources at the end of this book lists the copyright office's website.

There are different forms for different types of creative works, and it is important to use the proper one for registration whether it's done through the mail or online. These are all listed on the copyright office's website.

Duration of Copyright Protection Currently, the term of copyright for a particular work depends on several factors as outlined in the Copyright Term Extension Act of 1998 (CTEA), Pub. L. No. 105-298, 112 Stat. 2827 (1998). As a general rule, for works created after January 1, 1978, copyright protection lasts for the life of the author plus seventy years. In the case of an anonymous work, a pseudonymous work, or a "work made for hire," the copyright term is 95 years from the year of first publication or a term of 120 years from the year of its creation, whichever comes first.

Transfer of Copyright to Others

The rights to a copyright are transferable, usually by assignment or licensing. The transfer of exclusive rights, that is, where only the grantee (person to whom the rights are given) can use the rights, is valid only if made in writing and signed by the holder of the copyright, the grantor (person granting the rights). Transfer of nonexclusive rights need not be in writing. Remember though, whenever a copyright is transferred or licensed, it must be recorded with the Copyright Office.

Compulsory Licensing of Copyright

Compulsory licensing covers certain works that others can use after the payment of a fee set by the copyright office, instead of the copyright owner agreeing to the use. This practice is common in the music industry. Here's how it works: If an agency wants to use a musical piece in a commercial, notice is served on the owner of the copyright, and monthly royalties are paid to the owner. Cable and satellite television providers, like Comcast and DirecTV, obtain a compulsory license for the transmission of copyrighted works. Royalties are paid as a percentage of the gross receipts of the cable system to the Copyright Royalty Tribunal (a clearinghouse for accounting and disbursement of royalties) and later distributed to the owners.

Assignment of Rights

Many authors assign their rights to organizations who, in turn, authorize usage by others for a fee. Organizations such as ASCAP (American Society for Composers, Artists, and Publishers) hold copyrights for many musical works. Broadcasters and commercial users are required to pay a fee to ASCAP, which is then distributed to the owners for the use of material.

The "Works-for-Hire" Rule

When an employer, person or company has an employee or agent perform work, the employer is considered the author and the owner of the copyright of that work. Under copyright law this is called work "made-for-hire." In other words, when the work is made by an employee (work-for-hire), the actual person who created it does not own the copyright. The person who employed the worker does.

"Works-for-hire" include items produced by an employee within the scope of his employment. If an employee of the company is asked to photograph a product, the company is the owner of the copyright in the photograph and it is a work-for-hire. However, work created outside the scope of his employment is owned by the employee and not the employer. The concept or term also covers works specifically ordered or commissioned for a particular purpose, if there is an agreement in writing that the work was done for hire. However, a work-for-hire does not normally include routine professional services on behalf of a client, unless there is an agreement to the contrary.

Ownership problems can arise when an independent contractor is commissioned to create work. *108 Degrees, LLC v. Merrimack Golf Club, Inc.,* 2010 DNH 54 (2010), involved a golf course marketing deal that landed in the rough. 108 Degrees, LLC, was a marketing company who brought suit against the owners and operators of the Merrimack Valley Golf Club in Methuen, Massachusetts. They alleged that they breached a contract and a promissory note by refusing to pay for a new website that 108 Degrees designed [*2] for the golf club. In addition, 108 Degrees accused the Merrimack of infringing its copyright by launching a nearly identical website.

Merrimack argued that 108 Degrees cannot recover for copyright infringement because the website materials were "work made for hire" and as such belonged to the golf course, not to 108 Degrees. Typically the hiring party owns the copyright in "work made for hire," unless otherwise agreed in writing. In this case, the court said: "it is unclear from the complaint whether the website materials fall within the statutory definition of 'work made for hire.' Moreover, even if they do, the complaint alleges that the parties agreed in writing that 108 Degrees would own the copyright until it received full payment from the golf course, which if true would amount to a contractual resolution of the issue (in other words, that the parties 'contracted around' the work-for-hire doctrine)." This written exclusion is typically the way the work for hire rule is settled with independent contractors.

Under the Copyright Act of 1976, copyright ownership "vests initially in the author or authors of the work" (17 U.S.C. ß 201(a)). "As a general rule, the author is the party who actually creates the work, that is, the person who translates an idea into a fixed, tangible expression entitled to copyright protection. The Act carves out an important exception, however, for 'works made for hire.'" If a copyrighted work falls within that exception, then "'the employer or other person for whom the work was prepared is considered the author' and owns the copyright, unless there is a written agreement to the contrary."

The court reasoned that: "A copyrighted work 'comes within the work for hire doctrine if it consists of either (i) a work prepared by an employee within the scope of her employment or (ii) one prepared by an independent contractor on special order or commission.' Here, 108 Degrees created the website materials as an independent contractor, not an employee. Not every work by an independent contractor qualifies as a work for hire. The work must be specially ordered or commissioned for use as a contribution to a collective work, as part of a motion picture or other audiovisual work, as a translation, as a supplementary work, as a compilation, as an instructional text, as a test, as answer material for a test, or as an atlas, *if* the parties expressly agree in a written instrument signed by them that the work shall be considered a work made for hire."

As with many questions involving copyright law and the Internet, the courts are only starting to weigh in on whether a website can fall under one of the nine listed categories under the work-for-hire statute. It is possible that website materials might fall within the "other audiovisual work" category, at least if they "consist of a series of related images . . . together with accompanying sounds." And, of course, if they include the specific content listed in the statute (e.g., an instructional text, a test, or an atlas), then they also might qualify. "Because," as the court said, "the creation of websites can differ drastically from case to case," suggesting that "each website would have to be analyzed individually to determine if it could fall within the enumerated works."

And in any event, this court didn't need to address that issue, because the other statutory prerequisite has not been satisfied. That is, nothing in the complaint suggested that the parties had a written work-for-hire agreement. Merrimack pointed to language in the complaint that refers the website materials as "work prepared by the Plaintiff for the Merrimack Valley Golf Club." But the statute is clear, that is not enough. To satisfy the rule the "writing must precede the creation" of the copyrighted work, or at the very least must "confirm a prior agreement, either explicit or implicit, made before the creation of the work." In this case, 108 Degrees denies the existence of any such agreement.

The court in this case concluded: "Moreover, even assuming *arguendo* that the website materials qualified as work for hire, that would not necessarily resolve the issue of copyright ownership, because the Copyright Act allows parties to contract around the work-for-hire rules. (Hiring entity owns copyright in work for hire unless the parties have expressly agreed otherwise in a written instrument signed by them). Here, 108 Degrees alleges that the parties signed a promissory note acknowledging that 108 Degrees would own the copyright in the website materials until it received full payment from the golf course. Although the defendants vehemently dispute the validity of the note, the plaintiff's allegations must be accepted as true for purposes of resolving the [claim]."

The best way to avoid copyright ownership problems when dealing with independent contractors (including freelancers) is to have them sign a written document designating that all materials created by the freelancer are works "made for hire" and that the creator transfers and assigns all rights and interest to the company commissioning the work. Remember, the independent contractor must transfer rights, establishing that the work is made for hire in writing, or ownership problems may arise.

Copyright and Protection of Ideas

One very important point about copyright must be made clear, and I've said this before. Copyright does not protect an idea *per se*. It does, however, protect the *expression* of an idea. If the expression of the original idea is recognizable in another work, to the extent that an infringement is created, a lawsuit may result.

If Widget Manufacturing Company designed and built a new widget refurbisher, the company cannot copyright the machine. We saw earlier that devices may not copyrighted. If anything, the machine would need to be protected under patent law. However, to produce a brochure for its new product, Widget Manufacturing had a photograph taken of the machine. That picture could be copyrighted as it is an expression of the idea. But the copyright only protects the photo, not the widget. Let's take a closer look at this concept.

Copyright Does Not Protect Ideas *Per Se*

As we just saw in the Widget Manufacturing hypothetical, copyright is limited in scope. It does not protect an idea; a concept. Copyright protection does not cover "any idea, procedure, system, method of operation, concept, principle, or discovery, regardless of the form in which it is described, explained, illustrated, or embodied in such work" (17 U.S.C. section 102).

Copyright Protects the Expression of an Idea

Copyright may be used to stem an unauthorized expression of an idea. An expression of an idea can take almost any form. An advertisement, a photograph, a movie, a book, and even a video game can all be expressions of ideas. Unlike a patent, copyright protects only the expression—the tangible fixed form used to allow others to perceive the idea—not the idea itself.

Recall the case mentioned earlier—*Joshua Ets-Hokin* v. *Skyy Spirits, Inc.*, 225 F.3d 1068 (2000).

Ets-Hokin was a professional photographer in San Francisco. He shot a series of photographs for Skyy Vodka and ultimately produced and delivered three photographs of the Skyy bottle. As the court described the photographs: "the [Skyy] bottle appears in front of a plain white or yellow backdrop, with back lighting. The bottle seems to be illuminated from the left (from the viewer's perspective), such that the right side of the bottle is slightly shadowed. The angle from which the photos were taken appears to be perpendicular to the side of the bottle, with the label centered, such that the viewer has a 'straight on' perspective. In two of the photographs, only the bottle is pictured; in the third, a martini sits next to the bottle."

According to the contractual agreement between the parties (the application, or lack thereof, of the "Work-for-Hire" rule may be determined by mutual agreement through the terms of a contract) signed by Skyy, Ets-Hokin retained all rights to the photos and only licensed limited rights for Skyy's use. Skyy claims that it found Ets-Hokin's photographs unsatisfactory and hired other photographers to photograph their bottle.

Ets-Hokin brought suit against Skyy for copyright infringement among other causes of action. He alleged that Skyy used photographs taken by the other photographers that mimicked the photos he had taken. Specifically, he claimed that these other photographers infringed upon his photographs and produced virtually identical photos of the vodka bottle.

The court said: "Skyy argues, in a nutshell, that the commercial photographs of its vodka bottle are not worthy of copyright protection. We disagree. The essence of copyrightability is originality of artistic, creative expression. Given the low threshold for originality under the Copyright Act, as well as the longstanding and consistent body of case law holding that photographs generally satisfy this minimal standard, we conclude that Ets-Hokin's product shots of the Skyy vodka bottle are original works of authorship entitled to copyright protection. To put our holding in context, we summarize the historical treatment of photographs both as artistic expression and as the proper subject of copyright protection."

Here, the court showed that the Ets-Hokin photograph was "the expression" of the object or "idea", the Skyy Vodka bottle, and was protected under copyright. And the subsequent photographers that Skyy hired infringed upon Ets-Hokin's expression by making such a close copy of it.

Copyright and Digital Mapping

New technologies bring new challenges. In 2003, in conjunction with its advertising agency, Saatchi & Saatchi, Toyota began work on its 2004 model-year advertising campaign. The new campaign would involve, among other things, digital models of Toyota's vehicles for use on their website and in other media. These digital models would have advantages over the photographs Toyota had used previously. With a few clicks of a computer mouse, they could change the color of the car, its surroundings, and even edit its physical dimensions to portray changes in vehicle styling. Prior to this technology, Toyota had to produce photo shoots of new vehicles each time the manufacturer made even a small design change to their car or truck.

To produce these digital models, Saatchi and Toyota hired Grace & Wild, Inc. (G&W) which is now Ringside Creative in Detroit. In turn, G&W subcontracted with Meshwerks to assist with two initial aspects of the project; digitizing and modeling. Digitizing involves collecting physical data points from an object. For Toyota's vehicles, Meshwerks covered each car, truck, and van with a grid of tape and running an articulated arm tethered to a computer over the vehicle to measure all points of intersection in the grid. Based on these measurements, modeling software generated a digital image resembling a wire-frame model. Essentially, the vehicles' data points (measurements) were mapped onto a computerized grid and the modeling software connected the dots to create a "wire frame" of each vehicle.

At this point, however, the on-screen image remained far from perfect and manual "modeling" adjustment were necessary. Meshwerks personnel fine-tuned the lines on screen to resemble each vehicle as closely as possible. Approximately 90 percent of the data points contained in each final model were the result not of the first-step measurement process, but of the skill and effort its digital sculptors manually expended during the second step. As an example, some areas of detail, such as wheels, headlights, door handles, and the Toyota emblem, could not be accurately captured. Those details needed to be recreated as realistically as possible by hand, based on photographs. Even for areas that were measured, Meshwerks faced the challenge of converting measurements taken of a three-dimensional car into a two-dimensional computer representation; to achieve this, its modelers had to sculpt, or move, data points to achieve a visually convincing result. The purpose and product of these processes, after nearly eighty to one-hundred hours of effort per vehicle, were two-dimensional wire-frame depictions of each Toyota vehicle that appeared three-dimensional on screen, but were utterly unadorned—lacking color, shading, and other details.

With Meshwerks' wire-frame products in hand, G&W then manipulated the computerized models by adding detail. Next, G&W digitally applied color, texture, lighting, and animation for use in Toyota's advertising.

A dispute arose because, according to Meshwerks, its contract with G&W allowed for only a single use of its models as part of one Toyota television commercial. Meshwerks claimed that G&W improperly (in violation of copyright laws as well as the parties' agreement) reused and redistributed the models created by Meshwerks in many other media.

In *Meshwerks, Inc.* v. *Toyota Motor Sales U.S.A., Inc.*, 528 F.3d 1258 (2008), Toyota claimed that Meshwerks' wire-frame models lacked sufficient originality to be protected under copyright. Specifically, they argued that any original expression found in Meshwerks' products was attributable to the Toyota designers who conceived of the vehicle designs in the first place. Therefore, Toyota's use of the models could not give rise to a claim for copyright infringement.

The court stated: "The parties focus most of their energy in this case on the question whether Meshwerks' models qualify as independent creations, as opposed to copies of Toyota's handiwork. But what can be said, at least based on received copyright doctrine, to distinguish an independent creation from a copy? And how might that doctrine apply in an age of virtual worlds and digital media that seek to mimic the "real" world, but often do so in ways that undoubtedly qualify as (highly) original? While there is little authority explaining how our received principles of copyright law apply to the relatively new digital medium before us, some lessons may be discerned from how the law coped in an earlier time with a previous revolution in technology: photography."

The court went on saying:

As Judge Pauley admirably recounted in *SHL Imaging, Inc. v. Artisan House, Inc.*, photography was initially met by critics with a degree of skepticism: a photograph, some said, "copies everything and explains nothing," and it was debated whether a camera could do anything more than merely record the physical world. These largely aesthetic debates migrated into legal territory when Oscar Wilde toured the United States in the 1880s and sought out Napoleon Sarony for a series of publicity photographs to promote the event. Burrow-Giles a lithography firm, quickly copied one of Sarony's photos and sold 85,000 prints without the photographer's permission. Burrow-Giles defended its conduct on the ground that the photograph was a "mere mechanical reproduction of the physical features" of Wilde and thus not copyrightable. Recognizing that Oscar Wilde's inimitable visage does not belong, or "owe its origins" to any photographer, the Supreme Court noted that photographs may well sometimes lack originality and are thus not *per se* copyrightable. At the same time, the Court held, a copyright may be had to the extent a photograph involves "posing the said Oscar Wilde in front of the camera, selecting and arranging the costume, draperies, and other various accessories in said photograph, arranging the subject so as to present graceful outlines, arranging and disposing the light and shade, suggesting and evoking the desired expression . . . ." Accordingly, the Court indicated, photographs are copyrightable, if only to the extent of their *original* depiction of the subject. Wilde's image is not copyrightable; but to the extent a photograph reflects the photographer's decisions regarding pose, positioning, background, lighting, shading, and the like, those elements can be said to "owe their origins" to the photographer, making the photograph copyrightable, at least to that extent.

Central to the evaluation of this case is the fact that Meshwerks' digital wire-frame computer models depict Toyota vehicles without any individualizing features: they are untouched by a digital paintbrush; they are not depicted in front of a building, roaring down the highway, or climbing up a mountainside. In other words, Meshwerks' models depict nothing more than unadorned Toyota vehicles. The court explained: "the unequivocal lesson from *Feist* is that works are not copyrightable to the extent they do not involve any expression apart from the raw facts in the world. [i]n connection with the predecessor technology of photography, '[a]s applied to a photograph of a pre-existing product, that bedrock principle [of originality] means that the photographer manifestly cannot claim to have originated the matter depicted therein . . . ' " The upshot is that the photographer is entitled to copyright solely based on lighting, angle, perspective, and the other ingredients that traditionally apply to that art form. Exactly the same is true with the digital medium. The court explained: "[t]he facts in this case unambiguously show that Meshwerks did not make any decisions regarding lighting, shading, the background in front of which a vehicle would be posed, the angle at which to pose it, or the like—in short, its models reflect none of the decisions that can make depictions of things or facts in the world, whether Oscar Wilde or a Toyota Camry, new expressions subject to copyright protection."

The court summed it up best: "In reaching this conclusion, we do not for a moment seek to downplay the considerable amount of time, effort, and skill that went into making Meshwerks' digital wire-frame models. But, in assessing the originality of a work for which copyright protection is sought, we look only at the final *product,* not the process, and the fact that intensive, skillful, and even creative labor is invested in the process of creating a product does not guarantee its copyrightability. ('Even if the *process* is both expensive and intricate, an exact or near-exact duplicate of an original should not qualify for copyright.') This is not to say that [accurately reproducing an underlying image] requires no skill or effort; it simply means that such skill and effort does not suffice to invoke the highly advantageous legal monopoly granted under the Copyright Act. In the case before us, there is no doubt that transposing the physical appearances of Toyota's vehicles from three dimensions to two, such that computer-screen images accurately reflect Toyota's products, was labor intensive and required a great amount of skill. But because the end-results were unadorned images of Toyota's vehicles, the appearances of which do not owe their origins to Meshwerks, we are unable to reward that skill, effort, and labor with copyright protection."

We will certainly see more activity in this area with new technologies emerging every day.

The Fair Use Doctrine

All holders of copyright are susceptible to the "fair use doctrine," which permits certain copying of copyrighted material for purposes of criticism, news reporting, teaching, or research. Remember the Google case from the beginning of the chapter? Generally, however, copying for commercial use would violate the rights of the copyright holder. The fair use doctrine will not protect advertisers who try to use copyrighted material for commercial purposes without obtaining permission and paying for it.

Fair use was developed to balance authors' rights to protection of their copyrights and accompanying economic compensation against the public's desire for a free flow of ideas and information. It could be argued that, basically, the doctrine tries to achieve a safe area between copyright protection and freedom of speech. But it's a very narrow "safe area."

Defining "Fair Use" Protection

The main issue that the courts look to in determining if the use falls under the "fair use doctrine" is whether the usage substantially diminishes the value of the work.

One of the most notable examples of fair use was shown in the landmark case involving Universal City Studios and its suit against Sony. This case discussed a then-new area of copyright—copying by home video recorders—that Congress could not have conceived would occur when it enacted the first Copyright Act. Sony manufactured millions of its Betamax video tape recorders and sold them through many retail outlets. At the time Beta and VHS were the "new media" of the day.

Universal owned the copyrights to many of the movies, television programs, and other programming it broadcast over television stations across the country. In *Sony Corp.* v. *Universal City Studios*, 52 U.S.L.W. 4090 (U.S. Jan 17,1984) rev'g 659 F.2d 963 (9th Cir. 1981), Universal claimed that by Sony providing the means to copy or record these shows from television, people were violating copyright laws. Universal was essentially claiming contributory infringement in its suit because although Sony could not infringe on Universal's copyrights directly, Sony contributed to it through consumers who bought and used the video recorders to record movies. However, Universal's argument in court was not valid under the Copyright Act. Contributory infringement did not exist here anymore than it would for a camera manufacturer or a photocopy machine manufacturer.

Sony further argued that the video recorders allowed the consumer to time-record from television. This allowed the consumer to watch the show when it was more convenient, actually expanding the television viewing audience that would watch the program. Therefore, the copyright holder could not object to the home recording of copyrighted material. The key here was whether the home recording impaired the commercial value of the work now or in the future. In this case it was ruled that it did not.

The court determined, in a twenty-two-page opinion, that noncommercial home recording of copyrighted material broadcast over public television was fair use and did not constitute copyright infringement. "Noncommercial" is the operative word here because there would be no reduction in the market for the original work.

Commercial Use and Fair Use

Although every commercial use of copyrighted material without permission is a copyright infringement, noncommercial uses are a different matter. In order to uphold a claim of infringement through noncommercial uses, it must be shown that allowing the use could cause some harm or could damage the potential market for the work. If the copyrighted material is used for commercial use, that likelihood is presumed, but for noncommercial use it must be shown. Universal tried to argue that by allowing its shows to be recorded at home, "live television or movie audiences will decrease as more people watch Betamax tapes as an alternative." The court disagreed and Sony won.

Here's an example that relates to advertising directly. *The Miami Herald*, published by Knight-Ridder Newspapers, developed an ad campaign to promote the new format of its magazine-style television supplement to the newspaper. The Sunday supplement was introduced in the newspaper in November 1977. The campaign included print ads and television commercials.

The focus of the *Miami Herald's* campaign was to compare its television magazine to *TV Guide* magazine. The print ads showed the covers of both magazines in actual size, with a headline which read: "The *Herald's* new TV book. It's a little bit bigger and a little bit better." The message in the ad was that the *Miami Herald's* book was bigger, had more listings, was easier to read, and was more up-to-date than *TV Guide* magazine. In the television commercials, the message was the same (box 9.1).

Box 9.1

A typical *Miami Herald* ad for their new weekly book of television listings, based on the Goldilocks and the Three Bears theme, went like this:

Narrator: "This is the story of Sidney Bear, Cindy Bear, and Junior Bear. They all loved to watch TV, but ...."

Older man: "This TV book is too small."

Child: "This TV book is too big."

Older woman: "This TV section is just right."

Narrator: "It was the *Sunday Herald's* new TV book at no extra cost. The three bears loved the new, just-right size with its up-to-date and more complete listings. "Til one day this little blonde kid—uh, but that's another story. Something for everybody. Everyday of the week."

When Triangle Publications, the owner of *TV Guide* magazine, heard about these ads, it brought suit. In *Triangle Publications* v. *Knight-Ridder*, 626 F.2d 1171 (5th Cir. 1980), Triangle objected to the reproduction of a *TV Guide* cover in both print ads and television commercials. The issue was whether the use of the *TV Guide* cover in the Herald's ads was allowed under the fair use doctrine.

The court determined that the *Herald's* ads did not copy the essence of *TV Guide*; that is, the articles, schedules, and features contained inside. The *Herald* reproduced only the cover of the magazine. This, the court reasoned, was not enough to determine that the commercial value of *TV Guide's* copyright would be diminished. In fact, if the *Herald's* ads drew customers away from *TV Guide*, it would have been because of the validity of the message—the difference between the two publications rather than showing the *TV Guide* cover.

The court concluded by saying *TV Guide* "suffered no economic injury whatever from the alleged infringement of its copyright." The *Herald* won its claim of fair use. For a discussion of comparative advertising issues, which parallels this case, review chapter 6.

The Final Insult Example Paramount Pictures produced the movie *Naked Gun 33 1/3: The Final Insult*. Advertising to promote the movie included an image of Leslie Nielsen's smirking face superimposed on the body of a nude pregnant woman. Paramount superimposed Nielsen's face on a photograph that very closely resembled a photograph taken by Annie Leibovitz of actress Demi Moore that had run on the August 1991 cover of *Vanity Fair* magazine. The pregnant Moore, nude, was shown from the side, with her right hand and arm covering her breasts and her left hand supporting her stomach (ala Botticelli's Birth of Venus). Moore had a ring on her middle finger and was wearing a very serious expression.

In August 1993, Paramount hired the design firm, Dazu, Inc., to create and produce an advertising and promotional campaign for the upcoming movie. Dazu showed Paramount four ads with composite photographs of Nielsen's face in place of what had been the faces of Sharon Stone, Madonna, Jane Fonda, and Demi Moore.

Each proposed ad included a slogan that related to the March release date of the film. The composite photograph depicting Nielsen as the pregnant Moore slyly announcing: "DUE THIS MARCH." Paramount approved the concept and selected the composite of Moore's body and Nielsen's face.

Instead of copying the original photograph, Paramount hired another photographer to take the image of a nude pregnant woman, similarly posed. The photograph resembled, in great detail, Leibovitz's photo. Neilsen's face was then superimposed on the model's body.

Leibovitz v. *Paramount Pictures Corp.*, 137 F.3d 109 (2d Cir. 1998), was the case that resulted. Paramount claimed that its advertising was a parody of Leibovitz's original photograph. And as such, was a fair use. According to the court, the fair use doctrine "permits the use of copyrighted material without the owner's consent in a reasonable manner for certain purposes." Leibovitz argued that because the advertising was used for commercial purposes, Paramount could not use the fair use defense.

As we have seen in other cases, whether a use is "fair" involves:

1. The purpose and character of the work;
2. The nature of the copyrighted work;
3. The amount and substantiality of the work used; and
4. The effect of the use on the market for the original.

Although "parody" is not specifically mentioned in the Copyright statute as permissible fair use, courts have long afforded such works some measure of protection. The court reasoned that the *Naked Gun* ad was commenting on, and essentially making fun of, the original Leibovitz photograph. The court said: "[B]ecause the smirking face of Nielsen contrasts so strikingly with the serious expression on the face of Moore, the ad may reasonably be perceived as commenting on the seriousness, even the pretentiousness, of the original."

The court cautioned, however, that simply being different from the original did not necessarily mean a work "commented" on the original. In this instance however, the Neilsen photograph could be perceived as commenting, through parody, on the original photograph.

The court analyzed its position on the parody by stating:

A. First factor. We inquire whether Paramount's advertisement "may reasonably be perceived," as a new work that "at least in part, comments on" Leibovitz's photograph. Whether it "comments" on the original is a somewhat closer question. Because the smirking face of Nielsen contrasts so strikingly with the serious expression on the face of Moore, the ad may reasonably be perceived as commenting on the seriousness, even the pretentiousness, of the original. The contrast achieves the effect of ridicule that the Court recognized in *Campbell* would serve as a sufficient "comment" to tip the first factor in a parodist's favor. ("It is this joinder of reference and ridicule that marks off the author's choice of parody from the other types of comment and criticism that traditionally have had a claim to fair use protection as transformative works.")

In saying this, however, we have some concern about the ease with which every purported parodist could win on the first factor simply by pointing out some feature that contrasts with the original. Being different from an original does not inevitably "comment" on the original. Nevertheless, the ad is not merely different; it differs in a way that may reasonably be perceived as commenting, through ridicule, on what a viewer might reasonably think is the undue self-importance conveyed by the subject of the Leibovitz photograph. A photographer posing a well-known actress in a manner that calls to mind a well-known painting must expect, or at least tolerate, a parodist's deflating ridicule.

Apart from ridiculing pretentiousness, the ad might also be reasonably perceived as interpreting the Leibovitz photograph to extol the beauty of the pregnant female body, and, rather unchivalrously, to express disagreement with this message. The District Court thought such a comment was reasonably to be perceived from the contrast between "a serious portrayal of a beautiful woman taking great pride in the majesty of her pregnant body . . . [and] a ridiculous image of a smirking, foolish-looking pregnant man."

The fact that the ad makes a parodic comment on the original does not end the first-factor analysis, however, because the ad was created and displayed to promote a commercial product, the film. This advertising use lessens the "indulgence" to which the parodic ad is entitled. Paramount seeks to mitigate the negative force of the advertising purpose by arguing that the advertisement should be viewed as an extension of the film, rather than merely an advertisement for it. Paramount emphasizes the general jocular nature of the film, as well as the film's specific humorous treatment of pregnancy and parenthood.

Though the advertising purpose of a parodic copying should not be entirely discounted simply because the ad promotes a humorous work, there is some slight force to Paramount's argument. For those who see the movie, the parodic comment of the ad might reasonably be perceived as reenforced by the kidding comments of the movie concerning pregnancy and parenthood.

On balance, the strong parodic nature of the ad tips the first factor significantly toward fair use, even after making some discount for the fact that it promotes a commercial product. "[L]ess indulgence" does not mean no indulgence at all.

B. Second Factor. Though Paramount concedes the obvious point that Leibovitz's photograph exhibited significant creative expression, . . . the creative nature of an original will normally not provide much help in determining whether a parody of the original is fair use. The second factor therefore favors Leibovitz, but the weight attributed to it in this case is slight.

C. Third Factor. In assessing the amount and substantiality of the portion used, we must focus only on the protected elements of the original. Leibovitz is entitled to no protection for the appearance in her photograph of the body of a nude, pregnant female. Only the photographer's particular expression of such a body is entitled to protection. Thus, to whatever extent Leibovitz is contending that the ad takes the "heart" of the original, she must limit her contention to the particular way the body of Moore is portrayed, rather than the fact that the ad copies the appearance of a nude, pregnant body. Moreover, in the context of parodies, "the heart is also what most readily conjures up the [original] for parody, and it is the heart at which parody takes aim." Thus, the third-factor inquiry in the parody context concerns "what else the parodist did besides go to the heart of the original."

Paramount went to great lengths to have its ad copy protectable aspects of the Leibovitz photograph. Even though the basic pose of a nude, pregnant body and the position of the hands, if ever protectable, were placed into the public domain by painters and sculptors long before Botticelli, Leibovitz is entitled to protection for such artistic elements as the particular lighting, the resulting skin tone of the subject, and the camera angle that she selected. ("Elements of originality in a photograph may include posing the subjects, lighting, angle, selection of film and camera, evoking the desired expression, and almost any other variant involved.")

The copying of these elements, carried out to an extreme degree by digital retouching, took more of the Leibovitz photograph than was minimally necessary to conjure it up, but *Campbell* instructs that a parodist's copying of more of an original than is necessary to conjure it up will not necessarily tip the third factor against fair use. On the contrary, "[o]nce enough has been taken to assure identification," as plainly occurred here, the reasonableness of taking additional aspects of the original depends on the extent to which the "overriding purpose and character" of the copy "is to parody the original," and "the likelihood that the parody may serve as a market substitute for the original." That approach leaves the third factor with little, if any, weight against fair use so long as the first and fourth factors favor the parodist. Since those factors favor fair use in this case, the third factor does not help Leibovitz, even though the degree of copying of protectable elements was extensive.

At the trial, it became apparent that the use of the parody did not weaken the market for the original photograph. While the court did determine that Paramount copied more of the original photo than necessary to conjure up the parody, the first and fourth factors allowed the use. The court held that the advertising was a parody.

When a Fair Use Argument Does Not Protect Against Infringement

The fair use doctrine has been used to allow certain forms of parody, that is, when the "style of . . . [a] work is closely imitated for comic effect . . ." (*Webster's New Collegiate Dictionary* (Springfield, Mass.: Merriam-Webster Inc., 1999). But the advertiser must understand the limits of the doctrine. To determine whether the use made of a copyrighted work can be considered fair use, the following need to be considered:

- The purpose and character of the use, including whether such use is of a commercial nature or is for nonprofit educational purposes;
- The nature of the copyrighted work;
- The amount and substantiality of the portion used in relation to the copyrighted work as a whole; and
- The effect of the use upon the potential market for or value of the copyrighted work (17 U.S.C. section 107).

On the other hand, in the advertising area, a parody can fall outside the fair use doctrine when another company's theme, tag line, or primary characteristic is taken. Sambo's restaurants found this out when Dr. Pepper sued it for copyright infringement.

Dr. Pepper developed its *"Be a Pepper"* campaign in 1978. Within four years the company had spent over $100 million on the campaign and had realized tremendous results. Dr. Pepper was so pleased with the results that it planned for the campaign to run another ten years.

In many cases, success breeds imitation. Here, Dr. Pepper was the success, Sambo's was the imitation.

While the Dr. Pepper campaign was in its fourth year, Sambo's ad agency, Bozell-Jacobs, developed a campaign called "Dancing Seniors" that bore striking similarities to the Dr. Pepper campaign (see box 9.2).

The Sambo's commercials first aired in late 1980, and when Dr. Pepper learned of this in January 1981, it sued in *Dr. Pepper Co.* v. *Sambo's Restaurants, Inc.*, 517 F. Supp. 1202 (1981). Dr. Pepper held copyrights to its television commercials and to the "Be a Pepper" jingle. As a defense to the case, Sambo's claimed that it was entitled to parody the Dr. Pepper commercial under the Fair Use Doctrine.

However, any commercial use has a tendency to contradict the fair use doctrine. This is a very risky area for advertisers. Because of Sambo's use of the essence and substance of the Dr. Pepper commercial, it diminished the Dr. Pepper spot's value, uniqueness, and originality and took the infringement out of the fair use arena.

Dr. Pepper and Sambo's TV Commercial Comparison

Both commercials open with one person (the leader) dancing and singing the beginning of a jingle.

Dr. Pepper Original:	*Sambo's Version*
Leader sings: "I drink Dr. Pepper and I'm proud. I'm part of an original crowd."	Leader sings: "I eat at Sambo's Restaurants every day. I get a special deal on my dinner meal."

Both commercials use people dancing along with the leader and singing a chorus:

Dr. Pepper Original:	*Sambo's Version*
"Wouldn't you like to be a Pepper, too?"	"Don't you want to be a senior, too?"

Sambo's impact on the useful life of the "Be a Pepper" campaign was an infringement and Sambo's lost.

What about fair use of copyrighted material that was not another commercial? Parody or satirization is a common and legal practice in all forms of entertainment and social commentary under the fair use doctrine. However, it is not allowed in advertising.

Miller Brewing Company, its advertising agency Backer & Spielvogel, and comedian Joe Piscopo (the performer in the commercial) were sued by a rap music group, The Fat Boys. The case, *Tin Pan Apple, Inc.* v. *Miller Brewing Co., Inc.*, 737 F.Supp. 826 (S.D.N.Y. 1990), involved a television commercial that infringed the copyright of some of the Fat Boys' songs. Miller argued that the similarity between the Fat Boys composition was allowed under the Fair Use Doctrine because the commercial was simply a parody of rap music in general, and of the Fat Boys in particular. In Miller's argument, they discounted the fact that the music and action used in the commercial was "substantially similar," the test for copyright infringement, to the Fat Boys' songs and performances.

Miller tried to use a 1989 case where a federal court ruled that a song entitled "I Love Sodom," used in a skit on the television program *Saturday Night Live*, did not infringe the copyrighted song "I Love New York." This was clearly because the purpose of the skit was to satirize the way in which New York City had attempted to rectify its rather tarnished image through the use of a comprehensive advertising campaign. This form of parody was protected under the fair use rule because it was used for social satire, rather than commercial advertising.

Although the parody defense is viable in situations where parts of the copyrighted work are used for social comment or criticism, the defense did not apply in the *Miller* case because its use was solely for the purpose of promoting the sale of a commercial product; in this case, beer. Commercial advertising cannot use the doctrine of fair use to defend an illegal use of copyrighted material.

As we have just seen, the more unique the concept of the commercial, the greater the protection required against infringement. If the commercial is based on more general situations, greater latitude will be allowed. Any car commercial may use a showroom as its setting with a car salesman speaking to the audience. However, if the bulk of the commercial shows a salesman announcing claims about the car, which are obvious and blatant lies, and subtitles are shown (as in the past Isuzu commercials), the courts will be more inclined to consider this type of use an infringement.

The Big One Example Columbia Picture's 1997 movie *Men in Black*, grossed over $250 million at the box office in the United States and over $337 million in its international theatrical run. Merchandise licensing included posters, toys, video games, T-shirts, hats, games, greeting cards, and books. Furthermore, millions of copies of the single and musical soundtrack to *Men in Black* have been sold.

Michael Moore's documentary entitled *The Big One* (TBO) was advertised with posters that infringed the *Men in Black* (MIB) movie poster. *Columbia Pictures Industries, Inc.* v. *Miramax Films Corp.*, No. CV98-2793 ABC (AIJx), 1998 U.S. Dist. LEXIS 11325 (C.D. Cal., June 2,1998), was the case.

The movie *The Big One* opened on April 10, 1998. It was a documentary about the consequences of corporate America's focus on achieving maximum profits while turning a blind eye to the consequences, including plant closings, employee layoffs, and employee benefit reductions.

The advertising and poster used to promote the MIB movie featured Will Smith and Tommy Lee Jones wearing black suits, white shirts, black ties, and sunglasses. They carried over-sized weapons and had serious expressions. The copy read: "Protecting the Earth from the scum of the Universe." On the other hand, the poster for *The Big One* featured Michael Moore wearing essentially the same cloths, standing in front of a skyline of New York City. Moore's hair was disheveled and he was also wearing a black baseball cap. He was carrying an over-sized microphone and was smirking. The copy read: "Protecting the Earth from the scum of Corporate America."

The court discussed the requirements to establish copyright infringement: "Plaintiffs must prove: (1) that Plaintiffs owned the allegedly infringed work; and (2) that Defendants copied Plaintiffs' copyrighted work. 'Copying' is composed of two parts: (1) circumstantial evidence of the defendant's access to the copyrighted work; and (2) substantial similarity between the copyrighted work and the defendant's work. 'Substantial similarity' refers to similarity of expression, not merely similarity of ideas or concepts."

The court found that *The Big One* poster infringed the MIB poster. The court explained: "The TBO poster is substantially similar to the expressive ideas contained in the MIB poster in that both contain: (1) figures carrying a large object; (2) figures of a similar size with similar stances; (3) figures standing in front of a New York skyline at night; (4) a similar manner of expression; (5) similar color; and (6) an identical layout."

In addition to the poster infringement, the court also found that the TBO trailers infringed the MIB trailers. It said: "The MIB Trailers are substantially similar to the expressive ideas contained in the TBO Trailers. The trailers contain a virtually identical theme, format, pace, and sequence of events."

Miramax also attempted to use a fair use defense, claiming that its use of the copyrighted materials was a fair use. In support of their fair use argument, the defendants contend that the TBO Trailer pokes fun at the MIB image by suggesting that an unfit documentation may "assume the mantle of hero and do battle against the villains of corporate America, as the [*Men in Black*] do battle against aliens." The defendants argued that advertising for *The Big One* "does not merely use the original concept to promote itself or as a vehicle to satirize some other subject. Rather, [the] advertising directly targets [*Men in Black*] for comment."

The court explained: "The fair use defense permits courts to avoid rigid application of the copyright statute when, on occasion, it would stifle the very creativity which that law is designed to foster."

"The Copyright Act sets four factors for courts to consider in determining if a fair use defense exists in any given case: (1) the purpose and character of the accused use; (2) the nature of the copyrighted work; (3) the importance of the portion used in relation to the copyrighted work as a whole; and (4) the effect of the accused use on the potential market for or value of the copyrighted work."

Because of this, the court rejected the defendant's fair use defense. The poster and trailers were created for commercial purposes. The poster and trailers merely copied the bulk of the MIB poster and trailers and were clearly intended, according to the court, to get attention for *The Big One*.

The court stated: "In this case, The TBO Poster and Trailer do not create a 'transformative work.' The TBO advertisements cannot reasonably be perceived as commenting on or criticizing the ads for 'Men In Black.' The TBO Poster merely incorporates several elements of the MIB Poster: figures with a particular stance carrying large weapons, standing in front of the New York skyline at night, with a similar layout. Similarly, the TBO Trailer appears to be little more than an effort to 'get attention' for *The Big One* and 'avoid the drudgery in working up something fresh.'"

The TBO poster and trailer were designed solely for the purpose of attracting viewers to see *The Big One*. As such, Miramax has merely used the copyrighted work as a vehicle to poke fun at another target—corporate America. It has not used its advertising to comment on or criticize the copyrighted work.

Carazy Copyright Example Louis Psihoyos was a photographer who took the photo of Larry Fuente in front of his wildly decorated Cadillac called the Mad Cad. This was not your typical Cadillac. Fuente extended the tail fins of the car by several feet using a dazzling edifice of beads and rhinestones that look like flames rising into the air. The curly flames were really a mosaic of flamingoes, geese, ducks, and horses arranged one atop the other. The beads and rhinestones of many colors, including pink, gold, silver, and aqua, decorate these fins and the rest of the car.

The Examiner published a news magazine called *The National Examiner.* The Examiner claimed that it obtained a slide of Psihoyos' photograph from the publisher of the book: *Art Cars: Revolutionary Movement.* The Examiner maintained that it thought that the publisher had given authorization to reproduce the slide.

In its July 22, 1997, issue, the Examiner reproduced Psihoyos' photograph. The Examiner did not obtain permission from either Psihoyos or Fuente for the use the photograph. The photograph was used as part of a pictorial entitled "CARAZY: Take a ride on the wild side in kookie vehicles."

Along with the photo was the text: AMERICANS wheely love their cars, and some folks have even turned them into wacky works of movable art! They've let their imaginations run wild and used anything and everything to decorate their car-azy hot rods. So, next time you hit the road, see if you spot one of these awesome autos.

In *Psihoyos* v. *National Examiner*, No. 97 Civ. 7624 USM), 1998 U.S. Dist. LEXIS 9192 (S.D.N.Y., June 22, 1998), the Examiner contended that its use of the photograph was a fair use because it was being used for news reporting or commenting purposes. The court disagreed. The Examiner used the photo to create commercial interest in its magazine.

Moreover, the use adversely impacted the copyright owner's market for the original photograph. The court concluded that the Examiner's piece could compete with the original. According to the court: "Psihoyos states that the Examiner's piece adversely impacted the potential market for his work because he did not earn licensing fees from the Examiner and because the Examiner's piece can be used as a poster, reducing demands for the original. The Court agrees."

The Examiner's fair use argument was rejected as well. The court stated: "Fair use has been defined as 'a privilege in others than the owner of the copyright to use the copyrighted material in a reasonable manner without his consent.' Congress identified four factors, which are not intended to be exhaustive, to be used in evaluating a defense of fair use. These factors are: (1) the purpose and character of the use; (2) the nature of the copyrighted work; (3) the substantiality of the portion used in relation to the copyrighted work as a whole; and (4) the effect on the potential market for or value of the copyrighted work."

The court went on in detail:

> The central purpose of this investigation is to see . . . whether the new work merely "supercede[s] the objects" of the original creation . . . or instead adds something new, with a further purpose or different character, altering the first with new expression, meaning, or message. Although such transformative use is not absolutely necessary for a finding of fair use, . . . the goal of copyright, to promote science and the arts, is generally furthered by the creation of transformative works. Such [transformative] works thus lie at the heart of the fair use doctrine's guarantee of breathing space within the confines of copyright . . . and the more transformative the new work, the less will be the significance of other factors like commercialism, that may weigh against a finding of fair use. The Examiner contends this factor weighs in favor of finding fair use because its use of Psihoyos' photo is transformative. Specifically, the Examiner states that as "a news magazine with wide distribution," it used the picture for news reporting or commenting purpose. The Court disagrees.

The Examiner's use is not transformative, because its piece uses the photo to show what it depicts. It is clear from examining the Examiner's article that its purpose was not to comment on the Psihoyos photo but to use it "for precisely a central purpose for which it was created"—to show how an art car looks. Thus, the Examiner's use is not transformative.

The fact that the Examiner used the photo for a commercial rather than a nonprofit educational purpose also weighs against a finding of fair use. The Supreme Court has stated that: "the crux of the profit/nonprofit distinction is not whether the sole motive of the use is monetary gain but whether the user stands to profit from exploitation of copyrighted material without paying the customary price." Here, the commercial nature of the Examiner's use is undisputed. The Examiner has commercially exploited the Psihoyos photo to create news—a centerfold consisting of "car-azy hot rods."

The above facts demonstrated to the court that the Examiner's use does not constitute a fair use.

Copyright Issues Relating Specifically to Advertisements

Copyright law can, as in the Dr. Pepper case, be used against an ad or commercial derived substantially from another piece. This goes back to the "expression of an idea" concept discussed earlier: that is, if the other commercial takes the same basic feeling or premise. Devising a concept for an advertisement is an idea. A specific ad is an expression of that idea and will have copyright implications.

When an Ad Copies the Expression of Another Ad

To illustrate this point, let's look at *Kleier Advertising, Inc. v. Premier Pontiac, Inc.*, 921 F.2d 1036 (1990). This case centered around Kleier Advertising's syndicated advertising campaign that used a trouserless character wearing boxer shorts with the slogan "We'll Beat the Pants Off Any Deal!" The program was used primarily on billboards where actual scaffolding supported a life-size mannequin that implies that it's a billboard company employee working on posting the advertising display. The mannequin was wearing a hardhat and work clothes with its trousers down around the ankles exposing loudly colored boxer shorts. Kleier had previously obtained copyrights on the "Beat the Pants" advertising program.

In order to get a license to use Kleier's "Beat the Pants" campaign, a car dealership needed to pay Kleier an upfront license fee for one year within the dealership's marketing area (with the right to renew for another year for 15 percent of the initial license fee). In the Tulsa market the initial fee was $14,887.00 and the renewal fee was $2,233.05.

In December 1984, Lister Pontiac in Tulsa, Oklahoma produced its own billboard (through Stokely Outdoor Advertising, Inc.) with the slogan, "We'll Beat the Pants Off Any Deal in Town." Affixed to Lister Pontiac's billboard was scaffolding with a trouserless mannequin in boxer shorts wearing the same type of clothing and in the same working posture as the Kleier mannequin. Kleier alleges Lister Pontiac infringed on Kleier's copyright. The literal duplication of so many aspects of the Kleier campaign left little doubt to the court (or any reasonable person) that there clearly was an infringement.

The court agreed with Kleier and awarded them $17,120.05 (the licensing fee and renewal) for the infringement.

The Song Says It Best Example Country singer Aaron Tippin recorded the song "You've Got to Stand for Something" in 1990. The song peaked in popularity in February 1991, when it was the fifth-best-selling country music song in the United States. Although the initial copyright for the song listed Tippin and Buddy Brock as the only authors of the lyrics, in 1996 Acuff-Rose amended its copyright to list Brock's father, William Brock, as an additional author. According to Acuff-Rose (and William Brock), William Brock independently created the sentence "You've got to stand for something, or you'll fall for anything."

Acuff-Rose Music owned the copyright to the country song. In the song the lyrics repeat: "You've got to stand for something or you'll fall for anything."

Jostens was a manufacturer of custom rings. In December 1992 they launched a nationwide advertising campaign for its school class rings that used the theme: "If you don't stand for something, you'll fall for anything." The slogan was preceded by: "The song says it best."

In *Acuff-Rose Music, Inc.* v. *Jostens, Inc.*, No. 987135, 1998 U.S. App. LEXIS 21599 (2d Cir., September 4,1998), Jostens claimed that the line in the music could not be copyrighted, so there could be no infringement. The court said: "To qualify for copyright protection, a work must be original to the author. Originality does not signify novelty; a work may be original even though it closely resembles other works so long as the similarity is fortuitous, not the result of copying."

In this landmark case the court went on: "The sine qua non of copyright is originality. To qualify for copyright protection, a work must be original to the author. Original, as the term is used in copyright, means only that the work was independently created by the author (as opposed to copied from other works), and that it possesses at least some minimal degree of creativity. Originality does not signify novelty; a work may be original even though it closely resembles other works so long as the similarity is fortuitous, not the result of copying."

Referring to these prior uses of the saying, the district court decided that the phrase "enjoyed a robust existence in the public domain long before Tippin employed it for his song's title and in the key lyrics." It therefore concluded that the lines in Acuff-Rose's song lacked the requisite originality to warrant protection, in effect finding that, given the widespread popular usage of the phrase, William Brock most likely did not independently create the lyric lines of Acuff-Rose's song.

In its support, Jostens showed numerous instances when the line had been used that predated Acuff's song, including the Bible, Abraham Lincoln, Martin Luther King, Malcolm X, and Ginger Rogers. In 1985 popular singer/songwriter

John Mellencamp included a song in his album entitled "You've Got to Stand for Somethin'," which included the lyrics, "You've got to stand for somethin'/Or you're gonna fall for anything."

The court held that the phrase had been in existence in the public domain long before the Acuff copyright and that the line lacked the originality required for protection.

When There Is Similarity of Expression

In 1992, Honda's advertising agency, Rubin Postaer, came up with a new concept for the Honda del Sol convertible with its detachable rooftop. Rubin Postaer claimed that the commercial was initially inspired by the climax scene from the movie *Alien*, wherein the alien is ejected from a spaceship. From there, the agency began working on the storyboards for the Honda del Sol's "Escape" commercial. As the concept evolved into the helicopter chase scene, the commercial took on various internal project names, one of which was "James Bob," a play on words for James Bond.

While the commercial was initially approved by Honda in May 1992, actual production of the commercial did not begin until July, 1994. When casting began on the project in the summer of 1994, the casting director specifically sent requests to talent agencies for "James Bond"-type actors and actresses to star in what conceptually could be "the next James Bond film."

With the assistance of the same special effects team that worked on Arnold Schwarzenegger's movie *True Lies*, Rubin Postaer produced the Honda del Sol commercial. It featured a fast-paced helicopter chase scene featuring a suave hero and an attractive heroine, as well as a menacing and grotesque villain. When MGM first learned of the commercial they complained to Honda. MGM's position was that Honda's commercial infringed on the 16-film James Bond series in two ways: (1) by duplicating specific scenes from the sixteen films; and (2) by the male protagonist's possessing James Bond's unique character traits as developed in the sixteen films.

On January 15, 1995, in an effort to placate MGM's concerns Honda changed their commercial. They altered the protagonists' accents from British to American. They also changed the music to make it less like the James Bond theme. This version of the commercial was shown during Superbowl XXIX, where the San Francisco 49ers trounced the San Diego Chargers 49-26.

In *Metro-Goldwyn-Mayer, Inc.*, v. *American Honda Motor Co., Inc.*, 900 F. Supp. 1287 (1995), MGM claimed that the Honda commercial infringed their copyright in the James Bond films by intentionally copying numerous specific scenes from the films and infringed their copyright to the James Bond character as expressed in those films.

Honda responded that MGM was simply trying to gain a monopoly over the 'action/spy/police hero' genre which is contrary to the purposes of copyright law. The court said: "Defendants argue that the allegedly infringed elements identified by Plaintiffs are not protectable because: (1) the helicopter chase scene in the Honda commercial is a common theme that naturally flows from most action genre films, and the woman and villain in the film are but stock characters that are not protectable; and under the Ninth Circuit's *Sam Spade* decision, the James Bond character does not constitute the "story being told," but is rather an unprotected dramatic character."

The court also wrote: "In their opening brief, Plaintiffs contend that each of their sixteen films contains distinctive scenes that together comprise the classic James Bond adventure: 'a high-thrill chase of the ultra-cool British charmer and his beautiful and alarming sidekick by a grotesque villain in which the hero escapes through wit aided by high-tech gadgetry.' Defendants argue that these elements are naturally found in any action film and are therefore unprotected 'scènes à faire.' "

If you recall from earlier in this chapter, these film sequences would be only "scènes à faire" without James Bond. Yet, it is James Bond that makes a James Bond film.

The court wrapped up the issues by saying: "It appears that Defendants misconstrue Plaintiffs' claim. First, Plaintiffs do not allege that Defendants have violated Plaintiffs' copyright in the James Bond character itself, but rather in the James Bond character *as expressed and delineated in Plaintiffs' sixteen films.* To the extent that copyright law only protects original *expression,* not *ideas,* Plaintiffs' argument is that the James Bond character as developed in the sixteen films is the copyrighted work at issue, not the James Bond character generally."

Copying from the Internet

The video game market is enormous and very lucrative, and Sony, with its PlayStation console and games, is a market leader. The original console in the series, the PlayStation, was the first video game console to ship 100 million units, nine years and six months after its initial launch. Its successor, the PlayStation 2, was released in 2000. The PlayStation 2 is the best-selling home console to date, having reached over 155 million units sold as of December 28, 2012. Sony's follow-up, the PlayStation 3, was released in 2006 and has sold over 80 million consoles worldwide as of November 2013. Sony's latest console, the PlayStation 4, was released in 2013, selling 1 million consoles in its first twenty-four hours.

The Bleem emulator was PC software that effectively "emulated" the function performed by Sony's hardware console through a process of reverse-engineering the components in the console. Essentially, Bleem devised a computer program to perform these same functions on a personal computer.

The legality of the emulator was not at issue in *Sony Computer Entertainment America, Inc. v. Bleem, LLC,* 214 F.3d 1022 (2000). The issue was with the validity of the method by which Bleem advertised its product. In various advertising media, Bleem has included comparative "screen shots" of Sony PlayStation games. These show what the game looks like when played with a Sony console on a television screen, what it looks like when played with Bleem's emulator on a computer screen.

Screen shots on the packaging of video games is common since they convey to the purchaser exactly what the game will look like on a screen when it is played. In fact, the majority of the packaging of most typical video games is intricate artwork that evokes the spirit of the game.

In this case, Sony did not alleged that Bleem's depictions of the games were inaccurate or misleading, only that Bleem may not use those screen shots because they are Sony's copyrighted material.

Sony sued Bleem for a number of intellectual property violations. The only issue on appeal, however, is whether Bleem's unauthorized use of Sony PlayStation game screen shots in its advertising was a violation of Sony's copyright.

After reviewing all the aspects of the case, the court held:

Our conclusions with respect to Bleem's use of screen shots apply only to those screen shots that Bleem has generated by taking the actual images of Sony's games from a television screen. The entire premise of comparative advertising is that the consumer is being made aware of the true choices. To the extent Bleem merely approximates what the PlayStation games look like, by generating screen shots through a process of degrading a computer image, it is simply creating a simulation. If Bleem insists on generating simulated approximations of Sony's games, there is no need for Bleem to use Sony's copyrighted material whatsoever.

We conclude that it is a fair use for Bleem to advertise comparatively only between what PlayStation games *actually* look like on a television and what they *actually* look like on a computer when played with the emulator. It is in this context alone that the comparison is necessarily Sony-specific. Otherwise, Bleem must be content to make its comparison without using another's copyrighted material. We are persuaded by the need for Bleem to impose minimally upon Sony's copyright with respect to these screen shots because there is no other way to create a truly accurate comparison for the user. The way of simulations is a slippery one for Bleem and if it chooses to embark upon it, it must do so without the support of Sony's copyright. With that limitation in mind, we conclude that Bleem's use of Sony's copyrighted material was fair.

The distinction in this case revolved around Sony's copyright. The court reasoned that Sony's copyright covered the actual game, not the individual screen shots. So long as they were captured off of Bleem's console there was no infringement. This case involved a number of intricate issues beyond copyright, including fair trade and comparative advertising.

Legal Remedies

Obviously, one should not take the copyrighted work of someone else and use it without permission. Congress, in creating the Copyright Act, felt that there were two good reasons for making this unauthorized use illegal. First, the author may have future plans to license the work. And infringement could severely interfere with these plans. We saw this in the Dr. Pepper case. Second, the author may consider that commercial exploitation of his work may demean his creative efforts and thereby erode its credibility. This is especially true in the case of literary works, although we saw the advertising version of this in the Pufnstuf case.

As for damages, the copyright owner is entitled to recover the actual damages suffered by him as a result of the infringement, or any profits of the infringer that are attributable to the infringement (these are not taken into account in computing the actual damages). In establishing the infringer's profits, the copyright owner is required to present proof only of the infringer's gross revenue, and the infringer is required to prove his or her deductible expenses and the elements of profit attributable to factors other than the copyrighted work.

Statutory damages for all infringements involved in the action are another option. This provides awards in a sum of not less than $750 or more than $30,000 per infringement, as the court considers proper.

Where the court finds that an infringement was committed willfully, the court in its discretion may increase the award of statutory damages to a sum of not more than $150,000.

Additional remedies for copyright violation include injunction, seizure, impounding and destruction of infringing items, and in many cases attorney's fees. Indeed, advertisers should be careful where copyright infringement is concerned. The penalties can be very severe, as we have seen.

10 Trademark Regulation

I hate the man who builds his name
On ruins of another's fame.
—John Gay

Within twenty years after the Civil War, a Columbus, Georgia, pharmacist named John S. Pemberton had invented, manufactured, and sold a variety of products. These ranged from Globe of Flower Cough Syrup and Indian Queen Hair Dye to Triplex Liver Pills, Gingerine, and Extract of Styllinger.

Pemberton later moved to Atlanta where he created a drink that combined an extract of kola nut, fruit syrup, and extract of coco leaf. In 1886 he took his syrup to Jacob's Drug Store in Atlanta where, on a trial basis, he was allowed to sell his drink at the soda fountain. The drink became modestly popular with the patrons.

Eventually Pemberton became disillusioned with the drink and sold out to a man named Asa Chandler. Pemberton made $1,750. With his new product in hand, Chandler first advertised the drink as a "Wonderful Nerve and Brain Tonic and Remarkable Therapeutic Agent." By 1893 Chandler had sold 48,427 gallons of his tonic. A year later, soda water was added to the mixture, and it was bottled.

Chandler's tonic grew in popularity. In fact, the more a person drank, the more that person wanted. In part that was because of the caffeine and small amounts of cocaine that remained in the syrup after the brewing process. As sales of the drink grew, it became apparent to Chandler that he needed to market the product on a larger scale. So, in 1906 he hired the Massingale Agency in Atlanta to advertise his product. From that point on, Chandler's drink (which was named by the Jacob's Drug Store bookkeeper) soared into marketing history. The drink was Coca-Cola.

The strength and value of a trademark to identify goods and distinguish them from others cannot be overstressed. Trademarks have served primarily to identify the source of goods and services since the middle ages, and law has protected trademarks since the early seventeenth century. Trademark infringement law was imported from England into our legal system with the goal of preventing unfair competition through misappropriated marks. Although the initial attempt at federal regulation in the United States was declared unconstitutional (100 U.S. 82 & 25 L. Ed. 550 (1879)), trademarks have been protected under federal statute since the passage of the Lanham Act in 1946.

As Coca-Cola proved, a successful business gets that way by investing much of its efforts—and money—in building a favorable identity for itself and its products. This can be reputation, and in many cases it is goodwill. In today's parlance, we hear the phrase "brand" bandied about all too often. We think of Apple as a brand, and Nike as a brand. But the term "brand" is often confused with "brand name" by the consumer. A brand, in marketing terms, is actually the persona of the company, not the product. Coke is Americana, mom-and-pop, apple pie, and Little League. It's not carbonated sugar water. Nike is about the spirit of competition, not about shoes. In essence the product is what the company makes, but the brand is what they stand for; the place they hold in the mind of their consumer. The consumer's impression of what the brand stands for—what those in advertising work so hard to build and maintain—will draw first-time buyers and continue to bring back repeat customers. Therein lies the value of a brand.

Trademarks are an important part of indicating the source of the product, and therefore the brand that makes the product. They make the product recognizable and identifiable by the consumer. Often, the trademark can say more than any photo or amount of ad copy. The old adage claims that pictures speak louder than words. Well, a reputable trademark can speak louder than both. Take one of the top brands in the 1970s, Volkswagen. One Volkswagen ad ran the headline: "Here's What to Do to Get Your Volkswagen Ready for Winter." The rest of the page was blank—except for the Volkswagen logo; their trademark.

If we want to monetize it, according to Interbrand, Apple is the most valuable brand in the world. Google is the second most valuable. Coke is number three, down from being the number one brand in the world for thirteen years in a row. And these brands are manifested in their trademarks. A trademark truly is the symbol of the brand.

When a consumer sees a product with a particular trademark on it, that person should be able to rely on the image that the mark conjures up and trust the quality of a product that carries it. After all, trademark laws were created to support that trust. A trademark is intended to distinguish one manufacturer's goods from another's. That's why a company must protect its trademark, and also why a company must be careful not to infringe on another company's mark.

Qualities of a Trademark

There are many aspects of trademark law that advertisers must understand. One of the first concerns the qualities need to exist in a trademark. The following section discusses this important issue.

The Difference between a Trademark and a Trade Name

Under the Federal Trademark Act of 1946, trademarks may be registered, but trade names may not.

[A trademark is] word, name, symbol, or device or any combination thereof adopted and used by a manufacturer or merchant to identify his goods [or services] and distinguish them from those manufactured by others. [Trade names are] "individual names and surnames, firm names and trade names used by manufacturers, industrialists, merchants, agriculturalists, and others to identify their businesses, vocations, or occupations (Trademark Act of 1946, section 45, 15 U.S.C., Section 1127 (1976)).

To distinguish the two terms, a trademark refers to products or services, and a trade name refers to the business entity itself. For example, ConAgra Foods (the company) is a trade name while its product, Hunt's Ketchup, is a trademark; Ford is a trademark while Ford Motor Company (the manufacturer) is a trade name.

Types of Trademarks

The term "trademark" actually covers a number of marks of various uses. There are trademarks, service marks, certification marks, and collective marks. A trademark, as we have just discussed, is used in connection with a product.

A "service mark" is a type of trademark. Service marks are used to identify and distinguish the services of one individual or organization, even a unique service, from those provided by others. Service marks and trademarks serve essentially the same purpose and function in essentially the same manner except that service marks identify the source of services rather than goods. The term "service" applies only to services rendered to others; it does not apply to services that are solely for the benefit of the performer. These services are identified with an "SM" symbol. The category of service marks also includes slogans, titles, characters and symbols.

Another form of mark is called a "certification mark," which calls attention to the origin, material, nature, method of manufacture, accuracy, quality, or labor source of a product. Examples include the Good Housekeeping Seal of Approval, the mark used for the AFL-CIO, or the mark used by the cotton industry "cotton" to designate the 100 percent cotton composition of the item.

Collective marks, another form of trademark, are marks used to show membership in an organization or group. A collective mark has no relation to a specific product or service, but merely shows affiliation with the group. The marks used by the Elks' Lodge or the American Association of Advertising Agencies are prime examples.

Strong Marks versus Weak Marks

As far as trademarks are concerned, there are two strengths of marks: strong and weak. The law offers different protection for each type so it is important for the advertiser to be aware of the difference between the two types of marks.

Strong Marks Strong marks can receive protection under trademark law simply because they are distinctive. Marks in this category can include those that are suggestive of the product. A strong mark is coined or fanciful, such as "Google," "Xerox," or "Nike." "Apple" for computers, "Raid" for insect spray, and "Drano" for clogged drains are other examples of strong marks. Strong marks, while they are suggestive, are more than just descriptive of the product they are used with. The word apple meant little other than as a fruit until Apple Inc., started making computers under that name.

Weak Marks Weak marks do not automatically qualify as trademarks and will be permitted protection only if the Trademark Office allows it. A weak mark would be composed of words that praise or describe a quality like "best" or "premium." However, a weak mark, as such, will be granted protection as a trademark only if it has acquired a secondary meaning. This implies that the consumer makes an automatic connection between the product or service that the mark refers to and its source. The consumer must associate the product and the mark with the manufacturer. If this connection can be shown, then protection can be afforded the mark. For example, when you hear the term "Big Mac," what do you think of? McDonald's of course. Or, the name "Bug" (actually coined by consumers which stuck) in reference to the Volkswagen Beetle, is protectable. That's secondary meaning.

Another category of weak marks include the use of geographical names. Unless secondary meaning could be established, names using "Swiss" for watches, "Columbian" for coffee, "Florida" for oranges, and so on would not be protected under trademark law. These names only designate the geographic origin of the item, and a manufacturer cannot take such a designation for its own to the exclusion of others.

Weak marks also include surnames. Common names like Johnson, Smith, White, and Jones have probably already been trademarked at some time. If another company has already trademarked a surname, a manufacturer runs the risk of infringing on that mark. Even if the name is the person's legitimate one, it can still infringe on another's trademark.

Let's say that Smith's Oil begins manufacturing its product and trademarks the name. It runs a high risk that another trademark already exists under that name. If time goes by, and no claims are brought, consumers may become accustomed to associating Smith's Oil with the product. In this case, the name develops a secondary meaning. If another manufacturer begins selling an oil product under that same name, in the same marketing area, it would be infringing on Smith's trademark.

Marks that use descriptions of praise as trademarks also fall into the weak mark category. "Premium," "World's Finest," and others are very weak unless secondary meaning can be attributed to the trade name. However, this does occur, as we'll see later. Products such as Pabst Blue Ribbon beer, Gold Medal flour, and others have achieved this secondary meaning status through heavy and continued usage of the marks for many years within the market. As a result, they are protected under trademark.

Establishing and Registering Trademarks

We saw with copyrights, that those rights are established at the moment a piece is created. With trademark, it's a little different. Trademark rights are established by "using the mark in commerce." Specifically, 15 U.S.C. §1127 clarifies a "use in commerce" in the following way:

(1) On goods when:
  (A) it is placed in any manner on the goods or their containers or the displays associated therewith or on the tags or labels affixed thereto, or if the nature of the goods makes such placement impracticable, then on documents associated with the goods or their sale, and
  (B) the goods are sold or transported in commerce, and
(2) On services when it is used or displayed in the sale or advertising of services and the services are rendered in commerce, or the services are rendered in more than one State or in the United States and a foreign country and the person rendering the services is engaged in commerce in connection with the services.

So essentially, a trademark owner establishes rights to a mark by offering products for sale "in commerce" with the trademark used on the product. The same principle applies for services by advertising the mark "in commerce." Until 1989 federal trademark law said that a company must actually use a trademark before it could be registered. However, in 1989, the statute was amended to allow trademark registration by showing an "intent to use" the mark. Currently, many major brands often file such "intent to use" application, which establishes the owner's priority as the application date rather than the date of first use in commerce. The mark must still be used in commerce to gain protection.

In *Rescuecom Corp.* v. *Google Inc.*, 562 F.3d 123, U.S. App. LEXIS 7160; 90 U.S.P.Q.2D (BNA)1287 (2009), the "use in commerce" requirement was addressed.

Rescuecom is a national computer service franchising company that offers on-site computer services and sales. Rescuecom conducts a substantial amount of its business through the Internet and receives between seventeen thousand and thirty thousand visitors per month to its website. It also advertises over the Internet, using many web-based services, including those offered by Google. Since 1998, "Rescuecom" has had a registered federal trademark.

Google, as we all know, is the premier Internet search engine, through www. google.com. Using Google, a person searching for the website of a particular entity in trade (or simply for information about it) can enter that entity's name or trademark into Google's search engine and launch a search.

Rescuecom alleged that, through Google's AdWords program, potential purchasers of its services who search for its website on Google are misleadingly directed to the ads and websites of its competitors in a manner which leads them to believe that these ads or websites are sponsored by, or affiliated with Rescuecom.

In addition, Google displayed, offered, and sold Rescuecom's mark to Google's advertising customers when selling its AdWords advertising services. Google also encouraged the purchase of Rescuecom's mark through its Keyword Suggestion Tool. Google's utilization of Rescuecom's mark fits literally within the terms specified by 15 U.S.C. ß 1127. The court said: "According to the Complaint, Google uses and sells Rescuecom's mark 'in the sale . . . of [Google's advertising] services . . . rendered in commerce.' ß 1127. . . . Google's actions are a 'use in commerce' under the Lanham Act."

The court also reasoned: "If we were to adopt Google's argument, the operators of search engines would be free to use trademarks in ways designed to deceive and cause consumer confusion. This is surely neither within the intention nor the letter of the Lanham Act."

Registration of Marks

Trademarks are registered with the U.S. Patent and Trademark Office in Washington, D.C. To be clear, registration of the mark is not required in order to have enforceable rights, but registration does provide several advantages. Federal registration establishes national coverage for the trademark owner. Without this, a trademark owner's rights typically are limited to the states where it has been used in commerce. Federal registration also offers access to federal courts (in addition to state courts) and gives several procedural benefits during litigation.

The importance of registering a mark is that doing so notifies others that the owner of the mark "claims" the exclusive rights to its use. But registering the mark and using it in commerce are not enough to protect the mark owner's rights. Notice of registration must be used along with the mark.

Keep in mind that registering a mark does not create an unlimited legal right to ownership; rather it's a "claim" of ownership. To be protected, the mark must not infringe upon another's mark. We'll delve into this aspect more later in this chapter.

Length of Registration Once a trademark is registered, the claim is established for ten years. After obtaining registration, the company has six months to begin using the trademark in commerce. Registration may thereafter be renewed for unlimited ten-year periods. An application must be filed within six months before the expiration of a trademark.

Trademark Registers Trademarks can be recorded in one of the two registers of the Trademark Office: the Principal Register or the Supplemental Register. All applications for registration go first to the Principal Register. If the mark does not meet the requirements of that register, it is passed on to the Supplemental Register for possible acceptance. This is an automatic process used by the Trademark Office.

It is important to note that, unlike copyright, registering a trademark does not provide any right of ownership. Any such right exists through common law as a property right. Because of this, many marks that are not registered are still afforded trademark status. We'll see this in some of the cases that follow.

Also, some marks that are registered can have their trademark status revoked if challenged by a company that previously registered and used the same mark. The registers only provide a place where marks can be listed for public record. This doesn't mean that there are not good reasons to register a mark. Indeed there are, and we have already discussed some of them.

The Principal Register accepts only marks that meet certain standards, but keep in mind that the Trademark Office does not search for similar marks that have already been registered. The applicant must perform its own search or hire someone, such as a trademark attorney to do this. The Trademark Office only judges a mark against the standards of the office for acceptance, not against other marks already registered—that's the applicant's responsibility. Standards for acceptance include:

1. The mark must be distinctive;
2. The mark must not be immoral, deceptive, or scandalous;
3. The mark must not consist of a flag, emblem, or insignia of the United States or other country;
4. The mark must not consist of the picture or signature of an individual without prior consent;
5. The mark must not resemble another mark;
6. The mark must not be merely descriptive of the product;
7. The mark must not be geographically descriptive of origin; and
8. The mark must not be a surname.

The Supplemental Register is more lenient. All four of these requirements must be met for registration:

9. The mark must be unqualified for registration on the Principal Register;
10. The mark must be able to distinguish the product;
11. The mark must not fall into any category above for the Principal Register, except numbers 6, 7, or 8; and
12. The mark must have been used in commerce for one year without opposition from another trademark owner.

Marks that May Not Be Registered

There are a few areas that could disqualify a mark from registration. Let's take a closer look.

Confusing or Deceptive Marks. Marks cannot be registered that are "likely . . . to cause confusion, or cause mistake, or to deceive" (15 U.S.C., § 1052(d)).

This could also occur through the use of a similar or exact duplication of another trademark.

Marks That Are Descriptive of a Place or Function. Marks cannot be registered as trademarks if they are only functionally or geographically descriptive, or if the mark is only a surname. In other words, the mark must be distinctive.

Use of Flags or Insignias. Marks cannot use flags, coats of arms, insignia of cities, states, the federal government, or foreign countries.

Use of Names or Personal Identities. Marks cannot use the name, image, or signature of a person, unless written permission is given.

Use of Immoral Marks. Marks cannot be "immoral" or "scandalous" 15 U.S.C.,§ 1052(a)).

This includes names that are contemptuous or disparage a person, institution, established belief, or national symbol.

Notice of Registration

It is important to place a notice of registration along with a trademark. A notice of registration of a mark allows damages to be recovered if infringement of the mark occurs. Without that notice damages cannot be awarded; only the infringing usage of the mark may be stopped. Notice also lends credibility, which should help deter potential infringers. Registration notice also helps establish that the mark is a trademark rather than a generic term.

The Trademark Act states that "a registrant of a mark . . . *may* give notice that his mark is registered by displaying with the mark as used . . . the letter 'R' enclosed within a circle."

The act goes on to say: "[I]n any suit for infringement under this chapter by such a registrant failing to give such notice of registration, no profits or damages shall be recovered . . . *unless the defendant had actual notice of registration* . . . " (emphasis added), (15 U.S.C., section 1111).

Marks that are not yet registered, but for which application has been made, can be identified with a "TM." Be aware that it is legal to use a notice of actual registration "®" only after a certificate of registration has been issued.

The registration notice may be placed anywhere in relation to the mark and in any style. If a trademark is used more than once in an ad, it is not necessary for the notice to appear every time the mark appears, but it should appear with the mark that is used first or appears most prominently. Of course, the notice itself should be large enough to be readily recognizable and readable.

Another important consideration applies when using another company's trademark in another ad. Let's say Ford wants to reference Chevrolet's trademark. Ford must always use the appropriate notice with Chevy's mark. Also, when a company uses someone else's trademark in their ad, they must capitalize the mark. For example, use "Chevrolet" not "chevrolet." In other words, capitalizing lets the reader of the ad know that the mark is, a proper noun and, the trademark of another company. This may need to be clearly identified elsewhere in the ad if there is any chance of confusion, such as a credit line stating: "Chevrolet is the registered trademark of General Motors Corporation."

Using a Trademark Notice with a Mark that Has Not Been Registered

If a notice is placed with a trademark that is not registered, severe problems can result. Most importantly, the right to register the mark in the future can be lost. A trademark known as "Four Roses" is a good example. In 1925 Small Grain Distilling Company applied for and was granted the trademark "Four Roses" for its high-grade whiskey. "Four Roses" was a widely known brand name at the time.

Early in 1926 another company, Four Roses Products, began placing a notice of registration on its malt syrup product. The name "Four Roses" was used on the product packaging along with the notice "Trade-Mark Reg. U.S. Pat. Off." When Small Grain learned of this, it brought the case to court in *Four Roses Products Co. v. Small Grain Distilling & Drug Co.*, 29 F.2d 959 (D.C.Cir. 1928).

The fact was Four Roses Products had never received a registration of the trademark for "Four Roses." It had applied for registration but had been denied. Four Roses Products used the registration notice even though it knew it had no registration. The court determined that Small Grain's trademark of Four Roses was legitimate and Four Roses Products' mark was not. Essentially, Four Roses Products tried, through the use of the registration notice, to imply that its product was registered and authentic and that any other, including Small Grain's, was an infringement. This was not accurate.

Since Four Roses Products used the registration notice with an unregistered mark, it lost the case, had to pay damages for infringement, and lost any chance for future registration. As a side note, this must have been a heated case in court considering the time it occurred—not long after the 18th Amendment to the Constitution was adopted which repealed prohibition.

There is another reason to not use a registration notice if the mark has not actually been registered. That is, the right to stop another company from using the same mark can be lost. Fox Photo learned about this in 1972. Long before iPhones and digital cameras, the company provided photo film developing and finishing services to the public. A point of notoriety came in the chase scene in the 1985 movie *Back to the Future*, when the Libyan terrorists crashed their van into a Fox Photo booth at the Twin Pines Mall.

The Fox Photo logo consisted of a red fox running with the name Fox Photo across it. Fox Photo also used, as part of its logo, a red "R" in a circle. Sometime later, Harry Otaguro began publishing a photo magazine called *FOX*. Fox Photo decided that Otaguro's magazine infringed its trademark because of the similarity in the names and the fact that both products competed in the same category—photography. *Fox-Stanley Photo Products, Inc.* v. *Otaguro*, 339 F. Supp. 1293 (D. Mass 1972), resulted. Unfortunately Fox Photo had never registered the Fox Photo mark. That, however, did not deter it from placing a registration notice with the logo to imply registration of the mark.

Fox Photo lost its case at the outset simply because it did not own the trademark. Because it had used a registration notice on a mark that had not been registered, Fox also lost its right to be granted a trademark registration for its logo in the future.

What Does—and Doesn't—Cause Trademark Infringement

Uses that Cause Infringement

The most important concern in developing a new mark is establishing that it does not infringe on an existing mark. The new mark must not be the same as another existing mark or confusingly similar to an existing mark.

Believe it or not, there is no single place where the applicant can look to find a list of all trademarks. Simply checking with the Trademark Office isn't enough. One reason for this is that some marks may be registered in a particular state (we look at this later in the chapter). Another reason is that a mark may have been used for many years without being registered. The original mark would be allowed protection in many cases under common law (refer to the section "Trademark Registers" for an explanation). There are, however, professional trademark search services. These services are fairly thorough and use a number of sources to determine if the mark already exists as a trademark.

It is important to check new trademarks before putting them into use, as Goodyear found out. Today Bridgestone is the world's top tire producer. But Goodyear was the world's largest tire manufacturer in 1974 with net sales reached over $5.25 billion. A minor competitor, Big O Tire Dealers, manufactured a private label tire of its own. In late 1973, Big O named its line of tires "Big Foot." The name appeared on the sidewall of each tire.

In July of 1974 Goodyear adopted the name "Big Foot" for its new Custom Polysteel Radial tire. The name also appeared on the side of the tire. The firm hired a trademark search firm to investigate any existing trademark conflicts. None were shown. Feeling secure, Goodyear developed an advertising campaign to promote its new tire, Big Foot. Within a year, Goodyear had spent over $9.6 million on the advertising of this single product. Typical headlines from Goodyear ads were:

Bigfoot, the new Polysteel Radial.
Bigfoot. The Polysteel Radial that keeps its feet even in the rain. Only from Goodyear.

In August of 1974, Goodyear learned of the existing and previous trademark held by Big O Tires. Goodyear tried to buy the rights to use the name from Big O, but the offer was not accepted. When Big O refused the offer, it mentioned the possibility of a lawsuit if Goodyear did not stop using the trademark "Big Foot." As stated in court, Goodyear informed Big O president Norman Affleck, that if Big O did bring suit, "the case would be in litigation long enough that Goodyear might obtain all the benefits it desired from the term 'Big Foot.'"

In fact, Big O Tires did sue in *Big O Tire Dealers, Inc.* v. *Goodyear Tire & Rubber Co.*, 561 F.2d 1365 (1977). The problem occurred because Goodyear, through their search firm, failed to verify an existing trademark for "Big Foot." Since there was such a trademark, Goodyear lost the case.

At trial it came to light that when Goodyear learned of the Big O trademark, not only did it not discontinue its ad campaign, which claimed exclusiveness, it continued to willfully infringe upon the existing mark. Goodyear basically thumbed its huge corporate nose at Big O. Because of Goodyear's action and its disregard for Big O's trademark, the court awarded $678,302 in compensatory damages and $4,069,812 in punitive damages.

The Parody Example While it's not common to see trademark litigation involving parodies and satires, it's likely to see more actions in this era of head-to-head competitive advertising. The precise issue here is whether an advertiser may depict an altered form of a competitors trademark to identify the competitor's product in a comparative ad.

In the arena of trademark parody, intent can easily distinguish uses of trademarks that function to sell products from uses that seek to make a social or political commentary or an artistic expression. To that end, all that is needed is an "intent" to promote one's own product.

In the case of *Deere & Company* v. *MTD Products, Inc.*, 41 F.3d 39, U.S. App. LEXIS 33042; 32 U.S.P.Q.2D (BNA) 1936 (1994), we see a classic example of parody with an intent to promote one's own product. The line-drawing in this area is problematic when a mark is parodied for the dual purposes of making a satiric comment and selling a competing product.

John Deere, founded in 1837 in Moline, Illinois, is the world's largest supplier of agricultural equipment. For over one hundred years, Deere has used a leaping deer design as a trademark for identifying its products and services, accompanied by the slogan "Nothing Runs Like a Deere". Deere owns numerous trademark registrations for different versions of the Deere Logo. Although these versions vary slightly, all depict the static silhouette of a leaping male deer in profile. The Deere Logo is widely recognizable and a valuable business asset. In fact, Deere's net sales of equipment bearing the Deere Logo for the 2013 exceeded $37 billion. Deere has spent a substantial amount of money using the Deere Logo to advertise its products and services, including its related financial services and insurance operations.

MTD Products, founded in 1932, manufactures and sells lawn tractors. In 1993, W.B. Doner & Company, MTD's advertising agency, created a commercial that used the Deere Logo (without Deere's authorization) for the purpose of comparing Deere's line of lawn tractors to MTD's "Yard-Man" tractor.

MTD's commercial used an animated version of Deere's trademark and compared its product to that of Deere's. For the commercial Doner altered the Deere logo in several respects: The deer in the MTD version of the logo is proportioned differently than in the actual Deere Logo; the MTD Version also removed the name "John Deere" from their version of the logo, and made the logo frame more sharply rectangular.

As the court described it: ". . . the deer in the MTD version is animated and assumes various poses. Specifically, the MTD deer looks over its shoulder, jumps through the logo frame (which breaks into pieces and tumbles to the ground), hops to a pinging noise, and, as a two-dimensional cartoon, runs, in apparent fear, as it is pursued by the Yard-Man lawn tractor and a barking dog." MTD did not dispute that the Deere Logo was a distinctive trademark that is capable of being diluted and has acquired the required secondary meaning in the marketplace.

In ruling in favor of Deere, the court said: "Whether the use of the mark is to identify a competing product in an informative comparative ad, to make a comment, or to spoof the mark to enliven the advertisement for a noncompeting or a competing product, the scope of protection under a dilution statute must take into account the degree to which the mark is altered and the nature of the alteration. Not every alteration will constitute dilution, and more leeway for alterations is appropriate in the context of satiric expression and humorous ads for noncompeting products. But some alterations have the potential to so lessen the selling power of a distinctive mark that they are appropriately proscribed by a dilution statute. Dilution of this sort is more likely to be found when the alterations are made by a competitor with both an incentive to diminish the favorable attributes of the mark and an ample opportunity to promote its products in ways that make no significant alteration."

The Velvet Elvis Example A Houston, Texas, nightclub called The Velvet Elvis, owned by Barry Capece, was designed to be a recreation of the eclectic bars of the 1960s. The decor included velvet paintings (including one of Elvis Presley), lava lamps, beaded curtains, and vinyl furniture. The club was a parody of the faddish sixties bars, and Capece claimed that the name The Velvet Elvis was symbolic, and had no specific connection to Elvis Presley.

However, the advertising for the club made direct references to Elvis and Graceland, and used phrases like "The King Lives," "Viva la Elvis," and "Hunka-Hunka Happy Hour." Also, in many of the advertisements the "Elvis" portion of the logo "The Velvet Elvis" was very large in relation to the word "Velvet." The bar served a wide variety of food and liquor with menu items ranging from appetizers to full entrees. The menu included "Love Me Blenders," a type of frozen drink; peanut butter and banana sandwiches, a favorite of Elvis's; and "Your Football Hound Dog," a hot dog. Live music was also regularly featured at the bar. Its decor included velvet paintings of celebrities and female nudes, including ones of Elvis and a bare-chested

Mona Lisa. Other decorations included lava lamps, cheap ceramic sculptures, beaded curtains, and vinyl furniture. *Playboy* centerfolds covered the men's room walls. Magazine photographs of Elvis, a statuette of Elvis playing the guitar, and a bust of Elvis were also among the club's decorations.

The estate of Elvis Presley (EPE) sued the nightclub for trademark infringement and unfair competition in *Elvis Presley Enterprises, Inc.* v. *Capece*, 141 F.3d 188 (5th Cir. 1998), by claiming: "[T]he inclusion of its 'Elvis' trademark in the service mark 'The Velvet Elvis' coupled with Defendants' use of the image and likeness of Elvis Presley in advertising, promoting, and rendering bar services creates confusion as to whether EPE licensed, approved, sponsored, endorsed or is otherwise affiliated with 'The Velvet Elvis,' constituting unfair competition and trademark infringement under the common law and Lanham Act."

In determining if there was any likelihood of consumer confusion, the lower court considered The Velvet Elvis service mark and the club's decor separately from the nightclub's advertising and promotional materials.

The lower court determined that the bar's decor was a parody and that there was no likelihood that consumers would believe that the nightclub was owned or authorized by Elvis Presley's estate. In contrast, the advertising did not convey the style of the club's decor but only the association with the name. Because of this, the lower court found that the ads were likely to deceive people into believing that the nightclub was associated with the estate of Elvis.

The appellate court, however, did not agree with the lower court's separating the service mark in the decor and its use in advertising.

The court noted:

> The use of a mark in advertising is highly probative of whether the mark creates a likelihood of confusion in relation to another mark. Evidence of the context in which a mark is used on labels, packages, or in advertising material directed to the goods is probative of the reaction of prospective purchasers to the mark. Courts consider marks in the context that a customer perceives them in the marketplace, which includes their presentation in advertisements. In the case of a service mark, advertising is of even greater relevance because the mark cannot be actually affixed to the service, as a trademark is to the goods. Many prospective purchasers first encounter the mark in advertising, rather than on the product; therefore, the service mark cannot be isolated from the advertising in which it appears.

The appellate court also disagreed with the district court's determination that the nightclub decor was a parody. According to the appellate court, parody (an element in determining trademark infringement) was not relevant to this case. Since the Fifth Circuit had not yet considered parody in a trademark case, the court looked to the Supreme Court's interpretation of parody in the copyright context.

The Supreme Court noted:

> [T]he heart of any parodist's claim to quote from existing material, is the use of some elements of prior author's composition to create a new one that, at least in part, comments on that author's works. If, on the contrary, the commentary has no critical bearing on the substance or style of the original composition, which the alleged infringer merely uses to get attention or to avoid the drudgery in working up something fresh, the claim to fairness in borrowing from another's work diminishes accordingly (if it does not vanish), and other factors, like the extent of the commerciality loom larger. Parody needs to mimic an original to make its point, and so has some claim to sue the creation of its victim's (or victims') imagination, whereas satire can stand on its own two feet and so requires justification for the vary act of borrowing.

In this case the nightclub owner claimed that the nightclub's decor was a parody of the sixties—the Las Vegas lounge scene, the velvet painting craze, and possibly the country's fascination with Elvis. In court, the owner stated that he was trying to make fun of clubs like Hard Rock Cafe and Planet Hollywood. The court found that "Without the necessity to use Elvis' name, parody does not weigh against a likelihood of confusion in relation to EPE's marks." In other words, parody is not a defense to trademark infringement, but rather another factor to be considered, which weighs against a finding of a likelihood of confusion.

To this point, the court said: "This same need to conjure up the original exists when a parody targets a trademark or service mark. In the case of the standard likelihood-of-confusion analysis, a successful parody of the original mark weighs against a likelihood of confusion because, even though it portrays the original, it also sends the message that it is not the original and is a parody, thereby lessening any potential confusion."

The appellate court found that the nightclub's use of the name The Velvet Elvis, both in advertising and the interior decor infringed the trademarks owned by Elvis Presley's estate. The appellate court agreed with the district court that advertising for The Velvet Elvis created the impression that the bars theme was to pay tribute to Elvis Presley. The advertising campaign alone could cause consumers to believe that the nightclub was sponsored by (or associated with) Elvis Presley's estate.

The court stated: "Evidence of actual confusion is not necessary to a finding of a likelihood of confusion, but 'it is nevertheless the best evidence of a likelihood of confusion.' Actual confusion that is later dissipated by further inspection of the goods, services, or premises, as well as postsale confusion, is relevant to a determination of a likelihood of confusion. Initial-interest confusion gives the junior user credibility during the early stages of a transaction and can possibly bar the senior user from consideration by the consumer once the confusion is dissipated."

EPE presented witnesses who testified that they initially thought the Defendants' bar was a place that was associated with Elvis Presley and that it might have Elvis merchandise for sale. The witnesses all testified that, upon entering and looking around the bar, they had no doubt that EPE was not affiliated with it in any way. Despite the confusion being dissipated, this initial-interest confusion is beneficial to the Defendants because it brings patrons in the door; indeed, it brought at least one of EPE's witnesses into the bar. Once in the door, the confusion has succeeded because some patrons may stay, despite realizing that the bar has no relationship with EPE. This initial-interest confusion is even more significant because the Defendants' bar sometimes charges a cover charge for entry, which allows the Defendants to benefit from initial-interest confusion before it can be dissipated by entry into the bar. Additionally, the finding by the district court that the Defendants' advertising practices caused actual confusion shows that actual confusion occurred when consumers first observed the mark in commerce.

The court held that there was a likelihood that consumers would be confused by the nightclub's use of the mark The Velvet Elvis. The estate of Elvis Presley also owned a restaurant in Memphis. And, the court reasoned that the nightclub's use of The Velvet Elvis mark in advertising and in the bar showed an intent to build the market for the bar by trading on the name of Elvis. The appellate court overturned the lower court's ruling and held in favor of EPE.

A Fashionable Example In 2010, during the postgame show of the New Orleans Saints crushing of the Indianapolis Colts in Super Bowl XLIV, Hyundai Motors debuted a TV commercial that it described as "a humorous, socio-economic commentary on luxury defined by a premium price tag, rather than by the value to the consumer." The ad included a scene of a basketball decorated with a distinctive Louis Vuitton trademark pattern.

Hyundai's :thirty-second commercial was name "Luxury" and consisted of brief vignettes that showed policemen eating caviar in a patrol car; large yachts parked beside modest homes; blue-collar workers eating lobster during their lunch break; a scene of an inner-city basketball game played on a lavish marble court with a gold hoop; and a scene of the Hyundai Sonata driving down a street lined with chandeliers and red-carpet crosswalks.

The commercial's scene of an inner-city basketball game featured a basketball bearing marks similar (but not identical) to the Louis Vuitton marks.

In *Louis Vuitton Malletier, S.A.,* v. *Hyundai Motor America*, 10 Civ. 1611 (PKC), 2012 U.S. Dist. LEXIS 42795 (2012), Louis Vuitton characterized the scene as "a street-yard basketball scene in which it would use a basketball with markings copied from the design and colors of the [Louis Vuitton] Marks, altering them only slightly." In fact, the Louis Vuitton marks are known as the "toile monogram" and consists of a repeating pattern design of the letters "LV" with flower-like symbols on a chestnut-brown background.

According to Hyundai, the commercial sought to "emphasize" the "style, quality and amenities" of the 2011 Sonata, "a mid-sized Sedan priced at approximately $20,000." Hyundai, explained that its "Luxury" ad sought to "redefine the concept of luxury by communicating to consumers that Sonata offered 'luxury for all.' The commercial attempted to accomplish this goal by poking fun at the silliness of luxury-as-exclusivity by juxtaposing symbols of luxury with everyday life (for example, large yachts parked beside modest homes). The symbols of 'old' luxury, including the [Louis Vuitton] Marks, were used as part of the Commercial's humorous social commentary on the need to redefine luxury during a recession . . . The commercial poked fun at these symbols of 'old' luxury to distinguish them from [Hyundai] in an effort to challenge consumers to rethink what it means for a product to be luxurious." In Hyundai's argument, the ad sought "to distinguish [Louis Vuitton] from the common-sense Sonata."

To this point the federal anti-dilution statute "is designed solely for the benefit of sellers. Its purpose is to protect the owners of famous marks from the kind of dilution that is permitted by the trademark laws when a junior user uses the same mark in a non-confusing way in an unrelated area of commerce." It applies "regardless of the absence of competition or confusion." The 2006 amendments to the Trademark Dilution Revision Act (we will look at the TDRA later in this chapter) eliminated a requirement that a plaintiff prove actual dilution. A plaintiff need only establish likely dilution.

There are two types of dilution: blurring and tarnishment. The court explained: "[B]lurring is an 'association arising from the similarity between a mark or trade name and a famous mark that impairs the distinctiveness of the famous mark.' As noted, the statute states that blurring may occur regardless of actual or likely confusion, competition or economic injury. Under the TDRA, to successfully prove blurring, a plaintiff need not establish 'substantial similarity,' and a court considers the 'degree of similarity' as one of six probative factors."

The Louis Vuitton marks and the basketball design used in "Luxury" were virtually indistinguishable. They featured highly similar geometric designs stamped in gold, set against a brown background. When closely scrutinized, the design in the Hyundai commercial included the stylized initials "LZ," as opposed to Louis Vuitton's "LV." In fact, the "LZ" and the "LV" were portrayed in similar scripts and designs.

In this case, the context of the marks' use is important in a similarity analysis. Hyundai argued that, rather than making a side-by-side comparison of the designs, the context of its "Luxury" spot underscores the differences between Hyundai and Louis Vuitton. However, the brief appearance of the Louis Vuitton-like marks actually heightened the similarities. Without extremely close scrutiny, the elements of the Louis Vuitton Toile Monogram, and their overall effect, are virtually indistinguishable from Hyundai's stylized basketball pattern design. Add to this, the brevity of the basketball's appearance in the "Luxury" ad, totaling approximately one second, made it even more difficult to notice the minor. This similarity was clearly intended by Hyundai. The court said: "the ball's design was intended to 'register luxury with the snap of the fingers.' Considered in context, the ball's fleeting appearance in "Luxury" heightens the similarities between Louis Vuitton's marks and the Hyundai design."

The court concluded by stating: "Viewed in its entirety, Louis Vuitton has set forth evidence that satisfies each of the TDRA's six blurring factors. It also bears emphasizing that these factors go toward the ultimate question of 'whether an association, arising from the similarity of subject marks, impairs the distinctiveness of the famous mark.' The blurring inquiry does not require two companies to be in direct competition."

Protection for Specific Use

Keep in mind that a mark can only be registered for use within a specific category. A trademark can be used only with the product or product line that it was registered for. In other words, registering a mark for use with a specific product does not automatically allow that mark to be used with other products. Let's say Bonzo Company manufactures and owns a trademark for its line of cars. Their trademark can be used for it line of cars but it cannot use that trademark for a new line of dishwashers.

Palming Off Example The name Johnnie Walker has meant high-quality Scotch Whiskey since 1880, when the trademark was created. Since its inception, the name was heavily advertised and promoted. As a result, the name Johnnie Walker has gained an excellent and very recognizable reputation. I think I can safely say almost every adult knows the name "Johnnie Walker," and quickly associates it with whiskey.

In the early 1950s, Tampa Cigar Company began marketing one of its cigars under the name Johnnie Walker. This irritated John Walker & Sons (the whiskey company) enough to file a lawsuit: *Tampa Cigar Co.* v. *John Walker & Sons, Ltd.*, 222 F.2d 460 (5th Cir. 1955), 110 U.S.P.Q. 249 (Com. Pat. 1956).

Clearly, the use of "Johnnie Walker" on cigars was an infringement. Tampa tried to take advantage of the fame and reputation built on the Johnnie Walker name. In effect, Tampa Cigar tried to create the impression that the makers of the whiskey were the makers of the cigars. This practice is called "palming off."

Tampa argued that because the products were different, it should be allowed to use the name. "That," the court said, "we decline to do." While the products, whiskey and cigars, are different, they are often sold to the public at the same time and in the same stores. Bars, liquor stores, restaurants, markets, convenience stores all sell these items. Johnnie Walker whiskey and cigars could literally be placed side by side and sold to the same person at the same time. Even though the products were different, the cigar's use of the mark was an infringement.

Different Markets Example On the other hand, there are cases where no infringement exists. A good example of this can be seen in *Holiday Inns, Inc.* v. *Holiday Out In America*, 481 F.2d 445 (5th Cir. 1973).

Holiday Inns had developed a considerable reputation with the public for its chain of travel motels. Its reputation was one of consistent high quality. Keeping close watch over its marks of "Holiday Inn, Holiday Inns of America," and "The Nation's Innkeeper," Holiday Inns, Inc. guarded its service marks.

In 1966 another company opened a series of trailer parks under the name "Holiday Out" and "Holiday Out in America." Holiday Out registered its trademark on January 23, 1967, describing its business as "maintaining and operating campground facilities for campsite owners." When Holiday Inn learned of this, it filed a suit in July of that year.

The court found that they were totally different markets, and no proof was shown to validate Holiday Inn's claim of infringement. The court felt that allowing both trademarks to be used "is not reasonably calculated to cause confusion or mistake or to deceive." Holiday Out was allowed to retain its trademark.

Use that Doesn't Cause Infringement

Sir Speedy, a California corporation, operates a nationwide chain of 705 print shops, including 41 in the greater Chicagoland area. A Sir Speedy franchise requires that the operator agree to run the business in accordance with Sir Speedy's guidelines and pay royalties to Sir Speedy. In exchange, the franchisee becomes licensed to use the Sir Speedy trademarks and reputation to build its business.

The owner of Express Printing Company had operated as a Sir Speedy franchise from 1979 until 1994. At that time he voluntarily terminated his franchise with Sir Speedy and immediately opened Express at the same location, using the same phone number. In 1996, Sir Speedy granted a franchise to another person, who opened up just three blocks down the road from Express. After Sir Speedy was told about Express' yellow pages advertisement, it sent a letter to Express demanding that it stop referencing Sir Speedy in its advertising.

In *Sir Speedy, Inc.* v. *Express Printing Center*, No. 98C3762, 1998 U.S. Dist. LEXIS 11248 (N.D. Ill, July 17, 1998), the court viewed Express' yellow pages advertisement in context. The Express advertisement ran in the 1998–1999 Ameritech Yellow Pages, and was located on the same page, directly below a larger Sir Speedy advertisement. The phrase "formerly Sir Speedy" was in small type and placed below the much larger Express logo. "Indeed, it would take an extraordinary amount of oversight and a few Jordanesque leaps of logic to conclude that all Sir Speedy shops had become Express Printing Centers," the court reasoned.

In the case, the court stated: "Sir Speedy requests injunctive relief because of Mr. Matye's and Express' damage to Sir Speedy's goodwill. However, aside from this naked allegation, Sir Speedy puts forth no supporting evidence. Furthermore, and much to its detriment, Sir Speedy admits that treble damages will suffice for damage 'to Sir Speedy's goodwill, business, name, and mark resulting from Defendants' use of the name and mark since the time that defendants began his infringing use.' Sir Speedy also requests Express' gross receipts during the infringement period, to be used to calculate the damage to Sir Speedy's goodwill. Therefore, a legal remedy will be adequate for Sir Speedy, and the fact that money will compensate the loss in itself suggests that the harm is not irreparable."

Sir Speedy also argued that by stating that Express was formerly a Sir Speedy franchise, the company was subtly claiming that it could provide the same service as a Sir Speedy. The court rejected Sir Speedy's argument that the phrase "formerly Sir Speedy" could be read to mean that "Express Printing Center provides the same quality of service as Sir Speedy."

Express was not claiming to be a Sir Speedy franchise. The phrase simply noted that, previously, Express had been a Sir Speedy franchise, but that it was no longer.

The court summed up the issue of balancing the harms that each party may experience: "If this injunction is not issued, Sir Speedy claims that it will continue to suffer incompensable harm. It is imaginable that potential customers would be drawn away from the Sir Speedy of Deerfield and to Express Printing Center because of Mr. Matye's use of the phrase 'formerly Sir Speedy.' However, Sir Speedy's failure to present any evidence of this, as well as the fact that seven other print shops in the area have been using the same phrase in their advertisements for nearly a decade without Sir Speedy noticing, militates against such a finding. The potential harm to Sir Speedy, at worst, appears negligible."

"On the other hand, if this injunction is issued, specifically the portion which requires the changing of Express' telephone number, the harm to Mr. Matye would be disastrous. For over a decade, all of Mr. Matye's business has been acquired through the telephone, and correspondingly, the telephone number he has had for the last nineteen years. He has over one thousand customers who communicate with him only through that telephone number. If he is forced to change that number now, Express would likely be put out of business, and Mr. Matye, along with his six employees, would be unemployed."

Because Sir Speedy failed to sustain its initial burden, the court denied Sir Speedy's request for a preliminary injunction.

Playmate of the Year Example Terri Welles is a model and spokesperson who began her modeling career with *Playboy* magazine in 1980. In May of 1980 Ms. Welles appeared on the cover of *Playboy* magazine and in the December 1980 issue, was the "Playmate of the Month." Ms. Welles received the "Playmate of the Year" award in June of 1981. Since 1980 Ms. Welles has appeared in thirteen issues of *Playboy* magazine and eighteen special publications that were published by Playboy Enterprises, Inc. (PEI). Ms. Welles claims that since 1980 she has referred to herself as a "Playmate" or "Playmate of the Year," all with the full knowledge of PEI.

On June 29, 1997, Welles opened a website (www.terriwelles.com) that included photographs of herself and others, a fan club posting board, an autobiography section, and so on. The heading for the web site was "Terri Welles-Playmate of the Year 1981" and the title of the link page was "Terri Welles-Playboy Playmate of the Year 1981." The web site included a disclaimer at the bottom of most pages which stated that: "This site is neither endorsed, nor sponsored by, nor affiliated with Playboy Enterprises, Inc. PLAYBOY, PLAYMATE OF THE YEAR and PLAYMATE OF THE MONTH are registered trademarks of Playboy Enterprises, Inc."

Playboy owned the trademarks Playboy, Playmate, Playmate of the Month, and Playmate of the Year.

In *Playboy Enterprises, Inc.* v. *Welles*, No. 98-CIV-0413-K (JFS), 1998 U.S. Dist. LEXIS 9180 (S.D. Cal., May 21, 1998), 47 U.S.P.Q.2d 1186, the court found that Welles' use of the term Playmate of the Year 1981 was a fair use of Playboy's trademarks.

The court noted:

[T]he other trademarks such as Playmate are not only trademarks related to *Playboy* magazine, but they are titles bestowed upon particular models who appear in the magazine. From the papers submitted and oral arguments, it appears that the terms Playmate, Playmate of the Month, and Playmate of the Year are titles which Playboy magazine awards to certain Playboy models, who then use the title to describe themselves. Much like Academy Award winners, crowned Miss Americas, and Heisman Trophy winners, Playboy Playmates are given a title which becomes part of their identity and adds value to their name. Indisputably, these winners represent the awarding organization or sponsor, but the title becomes part of who they are to the public.

Moreover, it was learned that Playboy encouraged models to use the Playmate title for their own self-promotion as well as the promotion of Playboy's magazine. It was also determined that Welles was not contractually restricted from using the Playmate of the Year title in any way.

The court stated: "This case is not a standard trademark case and does not lend itself to the systematic application of the eight factors. In the case at bar, defendant has used the terms Playmate of the Year and its abbreviation PMOY on her website. She has also used the terms Playboy and Playmate as meta tags for her site so that those using search engines on the Web can find her website if they were looking for a Playboy Playmate. The problem in this case is that the trademarks that defendant uses, and the manner in which she uses them, describe her and identify her. This raises a question of whether there is a 'fair use' of these marks pursuant to 15 U.S.C. §§ 1115(b)(4) and 1125(c)(4). Terri Welles was and is the 'Playmate of the Year for 1981.' Plaintiff has conceded this fact and has not submitted any evidence for the court to conclude that PEI may prevent defendant from using that term to identify herself and her award, as noted above. PEI conceded that there are no contractual agreements between it and defendant which restrict her use of any of the marks. Thus, defendant has raised a 'fair use' defense which must be overcome by the plaintiff before a potential infringement under Section 43(a) of the Lanham Act or trademark dilution under Section 43(c) of the Lanham Act may be found."

A fair use (not to be confused with the Fair Use Doctrine as it applies to copyright) defense to trademark infringement arises when the trademark also describes a person, place, or an attribute of a product, the court found. The fair use defense prohibits the trademark owner from appropriating a descriptive term for its exclusive use and so prevents others from accurately describing themselves or a characteristic of their goods or services. Welles' use of disclaimers on her web pages confirmed that there was no attempt by Welles to confuse the public into thinking that her site was a Playboy-related site.

The court concluded: "It is clear that defendant is selling Terri Welles and only Terri Welles on the website. There is no overt attempt to confuse the websurfer into believing that her site is a Playboy-related website. In this case, then, defendant's use of the term Playmate of the Year 1981 'is descriptive of and used fairly and in good faith only to describe [herself]' (15 U.S.C. § 1115(b)(4))."

As such, the use of the abbreviation PMOY '81 is also permissible since it makes reference to her title as "Playmate of the Year 1981." Since the court finds that "PMOY '81" is a fair description of Ms. Terri Welles, it is not necessary to rule on whether the abbreviation PMOY is a protected trademark.

In addition, it is unclear that irreparable harm would ensue from the continued operation of Ms. Welles' website since plaintiff has not demonstrated that there is a likelihood of confusion. As such, the court, hereby, DENIES plaintiff's Motion for a Preliminary Injunction.

The FTC and Deceptive Trademark Uses

In addition to the Trademark Office's regulations, the FTC can become involved if the trademark or trade name used is deceptive. The FTC's concern is any form of deception of the consumer, whether in an ad or a name. Having a trademark registered does not protect it against causing other violations of the law. In cases where the name does fall into the deceptive or false advertising arena, the FTC can force the company to stop using the name.

A rental car company using the trade name "Dollar-A-Day Car Rental" was brought into court by the FTC in *Resort Car Rental System, Inc.* v. *FTC*, 518 F.2d 962 (9th Cir. 1975). It was shown that the name created an obvious impression to the public. The court said: "The 'Dollar-A-Day' slogan carries strong psychological appeal. Its connotations are obvious." The consumer could expect to be charged $1 per day for a rental car. This was certainly not true, however.

This case turned on the issue of deceptive advertising. The point here is that trademark registration did not create a shield to protect what was essentially a deceptive claim in the guise of a trade name. Dollar-A-Day was required to change its name.

Fair Use of Trademarks

In the early 1980s, Maurice Starr discovered fifteen-year-old Donnie Wahlberg, who immediately impressed him with his rapping skills, dancing ability and showmanship. Wahlberg recruited other members including his younger brother Mark (Mark chose to quit before they started recording), his best friend Danny Wood, schoolmate Jordan Knight, Jonathan Knight and Joey McIntyre. The group known as *New Kids on the Block* from Boston, Massachusetts began in 1984. They have sold more than eighty million records worldwide, making them one of the world's best-selling groups of all time.

Two newspapers, *USA Today* and *The Star*, conducted polls of their readers seeking an answer to a pressing question: Which one of the New Kids is the most popular?

USA Today's poll contained a picture of the New Kids and asked, "Who's the best on the block?" The polls listed a 900 number for voting and added: "New Kids on the Block are pop's hottest group. Which of the five is your fave? Or are they a turn off? . . . Each call costs 50 cents. Results in Friday's Life section."

The Star's poll, along with a picture of the group, asked: "Now which kid is the sexiest?" The poll, appeared in a page containing a story on a New Kids concert, also stated: "Which of the New Kids on the Block would you most like to move next door?"

In *The New Kids On The Block* v. *News America Publishing, Inc.*, 971 F.2d 302; 1992 U.S. App. LEXIS 16678; 23 U.S.P.Q.2D (BNA) 1534; 20 Media L. Rep. 1468; 92 Cal. Daily Op. Service 6474; 92 Daily Journal DAR 10292 (1992), the New Kids complained that the two newspapers were undermining their leadership over their fans.

With many well-known trademarks, such as Jell-O, Scotch tape and Kleenex, there are other nontrademark phrases available for describing the products (gelatin, cellophane tape and facial tissue). However, often there is no substitute description when many goods and services are effectively identifiable only by their trademarks. The court reasoned that: ". . . one might refer to "the two-time world champions" or "the professional basketball team from Chicago," but it's far simpler (and more likely to be understood) to refer to the Chicago Bulls. In such cases, use of the trademark does not imply sponsorship or endorsement of the product because the mark is used only to describe the thing, rather than to identify its source."

In this case, both *The Star* and *USA Today* referenced the New Kids only to the extent necessary to identify them as the subject of the polls. They did not use the New Kids' distinctive logo or anything else that wasn't necessary to make the message clear to readers. Nothing in the polls suggested joint sponsorship or endorsement by the New Kids. The court said: "The *USA Today* announcement implies quite the contrary by asking whether the New Kids might be 'a turn off.' *The Star*'s poll is more effusive but says nothing that expressly or by fair implication connotes endorsement or joint sponsorship on the part of the New Kids."

The New Kids argued that, even if the newspapers were entitled to a nominative fair use defense (again, this is not to be confused with the Fair Use Doctrine as it applies to copyright) for the newspaper announcements, they were not entitled to it for the polls themselves, which were money-making ventures separate from the newspapers' reporting businesses. In short, New Kids argued that a fair use defense is inapplicable where the use in question competes directly with that of the trademark holder.

The court stated: "The New Kids claim that *USA Today*'s and *The Star*'s use of their name amounted to both commercial and common law misappropriation under California law. Although there are subtle differences between these two causes of action, all that's material here is a key similarity between them: The papers have a complete defense to both claims if they used the New Kids name 'in connection with any news, public affairs, or sports broadcast or account' which was true in all material respects."

In this case, *USA Today*'s and *The Star*'s use of the New Kids' name was "in connection with" news accounts. *The Star* ran concurrent articles on the New Kids along with its 900-number poll, while *USA Today* promised a subsequent story on the popularity of various members of the singing group. Both papers also have an established track record of polling their readers and then reporting the poll results as part of a later news story. As a result, the New Kids' misappropriation claims were.

Slogans

In some cases slogans may be trademarked. But those situations are controlled by strict guidelines. Slogans, if they qualify for protection, fall into the category of service marks. A mark may consist of any slogan, but it is allowed protection only if it distinguishes the product.

In 2000, Ralph Nader turned out to be the person who turned the George W. Bush Presidential campaign into a win. Nader-voters who spurned Democrat Al Gore to vote for Nader ended up swinging both Florida and New Hampshire to Bush. In Florida, which George W. Bush carried by 537 votes, Mr. Nader received nearly one hundred thousand votes. In New Hampshire, which Bush won by 7,211 votes, Mr. Nader pulled in more than twenty-two thousand votes. If Gore had won either of those two states instead, Bush would have lost the 2000 election. If that had happened, we would not have had a U.S. President named George W. Bush. The result, however, was that Nader managed to turn two key states in favor of Bush, and he became the person who made G.W. Bush the forty-third President of the United States. Arguably, Nader turned out to be more important to Bush's campaign success, than financial contributors such as Enron's chief Ken Lay.

During that 2000 presidential campaign, Nader aired political TV advertisements that showed a series of items with prices for each. Phrases like "Promises to special interest groups: over $100 billion" filled the screen and all ending with a phrase "finding out the truth: priceless. There are some things that money can't buy."

In *MasterCard Int'l Inc.* v. *Nader 2000 Primary Comm., Inc.*, 00 Civ. 6068, U.S. Dist. LEXIS 3644, 2004 WL 434404 (S.D.N.Y. Mar. 8, 2004), the court ruled in favor of Ralph Nader and his presidential committee in a trademark infringement action brought by MasterCard International Inc. MasterCard claimed that Nader's use of its well-known "priceless" trademarked slogans "PRICELESS" and "There are some things money can't buy. For everything else there's MasterCard." infringed and diluted its two registered marks.

Although the court found that MasterCard's marks were strong and that Nader used the marks in his advertising, it nonetheless held that there was no likelihood of confusion because there was little similarity between MasterCard's credit card services and Nader's political campaign. The court also determined that there was no evidence of actual confusion or that Nader intended to confuse the public. Rather, Nader's advertisements were intended to criticize the role of financial contributions in politics.

Furthermore, the court reasoned that MasterCard had no case for its dilution claim because noncommercial uses of a mark are specifically exempted under the Federal Trademark Dilution Act (FTDA). While MasterCard argued that Nader's advertising was commercial in nature due to an increased number of contributions made to his campaign as a result of the advertising. Yet the court rejected MasterCard's argument, since the advertising merely expressed Nader's opinion on presidential campaigning. Even if Nader's use of MasterCard's marks was commercial, they failed to show that that use actually caused dilution of the distinctiveness of its marks. Finally, MasterCard failed to show that Nader's use of its marks created a likelihood of dilution.

"We Smile More" Example

Marriott began using the slogan, "We Smile More," as an advertising and promotional line in 1964. In 1968 the hotel chain applied for registration of the slogan as a trademark after it learned that Ramada Inns had begun using the same line.

The case went to trial in *In re Marriott Corp.*, 517 F.2d 1364 (C.C.P.A. 1975), where it was determined the slogan did qualify to be registered. A slogan does not have to be unique in verbiage to qualify. "[A] capability of identifying and distinguishing the source of goods or services is all that is required to support registration."

The court went on to say that "the function of a . . . mark is to indicate continuity of quality of services, i.e., that the quality of services rendered in connection with a particular mark is controlled by a single entity." Marriott showed that customers were aware of the slogan and recognized the mark as belonging to it. These consumers substantiated that they knew the slogan referred to Marriott, and only to Marriott. Indeed, the slogan indicated the source. The court allowed the registration of "We Smile More" as a trademark.

See the section on the Federal Trademark Dilution Act of 1995 that follows later in this chapter. The consideration of likelihood of consumer confusion (as was typical of the case here) is no longer a requirement for infringement.

The Slogan that's a Mouthful Example

Everyone in advertising will no doubt remember McDonald's campaign in the mid-1970s that used the slogan:

"TWOALLBEEFPATTIESSPECIALSAUCELETTUCECHEESEPICKLESONIONSONASESAMESEEDBUN."

McDonald's began using the slogan in its advertising in late 1974. It spent over $2 million in advertising, using the slogan as its theme through the end of 1975. The advertising campaign included almost every media available from TV, radio, newspaper, magazine, billboards, through point-of-purchase, contests, and premiums.

In essence, McDonald's saturated the market with

"TWOALLBEEFPATTIESSPECIALSAUCELETTUCECHEESE-PICKLESONIONSONASESAMESEEDBUN."

McDonald's applied for registration of its slogan as a trademark in 1975, and *In re McDonald's Corp.*, 199 U.S.P.Q. 490 (TTAB 1978), resulted. At the hearing the argument was made in opposition to the application that the phrase was no more than a descriptive list of ingredients of a Big Mac sandwich. However, the phrase is a unique "and somewhat catchy arrangement and combination which in its entirety creates a commercial impression quite different from that of the individual words as they are ordinarily used."

Through its massive advertising campaign, McDonald's also met the second requirement for registration, that of knowledge of origin by the public. At the time, everyone who knew the name McDonald's knew the slogan. There was little doubt the public knew that the phrase meant only McDonald's.

A Hog by Any Other Name Example

In 1969 Ronald Grottanelli opened a motorcycle repair shop and named it "The Hog Farm." Since then his shop was located at various sites in New York state. After 1981 Grottanelli began using the word "hog" in connection with events and merchandise for his shop. He also sponsored events known as "Hog Holidays" and "Hog Farm Holidays," and sold products such as "Hog Wash" engine degreaser and a "Hog Trivia" board game.

Beginning in the early 1970s, motorcyclists began using the term "hog" when referring to Harley-Davidson motorcycles. For several years the company tried to disassociate itself from the word "hog." The company wanted to distance itself from the connection between "hog" as applied to motorcycles and negative groups, such as Hell's Angels, who were among those associating the term to Harley-Davidson motorcycles.

However, in 1981, Harley-Davidson recognized that the term "hog" had significant financial value and began using the term in connection with its merchandise, accessories, advertising and promotions. In 1983 it formed the Harley Owners' Group, using the acronym "H.O.G." Four years later, in 1987, it registered the acronym in conjunction with various logos.

By 1979 Grottanelli started using his version of Harley-Davidson's bar-and-shield logo. In an ad he ran in 1979, he included a hand-drawn copy of the bar-and-shield logo, with the name "Harley-Davidson" displayed on the horizontal bar. When Harley-Davidson protested to this use, Grottanelli replaced the words "Harley-Davidson" on the horizontal bar of his logo with the words "American-Made." He also put a banner at the bottom of his logo with the words "UNAUTHORIZED DEALER." In 1986, Grottanelli began using his current logo, which adds an eagle's wings behind the shield. This addition, patterned after Harley-Davidson's bicentennial logo design mark, included an eagle above the shield. Grottanelli's 1986 version of his logo also features a drawing of a pig wearing sunglasses. Grottanelli acknowledged at trial that his version of the logo was "supposed to be similar, but confusing . . . [t]o a Harley-Davidson bar and shield."

Harley-Davidson, Inc. v. *Grottanelli*, 164 F.3d 806 (2d Cir. 1999), was the case where this all came to a head. In court, Harley-Davidson argued that it is entitled to trademark protection for the term "HOG" as it is applied to motorcycles because a substantial segment of consumers used the term to refer to Harley-Davidson motorcycles.

The court reasoned on this point: "Some decisions have invoked this principle to accord a company priority as to its subsequent trademark use of a term. See *National Cable Television Ass'n, Inc.* v. *American Cinema Editors, Inc.*, 937 F.2d 1572 (Fed. Cir. 1991), mark 'ACE'; *Volkswagenwerk AG* v. *Hoffman*, 489 F. Supp. 678 (D.S.C. 1980), mark 'BUG'. Whether or not we would agree with these decisions, they present a significantly different situation. Neither 'ACE' nor 'BUG' was a generic term in the language as applied, respectively, to a category of film editors or a category of automobiles prior to the public's use of the terms to refer to the American Cinema Editors and Volkswagen cars. By contrast, 'hog' was a generic term in the language as applied to large motorcycles before the public (or at least some segments of it) began using the word to refer to Harley-Davidson motorcycles. The public has no more right than a manufacturer to withdraw from the language a generic term, already applicable to the relevant category of products, and accord it trademark significance, at least as long as the term retains some generic meaning."

For all of these reasons, Harley-Davidson may not prohibit Grottanelli from using "hog" to identify his motorcycle products and services. Like any other manufacturer with a product identified by a word that is generic, Harley-Davidson will have to rely on all or a portion of its trade name (or other protectable marks) to identify its brand of motorcycles, for example, "Harley Hogs."

Then the court turned to Grottanilli's use of the Harley-Davidson logo. Grottanelli claimed that his use of Harley-Davidson's logo was a parody, and therefore allowed.

The court reasoned that that argument:

[I]s vulnerable not only because he uses it to market competing services but also because whatever protection is to be afforded a trademark parody must be informed by the Supreme Court's recent elucidation in the copyright context of parodies allegedly protected by the defense of fair use. See *Campbell* v. *Acuff-Rose Music, Inc.*, 510 U.S. 569 (1994), "[T]he heart of any parodist's claim to quote from existing material is the use of some elements of a prior author's composition to create a new one that, at least in part, comments on that author's works." The comment must have some "critical bearing on the substance or style of the original composition." The Supreme Court's parody explication as to copyrights, set forth in the context of an expressive work, is relevant to trademarks, see Robert S. Shaughnessy, Note, Trademark Parody, 72 Va. L. Rev. 1079 (1986), especially a trademark parody that endeavors to promote primarily non-expressive products such as a competing motorcycle repair service. Grottanelli's mark makes no comment on Harley's mark; it simply uses it somewhat humorously to promote his own products and services, which is not a permitted trademark parody use.

The court then looked at Grottanelli's use of his disclaimer as a defense. The court reasoned on this issue that: "Grottanelli gains no protection by coyly adding to his version of the bar-and-shield logo the wording 'UNAUTHORIZED DEALER.' We have alluded to commentary questioning the capacity of brief negating words like 'not' or 'no' in disclaimers adequately to avoid confusion. Whatever the worth of such disclaimers in other contexts, the use of the prefix 'UN' before 'AUTHORIZED DEALER' provides Grottanelli with no defense when used on signage designed to attract speeding motorcyclists."

The court concluded that Grottanelli was properly enjoined from using his current bar-and-shield logo or any mark that resembles Harley-Davidson's trademark, but reversed the lower court's ruling that enjoined his use of the word "hog."

Foreign Words Used as Trademarks

Another area to consider is the use of foreign words in trademarks. Some companies try to register marks using foreign words in place of the English version that they could not ordinarily register in English. If the words are descriptive of the product in that foreign language, then the United States will also consider them not qualified to be protected under trademark law. The guide should be that if the mark would not qualify in English, for whatever reason, it wouldn't qualify using another language either.

On another point, if a company desires to market its product in other countries, it must consider the trademark laws of those governments. They all vary and may have a large impact on the choice of a trademark. A specialist should be consulted in this case, since the requirements of foreign countries far exceed the scope of this book.

Genericide and Its Relationship to Trademarks
What Can Happen When a Mark Is Misused

Ultimately, when a mark is misused, it can be lost to the forgotten world of generic terms. The consumer may begin to consider a trademark as the name of the product line in general. Then the trademark no longer identifies and distinguishes the product of a particular manufacturer. Instead of standing for one particular brand name of product, the mark stands for the type of product. This is called "genericide."

When a trademark is not handled properly, it can be weakened to the point that it is no longer protected as a trademark. Therefore, an advertiser/marketer must be very cautious. The manufacturer's own promotion, labeling, and advertising are often at fault when this happens. Genericide has been the demise of many trademarks, which we now consider product lines, including "cellophane," "celluloid," "kerosene," "lanolin," "linoleum," "milk of magnesia," "dry ice," and (as we'll soon see) "aspirin," "thermos bottles," "escalators," and "PROMS." These trademarks were allowed to deteriorate to the point that they became synonymous with the product rather than the manufacturer.

The key to understanding the process is this: Genericide happens in the mind of the consumer, not to the product. When brand names are used as verbs by consumers rather than nouns, genericide can result. Today, we photoshop images. But Photoshop is a trademark and Adobe Systems is the owner. Adobe goes to great length to protect its mark and clarifies use of its name on its website: "Correct: The image was enhanced using Adobe® Photoshop® software. Incorrect: The image was photoshopped." Fortunately Photoshop has acquired secondary meaning to protect its mark. But the point is still the same . . . more on this later in this chapter.

Yet, there is something that the advertiser can do to control how the consumer perceives the trademark. The easiest way to avoid genericide and to protect a trademark would be to control misuses of their trade name (and therefore trademark). For example, in marketing trademark owners should encourage use of the word *brand* in connection with the name and product, i.e., "Xerox brand copiers" or "IBM brand computers," to forestall any assumption by consumers that the trademark is a generic term. The more the trademark owner attempts to control the use (and misuse) of its mark, the better.

The Headache that Aspirin Caused How many brands of aspirin can you think of? Bayer, Johnson & Johnson, Excedrin, Bufferin, and Anacin are some of the major ones. This is the problem that Bayer had to deal with in the early 1920s, because "aspirin" was originally a trademark.

"Aspirin" was the trademark for the drug acetyl salicylic acid, a powder that was patented by Bayer Company in 1898. In 1904 the name of the drug was changed to monoaceticacidester of salicylic acid. Bayer began allowing chemists, druggists, and physicians to make the powder into tablets for sale under names such as "Squibb Aspirin," "Smith, Klein & French Aspirin," or "United Drug Company Aspirin." United Drug, in particular, sold over nineteen million tablets in its first two years. The consumer could not possibly have known the manufacturer of the drug, only the name on the bottle.

In 1915 Bayer changed its policy and discontinued selling to other manufacturers. From that time on Bayer prohibited others from manufacturing or selling the drug. It began selling aspirin itself in tablets to the general public. Tablets were sold in tin boxes with a legend (see box 10.1).

Box 10.1

The Trademark "Aspirin" (Reg. U.S. Pat. Office) is a guarantee that the monoaceticacidester of salicylic acid in these tablets is of the reliable Bayer manufacture.

But it was too late; the harm had been done. Because of this change in policy, United Drug sued Bayer, claiming that the name *aspirin* had become a descriptive name, free for anyone to use. The case was *Bayer Co.* v. *United Drug Co.*, 272 F. 605 (SDNY 1921). While the druggists knew that aspirin was a trademark, the general public did not. Its only knowledge of the product was through the over-the-counter brands that were available, especially since many manufacturers had used the name alone in labeling and advertising—all allowed by Bayer.

Bayer understood that the term "aspirin" had become generic. When it began to sell to the public in 1915, its labels read: "Bayer—Tablets of Aspirin." This meant that the tablets were Bayer's make of the drug known as "aspirin."

The public could not have known that "aspirin" was a trademark for momoaceticacidester of salicylic acid; it thought that *aspirin* was the name of the drug. By allowing this confusion to occur, Bayer failed to protect the trademark as such, and the Trademark Office declared the trademark not valid as of 1918. The court in its decision agreed with both the Trademark Office and United Drug in determining that the name "aspirin" had become a generic term.

The Moving Stairway Trademark registration number 34,724 was issued to Charles D. Seeberger in 1900. The trademark was for the term "escalator." Seeberger had invented the device and assigned the trademark to the Otis Elevator Company a number of years later, which manufactured not only elevators, but escalators as well.

A typical ad for Otis from a 1946 issue of *Architectural Forum* magazine contained the following:

Obviously, the Otis name was treated as the trademark, and the names "escalator" and "elevator" were merely descriptive of the product. This was plain from the ad copy. As a result, the Haughten Elevator Company attempted, in the late 1940s, to have the name "escalator" declared generic (box 10.2).

Box 10.2

Otis (logo)

THE MEANING OF THE OTIS TRADEMARK.

To the millions of daily passengers on the Otis elevators and escalators, the Otis trademark or name plate means safe, convenient, energy-saving transportation. To the thousands of building owners and managers, the Otis trademark means the utmost in safe, efficient, economical elevator and escalator operation.

Haughten succeeded with its efforts in *Haughten Elevator Co.* v. *Seeberger*, 85 U.S.P.Q. 80 (Comm'r 1950). Here, the court determined that the term "escalator" was a generic term for a moving stairway. The court reasoned that the term "escalator" described any moving stairway made by any company. Otis, in large part, allowed this to occur through its literature and advertisements. The term "escalator" was not used by Otis to identify it as the originator and only source of an escalator. The word "escalator" became a generic term for any moving stairway. Trademark number 34,724, held by Otis, was cancelled.

The PROM that Never Was Most losses of trademark protection to genericide occurred in the years when marketing and advertising techniques were young. As we have seen, many early trademarks were lost because of poor handling. But today's company is still at risk when it comes to trademark protection as clearly seen in a recent example involving the computer revolution and one of its components, the "PROM."

High-tech aficionados love to use initials for the names of components. For computer memories, RAM stands for Random Access Memory, SAM for Simultaneous Access Memory, CAM for Content-Addressable Memory, ROM for Read-Only Memory, and PROM for Programmable-Read-Only Memory.

The Harris Semiconductor Division of Radiation, Inc. developed the first field programmable-read-only memory. Harris adopted the acronym "PROM" for the product and put that name on its merchandise. Soon after, other companies developed similar programmable-read-only memories and also used the designation "PROM." Harris attempted to stop the other manufacturers from using the name, claiming that "PROM" was a trademark for its own products. Harris then attempted to register the term "PROM" as its trademark.

When this occurred, Intel (one of the other competitors) brought an action to stop Harris from acquiring the trademark. In *Intel Corp.* v. *Radiation, Inc.*, 184 U.S.P.Q. 54 (TTAB 1974), the issue was whether the term "PROM" should be trademarked. Essentially, the court determined that "PROM" was merely the "descriptive letters [that] constitute the initials or abbreviations of the common name of the product."

In fact, the trade had already become well-acquainted with the term "PROM." The acronym had been used extensively by publications within the trade and in promotional materials of various manufacturers. It was common practice in the electronics industry to use abbreviations as an easy method for identifying the different components. It was also well known that these acronyms did not denote the manufacturer of the component. Indeed, "PROM" was only a descriptive name or acronym for the specific type of memory. Harris was not granted a trademark for the term "PROM"—it was a generic name.

How to Avoid Genericide

Al Ries and Jack Trout, in their classic ad book, *Positioning: The Battle for Your Mind*, extol the virtues of positioning a product so that the brand name becomes synonymous with the product. It's the basis for positioning strategy, and anyone in advertising knows it. Let's take a short step back to our Bayer case. In their book Trout and Ries use it as an example to discuss the power in a name: The tablets in a bottle of aspirin are Bayer. Not aspirin manufactured by a company called Bayer . . . The great strength of an established brand name is this close identification with the product itself. In the consumer's mind, Bayer is aspirin, and every other aspirin brand becomes 'imitation' Bayer.

The strength of positioning strategy cannot be questioned. But what is good for marketing may be terrible for protection of a trademark. We discussed this earlier in the chapter, but the advertiser must be careful not to destroy a trademark in the process of building brand awareness.

The best method an advertiser can use to avoid genericide is to treat a trademark as a trademark. In other words, distinguish it from the type of product. How can you accomplish this? For copywriters, a trademark should always be an adjective that modifies the product name. It is not a noun; the noun names the type of product. Actually, the trademark is a proper adjective modifying a proper noun—allowing both words to be capitalized.

As an example, let's take a fictitious company called Metropolis Manufacturing. It makes a car called the Metromobile. Now "Metromobile" is a trademark. In its advertising, to protect the trademark, Metropolis must not refer to its car merely as a Metromobile. It should refer to it as a Metromobile Automobile or Metromobile Car. (Also, note that a trademark is not a verb since you can't Metromobile to work.)

Here's the test to see if a trademark is treated as a trademark, therefore avoiding possible genericide. A typical advertisement headline to accomplish this might read: "Enjoy the Freedom of the Road in a Metromobile Car." If you eliminate the trademark, "Metromobile," does the remaining sentence make sense? Aside from the fact that it would be a horrible headline, it would read: "Enjoy the Freedom of the Road in a Car." The headline still makes sense grammatically. Compare this to an incorrect usage of the mark. If the type of product were left out, the headline would read, "Enjoy the Freedom of the Road in a Metromobile." Now remove the trademark from this version, and the headline would make no sense: "Enjoy the Freedom of the Road in a." The sentence must make grammatical sense if the trademark is removed.

But let's be realistic. Not all advertisers follow these rules. One reason is that some trademarks are so strong the consumer invariably knows exactly what product is being referred to. How is it that a consumer can Google a movie, smoke a Salem, use a box of Tide, drink a Coke, or wear Nikes? It happens because some trademarks are very well understood by consumers. They know exactly what product is being referred to when the term is used. This is the secondary meaning we discussed earlier. The consumer places the specific name with the trademark automatically in his mind. We saw this earlier when we discussed positioning. Yet, all trademarks are not so fortunate as to have that status. Only in cases where the specific term is understood so thoroughly can the advertiser feel secure that the trademark can stand alone. For new products, or lesser-known ones, habitual use of the trademark without mention of the generic product should be avoided. When Bayer first heard people ask, "What brand of aspirin do you use?" it should have seen what was coming.

Trademark Dilution

The Federal Trademark Dilution Act of 1995

The Federal Trademark Dilution Act of 1995 (Dilution Act) is the most recent major development in trademark law and it has significant impact.

The Dilution Act (Pub. L. 104-98) was signed by President Clinton on January 16, 1996, and became effective immediately. The act amended section 43 of the Trademark Act of 1946 (15 U.S.C. § 1125(c) (Supp. 1996)).

This new act created a significant change in the law of trademarks. Until the act was passed, use of a mark was only actionable, under federal law, if it caused a likelihood of confusion as to the source. Now dilution of a famous mark is actionable under federal law. (Take note that some of the cases discussed in this chapter were viewed under the likelihood-of-confusion standard if they were decided prior to the 1995 Act.)

Owners of "famous" marks are now able to get injunctions, under federal trademark law, that will stop uses that weaken their marks or willfully trade on the reputation of the mark, even if that use does not cause consumer confusion. The idea of trademark dilution looks to the substantial investment an owner makes in the mark and the commercial value of the mark itself. This ties back into the value of the "brand" we discussed early in the chapter. Even in the absence of actual consumer confusion, the power of a mark may be weakened by another's use.

Twenty-five states have also enacted dilution statutes. In general, the states have patterned their law after the Model State Trademark Bill (Model State Trademark Bill, § 12 (USTA 1964)), which in part provides: "Likelihood of injury to business reputation or of dilution of the distinctive quality of a mark registered under this Act, or a mark valid at common law or a trade name valid at common law, shall be a ground for injunctive relief notwithstanding the absence of competition between the parties or the absence of confusion as to the source of goods or services."

According to Senator Orrin Hatch, "a federal dilution statute was needed because only twenty-five states currently prohibit dilution, making national protection a 'patch-work system.'" Until the act was passed, the form and extent of remedies for trademark dilution varied from state to state. Some courts required a showing of likelihood of confusion. Other courts maintained that only noncompetitive, nonconfusing uses were prohibited.

Provisions of the Dilution Act The Dilution Act contains certain provisions regarding trademarks. The owner of a famous mark is entitled to injunctive relief against another's use of the mark or trade name if the use causes dilution of the distinctive quality of the mark. In addition, if the violator trades on the owner's reputation or causes dilution intentionally, then the court may award the violator's profits, actual damages, treble damages, and costs of the suit as specified in sections 1117(a) and 1118 of the Lanham Act (15 U.S.C. § 1125(c)(2)).

The owners of famous marks may now obtain an injunction against use of their marks if such use begins after the mark has become famous, and if the use dilutes the distinctive quality of the mark. Under the Act, "fair use" of a mark in comparative advertising, noncommercial use of a mark, news reporting and commentary are not actionable.

When Is a Mark Famous and Distinctive? One of the potential difficulties with the Act is determining when a mark is famous and distinctive. The Act sets forth eight guidelines to be used in determining whether a mark is distinctive and famous (courts can also add their own, as well).

The eight factors include:

1. The degree of inherent or acquired distinctiveness of the mark;
2. The duration and extent of use of the mark in connection with the goods or services with which the mark is used;
3. The duration and extent of advertising and publicity of the mark;
4. The geographical extent of the trading area in which the mark is used;
5. The channels of trade for the goods or services with which the mark is used;
6. The degree of recognition of the mark in the trading areas and channels of trade used by the mark's owner and the person against whom the injunction is sought;
7. The nature and extent of use of the same or similar marks by third parties; and
8. Whether the mark was registered under the Act of March 3, 1881, or the Act of February 20, 1905, or on the principal register.

Dilution of the Distinctive Quality of a Mark Does the use cause dilution of the distinctive quality of the mark? To help determine this, Congress amended section 45 of the Trademark Act by inserting a definition of dilution. The act defines dilution as "the lessening of the capacity of a famous mark to identify and distinguish goods or services, regardless of the presence or absence of 'competition between the owner of the famous mark and other parties,' or likelihood of confusion."

A plaintiff, then, needs to prove both the capacity of a famous mark to be identified and distinguished and a lessening of that capacity. The phrase "lessening of the capacity" does not create a clear line. So, it is likely that courts will look to cases that have interpreted state dilution statutes.

Courts will probably look to cases that have interpreted state dilution statutes. The legislative history of the Dilution Act provides that dilution "is designed to encompass all of the forms of dilution recognized by the courts, including dilution by blurring, by tarnishment and disparagement, and by diminishment" (H.R. Rep. No. 374, 104th Cong., 1st Sess (1995), reprinted in 1996 U.S.C.C.A.N. 1029).

The two most common forms of dilution are "blurring" and "tarnishment." Blurring involves the "whittling away of an established trademark's selling power and value through its unauthorized use by others upon dissimilar products." Hypothetical examples were given in the New York Statute: DuPont shoes, Buick aspirin tablets, Schlitz varnish, Kodak pianos, and Bulova gowns.

In addition, a trademark may be tarnished when it is linked to products of shoddy quality, or is portrayed in an unwholesome or unsavory context, with the result that the public will associate the lack of quality or lack of prestige in the defendant's goods with the plaintiff's unrelated goods. Some examples of tarnishment have been found when a mark's likeness is placed in the context of sexual activity, obscenity, or illegal activity.

Carve-Outs To deal with First Amendment concerns, the Dilution Act explicitly exempts certain trademark uses from liability. First Amendment groups had criticized the dilution legislation as endangering First Amendment rights. The criticism focused primarily on the fact that parody—traditionally regarded as a form of fair use under copyright law—is one type of potential trademark dilution. In response to this criticism, Congress carved out "fair use" of a mark in comparative advertising, "non-commercial" use of a mark, and news reporting and commentary from actionable uses.

Other Protections

As mentioned earlier, the act encourages federal registration of marks. The bill was amended to include federal registration as one of the nonexclusive factors a court may consider in determining whether a mark is "famous and distinctive." Essentially, the trademark office must determine a mark to be distinctive or to have acquired distinctiveness before it will be registered. It also reasons that federal registration is a valid step in establishing and protecting a famous mark.

Owning a federally registered trademark is a defense against an action brought under the common law or a state dilution statute. Therefore, federal registration of a trademark offers a new benefit—protection against later claims of dilution under common law or state laws. However, nothing in the new law prohibits an action under the Dilution Act against the owner of a federal or state registration.

The Dilution Act does not preempt existing state dilution statutes. State laws may continue to be applied in cases involving famous marks. For example, if a mark is not considered famous under the Dilution Act because its fame is limited to a particular state or region, an action may be available under state law.

The federal Act is different than many state dilution laws since it applies to only famous marks, while many state statutes do not contain such a limitation. In general, though, court decisions interpreting state statutes only extend protection to well-known marks. However, the Act allows for a nationwide injunction, which state dilution law does not. The Act also confers federal jurisdiction for dilution regardless of whether there are other Lanham Act claims asserted.

The SPAM Example

Here's an example of a case decided under a state dilution statute. In *Hormel Foods Corp.* v. *Jim Henson Prod., Inc.*, 73 F.3d 497, 37 U.S.P.Q. 2d 1516 (2nd Cir. 1996), the Second Circuit held that the New York Anti-Dilution statute was not violated. Hormel brought an action against Jim Henson Productions for naming a puppet character "Spa'am." The plaintiff alleged infringement and dilution of its trademark, SPAM.

According to the court, no likelihood of dilution existed by blurring—the parody was not likely to weaken the association between SPAM and the food. Nor was the SPAM mark "tarnished" by the movie's use of a character named Spa'am. Evidence showed that the character was likable and would not generate any negative associations. In addition, the parody was not being used to sell another product that would compete with Hormel.

The Cat in the Hat Example

Several cases have been decided under the Dilution Act. For example, in *Dr. Seuss Enters., L.P.* v. *Penguin Books U.S.A., Inc.*, 924 F. Supp. 1559 (S.D. Cal. 1996), the court held that the Dilution Act does not apply to parodies. Defendant, Alan Katz, wrote *The Cat Not in the Hat*—a parody based on the O.J. Simpson double-murder trial. The rhymes, illustrations, and book's packaging all imitated the unique style of the works created by Theodore S. Geisel (Dr. Seuss). As a result, Dr. Seuss brought this suit against the publisher and author seeking an injunction against publishing the book.

Penguin, the publisher of Katz's book, argued that the Act does not apply to its use of the mark because of the exception contained in § 1125(c)(4)(b), which permits "noncommercial use of a mark." Dr. Seuss argued, however, that Penguin's use cannot be accepted as noncommercial because the marks are used to make their books more entertaining, thereby selling more copies.

The court rejected Dr. Seuss' interpretation of the noncommercial exception by reasoning that an expressive use is not rendered commercial by the impact of the use on sales. The court quoted Senator Hatch who, in introducing the bill, defined the exception as including "parody, satire, editorial, and other forms of expression that are not part of a commercial transaction." According to the court, commercial speech is only that speech which is part of a commercial transaction. The court therefore held that the defendant's use is exempt from the reach of the Dilution Act.

The Ringling Bros. Example

The *Ringling Bros.-Barnum & Bailey Combined Shows, Inc.* v. *B.E. Windows Inc.*, No. 96 Cov. 4758 (SAS), 1996 WL 391886 (S.D.N.Y. July 11, 1996), situation dealt with issues of dilution through blurring of the mark's strength rather than dilution through tarnishment of the mark.

Ringling Brothers went after an injunction claiming dilution of its trademark phrase THE GREATEST SHOW ON EARTH by defendant's use of the name "The Greatest Bar on Earth" for a bar at the top of (what was until September 11, 2001) the World Trade Center in New York. Ringling Brothers' claims were based on the Dilution Act and the New York Anti-Dilution statute. The court decided that although the two marks appear similar at first glance, differences in the words chosen for each phrase and the products represented prevented dilution by blurring. The court also found that despite the famousness of the Ringling Brothers' mark, the defendant's mark was little known and thus would not cause dilution.

It's not clear from this case what exactly is the role state statutes played in reaching the decision.

Another Ringling Bros. Example

Another Ringling Brother's case, *Ringling Bros.-Barnum & Bailey Combined Shows, Inc.* v. *Utah Division of Travel Development*, Civil Action No. 96-788-A (E.D. Va. Sept. 10, 1996), dealt with whether the anti-dilution provision operates only where the allegedly diluting mark is identical to the famous mark, or whether it is also triggered where the diluting mark is only similar to the famous mark.

In this case, Ringling Brothers sought relief for use of the slogan THE GREATEST SNOW ON EARTH in connection with license plates, advertisements, and other promotions for Utah's resorts. The defendant claimed that the Dilution Act applies only to situations where the mark used is identical to the famous mark. Specifically, the defendant argued that language in the Dilution Act stating that the owner of a famous mark is entitled to an injunction "against another person's commercial use in commerce of a mark or tradename" refers only to use of the famous mark.

However, the court disagreed, and stated that "Congress chose to use plain and unambiguous language to make clear that a famous mark may be diluted by the use of 'a mark,' not 'the [famous] mark.'" Applying the statute to protect against the use of same or similar marks is consistent with Congress' goal of creating uniformity among states and conforming to international provisions already enacted.

The Impact of *Moseley* v. *V Secret*

A pivotal case occurred in 2003, in *Moseley* v. *V Secret Catalogue Inc.*, 537 U.S. 418 (2003), which held that a federal claimant must prove "actual" dilution (rather than a mere "likelihood of dilution") to win a dilution claim.

An army colonel sent a copy of an advertisement he found for a retail store, "Victor's Secret," to the corporation that owned the well-known national chain of Victoria's Secret stores. The colonel, who saw the ad was offended by what he perceived to be an attempt to use a reputable company's trademark to promote the sale of "unwholesome, tawdry merchandise." The well-known chain asked the small retail store owned by Victor and Cathy Moseley, located in a strip mall in Elizabethtown, Kentucky, to discontinue using the name. But they only changed the store's name to "Victor's Little Secret," which did not satisfy the owners of the Victoria's Secret chain.

The corporation owns the Victoria's Secret trademark, and it operates over 750 Victoria's Secret stores, two of which are in Louisville, Kentucky, a short drive from Elizabethtown. In 1998 their sales exceeded $1.5 billion and they spent over $55 million advertising the Victoria's Secret brand. Suit was then filed against the Moseley's, alleging, "the dilution of famous marks" under the FTDA.

The Supreme Court stated that:

Noting that petitioners did not challenge Victoria Secret's claim that its mark is "famous," the only question it had to decide was whether petitioners' use of their mark diluted the quality of respondents' mark. Reasoning from the premise that dilution "corrodes" a trademark either by "blurring its product identification or by damaging positive associations that have attached to it," the court first found the two marks to be sufficiently similar to cause dilution, and then found "that Defendants" mark dilutes Plaintiffs' mark because of its tarnishing effect upon the Victoria's Secret mark. It therefore enjoined petitioners from using the mark "Victor's Little Secret" on the basis that it causes dilution of the distinctive quality of the Victoria's Secret mark.

The Court went on by stating:

1. The FTDA requires proof of actual dilution.

    (a) Unlike traditional infringement law, the prohibitions against trademark dilution are not the product of common-law development, and are not motivated by an interest in protecting consumers. The approximately 25 state trademark dilution laws predating the FTDA refer both to injury to business reputation (tarnishment) and to dilution of the distinctive quality of a trademark or trade name (blurring). The FTDA's legislative history mentions that the statute's purpose is to protect famous trademarks from subsequent uses that blur the mark's distinctiveness or tarnish or disparage it, even absent a likelihood of confusion.

    (b) Respondents' mark is unquestionably valuable, and petitioners have not challenged the conclusion that it is "famous." Nor do they contend that protection is confined to identical uses of famous marks or that the statute should be construed more narrowly in a case such as this. They do contend, however, that the statute requires proof of actual harm, rather than mere "likelihood" of harm. The contrast between the state statutes and the federal statute sheds light on this precise question. The former repeatedly refer to a "likelihood" of harm, rather than a completed harm, but the FTDA provides relief if another's commercial use of a mark or trade name "causes dilution of the [mark's] distinctive quality." Thus, it unambiguously requires an actual dilution showing. This conclusion is confirmed by the FTDA's "dilution" definition itself. That does not mean that the consequences of dilution, such as an actual loss of sales or profits, must also be proved. This Court disagrees with the Fourth Circuit's Ringling Bros. decision to the extent it suggests otherwise, but agrees with that court's conclusion that, at least where the marks at issue are not identical, the mere fact that consumers mentally associate the junior user's mark with a famous mark is not sufficient to establish actionable dilution. Such association will not necessarily reduce the famous mark's capacity to identify its owner's goods, the FTDA's dilution requirement.

2. The evidence in this case is insufficient to support summary judgment on the dilution count. There is a complete absence of evidence of any lessening of the VICTORIA'S SECRET mark's capacity to identify and distinguish goods or services sold in Victoria's Secret stores or advertised in its catalogs. The officer who saw the ad directed his offense entirely at petitioners, not respondents. And respondents' expert said nothing about the impact of petitioners' name on the strength of respondents' mark. Any difficulties of proof that may be entailed in demonstrating actual dilution are not an acceptable reason for dispensing with proof of an essential element of a statutory violation.

The Trademark Dilution Revision Act of 2006

On October 6, 2006, President George W. Bush signed into law H.R. 683, the Trademark Dilution Revision Act of 2006 (TDRA), which alters the Federal Trademark Dilution law in several respects. Mainly, the law overrules the Supreme Court's 2003 decision in *Moseley* v. *V Secret Catalogue Inc.*

In contrast to a claim for trademark infringement, (which requires a claimant to prove "likelihood of confusion" between its trademark and a mark used by the defendant), dilution law requires no evidence of likelihood of confusion and gives famous mark-holders the power to prevent use of their marks even in unrelated fields.

The decision in *Moseley* imposed an unfairly high burden of proof to establish dilution, but did not provide clear guidelines on how to satisfy that burden. In contrast, H.R. 683 is the result of a concerted effort to lower the burden of proof for federal dilution claims and to clear up confusion among the courts on other issues that often present themselves in dilution litigation.

The TDRA includes the following:

1. It clarifies that only truly famous marks are entitled to protection against dilution and permits courts to "consider all relevant factors" (including several identified in the statute) in order to determine whether a claimants' mark is famous enough to be protected. Accordingly, marks possessing only "niche fame—that is, fame in a narrow cross-section of the consuming public—are not protected, contrary to some prior court decisions.
2. It emphasizes that famous marks that have acquired their "distinctiveness" (by developing "secondary meaning") are entitled to the same protection against dilution as marks that are inherently distinctive. This overrules a group of cases from the Second Circuit that barred dilution claims involving marks that were not inherently distinctive.
3. It emphasizes that "dilution by tarnishment" (defined in the statute as an association arising from the similarity between the claimants' famous mark and a mark used by another that harms the reputation of the famous mark) is actionable under federal law. Some courts had held that only "dilution by blurring" (association due to similarity that "impairs the distinctiveness" of the famous mark) was actionable.

The TDRA contains safeguards against overreaching by claimants as well. It excludes from liability "any fair use, including a nominative or descriptive fair use, or facilitation of such fair use, of a famous mark by another person other than as a designation of source." It also permits the use of famous marks in connection with comparative advertising, parody and criticism, news reporting, and for other "non-commercial" purposes.

On the one hand, only owners of demonstrably famous marks will be able to seek relief for dilution in federal court. This will bring the Lanham Act into balance with the common law roots of dilution, which traditionally has been viewed as an exceptional form of protection reserved for exceptional marks. Conversely, famous mark owners will now have the benefit of a significantly reduced burden of proof in attacking and seeking injunctive relief (and damages) for unauthorized use that threatens their marks and their products and services.

The Anticybersquatting Consumer Protection Act

With the exponential growth of the Internet, the Anticybersquatting Consumer Protection Act (ACPA), 15 USC §1125(D) "was intended to prevent 'cybersquatting,' an expression that has come to mean the bad faith, abusive registration and use of the distinctive trademarks of others as Internet domain names, with the intent to profit from the goodwill associated with those trademarks" (*Shields v. Zuccarini*).

The ACPA has been used to correct a number of issues inherent with the Internet. These include "cybersquatting," which occurs when a registrant obtains a domain name containing another's mark and subsequently offers to sell it to the mark. The ACPA has also been used to prevent domain registrants from improperly profiting from the commercial use of another's mark, such as by selling or displaying ads for products that compete with those of the mark holder at a domain that contains the mark. Further the ACPA has also been successfully used to prevent tarnishment of a mark by its use in the domain of a website containing pornographic or other materials that the mark holder does not want his mark associated with. Also, the ACPA has been used to combat gripe sites; websites that are critical of the mark holder which are set up at a domain containing his mark.

Prevailing with an ACPA claim, first requires that the defendant has been found to "register, traffic in or use" the offending domain name. Second, it must be established that the domain name was "identical or confusingly similar" to a "distinctive" mark, or identical, confusingly similar or dilutive of a "famous" mark.

In the case of the ACPA , a court can order the forfeiture or cancellation of the offending domain name or its transfer to the owner of the mark. The mark owner can also recover up to three times actual damages and obtain injunctive relief. Actual damages includes profits the domain name registrant made from his use of the mark, as well as losses sustained by the mark holder as a result of those actions. In lieu of actual damages, the mark owner can elect to recover statutory damages of between $1,000 and $100,000 per domain. In "exceptional cases," attorney's fees may also be awarded.

Shields v. *Zuccarini* Example

A pivotal case regarding the ACPA was *Shields* v. *Zuccarini*, 254 F3d 476 (3d Cir. 2001). Joseph Shields was a graphic artist who created, exhibited and marketed cartoons under the names "Joe Cartoon" and "The Joe Cartoon Co." Noted for his crude humor and tongue-in-cheek violence, Joe Cartoons were among the first widely distributed web-based productions of their kind. His creations included the popular "Frog Blender," "Micro-Gerbil" and "Live and Let Dive" animations. Shields licensed his cartoons to others for display on T-shirts, coffee mugs and other items, many of which are sold at gift stores across the country. He had marketed his cartoons under the "Joe Cartoon" label for many years.

On June 12, 1997, Shields registered the domain name joecartoon.com, and he has operated it as a web site ever since (other than a two year break on YouTube). Visitors to the site could download his animations and purchase Joe Cartoon merchandise. Joe Cartoon's web traffic had increased exponentially, averaging over seven hundred thousand visits per month.

In November 1999, John Zuccarini, a "wholesaler" of Internet domain names, registered five variations on Shields's site: joescartoon.com, joecarton.com, joescartons.com, joescartoons.com and cartoonjoe.com. Zuccarini's sites featured advertisements for other sites and for credit card companies. In essence, visitors were trapped in the sites and were unable to exit without clicking on a succession of banner advertisements. Zuccarini received between ten and twenty-five cents from the advertisers for every click.

The court clarified this case: "On November 29, 1999, the ACPA became law, making it illegal for a person to register or to use with the "bad faith" intent to profit from an Internet domain name that is "identical or confusingly similar" to the distinctive or famous trademark or Internet domain name of another person or company. See *15 U.S.C. ß 1125(d) (Supp. 2000)*. The Act was intended to prevent "cybersquatting," an expression that has come to mean the bad faith, abusive registration and use of the distinctive trademarks of others as Internet domain names, with the intent to profit from the goodwill associated with those trademarks."

As to Zuccarini's role, the court said: "Although Zuccarini's sites did not involve pornography, his intent was the same as that mentioned in the legislative history above—to register a domain name in anticipation that consumers would make a mistake, thereby increasing the number of hits his site would receive, and, consequently, the number of advertising dollars he would gain. We conclude that Zuccarini's conduct here is a classic example of a specific practice the ACPA was designed to prohibit. The district court properly found that the domain names he registered were "confusingly similar.""

The court awarded statutory damages in the amount of $10,000 for each infringing domain name and attorneys' fees and costs in the amount of $39,109.46.

Nissan v. Nissan Example

In the case of *Nissan Motor Co., Ltd.* v. *Nissan Computer Corporation*, 2002 U.S. Dist. LEXIS 6488; 61 U.S.P.Q.2D (BNA) 1839 (2002), we see a different result.

Nissan Motor Co., Ltd., is one of the six largest automobile manufacturers in the world. Nissan Motor Co. owns various registered trademarks using the word "Nissan" in connection with automobiles and other vehicles. The first such trademark was registered in 1959. Nissan North America also operates an Internet website at www.nissan-usa.com.

The defendant, Nissan Computer Corporation, was a North Carolina company in the business of computer sales and services. The company was incorporated in 1991 by Uzi Nissan. In 1995, the defendant registered a trademark for its Nissan Computer logo with the state of North Carolina.

Nissan Motor Co. (unlike Toyota) was not named after a real person. In 1928, Yoshisuke Aikawa founded the holding company Nihon Sangyo, which owned what would become the automobile manufacturer. Nissan, in fact, was an abbreviation of Nihon Sangyo, that was used on the Tokyo stock market.

In October 1999, the parties met to discuss the possible transfer of the nissan. com domain name. In the course of these discussions, Mr. Nissan stated that he would not sell the domain name except for several million dollars, and made a proposal involving monthly payments in perpetuity. It's no surprise that negotiations were unsuccessful.

The court, in this case, stated: "The domain name at issue 'consists of the legal name' of the owner of the corporation and the licensor of the 'Nissan' name, both of which are Mr. Nissan. Moreover, the fact that domain name consists of the surname of the owner of the corporation, distinguishes the instant case from traditional cybersquatting fact patterns. Here, the defendant registered 'nissan.com' and started the website in connection with its legitimate computer business. Additionally, the defendant does not have a pattern of registering famous trademarks and extorting them to the owners."

The traditional cybersquatting pattern is where a third party intentionally registers someone else's trademark, with the intent of preventing the rightful owner from using it as a domain name. This is usually with the intent of profiting by selling it to the trademark owner or otherwise taking commercial advantage of it.

In this case, the plaintiffs contended that, although courts should protect those who use their legal name as part of a business, when that name has already become famous as a trademark, a latecomer may not be allowed to use the name in a commercially confusing manner. The court reasoned that: "[a]lthough this Court has found that the defendant has infringed on the plaintiffs' trademark regarding auto related goods and services, that does not necessarily mean that the defendant's use of 'nissan.com' is cybersquatting. Indeed, the ACPA 'does not extend to . . . someone who is aware of the trademark status of the name but registers a domain name containing the mark for any reason other than with bad faith intent to profit from the goodwill associated with that mark.' The ACPA was intended to combat cybersquatting not trademark infringement. Accordingly, the defendant's infringement of the plaintiffs' trademark regarding auto related goods and services, does not establish that the defendant possessed the bad faith intent to profit from the plaintiffs' mark as required under the ACPA."

Essentially, the statutory requirement of bad faith under the ACPA favored the defendant. The court concluded: "The facts of the instant case do not present a situation where the defendant engaged in conduct that was meant to be outlawed as cybersquatting. Indeed, the facts of the instant case are readily distinguishable from those in which the courts have found actionable cybersquatting."

Trademarks under State Law

While the Trademark Act grants protection of trademarks on a federal level, the separate states can also grant trademark registration. As mentioned earlier, if the trademark will only be used within a state, a state registered trademark may be filed. However, state trademarks don't have the same level of protection as federally registered marks, as we saw.

In addition, trademarks for professional services may be registered by the state. This applies only to businesses that the state categorizes as "professional" (doctors, attorneys, certified public accountants, etc.). These firms, which are prohibited from using fictitious names, may trademark their firm name even though they are using surnames. The regulations of the respective state should be considered in these situations.

Contests and Lotteries 11

We are so busy measuring public opinion that we forget we can mold it. We are so busy listening to statistics we forget we can create them.

—*Bill Bernbach*

The summer of 1955 brought the era of the game show—long before "Wheel of Fortune" or "Jeopardy" were conceived. All across America people tuned in to watch an immigrant welder win a fortune through his knowledge of art or a file clerk dazzle the audience with her grasp of opera trivia—the common citizen getting the chance to become richer than his or her wildest hopes. The things dreams are made of—to win a fortune on such shows as "Twenty-One" (portrayed in the movie *Quiz Show*), "The $64,000 Question," "Tic-Tac-Dough," "Name That Tune," "Dotto," and "The Big Surprise." All for that moment of glory. As Andy Warhol put it: ". . . everyone will be world famous for fifteen minutes."

To assure honesty, the questions were guarded so that no one could discover them, or their answers. The audience was sure that contestants could not possibly have known what they would be asked. On many shows isolation booths were used so that the contestants could not get help from the audience. Some shows went so far as to lock the questions, and answers, in a bank vault, and then have them hand-delivered to the host by bank officials accompanied by armed guards.

The tension would build with each question, and the audience would sigh with relief after each correct answer. The appeal of the game show was what appeared to be the unrehearsed spontaneity of the shows (reality TV of that era), and that the contestants were masters of certain areas of knowledge, memory, and intelligence. These game shows were a spectacle to behold. The audiences became engrossed in the show, and they were just that—all show.

In July 1958, the Federal Communications Commission (FCC) was drawn into the scene when a contestant of "Dotto" complained that the show was rigged. Not much resulted from this investigation. The station denied any wrong-doing, and the case was dropped. But news had leaked out, and the game show scandal began to draw public attention. In late 1959, a subcommittee of the House Committee on Interstate and Foreign Commerce opened hearings on the matter.

Witnesses (previous contestants) who were called before the subcommittee testified that they were given the questions and in many cases the answers as well.

Some were given scripts to memorize. Even the theatrics of their responses were coached. Despair, agony, exuberance, elation were all prerehearsed to create the desired effect for the audience.

Good-looking contestants were promoted to increase the television audience; unattractive ones were routinely eliminated (or so the producers would try). Dr. Joyce Brothers, who subsequently became a well-known psychologist and advice columnist, was one such contestant. The producers of the game show tried to get her to lose the game, but her knowledge of boxing was so extensive that she answered every question they threw at her.

Quite obviously the game shows were fixed, and the advertising community was also involved. The advertisers and their agencies were the ones who were truly in control of the purse-strings. At that time, unlike today, it was common for a single advertiser to sponsor an entire show, therefore wielding a tremendous amount of control over the show and its content to the point where the advertiser actually directed the contestant briefing.

Since then, contests of every kind have drawn acute attention from the networks, the FTC, and courts alike. Sometimes they are called games, sweepstakes, games-of-chance, or just contests. Regardless of the name, the intention is obvious. The advertiser expects that the consumer will enter the contest and be drawn to its product.

In other words, contests generate interest because they get the consumer involved. They appeal to a basic human trait—the very human desire to get something for nothing. The real intent, then, is to transfer this desire to the product and, with that, increase sales.

Somewhere, right now, people are filling out entry forms and dreaming of what they'll do with the money if they win; winning an easy reward for little effort is a dream for many people. Yet, the odds of winning a contest are extremely low. For example, the odds to win first prize in the current *Reader's Digest* Million Dollar Payday Sweepstakes are about one in 49.5 million.

What does an advertiser need to be concerned with when creating and promoting a contest? Actually, the answer is very simple.

There are clear guidelines for advertisers who want to run a contest. If the contest is structured according to these guidelines, the games are legal. However, should a game fall outside the guidelines, it will be considered a lottery—which is gambling and is illegal (unless government sponsored and regulated). To prevent an illegal lottery, there are specific and stringent laws that control contests. This heavy regulation evolved because contests closely resemble lotteries by their nature. In the states that permit this form of gambling, it is very heavily regulated just like all forms of gambling including casinos. For the advertiser, a contest must not be allowed to cross over the line and become a lottery.

What Constitutes an Illegal Lottery

Today, many states have sponsored lotteries to raise funds for various government institutions. In California, for example, the proceeds from their lottery were intended to benefit public education. In Colorado, lottery profits were intended to benefit state parks and recreation areas. With the growth and popularity of these lotteries, many companies have jumped on the contest bandwagon. Companies that had not been involved with contests in the past have begun promoting their products through contests and sweepstakes of every kind. In this chapter we will not be considering casino gambling issues. Casino gaming is a niche area that is beyond the scope of this book. The true focus of this chapter is to understand how advertisers and marketers can keep their mass-consumer contests from becoming illegal lotteries.

In order to remain within the boundaries of a legal contest, it is important to understand what situations will be considered an illegal lottery so they can be avoided. The generally accepted definition of a lottery is "a chance or chances taken, for a consideration, in the hope or expectation that something would be obtained of greater value than that which was given up, but with the full knowledge that nothing at all might be obtained . . ." (*United States* v. *83 Cases of Merchandise Labeled "Honest John,"* 29 F. Supp. 912, at 915 (D.C. Md., 1939)).

The difference between a contest and a lottery is quite simple, and advertisers must understand the difference. Let's take a look at the three basic conditions that create a lottery:

- A prize must be offered;
- The entrant must give up something (consideration) in order to participate; and
- Winning must involve an element of chance rather than skill.

If one, or more, of these elements is missing, a lottery does not exist. All three are required for a lottery. Two elements occur in most all games of chance: a prize and chance. The tricky element, as you'll see, is consideration.

In the late 1930s the government confiscated 83 cases of merchandise marked "Honest John," "Wonder Store," and "Diamond Store." Each of these boxes contained smaller boxes with a number on each. On the main display case were small pull-tabs, which a consumer would remove to reveal a number underneath.

The consumer purchased a chance to remove one pull-tab for 1, 2, or 5 cents. After the pull-tab was removed to reveal a number, the consumer got the prize in the small box that had the same number on it. Each box contained a small amount of inexpensive candy and some other trinket. The value of the items in the prize boxes was only a few cents, and each box contained a prize of equal value.

Now the question is, was that a legal contest or an illegal lottery? That question was answered by the court in *U.S.* v. *83 Cases of Merchandise Labeled "Honest John,"* 29 F. Supp. 912 (D.C. Md., 1939). The court examined the three elements that needed to exist in order for this to be a lottery: a prize, consideration, and chance. In this case, "there is no single prize, no group of prizes, but a prize given for every chance that is taken."

In a lottery, the consumer takes a chance on winning a prize that is much greater than the price paid to participate. In this case there was no substantial difference between the amount of money that the participant paid and the value of what would be received. In essence there was no "prize" involved.

No chance was involved either, because all participants received an item for their participation in the game. This game, then, was a legal contest because it did not meet all three of the elements required of a lottery. This early case, however, defined the conditions of what constituted a legal contest and an illegal lottery.

Prize as an Element

Most games of chance end with a winner, or a couple of winners, who receive a prize. A prize is a special item given to the winner. It is also what is used to induce the consumer to enter the game.

Prizes can range from cash, to cars, vacations, merchandise, to just about anything. A number of years ago Zerex antifreeze (now owned by Valvoline), made by DuPont Corporation, offered as first prize in its contest a radiator filled with Zerex antifreeze. What made this prize worth winning was the fact that the radiator was installed in a new Rolls-Royce.

If every entrant receives a gift of equal value, and in the same way, then no "prize" is awarded. We saw this in the *83 Cases* case just discussed. If the gifts have different values (and if the other two elements also exist), the game is considered a lottery.

In the early 1900s, a company in Georgia named Purvis Investments offered a plan to customers. The plan involved offering a loan on very favorable terms to the first few people who mailed in an investment of a specific amount. However, the investment return was not as good as other savings institutions at the time. The main feature of the scheme was the possibility of obtaining a loan at better than average rates. That was the incentive for entering the "contest" and paying the investment amount. The customer's payment of the investment constituted "consideration."

When entries were received at the company, they were opened and numbered. But if a batch of entries were received in the same day's mail, it would be pure chance which envelope was opened first. So, we have the element of chance. When this scheme made its way to the courts in *United States* v. *Purvis*, 195 F. 618 (N.D. Ga. 1912), the court said, "it was of course a mere matter of chance as to which the . . . clerk . . . should take up first, as he opened and entered them."

The final element necessary for this to be a lottery was the existence of a prize. In this case the prize was an opportunity to obtain a loan on favorable terms. "It was the desire to obtain loans on the very attractive terms proposed . . . which made these contracts so much favored and which induced the purchase of these loan contracts," the court stated. The investment return itself was not particularly attractive. Better returns could have been achieved at other savings institutions. But the chance to obtain one of the loans was a thing of value. It also made this qualify as the element of a prize. The scheme was held to be a lottery.

Consideration as an Element

The next element of a lottery is consideration. If the other two elements exist but there is no consideration, then there is no lottery. But what is the definition of consideration? Many acts can constitute consideration. Even a forbearance (a promise to not do something) can be consideration. Yet, the most obvious form of consideration is money. There are others, and we look at those here.

It is extremely important to understand that what we are discussing are general rules under federal law. Each state, as well, has specific laws concerning what it feels qualifies as consideration in relation to a lottery. We'll look at these later in this chapter. Without exception, the advertiser should check into the laws of any state in which it intends to promote a contest.

As just explained, the exact definition of consideration varies from state to state. But generally, consideration can be money or anything of value. It can also be an act such as exerting substantial time and effort in some way. In Wisconsin, which is unique in this respect, consideration is defined by statute as "anything which is a commercial or financial advantage to the promoter or a disadvantage to any participant" (Wisconsin Statutes Annotated, section 945.01(2)(b)(1)(1981)). What this means is that some states (including Wisconsin) feel that any burden put on the participant constitutes consideration. But, generally, the requirement that a consumer visit the store to obtain game pieces is not interpreted as consideration.

Around 1950 George Wagner was the Postmaster of Garden City, New York. Mr. Wagner wanted to ban the mailing of a card that he felt constituted a lottery. Here's how the game worked. The consumer who received the card in the mail would remove the coupon portion which contained a number. Then the consumer kept the coupon and mailed the other portion of the card to the Garden City Chamber of Commerce.

Later, the consumer visited the stores that participated in the game. If the consumer saw an article in the store window that had the same number as the person's coupon, the store would give the item as a prize. In essence, this was a treasure hunt.

The question is, does the act of visiting stores create a consideration which would make this a lottery? That question was answered in *Garden City Chamber of Commerce v. Wagner*, 100 F. Supp. 769 (E.D.N.Y. 1951). The court agreed, on one point, with the Postmaster who brought the suit by stating: "consideration is present in the substantial amount of time and effort involved in examining the various prizes to ascertain whether one holds a winning ticket."

As seen earlier, consideration can take the form of a payment of money, purchase of a ticket, or the expenditure of substantial time or effort. The basis of the controversy in this case, however, is whether the act of visiting a store "actually involves an expenditure of substantial effort and time." The court ruled that it did not, saying: "[We] have found no case in which the element of consideration has resided in walking or driving to look in a window."

Generally, situations that are not classified as consideration include requiring participants to:

- Visit a store to enter;
- Return to store to learn of winners;
- Visit different stores;
- Witness a demonstration or take a demonstration ride; or
- Pay postage.

Once again, it is important to consult specific state statutes for exact current regulations.

Now let's look at typical situations involving consideration.

Use of Consumer's Name or Likeness as Consideration Requiring the authorization to use the name or likeness of a participant or winner could be held that consideration was given because there is consent to do something in the future. It is consideration notwithstanding the future performance aspects of the consent.

The Gift Enterprise as Consideration In many cases the consumer must purchase the advertiser's product to qualify for the contest. Then usually a proof of purchase in the form of a box top, wrapper, facsimile, or the like is sent in to register for the contest, or it is done online. This is known as a "gift enterprise."

Even though the price of the product remains the same, there is consideration because the consumer is required to do something. The consumer is required to make a purchase.

Therefore, a gift enterprise scheme involves the element of consideration. This explains the common "No purchase required" disclaimer used in many contests.

There is another situation that is very closely related to a pure gift enterprise. That involves games where a lottery is created when a customer must promise to buy a product to enter a game. A good example of this situation occurred in 1976, with a radio promotion called "Dial-a-Discount."

Don J. Plumridge Advertising in Washington, D.C., developed a radio campaign for one of its clients, Allyn's Pants Ranch (see box 11.1 for a typical commercial from the campaign). The concept of the game was pretty straightforward. The customer took a pair of pants to the counter where the Wheel of Fortune was spun. Wherever the wheel stopped was the amount of the discount off the purchase price of the pants.

Allyn's Pants Ranch Radio Commercial

Dial your own discount on a pair of pants. This is our Pants Ranch Wheel of Fortune. On it are various dollar amounts. Two dollars, three dollars, four, five, and ten dollars. After you purchase any pair of pants—and the Pants Ranch has over forty thousand to choose from—you get to dial your own discount. What you spin on the wheel is what you save on the purchase of your first pair of pants. If the wheel stops on "freebie," lucky you! Cause there's no charge. The pants are on us!

When the FCC found out about the game, a complaint was initiated: *In the Matter of Metromedia Inc.*, 60 F.C.C. 2d 1075 (1976).

The commission discussed the following: "Whether a 'Dial-a-Discount' participant's commitment to purchase a pair of pants alone [constituted] the requisite element of consideration, since if money has not yet changed hands, any participant may refuse to pay after spinning the discount wheel and return the pants to the shelf."

However, the game rules required this agreement to pay in order to participate, and therefore, consideration existed because there was an "agreement" to pay at least the regular price of a pair of pants in order to participate. This game was an illegal lottery because it required that the consumer purchase the pants without knowing, in advance, the amount of the discount. Metromedia lost the case and was required to pay a $16,000 fine for promoting an illegal lottery.

Free Airline Tickets as Consideration In *Consumer Protection Division* v. *Luskins, Inc.*, 706 A.2d 102 (1998), the office of the Attorney General of Maryland proceeded against Luskin's for an appliance store advertisement that offered consumers two free airline tickets for any purchase of $200 or more (see box 11.2). The state claimed that the offer violated Section 13-305 of Maryland's Consumer Protection Act that prohibits a person from notifying another person of eligibility to receive something of value if the purchase of goods or services is required.

The first print ad Luskin's ran included the following:

FREE* AIRFARE FOR TWO . . .

TO FLORIDA, THE BAHAMAS OR HAWAII.

* Buy an Appliance, TV, Stereo, VCR, or any Purchase over $200

And You'll Get a Big Gift For Two (Round Trip Airfares).

Buy Selected Items for $200-$299. Get Airfare for 2 To/From FLORIDA.

Buy Selected Items for $300-$399.

Get Airfare for 2 To/From BAHAMAS. Buy Selected Items over $400.

Get Airfare for 2 To/From HAWAII.

TICKETS MUST BE USED WITHIN ONE YEAR.

ASK FOR DETAILS.

* Vacations Premiums Offered Through Vacation Ventures, Inc. Which is not affiliated with Luskin's. Minimum Hotel Stay Required. See Store For Details . . . Applicable Taxes Apply. See Store For Details.

There were several versions of the television ad. All versions contained some form of disclaimer regarding the free airfare, typically, "minimum hotel stay required." The disclaimers, in fine print at the bottom of the screen, were shown only for brief periods. One advertisement stated, "Min. hotel stay req. Offered through Vacation Ventures, Inc. which is not affiliated [with] or guaranteed by Luskin's. Taxes apply. Details at store." Even the fastest speed reader could not have finished reading the statement before it disappeared from the screen.

The Luskin's ad stated that consumers would receive free airfare for two to Florida, the Bahamas, or Hawaii if the consumer purchased an appliance, TV, stereo, VCR, or any purchase over $200. The ads appeared in newspapers and on television.

Of the advertising, the court reasoned:

> Luskin's advertising campaign ran afoul of the definition set forth in section 13-301(1) by misleading consumers into thinking that they would receive free airfare when, in fact, they were given a travel certificate for a vacation program that would cost a minimum of "hundreds of dollars" to redeem. [E]ven if consumers had carefully read the advertisement, the disclaimer was ambiguous because "consumers reasonably could assume that they had to arrange for and pay for hotel accommodations themselves," which was not permitted under any of the travel packages. [T]he disclaimer did not dispel the impression that the "airfare primarily was conditioned upon the purchase of consumer goods at Luskin's and that any further condition or requirement would be secondary;" the cost of purchasing the consumer goods, however, became secondary, when compared with the cost of redeeming the travel certificate.

Sections 13-305 (a) and (b) of the Maryland statute stated as follows: "A person may not notify any other person by any means, as part of an advertising scheme or plan, that the other person has won a prize, received an award, or has been selected or is eligible to receive anything of value if the other person is required to purchase goods or services, pay any money to participate in, or submit to a sales promotion effort."

Luskin's argued that § 13-305(b) only applied in situations where individuals were notified by mail that they were specially selected to receive a prize. The court held, however, that § 13-305(b) applied since the statute clearly stated that a person may not notify any other person by any means that they had won a prize. The Luskin's promotion was illegal because it met each element of the statute:

1. Luskin's newspaper and television ads notified individuals;
2. The airline tickets qualified as something of value; and
3. Having to purchase a $200 item from Luskins qualified as a requirement to purchase goods.

Luskin's then argued that they were exempt under subsection (a)(3), which exempts offers of savings on consumer goods or services including one-cent sales, two-for-the-price-of-one sales, or manufacturers cents-off coupons. However, the court held that the Luskin's promotion did not offer any savings on consumer goods.

Presence at the Drawing as Consideration Here again there is a difference of opinion. But most states feel that requiring participants to be present in order to win a drawing is consideration.

Obstacles in Obtaining Entry Forms as Consideration If free entry forms for a game are offered but the company has irregular office hours, a problem can result. Also, if the participant must, let's say, purchase a newspaper to obtain entry forms, an illegal lottery exists. The purchase of the newspaper is consideration. In other words, entry forms must be made readily available, and a purchase must not be required in order to obtain an entry form. Otherwise, consideration is given.

The following case provides a good example of obstacles for participants. Dreem Arts, Inc., published a newspaper in Chicago called *Nightmoves*. The paper cost $2 and contained a game called "Pick and Play." The idea of the game was for the reader to pick the winners of upcoming professional and college football games. All upcoming games were listed, along with the point spread. Participants mailed in their entry blank listing the teams they picked to win. If an entrant picked ten winning teams, the prize was $1,000 in cash. Other prizes were available if a person picked at least four winning teams. The advertised contest rules were as follows: "Free contest entry forms are available at office of publisher. Please send stamped self-addressed envelope and free entry form will be mailed to you; a reasonable hand-drawn facsimile can be used—in addition to stores and newsstands, copies of Nightmoves are available at Chicago public libraries for your inspection (no limit to number of contest entries.) . . . No purchase necessary—tax liabilities for all prizes are the sole responsibility of winners."

Late in 1985 the Chicago Police Department confiscated newspapers from various locations, and *Dreem Arts, Inc.* v. *City of Chicago*, 637 F. Supp. 53 (N.D. Ill. 1986), was the result. A detective investigated the case and found that the *Nightmoves* offices had no sign displayed. The office was closed, and no employees were present. He was unable to obtain the "free entry form." The detective also tried to obtain an entry blank by mail, but none was ever received. Another detective visited over twenty-four Chicago libraries, none of which had ever subscribed to the newspaper.

If the consumer is allowed to submit a reasonable facsimile for an entry, no consideration exists. There is a problem, though, when the consumer can't get a copy from which to make a facsimile without buying something. That was the case here.

Obviously the publisher devised the rules to "purposely [make] it more difficult to obtain free entry forms than to pay the $2 newsstand price of *Nightmoves*." The court found that the obstacles in obtaining free entry blanks made this option inordinately difficult. Because the only realistic way to enter the game was to pay the $2 price of the newspaper, this was consideration, and that made the game an illegal lottery.

Scratch-and-Win and Consideration Treasured Arts, Inc. (TAI) sold the Treasured Arts Power Call Card for $2. The card allowed three minutes of long distance telephone time provided by United States Long Distance (USLD). The card was perforated so that it could be torn in half: one side was a "scratch-and-win" game piece, and the other side had instructions on how to receive the long distance time. With the "scratch-and-win" game, the purchaser could win prizes ranging from $1 to $50,000.

The Mississippi Gaming Commission (MGC) argued that the card constituted a lottery since the purchaser received nothing of value when purchasing the card. Therefore, the money paid for the card was actually consideration for an opportunity to play the game.

Here in *Mississippi Gaming Commission* v. *Treasured Arts, Inc.*, 699 So.2d 936 (Miss. 1997), we see an example of what was ultimately considered a legal promotion and not an illegal lottery under Mississippi law.

The relevant Mississippi Code (Miss. Code Ann. § 75-76-3) states that a lottery consists of: the offering of a prize; the awarding of a prize by chance; and the giving of consideration for the opportunity to win the prize. All three elements must exist to constitute an illegal lottery.

In analyzing the issues here, the court stated: "The parties are in disagreement as to whether a purchaser of a Card actually pays any consideration for the opportunity to chance to win a prize such that there is a violation of subsection (a) of the statute. TAI asserts that the consideration paid for the Card is paid for the card itself and not for the game piece attached. If true, this would mean no consideration is paid for the opportunity to win a prize and the product does not constitute a lottery. However, the MGC claims the purchaser of a Card is paying more than the maximum retail value for per minute long distance time, which results in consideration for the opportunity to win the monetary prizes offered by TAI."

MGC presented evidence from another long distance carrier, LDDS WorldCom. The evidence indicated the price LDDS WorldCom charged per minute with its PhonePass prepaid phone card, and what it claimed was the maximum typical retail value of the per-minute phone time on these types of cards, was $0.45. MGC contended that since the price of the card exceeded the usual price per minute for long distance time, consumers were giving something of value for the chance to win a prize.

On the other hand, Treasured Arts presented testimony from USLD that the actual price charged by USLD per minute for long distance time was $0.66. The Treasured Arts card sold for $2 and provided three minutes of long distance time. Therefore, each minute cost a fraction over $0.66. It was determined that (essentially) no additional consideration was paid by the purchasers of the card for an opportunity to win a prize.

The court stated: "In a capitalistic society competition is the axis on which a free market turns. The MGC's argument that a price charged by one long distance carrier which exceeds the price charged by another is necessarily consideration for an opportunity to win a prize is without merit. The lower court should have never considered the affidavit of [LDDS] as binding authority as to what 'the maximum retail value' of long distance service should be. Granted it is authority as to what LDDS WorldCom charges for its long distance time. But there is not one scintilla of evidence that what one company charges for long distance time is binding on another as the maximum retail value."

In affirming the lower courts decision, this court went on:

> The lower court granted summary judgment based on evidence that the Card had some value. The court stated that it mattered not whether the Card was worth $.66 or $.14, it was apparent it was worth something. The court then narrowed its only issue to whether the consideration paid for the Card, which had some value, amounted to the giving of consideration for the game piece, which granted the chance to win a prize. The court then granted summary judgment based on its finding that the Card was an item that had value and consideration was paid for it and concluded no consideration was paid for the game piece. The lower court refused to get into a dispute as to whether the consideration paid for the Card was adequate or not, reasoning that this Court had never done so.
>
> We disagree that the amount of consideration is not at issue . . . Nevertheless, the lower court reached the correct result based on the evidence in the record before this Court. The affidavit of Melley and the fact that the game pieces could be obtained free through the mail support TAI's Motion for Summary Judgment. The MGC provided no evidence in the record to constitute a genuine issue of material fact. Therefore, the Court holds that TAI was entitled to a judgment as a matter of law.

Consideration in the Internet Era During broadcasts of the wildly popular television programs "American Idol" and "Deal or No Deal," viewers were able to participate in two cash giveaways (games). The promoters of these Games, ran commercials during each television broadcast inviting viewers to enter the Games for a chance to win cash prizes. In the "American Idol Challenge," viewers were given a trivia question about the "American Idol" show. Viewers could enter the drawing by submitting the correct answer within twenty-four hours, through a text message for a ninety-nine cent fee or through the internet at no charge. Viewers were allowed up to ten entries, and, for each correct submission, the viewer entered a drawing, from which the eventual winner was chosen at random.

As a result of these games, Darlene Couch, Karen Herbert, Judy Schenker, Jodi Eberhart, and Cheryl Bentley entered but did not win a prize. As the court irreverently stated in *Couch* v. *Telescope Inc.*, 611 F.3d 629; 2010 U.S. App. LEXIS 13937 (2010): "Unsuccessful but undaunted, they turned to the high-stakes world of class action litigation. Seeking to represent a class of all individuals who paid the ninety-nine cent text message fee to enter the Games but lost, plaintiffs filed suit in federal court, claiming that the Games are an illegal lottery under *California Penal Code ß 319* and thus constitute unfair business practices."

Defendants, owned by Fox Broadcasting, claimed that the third element, consideration, was missing because the Games had a free method of entry (the Internet) available to all participants. But the important question is not whether some people could enter for free.

The offer of a free alternative method of entry does not change the fact that viewers who sent in text messages paid only for the privilege of entering the Games. They received nothing of equivalent economic value in return. As a result, the court held: ". . . the Court finds that Plaintiffs have sufficiently alleged that Defendants conducted illegal lotteries as defined by California law."

Chance as an Element

Chance is another element that must exist in order to qualify as a lottery. If chance dominates the game, rather than skill or judgment, it becomes a lottery. Chance is usually involved in games in which the participant must guess something to win—from guessing the number of beans in a jar to guessing the number of people that will attend a grand opening event. (There are other ways chance can create problems, and we look at those later.)

Chance is an interesting element. Pure chance is not the issue in most cases that have gone through the courts. Rather, the courts look to whether chance is the controlling factor in awarding prizes. For example, a dice game involves pure chance. On the other hand, a chess game involves pure skill. In the middle are card games, which are games of chance. They do not stop being games of chance simply because some element of skill is involved. Card games are still predominantly controlled by the luck of the draw.

One of my favorite examples of a game of chance involved a trade newspaper, the *United States Tobacco Journal*. The case occurred about 1900 and involved an advertisement for a game advertised in the newspaper (see box 11.3). It listed the prize to be awarded to the number of people who guessed next closest in descending order. At the end of the list were people who won $5 or a box of free cigars. In theory, over thirty-five thousand people could win something. Obviously, because of the newspaper's audience, the game was directed to retail sellers of cigars and other tobacco products. These retailers could make four estimates for every one hundred cigar bands sent in.

The game was sponsored by a cigar manufacturer, the Florodora Company. As part of the rules, the company allowed each Florodora cigar band to count as two for the purpose of entering the game. Suffice it to say that the purpose of Florodora was to increase sales of its brand of cigar. There is nothing wrong or illegal in this.

Box 11.3 **Florodora Company Ad**

The United States Tobacco Journal

SAVE OUR BANDS

Another free Distribution of $142,500.00 Will be made in December, 1903 Based on the Month of November, 1903 TO SMOKERS OF [Here follow the names of 30 brands of cigars.]

How many cigars (of all brands, no matter by whom manufactured) will the United States collect taxes on during the month of November, 1903? (Cigars bearing $3.00 tax per thousand) The persons who estimate nearest to the number of cigars on which $3.00 tax per thousand is paid during the month of November, 1903, as shown by the total sales of stamps made by the United States Internal Revenue Department during November, 1903, will be awarded as follows: To the person estimating the closest . . . $5,000 in cash.

Yet, the State of New York felt that the game was an illegal lottery, so they arrested the magazine publisher, Ismar Ellison. In many states, operating a lottery is a criminal offense; in this case it was a misdemeanor. The case was *People ex rel. Ellison* v. *Lavin*, 179 N.Y. 164 (1904). According to the elements of a lottery, this game provided for awarding prizes. It also possessed the element of consideration by requiring the dealer to purchase cigars from which to get the bands required to enter the game. "Therefore," said the court, "the only question presented by the case is whether the distribution is made by chance or not."

This game was a lottery because the outcome was based primarily on chance. That is not to say that there is no skill or judgment involved, but it is slight compared to the chance involved. "A lottery," said the court, "does not cease to be such . . . because its result may be affected, to some slight extent, by the exercise of judgment." In this case, the controlling factor in receiving a prize was chance, rather than skill or judgment.

Earlier in this chapter we looked at a case that involved picking the winners of upcoming football games. Surely chance is involved in that game, you may think. Not so. Let's look at a situation to explain why that is.

Charles Rich and Frank Camarrata ran a game for which they were essentially bookmakers. The two men solicited bets or wagers on the outcome of sporting events from horse racing to baseball. They also took bets on elections. A complaint was filed against these two men charging that they were operating an illegal lottery in *United States* v. *Rich*, 90 F. Supp. 624 (E.D. Ill. 1950).

The participant wagered an amount by placing a bet. The requirement of consideration was met. The participant also stood to win a large return if the right team won. That meant that the requirement of a prize was also present. What was left to be determined was whether the game involved chance. That was the issue that the court was left to ponder.

The court said about "chance" that ". . . the word has reference to the attempt to attain certain ends, not by skill or any known or fixed rules, but by the happening of a subsequent event, incapable of ascertainment or accomplishment by means of human foresight or ingenuity." Obviously, a blindfolded man pulling a winning ticket from a jar involves pure chance. Here, though, it's a different story.

The government argued that choosing the winner of a horse race or baseball game offered extremely narrow odds. Because of the huge amount of uncertainty, the winner could attribute the win to nothing more than a guess.

The court, however, felt that "there is always something more than a mere guess" involved, and they said: "The odds may often be long, and the chance of winning small so as to tempt the ignorant and the greedy to risk amounts small or large on the chance of getting a much larger return, and yet in every case there is a race or a game of skill or an election or something in which natural forces are involved and upon which knowledge, skill and judgment are brought into play."

In the case of a horse race, bets are placed on races that may be run quite some time in the future. Yet, the bets are placed based on information that can be obtained about the horses in advance. The stable that the horse comes from, the owner, the jockey, and the track are all considerations on which knowledge, skill, and judgment can be used to make a selection. There is no pure chance here as applied to lotteries. The government lost its case.

But chance in determining the winner is not the only way this element can be involved to turn a contest into a lottery. Chance is also created when the amount of the ultimate prize is unknown or undetermined. That is, when the amount of the prize is to be determined by some event yet to happen, like the dollar sales of a particular store on a certain day in the future. Another situation could exist when the prize depends on the number of people who ultimately enter the contest.

In 1963 Boris Zebelman was a car dealer in Gardner, Kansas. He developed a game to promote his dealership, which he advertised through the mail. He claimed that anyone who bought a car from him would become an "automobile owner representative." This rep would then submit names and addresses of others who would be potential buyers. For each person whose name was submitted and who purchased a car, also becoming a rep, the original rep would receive $100 in cash. Also, the original rep would receive $50 for each person whose name was submitted by the new participant, if that person bought a car and participated as a rep.

In other words, let's say Mr. Smith bought a car from Zebelman and became a rep. He would submit names of others including Ms. Jones. Now Ms. Jones buys a car and becomes a rep, and Mr. Smith receives $100. Then Ms. Jones submits the name of Mr. Adams, who buys a car and becomes a rep. In that case, Ms. Jones would receive $100, and Mr. Smith would receive $50.

If this sounds like a pyramid scheme, it is.

Zebelman was caught and charged with fifteen counts of running a lottery. The case was *Zebelman* v. *United States*, 339 F.2d 484 (10th Cir. 1964). The question here is tricky. Is chance involved? In the case of the original purchaser rep, the answer is no. In this phase of the game, chance is not the controlling factor. The person has control over this part of the game.

The chance element enters into the picture because "the original purchaser has no control over the payment or receipt of the $50 since it is the person whose name he submits that must locate another buyer." This situation requires, in large part, the element of chance, and this makes the scheme a lottery.

A Chance to Win Here's an interesting one. A group of car dealers (Classic Buick-GMC Truck, Inc., Bill Dodge Oldsmobile-Buick-Pontiac-GMC Truck, Inc., Westbrook Saturn, Inc., Infiniti of Falmouth, Inc., and Bill Dodge Ford-Lincoln-Mercury, Inc.) ran a promotion that said that any person who leased a new vehicle at one of their participating dealerships during a certain four-week period would win twelve monthly lease payments (paid by the dealership) if the local temperature equaled or exceeded 96 degrees Fahrenheit at the Portland, Maine, airport on a specified date.

The dealers also offered that any person, without purchasing or leasing any vehicle, could submit their name for a drawing during the same four-week period. The winner of the drawing would be eligible to receive $5,000 cash if the temperature reached or exceeded 96 degrees.

In *Classic Oldsmobile-Cadillac-GMC Truck* v. *State of Maine*, 704 A.2d 333 (Me. 1997), the court held the game to be an illegal game of chance under Maine law.

Under Maine law (17 M.R.S.A. § 330(2) (Supp. 1996), a game of chance is defined as:

A. A person stakes or risks something of value for the opportunity to win something of value;
B. The rules of operation or play require an event the result of which is determined by chance, outside the control of the contestant or participant; and
C. Chance enters as an element that influences the outcome in a manner that cannot be eliminated through the application of skill.

The dealership argued that the promotion was not an illegal lottery because it didn't require a purchase to participate. According to the second option, any person could submit his or her name and have the chance to win the $5,000 prize. However, the plan involved two promotions—one for those who entered into a lease agreement and one for those who did not. Under the plan, every lessee could win the lease payments if the specific temperature was reached, but the other entrants participated in a drawing in which only one person would win. The court found that these were two separate games. The promotion involving the vehicle lease constituted an unlawful game of chance.

The lease promotion involved an element of chance (the temperature on a future date at a particular location) that was outside the control of the entrants and one that could not be eliminated through the use of skill. The customer's lease and the twelve months of free lease payments constituted something of value. The only issue was if the entrant "staked or risked" any part of the lease consideration for the opportunity to win.

The dealership argued that purchasers of the lease agreements had not risked anything in the promotion because even if they did not win, they still had the car that they leased.

The court found:

This present promotion is designed to increase the number of cars leased by offering lessees the chance to win twelve free monthly payments. Plaintiffs hope to derive profit from an increase in business, and customers hope to win the monthly payments. The mutual element of gain that characterizes a wager is therefore present. Turning to the element of risk, plaintiffs acknowledge their risk but argue that customers have nothing of value at stake and no risk of loss. They argue that even if the customers do not win, they have the car that they have leased.

Plaintiffs ignore the obvious fact that if the prospect of winning induces anyone to enter into a lease, it follows inexorably that the lease consideration, in part, is provided for that chance. This is not a case in which the chance to win is gratuitously conferred after the parties make their bargain. By the express terms of the promotion, the chance to win is offered as part of the benefit of the bargain, even though the customer has the right to opt out. A customer responding to such an offer necessarily stakes some part of the consideration on the chance to win.

This was not a case where the chance to win was gratuitously conferred after the parties made their bargain, it was part of the deal, the court found.

Use of Skill as Opposed to Chance If skill or judgment is dominant, then the game is not a lottery. In games that ask for the "best letter," "best essay," or "best name," no chance is present. Also, as we saw in the *Rich* case involving sports games, skill or judgment is required because picking the winner is determined in part by the skill of the entrant.

As long as the winners are determined on the basis of a comparison of the skill of the entries, it is legal. In these games if a tie exists, both winners must receive prizes of equal value; otherwise chance enters into the picture again.

In 1912 the Armstrong-Byrd Music Company in Oklahoma City, Oklahoma, ran a promotion for a giveaway of one of its pianos. The company ran ads promoting the contest. The object of the game was to complete a puzzle by filling in spaces with numbers to make a total of fifteen. The puzzle was quite simple, but the challenge was to submit an entry that was the neatest or most unique design.

On May 10, 1912, a group of judges gathered together to pick the winner from the 6,500 entries. Most were simply filled in puzzles from the entry blank supplied in the newspaper ad. But a few were very original. One was actually made out of burnt wood, and another was embroidered on a pillow. The five most unique and original were awarded the promised prizes.

When the winners were notified of their prizes by mail, the Postmaster, H. G. Eastman, filed suit to stop what he considered an illegal lottery. The case was *Eastman* v. *Armstrong-Byrd Music Co.*, 212 F. 662 (8th Cir. 1914). The court determined that the contest winners were picked based on a use of their skill and judgment. As the court said, "There was no element of chance in this scheme or plan." This contest was not a lottery and therefore legal.

Noteworthy Case Studies Involving Contests and Lotteries

An Example of Third Party Benefit

This situation arose out of an allegedly misleading promotion by Direct American Marketers (Direct American). A disgruntled consumer, Theodore Zekman, claimed that because AT&T provided (and profited from the telephone calls) the "900" telephone number used by consumers to respond to Direct American's promotion, it was liable. The case was *Zekman* v. *Direct American Marketers, Inc.*, 695 N.E.2d 853 (Ill. 1998).

Mr. Zekman filed a lawsuit claiming that AT&T was secondarily liable for the allegedly fraudulent prize scheme promoted by Direct American. Under the promotion, consumers were sent a series of mailings that stated they had won either a large cash award or discount coupons. To collect the prize, consumers called a 900 number listed in the mailing. There were also instructions in the mailing on how to redeem the prizes by mail. Zekman made eleven phone calls in response to the various mailings and incurred a charge of about $8 to $10 dollars per call. The Illinois Supreme Court held that AT&T could not be liable under the Illinois Consumer Fraud and Deceptive Trade Practices Act for knowingly receiving the benefits of another's fraud.

The pertinent section of the statute reads:

> Unfair methods of competition and unfair or deceptive acts or practices, including but not limited to the use or employment of any deception, fraud, false pretense, false promise, misrepresentation or the concealment, suppression or omission of any material fact, with intent that others rely upon the concealment, suppression or omission of such material fact, or the use or employment of any practice described in Section 2 of the "Uniform Deceptive Trade Practices Act," approved August 5,

1965 (815 ILCS 510/2 (West 1992)), in the conduct of any trade or commerce are hereby declared unlawful whether any person has in fact been misled, deceived or damaged thereby.

The court stated: "[w]e agree with AT&T that the plain language of section 2 of the Act does not include anything that makes it unlawful to knowingly receive the benefits of another's fraud." The statute clearly contemplated that the entity perpetuating the misrepresentation was the entity liable under the statute. Using the canons of statutory interpretation, the court held that when a statute provided a list that was not exhaustive (including but not limited to), the class of unarticulated things must be interpreted as those things that are similar to the named things.

The court explained further: "The common feature of the forms of conduct listed in section 2 of the Act is that they involve actions directly done by the perpetrator of the fraud. Knowingly receiving the benefits of another's fraud, however, more closely resembles a form of secondary liability. We believe that a claim for knowingly receiving the benefits of another's fraud is not so similar to the enumerated violations of section 2 of the Act that the legislature intended for it to be a cause of action under the statute. With no clear indication from the legislature that such conduct violates section 2 of the Act, we cannot extend liability to those who knowingly receive the benefits of another's fraud."

Zekman then tried for liability on AT&T under section 2P of the Consumer Fraud Act, which deals directly with disclosures of conditions on offers of free prizes and gifts.

The relevant section states:

It is an unlawful practice for any person to promote or advertise any business, product, or interest in property, by means of offering free prizes, gifts or gratuities to any consumer, unless all material terms and conditions relating to the offer are clearly and conspicuously disclosed at the outset of the offer so as to leave no reasonable probability that the offering might be misunderstood.

Again, the Court stated: "[w]e believe that this provision clearly relates only to the person offering the free prizes, gifts or gratuities. The plain language of this statute does not pertain to those who knowingly receive the benefits of another's fraud."

Zekman also alleged that AT&T directly violated Section 2 of the Act by reviewing, revising, and approving Direct American's deceptive solicitations and recorded messages, and by billing Zekman for the 900-number calls in an allegedly misleading manner. In order to state a claim under Section 2, Zekman had to allege a deceptive act or practice by AT&T and that AT&T intended Zekman to rely on the deception. Illinois law also required that the fraud complained of be the proximate cause of the Zekman's injury.

The court maintained that AT&T did not cause Zekman's injury. In his deposition testimony, Zekman's acknowledged that when he received the mailings he did not know whether he had won a cash prize and that he made the 900-number calls in the hope of winning a prize. Zekman also understood that he would be charged for the calls and admitted that he heard the recorded message at the beginning of each call telling him that he could avoid any charges by immediately hanging up. As a result, clearly, there was no fraud on the part of AT&T.

You May Have Already Won: The American Family Publishers' Example

American Family Publishers was widely known for its television commercials featuring the late Ed McMahon and Dick Clark. Thirty-two states and the District of

Columbia joined in a $1.25 million settlement with American Family Publishers for violating state consumer protection laws (that covered contest and lotteries) by using deceptive advertising in connection with its sweepstakes.

Under the terms of the settlement, American Family agreed to revise its sweepstakes so that they would:

1. Only tell consumers that they were winners if they had in fact won;
2. Only tell consumers that they were among a select group that had a chance of winning a prize if the odds of winning were disclosed;
3. Tell consumers that no purchase was necessary to participate in the sweepstakes;
4. Clearly explain how to enter the sweepstakes without a purchase;
5. Make it clear to consumers who ordered magazines on an installment payment plan how much money was due each month; and
6. Not imply that consumers had a better chance of winning if they purchased magazines.

The states that joined in the settlement were: Alabama, Arizona, Arkansas, California, Hawaii, Idaho, Illinois, Kansas, Kentucky, Massachusetts, Michigan, Minnesota, Mississippi, Montana, Nebraska, New Hampshire, New Jersey, New Mexico, Nevada, North Carolina, Ohio, Oklahoma, Oregon, Pennsylvania, Rhode Island, South Dakota, Tennessee, Texas, Vermont, Virginia, Washington, Wisconsin, and Washington, D.C.

American Family Publishers still faces a number of actions involving its allegedly deceptive and unfair practices in connection with its sweepstakes and contests that have been consolidated to the federal district court in New Jersey (*In re American Family Publishers Business Practices Litigation*, No. 1235, 1998 U.S. Dist. LEXIS 12514 (judicial Panel on Multistate Litigation, August 12, 1998)).

The NCAA Final Four Example

The National Collegiate Athletic Association (NCAA) governs the athletic programs of the nation's colleges and universities. Many NCAA competitions have gained widespread popularity, particularly the women's and men's NCAA Division I basketball tournaments. Due to both the popularity of such events and the limited seating in sports arenas, demand for tickets often exceeds supply.

To distribute tickets to these events, the NCAA developed the following ticket-distribution system. The NCAA set the face value of the tickets to its events many months in advance. Would-be ticket purchasers submitted an application to the NCAA offering to purchase tickets for a particular event. Each applicant could submit only one application, but an applicant could submit multiple offers on a single application, though only one offer could be accepted. When submitting an application, the applicant must submit the face value of the tickets along with a nonrefundable handling or service fee for each offer. The NCAA used a random-selection program to accept offers from the pool of offers. Applicants whose offers were accepted received event tickets via overnight delivery. Applicants whose offers are rejected received refunds of the ticket price (though it may take several weeks or months). No applicant received a refund of the handling fee.

This ticket-allocation system was used for the 2009 NCAA Men's Final Four. The 2009 NCAA Men's Division I Basketball Tournament involved 65 schools playing in a single-elimination tournament to determine the national champion of the 2008–09 basketball season. It began on March 17, 2009, and ended with the championship game on April 6 in Detroit, Michigan, where the University of North Carolina defeated Michigan State to become champion.

The NCAA set the face value of the tickets at $150 each, and tickets were sold in pairs. Fewer than five thousand tickets were released for sale and several hundred-thousand people submitted offers. Each applicant could submit up to ten offers, but if one offer was accepted, the remaining offers were rejected. A handling fee of $6 was charged for each offer. If an applicant's offer was accepted, they would receive game tickets via overnight mail, and if that applicant had made more than one offer, they also received a refund of the total ticket price for the rejected offers. Applicants whom had all their offers rejected also received refunds of the total ticket price. No one received a refund of the handling fees.

In *George v. National Collegiate Athletic Association*, 945 N.E.2d 150, 2011 Ind. LEXIS 332 (2001), the plaintiffs submitted offers to the NCAA through their website to purchase tickets but their offers were not accepted. The court said: "They submitted their applications knowing both that the handling fee was nonrefundable and that there was a possibility demand would exceed supply and that the random-selection process would be utilized. Dissatisfied with not being able to purchase tickets, the plaintiffs filed suit."

The underlying basis for all of the claims in this suit was the allegation that the NCAA's ticket-distribution system constituted an illegal lottery under Indiana law.

"In sum," the district court said:

> it would stretch the definition of "lottery" beyond what the General Assembly intended to hold that the NCAA's ticket-distribution plan is a proscribed lottery under *Indiana Code section 35-45-5-3*. The NCAA creates the primary market by issuing tickets in the first place, and it sets the price for these events many months in advance. In setting the price, the NCAA reasonably calculates what the fair-market value at the time of the event will be. Moreover, the NCAA's ticket process is not materially different from the process utilized by the Indianapolis Colts in *Lesher*. We note, however, that our holding would not prevent a prosecutor or plaintiff from attacking a similarly structured scheme that is merely a ruse for a traditional lottery. Barring such a ruse, we conclude that where an event coordinator creates the primary market for event tickets, the fair-market value of the tickets is equal to their face value. In this case, there was no "prize" and hence no "lottery" because at the time applicants submitted to the NCAA their offers to purchase tickets, the market value equaled the face value of the tickets. Thus, as a matter of law, the NCAA's ticket-distribution plan is not a lottery.

However, this case was appealed to the U.S. Court of Appeals in *George v. National Collegiate Athletic Association*, 613 F.3d 658; 2010 U.S. App. LEXIS 1457 (2010). Here the result was quite different and illustrated the complexity of many contest/lottery issues.

The Court of Appeals felt that ". . . these retained 'service' or 'handling' fees, as well as the NCAA's use of the applicants' money, constitute consideration for a chance to win the right to purchase 'highly prized' tickets for priority seating at venues that 'are much too small to meet ticket demand' and that the NCAA's ticket-distribution system constitutes an unlawful lottery."

The court dug deeper stating "Plaintiffs allege that 'the number of applicants greatly exceeds the number of tickets on virtually every occasion,' that the NCAA falsely advertises the availability of certain seats and 'manipulate[s]' the purportedly random drawings 'to accommodate business needs,' and that the resale market value of the tickets is high due to their scarcity."

When the district court cited *Lesher (496 N.E.2d at 789-90)*, an earlier case that ruled that a distribution scheme for season tickets to Indianapolis Colts games did not constitute an unlawful lottery, the issues were different. In *Lesher*, the applicants submitted the face value of the tickets plus a handling fee. Winners were selected at random. Losers received a full refund of the ticket price and the handling fee. Defining a prize as "something of more value than the amount invested," the court in *Lesher* held that the applicants merely "invested the price of the tickets and received in exchange either the tickets or the entire amount invested," such that "those receiving tickets got nothing of greater value than those who received refunds." Because the court found that no prize had been awarded, it held that the scheme was not a lottery.

Here, people were required to invest the additional "service fee" of six to ten dollars per ticket or entry, which had no relation to the NCAA's actual cost in running the ticket-distribution process and was not refunded. In essence, win or lose, the service fee was forfeited by all entrants and retained by the NCAA. The result of this is that, the plaintiffs had argued the existence of consideration that was not present in *Lesher*, where the handling fee was refunded to those who did not get tickets.

Also, plaintiffs here argued the existence of a prize not present in *Lesher*. They specifically alleged that the scarcity of the tickets makes those tickets far more valuable than the cost of purchase.

The NCAA argued that the plaintiffs had not alleged an element of chance. The court appellate said: "In Indiana, the 'chance' element is met if 'the winning of a prize is dependent primarily on, if not solely, upon chance [rather than skill].' For an event in which the demand for tickets exceeds the supply and the right to purchase tickets is allocated at random, the element of chance is plain. Applicants for NCAA tickets do not obtain their reward through any exercise of skill or judgment. Nonetheless, the NCAA argues that its ticket-distribution scheme lacks any element of chance because a random drawing occurs only if the demand for tickets to a given event exceeds the supply. Therefore, an element of chance is not *necessarily* present. But Plaintiffs specifically allege that tickets are highly prized and that the venues hosting the events are 'much too small to meet ticket demand.' The fact that all applicants may win tickets for some events does not obviate Plaintiffs' claims that they paid money to enter drawings for valuable tickets where the demand for tickets *did* exceed the supply."

It was determined, in this case, that the plaintiffs had established all elements of a lottery. They paid a per-ticket or per-entry fee (consideration) to enter a random drawing (chance) in hopes of obtaining scarce, valuable tickets (a prize). The court ruled: "Plaintiffs have sufficiently alleged that the NCAA operated an unlawful lottery. Accordingly, the district court's order of dismissal must be reversed as to *all* counts remaining in Plaintiffs' Second Amended Complaint."

Entities that Have Regulation over Contests

There are basically four federal agencies with control over contests and how they are promoted. The U.S. Postal Service has control over any contest that uses the mail in any way. The Federal Trade Commission has control over any activity which is deceptive or unfair, including contests. The FCC controls any contest advertised over radio or television. The Bureau of Alcohol, Tobacco and Firearms (ATF) controls contests which affect those items. And, finally, each state has specific statutes that govern the use of contests, as do each of the television networks.

U.S. Postal Service

The first form of regulation over gambling activities took place in 1868 in the form of postal regulations (15 Stat. 194 (1868)). These laws were created in an attempt to curb the fraud and abuse in state-sponsored lotteries after the Civil War.

Under current law, it is a criminal offense to mail any advertisement of any lottery, gift enterprise, or similar scheme where prizes are awarded based on chance. Violation of this law carries a fine of $1,000 or two years in prison, or both (18 U.S.C., section 1302 (1982)). In addition, the Postal Service is authorized to issue a cease-and-desist order and refuse processing any such advertisement in the U.S. mail (39 U.S.C., section 3001, 3005 (1984 Supp.)). Violation of a cease-and-desist order carries a civil fine of up to $10,000 per day.

Contests that use the mail in any way must be approved by the General Counsel, Mailability Division, U.S. Postal Service, Washington, D.C. 20006. When I say "contests that use the mail," I mean anything from mailing entry forms to mailing notification to winners after the contest.

We've seen cases earlier where the Postal Service brought suit because the mail was used in the scheme. United States v. Purvis, Garden City Chamber of Commerce v. Wagner, Dreem Arts, Inc. v. City of Chicago, People ex rel. Ellison v. Lavin, and Eastman v. Armstrong-Byrd Music Co. are good examples of cases where the Postal Service became involved.

Until recently, a game of chance enclosed in a product package violated the postal lottery law unless it was disclosed clearly in the advertising and on the package that a person could enter the contest by merely sending in a "facsimile" in the form of a 3" × 5" card with the product's name or some other words or phrases written or printed by hand. However, in 1979 the Postal Service, by means of a "no action" letter, approved a promotion involving an in-pack game piece, if the package itself contained a notice of "no purchase necessary" and advised that a free game piece was available to persons who requested one by mail. In the view of the Postal Service this message offered potential entrants an accessible free entry alternative and that, therefore, persons who chose to enter by purchasing the package would be doing so voluntarily. In other words, the equivalent free entry offer eliminated the lottery element of consideration. Contrast this with the *Dreem Arts* case we looked at earlier, where it was much more difficult to obtain information with which to send in a facsimile entry.

Federal Trade Commission

The FTC, in 1925, began issuing cease-and-desist orders against lotteries. Since then the FTC has established rules that apply to contests. It requires the following:

- Disclosure of the exact number of prizes to be awarded;
- Disclosure of the odds of winning;
- Disclosure of the area within which the game will exist;
- Disclosure of the length of the contest;
- That all game pieces must be distributed to stores on a totally random basis; and
- That the game cannot end until all game pieces are handed out.

Also, any game that continues beyond thirty days must disclose the number of unredeemed prizes and revised odds on a weekly basis. Successive games must be separated by thirty days or the length of the previous game, whichever is shorter.

These rules do not apply to broadcast media; however, the same information must be made available to consumers. The company must disclose where the consumer can go, or write, to get complete contest information.

R. F. Keppel & Brothers operated a business which manufactured and placed in retail stores a candy game known as Break and Take. In the early 1930s, Keppel promoted its game in stores located near schools. It displayed the game in a way that would be attractive to children. The company earned about $234,000 a year from the game.

The game involved an assortment of wrapped candy. The participant would pay one cent and pick a piece of candy from the 120 pieces in the display. The candy would be opened to discover if it contained a penny as a prize, or a slip of paper with a purchase price of 1, 2, or 3 cents. In reality, only four pieces contained a penny. The other pieces of candy contained prices of 1 to 3 cents each. If the candy contained a ticket, that was the price that the participant had to pay. There was a possibility that the person could win back the initial penny investment and get the candy free. But the odds were very low.

Obviously, this game qualified as a lottery. All three essential elements were present: consideration, prize, and chance. Yet, the Federal Trade Commission brought suit in *Federal Trade Commission* v. *R. F. Keppel & Bros. Inc.*, 291 U.S. 304, 54 S.Ct. 423, 78 L.Ed. 2d 814 (1934), because of the game's effect on children. They were the audience to which the game was directed.

The Supreme Court, in upholding the FTC's decision, felt that "the method of competition adopted . . . induces children, too young to be capable of exercising an intelligent judgment of the transaction, to purchase an article less desirable in point of quality or quantity than that offered at a comparable price."

That is why the FTC became involved with the lottery. The method exploited children who were unable to protect themselves. The FTC, as we saw in chapters 2 and 3, concerns itself with deception and unfairness. As the Court said, "It would seem a gross perversion . . . to hold that the method is not 'unfair.'" Keppel lost the case.

In many cases, the FTC may issue a cease-and-desist order for games that are not deemed to be literally illegal lotteries. Remember that the FTC has the authority to stop any activity that is unfair or deceptive, even if it does not violate specific lottery regulations.

A good example of this involved the *Reader's Digest* Sweepstakes (not to be confused with the earlier case). Entry forms were mailed to members of the public. The entry forms contained a number and a ticket with the same number printed on it. The participant was to return the ticket to *Reader's Digest* where it would be compared against preselected winning numbers. If the number on the ticket matched a winning number, that prize would be awarded.

The intent of the sweepstakes was to build sales in its products. To promote its sweepstakes, *Reader's Digest* made claims about the contest, including:

- Participants only needed to mail in their ticket to receive their prize if they were winners;
- Participants had a reasonable chance of winning;
- All advertised prizes had been purchased by *Reader's Digest* prior to the contest;
- Consumers who received entry forms were "selected," "chosen," or were "one of the few people to be invited;"
- Entry forms were mailed on a limited basis; and
- 101,751 prizes were offered worth $999,000 (in January, 1969—a typical contest).

This well-known sweepstakes ran into trouble when the FTC stepped in and filed suit in *In the Matter of Reader's Digest Assn.*, 79 F.T.C. 696 (1971). The FTC took action, not because this was an illegal lottery, but because the sweepstakes was deceptive.

In reality, the claims that *Reader's Digest* made in its advertisements and promotion were not accurate. Participants were not "one of the few to be invited." In fact, hundreds of millions of copies of the *Reader's Digest* Sweepstakes entry forms were mailed to consumers. In the January 1969 contest, there were not 101,751 prizes worth $999,000. In reality there were 40,517 prizes worth $441,789.

Also, winners were required to do more than send in their ticket to receive a prize. They were required to do other undisclosed things—for example, submit to interviews by a private detective before being allowed to obtain their prize.

In addition, there was no "reasonable opportunity to win" in *Reader's Digest* Sweepstakes. The odds of winning first prize were about one in four hundred and eighty thousand. The *Reader's Digest* Sweepstakes was simply not what it was promoted to be. Because of the deception, the FTC issued a cease-and-desist order.

Generally, there are specific situations regarding contests that the FTC does not allow. The following list represents a general outline of practices that are prohibited by the FTC as they apply to contests:

- Making false representations of the value of a prize;
- Promising cash and awarding merchandise instead;
- Failing to follow contest rules as established; and
- Offering a number of prizes that differ from those advertised.

In addition, the FTC does have a rule governing contests in the food retailing and gasoline industries. Issued in the wake of complaints that games were allegedly rigged, the commission adopted a rule, that is almost impossible to live with, requiring that the game pieces must be updated frequently (16 C.F.R. 419). This is difficult in a game that might be run by as many as ten thousand retail gas stations.

Federal Communications Commission

Congress first attempted to regulate the airwaves under the Radio Act of 1927 (44 Stat. 1162 (1927). However, lotteries were not regulated in broadcast until the Federal Communications Act of 1934 (H. R. Rep. No. 72-2106, 72 Cong. 2d Sess. (1933). Later these regulations were made a part of the Criminal Code as Section 1304 (18 U.S.C., section 312 (1982).

Under current law, Section 1304, it is a criminal offense to broadcast by radio or television any advertisement for a lottery, gift enterprise, or similar scheme. Specifically, the statute prohibits: "Any advertisement of or information concerning any lottery, gift enterprise, or similar scheme, offering prizes dependent in whole or in part upon lot or chance, or any list of the prizes drawn or awarded by means of any such lottery, gift enterprise, or scheme, whether said list contains any part or all of such prizes . . . ." (18 U.S.C., section 1304).

A good example of this occurred in 1973. The University of Florida radio station WRUF in Gainesville, Florida, broadcast a radio commercial for its client, Shaw and Keeter Fordtown. Any person who purchased an automobile from the dealership received a prize (see box 11.4).

When the FCC learned of the commercial, it filed a complaint against the school. The FCC held that a violation of lottery restrictions was created with *In the Matter of University of Florida*, 40 F.C.C.2d 188 (1973).

All three elements of a lottery existed in this case. A prize was offered in the form of a savings bond. While every purchaser received a bond, values varied of the bonds considerably. Consideration existed since the consumer was required to purchase a car or truck before being eligible to win a savings bond. Finally, chance was present as to which bond would be won. Since the University of Florida created, produced, and aired the spot, it was required to pay a fine of $2,000.

In any case where broadcast media is involved the advertisement should include information on the following:

- Who may participate;
- Type of entries required;
- Where, when, and how the entry is to be submitted;
- Number and nature of prizes;
- The existence of duplicate prizes in the case of ties;
- The closing date; and
- Where complete contest details can be obtained.

Bureau of Alcohol, Tobacco, and Firearms

The ATF has jurisdiction over what's contained in, attached to, or printed on packages of certain tobacco products, such as cigarettes. The ATF view differs from the U.S. Postal Service's as to what constitutes a lottery. The ATF believes, for example, that the element of consideration exists even if no purchase of a tobacco product is required to take part in a contest. The statute in question is a section of the Internal Revenue Code of 1954 (26 U.S.C. 5723(c)), providing that no certificate or coupon representing a "ticket, chance, share or interest in or dependent, the event of a lottery" shall appear in or "on any package of tobacco products or cigarette papers or tubes."

The ATF also issues advisory letters involving the lottery aspects of proposed promotions. However, unlike the Postal Service, it has steadfastly refused to permit any kind of game promotion in which the game price is enclosed in the package with cigarettes or cigars.

State Regulation

Each of the states is in agreement as to what constitutes an illegal lottery, as we've discussed in the previous part of this chapter. They agree with the federal guidelines in most all cases. The difference shows up in how the states interpret the requirements. What constitutes "chance," "a prize," and especially "consideration" is where the states vary in some ways.

Each state has legislated specific requirements for contests. Current state statutes or amendments, regulation, or case law should be consulted before creating an advertisement involving a contest.

Network Standards

All major television networks have special rules to monitor ads that promote contests. Each has specific review procedures covering such advertising.

The advertiser of a proposed contest should present the storyboard and the game details, along with rules, entry prizes, game pieces, and any other elements to the network involved for approval.

Each network can be contacted for a set of guidelines that they follow. A list of the major networks contacts is included in the Index of Sources section.

Suggestions for Creating Contests

When developing contests there are certain items to consider. Here is a quick reference list of points to think about when developing contests and promoting them in ads. This is only a starting point; the specifics of the contest will determine what must be included.

Contest development should include the following:

- A description of the judging method;
- A statement that entries will not be returned;
- A statement that entries become the property of the company;
- A statement that winners will be notified by mail, if applicable;
- A statement regarding the limit on the number or frequency that a person may enter;
- A statement as to who may or may not enter the contest (e.g., children under 18, employees of the company);
- A list of places where the contest is void;
- A list of the prizes, including the retail value and cash substitute option if any;
- A clarification regarding whether certain prizes will only be given to parents or guardians, if a minor is the winner;
- A list of where entries may be sent, as well as where contest rules, a list of winners, and a list of prizes, may be obtained;
- A statement that the company reserves the right to use names and likenesses of entrants or winners for publicity purposes;
- A deadline (by final postmark date) for receipt of entries;
- Disclaimer of liability for any applicable taxes, licensing, or other fees on prizes;
- Disclaimer of liability for lost or stolen prizes;
- Disclaimer of liability for prizes supplied by others; and
- The termination date of the contest.

12 Guarantees and Warranties

The only things worth learning are the things you learn after you know it all.

—*Harry Truman*

When someone mentions the word "guarantee," most people think of a piece of paper that comes with their new car, dishwasher, or iPhone. In that case, the guarantee explains what the manufacturer will do if certain parts of the product fail within a certain time. This type of product guarantee is very common in today's market economy.

But there are other guarantees. Probably the most important and powerful one ever created was devised by a group of fifty-five men who met at a convention in Philadelphia. The first to show up for the meeting was a thirty-six-year-old educator from Virginia named Jim Madison. The others who joined the meeting later were people from business, government, shipping, farming, education, and law. In fact, more than half of them were lawyers.

The group had the task of creating a guarantee for a new product. It was a different, rather revolutionary product, so they had to consider new situations that might arise and what would happen if they came about. This group continued their meeting for almost seventeen weeks before they had ironed out the conditions of their guarantee. Finally, they were satisfied. And, then as with all good guarantees, they put it in writing so that anyone who needed to could rely on it, should a claim become necessary.

The guarantee that I have been discussing was written sometime ago—in 1791 to be exact. And it's still in effect today. It's called the Bill of Rights—the first ten amendments to the Constitution of the United States. It's a guarantee for the people, a guarantee of personal freedom. It is probably the most powerful (the *Magna Carta* being the only other that comes close) and yet misunderstood guarantee ever written.

Although most people don't consider the Bill of Rights to be a guarantee, it surely is one. It guarantees the people of the United States certain "inalienable rights" (as prescribed in the Declaration of Independence) that cannot be taken away or overlooked. Of all the cases that the U.S. Supreme Court hears involving constitutional liberties, most of them involve breaches of the Bill of Rights.

Since this chapter deals with guarantees, I thought it appropriate to start with the first ever written in this country. The Ninth and Tenth Amendments essentially say, "we mean what we said." Specifically, the Tenth specifies that powers not delegated are reserved. The Ninth guarantees "[T]he enumeration in the Constitution, of certain rights, shall not be construed to deny or disparage others retained by the people." For over two hundred years this guarantee was ignored until the Supreme Court used it to announce that the privacy of the bedroom involved an "unenumerated" right. Specifically, the issue was contraception.

The Eighth Amendment disallows cruel and unusual punishment, as well as excessive bail and fines. The Seventh guarantees the right to a jury trial in civil cases "where the value in controversy exceeds twenty dollars." The Sixth begins, "The accused shall enjoy the right to a speedy and public trial . . . ."

The Fifth Amendment declares two guarantees. The first specifies that no person "be subject for the same offense to be twice put in jeopardy of life and limb." Today we call this "double jeopardy." The other guarantee is that no person "shall be compelled in any criminal case to be a witness against himself." We call this "self-incrimination." This Amendment has caused the greatest amount of activity in the courts, from the "Communists-are-everywhere" era of Joe McCarthy and Richard Nixon to the "read-him-his-rights" era of the *Miranda* rule in 1966 (*Miranda* v. *Arizona*, 384 U.S. 436, 86 S.Ct. 1602, 16 L.Ed. 2d 694 (1966)).

The Fourth Amendment guarantees protection ". . . against unreasonable search and seizures." The Third touches on a person's right of privacy in his or her home. The Second Amendment specifies a guarantee that a "well regulated Militia being necessary to the security of a free State, the right of the people to keep and bear Arms shall not be infringed." This originally applied to the right of a State to create a government controlled militia and to keep and bear arms, not the individual citizen as most gun-rights proponents claim.

The First Amendment, although it lay dormant for over 130 years, guarantees freedom of speech, freedom of the press, the right of people to peacefully assemble, and the right to practice one's religion.

So there you have it. The first guarantee written in this country. And yet it wasn't unanimously adopted by every state until 1939. Massachusetts, Georgia, and Connecticut were the holdouts.

In reality all guarantees have the same purpose. They are intended as a protection. They give confidence to people who must rely on a claim. But the guarantees we are concerned with here are simpler. They are guarantees that involve the state of the marketplace, rather than the state of the Union.

In recent years, companies have turned to guarantees and warranties to create added value for their customers. Airlines, appliances, banks, cars, computers, hotels, delivery services and many others have developed strong guarantees for products and services and incorporated that fact into their advertising. Warranties and guarantees have increasingly become a part of many company's product benefits, which help position the company against the competition.

In the fall of 1986, American Express started an ad campaign promoting its "Buyers Assurance Plan." American Express would automatically extend the manufacturer's warranty on any purchases made on its charge card. In some cases the manufacturer's warranty was extended for up to a year. The campaign was intended to run for only four months, but it was so successful that it was continued through 1987. The plan was instituted because American Express was used mostly for such business and travel purchases as airfare, hotels and meals. But the company wanted to increase sales of retail merchandise with its charge card. As a result of the extended warranty, consumer use of the card increased considerably.

In 1983 Ford offered a lifetime service guarantee covering major repairs for as long as the customer owns the car. This was intended to offset Ford's negative service reputation among the public, with many claiming the letters F-O-R-D were really an acronym for "Fix Or Repair Daily."

In the spring of 1987, Lufthansa German Airlines began a program for first class and business class passengers guaranteeing to pay $200 for any missed connecting flights or late baggage due to the airline's fault. Passenger ticket sales increased, as a consequence, with only minimal claims filed.

Today, eBay's Money Back Guarantee states: "This is our way of reminding you that you can buy on eBay with complete confidence. You'll get the item you ordered or get your money back."

Advertisements that exclaim "money-back guarantee," "quality assurance," "customer satisfaction," or "extended warranty" have become strong marketing and selling tools. Entire ad campaigns are often built around them. Because of this, the advertiser must understand the legalities of promoting guarantees and warranties in its ads.

The Difference between a Guarantee and a Warranty

The terms "warranty" and "guarantee" are often used interchangeably. In reality there is very little difference between the two, but there is a distinction. To be technical, a warranty is an assumption by the seller of the quality, suitability, character, and performance of the product. On the other hand, a guarantee is the agreement that comes with the purchase of the merchandise that, if the product fails to live up to the claims, the seller will remedy the situation in some way.

A warranty is, simply put, a promise that becomes a contract between the manufacturer and the buyer. That contract goes into effect at the moment the consumer makes a purchase.

A guarantee is a promise that if something goes wrong with the product, the manufacturer will do certain things.

Let's say Canon claims that their digital camera is "free from defects in workmanship and materials." That's a warranty. If the camera turns out to be defective, the guarantee states that "if defective it will be repaired or replaced free of charge." The warranty states what the manufacturer claims the product will do. The guarantee states what the manufacturer will do if the product fails to live up to the warranty. Combine a warranty and guarantee, then advertise them and you can form the basis for legal action. For the rest of this chapter we'll roll "warranty" and "guarantee" together into the term guarantee.

The Scope of Warranties and Guarantees

Here, we will deal mainly with how guarantees should be advertised rather than discussing the legalities of developing guarantees. The balance of this chapter will be devoted to considerations about using guarantees in advertising. And the liabilities of deceptive or unfair practices when advertising warranties and guarantees.

Representations Made in Ads about Guarantees

When advertisements discuss product guarantees the advertiser must be concerned with how they make certain representations. When claims are made in an ad about the quality, results, or effects of guaranteed merchandise, the advertiser must do certain things—identify the guarantor and state the characteristics, performance, duration, conditions, and charges involved.

Identifying the Guarantor

In Maryland in the early 1960s, World Wide Television Corporation sold used television sets and appliances to the public. As part of its promotion the company advertised in newspapers and on radio, focusing on a guarantee for its products.

The company had a unique way of selling its products. World Wide's giant screen Olympic console televisions were controlled by a coin meter, called the "Metermatic Plan." Instead of making monthly payments for the appliance, the purchaser would insert coins in a box to turn on the unit, similar to a coin-operated laundry. The purchaser couldn't use the appliance unless money was put in. A typical ad stated that the products were guaranteed (see box 12.1).

Box 12.1   **World Wide Television Corporation Ad**

BRAND NEW GIANT SCREEN OLYMPIC CONSOLE TELEVISION

WITH ONE FULL-YEAR GUARANTEE including picture tube. Service is fully guaranteed! Service guarantee included! The Metermatic Plan is better because service is guaranteed.

In truth, the Olympic televisions were guaranteed by Siegler Corporation, the makers of the television, and not World Wide. Yet this was not stated anywhere in the ads, but only in the instruction booklet included with the television set. The implication in the ad was that World Wide was guaranteeing the television sets. The consumer could not have known the true identity of the guarantor until after the television was delivered. This was deceptive.

There's another unique thing about World Wide's service guarantee. Service was guaranteed because if the company didn't fix a broken set, it wouldn't be used by the consumer—and the company wouldn't get paid. That's the only reason service was fully guaranteed. The Federal Trade Commission (FTC), learning of the situation, filed a complaint, *In the Matter of World Wide Television Corp.*, 66 F.T.C. 961 (1964).

In that case the commissioner stated: "[World Wide's] products are not unconditionally guaranteed for one year. Said guarantee is subject to numerous requirements, limitations, and restrictions. The advertised guarantee fails to set forth the nature, conditions and extent of the guarantee, the manner in which the guarantor will perform . . . and the identity of the guarantor."

The commissioner ordered that World Wide could not claim its products were guaranteed unless the nature, extent, and duration were clearly stated. Further, World Wide had to clearly state the name and address of the actual guarantor.

Stating the Characteristics or Attributes to Be Guaranteed

An advertiser can build whatever guarantee it wants into a product. In other words, an advertiser may create the limits of any guarantee on its products. However, it must state the characteristics, attributes, and limitations in its guarantee. But simply using the word "guaranteed" alone and without clarification must always be avoided.

One of the earliest situations to establish this point involved the Parker Pen Company, founded in 1888 and still in business today. Parker manufactured quality fountain pens and sold them to the public. In 1946 Parker ran advertisements for its pens that contained a statement "Guaranteed for Life by Parker's." The specific terms of the guarantee were spelled out elsewhere in the ad: "Pens marked with a Blue Diamond are guaranteed for the life of the owner against everything except loss or intentional damage, subject only to a charge of 35 cents for postage, insurance and handling, provided complete pen is returned for service."

The FTC filed a complaint against Parker because it felt that by charging thirty-five cents a deception was created as to the "Lifetime Guarantee." The FTC claimed that the thirty-five-cent charge limited the guarantee. The case was appealed to the Federal Circuit Court of Appeals in *Parker Pen Co.* v. *FTC*, 153 F.2d 509 (C.C.A. 1946).

There the court voiced its opinion. "Ordinarily the word, guarantee, is incomplete unless it is used in connection with other explanatory words.' To say a pen or other object is guaranteed is meaningless. What is the guarantee? Is it a limited guarantee? Is it an unlimited guarantee? The answer to these questions gives meaning to the word 'guaranteed.' The same is true of the words 'Guaranteed for Life' or 'Life Guarantee.'"

In this case, Parker advertised its guarantee, claiming that it would make needed repairs during the life of the original buyer, if that person paid thirty-five cents per repair. There is nothing wrong with that. It clearly spelled out the terms of its guarantee. Parker won its case.

Specifying How the Guarantee Is to Be Performed

Another element of the claim that a product is guaranteed involves how the guarantee will be honored. In other words, what will be done if the product fails to perform as promised.

Capitol Manufacturing Company in New York offered watches represented as manufactured by Hamilton and Gruen Watch companies. In reality, Capitol did not sell Hamilton or Gruen watches, but rather cheap imitations. In its ads, Capitol made statements about its watches, including:

ELECTRA TWO-YEAR SERVICE GUARANTEE
We guarantee this watch for two years from date of purchase against defects in material and workmanship.

This guarantee appears to name a company called Electra as the guarantor. It claims that any obligations that the company has under the guarantee will be performed fully, satisfactorily, and promptly. The ad also states that the watch will operate properly for at least two years.

Capitol's guarantee came to the attention of the FTC. Since the guarantee did not specify how the guarantor would fulfill the guarantee, the FTC filed a complaint, *In the Matter of Capitol Mfg. Corp.*, 73 F.T.C. 872 (1968), charging that the guarantee was deceptive. The watches sold by Capitol were so cheaply made that "[f]ew, if any, . . . will operate for at least the two year period represented in the guarantee," The court stated.

The problem with this guarantee was its failure to state what Capitol would do if the watch broke within the two-year period. Would it repair the watch? Would it replace the watch? Would it refund the purchase price? None of this was stated. In truth, it wasn't going to do anything. This is probably how the FTC learned about the situation in the first place.

When any guarantee is claimed, the court said the: "manner in which the guarantor will perform . . . [must be] clearly and conspicuously set forth in immediate connection therewith." Since Capitol failed to provide this information with its guarantee, the FTC issued a cease-and-desist order.

Duration of the Guarantee

A guarantee should specify a limit as to the length of time it will be honored by the manufacturer. Advertisers can get into trouble with guarantees described as "for a season of use," or "for the year." The guarantee should specify when the time of the guarantee starts. For example, a statement such as, "guaranteed for one year from the date of purchase," leaves little to interpretation and is preferred.

Another way to list the duration of a guarantee is to state its termination date. Food products are commonly guaranteed in this way. Food generally lists an expiration date for the "guaranteed" use of the product such as "not good after . . ."

A common way to start the clock running on a guarantee is through a mail-in registration card or online registration. Many products are guaranteed only after a registration card is filled out and returned to the manufacturer or registered online through the manufacturer's website. Many home appliances, home theater components, cameras, and watches are commonly guaranteed in this way.

In the late 1950s, a sewing machine manufacturer placed ads in national consumer magazines including *McCall's* magazine. The manufacturer, International Stitch-O-Matic in Chicago, promoted its guarantee in their ads. The guarantee stated that the product was backed by a "money-back" guarantee on the entire machine for twenty-five years. When it turned out that this was false, *In the Matter of International Stitch-O-Matic Corp.*, 54 F.T.C. 1308 (1959), resulted. The guarantee claimed that the entire machine was covered for twenty-five years. In fact, only the motor was guaranteed, and for just one year. The Stitch-O-Matic guarantee had limitations, including time, which were blatantly misstated in its ads.

Stating Conditions of the Guarantee

In the late 1960s Universe Chemicals Incorporated, manufactured and sold a water-repellent paint by the name of "Kleer-Kote" and "Kolor-Kote." The sales demonstration of the product was quite impressive. Various items were shown to the prospective buyers, and they were told that the items were coated with Kleer-Kote or Kolor-Kote.

A piece of sheet metal, coated with Kolor-Kote, was shown, and the prospect was told that the paint would not crack, peel, or break even if the metal was bent. In another example, a treated brick demonstrated the repellent quality of the coating when water was poured over it. The coating was heated with an infrared bulb to demonstrate its heat resistance. A sieve was coated with Kleer-Kote and was shown to hold water without leaking.

The product appeared to be truly amazing, and the demonstrations were convincing. Kleer-Kote and Kolor-Kote even came with a "ten-year, unconditional guarantee." Unfortunately, the product failed to live up to its claims, and the guarantee turned out to be not much of a solution. The FTC became involved and filed *In the Matter of Universe Chemicals, Inc.*, 77 F.T.C. 598 (1970).

While the wording in the Kleer-Kote brochure stated that the product was "unconditionally guaranteed for 10 years," this was not the case. When a guarantee is claimed to be unconditional, it means just that: no conditions. If there are *any* conditions, the guarantee is not unconditional. In that case, it should be stated as a "limited guarantee" and then the limits must be specified.

Actually, in Universe Chemicals' case the company would only replace their product if defective. In certain cases the product was replaced, but in many cases the company refused. "The guarantee," said the commissioner, "was clearly not unconditional, and the conditions were not stated in the advertising."

Stating Charges Involved in a Guarantee

Western Radio Corporation manufactured pocket-sized radios and advertised them in such magazines as *Popular Science* in the mid-1960s. Its Radi-Vox transmitter was advertised with a "money-back guarantee." However, the company failed to inform the consumer that a service charge applied to the guarantee.

The case went to court in *Western Radio Corp.* v. *FTC*, 339 F.2d 937 (7th Cir. 1964). There, the court said the advertising had the capacity and tendency to mislead the public "by failure to disclose a service charge in connection with the advertised unconditional guarantee."

When a guarantee is advertised as a money-back guarantee, it means just that. Any guarantee must state "the terms and conditions of such guarantee . . . clearly and conspicuously . . . including the amount of any service or other charge which is imposed."

Problems with Advertising Guarantees

The most obvious problem encountered in advertising a guarantee is whether the ad creates a deception about the actual guarantee. When there is a difference between the guarantee and the way it is advertised or where it is a blatant falsehood, the FTC can step in.

Variations between an Advertised Guarantee and an Actual Guarantee

Montgomery Ward, founded in 1872 was up against rivals Sears, JC Penny, Macy's, Gimbels and Dillard's shopping mall presence in the 1960s. As it desperately tried to regain market-share, Montgomery Ward offered rebuilt car engines through its chain of retail department stores. In its advertisements the engines were promoted as having an unconditional guarantee. The customer would read the ad, go to the store, and purchase the engine only to learn later that the guarantee had quite a few restrictions.

The Montgomery Ward guarantee was not unconditional. It actually covered only a period of ninety days or four thousand miles (see box 12.2). The guarantee also contained other restrictions. For instance, the guarantee only provided for the following:

* Replacement of parts, no labor;
* A claim for engines installed by Wards;
* A claim if required checkups are made;
* A claim if damage was not caused by misuse or accident; and
* A claim if a valid certificate was on file.

Eventually, the FTC learned of Montgomery Ward's guarantee and a complaint was filed in: *Montgomery Ward & Co.* v. *FTC*, 379 F.2d 666 (7th Cir. 1967).

Montgomery Ward argued that it had a policy of honoring claims for defective merchandise even though its guarantee stated many restrictions. In fact, the court acknowledged that there was no evidence "that any customer had any claim under any guarantee . . . or that [Ward] failed to satisfy any claim under its guarantees."

Box 12.2 **Montgomery Ward Guarantee**

FOR A PERIOD OF NINETY DAYS from the date installed or four thousand miles (whichever comes first) we warrant this rebuilt assembly for passenger car service against defects in material and factory workmanship provided our installation and operating instructions are followed.

The point, however, was that Ward's actual guarantee placed many restrictions, which were not revealed in its advertising. Plain and simple, this is deceptive. If you'll recall from chapters 2 and 3, the FTC does not require a showing that actual deception occurred, only that the ad has the likelihood to deceive.

"The capacity [or under current interpretation, likelihood] to deceive," said the court, "involved in Ward's advertisements lies in the inducement to buy created by the unlimited, advertised guarantee." It is clear from this case that an advertiser must specify the terms of its guarantee in an ad, unless it truly offers an "unconditional" guarantee. The advertising of a guarantee must clearly express the actual guarantee that the consumer will get with the purchase.

False Statements Regarding a Guarantee

Certain industries place specific restrictions and requirements on guarantees of quality, origin, and authenticity of merchandise. Industries such as alcohol, tobacco, medicines, textiles, and others have such regulations. An advertiser should consult the specific regulations of these industries.

M. Reiner & Sons was a fur dealer in New York. In 1969 the company advertised and sold furs with the guarantee that the furs were authentic and in compliance with specific laws governing the fur trade (Fur Products Labeling Act, 15 U.S.C. § 69 et seq. (1988). The company claimed that the proper guarantee, as required by the Fur Products Labeling Act, was on file with the FTC.

It was learned later that this was not the case; therefore, a complaint was filed by the FTC: *In the Matter of M. Reiner & Sons*, 77 F.T.C. 862 (1970). The commission discovered that Reiner had no certificate of guarantee on file and therefore violated the law by creating a deception about its guarantee.

The commission stated that Reiner: "[F]alsely represented in writing that [it] had a continuing [guarantee] on file with the Federal Trade Commission when [it] in furnishing such guarantees had reason to believe that the fur products so falsely guaranteed would be introduced, sold, transported, and distributed in commerce."

As a result, Reiner was ordered to cease-and-desist from such practices.

Types of Guarantees

There are many different types of guarantees. Among the most common are money-back, satisfaction, lifetime, repair, limited, and refund or replacement guarantees. The type of guarantee offered is dependent on the manufacturer. Now let's take a look at each of these.

Money-Back Guarantees

This is one of the most common. A money-back guarantee means just that. If the consumer is not satisfied, a full refund must be given. This type of guarantee must be honored in a timely manner. If a customer asks for a refund, he must not be made to make numerous attempts to collect the refund.

This guarantee can be offered in a number of situations, and should be clearly stated in any ads as well as on the packaging of the product. Typical money-back guarantees clarify what the manufacturer will do under the following situations:

- If the consumer is not satisfied with the product;
- If it can be purchased elsewhere for less;
- If it fails to perform a specific job; and
- If it does not do its job better than its competition.

Satisfaction Guarantees

If an ad claims "satisfaction guaranteed," without any clarification, then the consumer is entitled to determine if the product satisfies or not.

In cases where the claim is "satisfactory-fit guaranteed" the consumer is still able to determine if satisfaction resulted from the purchase of the product. Satisfaction is a subjective judgment call, and the purchaser is allowed to use his or her judgment as to whether satisfaction exists.

Lifetime Guarantees

Lifetime guarantees are legal, but the terms of the guarantee should be clearly spelled out. The guarantee must be stated as "conditional" if charges are applied for service or replacement parts. A full disclosure of any conditions or service charges must accompany the guarantee. Terms such as "guaranteed forever" should not be used unless the manufacturer intends to live up to the claim, literally. The Sears Craftsman tool guarantee is a good example of a valid lifetime guarantee.

Claims that, in most cases, should be made include the following:

- Guaranteed to last through the ages;
- Guaranteed to give a lifetime of service;
- Guarantee of a lifetime;
- Guaranteed for a lifetime; and
- Guaranteed forever.

Repair Guarantees

Certain guarantees involve service repairs. These guarantees, usually found with appliances or automobiles, should be carefully explained. The following elements should be included in any repair guarantee:

- Time restrictions;
- Service charges;
- Cost of repairs;
- Party responsible for repairs; and
- Types of defects that are covered.

Limited Guarantees

As seen earlier, any guarantee that is not unlimited is limited. If a guarantee is claimed in an ad and it is not unlimited, then it must be called a limited guarantee.

A good example of a limited guarantee would be a computer hard drive. Typically the manufacturer provides that if the drive is defective it will be replaced. But no other obligations exist; the company cannot be made to pay for loss of the data that was on the drive.

Refund or Replacement Guarantees

Some guarantees may specify whether the manufacturer will refund the purchase price (sometimes pro-rated) or replace the item. The manufacturer may make this decision, but the term must be specified in the guarantee.

Guidelines for Advertising of Warranties and Guarantees

The FTC has developed specific guidelines that cover the many aspects of warranty and guarantee advertising. In addition, specific industry broadcast guidelines exist as well as guidelines for advertising on the Internet.

FTC Guidelines

The commission has guidelines to help advertisers avoid unfair or deceptive practices in the advertising of warranties and guarantees. These supplement the issues just discussed.

An advertiser generally is not required to state a warranty or guarantee offered on an advertised product, but is required only to disclose certain information if the guarantee is mentioned. An advertiser should mention that a product is warranted or guaranteed only if the seller or manufacturer "promptly and fully performs its obligations under the warranty or guarantee."

Written Warranties on Consumer Products If an advertisement for a consumer product costing more than $15 mentions a written warranty/guarantee, the FTC states: "The advertisement should disclose, with such clarity and prominence as will be noticed and understood by prospective purchasers, that prior to sale, at the place where the product is sold, prospective purchasers can see the written warranty or guarantee for complete details of the warranty coverage."

If an advertisement in a catalog or other solicitation for mail order or telephone sales mentions a warranty, the advertisement must prominently and clearly, in close proximity to the description of the warranted product or in a clearly referenced information section, set forth the full text of the warranty or disclose that prospective buyers can obtain complete details of the written warranty or guarantee free of charge upon specific written request from the seller or "from the catalogue or other solicitation."

Warranty Disclosure Requirements Originally the FTC required disclosure of virtually all warranty terms in ads mentioning guarantees. However, the FTC decided that to require disclosure of all guarantee terms in ads might deter advertisers from mentioning guarantee coverage at all. Since the Pre-Sale Availability Rule assures that guarantee terms are available to consumers at the store, the FTC also concluded such detailed disclosures in ads are not needed. Instead, the revised position recommends disclosure in guarantee ads promoting a product covered by the Pre-Sale Availability Rule 8, of the fact that the guarantee document is available for examination before purchase of the product.

There is a similar approach for mail-order, catalog sales and online ads. One provision calls for the disclosure of information sufficient to convey to consumers that they can obtain complete details on the written guarantee free upon specific written request, or from the catalogue or solicitation (whichever is applicable).

The FTC also states (concerning disclosures) that text in the ad will clearly and prominently specify that guarantee are available for inspection prior to sale.

Television ads will comply if the ads: "Make the necessary disclosure simultaneously with or immediately following the warranty claim. The disclosure can be presented either in the audio portion or in the video portion as a printed disclosure, provided that a video disclosure appears on the screen for at least five seconds."

However, the FTC states: "It may be necessary for multiple disclosures of the material limitations on a satisfaction guarantee to be disclosed in the audio portion of an advertisement, or to be disclosed for a longer period of time than five seconds in order for the disclosures to be clear and prominent."

Satisfaction Guarantees Satisfaction guarantees are very popular in advertising, particularly on television, in mail-order and on the Internet. The FTC states that "satisfaction guaranteed" claims should be used only if you plan to refund the full purchase price at the buyer's request. The guides also suggest that, if this type of representation is subject to material limitations or conditions (an express limitation of duration, or a limitation to products returned in their original packaging), the ad should disclose that limitation or condition.

"Lifetime" Representations The FTC suggests that use of the term "lifetime" in describing the duration of a guarantee or warranty can mislead consumers unless clarified as to the definition of "life." They require clarification of the life to which the claim refers, that is, whether or not it refers to the buyer's life.

Warranty Performance The FTC warns "that a warrantor or guarantor should ensure performance on advertised warranties or guarantees."

Industry Guidelines

All television networks have extensive guidelines pertaining to the advertising of warranties or guarantees. They will require clear and conspicuous disclosure in the commercial referring to a warranty or guarantee, whether the warranty is full or limited. For example, ABC requires that the ad disclose: "specific duration, major limitations (e.g., parts excluded or costs or responsibilities the customer must undertake), and 'see dealer for details'" statements. Under NBC's broadcast standards requirements, the ad must disclose: "the nature and extent of the guarantee; the identity of the guarantor; the manner in which the guarantor intends to perform; information concerning what a purchaser wishing to claim under the guarantee need do before the guarantor will perform pursuant to its obligations under the guarantee."

Internet Service Providers also have rules for advertising of guarantees. Facebook, Yahoo and many others follow similar paths when guarantees are included in offerings through their services.

The Magnuson-Moss Warranty Act

When Congress enacted the Magnuson-Moss Warranty Act (15 U.S.C. § 45 (1988)), it gave the federal government a potentially dominant role in warranty/guarantee law. While the act still hasn't lived up to initial expectations, it is, nonetheless, a major force to be reckoned with when offering a warranty or guarantee on a product or service. An initial determination should always be made whether the Magnuson-Moss Warranty Act applies. Magnuson-Moss is applicable to written warranties.

Essentially, there are two types of written warranties under the act: "full" and "limited." If you decide to offer your customers a "full" warranty, it means, among other things, that:

- You will fix or replace a defective product for free within a reasonable time;
- You won't require your customer to do anything unreasonable to get warranty service;
- Your warranty is good for anyone owning the product during the warranty period; and
- You will give your customer the choice of a new product or his or her money back if the product can't be fixed or hasn't been fixed after a reasonable number of attempts.

If you offer a "limited" warranty, it means you're offering less than what a full warranty provides. For example, a limited warranty may cover only parts and not labor, or cover only the first buyer, or charge for handling.

If a manufacturer or retailer offers a written warranty, the Magnuson-Moss act demands substantial analysis and compliance.

To get a copy of the Magnuson-Moss Act, implementing regulations, and explanatory pamphlets on the law, you should write to: the FTC, Washington, D.C. 20580, or check their website at: www.ftc.gov.

13 Special Areas of Advertising Concern

Consumers do not buy products. They buy product benefits.

—*David Ogilvy*

A tall, powerful woman in a black dress marched into a saloon in Medicine Lodge, Kansas, one evening in 1890. For many days prior, she had stayed outside the saloon reading the Bible—intently praying for the close of the saloon. The woman had good reason for her vigil. Her drunkard husband had died shortly after their marriage, leaving her a lonely and angry widow. At the time, Kansas was a "dry" (no alcohol) state, but the law was not effectively enforced.

When her prayers did not work, she turned to violence. The male patrons ran from the saloon, frantically stumbling, as she smashed the place to pieces with her axe. The well-placed blows struck by Carry A. Nation echoed far beyond the small town in Kansas. Around the beginning of the twentieth century there was increasing government regulation in many areas. Congress had begun to pass laws to protect the public from harmful foods and drugs and to conserve the nation's natural resources. The monopolies created by the Morgans and Rockefellers were beginning to be broken up. All this allowed the prohibition movement to catch fire as well.

It was not a new movement though. By the 1850s, prohibition laws were in effect in thirteen states. The forces behind the movement had roots in religious fundamentalism and support from the Women's Christian Temperance Union, founded in Ohio in 1874. In many states, local counties had the ability to vote themselves dry. And many did in West Virginia, Maryland, Illinois, Georgia, Missouri, and Mississippi. But neighboring counties could still supply the product—and they did.

The temperance drive gained new momentum after 1900, however. Beer and whiskey sales had grown rapidly among the large numbers of Irish and German immigrants. And, as would be expected, this brought about an anti-foreign ring to the cries for prohibition. And as women gained the vote for the first time, the temperance drive grew also.

The Committee of Fifty, formed in 1893 to study the "liquor problem," led the battle. The committee investigated the nation's poverty, crime, mental disease, and family decay and traced them all to alcohol use. They believed that national prohibition was the only answer because temperance—a supposed result of education and self-control—had not worked.

Congressmen and even president William McKinley had started to listen to the prohibitionists, and a nationwide law prohibiting alcohol sales went into effect. All this exasperated a man named Adolphus Busch, who personally took his argument to the president. Unfortunately, the president was a Methodist who as early as 1867 had been identified with "total abstinence."

If any single person energized the prohibition movement it was Adolphus Busch. He had the most visible profile, and his kingly demeanor and pro-German sentiments offended many Americans. Closely identified with his company, Anheuser-Busch Brewery, he became a prime target of the prohibitionists. Leading the industry as he did, he also had the most to lose; a long string of his descendants depended on beer for their livelihood. Adolphus had no intention of permitting the empire he had built for his children to be legislated out of existence. And it wasn't.

The stage was set when, nine days after his inauguration, president Roosevelt recommended that Congress officially sanction the return of beer. "I deem action at this time," he said, "to be of the highest importance." Congress—they were thirsty too—quickly approved a law authorizing the sale of beer with a 3.2 percent alcohol content. Moments after Roosevelt signed the beer bill, Busch sent a telegram praising him for his "wisdom and foresight" and for restoring to the "American people an old and time-honored industry." Prohibition had survived for a little over thirteen years.

Prohibition ended on April 7, 1933, with a raucous, national street party. It was a coast-to-coast party unlike anything this country has ever seen. Not even the celebration that followed the armistice ending the Great War (now known as World War I) or Lindbergh's solo flight across the Atlantic had compared. Beer was back, and Anheuser-Busch screamed the fact in full-page advertisements.

True to form, the company tried to hit upon a good advertising gimmick to celebrate beer's return. They picked a masterpiece. One that would become one of the most famous brand symbols in the world—a team of high-stepping, solemnly majestic, champing at the bit, Clydesdale horses pulling a beautifully detailed red and yellow beer wagon assembled "for advertising purposes."

The first truck out of the Busch plant had headed for the airport, carrying cases of the new Budweiser for president Roosevelt and the governor of New York. When the beer arrived in New York City and in Washington, D.C., it was loaded onto wagons drawn by teams of Clydesdales. In New York the horses caused a sensation as they clamored down Fifth Avenue and stopped at the Empire State building. In Washington, the team pulled up to a White House already deluged with similar shipments from other brewers.

Within 9 months, the required thirty-six states had ratified the twenty-first amendment, thereby repealing the eighteenth. But prohibition had taken a heavy toll on the nation's breweries. Of the 1,392 in operation in 1914, only 164 remained. For Anheuser-Busch the cost had been a staggering $34 million. But they had survived.

There are a number of special areas that concern advertising. We'll look at those in this chapter, starting with alcohol advertising.

Alcohol Advertising

Here we examine current restrictions on the advertising of alcoholic beverages, which are subject to oversight from the FTC, the ATF, state and county governments. Guidance and regulation is also provided by trade organizations and the television networks

The Federal Government's Role

As for the federal government, the Federal Communications Commission does not forbid the advertising of alcoholic beverages in broadcast media. On the other hand, the Federal Trade Commission and the Bureau of Alcohol, Tobacco, and Firearms have joint authority over the advertising of alcoholic beverages.

The Overboard Ad Example An advertisement showed a sailing boat at sea. Almost all of the young adults on board were holding bottles of Beck's beer, with several of them sitting on the edge of the boat, where there was no railing. The complaint, *Beck's North America, Inc.*, CCH Trade Regulation Reports ¶ 24,481, filed by the FTC charged that the advertisements constituted unfair acts or practices in violation of the FTC Act because they were likely to cause substantial injury to consumers. In addition, boating safety experts such as the United States Coast Guard stressed that boating accidents were greatly increased by the consumption of alcohol, the FTC said.

The case was settled and the agreement prohibited Beck's beer from producing television ads that depict a person having consumed or consuming alcohol on a boat while engaging in activities that pose a substantial risk of serious injury or that depict certain activities that would violate boating safety laws.

The White Russian Example Another case, *Allied Domecq Spirits & Wines Americas, Inc.*, Trade Regulation Reports ¶ 24,482, involved an advertisement claiming that Kahlua White Russian (a premixed cocktail) was a "low alcohol" beverage. According to the FTC, the beverage was not a low alcohol beverage because it contained 5.9 percent alcohol by volume, an amount equal to or greater than many other alcoholic beverages. A Kahlua White Russian had substantially more alcohol (ounce for ounce) than many beers, malt liquors, and wine coolers.

The United States Bureau of Alcohol, Tobacco, and Firearms sets the limit that can be claimed to be low alcohol at 2.5 percent by volume. Again, this case was settled. And the consent order prohibits Kahlua from representing that any alcoholic beverage containing 5.9 percent by volume is a low alcohol beverage. The order does not prohibit the company from making truthful comparative claims about the alcohol level of its products, however.

ATF's Role: Regulation Issues with Alcohol Advertising The other important federal agency having jurisdiction over the advertising of alcoholic beverages is the Bureau of Alcohol, Tobacco, and Firearms. The ATF groups alcoholic beverages into three major beverage groupings: malt beverages, wine, and distilled spirits and treats each group differently.

1. Malt beverages:

Under the Federal Alcohol Administration Act, a malt beverage is: A beverage made by the alcoholic fermentation of an infusion or decoction, or combination of both, in potable brewing water, of malted barley with hops, or their parts, or their products, and with or without the addition of [certain additional ingredients] (Federal Alcohol Administration Act, 27 CFR 7.20).

Malt beverages are low in alcohol content as a percentage of volume and occasionally escape regulations aimed at alcoholic beverages in general.

The ATF does not allow advertising the alcoholic content of malt beverages and does not allow any product containing less than one-half of one percent alcohol by volume to be called "beer," "lager beer," "lager," "ale," "porter," or "stout."

2. Wine:

Includes grape wine, sparkling grape wine, citrus wine, aperitif wine, raisin wine, and sake.

3. Distilled spirits:

Includes vodka, whisky, gin, brandy, rum, tequila, cordials and liqueurs, flavored spirits as well as imitations of any of these.

According to the ATF, the following rules must be followed:

- All ads must include the name and city of the manufacturer and the designation of the type of product involved;
- The ad may not make any false or misleading statements in any material respect or one that disparages a competitor's product;
- An ad may not make any statement that the manufacturer's beverage has intoxicating properties;
- Ads may not make any representation that the product has medicinal or therapeutic effects;
- Alcoholic beverage ads may not use any statement, design or representation regarding analysis, standards, or tests that may be considered misleading;
- An ad may not make a statement that's inconsistent with the product's label;
- An ad may not make any guarantee that is misleading; and
- An ad cannot use official flags, government insignia, or statements that can be construed as relating to the armed services.

In addition, there are other specific requirements regarding each type of alcoholic beverage.

State Controls

The most extensive control over advertising of alcohol comes from the individual states. They have restricted advertising on billboards, in circulars, and on radio and television. Displays on retail premises, newspaper and magazine advertising, retailer novelties, consumer novelties, premium offers, cents-off offers, samples, contests, and refunds are also considered state issues. It is important for any advertiser to investigate the specific regulations in any state in which he advertises. The detailed regulations of each state are too overwhelming for discussion in this chapter.

The Twenty-first Amendment to the Constitution gives the states some special powers. In *Capital Cities Cable, Inc.* v. *Crisp*, 467 United States 691, 104 S.Ct. 2694, 81 L.Ed. 2d 580 (1984), reversing *Oklahoma Telecasters* v. *Crisp*, 699 F.2d. 490 (10th Cir. 1983), the United States Supreme Court ruled against Oklahoma's advertising ban requiring cable television operators to screen out alcoholic beverage advertising that was part of the out-of-state signals they retransmitted by cable to their subscribers. The main reasoning behind the Court's ruling was that since cable television operates under FCC regulations, Oklahoma must follow federal law. In addition, Oklahoma's ban ran against established FCC regulations and their goal of making the benefits of cable television available nationally.

Two other important cases have upheld state control of liquor ads. In *Queensgate Inv. Co.* v. *Liquor Control Comm'n*, 459 United States 807, 103 S. Ct. 31, 74 L.Ed. 2d 45 dismissing appeal from 69 Ohio St. 2d 361, 433 N.E. 2d. 138 (1982), the United States Supreme Court dismissed an appeal from an Ohio state court's ruling upholding an Ohio regulation prohibiting retail liquor permittees from advertising the price of alcoholic beverages off their premises. The Fifth Federal Circuit then followed that precedent and upheld Mississippi statutes and regulations banning liquor ads on billboards, in print, and over the air within the state in *Dunagin* v. *City of Oxford, Mississippi*, 718 F.2d. 738 (5th Cir. 1983).

City Ordinances

An ordinance in the City of Oakland, California, stated: "No person may place any advertising sign for alcoholic beverages or tobacco products in publicly visible locations." "Advertising sign" was defined as "any sign, poster, placard, device, graphic display, or any other form of advertising directing attention to, or otherwise pertaining to, a commodity, service, business, or profession which is not sold, produced, conducted, or offered by any activity on the same lot." The ordinance was challenged in court by Eller Media, an outdoor billboard company. The court in *Eller Media Co.* v. *City of Oakland*, No. C98-2237 FMS, 1998 United States Dist. LEXIS 13319 (N.D. Cal., August 28, 1998), characterized the restriction as "off-site" advertising, as opposed to "on-site" advertising at liquor retail locations.

In addition, the ordinance did not apply to:

1. Alcoholic beverage advertising in commercial business districts;
2. Ads inside premises that lawfully sold alcoholic beverages;
3. Ads on commercial vehicles used for transporting products;
4. Ads in conjunction with temporary alcoholic beverage licenses;
5. Ads on taxicabs; and
6. Signs adjacent to and facing an interstate highway.

Prior to enacting the ordinance, the City of Oakland held public hearings during which it received testimony from school children, parents, teachers, nonprofit groups, and social scientists regarding the effect of alcoholic beverage advertising on underage drinking. The city also reviewed scientific literature that drew a direct correlation between a teenager's exposure to alcohol advertising and his or her propensities to "drink, drink heavily, and drink in hazardous situations such as in conjunction with driving." One report found that adolescents who suffered heightened exposure to alcohol advertising were more likely to associate drinking with attractiveness, athleticism, and success.

The court found that the purpose of the ordinance was to protect minors from the detrimental effects of alcohol consumption. The city tailored the ordinance to only include "off-site" billboards because of their ability to attract the attention of children. The court also found that the exceptions to the ordinance were crafted so as to leave other media available to advertisers, while limiting advertising in areas most likely to attract the attention of minors.

The federal district court upheld the ordinance passed by the City of Oakland that prohibited certain types of advertising for alcoholic beverages. The court ruled that the advertising restrictions in the ordinance advanced a substantial government interest and were narrowly tailored to serve that interest.

The Beer Institute

Beer is a legal beverage meant to be consumed responsibly. Its origins are ancient, and it has held a respected position in nearly every culture and society since the dawn of recorded history. Advertising is a legitimate effort by brewers to make consumers aware of the particular types, brands, and prices that are available.

Three basic principles which have long been reflected in the policies of the brewing industry continue to underlie these guidelines. First, beer advertising should not suggest directly or indirectly that any of the laws applicable to the sale and consumption of beer should not be complied with. Second, brewers should adhere to standards of candor and good taste applicable to all commercial advertising. Third, brewers are responsible corporate citizens, sensitive to the problems of the society in which they function, and their advertising should reflect that fact. Brewers strongly oppose abuse or inappropriate consumption of their products.

The Beer Institute's advertising and marketing codes are available online through: http://www.beerinstitute.org.

The Wine Institute

The voluntary code originally created in 1978 governing wine producers is from the Wine Institute. Since all the members of the Wine Institute are located in California, the code only governs wines produced in that state. Check the Wine Institute's website at: www.wineinstitute.org. They have a comprehensive list of reference materials on wine and related item advertising and marketing issues.

Distilled Spirits

Under the ATF rules alcoholic content by proof must be stated for all distilled spirits. It may be stated in terms of percentage by volume for cordials and liqueurs, cocktails, highballs, bitters, and other specialties as approved by the ATF. The words "bond," "bonded," "bottled in bond," "aged in bond," or synonymous terms cannot be used unless they appear on the label pursuant to ATF regulations. "Pure" can only be used if part of the name of the permit holder or retailer for whom the distilled spirits is bonded. The words "double distilled" and "triple distilled" are strictly forbidden.

The Distilled Spirits Council of the United States (DISCUS) is the voluntary authority that governs the advertising of distilled spirits. Check their web site at: www.discus.health.org.

TV Network Guidelines

Wine and beer ads (but not those for distilled spirits) may appear on the major television networks. NBC forbids the advertisement of alcoholic beverages as "necessary to maintain social status, obtain personal achievements, relieve stress or as a solution to personal problems."

On-camera consumption of alcohol is strictly forbidden. Ads for liquor outlets are acceptable to NBC if there is no reference to unacceptable wine or distilled spirits. Ads on NBC for airlines and restaurants may make incidental reference to cocktails, but advertising of mixed drinks is not acceptable, nor is the use of terms like "martini" or "Bloody Mary." Glassware associated with distilled spirits is not an acceptable prop to NBC, except in relation to the "incidental reference" mentioned above. NBC will review advertisements alerting the public to the dangers of alcohol abuse on a "case-by-case" basis.

ABC has a very similar set of guidelines; one minor difference is that ABC prohibits even the incidental display of cocktail props.

CBS has a policy against direct or implied references to excessive consumption of beer and wine.

For more details on all TV network alcohol advertising, refer to their websites listed in the Index of Sources.

Tobacco and Cigarette Advertising

Each year, heroin and cocaine together cause the death of approximately five thousand Americans. Yet, this tragedy is dwarfed by the Surgeon General's conclusion that cigarette smoking is responsible for over four hundred and eighty thousand unnecessary deaths each year in this country alone. According to these numbers, almost one out of six deaths in the United States can be traced back to cigarette smoking. Although smoking among adults dropped from 40 percent in 1965 to 29 percent in 1987, approximately fifty-five million Americans still smoke.

A Controversial Product

The controversy over cigarette advertising continues to grow. Critics condemn all types of advertising and promotion used to market cigarettes. On the other hand, many industry voices claim advertising is highly overrated as a factor in causing people to smoke. They cite peer pressure and parental role-modeling as more relevant causes.

Here we'll take a look at some of the concerns about cigarette marketing and advertising in more depth. First, there is the concern over the scope of cigarette advertising. In 2011 the tobacco industry spent close to $8.4 billion (that's about $23 million a day) for advertising and promotion.

The vast majority of new smokers are teenagers or younger. By one estimate, 60 percent are under the age of fourteen. This statistic is a cause for particular concern over the effects of cigarette advertising on children and teenagers.

The tobacco industry, on the other hand, has argued that advertising informs consumers about brand differences and leads to brand switching rather than to smoking initiation. Critics emphasize advertising's role in the glamorization of smoking, attracting new smokers, and impeding the efforts of smokers to quit. There simply is no way to determine which view is provable.

Since most smokers merely switch among the brands of Philip Morris and R. J. Reynolds, who control approximately two-thirds of the United States cigarette market, this seems to validate the critics' charges that the goals of advertising and promotion are somewhat broader than would be guessed.

Legal Issues

In recent years there has been much activity in the courts regarding the advertising of tobacco and cigarettes. The most visible of which may have been the Joe Camel Case. There has also been a great deal of activity in other government bodies, including individual states.

The Joe Camel Example In May 1997 the FTC alleged that R. J. Reynolds, through its Joe Camel advertising campaign, unlawfully caused or was likely to cause substantial and ongoing injury to the health and safety of children and adolescents under the age of eighteen. The agency sought an order: (1) prohibiting Reynolds from advertising to children Camel cigarettes through the use of themes or images relating to "Joe Camel;" (2) requiring that Reynolds disseminate public education messages discouraging persons under eighteen from smoking; and (3) requiring the company to collect and make available data concerning the sales of each brand of its cigarettes to persons under eighteen and each brand's share of smokers under eighteen.

On January 27, 1999, the Federal Trade Commission announced that it dismissed the case against R. J. Reynolds Tobacco Company for its Joe Camel advertising campaign. The Commission decided that the result it sought was accomplished by the recent multistate tobacco settlement and revisions of the United States Department of Health and Human Services' data collection methods.

The November 23, 1998, Master Settlement Agreement with forty-six attorneys general and five major cigarette companies covered the first and second issues.

That agreement, the Commission said: "Specifically bans the use of all cartoon characters, including Joe Camel, in the advertising, promotion, packaging, and labeling of any tobacco product . . . [and] the settlement requires the tobacco companies to help finance a national public education fund designed to carry out on a nationwide basis sustained advertising and education programs to counter underage usage of tobacco products and to educate consumers about the causes of prevention of diseases associated with the use of tobacco products."

As it relates to the third issue, the FTC said that the "Substance Abuse and Mental Health Services Administration of the United States Department of Health and Human Services is revising the protocol for its annual national household survey on drug abuse to add specific questions to elicit brand share of smokers under eighteen."

The Food and Drug Administration A number of tobacco companies, convenience store retailers, and advertisers recently challenged FDA rules that restricted the sale, distribution, and advertising of tobacco products. As a result, the Fourth Circuit has determined that the Food and Drug Administration does not have jurisdiction to regulate tobacco products in *Brown & Williamson Tobacco Corp.* v. *FDA*, No. 97-1604, 1998 United States App. LEXIS 18821 (4th Cir., August 14, 1998). The court reasoned that Congress (by its creation of the Food, Drug and Cosmetics Act) had not intended to allow the FDA the right to regulate tobacco products.

The FDA asserted jurisdiction over tobacco products under the "drugs" and "device" definitions in the Act. The Act defines "drugs" as "articles (other than food) intended to affect the structure or any function of the body of man or animals." "Device" is defined as an article which is intended to affect the structure or any function of the body of man or other animals, and which does not achieve its primary intended purposes through chemical action within or on the body of man or other animals and which is not dependent upon being metabolized for the achievement of its primary intended purposes (21 U.S.C. § 321(h)(3)).

According to the FDA, tobacco products fit under the Act's definitions because they were "intended to affect the structure or any function of the body." The FDA claimed that tobacco products were "combination products consisting of nicotine, a drug that causes addiction and other significant pharmacological effects on the human body, and device components that deliver nicotine to the body."

The court, however, reasoned that it was not Congress' intent to grant the FDA the authority to regulate tobacco products. The provisions of the Food, Drug, and Cosmetics Act did not support bestowing that authority, the court found. During its rulemaking process regarding tobacco products, the FDA found that tobacco products were "dangerous," "unsafe," and the cause of "great pain and suffering from illness such as cancer, respiratory illnesses, and heart disease."

However, the court stated:

> The FDA has proposed to regulate tobacco products under a statutory provision that requires conditions on sale and distribution which provide a reasonable assurance of safety. According to the FDA, a determination of safety under the Act requires consideration of the risks of a product compared to the "countervailing effects of use of that product, including the consequences of not permitting the product to be

marketed." Thus, the FDA concluded that withdrawal of tobacco from the market poses significant health risks to addicted adults which outweighs the risks of leaving tobacco products on the market. But that test is contrary to the statute. A statutory provision, provides that safety and effectiveness are to be determined by "weighing any probable benefit to health from the use of the device against any probable risk of injury or illness from such use."

Analyzing the statute shows that the FDA must strike a balance between the risks and benefits of the use of a certain product, not weigh the risks of leaving a product on the market against the risks of taking it off the market. The FDA was unable to state any real health benefit derived from leaving tobacco products on the market. "[B]ased on the FDA's characterization of tobacco products as unsafe, it is impossible to create regulations which will provide a reasonable assurance of safety. Thus, the FDA cannot comply with the terms of the very statutory provision it has chosen as its basis for regulation," the court concluded.

Preemption Issues: The Chicago Tobacco Ordinance In *Federation of Advertising Industry Representatives* v. *City of Chicago*, No. 97C7619, 1998 United States Dist. LEXIS 11777 (N.D. Ill., July 29, 1998), a Chicago ordinance that restricted advertising of both cigarettes and alcohol in any "publicly visible location" was preempted by the Federal Cigarette Labeling and Advertising Act (15 U.S.C. §§ 1131-1341).

The Federal Cigarette Labeling and Advertising Act established a comprehensive set of restrictions on cigarette advertising and labeling as they related to the health effects of smoking. The Act was designed to ensure that consumers received adequate, clear, uniform information about the dangers of smoking. In the interest of such uniformity, the Act contained an express preemption clause which stated: "No requirement or prohibition based on smoking and health shall be imposed under State law with respect to the advertising or promotion of any cigarettes the packages of which are labeled in conformity with the provisions of this chapter."

The Chicago ordinance stated: "No person may place any sign, poster, placard or graphic display that advertises cigarettes or alcoholic beverages in a publicly visible location. In this section, 'publicly visible location' includes outdoor billboards, sides of buildings, and freestanding signboards."

The ordinance also had ten exceptions that permitted advertising within retail premises, on city buses, at the major sports stadiums, and on interstate highways.

The court decided that it did not need to look beyond the express language of the preemption statute to find that the Chicago ordinance was preempted under the federal law. The ordinance clearly contained a "prohibition" and it was "with respect to the advertising and promotion of cigarettes." The contested issue was whether the ordinance's prohibition was "based on smoking and health."

The city argued that the purpose of the ordinance was to reduce sales of cigarettes to minors and, thus, the ordinance's prohibition was not "based on smoking and health."

The city argued: "The Ordinance explicitly states that its purpose is to reduce illegal transactions, that is, cigarette sales to or purchased by minors. Furthermore, the preamble is focused on illegal transactions, not health, and on the connection between outdoor advertising and illegal activities. Indeed, the very first section of the Ordinance recites that it is unlawful for any individual under the age of eighteen to purchase or be sold cigarettes. All of the recitals, or "whereas" clauses, deal with the illegality of cigarette sales to or purchases by minors, the degree of cigarette consumption by minors, the extent of outdoor advertising of cigarettes, the unique nature of cigarette billboards, the relationship between advertising of cigarettes and consumption of cigarettes, and the need for the Ordinance. Nothing in the recitals indicates that the purpose of the Ordinance, vis-à-vis cigarettes, is anything other than preventing illegal transactions."

The court rejected the city's arguments, finding that the real reason the ordinance was passed was the link between smoking and health. The reason it was illegal to sell cigarettes to minors in Illinois in the first place was because the legislature's desire to protect minors from the health risks associated with smoking. The court rejected the city's attempt to narrowly define the purpose behind the ordinance.

Because the ordinance prohibited cigarette advertising that was based on smoking and health, the court found that the ordinance was preempted by federal law.

The Vermont Ordinance In Vermont, a city ordinance that restricted retail tobacco advertising was preempted by federal law. Similar to the City of Chicago ordinance, the court in *Rockwood* v. *City of Burlington*, No. 2:98-CV-223, 1998 United States Dist. LEXIS 15021 (D. Vt., September 21, 1998), found that the Vermont ordinance was a "requirement or prohibition" "based on smoking and health . . . with respect to the advertising or promotion of any cigarettes." The court rejected the city's argument that the ordinance was enacted for the purpose of reducing the illegal sale of tobacco to minors.

The relevant part the ordinance prohibited:

(a) Point-of-sale advertising of tobacco products by any means other than a maximum of two black and white, text only, 12 by 14 inch signs (Tombstone Signs) in or on any retail establishment where tobacco products are offered for sale. The text could not exceed one inch in height, and could include only the brand name, description of the product, tar and nicotine content, price, and any warnings required by law. The Ordinance made it unlawful for city retailers to use any promotional items inside or outside their stores, such as clocks, grocery dividers, display racks, ashtrays, trash cans, catalogues, uniforms, T-shirts, or other clothing;
(b) Any tobacco advertising within one thousand feet of a school;
(c) The distribution of free samples of tobacco products or coupons redeemable for tobacco products;
(d) Any manufacturer, distributor, or retailer from sponsoring any athletic, musical, artistic, or other social event using a tobacco product brand name, logo, motto, or image; and
(e) Self-service displays of cigarettes or tobacco products.

The stated purpose of the ordinance was to decrease the illegal use of tobacco by minors. However, after reviewing the records of city council meetings and other public hearings held in connection with the ordinance, it became clear that health concerns were an important component of the city's concerns. The court stated: "It strains credulity to adopt the rationale that the City's Ordinance is unrelated to smoking and health, merely because the City has stressed its purpose of reducing illegal activity by minors. Clearly the dominant reason that lawmakers in Vermont as elsewhere seek to restrict the use of tobacco products by minors is the grave concern that addiction to nicotine in their youth will have long-term health consequences for them."

The court also rejected the city's argument that the ordinance did not regulate cigarette advertising within the meaning of the preemption statute. This, it claimed, was because it regulated the location and format of the advertising, but not its content, and did not limit the ability of cigarette manufacturers and vendors from advertising in the mass media. The court found, however, that one section of the ordinance specifically prescribed the content of tobacco product advertising signs as well as limiting their location. The text of the signs could only include the brand name, description of the product, tar and nicotine content, price, and any warnings required by federal law. On the other hand, the preemption statute made no distinction between prohibitions on advertising language and advertising locations.

This case also involved commercial speech issues. The court found that the city ordinance could not withstand First Amendment scrutiny since it restricted advertising of a lawful activity that was not misleading. There was no evidence that the tobacco companies targeted their advertising specifically to minors. And the court reasoned that the state had a valid state interest in reducing illegal (underage) smoking and that restricting tobacco advertising could possibly advance that interest.

The ordinance failed the *Central Hudson* (*Central Hudson Gas & Electric Corp.* v. *Public Service Commission of New York*, 447 United States 557 (1980)) test because it was not narrowly tailored to serve the city's asserted interest. The ordinance completely banned publicly visible tobacco advertising within one thousand feet of a school. It restricted point-of-sale advertising to two black-and-white signs in a retail establishment, and limited what could be displayed on the signs. Further, the ordinance banned sponsorship advertising and the distribution of free samples. None of these provisions were narrowly tailored to affect advertising targeted at minors, the court determined. The court found that there was not a "reasonable fit" between the ordinance and the city's interest in reducing underage smoking.

State Attorneys General Actions In 1998 nine state attorneys generals (California, Colorado, Massachusetts, New York, North Carolina, North Dakota, Oklahoma, Pennsylvania, and Washington) negotiated with tobacco companies on advertising restrictions that would not require Congress' involvement. On November 16, 1998, a proposed $206 billion agreement was announced. According to the agreement, Brown & Williamson, Lorillard, Philip Morris, and R. J. Reynolds agreed to fund a $1.5 billion antismoking campaign.

The settlement requires that the companies pay $25 million per year, for ten years, to a foundation that will study programs to reduce teen smoking and substance abuse as well as study the prevention of diseases associated with tobacco. Another element provides that the foundation will carry out a nationwide, sustained advertising and education program designed to reduce youth smoking and educate consumers. The foundation will also commission studies, fund research, and publish reports on youth smoking and substance abuse.

As it related to tobacco advertising:

- The settlement bans use of cartoons in the advertising, promotion, packaging, or labeling of tobacco products.
- The settlement prohibits targeting of youths in advertising, promotions, or marketing.
- The settlement bans industry actions aimed at initiating, maintaining, or increasing youth smoking.
- The settlement requires companies to: (1) develop and regularly communicate corporate principles that commit to complying with the Master Settlement Agreement and reducing youth smoking; (2) designate an executive level manager to identify ways to reduce youth access and consumption of tobacco; and (3) encourage employees to identify additional methods to reduce youth access and consumption.
- The settlement bans all outdoor advertising, including billboards, signs and placards in arenas, stadiums, shopping malls, and video game arcades, and limits advertising outside retail establishments to fourteen square feet.
- The settlement bans transit advertising of tobacco products and allows states to substitute, for the duration of billboard lease periods, alternative advertising which discourages youth smoking.

- Beginning on July 1, 1999, the settlement bans distribution and sale of apparel and merchandise with brand name logos, including caps, T-shirts, backpacks, and the like.
- The settlement bans payments to promote tobacco products in movies, television shows, theater productions or live performances, live or recorded music performances, videos, and video games.
- The settlement prohibits brand-name sponsorship of events with significant youth audience or team sports, such as football, basketball, baseball, hockey, and soccer and prohibits sponsorship of events where paid participants or contestants are underage. Bans tobacco brand names from stadiums and arenas.
- The settlement limits tobacco companies to one brand-name sponsorship per year after current contracts expire or after three years, whichever comes first.
- The settlement limits distribution of free samples to facilities or enclosed areas where the operator ensures no underage person is present.

On September 17, 1998, tobacco companies agreed to pay $1.7 billion to the state of Florida and accept additional advertising restrictions as part of that state's antismoking lawsuit. New advertising restrictions in Florida cover merchandise promotions such as Marlboro T-shirts and an agreement to not pay to have tobacco brands shown in movies.

In its antitrust case against tobacco companies, the State of Washington settled with two of the defendants on October 2, 1998. The settlements involved Smokeless Tobacco Council, Inc., and United States Tobacco Co. Here, United States Tobacco agreed to stop all billboard and transit advertising of tobacco products.

The company also agreed not to oppose legislation banning tobacco vending machines except in adult-only facilities, and legislation that would strengthen penalties for selling tobacco to minors. The company also agreed pay the state $2 million for reimbursement of legal costs.

Products Liability Lawsuits

A final economic disincentive is the threat of product liability suits. We looked at this subject in detail in chapter 8. A jury verdict in 1987 went against tobacco interests in *Cipollone* v. *Liggett Group, Inc.*, 789 F.2d 181 (3d Cir. 1986), cert. denied, 479 United States 1043, 107 S.Ct. 907, 93 L.Ed. 2d 857 (1987), producing three major results:

- The monetary award of $400,000;
- The release of extensive and previously confidential strategy and research documents from company and Tobacco Institute files, paving the way for future cases; and
- The willingness of a jury to determine that cigarette advertising has made express warranties about health aspects of cigarettes and that these contributed to the person's smoking and death.

In several cases, including *Cipollone*, courts did not allow the introduction of evidence of company failure to warn and negligence after 1966 (when the Cigarette Labeling and Advertising Act took effect). Both the likelihood and magnitude of awards in the future will depend on judicial clarification of:

- Underlying liability theories (risk-utility concepts, implied warranties); and
- Admissibility and weight given to the conduct of both the smoker and the cigarette company after 1966.

A number of jurists and legislators have subsequently expressed the conviction that Congress, by mandating a particular warning, could not possibly have intended to shield tobacco companies from all responsibility to warn consumers or to give companies license to fail intentionally to disclose important health information by mandating a particular warning.

The ultimate irony is: the cigarette companies can now escape liability for their deceptive ads because the federal courts have misinterpreted a law which was intended to impede the use of this death-dealing product by giving consumers more, not less, information.

However, until Congress acts or the Supreme Court overturns lower court decisions, consumers' injuries resulting primarily from smoking in the period after 1966 may be immune from recovery under products liability theories at least.

Effects of *Price* v. *Philip Morris, Inc.* In *Price* v. *Philip Morris, Inc.*, 219 Ill. 2d 182; 848 N.E.2d 1; 2005 Ill. LEXIS 2511; 302 Ill. Dec. 1 (2005), the plaintiffs represented 1.14 million consumers who purchased and used Cambridge Lights and Marlboro Lights cigarettes in Illinois for personal consumption between their introduction and February 8, 2001.

After a bench trial in the circuit court, the court found defendant, Philip Morris USA, Inc. (PMUSA), liable for fraud in violation of the Consumer Fraud and Deceptive Business Practices Act (815 ILCS 505/1 et seq.), and the Uniform Deceptive Trade Practices Act (815 ILCS 510/1 et seq.), and awarded the estimated 1.14 million members of the plaintiff class compensatory and punitive damages, attorney fees, and prejudgment interest totaling $10.1 billion.

This case revolved around many issues but primarily the focus was over descriptions used on the cigarette packages. The decision of the circuit court was addressed on this appeal. The court concluded in a seventy-page opinion, that the FTC could, and did, specifically authorize all United States tobacco companies to utilize the words "low," "lower," "reduced" or like qualifying terms, such as "light," as long as the descriptive terms are accompanied by a clear and conspicuous disclosure of the "tar" and nicotine content in milligrams of the smoke produced by the advertised cigarette. Further, the FTC forbade the representation of tar ratings as "a numerical multiple, fraction or ratio of the tar or nicotine ratings of any other brand," but specifically allowed the "express or implied representation" that a cigarette was "low," "lower," or "lowest" in tar and/or nicotine. Thus, the court held that plaintiffs' claim is barred by section 10b(1) of the Consumer Fraud Act.

The court stated:

> At oral argument, plaintiffs' counsel noted that the circuit court made two separate findings of fraud: (1) a finding that PMUSA's use of the terms "light" and "lowered tar and nicotine" was fraudulent and deceptive based on the known phenomenon of compensation, and (2) a finding that the members of the plaintiff class were defrauded because PMUSA failed to disclose that its "light" cigarettes were more mutagenic than full-flavor cigarettes. Counsel argued that, even if this court were to reverse on the merits of the first claim, the second portion of the circuit court's judgment must still stand.
>
> ———We have not reached the merits of either aspect of plaintiffs' fraud claim, having found the entire claim barred by section 10b(1) of the Consumer Fraud Act. However, our discussion thus far has focused on the PMUSA's use of the disputed terms. The question we must next address is whether, even if the use of the terms was specifically authorized by the FTC, a claim may be brought under the Consumer Fraud Act based on PMUSA's describing more mutagenic cigarettes as "light" and as

delivering "lower tar and nicotine." For two reasons, we find that the claim of fraud based on increased mutagenicity cannot stand.

The reasons for this were two-fold. First, plaintiffs' claim regarding mutagenicity was linked to their claim that the terms "lights" and "lowered tar and nicotine" were fraudulent and deceptive. Even though the circuit court found that members of the class understood those terms as to an implied claim of safety and relied on this understanding, their Consumer Fraud Act claim is barred by section 10b(1). It was clear that the FTC had defined both terms as meaning 15 milligrams or less of tar. Because PMUSA was specifically authorized to use these terms on its labels and in its, any claim based on the use of these terms was barred by section 10b(1) of the Consumer Fraud Act.

Second, plaintiffs' mutagenicity claim was based on PMUSA's failure to make additional disclosures beyond those required by federal statute and the voluntary agreement with the FTC: the tar and nicotine content in milligrams and the mandatory warning label. Effectively, the claim was barred by finding compliance with disclosure requirements of federal statute to be a defense to liability under the Consumer Fraud Act.

The court said: "Plaintiffs note that the FTC has never adopted a trade regulation rule approving the use of descriptors such as "light" or "low tar," and that the FTC has never stated that the use of such descriptors has been "substantiated" by any cigarette manufacturer. Further, plaintiffs argue that PMUSA has never claimed to have any proof that its "Lights" are safer than regular cigarettes. These statements are true, but do not resolve the question whether the FTC has specifically authorized the use of these terms."

However, the court stated: "We conclude that the specific authorization required to trigger the exemption of section 10b(1) does not require formal rulemaking or official definitions. It is sufficient if the authorization proceeds from regulatory activity, including the resolution of an enforcement action by means of a consent order. The consent order provides express authority for the party that was the target of the enforcement action to engage in the conduct described in the consent order. In addition, a consent order entered into by the FTC with one member of a regulated industry, which is published pursuant to statute, provides implied authority for other members of the regulated industry to engage in the same conduct. It would elevate form over substance to say that FTC specifically authorized American Brands to use such descriptors so long as certain conditions were met, but did not thereby specifically authorize other members of the industry to act accordingly. Thus, while the authorization given to American Brands was express, the authorization given to the rest of the industry was implied, but no less specific. The necessary degree of specificity is provided by the language of the consent orders and by the FTC's long-standing use, if not formal adoption, of the definition of "low tar" as meaning 15 milligrams or less of tar per cigarette."

Because PMUSA was specifically authorized to use the disputed terms without fear that the FTC would challenge them as deceptive or unfair, they were exempt from civil liability under 10b(1) of the Consumer Fraud Act for the use of the. The court found no evidence in the record that PMUSA had failed to use these terms in compliance with the terms of the consent orders.

The court, in its conclusion clarified its position:

The increased mutagenicity of the smoke delivered by Marlboro Lights and Cambridge Lights cannot be a separate basis for a claim under the Consumer Fraud Act because, even if the terms "light" and "lowered tar and nicotine" do convey a message of safety, their use is specifically authorized by the FTC. In addition, any claim of fraud based on PMUSA's failure to disclose increased mutagenicity is barred by this court's long-standing rule against imposing additional disclosure requirements beyond those established by statute or agency regulation.

————Plaintiffs' claim under the Deceptive Practices Act must also fail. Section 4 of the Deceptive Practices Act exempts from liability "conduct in compliance with the orders" of a federal agency. Because we have concluded that the 1971 and 1995 consent orders provided specific authorization to all industry members to engage in the conduct permitted by the orders, these orders fall within the scope of section 4, even though PMUSA was not a party to either consent order.

————We have resolved the present case entirely on the basis of state law by construing and applying an exemption clause in a state statute. We do not address PMUSA's arguments that this action is expressly or impliedly preempted by federal law. Operation of section 10b(1) is not dependent on the intent of Congress. Rather, it is dependent on the intent of the Illinois General Assembly to allow regulated entities to engage in commercial conduct that might otherwise be alleged to be fraudulent or deceptive without risk of civil liability, so long as that content is specifically authorized by the regulatory body.

————Finally, we share the concerns expressed by plaintiffs and their *amici* about the devastating health effects of smoking and, in particular, the scourge of smoking among young people. We emphasize that because this action is barred by section 10b(1) of the Consumer Fraud Act, it is unnecessary to reach the merits of plaintiffs' claim that PMUSA intentionally deceived the public. Our resolution of the present case is in no way an expression of approval of PMUSA's alleged conduct. Nevertheless, as justices, our role is to apply the law as it exists, not to decide how the law might be improved. We must defer to the policy of the legislature as expressed in the language of the Consumer Fraud Act. Therefore, plaintiffs and others who would seek to alter the conduct of tobacco companies must take their case to the General Assembly, where they might seek amendment of section 10b(1); to the FTC, where they might seek changes in regulations; or to Congress, where they might seek amendments to the Labeling Act.

In closing: "We reverse the judgment of the circuit court and remand with instructions to dismiss pursuant to section 10b(1) of the Consumer Fraud Act."

United States Currency Restrictions for Advertisers

One area of concern for advertisers is the use of certain elements in advertising; in this case money. The use of United States currency in an ad has been a major issue for advertisers to deal with. Over the years I have seen numerous times the misuse of money in advertising. It's an often misunderstood item depicted in ads.

During the Civil War the first large issuance of paper money in the United States was made. As a result, a law (18 U.S.C. §474) was enacted to protect the uncontrolled counterfeiting that went with the wartime economy. At the time the law provided criminal liability for printing, photographing, or making any impression "in the likeness of any obligation or other security, or any part thereof . . . " In other words, you could not photograph or copy any money or part of it.

However, in 1958 Congress enacted another law that allowed the "printing, publishing . . . of illustrations of . . . any . . . obligation or other security of the United States . . . for philatelic, numismatic, educational, historical, or newsworthy purposes in articles, books, journals, newspapers, or albums . . . ." Yet, this law limited how currency could be reproduced to avoid counterfeiting. The reproduction could only be in black and white, larger or smaller than actual size, and the negatives and plates had to be destroyed immediately after use.

The government, however, did not allow reproduction of currency for commercial advertising purposes to fall under this exception. In 1984 the United States Supreme Court made a decision in *Time, Inc.* v. *Donald T. Regan, Secretary of the Treasury, et al*, 468 United States 641, 104 S.Ct. 3262, 82 L.Ed. 2d 487 (1981), which changed that. In that case, *Sports Illustrated* had used a color photograph of $100 bills pouring into a basketball hoop.

Time argued that Section 504 was unconstitutional in that it was a violation of free speech because the government could determine what was acceptable content or subject matter. The Court ruled in favor of Time in part.

In 1985 the Treasury Department formulated a policy statement regarding use of currency in ads. The policy stated that the Department would: "[P]ermit the use of photographic or other likenesses of United States and foreign currency for any purpose, provided that the items were reproduced in black and white and were less than three-fourth of, or greater than one and one-half times the size, in linear dimension, of each part of the original item. Furthermore, the negatives and plates used in making the likeness must be destroyed after their use. This decision will, for the first time, permit the use of currency reproduction in commercial advertisements, provided they conform to these size and color restrictions."

As a result, reproduction of currency is allowed in advertising under two conditions:

* It is not reproduced in full color; and
* It is reproduced less than three-fourth or more than one and one-half the size of the original.

Note: violating this law is a felony.

Considerations When Advertising Professional Businesses

Attorney Advertising

The first state to adopt an ethics code for attorneys was Alabama in the late nineteenth century. This specifically allowed newspaper ads to be used by members of the Alabama bar. However, in other states the practice was not allowed. In fact, a Denver, Colorado, attorney was suspended for six months by the state Supreme Court in *People ex rel. Maupin* v. *MacCabe*, 18 Colo. 186, 32 P. 280 (1893), for running a newspaper ad which claimed: "Divorces legally obtained very quietly, good everywhere." The Court noted in that case, "The ethics of the legal profession forbid that an attorney should advertise his talents or his skills as a shopkeeper advertises his wares."

In 1908 The American Bar Association published its Canons of Professional Ethics, which discussed attorney advertising. Cannon 27 (1908) stated, in part, ". . . solicitation of business by circulars or advertisements, or by personal communications, or interviews, not warranted by personal relations, is unprofessional."

It was not until 1977 that a major change occurred regarding attorney advertising. The landmark decision was the case of *Bates* v. *State Bar of Arizona*, 433 United States 350, 97 S.Ct. 2691, 53 L.Ed. 2d 810 (1977). Here, the United States Supreme Court upheld the First Amendment right of attorneys to advertise their services. However, the *Bates* case did not grant carte blanche to attorneys to advertise in any manner they wanted. The Court stressed that attorney advertising must not be false, deceptive, or misleading. They noted: "As with other varieties of speech, it follows as well that there may be reasonable restrictions on the time, place and manner of advertising."

The state bar associations greeted *Bates* with little enthusiasm. In fact, they limited *Bates* to its facts, which essentially allowed price advertising of certain routine legal services.

Even though *Bates* dealt with advertising by attorneys, it led the way for advertising by all professionals. Accountants, attorneys, doctors, dentists, pharmacists, and other professionals have been using advertising to attract clientele ever since.

In 1978, *Ohralik* v. *Ohio State Bar Association*, 436 United States 447, 98 S.Ct. 1912, 56 L.Ed. 2d 444 (1978), decided the question of direct solicitation. The Court stated that truthful, restrained advertising of prices for routine legal services was not unprofessional conduct. However, the Court also indicated that states have a legitimate interest in protecting the public from attorney advertising involving fraud, undue influence, or intimidation.

The Court said:

> By discussing the origin and impact of the nonsolicitation rules, I do not mean to belittle those obviously substantial interests that the State has in regulating attorneys to protect the public from fraud, deceit, misrepresentation, overreaching, undue influence and invasions of privacy. But where honest, unpressed "commercial" solicitation is involved—a situation not presented in either of these cases—I believe it is open to doubt whether the State's interests are sufficiently compelling to warrant the restriction on the free flow of information which results from a sweeping nonsolicitation rule and against which the First Amendment ordinarily protects.

The Supreme Court went further in another landmark attorney advertising case, *In re R.M.J.*, 455 United States 191, 102 S.Ct. 929, 71 L.Ed. 2d 64 (1982). The Missouri Supreme Court's Advisory Committee tried to disbar an attorney for violating attorney advertising regulations by using direct mail and advertising his expertise in his area of practice (personal injury) using wording that varied from that allowed by the code. The Missouri Supreme Court upheld the constitutional validity of these rules and reprimanded the lawyer. The United States Supreme Court, however, reversed this decision by saying:

> Truthful advertising related to lawful activities is entitled to the protection of the First Amendment. But when the particular content or method of the advertising suggests that it is inherently misleading or when experience has proved that in fact such advertising is subject to abuse, the States may impose appropriate restrictions. Misleading advertising may be prohibited entirely. But the States may not place an absolute prohibition on certain types of potentially misleading information, e.g., a listing of areas of practice, if the information also may be presented in a way that is not deceptive. Thus, the Court in Bates suggested that the remedy in the first instance is not necessarily a prohibition but preferably a requirement of disclaimers or explanation . . . Although the potential for deception and confusion is particularly strong in the context of advertising professional services, restrictions upon such advertising may be no broader than reasonably necessary to prevent the deception.

The Court went on: "Even when a communication is not misleading, the State retains some authority to regulate. But the state must assert a substantial interest and the interference with speech must be in proportion to the interest served . . . Restrictions must be narrowly drawn, and the State lawfully may regulate only to the extent regulation furthers the State's substantial interest."

In this case the Court clearly stated the broad parameters of an attorney's—and by inference any professional's—right to advertise.

The United States Supreme Court continued to show little patience for state restrictions on an attorney's right to advertise truthfully as demonstrated in its decision in *Zauderer* v. *Office of Disciplinary Counsel of the Supreme Court of Ohio*, 471 United States 626, 105 S.Ct. 2265, 85 L.Ed. 2d 652 (1985). Because of this ruling, attorneys may use accurate illustrations in their ads, as well as nondeceptive claims in ads that openly solicit specific types of clients. However, the decision requires some attorney ads to contain certain disclosures.

In 1981 Philip Zauderer, an attorney in Columbus, Ohio, began placing ads in Ohio newspapers. One ad included a line drawing of the Dalkon Shield, along with problematic copy (see box 13.1), and Zauderer's firm name, address, and phone number for "free information." Zauderer received over two hundred inquiries from the ad and ultimately initiated lawsuits on behalf of 106 women. Another ad noted Zauderer's availability to represent people charged for drunk driving. That ad contained the phrase: "full legal fee refunded if convicted of drunk driving."

Box 13.1   **Philip Zauderer Ad**

DID YOU USE THIS IUD?

The Dalkon Shield Intrauterine Device (IUD) is alleged to have caused serious pelvic infections resulting in hospitalizations, tubal damage, infertility, and hysterectomies. It is also alleged to have caused unplanned pregnancies ending in abortions, miscarriages, septic abortions, tubal or ectopic pregnancies and full-term deliveries. If you or a friend have had a similar experience do not assume it is too late to take legal action against the Shield's manufacturer.

Our law firm is presently representing women on such cases. The cases are handled on a contingent fee basis of the amount recovered. If there is no recovery, no legal fees are owed by our clients.

The Ohio Supreme Court publicly reprimanded Zauderer after ruling that the ads violated several rules in the state's Code of Professional Conduct. On July 29, 1982, Ohio's Office of Disciplinary Counsel (ODC) charged Zauderer with several disciplinary violations because of these ads. The case claimed that the drunk-driving ad violated Ohio Disciplinary Rule 2-101 (A), saying that it was "false, fraudulent, misleading, and deceptive to the public." The rational for this was that it offered representation on a contingent-fee basis in a criminal case, a violation under another disciplinary rule.

The complaint also charged that the line drawing in the Dalkon Shield ad violated Disciplinary Rule 2-101(B), which forbid use of illustrations in attorney ads and limited the kind of information in such ads to an established list of twenty items. In addition, the ODC claimed that the ad violated another disciplinary rule forbidding a lawyer from "recommending employment, as a private practitioner, of himself, his partner, or associate to a non-lawyer who has not sought his advice regarding employment of a lawyer." Another rule stated that a "lawyer who has given unsolicited advice to a layman that he should obtain counsel or take legal action shall not accept employment resulting from that advice."

The case also dealt with another rule that required ads mentioning contingent-fee rates to "disclose whether percentages are computed before or after deduction of court costs and expenses." The failure to inform clients that they would be liable for costs (as opposed to legal fees) even if their claims were unsuccessful made the ad "deceptive."

It was never alleged that the Dalkon Shield ad was false or deceptive. In fact, the ODC stipulated that the information and advice in the ad relative to Dalkon Shield litigation was not false, fraudulent, misleading, or deceptive and that the line drawing accurately depicted the Dalkon Shield.

The Court said: "Because all advertising is at least implicitly a plea for its audience's custom, a broad reading of the rules applied by the Ohio court (and particularly against self-recommendation) might suggest that they forbid all advertising by attorneys—a result obviously not in keeping with our decisions in *Bates* and *In re R.M.J.* Because appellant's statements regarding the Dalkon Shield were not false or deceptive, our decisions impose on the State the burden of establishing that prohibiting the use of such statements to solicit or obtain legal business directly advances a substantial governmental interest."

The Court concluded by saying the state did not meet that burden in this instance: "An attorney may not be disciplined for soliciting legal business through printed advertising containing truthful and nondeceptive information and advice regarding the legal rights of potential clients."

Ohio's laws regarding the use of pictures or illustrations in an attorney's ad was invalid for similar reasons. The likely purpose behind the restrictions was to ensure that attorney ads are "dignified." However, the court said it was "unsure that the State's desire that attorneys maintain their dignity in their communications with the public is an interest substantial enough to justify the abridgment of their First Amendment rights."

Zauderer was unsuccessful with the disclosure issue. The problem here involved a failure to include in the Dalkon Shield ad "information that clients might be liable for significant litigation costs even if their lawsuits were unsuccessful." The Court noted that Ohio's disclosure requirements do not prevent lawyers from advertising. Rather, lawyers are required by these rules to "provide somewhat more information than they might otherwise be inclined to present."

Specifically, the Dalkon Shield ad said that "if there is no recovery, no legal fees are owed by our clients." The drunk-driving ad said "full legal fee . . . refunded . . . ." However, the ads failed to mention the subtle distinction between "legal fees" and "costs." The problem with this technical point was that a layman might not be aware of the distinction between "fees" and "costs." Therefore, the United States Supreme Court affirmed the Ohio court's reprimand of Zauderer to the extent that it was based on the omission of material information concerning his contingent-fee arrangements in the Dalkon Shield ads and his terms of representation in the drunk-driving ads.

The FTC's Role in Attorney Advertising It's not surprising that the Federal Trade Commission has actively encouraged truthful attorney advertising as well as truthful professional advertising in general. As we learned earlier in chapters 2 and 3, the FTC is authorized to prevent unfair methods of competition and unfair or deceptive acts or practices in or affecting commerce. Under this mandate, the FTC encourages competition among professionals to a great extent. In recent years, the FTC has been looking into the competitive impact of restrictions on business arrangements that such state-licensed professionals as attorneys, doctors, and dentists can use. The commission's goal in that effort has been to urge the removal of those restrictions that restrain competition, raise prices, and hurt consumers without offering benefits.

In November 1984, for example, the FTC prepared a report, "Improving Consumer Access to Legal Services: The Case for Removing Restrictions on Truthful Advertising." Some thirty-two hundred lawyers in seventeen states were surveyed to find out if restricting attorney advertising affected the availability of legal services and the prices that consumers paid for these services. One of the main conclusions of the report was that ". . . restrictions on the manner, content, and form of lawyer advertising have limited the flow of information to consumers about lawyers and their services." The report also found "convincing support for the proposition that greater flexibility to engage in nondeceptive advertising will be associated with lower prices for consumers of legal services."

The FTC also plays a significant part in the area of professional advertising by offering recommendations to the state licensing authorities.

For example, in 1984 two Iowa attorneys televised three commercials that contained:

- More than a single nondramatic voice;
- Background sound;
- Visual displays other than words and numbers; and
- A list of four fields of practice which they would handle on either a percentage basis or a contingent fee basis.

While not alleging or demonstrating that these ads were false, misleading, or deceptive, the Iowa State Bar Association's Committee on Professional Ethics and Conduct obtained a temporary injunction and sought to permanently stop the attorneys from using these commercials to advertise their legal services.

It was charged that the three spots violated Iowa's Code of Professional Responsibility for Lawyers since they "contain more than a single non-dramatic voice, have background sound and visual displays of two or more people characterizing themselves as clients which make laudatory comment as to the defendants' services," and because they "list four areas of practice and contain no disclaimer."

As a result, the FTC urged the Iowa court not to restrict competition unnecessarily by limiting truthful, nondeceptive information. The commission listed three reasons why these ads were not deceptive:

- The ads did not make any misleading or deceptive statements or claims, nor was there any evidence on which the Iowa Supreme Court could base such a finding.
- A study submitted by the attorneys established that the public did not perceive the advertisements to be misleading or deceptive; and
- There was no evidence "in the record to support the premise generally that the technique of using dramatizations, background sounds or more than one non-dramatic voice" in a television commercial is inherently misleading. The FTC noted that the plaintiff's witness "testified that in his professional opinion, the use of such format and techniques was not inherently misleading or deceptive."

The FTC also stated that the American Bar Association's Commission on Advertising found no support that the use of graphic dramatizations and music in lawyer advertising is inherently misleading or potentially more misleading than advertisements which do not contain those elements.

Many state and local bar associations have used television commercials containing dramatizations, graphics, and music to advertise the availability of bar association-sponsored lawyer referral services. Therefore, the commission disagreed that a commercial featuring clients making laudatory comments about the attorney's services warranted an injunction. "All advertisements are, to some degree, self-laudatory," stated the commission.

As mentioned earlier, the FTC also offers advice to other professions. Generally, these comments also promote the FTC's strong opposition to restrictions on any truthful professional ad. For example, the New Jersey State Board of Dentistry proposed rules that would forbid "any statement offering gratuitous services or the substantial equivalent thereof." The FTC responded by stating that "a number of provisions in the proposed advertising rules would restrain truthful communication and thereby inhibit competition."

In fact, the FTC noted that this provision isn't needed to protect consumers: "To the contrary, truthful advertising of the availability of free services can be of great benefit to consumers and, in addition, such offers can be a valuable professional tool for new practitioners who are trying to establish themselves. While we are aware that there is a potential for deceptive schemes in the use of such advertising we believe that a total ban on the offering of free service is overly restrictive and unnecessary."

The ABA Code Since the *Bates* decision, the American Bar Association (ABA) adopted its new Model Rules of Professional Conduct in 1983, which included rules dealing with attorney advertising.

Other Professions

It is important to understand that while *Bates, In re R.M. J.*, and *Ohralik* dealt with attorney advertising, the same principles are applicable to advertising by all professionals. Indeed, it was in the United States Supreme Court's ruling in *Virginia State Board of Pharmacy* v. *Virginia Citizens Consumer Council, Inc.* 425 United States 748, 96 S.Ct. 1817, 48 L.Ed. 2d 346 (1976), where the court overturned a Virginia statute forbidding licensed pharmacists from advertising prescription drug prices. And, for example, in December 1978, the United States District Court for the Eastern District of Louisiana held that truthful newspaper advertising concerning the availability or cost of routine dental services was commercial speech protected by the First Amendment, finding a statute unconstitutional to the extent it restricted such advertising.

Political Advertising

Certainly, under the First Amendment to the United States Constitution no other form of speech enjoys more protection than does political advertising. Political advertising items such as posters, leaflets, and buttons have long been staples of our political system. Beginning with the campaign of John F. Kennedy, television advertising has come into its own as the dominant form of political advertising. Today political candidates spend tremendous sums of money on television ads as well as print, outdoor and Internet.

If you produce political advertising, you should be aware of an important federal statute—the Federal Election Campaign Act (FECA) of 1971 (Federal Election Campaign Act of 1971, 2 U.S.C. §431 (1982), P.L 92-225, 86 Stat. 3). Sections of this act, for example, discuss the disclosures a candidate should make in his or her ads, the time availability of the media, the contribution of services by an ad agency to a candidate, and many other relevant issues.

According to the FECA, ads involving a political candidate (or request for contributions to a campaign) must clearly name the candidate, authorized political committee, agent, or other person who paid for the ad. Campaign ads and other literature published by a political committee or person that are not authorized by a candidate to publish the material must also include notice that they are not authorized by the candidate.

The FECA requires broadcasters to allow reasonable access or allow candidates to buy reasonable amounts of time for federal elective office. On the other hand, newspapers and magazines aren't required to make space available to candidates.

The Federal Election Commission (FEC) was created by 1974 amendments to the FECA. The FEC regulations define "contribution" or "expenditure" as including any "direct or indirect payment distribution, loan, advance, deposit or gift of money, or any services . . ." This includes any materials or services that ad agencies offer to a candidate without requesting payment.

Ad agencies should also be aware of one important financial pitfall. If a candidate fails to pay an advertising agency, the agency must try to collect the debt or else the sum will be considered a political contribution.

The candidate, the candidate's ad agency, and the media should be aware of the American Association of Advertising Agencies' guidelines for political advertising. See the Index of Sources for their website.

Political Advertising and the First Amendment

Political advertising enjoys such an amazingly broad protection under the First Amendment that these ads are not reviewable by the Federal Trade Commission. For that matter, they are not reviewable by anyone else, either. Nevertheless, there are some limitations that can be placed on political advertising, specifically concerning where it is displayed. In 1984, for example, the United States Supreme Court ruled that a city's total ban on the posting of signs, including political signs, on public property did not violate the First Amendment. The case was *Members of City Council* v. *Taxpayers for Vincent*, 459 United States 1199, 105 S.Ct. 2265, 85 L.Ed. 2d 652 (1984).

In that case, Roland Vincent had run for the Los Angeles City Council. Some of his backers hired a political sign company to make and post signs with Vincent's name on them. The signs read: "Roland Vincent—City Council," and were attached to utility poles.

Acting under a town ordinance, city employees routinely removed all posters (including the political signs for Roland Vincent) attached to utility poles and similar objects.

On March 12, 1979, taxpayers and the political sign company filed suit in United States district court, seeking an injunction against enforcement of the ordinance as well as compensatory and punitive damages. However, the district court concluded that the ordinance was constitutional.

The United States Supreme Court agreed with the district court's decision saying that: "The problem addressed by this ordinance—the visual assault on the citizens of Los Angeles presented by an accumulation of signs posted on public property—constitutes a significant substantive evil within the City's power to prohibit."

The Court continued:

As recognized in *Metromedia, Inc.* v. *San Diego*, 453 United States 490, 101 S.Ct. 2882, 69 L.Ed. 2d 800 (1981), if the city has a sufficient basis for believing that billboards are traffic hazards and are unattractive, "then obviously the most direct and perhaps the only effective approach to solving the problems they create is to prohibit them" . . . As is true of billboards, the esthetic interests that are implicated by temporary signs are presumptively at work in all parts of the city, including those where appellees posted their signs, and there is no basis in the record in this case upon which to rebut that presumption. These interests are both psychological and economic. The character of the environment affects the quality of life and the value of property in both residential and commercial areas. We hold that on this record these interests are sufficiently substantial to justify this content neutral, impartially administered prohibition against the posting of appellees' temporary signs on public property and that such an application of the ordinance does not create an unacceptable threat to the profound national commitment to the principle that debate on public issues should be uninhibited, robust, and wide-open.

Broadcast Advertising

The FCC's Regulatory Role

Most restrictions that apply to advertising in print media apply to broadcast advertising as well. However, there's one major difference between advertising on television or radio and advertising on any other medium: Broadcasters operate under a license issued by the Federal Communications Commission. Congress created the FCC in 1934 with the institution of the Communications Act. This act was designed to regulate "interstate and foreign commerce in communication by wire and radio so as to make available, so far as possible, to all the people of the United States a rapid, efficient, nation-wide, and world-wide wire and radio communications service . . ." (The word "radio" also applies to television.) The Act authorizes the FCC to "make such regulations not inconsistent with law as it may deem necessary to prevent interference between stations and to carry out the provisions of [the] Act."

There are over ten thousand licensed radio and full-service television stations in the United States. More than nine thousand of these operate commercially and are supported by advertising revenues, the remainder are nonprofit, noncommercial stations.

The FCC's main authority lies in the fact that it has the power to grant applications to construct broadcast stations and license stations. The requirement that needs to be met, in the FCC's view, is whether these grants will serve the "public interest, convenience, and necessity."

Therefore, advertisers should be keenly aware of the following areas, as they directly affect advertising.

False or Misleading Advertising The Federal Trade Commission (FTC) has the main responsibility for protecting viewers and listeners from false, deceptive, or misleading advertising (see chapters 2 and 3). Yet, the FCC expects licensed stations to be diligent in seeing that such ads are not aired. Because of this the FCC and the FTC have an agreement whereby they exchange information on matters of common interest.

Commercial Volume The FCC has a policy statement which advises licensees that objectionably loud commercials are contrary to the public interest. According to the FCC, licensees are responsible for making sure that objectionably loud commercials are not aired.

Subliminal Ads The FCC strongly believes that the use of subliminal techniques in advertising is contrary to the public interest since, by their very existence, they're intended to be deceptive. This would also be a violation of the FTC Act.

Tobacco Ads Federal law prohibits the advertising of cigarettes and little cigars on any medium that falls under the FCC's jurisdiction. However, broadcast advertising for other tobacco products such as pipes, smoking accessories, or cigarette-making machines is not forbidden.

Sponsor Identification of Advertising A station that broadcasts paid-for material must announce that it's paid for or sponsored, and by whom.

Despite its concerns with various aspects of broadcast advertising, the FCC is forbidden from censoring broadcast material including advertising. Accordingly, the FCC can't require its licensees to accept or reject ads for a particular product (unless Congress has passed a law forbidding its advertising, as in the case of cigarettes). In addition, the FCC cannot take actions against "offensive advertising," unless it's found to violate a specific law or regulation.

Food and Drug Advertising

The FTC and FDA operate under a longstanding liaison agreement that divides the responsibilities between the two agencies. The FDA has primary responsibility for labeling, and the FTC has primary responsibility for advertising claims. Because of their shared jurisdiction, the two agencies work together.

Dietary Supplements

Nutritional Health Alliance, a nonprofit health association, brought a First Amendment challenge to FDA regulations that required FDA authorization in order to make health claims on labeling of dietary supplements. The regulations stated that the FDA would only allow health claims that were supported by scientific evidence. The regulations also set forth a timetable for submitting potential claims to the FDA for approval.

In *Nutritional Health Alliance* v. *Shalala*, 144 F.3d 220 (2d Cir. 1998), the court found that the First Amendment challenge was not appropriate because the plaintiff had not alleged any particular health claim that it wished to promote. Without a specific statement or claim to evaluate, the court could not determine if the proposed claim passed the first requirement of the *Central Hudson* test of truthful and nonmisleading speech.

The court stated: "[W]ithout a specific proposed health claim to review, on evidence of record before the FDA, we cannot determine whether the 'significant scientific agreement' requirement actually bars any truthful, non-misleading speech. In particular, we note that the parties have here argued at length over whether hypothetical health claims would, when combined with disclaimers of FDA acceptance, be misleading. That question seems to turn in part on whether the claims would confuse consumers with respect to possible side effects. And this issue is particularly difficult to resolve in the abstract and without a full record."

The court also determined that the FDA prior approval requirement for health claims in connection with dietary supplements was not an unconstitutional prior restraint of commercial speech. Because the prior restraint involved issues of health and safety, the court found that a 540-day prior restraint was acceptable. It granted a limited, but reasonable, time within which the FDA could evaluate the evidence of particular health claims. The waiting period also allowed for the development of a record on the matter so that a court could determine whether the regulated speech, was, in fact, truthful and non-misleading.

FTC Guidelines

Due to the growth of the dietary supplement market, and to help ensure that advertising for dietary supplements is truthful and not misleading, the FTC released *A Guide for the Dietary Supplement Industry*. This guide describes the basic principles of the law and uses examples from the supplement industry to illustrate those principles. The guide should help resolve uncertainty about the connection between the FTC's advertising policy and the Food and Drug Administration's regulation of labeling under the Dietary Supplement and Health Education Act.

The guide explains how the FTC identifies advertising claims and how it evaluates the adequacy of the substantiation for those claims. It also covers consumer testimonials, expert endorsements, and adverting claims based on historical or traditional use of supplements.

The Pay-Per-Call Number Rule

The Federal Trade Commission's Pay-Per-Call Number Rule (16 CFR Part 308) formerly known as the "900 Number Rule" enacted in 1993, took the guesswork out of these calls by requiring certain information in ads and preambles for pay-per-call number services. This is in addition to the protections under the Federal Communication Commission's own Pay-Per-Call Number Rule that governs telephone company practices.

Pay-Per-Call Number Ads

All print, radio, and television advertisements for pay-per-call number services must include:

1. The total cost of the call if there's a flat fee.
2. The per-minute rate if the call is charged by the minute, as well as any minimum charge. If the length of the program is known in advance, the ad also must state the total cost of the complete program.
3. The range of fees if there are different rates for different options. The ad also must state the initial cost of the call and any minimum charges.
4. The cost of any other pay-per-call number to which you may be transferred.
5. Any other fees the service might charge.

This information can't be hidden in small print: The cost of the call must be next to the pay-per-call number and printed in a size that's at least half the size of the pay-per-call number. In a television ad, an audio cost disclosure must also be made.

The Preamble

When a caller dials a pay-per-call number that costs more than $2, they should hear an introductory message or "preamble." They can't be charged for this message. It must briefly describe the service, the name of the company providing the service, and the cost of the call. It also must state that anyone under the age of eighteen needs parental permission to complete the call. Once this information is provided, the caller must be given three seconds to hang up without incurring any charge.

Exceptions to the Rule

The Pay-Per-Call Number Rule does not apply if to a pre-existing contractual agreement with an information service.

The Rule also excludes calls charged to a credit card. However, the bills for such calls would be covered by the dispute resolution procedures of the Fair Credit Billing Act.

Children

The Rule essentially prohibits companies from promoting pay-per-call numbers to young children. Some companies have promoted pay-per-call numbers to children, encouraging them to pick up the phone to talk to a cartoon character. Under the FTC Pay-Per-Call Number Rule, companies are prohibited from advertising or offering pay-per-call services to children under age twelve unless the services are truly educational in nature.

Preambles for all pay-per-call number services must state that if the caller is under age eighteen, parental permission is required to make the call.

"Miss Cleo" Couldn't See the Future Very Clearly

In infomercials that flooded the late-night airwaves between 1999 and 2002, Miss Cleo (actually Youree Dell Harris who passed away in 2016) promised to provide mystical insights into love, money, and other mysteries. Ms. Harris claimed to be a Jamaican mystic, but her birth certificate (introduced as evidence in a civil case in Florida) showed that she was born in Los Angeles to American parents. Ms. Harris invoked her Fifth Amendment right against self-incrimination in that case. What a surprise.

The FTC filed a complaint in *FTC v. Access Resource Services, Inc.* FTC File No. 012 3084. Civil Action No.: 02-60226 CIV (2002), in federal district court in February 2002, against ARS, PRN, and their officers, Steven L. Feder and Peter Stolz. The FTC alleged that the defendants engaged in deceptive advertising, billing and collection practices. The complaint specifically alleged that they misrepresented that consumers:

1. Would receive psychic readings at no charge;
2. Would not incur costs when they remain on the telephone with the psychic readers; and
3. Were obligated to pay charges for calls made to the defendants' audiotext numbers that consumers were not obligated to pay.

The complaint also alleged that the defendants repeatedly called consumers without providing them with a reasonable method of stopping the calls. And that the defendants violated the Pay-Per-Call Rule by failing to disclose the cost of the calls in their ads, and by threatening consumers with adverse credit reports before conducting reasonable investigations of the billing error notices from consumers.

The defendants' entire operation was permeated with fraud. According to the complaint, the defendants misrepresented the cost of services both in advertising and while providing services; billed for services that were never purchased; and engaged in deceptive collection practices. The defendants harassed consumers with repeated, unwanted, and unavoidable telemarketing calls that consumers could not stop. The FTC also alleged that the defendants often responded to consumers' inquiries with abusive, threatening, and vulgar language.

The case was settled when the operators of Miss Cleo's Psychic Hot Line agreed to cancel $500 million in customer bills, return all uncashed checks to customers and pay a $5 million fine. The landmark settlement outshines previous FTC settlements.

Although Miss Cleo faded from the airwaves (and from public view) she didn't go hungry. In three years, it's estimated her service billed $1 billion through nine hundred numbers and credit cards, and collected about half of that.

Under the deal, Florida-based Access Resource Services, Inc. (ARS) and Psychic Readers Network, Inc. (PRN) agreed to stop all collection efforts and forgive an estimated $500 million in outstanding consumer charges as part of the FTC settlement.

"The lesson in this case is that companies that make a promise in an ad need to deliver on it—whether it's about availability, performance, or cost," said J. Howard Beales III, Director of the FTC's Bureau of Consumer Protection. "I'm no psychic, but I can foresee this: If you make deceptive claims, there is an FTC action in your future."

The settlement prohibited the defendants from misrepresenting any material fact in connection with the sale of any pay-per-call or audiotext service; permanently banned them from calling consumers to solicit the use of any of the defendants' services without providing consumers with a reasonable method stop receiving such calls; and prohibited them from violating any part of the Pay-Per-Call Rule.

Besides the FTC action and a civil suit in Florida, Ms. Cleo and her handlers also settled pending charges in Arkansas, Illinois, Indiana, Kansas, Missouri, Oklahoma, Pennsylvania and Wisconsin.

The Telemarketing Sales Rule

On August 16, 1994, President Clinton signed into law the Telemarketing and Consumer Fraud and Abuse Prevention Act (TCFAPA) (15 U.S.C. 6101-6108).

This law directs the FTC to develop rules that would prohibit deceptive and abusive telemarketing acts or practices. The Telemarketing Sales Rule grew out of the TCFAPA and relates directly to advertising and marketing practices.

Section 310.3 defines what constitutes a deceptive telemarketing act or practice:

(1) Before a customer pays for goods or services offered, failing to disclose, in a clear and conspicuous manner, the following material information:
   (i)   The total costs to purchase, receive, or use, and the quantity of, any goods or services that are the subject of the sales offer;
   (ii) All material restrictions, limitations, or conditions to purchase, receive, or use the goods or services that are the subject of the sales offer;
   (iii) If the seller has a policy of not making refunds, cancellations, exchanges, or repurchases, a statement informing the customer that this is the seller's policy; or, if the seller or telemarketer makes a representation about a refund, cancellation, exchange, or repurchase policy, a statement of all material terms and conditions of such policy;
   (iv) In any prize promotion, the odds of being able to receive the prize, and if the odds are not calculable in advance, the factors used in calculating the odds; that no purchase or payment is required to win a prize or to participate in a prize promotion; and the no purchase/no payment method of participating in the prize promotion with either instructions on how to participate or an address or local or toll-free telephone number to which customers may write or call for information on how to participate; and
   (v)   All material costs or conditions to receive or redeem a prize that is the subject of the prize promotion;
(2) Misrepresenting, directly or by implication, any of the following material information:
   (i)   The total costs to purchase, receive, or use, and the quantity of, any goods or services that are the subject of a sales offer;
   (ii) Any material restriction, limitation, or condition to purchase, receive, or use goods or services that are the subject of a sales offer;
   (iii) Any material aspect of the performance, efficacy, nature, or central characteristics of goods or services that are the subject of a sales offer;

(iv) Any material aspect of the nature or terms of the seller's refund, cancellation, exchange, or repurchase policies;

(v) Any material aspect of a prize promotion including, but not limited to, the odds of being able to receive a prize, the nature or value of a prize, or that a purchase or payment is required to win a prize or to participate in a prize promotion;

(vi) Any material aspect of an investment opportunity including, but not limited to, risk, liquidity, earnings potential, or profitability; or

(vii) A seller's or telemarketer's affiliation with, or endorsement by, any government or third-party organization;

(3) Obtaining or submitting for payment a check, draft, or other form of negotiable paper drawn on a person's checking, savings, share, or similar account, without that person's express verifiable authorization.

(4) Making a false or misleading statement to induce any person to pay for goods or services.

Section 310.6 discusses exemptions:

The following acts or practices are exempt from this Rule:

1. Telephone calls initiated by a customer in response to an advertisement through any media, other than direct mail solicitations; provided, however, that this exemption does not apply to calls initiated by a customer in response to an advertisement relating to investment opportunities, goods or services described in §§ 310.4(a)(2) or (3), or advertisements that guarantee or represent a high likelihood of success in obtaining or arranging for extensions of credit, if payment of a fee is required in advance of obtaining the extension of credit;

2. Telephone calls initiated by a customer in response to a direct mail solicitation that clearly, conspicuously, and truthfully discloses all material information listed in § 310.3(a)(1) of this Rule for any item offered in the direct mail solicitation; provided, however, that this exemption does not apply to calls initiated by a customer in response to a direct mail solicitation relating to prize promotions, investment opportunities, goods or services described in §§ 310.4(a)(2) or (3), or direct mail solicitations that guarantee or represent a high likelihood of success in obtaining or arranging for extensions of credit, if payment of a fee is required in advance of obtaining the extension of credit.

The Consumer Financial Protection Bureau

Until recently, banks and other financial institutions (aside from debt collectors), were excluded from the FTC's authority. For a long time, there was no entity specifically charged with protecting consumers from deceptive and unfair conduct by banks, mortgage lenders, and other financial institutions. The Consumer Financial Protection Bureau (CFPB) was, as a result, established to fill that regulatory gap. The new agency has rulemaking, supervision, and enforcement authority over a wide range of the financial services area under the Consumer Financial Protection Act § 1031(d)(2).

The CFPB's first public enforcement action involved Capital One overcharges due to deceptive marketing of credit card "add-on" products including payment protection and credit monitoring services. Capitol One agreed to pay between $140 million and $150 million to 2 million customers and $60 million in penalties. In another case, the CFPB obtained a huge credit card deception consent order with Bank of America involving a settlement of $727 million in consumer refunds and $20 million in penalties. The Bank of America matter was the result of deceptive marketing of their credit card protection services and also unfair billing practices.

Both the CFPB and the FTC have authority to stop unfair and deceptive conduct, but the CFPB can also regulate "abusive" conduct. In other words, an "abusive" practice is one that:

(1) materially interferes with the ability of a consumer to understand a term or condition of a consumer financial product or service; or

(2) takes unreasonable advantage of:

   (A) a lack of understanding on the part of the consumer of the material risks, costs, or conditions of the product or service;

   (B) the inability of the consumer to protect the interests of the consumer in selecting or using a consumer financial product or service; or

   (C) the reasonable reliance by the consumer on a covered person to act in the interests of the consumer.

Essentially, "abusive conduct" exploits many consumer behaviors that are predictable, but not necessarily rational. To put it another way, the CFPB has authority to act on behavioral errors, such as overestimating their future ability to pay when borrowing money or underestimating how often they will overdraft their accounts. Contrary to the FTC's the "unfairness" and "deceptiveness" standards, the CFPB places the burden of reasonableness on the lender. Arguably, when it comes to matters of mortgages, lending and banking the vulnerability of consumers is far greater when it involves matters of their financial security than when they want to buy the new Xbox 360. I think this is a good argument.

Notes on Cites

In this book, you will notice that each case has a citation (cite) following the name of the case. For those who have a background in law, these cites are all too familiar. But for those who do not, they represent some unknown code. Here is how to decipher the code.

Citations indicate where the specific court opinions can be found, should you wish to read the entire court opinion. A typical cite may look like this: *Dawn Donut Co.* v. *Hart's Food Stores, Inc.*, 267 F.2d 358 (2d Cir. 1959).

The name of the case appears first: *Dawn Donut Co.* v. *Hart's Food Stores, Inc.* The first number following, indicates the volume of the reporter: 267. The next series indicates the name of the reporter: F.2d (in this instance: Federal Reporter, second series). The next set of numbers shows the page where the case begins: 358. In parentheses is the circuit court where the case was decided and the date it was decided.

The various sources are cited by abbreviations as we saw above. The following is a list of the most common published sources used in this book:

U.S.	United States Supreme Court Reports
F.	Federal Reporter (decisions by the Circuit Court of Appeals)
F.2d	Federal Reporter, second series
F. Supp.	Federal Supplement (decisions of the United States District Courts)
F.C.C.	Federal Communications Commission Reports
F.T.C.	Federal Trade Commission Reports
U.S.L.W.	United States Law Weekly
U.S.P.Q.	United States Patent Quarterly
A.	Atlantic Reporter
A.2d	Atlantic Reporter, second series
N.E.	North Eastern Reporter
N.E.2d	North Eastern Reporter, second series
N.W.	North Western Reporter
N.W.2d	North Western Reporter, second series
P.	Pacific Reporter
P.2d	Pacific Reporter, second series
S.E.	South Eastern Reporter
S.E.2d	South Eastern Reporter, second series
S.W.	South Western Reporter
S.W.2d	South Western Reporter, second series
S.	Southern Reporter
S.2d	Southern Reporter, second series

In addition, each state court system has its own reporters and digests where cases are recorded. While there are far too many to list here, I will give a few examples of the basic California sources. A complete list of abbreviations for all states can be found at any law library.

Cal.	California Reports (series one through three)
Cal.App.	California Appellate Reports (series one through three)
Cal.Dec.	California Decisions
Cal.Rptr.	California Reporter

Court decisions may be found in any law library. The Internet also allows you access to court opinions through LEXIS (www.lexis.com) and Find Law (www.findlaw.com). Federal Trade Commission cases may be found through www.ftc.gov.

Glossary

Advertising Terms

Body copy The text copy in an advertisement other than the headline.

Comparative advertising An advertisement or campaign that compares the advertiser's product or service to that of a competitor either by name, implication, or reputation.

Comprehensive layout A rough depiction of an advertisement to show basic placement of elements. Used to represent what the final advertisement will look before it is produced.

Deceptive advertising Advertising that, in any way, creates a false, misleading, or deceptive message within the mind of the average consumer to which the ad was directed.

Endorsement A claim, either implied or express, by a person or entity of significant standing, image or reputation in support of an advertiser, his product or service.

Freelancer An independent contractor. A person who is not an employee of either the principal or agency, but sells his work or services to various parties on a project basis.

Genericide The term used to describe a situation where a trademark is allowed to be used improperly so that the mark loses its status as a mark (which is owned) and therefore becomes a generic item.

Good will The value of a business in patronage and reputation above and beyond its tangible assets.

Look-alikes One person who bears a strong resemblance to another. Usually used in the context of a person who looks very much like a specific celebrity. The look-alike is used (as if he were the actual celebrity) in advertising to enhance the advertiser's image and promote a product or service.

Marks A trade mark or service mark. The physical combination of symbols and words which make up the trademark.

Palming-off The practice of creating the false impression that the advertiser's product is actually made by a manufacturer of greater reputation, thereby trading on another's image and status.

Puffery Exaggerated sales talk or boasting by an advertiser about the quality of his product or service. Puffery claims have no material way of being proven or disproven.

Qualifying language Language used in an advertisement to clarify or offset another claim in the same ad which would otherwise be deceptive if taken on its own merit. Qualifying language must have the same weight and visibility as the otherwise deceptive statement.

Royalties The share of the proceeds from his work, usually a specified percentage, paid to an author or artist.

Service marks A trademark used in connection with a business that sells a service, as opposed to a product to which a trademark can be affixed. See also: trademark.

Small print Also called a disclaimer: Small type used to clarify a previously mentioned point within an advertisement.

Storyboard A depiction, in drawn form, of what a final television commercial will look like. Usually drawn scene-by-scene to depict the sequence of the final commercial.

Testimonial A statement testifying to a person's or company's qualifications, abilities, and character or to the value of some product or service.

Trade secret A proprietary fact, process or item of knowledge gained through a working relationship with a company that would not be commonly known to the public.

Trademark A mark used in connection with a product or service to which value attaches, and which is owned by the company as a property right.

Voice-Over The narrated voice portion of a television or radio commercial.

Legal Terms

Actual damages Compensation for actual injury or loss suffered by the plaintiff.

Bailment A delivery of goods or personal property for the execution of a contract, usually for the benefit of both the bailor (one who delivers) and the bailee (one who receives). Example: Bailor parks her car in a parking garage. Bailee provides parking space.

Basis of bargain That on which any affirmation of fact or promise relating to goods sold is based, creating an express warranty.

Breach of contract   Failure without legal excuse to perform a promise which forms the whole of part of a contract.

Breach of warranty   Failure without legal excuse to meet the obligations created by the representations or promises made contemporaneously with a sale.

Cease-and-desist order   An order of an administrative agency or court prohibiting a course of conduct from continuing.

Class actions   A legal action by or on behalf of a large group of persons who are similarly interested in the matter. Available in federal and most state courts. Usually, the number of plaintiffs must be so numerous that it would not be practical or possible to bring separate suits. Also called "representative action."

Common law   The body of law that comes from the decrees of courts and hence the customs of the people, as opposed to laws created by state legislatures or the Congress in the form of a statute.

Compensatory damages   An award in an amount sufficient to compensate for the injury sustained and no more.

Consent   Voluntary agreement by a person with sufficient mental and legal capacity who is not acting on the basis of fraud or under duress.

Consideration   A giving over of a sum, right, interest, or benefit in return for the promise of another in creating a contract. Consideration may also be a promise or forbearance, detriment, or loss again given up as part of the contractual agreement.

Contract   An agreement by which the parties promise to do or not to do that which is the basis of the contract. Lit. I promise to do this if you promise to do that.

Damages   Financial compensation which may be recovered through the courts by a plaintiff who has suffered loss, detriment or injury as a result of the unlawful act, omission, or negligence of the defendant.

Foreseeability   Reasonable anticipation that an act or failure to act may result in injury or harm.

Fraudulent concealment   The deliberate failure to reveal a material fact with the intent to defraud.

Injunction   A court order issued at the request of one party to an action against another party in that action to refrain from an act. May be temporary pending the outcome of the action, or may be made permanent as a part of the decision of the court.

Jurisdiction   The legal right by which courts exercise their authority over parties and subject matter. May also literally refer to the physical location or boundaries where the courts or law enforcement agencies may exercise their authority.

Liability   Legal responsibility for the consequences of an action or inaction which may give rise to the award of damages to an injured party.

Merchantability (fitness for a particular purpose)   In sales context that the article sold is fit for the purpose it is sold when used in the ordinary way normally to be expected.

Monetary damages   Also can be called pecuniary damages. Those damages that can be calculated and compensated by an award of the court in the form of the payment of money.

Prior restraint   The concept that under the First Amendment to the United States Constitution a publication cannot be prohibited unless extreme circumstances require. The corollary concept is that if anyone is harmed or defamed by the publication, that party is free to pursue damages in a libel action after the fact.

Products liability   The concept that manufacturers are responsible for the goods they produce when defects in those products cause injury to the purchaser or user.

Public domain   The status of publications, products or processes that are not protected under patent or copyright and hence belong to the public rather than the creator, writer, inventor, or developer.

Punitive damages   Also called exemplary damages. An amount awarded by the court over and above the damages required to make an injured party whole where the injury was caused by particular malice, fraud, or deliberate conduct on the part of the party at fault. These damages are intended to punish the party at fault, comfort the injured party, and set an example to society as a whole in an effort to deter future similar acts.

Quantum meruit   The concept that no one should benefit unjustly from the labor of others under which a court will award a reasonable amount under an implied contract.

Reasonable man   An imaginary individual used by the court to determine if an injured party's conduct or expectations were that of the average person in similar circumstances. The standard one must have in mind to avoid liability for negligence.

Recision   In contract law the right to cancel a contract when a certain kind of default by the other party occurs. Note: Not every default creates a right to rescind the contract.

Regulation   A set of rules set out by an agency of either a state or the federal government, that is a department, at the direction of the legislative body in the form of a statute.

Remedies   The recourse available an injured party either by contract or by order of a court to rectify a wrong or injury whether by an award of money or an order to do or not to do something.

Restrictive covenants Agreements to refrain from doing something specified in the agreement. May be used in deeds, but for purposes of this book refers to employment contracts where an employee promises not to compete with the employer, in the event the employment is terminated, for a certain period of time within a certain geographic area. A restrictive covenant will only be enforced by the courts if it is reasonable.

Sole liability clause In a principal/agency relationship, a provision in a contract with a third party where the agent assumes full liability for any breach of the contract. Specifically, in advertising, sole liability clauses are commonly found in media contracts entered into between the media and the agent whereby the agent agrees to be fully liable for the debts incurred on behalf of the principal.

Specific performance A provision in a contract or an order by a court that money damages will not suffice to compensate an individual for losses incurred as a result of the breach of a contract. In these cases, the breaching party must actually perform the promise made in the contract.

Standing The concept that a party has sufficient stake in a matter to take it to court. Lit. Standing to sue.

Statutes An act of a state legislature or the federal Congress that creates a law requiring or prohibiting certain actions by citizens.

Strict liability in tort The concept that everyone involved in the manufacture and sale of a product is liable for any injury received by a consumer as a result of a defective product that is expected to and does reach the user without substantial change after manufacture or assembly.

Warranty A statement or representation made by a seller of goods, contemporaneously with and as a part of the contract of sale having reference to the character, quality, or title of goods and by which the seller promises to insure that certain facts are or shall be as they are represented.

Advertising Regulation Resources

American Advertising Agency Association
http://www.aaaa.org/Pages/default.aspx

Advertising Self-Regulatory Council (ASRC)
http://www.asrcreviews.org

ABC Advertising Guidelines
http://abcallaccess.com/wp-content/uploads/2014/01/Advertising-Guidelines-2013.pdf

CBS Advertising Guidelines
Contact CBS Corporation
CBS Headquarters
51 W. 52nd Street
New York, NY 10019-6188

Copyright
http://copyright.gov/eco/

Fox Television Advertising Guidelines
http://www.fox.com/sites/default/files/FBCADVERTISERGUIDELINES FINAL2013-2014.pdf

NBC Advertising Guidelines
http://nbcuadstandards.com/files/NBC_Advertising_Guidelines.pdf

Index

About the Author

Dean Keith Fueroghne has been an advertising professional for over forty-five years. Starting as an art department intern in 1967, he has held art director, copywriter, advertising manager, creative director, and vice president/general manager positions for a number of national and international advertising agencies including Bozell/Jacobs, DDB/Needham, and Ogilvy & Mather. He was also president and creative director of his own advertising agency, Mousetrap.

Fueroghne has undergraduate degrees from the University of California, Berkeley, and Thomas Edison State University. He studied law at the University of California at Los Angeles, while combining it with his daily involvement in the advertising business.

Fueroghne taught advertising law at the University of California at Los Angeles, and was also an adjunct professor at Pierce College. He consults with law firms across the country on advertising law cases and serves as an expert witness in the field. He and has lectured and written extensively on the subject.

The author may be contacted at: dean@deanfueroghne.com
www.deanfueroghne.com

Printed in the USA
CPSIA information can be obtained
at www.ICGtesting.com
LVHW081525280824
789525LV00005B/159